# The Transformation of Political Culture

## *Massachusetts Parties, 1790s-1840s*

D0166290

Ronald P. Formisano

New York Oxford
OXFORD UNIVERSITY PRESS

Copyright © 1983 by Oxford University Press, Inc.

First published by Oxford University Press, New York, 1983
First issued as an Oxford University Press paperback, 1984

Library of Congress Cataloging in Publication Data
Formisano, Ronald P., 1939-
The transformation of political culture.
Bibliography: p. Includes index.
1. Political parties–Massachusetts–History–19th century.
2. Political parties–Massachusetts–History–18th century.
3. Massachusetts–Politics and government–1775-1865. I. Title.
JK2295.M42F67 1983 324.2744'009 82-14517
ISBN 0-19-503124-5
ISBN 0-19-503509-7 (pbk.)

Printing (last digit): 9 8 7 6 5 4 3 2 1

Printed in the United States of America

## Acknowledgments

My sense of debt and gratitude continues to teachers, advisors and old friends who had little to do directly with this book, but much to do with me at times when it mattered: Lee Benson, William Bossenbrook, Raymond Miller, Robert Skotheim, and John Weiss. Student research assistants, funded largely by federal work-study and partly by department resources at Clark University, have been essential to data gathering and in some cases analysis, especially Gail Campbell, Babette Ceccotti, Andrew Draves, Mary Malloy, Ronald Petrin, Karen Sabasteanski, and David Saltman. Barbara DeWolf's work as a research assistant, made possible by Jeffrey Nelson, was funded by the Clark University history department and my savings—an excellent investment. I am grateful to Roxanne Rawson, Rene Baril, and Terry Reynolds of Clark University for typing large portions of this manuscript.

At an early stage the Inter-University Consortium for Political Research provided assistance, notably Jerome Clubb and Erik Austin, the latter giving generously of his own time and expertise in data processing. Alan Larsen, director of Clark University's Computer Center, not only made a "dependent user" feel comfortable but assisted substantially in data processing and analysis. My government department colleague John Blydenburgh also helped with interpretation of computer printouts.

Many men and women working at libraries and research institutions from the Library of Congress to the Northampton Historical Society aided my research. I want to thank especially: Stephen Riley and Winifred Collins at the Massachusetts Historical Society; Elizabeth Matkov, formerly at the Massachusetts State Library and James Parla at the Library Annex; Stanley Greenberg at the Forbes Library, Northampton; Elizabeth Johnson formerly at the Worcester Historical Museum; Ellen Mark formerly at the Essex Institute; and staff members of the libraries of Harvard University and the Rare Book Room of the Boston Public Library.

The American Antiquarian Society has a special relation to this book, since I have had the good fortune to teach and live near it in the past decade. AAS also gave me a fellowship enabling me to spend the better part of 1976–77 there as an NEH fellow in residence. Present and former members of the staff helped with consistent intelligence and good will, including: William Joyce, Nancy Burkett, Mary Brown, Georgia Bumgardner, Joyce Tracy, Kathleen Major, Marie Lamoureux, Carol Kanis, Carolyn Allen, Mark Savolis, Dorothy Beaudette, Richard Anders, Audrey Zook, Margaret Donoghue, John Hench, Frederick Bauer, Jr., and Marcus McCorison.

In various ways an important intellectual life has existed at AAS which has aided this book directly and indirectly. William Joyce, former AAS Manuscript Curator and Education Officer, now at the New York Public Library, helped make research at AAS especially rewarding through countless conversations with me and other fellows.

In 1974 David Fischer of Brandeis University and I organized an informal seminar of scholars throughout the region interested in social and political history 1750–1850, and it has met several times a year at AAS. At least two chapters of this book took shape as papers presented in that forum, the kind of gathering, I believe, in which the historical profession is seen at its best. Exchanges with Fischer, Richard D. Brown, George Billias, Richard Curry, Kent Newmyer, David Hall, and others in and out of the seminar made for a stimulating intellectual environment. In recent years Bill Joyce took over organizing the seminar, a task now continued by John Hench. Thanks to all who have been a part of it.

In 1972–73 a National Endowment for the Humanities younger humanists' fellowship permitted intensive research to begin on this project. In 1979–80 a Clark University sabbatical and a fellowship from the Charles Warren Center, Harvard University, gave me the chance to draft most of the manuscript. The year at the Center was marked especially by David Donald's consideration, and by conversations with other fellows, especially with Michael Perman who was one office away.

Individual chapters of the manuscript benefited from readings by John Zeugner, George Billias, Paul Lucas, Cynthia Enloe, and Kenneth Moynihan.

Readers of the entire first draft have given special services and deserve special thanks. James MacGregor Burns, Richard D. Brown and Joel Silbey rendered detailed written analyses and offered many helpful suggestions and provocative comments. Paul Bourke, while in the United States a short time from Australia, plunged into the thing and shared his critical response in several useful conversations. My old friend William Shade took on the "thickness" of the manuscript almost page by page, and favored me with comments that were not only the most critical received but also the most humorous. In many instances I stubbornly overruled the advice of these fine scholars and have clung to the error of my ways. Yet the final result must be better for their criticism and appreciation.

Thanks to Gail Filion of Princeton University Press and to Sheldon Meyer of Oxford whose appreciation of the manuscript was most gratifying. Sheldon Meyer's initial response came at a pivotal moment and was very important to me.

Otto Sonntag, though I have never met him, is very much a part of this book through his extraordinarily meticulous and erudite editing. It was a stroke of luck that the manuscript came under his care. Leona Capeless of Oxford guided me and the book through its final stages.

*Chebeague Island* R. P. F.
*August 1982*

## Contents

# Introduction

# I. Party Mobilization in the Nineteenth Century: The United States

Since the mid-1960s American political parties have declined as institutions commanding the loyalty of masses of voters. Ticket splitting has flourished in federal and state elections, and the number of those calling themselves "independents" approaches the percentage of the electorate who identify with either major party. Perhaps the outright rejection of partisan politics by millions of voters and nonvoters has not been greater in American history—not, at least, since the 1830s, when organized parties became the principal institutions for mobilizing mass participation in political life. The reverse parallels between the present party deterioration and the original era of party formation are striking. Patterns of behavior which are now falling into disuse were then taking hold and spreading vigorously. By 1840 or so, voters had come to identify with political parties on a scale that made the whole phenomenon something new under the sun. Now, amid the decay of party feeling and an even deeper distrust of the political system, it may be useful to investigate the process by which mass partisan loyalties formed.

This book proposes that party development in the United States extended from the 1790s to the 1840s. In contrast, most histories of party formation examine either the Federal-Republican or the Whig-Democratic era, and mostly the former. But the Federal and Republican parties lacked important attributes which the Whigs and Democrats possessed, and as the first "experimental" parties they did not become institutions with lives of their own. Not only did the Whig and Democratic organizations differ in scale, style, structure, and appearance, but, most important, citizens' perceptions of parties and their expectations of politics had changed. From this point of view, party formation can be seen as reflecting and causing an overall change in political culture.

"Political culture" refers to all those parts of a culture which are political, but it means especially those aspects of political life that are "obvious and universal facts which," as John Stuart Mill once said, "every one sees and no one is astonished at, [and] it seldom occurs to any one to place upon record." In a similar vein Louis Wirth once asserted that "the most important thing . . . that we can know about a man is what he takes for granted, and the most elemental and important facts about a society are those that are seldom debated and generally regarded as settled."[1] While political culture can thus be expressed quite tangibly, it is revealed best in the "taken-for-granteds."

The rise of political parties is a process much associated with the full flowering of Democracy in the United States—at least for adult white males. For most of this century, historians attributed the advance of democracy to heroic presidents or to such causes as the western frontier or industrial capitalism.[2] Since 1945, parties and party competition have attracted praise for promoting expansion of the suffrage and involvement of ordinary citizens in politics. In the Cold War era, particularly, many social scientists celebrated the "two-party system" as the major engine of democracy, and offered the American past to emerging new nations as a model for emulation. This study, however, has not proceeded from the assumption that parties and democracy are causally related; nor does it assume that Democracy experienced only unqualified progress during the years from George Washington, John Adams, and Thomas Jefferson to William H. Harrison, John Tyler, and James K. Polk.

Recently some historians and political scientists have associated the notion of "modernization" with party development, which is not surprising, since a host of other historical processes have been covered by this capacious conceptual umbrella. It should be clear above all, in the chapters that follow, that this study attacks the foundations for positing a dichotomy between traditional politics and party politics. The political culture of mass parties contained many innovations, but it also incorporated old patterns of influence as well as ancient habits of deference.[3] Thus, while it can be said that parties had assumed their "modern" form by the 1840s in that their basic character had been cast by then, Whig-Democratic political culture still possessed much that was traditional.[4]

Mass parties originated in the United States. Not until the 1880s did similar parties appear elsewhere in the world. In England, parties of notables and influentials dominated a limited, deferential, and influence-ridden electorate for most of the century. The years following the reform bills of 1832 and 1867 did not exhibit partisan politics, but from 1876 to 1886 the groundwork began to be laid for mass organizations. In the 1880s, too, party structures took shape in Norway and Sweden in a fashion very similar to that which had appeared in the United States half a century earlier. At the same time, in faraway but Anglo-Protestant and bourgeois Australia, parties replaced factions in the state of New South Wales.[5]

What propelled masses of average citizens to vote and, if only for certain seasons, to take an intense interest in politics?[6] Conditions varied from country to country, but in most nations where mass parties came into being citizens were moved usually by conflicts over national choices in foreign relations or economic policy. These *agenda-setting* choices tended to be many sided in their social impact. A financial issue, such as the tariff, could activate not only regional and occupational groups but also religious, cultural, and status groups. In all the countries just mentioned, moreover, *social movements* emanating from struggles for cultural dominance or from the clash of values between religious groups (Catholics versus Protestants or evangelical-fundamentalists versus secular cosmopolitans) often preceded, paralleled, or flowed directly into political party mobilization.[7]

Four "critical lines of cleavage" have shaped the party systems of Western democracies, according to S. M. Lipset and S. Rokkan. The Industrial Revolution largely created two of these "cleavages," one involving the clash of social classes and another involving different propertied groups. Before industrialization, however, two earlier lines of division had sprung from the "National Revolution," and both of these seem roughly relevant to the United States, where parties had formed in a new nation and before the Industrial Revolution. The first American parties, indeed, emerged precisely during the era when "securing the Republic" and issues of early national development dominated politics. Lipset and Rokkan maintain that in many Western countries the "National Revolution" gave rise to a conflict between a *central,* dominating, nation-building culture and the *peripheral* subcultures of ethnically, linguistically, or religiously distinct provincial populations resistant to state centralization. The other division pitted the centralizing nation-state against the historical corporate privileges of the church or otherwise involved, as in the United States, the struggle of *core* religious groups to remain dominant, while religious minorities fought against discrimination or sought to defend their practices or to extend their values.[8]

In Norway, for example, the nineteenth-century struggle between Center and Periphery played an extremely important role in shaping the first mass organizations and coalitions. Though it lacked a large aristocracy,

Norway had a long tradition of bureaucratic rule and a "strong urban patriciate, partly of foreign birth, well integrated into the European commercial network." In the middle of the nineteenth century the "regime of the officials" began to try to centralize the country, and in the 1860s and 1870s "several waves of mobilization" rose in opposition, especially from the relatively isolated peasantry and from groups throughout the country who felt their religion and culture to be at odds with those of the centralizing elites. By the early 1880s a parliamentary opposition had formed, consisting of a coalition between bourgeois urban radicals and masses of peripheral peasantry. Mass organization and counterorganization by conservatives drove tension so high that even civil war seemed possible until both sides agreed to compete within the law. In the next two decades "issues of nation-building" (which were also economic, cultural, and religious) intensely divided a growing electorate into parties of the right Center and the left Periphery, while economic development and urbanization also increased. These issues caused internal divisions and realignments in the original coalitions, especially in the Periphery. And until 1905 and the dissolution of "union" with a historically dominant Sweden, the question of Norway's relation to Sweden was perhaps the major constitutional issue of the early period of mass-party politics in Norway.[9]

Historians of early U.S. politics can agree, certainly, that the process of nation forming laid the bases for the development of parties. Though the U.S. had no national church, conflict between dominant and lesser religious groups was extremely important to politics in certain states, and particularly in New England, where Connecticut and Massachusetts possessed formally established churches until 1818 and 1833. Though Lipset and Rokkan's two lines of division cannot be applied directly to the U.S., they can be adapted to discern rough patterns of alignment between Center and Periphery in many states, and to a degree in the country at large. Michael Hechter defines the *"core"* as the "dominant cultural group which occupies territory extending from the political center of the society (e.g., the locus of the central government) outward to those territories largely occupied by the subordinate, or peripheral cultural group."[10] In this study, Center and Core will be used less as geographic concepts—though they often had spatial relevance—and more as ideological ones. Center groups will be those economically and politically aggressive groups wishing to strengthen governmental power and to use the state to promote development; Core groups will be more or less the same as the Center groups considered as culturally or religiously dominant groups seeking to maintain or extend their values over out-groups or minorities which the paternalist Core usually regard as subordinate or inferior. Those out-groups resisting the political, economic, or cultural hegemony of the Center/Core will be regarded as peripheral. It is not claimed here that this is the only way of looking at early U.S. politics, only that it is one approach that permits some comparison with the process of party formation in other Western liberal regimes.

In the 1790s the centralizing, pro-English, and Anglicizing elites of New England and the Middle States controlled the national government and energetically pushed the new Union as far as it would go toward statism and alliance with England. To what extent the federal government would actually function as a central government was *the* issue of the 1790s. It fused with the question of relations with England, as Anglophiles and centralizers coalesced as "federalists" (the party of order), opposed by "republicans" (the party of liberty) who reacted against the government's taking form and acting as a central government. The individualist gentry of the slaveholding South joined with northern representatives of religious, cultural, and status minorities in the Middle and Eastern states under the leadership of the Virginians Madison and Jefferson. In 1800 Jefferson's victory in the presidential electoral college represented a successful "mobilization of the periphery."[11]

Soon national politics became filled with ironies. The New England Federalists, defeated in 1800 in part because they promoted an active central government, soon after drifted into sectionalism and took up the defensive banner of states rights. Federal disaffection arose principally because of Republican foreign policy and its impact on maritime commerce. As the Napoleonic Wars raged throughout this era, and as England and France struggled for Atlantic supremacy, neither great power respected American's neutral rights and both did what they could to interrupt all trade with their adversary. Yankee merchants were willing, however, to run the risks, take the inevitable losses, and bank the still larger profits. Presidents Jefferson and Madison preferred to keep American ships at home, to punish England and France, and to force them without war to respect American neutrality. Eventually Madison and the Republicans would go to war with England (1812–1815), ostensibly over the issue of maritime rights, and fight rather ineptly what amounted to a second war of independence. Though perhaps necessary to the development of American national identity, this war drove bitter New England Federalists to the brink of secession, while, again ironically, it made the Republicans aware of the need for a stronger central government.[12]

Though thrown into an unfortunate and unnatural posture athwart American nationalism from 1807 to 1815, the Federalists had preferred "energy in government," along with rapprochement with England. By "energy" they meant something similar to power, except that to most early republicans the word "power" held negative connotations and was incompatible with liberty.[13] Federalists perhaps talked most about energy during the period 1800–1806, justifying their policies of the 1790s–from funding system to Jay Treaty and Sedition Law–as the necessary actions of government. And when the outrage of embargo and the pain of unwanted war had passed, "energy" was still important to Federalism even in its twilight years.

To Republicans "energy" was a red flag of danger. "I would as soon give my vote to a Wolf to be a shepherd, as to a man, who is always contending for the *energy of government,"* said the Republican and Baptist leader John Leland in 1802. But Republicans had a shibboleth of their own–"economy." Comparing Jefferson's administration with the preceding ones, Republicans found "economy instead of extravagance–saving in the room of wasting–diminishing taxes and not increasing them–lessening salaries and not swelling them–recalling foreign agents, and not sending them where they can be of no service–disannuling useless courts." "Economy," said the Federalist Josiah Quincy about the Republicans in 1805, "is the first and last of their political commandments." Even in 1812 a Federalist gave the same diagnosis: "The democrats have acquired the power by clamouring against armies and navies and everything which would accumulate influence to the nation–economy has been their watchword in every measure under the former federal administrations."[14]

More positively, Republicans championed "rights" and "liberty." According to one early-nineteenth-century observer, the Republicans desired "the most absolute liberty of individual action consistent with the public peace and respect for the rights of others." If the Federalists were the party of "law," then the Republicans were the party of "liberty."[15]

The Federalists, too, valued liberty, but they abhorred the Republicans' concept of "negative liberty," which, as Linda Kerber has observed, emphasized "individual immunity from restraint." Massachusetts's Federalist legislature warned in 1804, "Liberty and equality, as defined by those Utopian Philosophers who have adopted the scheme that *love* and *reason* impose upon each individual every necessary restraint . . . , are highly calculated to undermine all rational liberty, to prostrate all civil society, and to blot from the face of the earth all sorts of Government." Another Federalist put it more sharply: "Real liberty is not the power of doing what we please, but is a system of RESTRAINT, by which we are PREVENTED from injuring another in property of person, and are in like manner ourselves protected from his violence and injustice. Real liberty is a code of laws, containing COMMANDS, PROHIBITIONS, and MENACES, in which the will of individuals is so far from being CONSULTED, that it is directly CONTROLLED."[16]

In the classic manner of conservatives throughout history, Federalists called upon "tradition, a divine order, [and] contractual arrangements" as unimpeachable sanctions for the standing order.[17] Most essentially they cherished society as an absolute value in itself, transcending individuals or any of its component parts. Federalists viewed society as an organic whole of unequal but interdependent orders. "Society is bound together by ties, which make the cause of any one considerable class of society, the cause of all."[18] This social "wholism" and its corollary belief in the "harmony" of class interests remained a powerful American ideology throughout the nineteenth century. In the 1830s and 1840s, Whigs would also defend the harmony of interests between workers and capitalists, as would other defenders of the status quo during post–Civil War industrial strikes.

The Jeffersonian Republicans, in control of the government for more than a quarter century of peace and war, gradually adopted some of the centralizing policies of their opponents, especially as a result of trying to conduct a war. The Republicans soon advocated a national bank, tariffs, internal improvements, a stronger navy, and other federal measures. With the end of the war and of the long foreign-policy crisis, sectionalism and partisanship collapsed in an era of "good feelings." In some states partisan divisions persisted, but in the mid-1820s, with the election of a New England president, and a Republican who happened to be the son of John Adams and a former Federalist, the old partisan identities, such as they were, completely dissolved.

The first parties, in any case, had not become established as ends in themselves. While some members of the Federal-Republican generation were precocious partisans seeking to regularize political competition with permanent organizations, most early republicans regarded parties as means to ends. Opposition outside of the group of central officeholders was regarded not as healthy criticism of an incumbent administration but as opposition to "government" or "the government." The goals of Federalists and Republicans in power were the same–to eliminate and absorb their opponents. It was fitting that the era should be closed with the presidency of John Quincy Adams, a restless and introspective Puritan who always held parties lightly and who would not even use the appointive power of his office to aid his own re-election.[19]

The lack of institutionalized parties had been particularly evident on the national scene. Of course, interstate planning among like-minded elites influenced national politics, but congressional voting blocs and voting in the electoral college possessed a pronounced sectional basis. National organizations and campaigns as such did not exist. Republicans used the congressional caucus to nominate presidents, while some Federal leaders from different states held two secret meetings, one of which had no nomination at all. Foreign-policy crises in the 1790s and again in the period 1807–1815 had done most to create ideological conflict and to articulate divergent views of domestic policy. When the pressure from outside abated, the differing views of the good society which fueled Federal-Republican competition did not suffice to sustain even the rudimentary level of partisanship attained within the federal arena.[20]

In the states it was different. In Massachusetts, Delaware, Maryland, New Jersey, and Vermont, and in other states in the principal cities and towns, partisan consciousness had grown, and often at least one party and sometimes two had reached rather high levels of development: as parties-in-office, as organizations, and as parties-in-the-electorate. Yet even in the states, these experimental parties did not mature into the kind of political institutions that were to become widespread in the United States by the 1840s.

The period from the 1780s to the 1820s possessed almost a split personality: intensely passionate in partisan conviction but inhibited by powerful antipartisan assumptions about the nature of politics and society. While Federalism and Republicanism pulled the men of that early republican generation toward opposite poles, powerful moderating or centrist tendencies acted as a counterforce. Since party competition was dominant during the rest of the nineteenth century, historians have tended to minimize the significance of the centrist ethos which rivaled partisanship during the first quarter of the nineteenth century. Centrism and antipartyism were expressed especially in a mode which might be called the *Politics of the Revolutionary Center.*

This pattern of politics not only characterized the early republican era in the United States but has flourished in other new nations and has resulted from the quite natural popularity of the military and political leaders of anti-colonial wars for national independence. The warriors and "politicians," that is, the statesmen and public men of the Revolution (in an age when "politician" served as a synonym for "statesman"),[21] provided much of the leadership of both the Federal and the Republican parties. Military heroes or men who were thoroughly identified with the Whig-patriot cause and active in the revolutionary state governments or Continental Congresses, and who possessed a modicum of political ability or ambition, enjoyed long careers in politics. Many of these men could in most states be found as popular consensus candidates enjoying bipartisan support, especially for the higher elective offices in the gift of the people.

The Politics of the Revolutionary Center may be seen to have operated especially in the choice of state chief executives. Their office varied from state to state in its power and prerogative, but in most states it was undoubtedly the most important post *symbolically*. A particularly striking feature of post-Revolutionary New England, for example, was the peculiar longevity of certain governors, despite the reality of annual elections. In most cases these were war veterans or Whig patriots with an image of being "above parties."

In Massachusetts, the Federalists Caleb Strong (1800–1807, 1812–1816) and John Brooks (1816–1823) between them won election to sixteen terms. In Connecticut, different men held office during stretches running from 1787 to 1795, from 1798 to 1809, from 1813 to 1817, and from 1816 to 1826. Oliver Wolcott, the last in this series, had served also in 1796–1797. In Rhode Island, a man named Fenner governed for almost all the years from 1790 to 1811: Arthur Fenner from 1790 to 1805, when he died in office, and his son James from 1807 to 1811. In Vermont, Thomas Chittenden (1777–1788, 1790–1797), Isaac Tickenor (1797–1807, 1808–1809), and Jonas Galusha (1809–1813, 1815–1820) played roles about as important as those of New Hampshire's John Taylor Gilman (1794–1804, 1813–1815), John Langdon (1805–1808, 1810–1811), and Samuel Bell (1819–1823). Some of these men at times in their careers either acted as partisans or were attacked by partisan oppositions, but most of them were of the type whose candidacies tended, as Fisher Ames said of one such leader, to "kill faction."[22]

The broad popularity of these men usually rested on a solid foundation of identity with the Revolution. New Hampshire's John Gilman, who served fourteen terms as a governor and was a candidate in twenty different years, had seen limited military service, but was extremely active in New Hampshire's Revolutionary government and in the drive for independence. In 1788 he led the fight for ratification of the federal constitution, and though he was a Federalist, Gilman's success was attributed to his "popular manners . . . and . . . general fairness . . . rather than any deep-rooted attachment to federal views of government,"[23]

The Republican opposition to Gilman did not make a respectable showing until in 1802 it nominated John Langdon, a popular, romantic figure of the Revolution. In 1774 Langdon had joined a small raiding party against the British, and thereafter he held many public offices, served in the Continental Congress (1775–1776), supplied the Continental navy with several vessels built at his shipyard in Portsmouth, was elected senator from New Hampshire, and as president pro tem of the Senate had the honor of announcing George Washington's election to the presidency. Langdon was thoroughly identified with every phase of the Revolution and with the making of the new nation. His Republican supporters made extensive use of his Revolutionary record in appealing to voters, while also downplaying his partisan preference. As governor, in fact, Langdon pursued a moderate course in appointments. During his last term, in 1810–1811, partisan warfare heated up as it did elsewhere, and the old patriot, nearly seventy, retired to private life.[24]

New England's undisputed master of the "middle road" was Arthur Fenner of Rhode Island. A highly practical and ambitious merchant of Providence, Fenner traced his descent to one of the state's founding families. But other than his having served on a Whig "Committee of Inspection" in 1774, little is known of his activities on behalf of the patriot cause. What is well known is the political skill by which Fenner, although an anti-Federalist and "country" party leader, led a nonpartisan coalition in 1790 to bring Rhode Island into the Union. For the next fifteen years, Fenner won election as governor because of his ability to reconcile Federalists and Republicans, not to mention the jarring interests of rival towns, economic interests, and family clans. Described by a recent historian as "wily and politically indestructible," Fenner could, it seems, be removed from office only by death. In 1807 his son James briefly revived Fenner's coalitional politics and again reduced the gubernatorial election to an uncontested ritual. Meanwhile, Rhode Island politics was a crazy quilt, as "Federalists" prevailed in the election of some federal and state offices, and "Republicans" in others. When the Federalists won a seemingly clear-cut victory over the younger Fenner in 1811, they did it on a wave of anti-embargo and antiwar sentiment. It was perhaps equally significant that their standard-bearer William Jones (1811–1817) was a military veteran of the Revolution who had served as an army lieutenant, a captain of marines, a privateer, and a diplomat.[25]

Centrism and the political magic of the Revolutionary aura were not confined to New England. New York's great leader George Clinton, seven-time governor (1777–1795, 1801–1804), twice vice-president, and founder of a powerful political family, had also been a soldier of the Revolution before he was war governor of New York. And despite his nephew and successor De Witt Clinton's reputation for promoting the spoils system, a reputation not wholly deserved, George Clinton was moderate and conformed to prevailing standards in his handling of appointments.[26]

In Pennsylvania from 1790 to 1808, a nominal Federalist and then a nominal Republican were elected governor, but the "Federalist" usually behaved more like a Republican, and the "Jeffersonian" held many positions and ideas more characteristic of a Federalist. Both were elected to the constitutional maximum of three terms. Both were men of the Revolution who enjoyed enormously wide appeal.

Thomas Mifflin, though a merchant of Quaker background, became involved with the patriot cause as early as the Stamp Act crisis. One of the youngest and most radical members of the First Continental Congress, he was called by no less a rebel than John Adams the "animating soul of the revolutionary movement." After having served as an aide to Washington and as quartermaster general, Mifflin devoted himself to state politics and also served in the Continental Congress. He supported the new Constitution in 1787 and became Pennsylvania's first governor elected under the new order of things. Though often labeled a Federalist, Mifflin steered a middle course through the issues which divided Federalists and Republicans in the 1790s. Mifflin's recent biographer found it impossible to classify this handsome, charming, and accommodating man, concluding that "the party label did not count where so popular a political figure in Pennsylvania was concerned."[27]

Mifflin's successor, however, Thomas McKean, has often been called "the first Jeffersonian governor elected in the United States." Indeed, historians have pointed to his 1799 victory as a forecast of Republican success in 1800. Yet a close student of Pennsylvania politics has described McKean as a political chameleon who was "aristocratic at heart," and one of the most fundamentally conservative men in the state. Of Scotch-Irish background and from a family of unsuccessful tavern keepers, McKean rose with the American cause in the 1760s and was by the 1770s occupying an astonishing number of high offices in both Pennsylvania and Delaware. McKean was perhaps the leading practitioner of plural office holding on the continent: "All through a startling succession of political metamorphoses and governmental realignments . . . he remained firmly in office. And he loved high station with a fierce devotion."[28] Historians have differed on the extent to which McKean as governor removed Federalists from office, and none have found it a simple matter to summarize his political career. In 1805 he won re-election to a third term over the strong challenge of Simon Snyder, another Republican. McKean attracted both Federalist and Republican votes and carried several counties which had gone to his "Federalist" opponent of 1799. One constant of McKean's popularity, however, was his friends' claims that he was one of "the boys of '76."[29]

Across the border in "Federal Delaware," a reputation as a man of the Revolution was equally potent in aiding candidates standing for high office. The Republican opposition made effective use of political leaders with attractive Revolutionary War records, notably Congressman John Patten and the first Republican governor, David Hall. When a military hero was not available, their gubernatorial nominees were the next best thing: in 1802 they chose Caesar Augustus Rodney, nephew of the Revolutionary War governor of the same name; and in 1805, after Federal victories, they nominated "the son of Delaware's foremost Revolutionary martyr, Colonel John Haslet . . . killed at the Battle of Princeton."[30]

The appeal to the Revolutionary mainstream by Federalists and Republicans expressed in part the antipartisan tendencies of the political culture. At the same time many states were already heterogeneous in social composition, containing various and often antagonistic cultural, religious, status, economic, and geographic groups. And the alignment of these groups as between Federalists and Republicans tended to polarize, as in the nation, between Core (or Center) and Periphery.

In Massachusetts and Rhode Island, one readily sees a geographic pattern of political alignment, with the commercial centers and ancient cores tending toward Federalism. In New Hampshire, however, Republicans tended to be stronger in the coastal towns than in other regions. Indeed, Republicans did well elsewhere in many of the growing and rapidly changing ports, and especially in towns where small manufacturing had begun. Within the cities of Philadelphia and New York, Federalism remained strong the longest in the oldest and wealthiest wards. Baltimore, a boom town filled with outsiders and new wealth, turned to Republicanism early, but while supporting Jeffersonian policy in national affairs, Baltimore's Republicans fell into disarray on state and local issues. In such states as New Jersey, Delaware, Virginia, and North Carolina, Federal strength had a distinct regional cast. But the Core-Periphery conflict was not only geographic. It usually expressed several heavily overlapping lines of division: geographic, cultural, religious, status, or economic.[31]

Cultural and religious division appeared to shape Core-Periphery alignments as frequently as did any other division. In New England the dominant Congregational churches were strongly Federal, while dissenting religious groups, especially the Baptists and Methodists, gave the Republicans their surest sources of support. In Pennsylvania the Scotch-Irish and Germans swelled Republican majorities, while English-stock Quakers there and in New Jersey were staunchly Federal. Cultural and religious groups which enjoyed the highest status and which tended to dominate more recently arrived or historically subordinate peoples tended, in short, to be Federal, whereas those groups "beyond the pale" of core culture, core religion, or core status were peripheral and tended to be Republican.[32]

In Delaware the core English stock lived downstate on the richest agricultural land in Kent and Sussex counties. Originally Anglican, the growing population there turned increasingly to Methodism. Delaware remained one of the few states in which Federalism survived well into the nineteenth century, and it did so in Kent and Sussex, which Jefferson once characterized as virtually "counties of England." Meanwhile, Republican majorities came from upstate New Castle County, which the historian of early Delaware called "the Rhode Island of Delaware–the county that was otherwise." New Castle was heterogeneous in its social and cultural life, receiving a continuing in-migration of Scotch-Irish Presbyterians and other non-English groups, and possessing, as lower Delaware did not, rising ports and cities, water power, and manufacturing.[33] Thus in Delaware, an English, agrarian, Methodist, and downstate Core regularly opposed a non-English, non-Methodist, upstate, manufacturing, and commercial Periphery.

By the 1820s, when the last remnants of Federal-Republican competition died away, national political life had long been dominated by the Republican establishment. At the same time that the men of the Revolution aged and left the political arena, the social environment began to change in ways that would make possible an institutional development of party organizations not possible in the Federal-Republican era. In addition, attitudes to political party competition changed as the growing class of professional politicians increasingly believed that the partisan rivalry of 1800 to 1815 had had beneficial results for the welfare of the Republic.

The 1820s were among those watershed decades in which several different eras seemed to die and to be born and during which a confluence of material and spiritual changes combined to launch society and politics in new directions. In the mid-1840s Ralph Waldo Emerson looked back and decided that the period from about 1820 to 1840 had been an age of "great activity of thought and experimenting," and one in which the world had changed greatly. Many of his contemporaries agreed, and many later observers have also concurred.[34]

Amid many kinds of changes, those associated with what historians have called the transportation and communications "revolutions" probably did the most to create the technical potential for mass political organizations. The difficulty of travel in the United States of 1800 is well known. By 1840 great improvements had been made, even before the creation of an extensive railroad network. And the speed with which mail and news traveled increased greatly *before* the invention of the telegraph. The growth in the number of post offices was an indicator of many changes: better roads, more rapid systems of travel by land and sea, increased commerce, greater interdependence, and, of course, a greater volume of mail. From 1790 to 1828 the population of the country grew 3.3 times, but post offices multiplied 107 times, from 75 to almost 8,500. In 1790 there was one post office for every 52,389 persons—forty years later one for every 1,597 persons. And while the amount of correspondence also burgeoned, newspapers formed by far the heaviest component of the mails. In the same period the number of papers published went from 92 to 861—and in 1840 the figure was over 1,400. In Massachusetts over 90 newspapers were published in 1840, an average of one for every 2,000 voters, a ratio well below the national average.[35]

Newspapers became essential to the organization of parties, as vehicles of intraparty communication, as proselytizing agents, as a kind of public-address system to supporters, and sometimes as forums for debating controversial issues. Editors and publishers rose in political power and status, and usually were part of or close to the inner circles of leaders who ran factions and parties.

Indeed, post offices and newspapers provided basic building blocs of political patronage. By the 1830s party politicians had gone far toward tying together these elements of the communications and patronage systems into political engines.[36] This process, while gradual throughout the years from 1800 to 1830, accelerated after Andrew Jackson's inauguration in 1829 and especially during his second term as the Jacksonian, or Democratic, Republicans prepared to elect Martin Van Buren to the presidency.[37] Of course, other branches of the federal government also became important patronage networks by which to reward loyal partisans and to put them into positions of influence to promote the party's cause. For example, the Customs Service, the Internal Revenue Service, Land Office, and the Indian Bureau, some of which had been politicized earlier, all became thoroughly exploited. The Jackson administration's support of Isaac Hill's Concord Regency in its attempt to politicize the Portsmouth branch of the Bank of the United States became one of the precipitating causes of the "Bank War."[38] But the Post Office, extending as it did throughout the land, and constituting a nodal point for the transmission of information, best reflected the uses made of patronage and new communications capacities in the organization of parties.

In the 1820s the vast majority of citizens had lost interest in politics. They had never voted much in presidential elections anyway, and now they involved themselves only sporadically in state and local affairs. The presidential contests of 1828 and 1832 awakened some significant voter interest, however, and began a process, culminating in 1840, by which most citizens would place great importance on presidential elections.[39] This attentiveness to national affairs initially resulted less from an expanded suffrage or improved communications than from the emergence of an opposition to Adams's administration (1825–1829) which used anticentralizing and antistatist appeals similar to those of the Jeffersonian Republicans in the 1790s. Portrayed as a man of the new West and as a hero of the people, the slaveholder Andrew Jackson occupied the presidency in 1829 as a result once again of the mobilization of the Periphery against a presumed threat from a hegemonic Center. While John Quincy Adams and his secretary of state Henry Clay were economic nationalists, the actions of the federal government were hardly aggressive under the second Adams. Although his inaugural raised the specter of a "consolidating" (that is, centralizing) state, his administration was pitifully weak in dealing with the onslaught of its opponents, and the threats against which the Periphery mobilized from 1825 to 1828 were in large part of politicians' manufacture. Once again a sectional division in the presidential electoral vote quite like that of 1800 occurred, and a triumphant antistatist Periphery took over the appointive power. Political parties, however, were not yet organized.

To the extent that political factions did call forth citizens' energies, they met with stiff competition after 1828 from a great variety of social movements, most of which were short-lived, some of which became political, and which together represented an extraordinary development of new forms of public participation by average citizens. The complex relationship between social movements and political-party formation in Massachusetts will be explored in later chapters. Suffice it to say here that a major social movement such as Antimasonry represented something new in American public life and that it was created in part by the same conditions out of which political parties developed. Furthermore, in the northern states social and religious movements succeeded in awakening and activating citizens and in provoking disagreements over group values and life styles, and hence they contributed significantly to preparing masses of the citizenry for mobilization by crusading political parties. This pattern of social movements preparing the way for mass parties was repeated in general in England, Scandinavia, and elsewhere in the 1870s, 1880s, and 1890s.

During Jackson's first administration (1829–1833) the various juntos, factions, and out-groups which had coalesced behind the "Caudillo" strengthened their positions in their respective states with federal patronage. Jackson, meanwhile, assumed a posture as defender of the Republic and of the liberties of the states and people. In part because of his assertive personality, in part because of the skillful choice of issues by the politicos around him, and in part because developments in communications and suffrage had created a potential audience, Jackson attracted popular attention to broad national issues and to presidential elections. During his "war" with the Bank of the United States (1832–1836), the president emerged as a heroic popular tribune, striking down an aristocratic, centralizing, Anglicized institution, personified by the arrogant Nicholas Biddle of Philadelphia. Millions of Americans believed he saved the Republic. Other millions disagreed, however, and saw Jackson and his "spoilsmen" as a graver danger. During 1834, the National Republican opposition to Jackson, which had joined Henry Clay's presidential ambitions and the Bank issue in 1832, and had lost on both counts, reorganized itself as the Whig party.

The great English prime minister Benjamin Disraeli once said that "in times of great political change and rapid political transition it will generally be observed that political parties find it convenient to re-baptize themselves." The early 1830s were surely times of change on both sides of the Atlantic, therefore, because the English Tory party changed its name to the "Conservative" party (1830–1832), and soon thereafter National Republicans took on the Whig label. Both the Tories and the Nationals, however, were primarily legislative parties, and neither was well developed as a mass organization or a party institution.[40]

In the early Republic the term "old Whig" served as a synonym for "patriot," and hence the christening of 1834 brought the opposition to "King Andrew," as they called him, squarely into line with the Revolutionary Center. The Federalists had recognized that the Republicans or "Democratic-Republicans" enjoyed the advantage of a more popular name, and responded with an eclectic, latitudinarian, and pragmatic approach to the entire matter, often calling themselves anything but Federal and sometimes "Republicans." Whigs eventually also came to see their name as something of a liability, if not an anachronism. Indeed, by the late 1830s, though all parties major and minor appealed to the electorate as true representatives of the Revolution, the politics of the Revolutionary Center no longer provided the powerful centripetal pull in American politics that it had once had.

In 1836 the presidential election was still not fought out between two organized, coherent, national political parties, but in the states party competition had appeared in most places during the years 1834 to 1836. William Shade has identified two "phases" of development in the formation of state parties throughout the United States. Phase I ran from 1824 to 1836, and during it voter turnout varied greatly (in part because suffrage restrictions still existed) and vote distribution showed wide swings in voter preference. In all sections and in all kinds of states, various and erratic patterns of voter behavior can be found. Shade has placed emphasis on the state-centeredness of politics and on the usually important role played in these years by state-house cliques and juntos. In Congress, too, high cohesion existed within state delegations, so much so that sectional and "party" alignments were in large part simply artifacts of state interest. Between 1834 and 1840, however, partisan organization extended rapidly throughout most states.[41]

Shade identified the years 1836 to 1853 as Phase II, or the "stable" phase, of the new party system. But he also emphasized that party institutions remained incomplete in many ways until well into the 1840s—and in some ways beyond that. It will be evident in the description of Massachusetts's party formation in Chapter XI that any reminder concerning the gradual evolution of rationalized and disciplined organizations is well taken.

By the late 1830s the party divisions among sections and social groups had once again roughly revived the old Core/Center versus Periphery cleavage, except that in the new party system the sectional imbalance that had characterized Federal-Republican politics had disappeared. In the northern states, the Whigs represented the Core particularly in cultural terms, as the party of English-stock and evangelical Protestants. The Democrats still gathered together a diverse army of subcultures historically dominated by the English or otherwise alien and antagonistic, such as the kers," the Scotch-Irish, and Germans. In the South the Whigs towns and counties of the Center, where commerce and a n outlook flourished, while Democratic votes came most m the backcountry. In the North and the South, for different reasons, and with many variations, the Whigs tended to be strong in Core and Center while Democrats seemed characteristically associated with the upcountry, backcountry, or highlands.[42] In Massachusetts the geography of parties had changed somewhat by 1840, but key vestiges still remained of the Periphery's ancient resistance to the "haughty" culture and morality of the Core and the political or economic domination of the Center.[43]

Massachusetts is an excellent place in which to conduct an intensive examination of these processes. In the early national period it contained about as much ecological variety as could be found in any northern state. Agricultural and maritime at the beginning of the nineteenth century, it led the nation in building factories and, the claims of Samuel Slater and Rhode Island aside, was the nursery, if not the birthplace, of the Industrial Revolution in the United States. Eager to catch up with New York City, which had been boosted far ahead by the Erie Canal and other advantages, Boston capitalists early set about building railroads, and by 1850 Massachusetts was being superbly served by the iron rail. But one must be careful not to read back or to claim too much for industrial change up to 1840. The transformation of political culture largely preceded the Industrial Revolution, which was more of an evolution anyway. Economic change came gradually; the emergence of parties as institutions was sudden by comparison. The Commonwealth of Massachusetts, at any rate, beckons the political and social historian of nineteenth-century America because of its early social and economic complexity, its leadership in intellectual and cultural trends, and its galaxy of outstanding individuals in all areas of life.

Given that a study of political culture seeks above all the obvious facts that no one bothered to record, the taken-for-granteds, it follows that historical inquiry into political culture requires an abundance of local sources regarding community life. This Massachusetts possesses, along with superb research institutions almost everywhere. By the same token, the existence of many books about Massachusetts in many related historical fields provided additional incentive for such a history.

Most important, perhaps, Massachusetts was a showcase of the major political and social movements of the early nineteenth century. The Federal and Republican parties were as well developed as anywhere else in the country, and the fact that the state ran against the national grain by favoring first the Federalists and then the Whigs made it especially interesting.[44] Though it may have been more ethnically homogeneous and Yankee than any other large state, lacking the diversity of New York or Pennsylvania, its Puritanism had contained early on, as Perry Miller once observed, the seeds of its own decomposition. Until 1833 the state by constitutional law possessed an established church, but disestablishment was almost a practical reality after 1824, and before then great changes had taken place in religious life. As in other states, religious revivalism and an aggressive evangelicalism flourished in the 1820s, and soon thereafter these impulses fed social movements and influenced politics. Antimasonry never became as strong as it did in Vermont, Pennsylvania, or New York, but for a time it provided the major political opposition to the state's ruling establishment. Nor did the Workingmen's movement become as strong as it did in New York City or Philadelphia, but trade unions and a Workingmen's party did struggle into being and articulated a view of American "progress" radically different from the ideology of the dominant capitalist entrepreneurs, who ruled the majority Center party and who were not without influence in the party of the Periphery. Finally, in the 1830s in Massachusetts, as in other northern states, social movements subsided or flowed into major-party coalitions as the latter came to be the main channels absorbing and directing the hopes and fears of tens of thousands of voters.

The transformation of political culture which took place between the 1790s and 1840s was for the most part as complete in Massachusetts as it was anywhere else in the United States. Certainly the state's economic development and social complexity, which historians and social scientists have posited as preconditions for the emergence of organized party politics, compared favorably with any other state's.[45] What it lacked in ethnic diversity it made up for in religious fragmentation and economic growth and complexity. Whatever the necessary causes of the change, however, it happened.

Ideas of party and attitudes toward party competition changed. "Party" became accepted, even as the thing itself changed and as perceptions of "party" then caught up with the reality.

Political participation changed. The number of voters grew immense. A minority constituted the "political stratum" who participated in public business beyond merely voting or holding opinions,[46] but the size of this segment of the electorate was larger than ever before. Mass attitudes to "party" shifted, and men's expectations of politics and political leaders were also different from what they had been in the 1790s. Although attitudes and expectations from the past lingered, they now were part of a new political culture.

Habits of deference in a highly class- and status-conscious society had persisted well into the 1820s. Those with wealth, talent, and economic power were expected to exert influence over those dependent on them, and their influence often radiated through several networks of kinship, interest, and affiliation. The rank and file of the electorate were highly visible in their partisan choice in the mostly open voting. This condition normally enhanced the influence of the powerful and prominent, though open voting could also enforce group and subcommunity pressures which sometimes operated against influence coming from above in the social hierarchy. On balance, however, open voting probably aided those who controlled social resources. The persistence of deference and influence needs to be stressed because historians have too often assumed that party competition uniformly operated as an egalitarian solvent of these "traditional" patterns. In fact, political organizations often smoothly assimilated deference and influence to do the work of "party."

The Whig and Democratic parties, in contrast to the Federal and Republican, acquired a life of their own. They were not merely means to an end, but also became ends in themselves. Whereas public men and local influentials earlier had committed themselves to "electioneering" (their word) only intermittently, and had engaged in sporadic ad hoc "exertions" to try to shape the outcome of elections, in 1838–1840 political men—some of them professionals of the new breed—engaged in what may properly be called *campaigning*. The infrastructures of each party's campaigns were their convention systems, by which they generated nominations, resolutions, public appeals, and images and with which they often resolved intraparty disagreements and rivalries. The convention system of 1840 *looked* totally different from the informal meetings and caucuses of the Federal period. It operated ostensibly from the bottom up rather than from the top down. Yet its inner control still nestled in tight circles of powerful men, and the convention system, at least in Massachusetts, took much longer to develop than historians have supposed. Parties used mixed caucuses, consisting of their elected legislators joined by prominent leaders especially from unrepresented towns, which maintained the influence of the legislature for a very long time. Thus, new and old styles coexisted in the political culture of organized, mass parties.

The story told here obviously is far from being one of the Triumph of Democracy through parties, but neither is it one of its betrayal. Parties were less creators than creatures of democratic politics, and as such they acted both to sustain and to block the full and fair operation of representative government. The social movements of protest and reform which arose in the 1820s and 1830s contributed more to the health of democracy as they sought more directly than parties to bring the practices of public life into line with the professions of republicanism. In the 1850s, too, after party organizations had seemingly established an unassailable command of the routine political life of the state, a populist revolt of massive proportions overthrew the dominant Whigs and unhinged, for a time, the very system of party politics itself. Though filled with apparently contradictory impulses of reform and intolerance, the populism of the 1850s resulted in an extension of democratic institutions and of the state's protection to less favored socioeconomic and other groups. The collapse and disappearance of the Whig Party in the 1850s also indicated the incompleteness of parties as institutions and systems. The parties had acquired lives of their own, but the citizenry still possessed the capacity to undo what had been done in its name.

A Deferential-Participant politics was not replaced overnight by democratic, party politics, and the new politics was a synthesis, a blend of deference, influence, party, and egalitarianism. The history of its growth shows forcefully that not all change is for the better and that politics can become more democratic in some ways while at the same time becoming less democratic in others. It is difficult to see the "modernization" of politics in all of this, at least in the sense that this term is usually given, though a distinct secularization of public life did accelerate in this period.[47] There was, above all, no linear, positive relation between the passage of time and a liberating growth of democracy. Some things are gained, some things are lost. The case of Massachusetts illustrates the inadequacies of a celebratory, progressive approach to political culture.

## II. The Contours of Political Change in Massachusetts, 1790s–1840s

Everyone agrees that eighteenth-century political life differed from that of the nineteenth century. Thomas Hutchinson or John Hancock lived in a world different from that of George Bancroft or Edward Everett, separated not only by modes and styles of conducting politics but also by a social and physical environment whose distinguishing feature seemed to be the rapid pace of change. Disagreement arises about the timing and nature of the shift from one political world–implicitly aristocratic, overtly elitist, deferential, relatively stable, consensual, and devoid of political parties–to another–professedly democratic, self-consciously egalitarian, expansive, pluralist, and organized into political parties. Since parties are deemed to have been instrumental in this Great Change, there have naturally arisen various interpretations of their nature, and different estimates of just when parties emerged which were truly characteristic of nineteenth-century political culture.

This chapter seeks to show first of all the broad contours of change from the eighteenth century to the nineteenth. It assembles several indices of political activity which describe primarily the behavior of electorates and legislatures. By examining over time such things as voter turnout, town representation, incumbency, and number of bills passed, one can see that political activity throughout society was highly interrelated and that it seemed to rise and fall simultaneously in busy seaports and in remote country towns, among political elites who thought frequently about politics and among farmers and average citizens who usually gave little attention to public affairs. The data presented here do not, however, explain change; rather, they describe its broad outlines. The indices portray in skeletal fashion the stages of the gradual evolution of political parties and some of the differences between the Federal-Republican and Democratic-Whig periods.

The characteristic features of classic nineteenth-century party politics do not fully appear until the later period. The Federal-Republican parties or interests approached the later pattern in several ways but did not become entrenched institutions. This hypothesis is suggested, though not proved conclusively, by the evidence in this chapter. Subsequent chapters will elaborate the qualitative differences between the transitional Federal period and the Democratic- and Whig-party era. A summary of the main features of eighteenth-century political culture, which has been well described by several scholars, can put what is to follow in perspective.

### The Eighteenth Century

To speak of eighteenth-century *Massachusetts* political culture is to invoke a realm of thought and activity in which very few persons actually dwelt. Those few were a select group, drawn largely from the colony's gentry and leaders. The central government touched the lives of the populace infrequently and lightly; only occasionally did it command an aroused attention from active citizens. Towns acted often as units–ideally, as unified moral communities. Social structures and ideology thus precluded and inhibited the growth of political parties of the type which formed in the nineteenth century. Accordingly, most studies of eighteenth-century Massachusetts testify directly to the absence of organized parties, while some provide evidence leading indirectly but inexorably to that conclusion.

To most citizens of Massachusetts "the central government mattered little," Robert Zemsky has observed, "because the central government did little." The "business of government" was "confined to the military defense of the province, the umpiring of disputes between citizens, the supervision of unincorporated areas of settlement, and the maintenance of the province's governmental establishment. Hence only three issues regularly invited legislative activity: revenues, appropriations, and the currency." Some citizens at times became excited about state policy, but normally the provincial elites made most decisions along well-established lines.[1]

In the natural order of things, government simply reflected society or, as John Adams said in 1775, "should be in miniature an exact portrait of the people at large."[2] Nowhere was the organic unity of government and society better expressed than in the corporate life of the town, a civic community "coterminous with that of the church."[3] Social, political, and moral leadership were relatively undifferentiated in the towns, where the basic hierarchy of society was held together by the deference which the lower orders paid to the higher. Every town of any pretensions had a recognizable gentry, "who lived in houses of superior size and furnishings, tended to occupy the leading positions in local government, and sat in the best pews in the meeting house, generally elevated above the level of the rest." Special pews did not signify a hereditary nobility, which Americans repudiated; rather, they were "given by a sort of civic contract, to lapse if the recipient's heirs failed on their part." While the towns therefore sought "the greatest possible measure of stability and permanence in social rank," provincials nevertheless insisted that rank and status "to be maintained, had always to be earned anew." It is useful, too, to remember here J. R. Pole's insight that the deferential order did not produce class strife. As the townsman gaves respectables deference voluntarily, he simultaneously valued his own independence, which he did not regard as compromised. Deference might, on the contrary, "have been thought of as an affirmation of his own position, a voluntary expression of self-respect. It is probably because the offer of social deference has seemed to be inseparable from submission and servility to later generations of Americans that they have had so much difficulty in comprehending the fact that in the eighteenth century it was compatible with a very vigorous notion of one's own importance."[4]

The chief practical result of deference was stability of leadership. Townsmen elected the same men, or members of the same core families, to town and state offices for years and decades. Churches still cherished the ideal of the "settled" pastor, and long ministries were common through the second half of the eighteenth century. Similarly, the same men and family names appeared for long stretches on the rolls of town selectmen, moderators, state representatives, and other elected officials.[5]

In such a corporate and deferential environment, political parties found no habitat. The close-knit towns placed a premium on consensus, not on pluralism. While they sometimes experienced bitter divisions, they regarded these as aberrations to be resolved by deliberation.[6] In their behavior within the legislature during the eighteenth century the towns displayed their inner direction and corporate spirit. Towns often simply did not bother to send representatives to the General Court. When they did, uncontested elections for representatives were common, absenteeism was high (delegates stayed a short time, then went home), and for most of the century, though most towns were entitled to at least two delegates, on the average only about four towns a year sent more than one delegate. Michael

Zuckerman logically attributed this to the "sense of an undivided town interest that a single representative sufficed to speak for."[7] Thus it is easy to see that separate party interests would not develop within the towns—and that the same set of conditions prohibited parties from developing among the towns or within the legislature.

The legislature, to begin with, was not institutionalized.[8] Given the underrepresentation and absenteeism just mentioned, the extensive discontinuity of the legislators' tenure would undercut the formation of regular patterns of politicking. Most legislators were, in Zemsky's words, "backbenchers" or "localists" who tended to view all political problems in terms of their own constituencies. Rates of incumbency were low and turnover was high. Consequently, though alliances did form in the legislatures, "they were invariably small, close-knit, and ephemeral." The legislators, like elites and voters, generally "remained independent, being neither disciplined nor organized by the exigencies of party politics."[9]

Only a limited stratum of the populace even participated in politics—a slice of the upper and middle classes of male freeholders—and then sporadically. Apathy generally prevailed among citizens until they perceived a threat to their immediate interests. Then "they threw themselves into the political process, usually with success as politicians moved to placate them. After short bursts of activism citizens generally subsided to their normal apathy."[10] In the legislature, towns showing the most political activity in the period 1757–1764 tended to be large and among the most advanced economically.[11] A great many towns, and a great many citizens, simply exhibited no sustained political interest at all.

Combinations in politics were not only transient and undeveloped but were held in explicit contempt and fear by citizens and leaders alike. "Party" and "faction" were synonymous terms of opprobrium: political leaders frequently described their enemies' acts with these epithets. Yet the accusations suggest that somewhere, to some degree, the act and entity existed. The question thus becomes, To what did "party" refer *in the eighteenth century?*

Occasionally the term referred rather innocuously to parties to a dispute or disagreement, which might be of several years' duration. In 1757, for example, the town of Watertown split in two in its choice of representatives. The town "for some years past," the selectmen explained, "has been divided into parties nearly equal in number and as these contentions have been so sharp . . . that some of each party have done everything in their power to procure one of their own party to represent the town." But this contention had originated in 1754 when the town's meeting house had burned and disagreement had arisen over whether to repair the old building or erect a new one at some other place. The town was divided along personal and "geographical" lines—hardly a matter of political parties.[12]

For our purposes, "party" in the eighteenth century most pertinently referred to networks of "influence," "connection," or even "corruption" in the senses these terms had originally acquired in British politics during the preceding century.[13] "Influence," for example, could be that patronage by which executives sought to make sure that their placemen in a popular assembly swung enough weight to give a colonial governor control.[14] Governor Bernard of Massachusetts tried to establish such power in the 1760s, but his attempt, like that of all late colonial executives, ended with the legislature defiantly insisting on autonomy. Brennan has shown that the patriotic opposition to Bernard focused especially on the practice of plural office holding among the governor's connections but that after 1775, when the patriots moved into the government, they continued the custom of plural office holding in good eighteenth-century fashion. No less a radical than Samuel Adams defended this practice on the grounds that the offices were no longer "the Gift of the Crown, but of the People, [so] there was no Impropriety."[15] Of course, the quintessential case of the eighteenth-century party as "connexion," and indeed as nepotism, was the network which Thomas Hutchinson created while lieutenant governor in the 1760s and early 1770s. Gordon Wood has captured the intense fears which Hutchinson's "party" machinations aroused in patriots already tending toward rebellion:

> Not only had Thomas Hutchinson grasped the most important offices into his own hands, but his numerous relatives and hirelings had been placed in strategic positions throughout the community—all so connected and interrelated that it could only be a gigantic pattern of conspiracy. . . . For John Adams it was only the "Character and Conduct" of Hutchinson and his vast machine that "have been the Cause of laying a Foundation . . . of perpetual Struggles of one Party for Wealth and Power at the Expense of the Liberties of this Country, and of perpetual Contention and Opposition in the other Party to preserve them." "Is not this amazing ascendency of one Family," asked Adams, "Foundation sufficient on which to erect a Tyranny."[16]

Patronage was the key, according to Bernard Bailyn, to building "an effective 'interest' or 'party' that could stand firm for law and the needs of government." Thus the nucleus of "party" began at the top of the government, where several of Hutchinson's relatives and close associates occupied important positions. At the lowest levels of government, Hutchinson sought to manipulate "choices for the militia officers, lesser judgeships, and other local offices." Power operated by punishment and reward, using office, economic opportunities, bribery, or official recognition. It was also vital that the faction elect "the proper people" to the legislature and that "once elected, they attend."[17]

But Bailyn has shown, too, the limits of Hutchinson's "party," which loomed so noxiously large in patriot eyes. Hutchinson had less and less success, for example, in getting "the proper people" or a court party elected to the legislature. Indeed, after the Stamp Act he saw "the progressive elimination from the Assembly of the friends of government." Most crippling, however, to Hutchinson's attempt to create an interest or party was "the insufficiency of patronage in a world assumed to be dominated less by public opinion than by the manipulation of 'interests.' Bernard had put the point succinctly: 'If punishments and rewards are the two hinges of government as politicians say . . . this government is off its hinges, for it can neither punish nor reward.' "[18]

These, then, were the contemporary meanings of "party," but historians have also used the term to refer to other eighteenth-century groupings similar to "interests" which they claim possessed, if only implicitly, distinct ideologies. Several scholars have found that from the 1740s through the 1780s political divisions recurred along cosmopolitan-commercial versus localist-country lines. Cosmopolitans embraced change and the secularization of society; their towns were more complex, economically and socially. Localists tended to live in less developed towns and to resist modernity and to cling to more traditional ways. Scrutiny of the extant roll calls in the legislature for these decades (there are few) has revealed rough divisions among towns along socioeconomic lines.[19] This recurring cosmopolitan-localist polarity, however, threw into conflict not any persisting or durable political parties but, rather, factions and unstable coalitions. The dichotomy should not be transformed by the alchemy of semantic anachronism into party politics.

Eighteenth-century assumptions about the relation between government and society also shaped the new Massachusetts constitution of 1780. Its "conservative republicanism" reflected the Whig aim of providing for the institutional representation of different social "orders." The document spelled out a distinctly hierarchic and graded set of property qualifications for office holding and voting, making some suffrage restrictions in fact higher than before. They were not, however, strictly enforced, and were soon liberally interpreted. The idea of the town as a corporate unit also continued, though it was beginning to be challenged by the idea of the individual citizen.[20] Basic views of the government's relation to society may have been beginning to change in this period, and political practice in some ways already departed from paper ideals, but the document itself expressed the Commonwealth ideal of a polity still inhospitable to parties.[21]

The practice of politics in the 1780s has aptly been characterized as "politics without parties."[22] Politics in the 1780s can indeed hardly even be called "preparty," that is, it was not preparty in the sense of being preparatory or immediately transitional to party politics. The transition began in the late 1790s and after. Rather, this partyless politics remained wholly within eighteenth-century molds. Its general features were the following.

*Legislative Blocs.* In the legislature a pattern of cosmopolitan-commercial versus localist cleavage appeared as before, particularly on fiscal issues. However, on a wide range of issues concerning commerce, protective tariffs, social and institutional structure, the land system, and the legal code," substantial consensus existed. As in the preceding forty years, roll call votes were rare events.[23]

*Uncontested or Low-Turnout Elections.* Elections, from the gubernatorial level on down, often went uncontested. State, local, and, after 1788, federal elections came at different times during the year, and voter turnout was extremely low for all types. In 1785 in a "contested" gubernatorial race, 11 percent of the potential voters cast ballots. In 1786 angry debtor farmers in central and western Massachusetts, made desperate by economic depression, mortgage foreclosures, taxes, and an unsympathetic legislature, marched on county courthouses and gathered in armed bands to prevent courts from sitting. After a rash of protest conventions, mobs, and sporadic violence, the state government in the winter of 1786–1787 sent out a small army of militia to crush the insurrection–known as Shays Rebellion, after a former Revolutionary War captain prominent among its leaders. Even after near civil war, the 1787 state election, which was something of a referendum on whether to be lenient or harsh toward the rebels, achieved a decade-high turnout of only 28 percent. In 1788 and 1790 the first congressional elections attracted 13 percent and 16 percent of the potential electorate. In lesser elections even lower rates prevailed.[24]

*Nonparticipation and nonrepresentation of Towns.* In 1780 and 1785 almost one-third of the towns and plantations submitted no election returns at all; in 1787, one-fifth. Throughout the eighteenth century, furthermore, many small towns did not want to incur the expense of sending a representative to the General Court. Zuckerman estimated that in at least two-thirds of the years from 1723 to 1766 more than one-third of the towns declined to send a deputy, and "for the eight years for which the most reliable records are available–the years from 1767 to 1774, a time . . . of high excitement and extraordinary provincial political activity–the percentage of towns with so much as a single representative of their own in the House never once exceeded fifty-three percent."[25] From 1780 to 1800 the proportion of unrepresented towns to the whole never fell below 40 percent and frequently climbed to over 50 percent.[26] Perhaps no better measure exists of the widespread inattention to the central government.

*Noncompetitive Elections.* In 1780, 1785, and 1787, over one-third of the towns that did vote gave one candidate over 90 percent of their votes. Small, relatively isolated towns tended either not to submit returns or to vote disproportionately for one candidate.[27] In 1796 the federalist Fisher Ames observed of a town's big antifederalist vote: "When they go wrong, our folks appear as a militia." In 1801 the citizens of the Connecticut Valley county of Hampshire similarly exhibited the ancient power of the "friends and neighbors" effect–twenty towns in the vicinity of Northampton, the residence of Governor Caleb Strong, voted unanimously for Strong's re-election.[28]

*Lack of Issue Continuity.* To the extent that groupings did develop in the legislature around fiscal issues in the 1780s, these fell apart later in the decade, after the state solved its financial problems.[29]

*Office-Specific Elections.* Elections for state officers or Congress bore little relation to one another or to divisions among representatives in the General Court. In town elections, consensual patterns of politics remained pervasive throughout the eighteenth century.

*Peripheral Eruptions.* Localist attempts to shake off centralist policies of cosmopolitans had a strong potential for illegal, violent resistance. Shays Rebellion was in this sense an alternative to political opposition.[30]

*Deference, Influence, and Connection.* Commercial and professional elites who lived in cosmopolitan towns tended to dominate state offices and policies. Candidates for governor of the new state had personal followings, and electoral coalitions remained volatile.

The pre-eminent post-Revolutionary leader was John Hancock, whose style in politics in no way resembled that of the later party politician, but instead belonged to that of the eighteenth-century Great Man. Hancock was one of the early and most successful practitioners of the popular politics of the Revolutionary Center, combining an odd mixture of republican and aristocratic elements. He won office consistently after the Revolution as a compromiser who successfully projected himself above "the violence of parties." Hancock "won power by 'forming a Coalition of Parties and confounding the distinction between Whigs and Tories, Virtue & Vice.' "[31] Yet Hancock's style has not been appreciated for the insights it provides into eighteenth-century political culture, and the man himself has often been deprecated for lacking intelligence. A blunt country farmer allegedly told him after the Revolution, "I remember we used to say that you found the money and Sam Adams the brains."[32] Historians have tended to remember the epithet about Hancock attributed to John Adams's sharp tongue—"the empty barrel." But even in a passage belittling Hancock with faint praise for his "picturesqueness," Henry Cabot Lodge grasped some of Hancock's political-cultural importance:

> Everything about him was picturesque, from his bold handsome signature, which gave him an assured immortality on the Declaration of Independence, to his fine house. . . . He was the Alcibiades, in a certain way, of the rebellious little Puritan town; and his display and gorgeousness no doubt gratified the sober, hard-headed community which put him at its head and kept him there. He stands out with a fine show of lace and velvet and dramatic gout—a real aristocrat, shining and resplendent against the cold gray background of everyday life in the Boston of the days after the Revolution, when the gay official society of the Province had been swept away.

If there had been a party of hedonism in Massachusetts Bay, Lodge convinces one, Hancock would have led it: "At the side of his house he built a dining hall, where he could assemble fifty or sixty guests; and when his company was gathered he would be borne or wheeled in, and with an easy grace would delight everyone by his talk and finished manners."[33]

Although he was first of all a hero of the Revolution with a "surpassing reputation for patriotism," Hancock's "unparalleled popularity" rested on quite traditional qualities—his "affable manners" in the mode of the "by gone colonial aristocracy" and his largesse toward the populace. "His wealth, being freely used in the subtler forms of generous, not to say prodigal hospitality, in no wise lessened his reputation. For his purse was always open to his 'friends.' "[34] His gifts to the people also sustained his image of "sacrificial patriotism."[35] Hancock understood as well the uses of patronage, especially with regard to justices of the peace, and he built his connection much in the style of royal governors earlier. His greater success and popularity should not obscure the fact that in political technique Hancock was far closer to Hutchinson and other eighteenth-century notables than he was to nineteenth-century politicians—even those of the Federal and Republican variety. The Revolution had made a difference, of course, and Hancock's role in it–as well as the mythic images of that role–ensured him a popular appeal which he cultivated with his purse and "picturesqueness."

### From the Eighteenth to the Nineteenth Century

After 1800 political life changed and for a time displayed activity on a scale not seen before. The period 1805–1815 in particular exhibited a spectacular outpouring of political interest, politicking, and, above all, voting in state elections. In the 1820s public attention fell off and the apathetic ways of the past returned. Then, sometime in the 1830s, political activity rose again at all levels, and with it political party organizations entrenched themselves to stay, both in the structure of government and, to an unprecedented degree, in the emotions of the people.

The rest of this chapter merely tries to describe those changes in gross outline, by giving a sense, first, of the general character of politics during the years 1800–1840, and, second, of the differences between the period 1800–1824 and that of the 1830s and 1840s.

The best-known contrast between eighteenth- and nineteenth-century politics springs from the striking rise in voter participation after 1800. In Massachusetts it rose rapidly after 1804 in state and presidential elections. Dropping after 1815, turnout followed a trend roughly like that of many other states, climbing steadily upward again after 1830.[36]

During the Whig-Democratic era the state's turnout peaked in 1840 and then leveled off below the national average–in 1840 the latter stood at 80.2 percent, Massachusetts's at 66.7 percent. The Commonwealth's 1840 turnout was the second lowest in New England, and only three states in the nation (not counting South Carolina) had lower rates. These comparisons are based, however, on the percentages of adult white males who voted.[37] Most states had eliminated, while Massachusetts had kept, a small tax-paying qualification for voting. Assessors' lists functioned, in short, as primitive voter registration lists, and, as will be seen below, it was not easy in some parts of the state for the transient or poor to vote.

High levels of participation did not prevail, however, in all kinds of elections. Turnout usually fell, as it did in later times, in balloting for state representatives, in special elections, or in referenda on constitutional amendments. Local elections also attracted fewer voters.[38] Yet participation at all levels rose high above the routines of eighteenth-century politics, and even those elections which at most times excite lower interest compare favorably with their counterparts in later periods of American

Figure 1. Voter Turnout in Governor's Elections, Annually, 1798–1853[a]

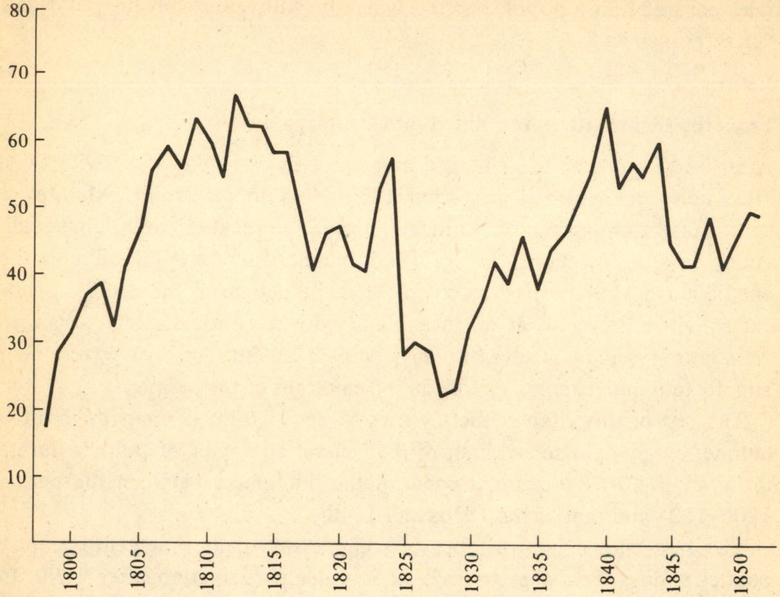


[a]percent adult males voting

history. Overall, the figures describing turnout suggest that something basic was changing in citizens' attitudes toward public life, politics, and political organizations. Thus the turnout line signals a basic change in political culture.

In the surge of political activity, nonrepresentation in the house of representatives became a thing of the past. The tides of mobilization may be seen crudely in the oscillating size of the house from 1800 to 1850. The contrast with earlier legislatures is as striking as the explosion in voter turnout. In 1810 the house numbered about 650, causing one observer to call it "a monstrous body of Legislators."[39] But the worst was yet to come: in 1812, small towns now being aided by the state treasury, the legislature's size peaked at 749. Later legislatures were smaller, and after 1820 Maine separated from Massachusetts. Although representation fell dramatically in the 1820s, along with voter turnout, when representa-

**Figure 2.** Size of House of Representatives, 1800–1853: number of members[a]

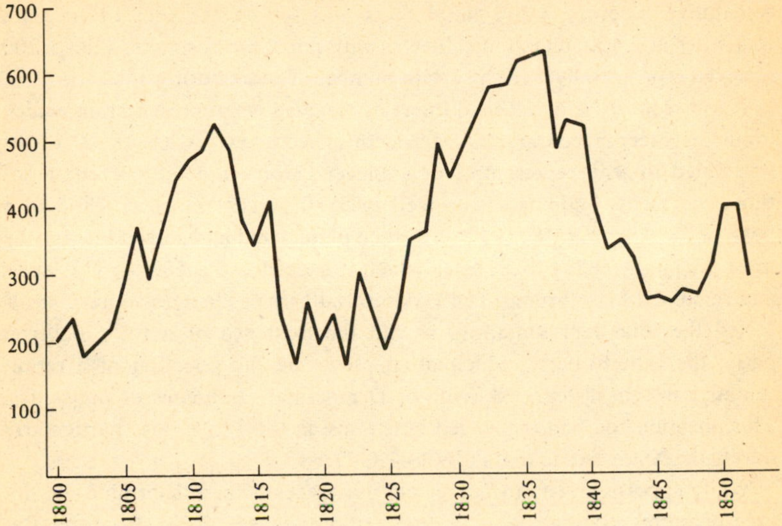


[a]excluding Maine

tion climbed again in the 1830s, the size of the house actually increased in comparison with the representation from Massachusetts proper before 1820. For purposes of comparison, only the numbers of Massachusetts representatives, excluding Maine, are presented in Figure 2. Thus, from 1800 to 1840 the contours of participation, as exhibited in voter turnout and in the size of the legislature, showed a decidedly similar pattern—activity came after 1804 and peaked about 1810–1815, and was followed by valleys of inattention in the period 1816–1830 and by reactivation in the years 1835–1840.

Though the legislature's size reflected dramatically the overall shift in political culture, its usefulness as an index is limited because it was influenced not only by the general degree of interest but also by changes in the rules governing its composition. For example, the decline in size following the peak of 1836 came in response to a doubling of the unit of representation in a deliberate effort to reduce the body. Similarly, the decline after 1840 followed ratification of the Thirteenth Amendment of the state constitution, which shifted apportionment from the historic unit of number of polls (males over 16) to that of population, allowing one representative to every 1,200 inhabitants and setting the unit of increase thereafter at 2,400 inhabitants. Towns with populations smaller than 1,200 received representatives for a certain number of years during a decade.[40]

Another measure of political interest, then, is town representation, which in the eighteenth century had frequently been low. After 1800, towns scrambled to send representatives as never before, and the percentage of those represented climbed from well over 60 percent in 1805–1806 to a peak of 82 percent in 1811–1812. It then plummeted and stayed low for the most part until 1827–1828, after which it exceeded the 1805–1812 levels and remained high through 1843. After 1840, rules changes somewhat affected the total representation, as did the existence of a third political party, the Liberty party, which often prevented the selection of a representative in that it deprived Whig or Democratic candidates of majorities. This phenomenon had influenced house size in the 1830s, too, particularly during the Antimasonic years (1831–1834).[41]

While apportionment and other circumstances helped determine the degree of representation, political competition between Federalists and Republicans led to the first great impulse of attentiveness. The contest for political power created unprecedented interest in the May meetings at which representatives were chosen, after the balloting for state executives and senators in April. In the cost-conscious towns the issue frequently became whether to send representatives or, if a town was entitled to several, how many. Partisan maneuvering often hid behind such procedural debates; Federal minorities in sure Republican towns tended to complain of expenses, as did Republican minorities in Federal strongholds. As early as 1800, partisan newspapers urged towns to take care to elect the right representatives; by the end of the decade, each side commonly found instances of their opponents' zeal carrying them "a step beyond the law" in claiming more representatives than allowed.[42] Partisan struggle might thus prevent some towns from sending any delegates while prompting others to send more than their share.

Republicans complained most about Federal-controlled Boston, charging that Federal assessors there invented "a new doctrine of transmutation" and learned to count even the dead as ratable polls. Over the protests of Republican legislators and newspapers, the state supreme court in fact decided in early 1811 that aliens, of which there were many in Boston, were not voters but could be counted as ratable polls for purposes of representation.[43]

During that same year, the only one of the period during which the Republicans solidly controlled both houses and the governorship, the Republican legislators expelled six "Federal Republican" representatives-elect from Gloucester, because some well-off "patriotic citizens" of that town had posted bonds assuring the town that if it elected the full number of representatives (six), the town would not bear any extra financial cost. The Republican majority said this amounted to improper influence, and it would not seat the Gloucester men (the town, incidentally, had earlier been Republican and had recently switched to Federalism). The case was significant for what it revealed about a town's typical stinginess, about the importance of local influentials, and about the variables affecting representation. Federalist protests revealingly emphasized that such practices were common in all manner of towns.[44]

Perhaps to remove influences of this sort, and no doubt to encourage representation from such outlying areas as Maine and Berkshire County where Republicans were numerous, the 1811 legislature passed a law providing that representatives' expenses be paid out of the Commonwealth's treasury. The effect of this was immediately apparent the next year, when 749 representatives were chosen. Many of the new representatives that year came from towns in Maine recently incorporated by the Republicans. When the Federalists regained control of the legislature the next year, however, they repealed the provision for state pay. In 1825, finally, with partisan strife stilled, a nominally Republican legislature again shifted the payment of delegates' expenses to the state.[45] Thus when political interest revived soon afterward there was all the greater incentive for towns to maximize their representation.

It should be pointed out that except during periods of intense partisan strife—for example, in the years 1810–1812—the actual attendance of legislators varied considerably and was usually much lower than the numbers actually elected. Though attendance rates overall probably improved after 1800, it was also true, as a contemporary observed, that "everyone . . . knew that . . . a great part of the members did not remain in their seats long enough to render service. They went home early in the session to save their towns from the burden of paying for their attendance, and left the business to be transacted by the representatives of a few towns." The latter tended to come heavily from the eastern coastal area, while in the western part of the state the most economically and socially advanced towns logged the best attendance records.[46]

Despite these qualifications, the towns' attitudes toward representation had changed dramatically from those prevalent in the eighteenth century.

**Figure 3.** Town Representation, 1782–1853: percentage of towns represented in House annually, First Session

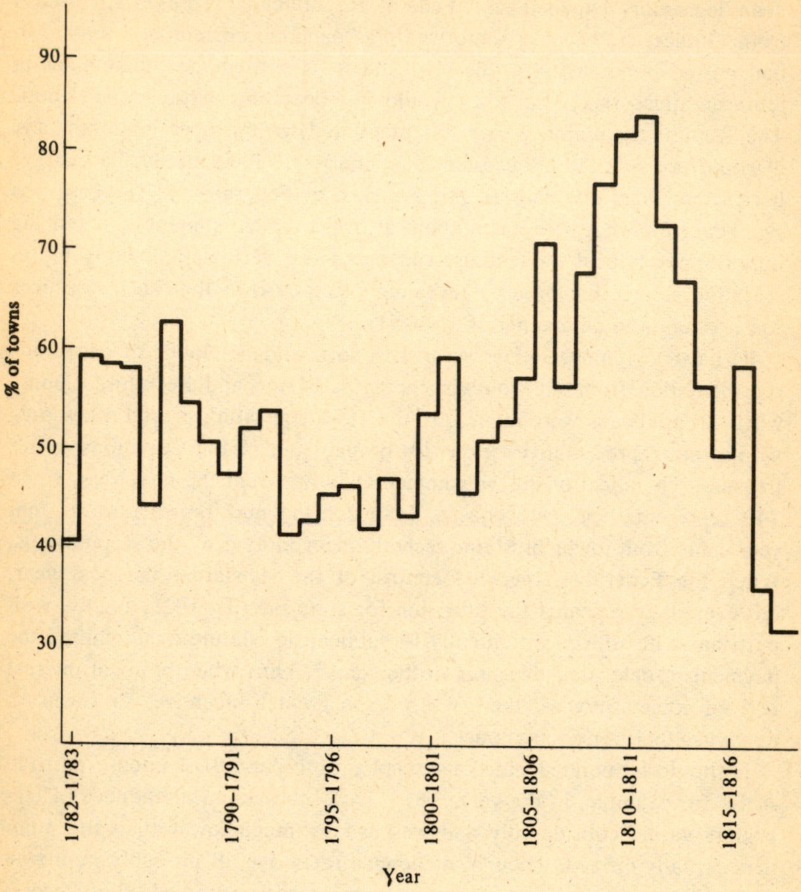

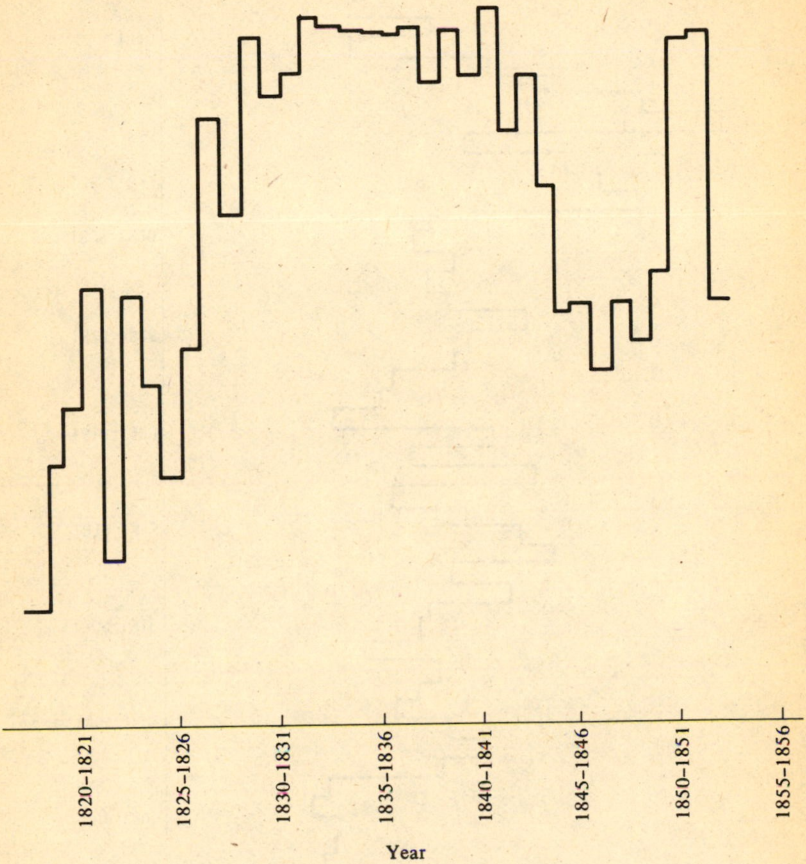
1820–1821
1825–1826
1830–1831
1835–1836
1840–1841
1845–1846
1850–1851
1855–1856
Year

Figure 4. General Court, Total Business, 1790–1844

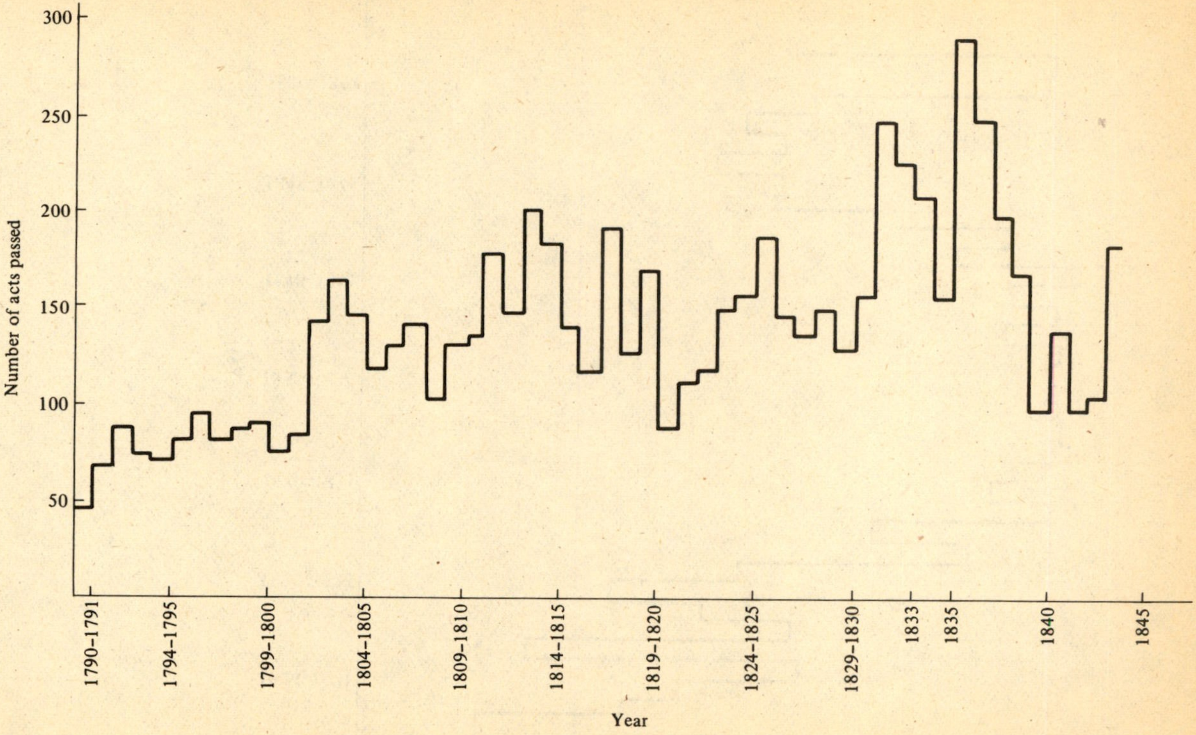

With increased participation, individual citizens and groups also stepped up the actual demands made on state government. After 1800 the amount of business done by the legislature rose above earlier levels, and the number of acts passed by the General Court tended to be highest during the years 1811–1815 and 1830–1837, roughly paralleling the high points registered by other indices of participation and attention.

Indeed, the roughly similar contours over time of the rates of voter participation, town representation, and legislative activity suggest a political system of considerable cohesion and interrelatedness. In addition Figures 1–4 chart, in a sense, the passage of Massachusetts's political culture from an eighteenth-century polity of normally low participation to the much higher levels of citizen activity associated with nineteenth-century politics.

### The Case for Parties, 1805–1815

The outpouring of voters in the period 1805–1815 has constituted an important part of the case that many historians have made for the existence of a "first party system" during the years from the 1790s to the 1820s. Great emphasis has recently been placed on *party competition* and *organization* as independent variables, while such things as voter turnout and legislative activity have been regarded as dependent variables. That is, organized competition acted as a dynamo generating voting and other kinds of participation. Although historians have not devised a way of measuring organization and treating it quantitatively, the historical literature certainly shows that organizational efforts by Federalists and Republicans rose and fell roughly in the same pattern as did the other indices of participation already examined.[47] Historians who stress the modernity of the Federalists and Republicans, their potency as organizations, and their break with earlier politics tend to give the party organizations most of the credit for stimulating voter turnout and political excitement generally. This book takes a different view. It maintains, instead, that organization, while having some independent effect on voting, was itself a dependent variable influenced in the short run by political events in the nation and state, and in the long run by changing social conditions and communications technology.[48]

Later chapters will consider in some detail both the Federal-Republican and the Democratic-Whig organizations, and will show the basic differences between them. The chiefly quantitative evidence being considered here, however, offers grounds for seeing both divergence and similarity between the two periods, and at first glance it provides an understanding of why many observers have chosen to emphasize the existence of well-established parties before 1820.

The simple division of the statewide vote for governor during the years 1800 through 1845 displayed features that focus attention on the elections from 1805 to 1815. Observing the annual state elections during 1800 to 1820, when Maine was part of Massachusetts, one notes that elections from 1805 through 1812 were closely contested: the percentage differences between the parties ranged from only 0.9 percent to just over 3.0 percent (Appendix II, Tables 1 and 2). When Maine is excluded and the fourteen counties that remained Massachusetts are observed from 1800 through 1826, a less competitive pattern emerges, but the years 1805–1812 still stand out because they brought a string of relatively close elections, in which the percentage difference between the parties was under 10 percent (Appendix II, Tables 3 and 4). Moreover, comparing the gubernatorial vote for parties appears to indicate that the earlier period generated closer elections for more years than did the period 1827–1848. The percentage differences between major parties fell blow 10 percent only in 1836, 1839, 1841, 1842, and 1843 (Appendix II, Tables 5 and 6).

Like the state division of voters among parties, interyear correlations of partisan percentages for counties and townships also show more stability in the earlier period. County correlations for the Federalist and Republican gubernatorial votes are quite high from 1800 through 1819, though it should be added that high correlations for a low number of cases (fourteen) are not necessarily significant. *Township correlations,* however, involving approximately three hundred towns, are just as high for the years 1800–1824. From 1805 through 1820 both the Federal and Republican interyear correlations never fall below .900. Later parties reached comparably high correlations only after 1826, and those were slightly lower (though all above .870) than those of the Federalists and Republicans. Correlations of the presidential vote show a similar pattern (Appendix II, Tables 7 and 8).

What does this mean? The correlations suggest that areas of Federalist support, for example, remained fairly constant during the quarter century from 1800 to 1824 and that towns voting strongly Republican in 1800 were likely to be doing so in 1811, 1820, and 1824. From this it can be inferred that *individuals* in the towns tended to vote along the same lines through the years and that these voters may thus be said to have been demonstrating party loyalty.[49] Such a conclusion and such a chain of inference are common in the literature of political history.

Yet the existence of party loyalty cannot be established solely by quantitative evidence. While extremely helpful in establishing the contours of political behavior, indices such as those examined here take on meaning within their historical and cultural context. Party loyalty is essentially a matter of names, symbols, and identities, and the historian needs to know what these were and to determine what candidates called themselves, what the names meant, and how far and deeply party consciousness pervaded the electorate. Correlations alone do not "prove" these things, though they do provide clues about when to look for relevant evidence. There were regions of Massachusetts, for example, which always found themselves on opposing political sides from the 1780s to the 1810s and 1830s and down to the late nineteenth century—but that does not necessarily mean that political organizations or the same party loyalties continuously existed in those regions.

Let it be granted, however, that the interyear correlations, along with turnout and other data, create a strong presumption in favor of the "first party system" thesis, especially for the years 1805–1815. Other quantitative evidence argues in favor of the view that the Democratic-Whig era constituted the more radical break with the eighteenth century.

In Massachusetts, as in other states and in the nation's capital, party organization tended to originate in the legislature and to be organized from the center outward. A good deal is known about the organizational offshoots which concentrated on contesting elections, but unfortunately there exist no studies of the Massachusetts General Court as an institution or of party development within the legislature.[50] It has been possible, however, to make a simple count of the frequency of roll-call votes in the legislature after 1800. Such votes were rare in the eighteenth century and their number remained low through the first three decades of the nineteenth, rising slightly in 1806, 1808, and 1811, and falling off after that. There appear to have been roll calls during only one year from 1815–1816 to 1825–1826, but scrutiny of the manuscripts in the Massachusetts Archives indicates that some roll calls were taken during that time and that records of them did not survive. Thus, though the data are incomplete because of vagaries in the sources, it is safe to say that roll calls in the Federal-Republican era remained infrequent and uncharacteristic. After 1834, however, the legislature, influenced by Whig-Democratic partisanship, departed from eighteenth-century practice and held many more roll-call votes.

Information depicting *incumbency* patterns in the General Court presents a similar picture of change after 1820. Banner claimed that changes in incumbency ratios unsettled politics after 1804, as turnover rose and

Figure 5. Roll–Call Votes in Massachusetts House, 1790–1848

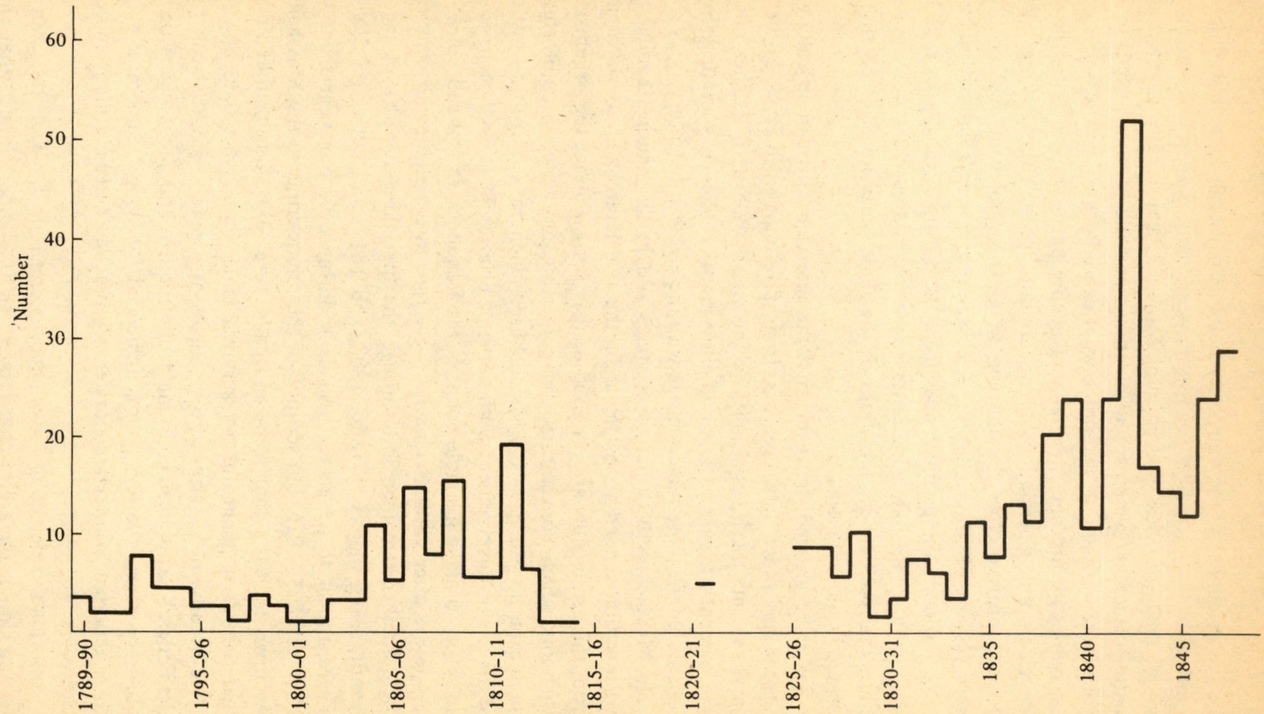

unpredictable new members showed Federal party managers the "p[illegible] of republicanism."[51] But Figure 6 shows that incumbency levels did no[illegible] go down substantially until after 1815. Turnover then remained high (though political interest was low), and in the 1830s rose still higher, depressing incumbency further.

This way of measuring incumbency does not take into account the fact that many men did not return to the legislature in consecutive years but served several times, say, in the course of five years or a decade. Thus a consideration of incumbency over several years can correct the tendency of annual readings to exaggerate turnover, and it provides another way of contrasting different periods. A calculation of "actual turnover" for three periods, 1800–1803, 1809–1812, and 1835–1838, for five selected counties resulted in very similar findings for all five counties. Four of the five had higher rates of turnover in 1809–1812 than in 1800–1803, and all five had still higher turnover in 1835–1838 (Appendix II, Table 9). These findings and Figure 6 both suggest that while nineteenth-century patterns quickly became different from those of the eighteenth century, the late 1830s also differed significantly from the Federal-Republican era.

The most dramatic divergence between the Federal-Republican and Whig-Democratic periods arises from a consideration of competitiveness within towns, that is, of the degree to which towns voted for a party. In the 1790s, as noted earlier, some towns still voted as whole units, and they continued to do so into the early 1800s. A look at changing patterns of competitiveness from 1800 through 1844 can be revealing.

"Competitiveness" is a relative concept, and political scientists give it varying definitions. In general it is a relationship between two leading political rivals, and measures of it give a sense of whether each election is up for grabs or whether one party usually wins and the runner-up ordinarily has little chance of winning.[52] Criteria of competitiveness vary, but many observers maintain that a habitual percentage of 60 percent or more renders an election unit noncompetitive. A more conservative approach has been adopted here; three higher thresholds of competitiveness have been used and graphed across time—80 percent, 75 percent, and 65 percent (Figures 7, 8, 9). The prominent feature of all three measures is the contrast between the years 1800–1824 and the Democratic-Whig era. The data suggest that consensual traditions remained relatively strong in many of Massachusetts's towns and cities through the first three decades of the nineteenth century but deteriorated rapidly thereafter.

Another way of approaching competitiveness is to look at the distribution of towns in given years grouped according to their degree of support

Figure 6. Massachusetts House Incumbency, 1790–1844: percentage of members returned each year from

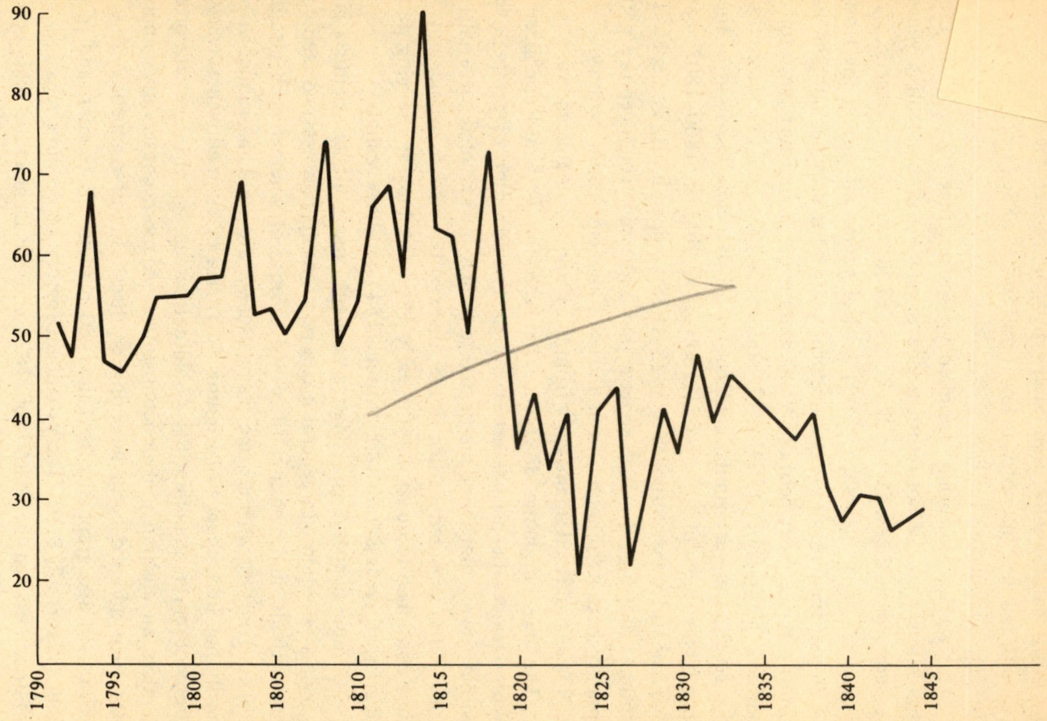

**Figure 7.** Party Competition in Massachusetts Towns, 1800–1844: 80% threshold of noncompetitive towns

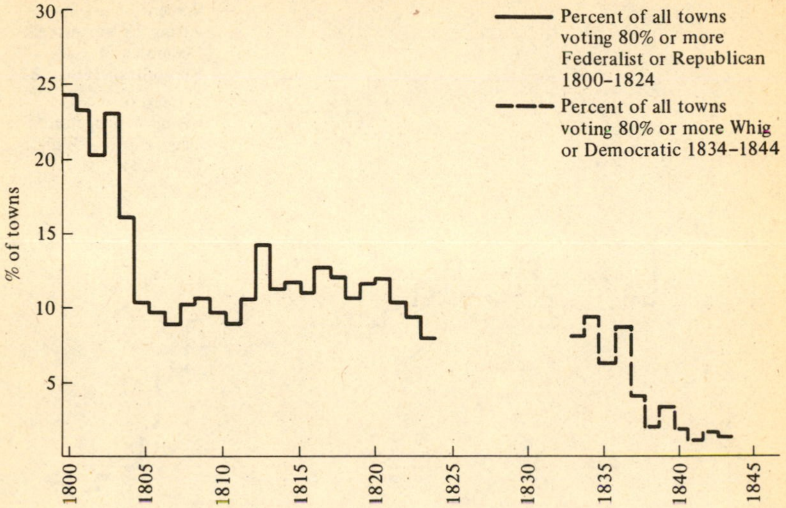


for a particular party: 0–19 percent, 20–39 percent, 40–59 percent, 60–79 percent, and 80–100 percent. When these cross-sectional distributions are arranged in histograms, a contrast just as dramatic appears between the Federal-Republican and Whig-Democratic eras.

The patterns in these histograms reveal rather striking differences between the Federal-Republican and Whig-Democratic eras. The 1800 histograms are almost U-shaped, while the curves of 1805–1815 are much flatter than the peaked, dramatic curves of 1840 and of 1844. Of course this reflects the tendency of more and more towns to become less one-sided and of internal competition to grow as traditions of consensus weakened steadily.[53]

If towns were more lopsided in the period 1800–1824 than in 1840–1844, were the masses of voters more imbued earlier with partisan loyalty? It is difficult to say, but in earlier years towns, and individuals, were also more erratic in their voting, despite the high interyear correlations observed for the Federal-Republican period. Indeed, Figures 10, 11, 12 and

**Figure 8.** Party Competition in Massachusetts Towns, 1800–1844: 75% threshold of noncompetitive towns

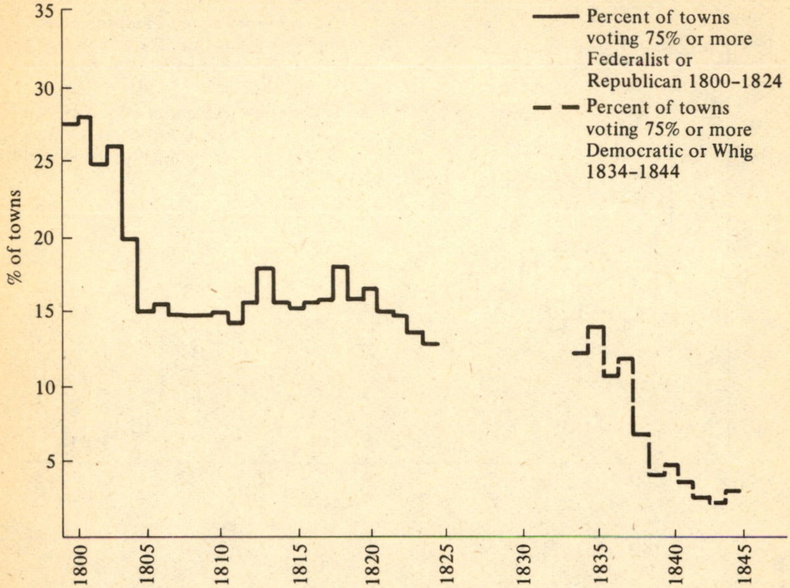


13, which show the extreme tilt of many towns, suggest that the high interyear correlations obtained then are to some degree an artifact of the extreme values of those distributions. This inference is supported by the standard deviations, which fall from almost 34.00 points in 1800 to just over 21.00 points by 1811 and 1820, then after rising briefly fall to 22.00 again in 1831 and keep falling after 1834 until they go below 14.00 in 1844. Thus, there was a greater amount of variance during the period 1800–1820 and further reason to believe that the interyear correlations then are artificially high (Appendix II, Table 10). The question whether earlier voters were more partisan than were post-Jacksonian voters is not easily resolved by quantitative data, and some of the ways in which the early national period looks more partisan may be matters of appearance only.

**Figure 9.** Party Competition in Massachusetts Towns, 1800–1844:
65% threshold of noncompetitive towns

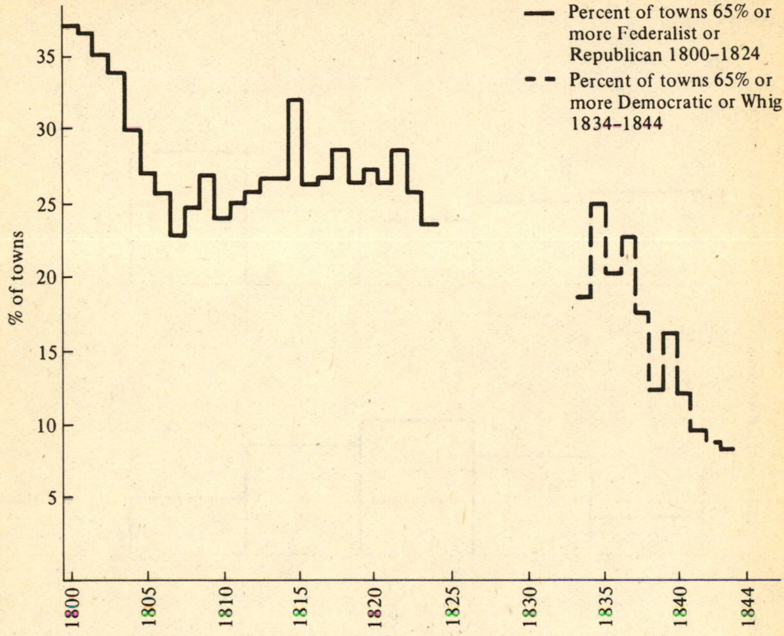


## Conclusions and Questions

The data assembled here in graphs, tables, and histograms have imparted information and raised questions. That the nineteenth-century world of politics differed from that of the eighteenth century is beyond doubt: the difference between a small pony and a full-grown hippo is obvious even if one is looking only at the skeletons. That political culture changed in the first several decades of the nineteenth century is a reasonable conclusion to draw from the foregoing. How, just *when,* and why it changed are questions that will be explored in the pages that follow. The quantitative evidence bearing on the issue of whether the Federalists and Republicans constituted a "first party system" has turned out to be somewhat incon-

**Figure 10.** Distribution of Federalist Vote, Governor, 1800, 1805, 1811, 1815.

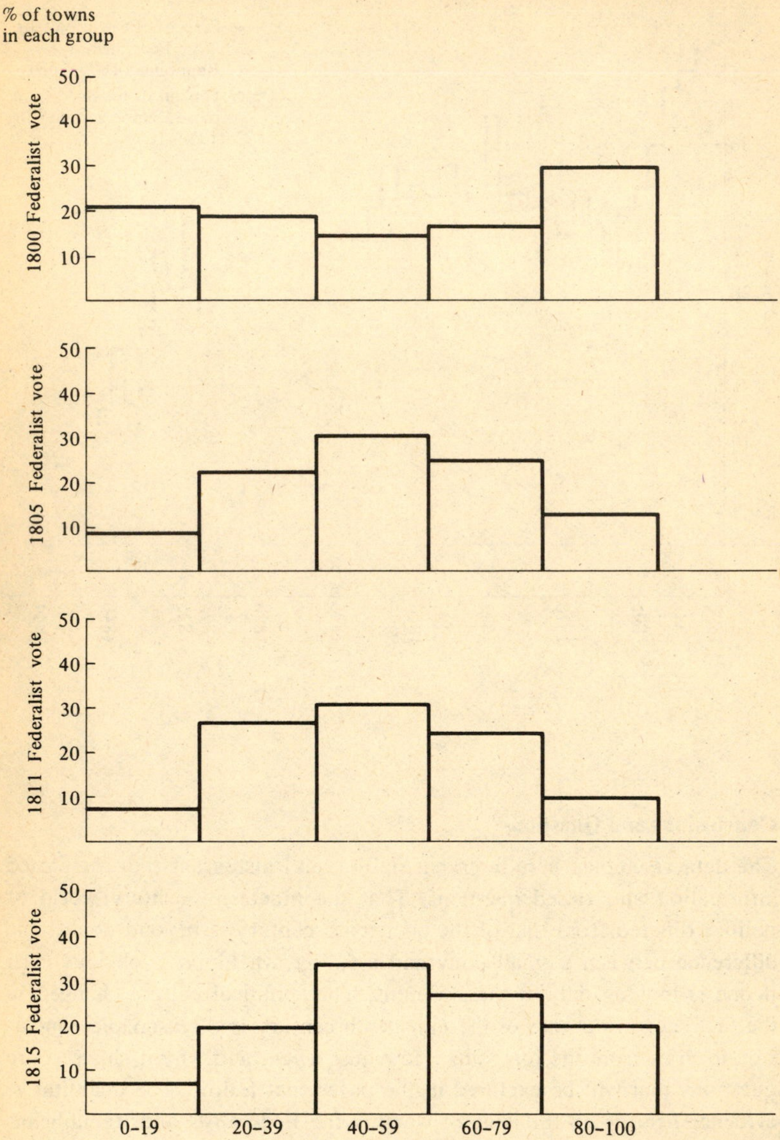

**Figure 11.** Distribution of Republican vote, Governor, 1800, 1805, 1811, 1820

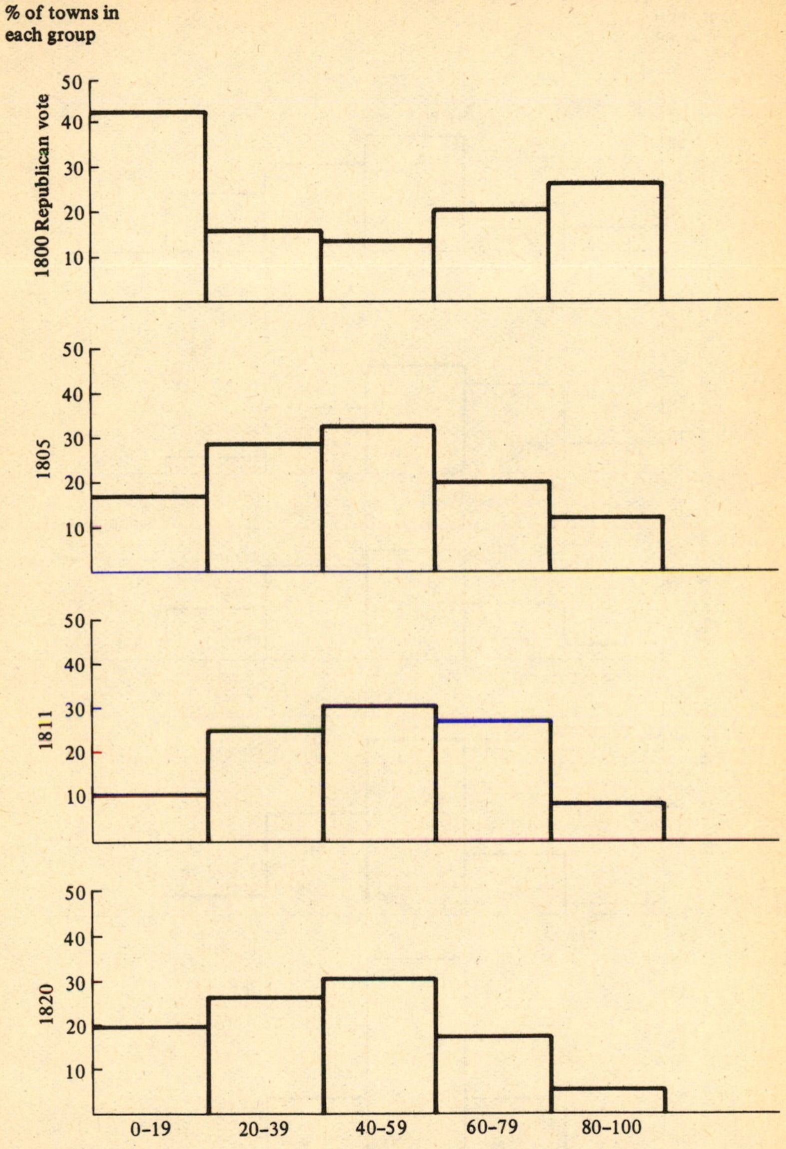

Figure 12. Distribution of Federalist vote, Governor, 1820, 1824, and Whig vote, 1834, 1840, 1844

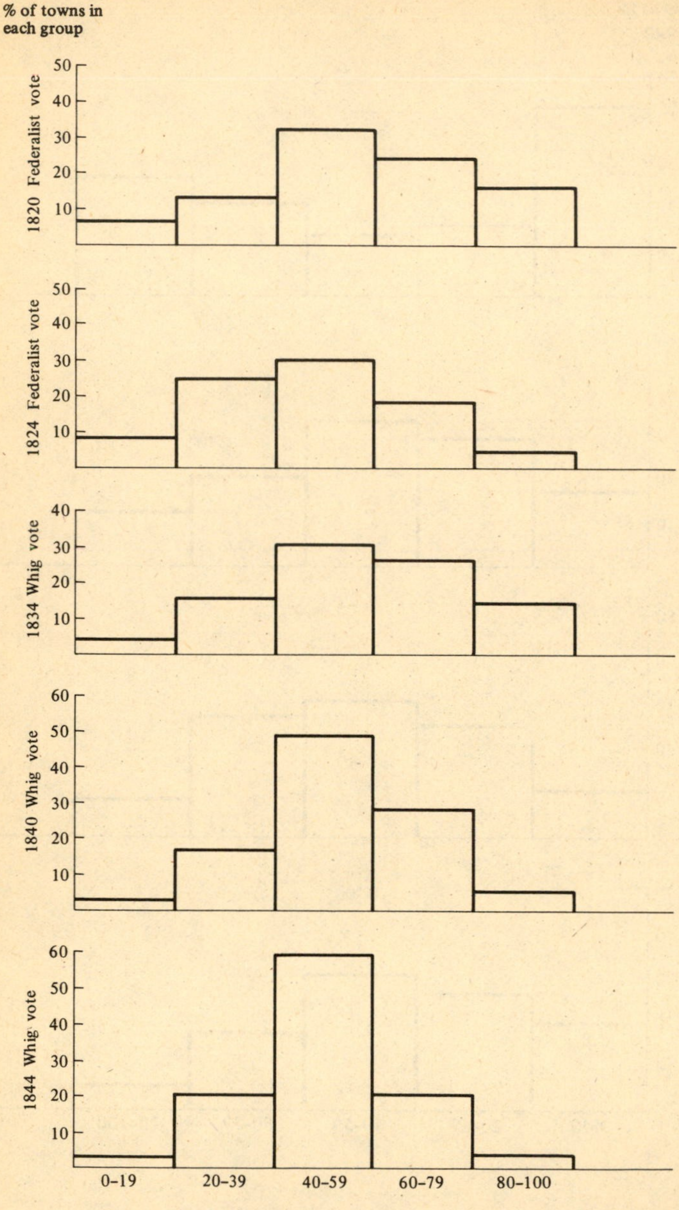

**Figure 13.** Distribution of Republican vote, Governor, 1815, 1824, and Democratic, 1834, 1840, 1844

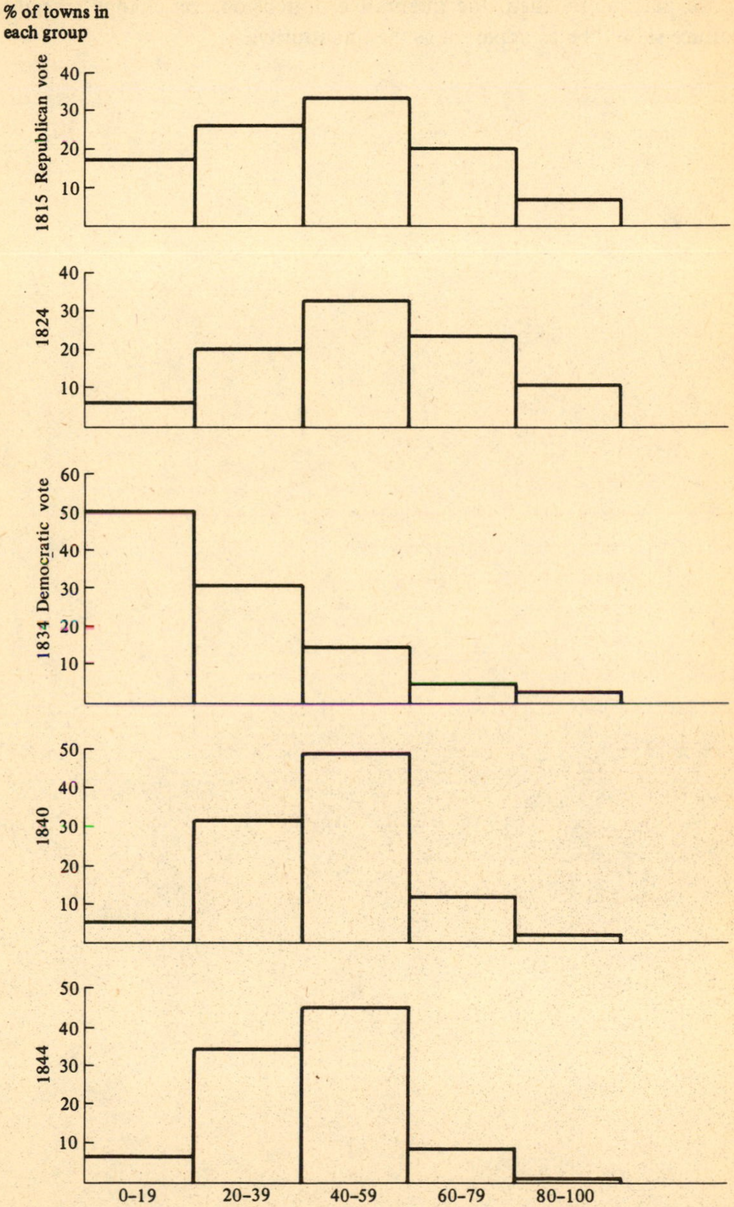

clusive. In subsequent chapters the nature of those early, transitional parties will be explored and eventually compared with the Whig and Democratic parties. By then, the qualitative dimensions of change in political culture should be as apparent as the quantitative.

**PART ONE**

# Federalists and Republicans: *The Revolutionary Center*

## III. The Politics of the Revolutionary Center

> The Patriot Samuel Adams [former Governor] . . . lived in Winter Street. . . . In 1800 Gov. Strong being chosen and the usual Election Sermon was to be preached. The Procession moved from the Present State House, Beacon Street, and passed down Winter Street—when opposite the Patriot Adams House—Mr. Adams at his Front Door made a respectful bow to Gov. Strong—who immediately left the Procession. . . . Gov. Strong went to Mr. Adams and with a sincere and hearty shaking of hands expressed a few words and then resumed his place in the Procession. This was emphatically a Great Event. Mr. Adams was a Patriot of the Revolution and held to his Democratic or Republican Principles. Mr. Strong though not so conspicuous a character—yet he was also a Great Spoke in the Revolutionary Wheel—and imbibed and carried with him in all matters the Federal Principles. Thus, then, two Antipodes in Politics, were Brothers, they were Americans, they loved their Country, and took different Roads to gather materials for building her imperishable Fame.
>
> —Marginalia by Thomas Jackson of Boston, February 8, 1841, in Alden Bradford, *Biography of the Hon. Caleb Strong* (1820), Widener Library.

### The Sacred War

The Revolution divided the people of the colonies into passionate factions, and in some places division flared into violent civil war. Yet by the end of the eighteenth century most Americans revered the Revolution as a Sacred War. Though they might disagree about the implications of its heritage, the event itself was a fountain of meaning for the national identity and a point of universal consensus for an already diverse population. Historians have neglected, however, the presence of the Revolution in everyday life up to the Civil War, and especially its influence on political life through the early national period.

It was not only that Federalists and Republicans were, despite their ferocious political competition, all republicans, sharing a basic ideological heritage, but also that service in the Revolutionary War or in public life in the 1770s and 1780s identified a man inextricably with the center of politics, whatever his views on particular issues. This powerful fact of political life has been obscured both by partisanship and by Federals and

Republicans who themselves took it for granted. While the rivalry of "Jacobin and Junto" was real, as were Republican fears of monarchy and Federalist fears of anarchy, both sides knew that the populace revered the Revolution and that political success depended on an appeal to the Revolutionary Center.

That the Revolutionary generation occupied the presidency for this period has long been obvious. Less well recognized has been the legitimacy that the Revolutionary mantle conferred on public officials of all kinds, and especially on state executives. The most popular governors of the early national era represented the legacy of the Revolution or personified it in their careers. As a result Revolutionary Center politics contributed to an ethos at odds with a party system.

The Revolution stayed with Americans for a long time, and references to it did not necessarily decline with time. Orators, novelists, popular writers, historians, and politicians all drew heavily on its events and heroes for example and imagery. By 1820 only four of the signers of the Declaration of Independence still lived, and combat veterans were in short supply. But communities across the nation made do with the "heroes" they had, no matter how minimal their connection with the actual war. Indianapolis regularly included in its Fourth of July celebration an old soldier who had actually been a British mercenary![1]

A Revolutionary past helped open the door to high state office. As an unschooled Massachusetts maverick observed in the 1790s, after revolutions establish free governments the few leading men in that project "can neaver [sic] receiv compensation & honours anough from the people for their services, & the people being brought up from their uths to reverance and respect such men they go on old ways & neglect to search & see for themselves & take care of their own interists. . . . They redily hear to measures proposed by grate men who they are convinced have done them good services."[2]

Thus it was that several members of the Revolutionary generation dominated Massachusetts's elections for governor, not only in the late eighteenth century but well into the nineteenth. In the 1780s and 1790s John Hancock and Samuel Adams occupied the executive chair for a total of fifteen years; Bowdoin and Sumner, the latter dying in office, another five. From 1800 through 1822 two Federalists, Caleb Strong and John Brooks, won election to fifteen terms. While three different Republicans won office during that period, two of them, significantly, died in office. The Politics of the Revolutionary Center relied heavily on men of the Revolutionary generation or on those who followed quickly in their footsteps. Strong,

Brooks, and their rivals resembled one another and their counterparts in other states more than they differed from them, whatever their party association. They were heroes of the Revolution and symbolized the Revolutionary Center. Those who best symbolized it proved the most popular and enduring candidates, provided they were blessed with long lives and a willingness to keep "standing" for office.

The most popular leaders had an image of not lusting after office and not liking political dealing. Several in fact possessed moderate temperaments which helped lift them above contending parties in the public eye. As an early historian observed of Strong and Brooks, though they were "of" the Federal party, "they could not justly be considered party-men."[3]

It may be objected that popular middle-of-the-roaders are not at all unusual even in a normal, two-party system in which parties are always bidding for independent or moderate votes. During the heyday of parties in late-nineteenth-century Massachusetts, for example, the minority Democrats tried to overcome their lack of numbers by nominating Republicans or independents for high office: "Elderly judges were in particular demand."[4] Early national politics differed in many ways, however, the most vital being that both parties pursued a centrism derived from the Revolution.[5] The most effective candidates for high executive office combined moderation and a reputation for having been "tried," as a Republican newspaper put it in 1800, "in the fiery furnace of our late glorious revolution, and been found faithful."[6]

The Revolution's aura lingered over both the ceremonial and the commonplace. It hardly surprises that Fourth of July orators addressed themselves to the Spirit of '76, but many other speakers on all kinds of occasions, public and private, also recalled "the glorious era . . . [when] men of purest and most active patriotism came forward into the public service."[7] Reverence for the Revolution continued unabated in the 1820s. Indeed, it may have increased as the last giants of the past slipped away—or departed spectacularly, as when John Adams and Thomas Jefferson both died on July 4, 1826. As ordinary Revolutionary veterans became fewer and more infirm, they seemed in even greater demand. Lafayette's visit in 1825 had something to do with this, but deeper impulses were already at work. The quickening of social change also may have helped in that it increased the sense of distance from the Revolutionary world. As transportation and communications improvements thrust men forward into a new present, "men talked much of the past." And the Revolution loomed largest in that past.[8]

In 1831 when William H. Seward made a political visit to Boston Antimasons, his hosts led him about from shrine to shrine of the Revolution and identified themselves with its sacred principles. Sixty years later Thomas Wentworth Higginson recalled what Revolutionary memories were like for a boy in Cambridge in 1830. The town, he said, "was especially full of its asociations." Here the first provincial congress met, there the committee of safety, here on February 1, 1775, the second provincial congress.

> In Christ Church . . . the company of Captain John Chester was quartered, after the battle of Lexington, and a bullet mark in the porch still recalls that period. . . . All these things were traditional among Cambridge boys. . . . We all knew the spot where Washington took command of the army. . . . We played the battle of Bunker Hill on the grass-grown redoubts built during the siege of Boston. . . . Moreover, there still lingered one or two wounded veterans whom we eyed with reverence. . . . The houses of Tory Row still stood in isolated dignity, some of them suspected . . . of being connected by secret underground passages.[9]

The Revolution's aegis protected veterans who held minor government sinecures, often until death or advanced infirmity. In one case, immunity from removal even extended to a hero's son. As late as 1836, Revolutionary "veterans" were made much of on holidays and regularly rounded up by political organizers to decorate party rallies.[10] An observer of an 1835 Bunker Hill celebration in Worcester County said "there were two or three pews stuffed full of survivors," four of whom had been at Bunker Hill, and he supposed they "will be carted about the country as long as their bones hold together."[11]

Time dictated that Revolutionary symbols and meanings would change, but from the 1780s to the 1820s those symbols remained powerfully effective in political rhetoric. Candidates, factions, and parties used them in a variety of ways. Both Republicans and Federalists claimed to be the true party of the Revolution, just as both claimed to be true to the Constitution. The Federalists, however, favored their image as the constitutional party while the Republicans more often defined themselves as "the party of the revolution." It was characteristic of nascent Federalist partisans in 1798 to don Revolutionary black cockades as emblems "of their attachment to government." It was just as typical of Republicans to accuse Federalists of betraying the Revolution: "There is not a single principle of the revolution," said a Republican in 1805, "which is not in direct opposition to their politics."[12] Republicans appealed far more to the Revolution as an action establishing liberty, and they liked to idolize Revolution makers like Samuel Adams and John Hancock. The Federalists appealed more to the Revolution as part of an extended process which created the American government, and they celebrated Revolution consolidators like Hamilton. Both parties revered Washington, of course, but Republicans tended to exalt "the Revolutionary general" while Federalists preferred "the cold and correct President."[13]

In the rivalry for possession of the Revolutionary Center, Fourth of July celebrations became politicized, and Republicans and Federalists held separate festivities, even in small towns. Republicans used the occasion to stir up Anglophobia, as the Democrats would do later, and a Federalist orator in 1812 blamed the war of that year on the tendency of one party to "monopolize this anniversary" with hatred for England and thereby to ensure the "success of their party."[14]

Yet while Republicans and Federalists embraced different elements of the Revolutionary tradition, the fact remains that the struggle for legitimacy promoted centrist appeals which inhibited the forming of well-defined political parties. Republicans frequently tried to attract votes from "honest Federalists," while their opponents appealed similarly to "considerate Republicans"—and both often spoke directly to "moderates," or "independents," or the "uncommitted."[15]

In the antiparty ethos, both centrist tactics and the novelty of parties made for fluidity in partisans' self-identification. This latitudinarian attitude toward political names lasted through the period, but the 1800 election for governor perhaps marked its apex.

The last of the eighteenth-century governors had died in office. Moses Gill, the lieutenant governor, wished to be elected governor in his own right, and his supporters urged voters to look to men from "the time that tried men's souls" and called him "a venerable PATRIOT of seventy-six." But the caucus of "Federalist" legislators and notables wanted Caleb Strong of Northampton, a former United States senator and also a man of '76. To oppose Strong, the "Republicans" nominated Elbridge Gerry, also a patriot, and the ensuing contest was not at all one between two organized parties.[16]

Each side portrayed its candidate as a Revolutionary hero and as a centrist moderate. The Boston *Columbian Centinel* (the leading Federal paper), compared Strong to that well-known "Republican Federalist" George Washington, while another supporter said that Strong was "a friend to Christian piety," but "no party man." One of Gerry's supporters, calling himself a "Real Federalist," claimed that Gerry, not Strong, truly represented the "principles of '75." While Strong was pursuing a lawyer's trade in a time of peril, Gerry was showing "Washington the *hero and sage* of America . . . his worth." Furthermore, Gerry had never been "a tool of party." Another writer called Gerry an "enemy to Faction" and said he knew "of no person more likely to banish all party distinctions." Gerry was, in short, "an undoubted republican . . . a decided Federalist and an honest man."[17] Such eclecticism reflected not opportunism but a situation in which parties as institutions had never existed and in which men were still sorting themselves out. Gerry opposed Strong, but warmly favored the re-election of his good friend President John Adams!

### The Federalists of the Revolutionary Center

Caleb Strong won the 1800 election and also won re-election for the next six years. Narrowly defeated in 1807, he refused nomination in 1808, but returned in 1812 to run against the incumbent Gerry. Regaining office, Strong presided over the state during the War of 1812, but he refused nomination in 1816 and retired.

Smallpox had impaired his sight and prevented him from being a military man, but Strong was nevertheless a hero of the Revolutionary Center. Among his political assets were his western Massachusetts residence (Northampton) and connections with the Connecticut Valley "River Gods," his Calvinist piety, his gentlemanly demeanor, and, not least, his thoroughgoing association with Revolutionary patriotism. When the Revolution had come to Northampton, Strong had been a young lawyer and selectman. He served throughout the conflict on the town's committee of public safety and continued in public life as state legislator, constitutional-convention delegate, councilor, state senator, and county attorney, while declining a seat in the Continental Congress and appointment to the state supreme court. He attended the Philadelphia convention in 1787 and though he left early gained a reputation as a staunch supporter of the Constitution, which he backed in the state ratifying convention. Chosen United States senator in 1789, Strong supported the policies of Washington and Hamilton, but while consistently sharing "federalist" views, he lacked the "domineering temper and asperties" of the high Federalists. Throughout his career of public service interspersed with retirements and "calls" to return, Strong displayed a moderation exemplified by his graceful greeting to Samuel Adams during the 1800 Election Day procession.[18]

Strong's moderation did not please ardent Federalist partisans, yet they recognized its value in producing majorities at the polls. As George Cabot observed in 1804, "there is no energy in the Federal party, and there could be none manifested without great hazard of losing the state government." Some of our best men, he added, were in office not because they possessed the right principles but because they did not act on them. *"They are permitted to have power, if they will not use it.* It is happy for us that we have a governor whose consummate prudence conciliates opponents without detaching friends, but he will cease to be popular the moment he dares to act with vigor."[19] Strong's reluctance to act made him just the right man to lead Massachusetts during the years of the unpopular War of 1812, when popular sentiment supported his foot-dragging and lack of cooperation with the national government's war effort.

Strong's supporters emphasized that he was a consolidator of the Revolution. He was, said his eulogist, no firebrand, but, like Washington, was steady, sober, and persevering. Firm in his opposition to the English, he was yet one revolutionary who "never denied the necessity of social order and constitutional authority."[20]

The Governor's piety and his "country" roots gave his friends ample opportunity also to dwell on his "unostentatious, republican simplicity." In 1805 Josiah Quincy urged Strong's re-election as a man of "humble, modest, intelligent deportment, abounding with unostentatious goodness, kind manners, and a countenance and conduct the most benevolent and attractive." Some sophisticated Federalists considered Strong a country bumpkin, but Quincy turned any possible prejudices against Strong on those grounds into an invidious comparison with Strong's Republican rival that year, James Sullivan:

> I know it has been said, that Gov. Strong is too frugal, that he rides down to Boston in the stage, or in a sulkey. That he does not dine the members of the General Court, in Boston, as often as Gov. Hancock did. And we are told that things will be mightily altered when Judge Sullivan sits in the chair; who lives in a great house, in the capital, and has already very frequently . . . entertained, very splendidly, all the leading republicans of both branches; and moreover . . . to exemplify, when he gets into the chair, *sound republican principles,* has, since the last election, got a superb equipage, and put his servants into new livries, all in green, trimmed, if I am not misinformed, with lace.[21]

When Strong retired from office in 1816, the Federalists turned to a man of even plainer republican simplicity. John Brooks, who thereafter won election for seven terms, was an authentic Revolutionary War hero and came to personify the nonpartisan "Era of Good Feelings" in Massachusetts. Although an easterner from Medford, Brooks had, like Strong, local roots and had maintained them while serving as a public official.

The son of a farmer, trained as a physician, Brooks was unusual even among post-Revolutionary executives in the fullness of his military career. At twenty-three he had captained some minutemen who harassed the redcoats in April 1775, on their costly retreat from Lexington and Concord, and had served with distinction throughout the war. He fought Burgoyne at Saratoga, wintered at Valley Forge, stood by Washington during the darkest hours, and by 1783 was a lieutenant colonel on the inspector general's staff. In 1786 Brooks marched again, as a major general of the Middlesex militia, called out to show force against the Shays rebels. In 1791 Washington appointed him federal marshal for Massachusetts and in 1792 a brigadier general of the U.S. Army.

In succeeding years Brooks's name frequently appeared before the public: as president of the Society of Cincinnati, the Massachusetts Medical Society, the Massachusetts Bible Society, and the Washington Monument and Bunker Hill Monument associations. In 1816, therefore, he was relatively new to electoral politics but enjoyed a quick and enduring success. After his inaugural the house welcomed him as "a patriot of the same school" as Governor Strong, "who had so ably contributed to the establishment of a free and enlightened form of government."[22]

Brooks encouraged the growth of "good feelings" by being "not exclusive in his appointments to public office"; his opponents could not charge that "he conducted as the head of a party." And when President Monroe came to Boston in 1817 on his visit of reconciliation, he said that he had read Brooks's latest inaugural with complete approval. So it was that Brook's "very name seemed to disarm party spirit with talismanic power."[23]

Brooks resembled Strong in his lack of close ties with the "Essex Junto" Federalists, and he seems to have been regarded as standing closer to the western Federalists and being more a representative of the Orthodox Congregationalists. The importance of Brooks's image as a country moderate and a pious Christian in the Strong mode was suggested by what happened after he decided to retire. In 1823 the Federalists nominated an urbane Boston Unitarian associated with Federalist partisanship, Harrison Gray Otis, and went down to a defeat that was the beginning of the end for them as a coherent political force.[24]

The Federalist demise of 1823–1824 was foretold during the last days of Brooks's reign by a Federalist offended by Brooks's moderation. "Our politics here are rapidly changing," this critic said, "and we only want some call on the Passions of the People to produce a change in the Rulers of the State. The great moderation & mediocrity of all that composes the

Executive . . . will for sometime insure his Reelection. What used to be the Federal Party died long since by Suicide."[25]

It was no accident that this jaundiced view of Brooks in 1822 came from Christopher Gore, the only other Federalist governor in this period, who won office briefly by defeating a Republican partisan in 1809 but who failed of re-election in two attempts against a Revolutionary Center Republican.[26]

Though talented, rich, and high-minded, Gore lacked the basics to become a commanding figure of the Revolutionary Center. He was too little a man of the Revolution and too much of a partisan. Nevertheless, Federalist campaigners claimed the Revolutionary mantle for Gore, pointing to his associations with Hancock and Washington and boasting that his public life was "begun in arms, in defense of the Liberties of his . . . Country."[27] The only military service which Gore had performed, however, was clerking for an artillery regiment during 1776–1778, preparing its payroll, and writing its colonel's reports while he finished his senior year at Harvard and then studied law. His political career began in the late 1780s when as a young lawyer of reputation he emerged as an ardent proponent of a strong federal government. Apart from becoming known as strongly federalist, anti-French, and anti-Jeffersonian, Gore distinguished himself primarily by amassing a great fortune while still a young man. He then quickly and smoothly assumed the posture of an eighteenth-century Great Man, becoming known for his magnificent residences, liveried servants, and fine coaches and carriages. That Gore enjoyed political success, too, testifies to the continuing strength of deference and the limits of democratic impulses after 1800. But Gore's failures in politics also reveal his lack of a genuine base in the Revolutionary Center.

Tradition and historians have linked Gore's serving only one term to his aristocratic character, and especially to a single incident in his year as governor. The story has been often told how Gore and his wife went off on an extended tour through the Commonwealth in grand style, sitting "in an open carriage, upholstered in red hammer cloth and pulled by four long-tailed bays; the coachmen and outriders wore bright livery, and the Governor's aides formed a mounted escort." Federalists greeted them with parades, salutes, and toasts, but Republican newspapers compared him to "an English prince or noble, dashing down among his tenants before an election." Historians have attributed Gore's defeat to a presumed offense given in this manner to the democratic sensibilities of his constituents.[28] While it is impossible to know how the tour affected the next two elections, it does deserve to be remembered as epitomizing the man's character.

Republican newspapers made the most of Gore's English tastes and often descended to calling him a Tory. Gore's family had in fact been divided by the Revolution; his brother Samuel, a brawny artisan, was an active Son of Liberty, while his father, John, was so devoted to the royal governor that in 1776 he received the Revolution by fleeing to Halifax. John, son of a carpenter, had been a merchant-mechanic whose livelihood depended on the patronage of Tory aristocrats; he painted coaches and designed coats of arms for colonial officials and gentry who came to him from as far away as Philadelphia. Though the elder Gore returned after the war and became a citizen, his son Christopher was always haunted by the charge of Toryism.[29]

His obvious Anglophilia not only invited such accusations but also worked against his enjoying popularity as a figure of the Revolutionary Center. Gore's career had little of the heroic about it, except when it came to making money and using it to gain status at the top. He served as a representative in the General Court for two terms and as a "federalist" delegate to the state convention of 1788. President Washington rewarded Gore's strong-government views by appointing him U.S. district attorney, a post which Gore held for several years but which began with a controversy that revealed Gore's elitism. Though other members of the legislature who had received federal appointments had resigned their seats, Gore did not. The state constitution, he observed correctly, prohibited multiple holding of state offices but said nothing about federal offices. The legislature, however, believed that the spirit of the constitution should apply to a man holding both state and national office simultaneously, and the legislators pressured Gore into resigning.[30]

While never a "popular" man like a Hancock or Strong, Gore was admired by his contemporaries for his intelligence and skills as a lawyer and above all for his great wealth. Gore first made money in law by settling the estates of former loyalists in Nova Scotia and by establishing good relations with merchants in Britain. He was especially skilled in suits involving debt collection, and he enjoyed the patronage of rich London merchants. But real riches came to Gore by speculation in government securities in partnership with the notorious Andrew Craigie. With aid from the Massachusetts State Bank (established 1784) and from Hamiltonian financial policy, Gore became the richest lawyer in Massachusetts. By 1789 he had already bought a Boston mansion with stables and separate kitchens, staffed it with four servants, and begun to indulge his taste for fine horses and carriages. Soon even John Adams would regard the Gores as part of a newly risen "nobility."[31]

The coach painter's son not only acquired wealth and its accoutrements but also turned himself into a rich gentleman who successfully acted the part of a Great Man, "cold and correct," with all the pretensions of the *haut bourgeois*. The young Daniel Webster, who never had a small opinion of his own person, found Gore impressive enough to be overawed and felt lucky to be chosen to apprentice in his law office. His peers seemed to regard Gore not as a nouveau but as a natural representative of the upper class, and historians have logically done the same. Perhaps his ardent support of "high Federalist" policies throughout the period reinforced the social position Gore assumed. But arrival at the heights of social class did not make Gore the complete popular leader, as it might have made a similarly able man in the eighteenth century–the Revolutionary mantle was lacking.

Gore was the classic Federalist: he called for strong measures against Shaysites in the 1780s; strongly criticized the Democratic-Republican societies of the 1790s; supported Jay's Treaty; advocated close ties with Britain; opposed Jefferson and criticized slaveholder domination of the national government; and completely identified with Federalist commercial maritime interests and their opposition to Republican foreign policy after 1806, the embargo, and war with England. In 1796 Gore left the country to serve as a claims commissioner on the Anglo-American board created by the Jay Treaty, and in the next eight years he would visit the United States only once. When he did return, in 1804, Gore took up residence at a magnificent country estate which he built in Waltham. There he lived, according to his biographer, in the style of an English country lord. His church was fittingly Boston's King's Chapel, which during Gore's long membership changed from Episcopalianism to Unitarianism.[32]

In 1804 Gore also plunged into efforts to elect Federalists to office and served several terms as a member of the Federalists' secret state central committee. Disdainful of popular prejudice, as ever, Gore boldly undertook the defense of Thomas Selfridge, a Federalist lawyer who had shot and killed the eighteen-year-old son of the Republican Austin when the young man had attacked him on the street with a cane. The trial attracted enormous attention, and when Selfridge was acquitted the Republicans loudly denounced the Federalist judge and the defendant's influential lawyers. The reaction, however, did not keep Gore from being elected state representative and then senator from Federal Boston. In the legislature he emerged as a leading opponent of Jefferson's foreign policy, and in 1808 Gore ran for governor against the Republican incumbent

James Sullivan and lost. Sullivan died in office, and Lieutenant Governor Levi Lincoln, a more partisan Republican, became Gore's next opponent in 1809. John Adams observed, "Both candidates are unpopular. Party alone will decide. . . ." With the aid of economic hardship and great discontent caused by the embargo, Gore beat Lincoln. This was to be his only triumph for a major electoral office. With the embargo removed and commerce revived, Gore could not gain re-election in 1810 or 1811 against the old patriot Elbridge Gerry.[33]

Competition for legitimacy within the Revolutionary Center tradition was particularly intense during these years, in part because the Republicans freely appealed to anti-British sentiment as a weapon against Gore. The Federalists countered this by associating Gore with the Revolution, Washington, the Constitution, and Christianity. But Republicans probably had the better candidate and a highly vulnerable target in Gore. "Whose carriage is that," asked Boston's leading Republican newspaper, "that rolls so majestically through the street, decked in scarlet and gold? One might as well elect the Duke of York."[34]

Gore's defeats did not end his political career. In 1813 Governor Strong appointed him to a vacant Senate seat, and a Federalist legislature, appreciative of Gore's well-known opposition to the War of 1812, enthusiastically endorsed him. In Washington, Gore continued his sustained criticism of the war against England. He warmly approved, though he did not attend, the Hartford Convention. When the war was over and partisan feelings were rapidly declining, Gore stayed in the Senate little more than a year, then resigned in 1816, well before his term was out. Sickness speeded his withdrawal, but it was also fitting that Gore retired from politics as party heat cooled in the "Era of Good Feelings."[35]

## The Republicans of the Revolutionary Center

The two principal Republican challengers of the Federalists during the years before 1812 were Elbridge Gerry and James Sullivan. Both personified the Revolutionary Center. Both were moderates. Though after 1810 Gerry became embroiled in partisan warfare, the overall careers of these two men are strikingly similar to one another and, indeed, to those of their Federal counterparts Caleb Strong and John Brooks.

James Sullivan first entered the lists against Strong in 1804. His victory three years later represented a vindication of moderation and a triumph of Revolutionary Center politics. While a more complicated man than Strong or Brooks, Sullivan also enjoyed a close identification with the

Revolution. In its formal reply to his inaugural address, the senate, even though Federal, immediately acknowledged the "conspicuous part, which your Excellency was called to act, on the great theater of our revolution." At the same time Sullivan seemed to embody all the traits often associated with Republicans: he was a liberal in church-state relations and civil liberties, a self-made man and entrepreneur, an intellectual, and very much an "outsider."[36]

Sullivan, like Strong, was a public-political man of the Revolution, not a military hero. Physical disability, in this case lameness, had kept him out of warfare. It is significant that the early biographers and eulogists of Strong and Sullivan are the source of information about their handicaps, while twentieth-century historians have ignored them. But in the nineteenth-century it was important to explain how a public man could have been eminent in the Revolution without having borne arms.

Sullivan was thirty when the Revolution began, and king's counsel for York County in his home district of Maine. He rapidly became identified with the "patriot" party and served in the provincial congress of Massachusetts and on many committees, including the committee of safety. Appointed to the state supreme court in 1776, he moved in 1778 to Groton and served throughout the war as jurist and legislator. On resigning from the bench in 1782, he moved to Boston and was promptly elected to Congress. During the 1780s and 1790s Sullivan usually allied himself with John Hancock, and in 1790 the governor appointed him attorney general. In that office Sullivan earned a reputation as a liberal in championing the rights both of religious dissenters against the Congregational establishment and of editors accused of sedition or libel. In religious matters, according to one authority, Sullivan "was equalled only by Levi Lincoln as an advocate of liberal interpretation of the Constitution."[37]

By the time of his election as governor, the lame youth from the Maine woods typified the Republican as outsider risen to wealth, respectability, and learning. He had made money as a lawyer and was a leading promoter of the Middlesex Canal. He was one of the first members of the American Academy of Arts and Sciences and a patron of the theater in a town where ministers denounced performances of Shakespeare as immoral. His career even contained a dash of radicalism. In 1793 he had joined Boston's Constitutional Society (one of the Democratic-Republican societies which Washington denounced), and though he resigned after two years, the man's credentials as a representative Jeffersonian could seemingly not have been better.[38]

Yet Sullivan can no more be described as a partisan than can Caleb

Strong. In 1800, for example, he wished for a reconciliation of Jefferson and Adams and for a union of "constitutionalists" to oppose Hamilton and the high Federalists. His early biographer said that although he unequivocally backed Jefferson in 1800, "his correspondence shows that he had never been in full fellowship" with either Federalists or Republicans.[39] Though a confidential ally of Hancock, Sullivan supported the federal Constitution in 1787 and later continued as attorney general, after the Federalists had taken control of the state government. Indeed, from the 1780s onward Sullivan's career was marked by moderation and attempts to mediate between intense partisans. He opposed the Shaysites, but also earned thanks from some of the rebels by undertaking their legal defense. Similarly, as attorney general under the Federalists, Sullivan dutifully prosecuted a libel case against a Jeffersonian editor but then took to the newspapers to criticize the principle involved. Still, Sullivan was not, as he sometimes claimed, neutral in politics. When his son William announced himself in a Fourth of July oration in 1802 as a Federalist, giving "great offence to the republicans," the father published a series of letters in Boston's leading Republican newspaper, so "that there will be no misapprehension of his own political views."[40]

Sullivan's moderation was nowhere more clearly evident than in religious matters, in which, according to William G. McLoughlin's revisionist view of Sullivan and the Republicans generally, he took a position "squarely between that of the ardent Federalist defenders of the establishment (lay and clerical) and the ardent opponents of the system, the dissenters."[41] Personally a "moderate Calvinist" who changed gradually to Unitarianism, Sullivan from the 1780s on consistently defended majority rule in the churches and favored the parish over the church, but never advocated separation of church and state. He defended the rights of dissenters and took every opportunity to criticize the Federal clergy's mixing in politics, but Sullivan wished to make the Standing Order tolerant, not to overthrow it. In his first inaugural (1807) Sullivan said that the Massachusetts constitution "excludes all persecution and intolerance on principles of religion and modes of worship," but he proposed no laws to relieve the grievances of dissenters. Sullivan reflected well what McLoughlin called the Republicans' "studied ambiguity on the question of religious taxes."[42]

In politics, too, Sullivan was an eighteenth-century moderate. Far from accepting parties, he recommended in 1802 that the Jefferson administration make "every exertion . . . to destroy the lines of party distinctions." "I am gratified," he wrote to Congressman William Eustis, "when I see members sometimes voting with one side and sometimes with the other." He also urged that Jeffersonians do everything possible to placate New England *sectional* interests in order to remove the grounds of "party division."[43]

As governor, Sullivan pursued a centrist course consistent with his eighteenth-century antipartisan attitudes. Though the high Federalists never trusted him and contemptuously scorned him as "whiffling," even they recognized his lack of partisanship and his distance from what they called "violent Democrats," such as Levi Lincoln.[44] Meanwhile, Sullivan, in his public statements and in his patronage policy, appealed to moderates on both sides. Like others of his type, he did not believe in the patronage ethics of a party system. As he said to Eustis in 1802, removing men from office for their opinions "is a species of tyranny of which we have loudly complained." And he went further: "To withhold offices from men who are satisfied with their country's constitution, because they do not love the present administration, when they are *better* qualified than others, would be no less than a militation with the principles of a free government." As governor, Sullivan apparently made good his word, and Republicans complained of his helping Federalists to get federal jobs by sending letters to the president "without consulting his friends . . . he has repeatedly erred in the same way." On the other hand, Sullivan fed office-hungry Republicans by reorganizing the courts of sessions and claiming the right to specify attorneys for the Commonwealth at the expense of county courts, all of which provided places for political brethren, as did his commissioning of many new justices of the peace.[45]

In 1808 he again demonstrated his concern for New England interests. After the passage of the embargo, deeply hated in Massachusetts, Jefferson allowed the governors of states that consumed more flour than they produced to issue "certificates of confidence" for flour they needed to import in order to prevent any hardships. The administration asked the governors to route certificates to "merchants in whom you have confidence." Sullivan issued so many of these certificates that one Federalist merchant described his as "unnecessary." Christopher Gore crowed that "Sullivan gives a Certificate to whomever applies for permission to import Flour; his son George taking only one dollar for the Certific." By the fall of 1808 this practice was so notorious that President Jefferson asked Lieutenant Governor Levi Lincoln to investigate the matter for him, observing caustically that "Governor Sullivan's permits are openly bought and sold here and in Alexandria, and at other markets."[46]

Though Federal hard-liners remained unappreciative of Sullivan, they clearly had little to fear from him. Back in the 1780s Samuel Adams had criticized Sullivan's mentor John Hancock for his "lavish hospitality and profuse expenditure," and similarly Josiah Quincy later contrasted the allegedly pretentious style of Sullivan with the "republican simplicity" of Caleb Strong. Sullivan patterned himself on the Hancock model, and at his Boston residence after 1783 he gave gala "hospitalities." The onetime outsider from Maine also dressed meticulously "in accordance with the prevailing fashion . . . with great care and elegance. His hair was daily powdered, and his lace ruffles, silk stockings, polished shoes and buckles, were always scrupulously neat."[47] This was a man who could, while telling about his fears of Federalists' regaining national power and changing the Constitution, complain that the people are incapable of self-government "and cannot maintain social order, unless, to use [Fisher] Ames' expression, the steel is in the hands of the civil magistrate, in the form of a bayonet."[48]

### Elbridge Gerry and the Irony of Antipartisan Politics

After Levi Lincoln's defeat by Christopher Gore, the Republicans nominated the Founding Father Elbridge Gerry, and in doing so they placed themselves squarely on the Revolutionary Center and also put forward even more of an antiparty man than Sullivan. Thanks to George A. Billias's superb recent biography, Gerry can now be understood fully in the context of his time. Earlier commentators were not only overly impressed with the superficial aspects of his career but accused Gerry of "inconsistency" because of their own anachronistic belief in the advanced state of parties in the early Republic.

Gerry's career as a public man of the Revolution, signer of the Declaration, Constitution maker, presidential envoy, and diplomat is well known. It showed, as Billias put it, "a rather remarkable adherence to the beliefs of the men of '76."[49] But Gerry's attitudes toward party and his stormy career illuminate brilliantly the politics of the Revolutionary Center in its complexity and contradictions, far more, for example, than does James Sullivan's consistent moderation. Gerry's career, including the partisanship of its last phase, after 1810, shows more clearly the continuance of a nonparty and antiparty ethos from the eighteenth century.

Gerry has often been thought of as an eccentric. "Poor Gerry," his friend Abigail Adams once said, "always had a wrong kink in his head." The merchant from Marblehead signed the Declaration but did not, alas, sign the Constitution. The fact is that Gerry as a congressman during the first two Congresses became a strong supporter of the new government. Anyone wishing to see continuity from the factions of the 1790s to the Federalists and Republicans later must contend with Gerry's independent stance, his support of Hamiltonian finance, and his simultaneous friendship with Hancock and Sullivan. According to Billias, Sullivan was Gerry's closest political adviser during his congressional years. As a presidential elector in 1796, Gerry voted for his friend John Adams but meanwhile hoped to reconcile Adams and Jefferson. In the late 1790s he came to fear Hamilton and the Federalists who sought war with France as a great danger to republican institutions, but stuck by Adams in 1800 even as he accepted the Massachusetts Republicans' nomination for governor, still hoping, however, for an Adams-Jefferson rapprochement.[50]

Gerry's moderation, antipartyism, and relationship with John Adams helped make sure that the 1800 gubernatorial election was no party contest.[51] In 1801 Gerry again just barely lost to Strong while partisan labels remained ambiguous. Fisher Ames had even feared that the defeated Federal president Adams would be "the jacobin candidate" for governor. Gerry's friends, however, put him forward as a "no party man" and "an inflexible patriot of 1775."[52] Gerry then retired from politics for a few years, surfacing in 1804 to act as presidential elector for Jefferson. The bitter contention which arose over Republican foreign policy after 1806 brought Gerry back into politics and into a contest for the governorship. In the Gerry-Gore test of 1810, political organizations mobilized voters to a degree unknown ten years earlier, but the struggle was in essence a competition to capture the Revolutionary Center. Gerry's reputation for patriotism and his Republican partisans' use of the Revolutionary aura helped propel Gerry into office. The Federalists, to be sure, claimed this heritage for Gore, but Gerry's credentials far outweighed Gore's as the "STATESMAN and the PATRIOT *of the Revolution,* whose talents and firmness were conspicuous in those *'times that tried men's souls.'* " Gerry was the " 'VETERAN OF THE REVOLUTION, THE SAGE OF '76.' " Even the Federalist senate, in replying to Gerry's first inaugural, recognized in the new governor "the man who so eminently contributed by his revolutionary services, to establish the independence, and secure the peace and prosperity of our country."[53]

During his first term Gerry acted as the moderate and nonpartisan centrist he had always been. His inaugural echoed Jefferson's inaugural of conciliation by inviting men of all political positions to unite. The lesson of our Revolution, he said, showed that union was vital to liberty: "Had a party spirit then prevailed, it would have been fatal. . . ." He asked every friend of his country to recognize " 'that an house divided against itself cannot stand' " and to "determine for himself to relinquish a party system, and the practices of misrepresenting, and unjustly reprobating, his political opponents." Gerry did more than talk. He kept Federalists in office who might have been replaced, and he ignored insults hurled at him by arrogant Boston Federalists–all to the dismay of some hard-line Republicans. A number of the latter even feared that the Federalists would nominate Gerry in 1811 in order to try to split the Republicans.[54]

In a short time such fears totally evaporated. The 1811 election grew exceedingly acrimonious, and Gerry came into office for his second year bristling with anger at the Federalists, whom he accused of reviving party spirit. This signaled the end of Gerry's centrism and the start of an extraordinary partisan administration, highlighted by the Republicans' attempt to cripple Federalist electoral strength with changes in election districts–an attempt that gave rise to the term "gerrymander," though the practice had a long history. The significant thing about Gerry's second inaugural, however, was that he announced his own dramatic shift under an *antiparty* banner. He still saw himself as a no-party man, now forced to act by the irresponsibility of a fanatical party. This was not hypocrisy but the natural perception of an eighteenth-century man who did not accept political parties as normal.

During 1811, besides gerrymandering state-legislative and congressional districts, the Republican legislature passed a number of "reforms" which their leaders had demanded for years. This legislation sought to open up the traditional establishment by making several institutions less exclusive and more representative of a broader range of social groups. From the legislature, therefore, came laws liberalizing the religious tax law, widening banking opportunities, broadening the directorship of Harvard College, and reorganizing the courts. At some points "reform" became political warfare, for example, when the lawmakers gave the governor new appointive powers within the court system and also authorized him to appoint new sheriffs, justices of the peace, and inspectors. And amid the howls of the Federalists, the legislature blatantly gerrymandered election districts for the state senate. Though the Federalists had played similar games, they had not done it so obviously.[55] The Republican majority also removed all restrictions on voting in town elections in the expectation that this, too, would aid their cause, and for the same reason it incorporated many new towns. Gerry probably had little to do with originating these measures, since pressure groups for some of them had existed for years and since he had shown little interest in most of them previously.[56] Yet Gerry shared at least the spirit of the Republican crusade. Stung by rabid Federalist criticism in the press and in an anonymous threatening letter, Gerry ordered his attorney general to examine Boston newspapers for libel and to bring offenders to trial. Though his administration secured only ten indictments and three convictions, Gerry pressed hard on this front, denouncing the licentiousness of the press and calling for stiffer laws.[57] His attitude to the press, like that of most of his contemporaries, both Federal and Republican, revealed that he did not think in terms of a legitimate opposition. Gerry had not so much changed abruptly into a partisan politician as remained fiercely committed to earlier ideals.

The great contrast between Gerry's two terms demonstrated powerfully the irony of antipartisan politics. While Gerry's second term broke sharply with his first—"as different as night and day," according to Billias—Gerry carried earlier antipartisan beliefs into the anti-Federalist outburst of 1811–1812. Gerry had always believed that the extreme Federalists posed a constant danger to Republican institutions. In the spring of 1811, Boston Federalists triggered this fear in Gerry by holding a mass meeting and issuing bold and inflammatory protests against the most recent laws governing trade with Great Britain and France.[58] Gerry reacted by claiming that he had tried to act in the past year with "impartiality, moderation, and justice" and that this seemed "to have allayed that unrelenting party spirit, which when indulged, has never failed (on the ruins of liberty) to establish despotism." But a few towns, and especially "our metropolis," including many of its respectable citizens, had rejected moderation. Boston, indeed, had passed resolutions not only denouncing laws of the United States as tyrannical and oppressive but claiming that any citizen might construe them as he wished. The Federalists had, in fact, made a veiled threat by calling for measures "short of force" and for the election of officers who would "oppose by peaceable, but firm measures, the execution of the laws, which if persisted in must and will be resisted." Gerry pounced upon this; he exclaimed that if these things could be, then "our constitutions are nullities, our constituted authorities are usurpers, and we are reduced to a state of nature."[59]

Gerry flatly announced that his appointments policy would change. In the past year he had reappointed every officer "who has been correct in his conduct . . . disregarding his politics." But no executive could be expected to neglect his "sacred obligations" to the point of keeping in office those who would "abuse the influence of their public characters, by sanctioning resistance to law, or by other such conduct, as will beguile peaceable and happy citizens into a state of civil warfare." His patronage policy became immediately partisan in several areas.[60]

In spite of all this, Gerry still closed his message with a prayer to God to banish party spirit forever and to induce all sides to embrace each other as Christian brethren. Even several months later, on January 8, 1812, Gerry delivered another legislative message which, while hostile to extreme Federalists, invoked yet more strongly the antiparty ethos of Jefferson's first inaugural. Anticipating now that war with Great Britain lay ahead, Gerry asserted that no reason remained for the continuance of party spirit. Only the remnants of an "anti-revolutionary party" or "royalists" who had taken on the name "Federalists" kept alive party spirit. Gerry complained of "internal enemies" and of a "polluted press, that flaming Ætna of party spirit."[61] Yet even while making an immoderate attack on his opponents, Gerry simultaneously called for a dissolution of parties: "Since . . . there no longer exists a cause for party spirit, in regard . . . to the *Federal Constitution,* or to the *two great Belligerents;* since our disputes with one are adjusted in part, and the residue thereof is in a train of amicable negotiations; since our concerns with the other are reduced to a point, which presents to us this choice, the alternative of *justice or war,* does not our country demand of us, *as her right,* to immolate contention on the altar of liberty, and to consecrate at her shrine a COALITION OF PARTIES?" Most Federalists, of course, did not regard war with England as acceptable, but Gerry obviously saw no validity in that view. "For the honor of the nation . . . let us now terminate an unnatural, dangerous, and disgraceful *spirit of party,* and again convince our internal and external foes, 'that we are all *Republicans,* that we are all *Federalists.*' "[62]

Historians have thought that Gerry's partisanship cost him re-election to a third term. While that idea fits well with the thesis presented here, the election was close and turnout very high, making it difficult to weigh the impact of the Republicans' policies. They certainly stirred voters, but so did the approaching war with England. Whatever the reasons for the election's outcome, a reputation for partisanship could be a liability for public men during this period.

This seems to have been the case with Levi Lincoln, the unsuccessful Republican candidate of 1809. On the one hand, Lincoln fit the model of the Revolutionary Center public man. A 1772 Harvard graduate and lawyer, he had just settled in the small town of Worcester when his public life began with the Revolution. After a short tour in the army besieging Boston, he returned to serve on Worcester's committee of correspondence and became an ardent patriot propagandist, writing a popular newspaper series known as "A Farmer's Letters." Lincoln then held many local and state offices and won election to Congress in 1800. He also gained fame as an able trial lawyer; in the 1780s he had worked together with Caleb Strong in presenting arguments that helped bring slavery to an end in Massachusetts.[63]

By the time of his election to Congress, Lincoln had emerged as an outspoken critic of the Adams administration and as one of New England's leading Jeffersonians. In 1801 Jefferson appointed him U.S. attorney general, and he served in that office until 1804, then returned to state politics and won election to the governor's council. In 1807 and 1808, Lincoln became lieutenant governor, then acting governor on Sullivan's death, before failing of re-election in his own right. By 1809, Jefferson's embargo had revived a sinking Federal party throughout New England, and Lincoln had not been as conciliatory toward the opposition as Sullivan had been.[64] When it fell to President Madison in 1812 to nominate a Supreme Court justice, Jefferson suggested his old friend Lincoln as the foremost New England candidate for the post, but Lincoln refused because of failing eyesight. He spent his last years as a gentleman farmer in Worcester, venerated as an aged patriot, learned man, and scientific farmer.

Though Lincoln's career was successful by any measure, he failed to emerge as a popular leader of the Revolutionary Center. He never won the governorship on his own, and the Republicans nominated him only during his incumbency. The Federalists, meanwhile, detested Lincoln for his extreme Republicanism, thinking him radical in beliefs and fanatical as a partisan. Yet Lincoln was neither a radical nor a fanatic. He had risen to the heights of social respectability by hard work and an advantageous marriage into a prominent Federalist family of Worcester. His farm resembled, according to contemporaries, an English manor, and Lincoln conducted himself as a public-spirited member of the local gentry. In 1809 John Adams described him as "one of our old whigs and a man of sense and learning." Yet Adams knew, too, that Lincoln was unpopular, and mentioned in particular his having given offense to the clergy and grieved "multitudes of our good Christians."[65] This occurred in a pamphlet of 1802 which Lincoln wrote attacking the Federal clergy for political meddling, and defending Jefferson and the Republicans against charges of irreligion. But what made Lincoln so offensive to Federalist leaders was less his anticlericalism than his role as an adviser to Jefferson on patronage matters in Massachusetts and New England. For a time Lincoln had great power to decide who would keep, lose, or gain office. Both he and

Jefferson wished to follow a policy of moderation, and neither wished to give credence to Federalist charges that Jeffersonians were mere office seekers. But Jefferson knew that the pressure for removals would be great, and some Republicans did agree with Jacob Crowninshield of Salem, who avowed that "Mr. Jefferson ought to displace every federal officer in Massachusetts." Jefferson told Lincoln, however, that appointments would depend on "deaths, resignations, and delinquencies." But, he added, any Federalist officeholder who engaged in electioneering against the administration would be fair game for removal. In 1802 Jefferson asked Lincoln to identify for him such "prominent offenders in your state in . . . the present election. I pray you to seek them, to mark them, and be quite sure of your ground that we may commit no error or wrong, and leave the rest to me."[66] Lincoln's role as majordomo of Jeffersonian removals and appointments in Massachusetts explains a good deal of the Federalist hatred of Lincoln, and of his reputation as a partisan.

Yet Lincoln was in part a man of the eighteenth century and shared with men like Sullivan and Gerry an antiparty ideal. With Jefferson he looked forward to a dissolving of party spirit and to "the great desideratum, the coalition of parties."[67] Lincoln, however, was not fundamentally an antipartisan. His essays attacking the Federal clergy, for example, showed a cast of mind that set him apart from Sullivan and Gerry. Though capable of appealing to moderate Federals and of lamenting the "virulence of party," he took for granted the existence of Republicans and Federalists as groups in conflict. The *Letters to the People* did not posit a permanent two-party system, but they implied a degree of dichotomous thinking not found among the moderate centrists.[68] As elections in the early 1800s became more fiercely contested, and as Lincoln himself became more frequently an object of Federalist vituperation, his attitudes hardened. He criticized the Republicans for being "too timid and accommodating to their enemies. To those who never will accommodate, but on the terms of an unconditional surrender, there can be no reconciliation, consistent . . . with the preservation of the existing republican system. . . ." By 1805 Lincoln was denouncing "third party men" who, he said sarcastically, had failed to get a man elected to office after describing him as unfit to hold it. Lincoln was "convinced that the republican success depends on a *steady* and faithful adherence to their old men, principles and measures." This was nothing less than disdain for centrism and moderation.[69] Yet Lincoln should not be pigeonholed simply as a party man. Even he shared in some of the ambivalence toward party that characterized the men of his generation; like them, he also lacked any perception of an institutionalized party system. His career, to the extent that it differed from that of a Strong or a Sullivan, helps to illuminate the elements of success for a popular leader of the Revolutionary Center.

A search for qualities making for popularity necessitates a focus on men who won the highest state office. Yet the careers of other leaders, such as Lincoln, who did not become popular chief executives or who served near the top, also demonstrates the power of the Revolutionary heritage and the appeal of moderation. This was particularly true of Republican nominees, as might be expected, since the Republicans were a challenging minority with a greater need to establish legitimacy. Revolutionary service alone was not sufficient to elect Republican hopefuls. In 1817, for example, the Republicans put forward General Henry Dearborn, who was not only a "soldier of the Revolution" but also commander in chief of the army in "the second contest for independence [War of 1812]." But the Federal incumbent at this point was John Brooks, and Dearborn must have appeared to many to have a me-too quality.[70] The Republican strategy oscillated between two poles: that of nominating men thoroughly identified with their cause (Lincoln's advice) and that of backing moderate centrists. The latter was, as argued here, the more successful. In pursuing this strategy, Republicans showed a flexible and pragmatic willingness to push forward, in the first or second places on their state ticket, men identified with neither party, or former Federalists, or even a man who still considered himself a Federalist.[71]

## The Last of the Old Patriots: William Eustis

After Gerry's defeat in 1812, the Republicans, no matter whom they nominated, could not dent Federal command of the chief executive's office. When they finally did break the grip of the Federalists on state elections, they did so with a man of the Revolutionary Center.

During the "Era of Good Feelings," the Republicans made only half-hearted efforts to defeat John Brooks and, incidentally, to elect William Eustis, whom they offered three times (1820–1822) before he won in 1823. When Brooks declined to be a candidate, the way lay open to Eustis. The Federalists cooperated by nominating a man far less popular than Brooks, Harrison Gray Otis. The Boston Federalists loved Handsome Harry, and the seacoast mandarins of the Federal establishment knew he was essentially a moderate who deserved the office. But aside from other drawbacks Otis had a reputation as a partisan and was too much of an eastern Federalist to unite his own political friends. More to the point here, Eustis was now the better candidate, standing almost in the succession to the Revolutionary Center.

In 1823 the Republicans' address to the electors said virtually just that. Observing that in recent elections "the republicans" had made only "feeble" efforts, they conceded that the Federal administration had been moderate. Furthermore, "the public services of the chief magistrate in the revolutionary war, were felt and acknowledged by the people. Having aided in the establishment of American freedom, although associated with its enemies at a season of peril, he was still believed to be a friend and supporter of . . . American freedom. . . . Hence his political identity with the federal party was considered rather nominal than real, and his election was not zealously contested by the great body of the republican party of the State."[72] But after Brooks had bowed out, the question of whom to elect was "free and unencumbered." And the Republican argument came simply to this: Otis was no Brooks, Eustis *was*.

After Eustis's election a leading Republican paper attributed his victory to the coming of age of a new generation of voters who were moved by two powerful influences. One was the popularity of "Democracy"; the other was the persisting influence of the American Revolution, whose examples taught the love of liberty and union and thus had turned the new generation against Federalism. The young saw in the latter a mere British faction while "Democracy is the cause of the Revolution, of mankind."[73] However young voters cast their ballots in 1823, this editorial placed Eustis's election victory squarely in the Revolutionary Center.

It was fitting that Eustis should have been the last governor of the Federal-Republican era in Massachusetts, because he was so much a man of the Revolution and of the Center. The son of an eminent physician, Eustis attended Harvard and then studied medicine with the Revolutionary hero Dr. Joseph Warren. When Warren fell at Bunker Hill, Eustis continued his work throughout the war as a patriot physician. In the legislature in the early 1790s, Eustis became identified with support for religious dissenters and joined the Constitutional Society. Yet his peers believed that Eustis was a Federalist at heart, and even Fisher Ames claimed that Eustis was a moderate who went into the democratic movement "to prevent greater mischief."[74] In 1800, as a candidate for state representative and then for Congress, Eustis successfully appealed to both Republicans and Federalists—he was the only Jeffersonian whom Boston sent to Congress that year. His stint from 1801 to 1805 drew praise from James Sullivan for its nonpartisanship. Eustis's friendly relations with Federalists, on the other hand, irritated Levi Lincoln, who described the good doctor as "pleasant and accommodating, as usual, to all, apparently the object of attention of both parties."[75] Eustis was Republican enough for Madison to appoint him Secretary of War in 1809 and later, in 1813, minister to the Netherlands.[76] Eustis again represented Boston in Congress from 1819 until his election as governor.

In 1823, as in 1800, the Republicans believed that both Federalists and Republicans would support "the Patriot and supporter of the American Revolution." The nominating convention claimed that he now held his congressional seat "by the almost *unanimous vote of the Federalists and Republicans of his District.*"[77] After a convincing re-election victory over a weak Federalist opponent in 1824, Eustis might have held office for a long time if he had wished. But he was seventy-two years of age by 1825, and in February the eulogists once more lamented, "Another patriot of the revolution is gone."[78]

Eustis had enjoyed wide popularity as governor, despite his having come into office with an inaugural address blistering with criticism of Federal actions during the War of 1812. In his appointments, however, Eustis was conciliatory. Before taking office, he had assured the retiring Brooks, an old crony of his, that he would "not make more removals than the public good required." Though initially alarmed by Eustis's inaugural, some Federalists holding state offices grew relieved as they kept their jobs. Indeed, Eustis continued his pattern of social relations and friendships with both Republicans and Federalists.[79]

Finally, Eustis was no harbinger of an egalitarian era but, rather, still very much a man of the eighteenth century. He had, according to a contemporary, an "aristocratic bearing." On returning from the Netherlands, he bought a mansion in Roxbury built around 1750 by Governor Shirley. It was an elegant building, with extensive servants' quarters, a large lawn and landscaped grounds, and was "suitable for a mansion of a governor." Before taking office, Eustis rode around in a one-horse wagon, but afterwards he "kept a very handsome coach." Eustis also entertained guests at dinners and parties in a style reminiscent of that of his friend Governor Sullivan and of the latter's mentor Governor Hancock.[80]

## The Center Is All: Levi Lincoln, Jr.

While Massachusetts was witnessing election contests between Republicans and Federalists in 1823 and 1824, most of the nation's politics had long since collapsed into a "Republican ascendancy" in which most important political struggles took place between different factions of Republicans.[81]

In 1824–1825 the old divisions finally departed from Massachusetts, or at least they no longer structured electoral competition as they had for some two decades. John Quincy Adams's election to the presidency, by putting a Massachusetts man back at the nation's helm, gave the final blow to the almost atavistic political rivalry which had outlived its reason for being. In the 1825 election, Republicans and Federalists united on a single candidate for governor, and the Center became all—at least at the top. This consensus governor, furthermore, though not of the Revolutionary generation, won re-election for eight consecutive terms in the manner of the popular Revolutionary Center leaders. It was at once ironic and most appropriate that the union of Federalists and Republicans finally came to Massachusetts under the titular leadership of Levi Lincoln, Jr.[82]

The irony lay not only in the fact that the son did what the father had scorned to do, but also in the fact that Levi the younger had himself started political life as something of a partisan. Born in Worcester in 1782, Lincoln had no connection with the Revolution except his father's name. The Harvard graduate and young lawyer entered the state senate in 1812 at the height of partisan acrimony, urged that Massachusetts give stronger support to the war effort, and denounced the Federalists' Hartford Convention. Lincoln adjusted, however, to the new currents abroad during the "Era of Good Feelings," and by the time of the constitutional convention of 1820 he was already emerging as a moderate. Indeed, two years later his "tact and independence" won him election as speaker of the house, though that body was Federalist. He made an excellent running mate for Eustis the next year, and after a brief stint as lieutenant governor Eustis appointed him to the state supreme court. While he was on the bench, Eustis died and the Republicans asked him to be their gubernatorial nominee in 1825. Lincoln himself aided the process of coalition by insisting that he would not accept a nomination from only one party. He became essentially a Republican nominee, however, in whom the Federalists acquiesced.[83] At the polls, voter turnout fell by almost half, but Lincoln gathered over 35,200 of some 37,400 votes cast, or 94 percent.

Not until the fall of 1831 did any serious opposition to Lincoln materialize, and even at that no single candidate opposing him ever received more than 30 percent. But his own vote fell to 53 percent in 1832, while *two* challengers got 24 percent and 23 percent each, and Lincoln decided to leave the governorship. Significantly, he did not at all retire from politics, which shows the emphasis he had placed on centrist politics and on being a consensus chief executive. He went on to several terms in Congress, to the collectorship of Boston (1841–1843), and to the state senate, and in 1848 he became Worcester's mayor after its incorporation as a city. Like so many other Republicans of the Center, Lincoln, who was described as "retaining the manners of the first part of the century . . . 'a gentleman of the old school,' " became a Whig. Indeed, his governorship effected the transition from Republicanism to National Republicanism, and thence to virtual Whiggery in its ideology and policy. More will be said about Lincoln's governorship in later chapters; it need only be observed here that by the late 1820s it was basically a National Republican, proto-Whig administration with which former Federalists and centrist Republicans felt quite comfortable. That development grew logically out of the Republicans' centrist strategy, which had succeeded, in the end, all too well.

# IV. "Party Spirit" and Party: Changing Meanings and Attitudes

The Politics of the Revolutionary Center prospered in a climate of hostility to political parties. It is well known that this antiparty milieu flourished throughout the presidencies of the Founding Fathers and continued to influence political leaders and citizens until well into the 1830s.[1] Indeed, antiparty sentiments have flowed as an undercurrent throughout American history, surfacing especially in periods of party realignment and becoming quite familiar to Americans during the past decade and a half of advanced party decay.[2] If parties are not disappearing today (partly because they are kept alive by artificial life-support systems), the period of extended realignment since the mid-1960s has served to heighten the antiparty strain whose tendency is already to be more intense at times when voters shift about and create new majorities and new minorities. Thus the unusually severe antipathies of the present perhaps come closest in scope and depth to the antipartisan disposition with which Americans first responded to parties during their long genesis.

Political leaders and average citizens overcame their consensual ideals to act in a partisan manner and ultimately to create political organizations, to vote for party candidates, and to work and vote for parties as institutions. Even Federalists and Republicans did this, to a degree, though some of them rationalized partisan action as a means of re-creating unity and consensus in the body politic. By the 1820s, political leaders went beyond the awkwardness of justifying themselves by earlier and inherently contradictory ideals, and began promulgating the virtues of parties and party competition. Some of these men were, significantly, the same ones who touted competition as the best stimulus for economic development.[3] Having come through the passionate struggle of the years before 1815, they drew a positive moral from a situation that had once seemed deplorable but inevitable. This shift from tolerating parties as necessary evils to accepting them as positive goods took place primarily among political leaders, of course, and especially among those whose careers were becoming like those of professional politicians.[4]

This important transition, which both reflected and helped create a shift in political culture, contained within it another important change in perception: not only did new attitudes to "party" arise, but ideas of the thing itself also changed.[5] What Federalists and Republicans had meant by "party" differed from what was meant in the 1840s. This change was necessarily more general, since most citizens shared the same images and metaphors by which they understood the meaning of party, whereas the acceptance of parties was initially limited to public men and political cadres. Politicians unveiled the new doctrine of party's benevolence in the 1820s, and the parties to which it referred were the Federalists and Republicans. By the 1830s, tolerance and acceptance of "party" were far greater than they had been when those early parties formed. After the Whig and Democratic parties became accepted realities, however, another change ensued. Images of "party" by the 1840s were not what they had been in 1810 or even in 1823. Since the thing itself had indeed changed, the "pictures in the mind" which men held of it, to paraphrase Walter Lippmann, had naturally changed as well.

In the Federal-Republican era, the terms "party" and "party spirit" often served the same purpose and were used interchangeably (as were "party" and "faction," though the latter seems to have been more common in the 1790s and earlier). In 1796 Washington had warned against the baneful effects of the "spirit of party," and antipartisan expression after 1800 continued to possess a very eighteenth-century tone and vocabulary. Denunciations of party or parties did not seem to have in mind the kind that came later. Men focused on a cast of mind, an attitude, a disposition, or an emotion. They spoke of the "violence of party spirit," figuratively suggesting a great impersonal force that swept all before it. But though this power was often compared to such natural forces as wind, storm, or fire, at bottom the imagery suggested that men chose to set it loose.

Parties have always been compared to churches. In 1810 "party" was thought of as a community or subcommunity of belief which engendered concerted action and excessive zeal and single-mindedness in public affairs. Its counterpart in religion was a sect. Any means adopted in pursuit of the group's goals, however, were not confused with party itself. Later on, when parties acquired more or less permanent organizations and a much more predictable relation to the structure of government, the analogy with churches still held. Only now parties resembled churches not in their sectarian nature but in their capacity as organized institutions.

## Seasons and Rites

In the early nineteenth century, political culture retained not only an inherent bias against parties but also many of the forms and style of an agricultural and theocratic society. Ceremony, celebration, and sermon remained conspicuously alive. Despite the upwellings of mass politics after 1800, the rituals of public life displayed a very traditional manner. Days of "Public Fasting and Prayer," called by proclamation of the governor, were held frequently in the first three decades but became relatively rare after 1830. Although by the 1790s both public officials and ministers had turned such "days" to political purposes, they ranked as important events in the Federal period and were among the many signs that political life was far from wholly secularized.[6]

The season of "electioneering" came not in the fall but in late winter and spring, and not for presidential elections but for state offices and representatives to the General Court. Politics quickened for congressional and presidential balloting, but the most intensely political season of the year arrived after nominations for the April state election were put forward in early or mid February. The several weeks of electioneering that followed were known as the "snake season," because "it was said the season thawed out the snakes."[7]

The centerpiece of the political year was the "General Election Day," a ritual of transference and inauguration whose antecedents went back to 1634. The polling for governor, lieutenant governor, and state senators occurred annually in town meetings on the first Monday in April, and the house of representatives election usually took place at least ten days before the last Wednesday in May. On the latter date, which was General Election Day, the new government took office amid considerable fanfare. The members of the senate and the house organized themselves in order to choose presiding officers in the morning, then in the afternoon went in procession with the executive to religious services and for the preaching of an Election Sermon. In 1812 Governor Strong's mere arrival in Boston occasioned bell ringing, artillery salutes, and a nearly mile-long escorting cavalcade of carriages and horsemen, and, when his carriage struck the pavement in Boston, "a spontaneous plaudit from an immense population welcomed the Patriot to the town." On such days crowds of all ages gathered from town and country all week long for the celebration. Those who did not come to Boston even in remote rural areas regarded the day as "*the* great holiday of the year, for all classes." On Boston Common, servants, including many blacks, colored persons, and apprentices, enjoyed a holiday of games and liquid stimulants. It was a "gala day, when persons of all ages, complexions, and tongues" mixed in sport and relaxation. Blacks and coloreds seem to have enjoyed their fullest latitude on General Election Day, and this aspect of the celebration as a holiday for the lower classes and castes was known as "Nigger 'Lection."[8]

Just afterwards, during the first week of June, the Ancient and Honorable Artillery Company of Massachusetts held its annual election, and the citizens enjoyed a day at least as colorful. In 1821 some ten thousand persons congregated in sunny weather for an "unusually splendid" artillery election, with a hundred muskets in line, artillery pieces, and a rainbow of uniforms. After breakfast the company paraded to the state house, then to the First Church for the Artillery Election Sermon, then to Faneuil Hall for dinner and endless toasts. The company finally marched to the Common for its "election," and the governor's ceremonial bestowing of insignias on new officers. After escorting the governor back to the state house, the company retired once again to Faneuil Hall for business and another meal. A U.S. military band provided music on this occasion, and again all kinds of persons mixed festively in Boston's streets and parks.[9]

In 1831 the most important of these spring rites was shifted by a constitutional amendment moving Election Day from May to the first Wednesday in January and fixing state elections on the second Monday in November.[10] The Artillery Company Election, along with Harvard's commencement, continued to be a major spring festival, but in the 1820s and 1830s, with the growth of travel and communications facilities, with the spread of manufacturing, and with the advent of religious disestablishment and other social and economic changes, many old customs died or became modified. Nowhere was this kind of transition abrupt, and the construction of a railroad through a village did not change life radically for all the inhabitants of a rural town. In Berkshire County the traditional "court days" persisted well into the 1830s as busy social occasions on which country folk gathered to do business, trade gossip, and talk politics.[11] But the change of General Election Day to the deep cold of midwinter symbolized the passing of the old political culture, though the new had not yet come fully into being.

It signaled a society becoming less tied to nature's seasons and a state government pragmatically pursuing economic development. It implied the great value now put on "organization" in all spheres of life, a word which would become, by the mid-1830s, the foremost shibboleth of political competitors. Indeed, images and connotations of organization became important in the new popular meanings of "party," which differed substantially from what "party spirit" had evoked earlier.

**Belief and Action: The Problem of Evidence**

Historians do not disagree about the existence of antipartisan attitudes among Federalists and Republicans. "Party" was something one denounced and accused one's opponents of promoting. "Party spirit" in excess was a great danger to the Republic, especially if one's opponents were left unchecked to follow their worst impulses. Meanwhile, however—and this is what leads scholars to disagree—both sides built political organizations, out of necessity and in spite of their antiparty ideals. Therefore, say defenders of the "first party system" thesis, look at the actions of the first party builders and not at their rhetoric. The next chapter deals specifically with political organization in order to test that part of the proposition. Aside from formal organizations, however, there is also all the informal partisanship of the Federal-Republican period, which startled contemporaries and which has fascinated historians because of what it seems to reveal about states of mind. What does one do with all of this partisan behavior if one cannot call it the action of "parties"?

Even the evidence of antipartyism can be used as a two-edged sword to justify the claim that parties existed, and it has appeared, in fact, in support of the argument that political parties functioned in the 1770s and 1780s. Thus, a condemnation of the "evil of party spirit" may be quoted to show both the feeling against party and the presence of party. A reference, however negative, to the "party spirit now raging" presents this problem of ambivalent evidence even more sharply. Party is hated, but there it is, or was.

The problem begins to be resolved when one treats separately the questions of the acceptance, the existence, and the character of parties. Antipartisan rhetoric does say much about whether or not party is accepted. Furthermore, *partisanship does not necessarily imply the acceptance of parties themselves*. As Austin Ranney has warned, "we cannot conclude that a person's preference for one party over the other means that he approves of parties *in general* as desirable institutions."[12] Ranney is speaking here of the long sweep of American party history in which parties have been established institutions. His point would seem to have even greater pertinence for the period before the 1830s, when parties did not enjoy such advantages. Ranney's observation can be extended: partisanship does not necessarily imply the presence of party organizations or institutions, though it does obviously indicate the presence of partisan mentalities.

Though Federalists and Republicans disturbed communities as if they were Montagues and Capulets, no one in Massachusetts during that time seems to have spoken out directly in favor of the blessings of political parties. If anyone publicly defended "party" or "party spirit" as inherent goods before 1815, it was a rare event.

Precocious partisans in other states occasionally praised the benefits of party, one of the earliest and best known cases being that of the southern Federalist Robert G. Harper, who in 1798 declared to Congress that party spirit and the contention of two parties could produce a middle course contributing to the public good. According to his biographer, this speech "made him almost unique in Federalist circles and probably in advance of the thinking of most Republicans."[13] Such opinions appeared rarely in Massachusetts, however, in public or in private.

Even in private it was unusual for political leaders to argue the virtues of party. Federalists and Republicans did discuss frequently the need for organization, but not many Federalists, for example, went as far as Fisher Ames did in 1799, saying that even the Jacobins served "the good cause by the violence of their attack, which makes good men enough afraid of their success, to rouse their own energies, and to oppose passion to passion. In this way, as our government is ever in danger of falling by party, it is fated to be saved and to live, if it shall live, by party. Its bane must be its diet." By 1801 Ames had moved even further beyond such stoicism as he urged fellow Federalists to unified action: "Party is an association of honest men for honest purposes, and, when the State falls into bad hands, is the only efficient defense; a champion who never flinches, a watchman who never sleeps." But, Ames continued, "the federalists are scarcely associated. . . . Is it not, therefore, proper, and indispensably necessary, to be active, in order to prevent the dissolution of the feeble ties by which the federal party is held together?"[14] Ames was exceptional, and such views were not, in any case, for public consumption.

Privately, political leaders in Massachusetts did frequently reveal that they possessed partisan mentalities. Like the Republican Levi Lincoln and the Federalist Christopher Gore, many men showed a disposition to draw the lines sharply between "us" and "them." When Joseph Story, as a young lawyer, replied to a question from a Boston gentleman about his politics that he was neither Federalist nor Jacobin but sui generis, the gentleman shot back, "He that is not with us, is against us." Nathaniel Ames, brother of the Federalist Fisher Ames, drew a sharp distinction between "enlightened Republicans" and "weaker brethren" who entertained "an idea of uniting all parties by soothing milk and water." He called these "the milky class," and one completely wrongheaded man he called "a still weaker tool of the Fudderalists." Many Federalists in turn regarded their moderates with as much scorn: George Cabot called them "the small Federalists," while Stephen Higginson equated an attempt "to build up a party of moderate independent men" with an invitation to unite "All the timid wavering and temporizing of both Feds and Jacobins." As a young lawyer in 1808, Leverett Saltonstall eagerly accepted on short notice an invitation to give a Federalist Fourth of July oration, because he wished to make his mark and gain acceptance as a partisan. He described the oration as "very federal, but not virulent. My own party appear pleased. Had I been very moderate and only tinged it with federalism, the demo's would have misrepresented it, and it would not have made warm friends among the feds." No one familiar with the partisan rage of the early national period will readily disbelieve the anecdote about two close friends of opposite politics who quarreled over the 1807 state election and for forty years "had no further intercourse" until one of them lay on his deathbed and his ancient friend undertook a long journey to make a final peace. Well might John Adams in 1809 describe the partisan mentality at its worst: "Whatever vices there are, Federalism and Republicanism will cover them all."[15]

All of this is well known, as is the alleged tendency of Federalists and Republicans to avoid one another socially. In Boston the Federalists dominated the "aristocracy," and through the years tradition has remembered the genteel lady's observation that in Beacon Hill drawing rooms one was as likely to meet a cow as a Republican.

Local histories, whose general disregard of political parties is in keeping with the antipartisan substrata of bedrock just beneath the surface of American life, frequently made some kind of reference to Federal and Republican party excitement, while they presented huge compendia of antiquarian items which otherwise gave not a hint that such a thing as political parties ever existed. Yet at least one local historian, whose able community study did discuss political affairs in detail, expressed the opinion that the apparently all-consuming Federal-Republican divisions had perhaps been exaggerated. Many persons simply refused to be drawn actively into partisan disputes.[16]

Even if its social influence was exaggerated, the excitement served to transform political behavior, and "party spirit" carried voters to the polls in unprecedented numbers. The most important aspect of all this, however, was that the partisan mentality was still perceived in eighteenth-century categories. The new activity and the old understandings were sometimes joined, as in an 1806 *Voters' Guide,* published by a Federalist, which was both a practical and a philosophical guide to government for the average citizen. Though it was not a partisan tract, its very appearance reflected changes in politics and perhaps the need to find new ways to instruct a citizenry no longer quite as deferential as in the past. The elegant little manual offered "knowledge" about election laws, voter and candidate qualifications, and the like, in order to avoid the evils of unfair elections in which wicked men might take advantage of voter ignorance. This was now urgent "on account of the party spirit which prevails in the state" and "its tendency to corrupt your elections." "When it rages with violence, truth and reason are disregarded," and unless voters learned their rights and privileges, "corruption" would destroy the constitutional safeguards of free elections. The *Guide* devoted an entire chapter to the "fatal consequences of party spirit" and began it with copious quotations from "Burgh." James Burgh (1714–1775) was one of the English "commonwealthmen" who so profoundly influenced American revolutionaries; he "wrote perhaps the most important treatise which appeared in England in the first half of the reign of George III."[17] The *Guide*'s thinking about parties, in short, was firmly rooted in the eighteenth-century antipartisan perspective.

Throughout the early national years both Federalists and Republicans, like the *Voters' Guide,* denounced "party spirit," not organization or system. By 1811 and 1812 election contests brought forth much planning and coordination, but a Federal newspaper typically denounced office seekers carrying "their party distinctions through all the grades of office from the President to the lowest town officers" as a manifestation of "Party Spirit."[18]

As late as 1823, eighteenth-century antipartisan ideology could still provide the framework for a discussion of the merits of party. Such a discussion was itself more unusual than the ideas it revealed. "A Subscriber" to the Salem *Observer* began the debate by rejoicing that the "useless distinctions *federalist* and *democrat*" were becoming obsolete. "Another Subscriber" disagreed, and then the editors contributed their own views on "Party Spirit." Arguments on all sides contained nothing unusual. The critic of party covered familiar territory and focused on the corruption of elections by *"the spirit of party, caucuses, and the arts and intrigues of office seekers* and their adherents." Party was but another name for faction. Parties were selfish and inconsistent, necessarily tended to render men wicked, and destroyed the peace of society. The editors, however, struck a theme which pointed more to what party would become: *"They feel no responsibility*. Their acts are performed by such numbers, that no one feels himself accountable for their conduct." The defender of parties, ironically, argued more in eighteenth-century terms than did any of the others. Claiming that it was human nature to be divided into parties, he said that party was not another name for faction, that faction was rather the abuse of party. To illustrate, he offered several extracts from Jonathan Swift's *Examiner* of 1711, which heaped scorn and ridicule on "A Man of No Party!" Swift had argued that everyone was of some party whether he admitted it or not and that a no-party posture was cowardly and hypocritical. Swift, however, seemed to be discussing not political parties, at least not those of the nineteenth century, but rather the universality of interest and ideology and the inevitable development in politics of differences generated by them.[19] Federalist and Republican political leaders attended legislative caucuses, nominating meetings, state and county committee meetings and organized the writing of ballots and the encouragement and mobilization of voters. But these things did not seem to be what men had primarily in mind when they thought about "party spirit."

Prevailing modes of thought rested on traditional foundations and assumptions. No image of an organization or institution gave "party spirit" its fearful reputation, and men could still define it as one might today define "subjectivity," "interest," or "ideology." The techniques and stratagems used to contest elections appeared to be ephemeral by-products of the vicissitudes of party spirit.

Evidence showing the perception of party as party spirit may be found abundantly in early-nineteenth-century Massachusetts. Some way is needed of tracing more precisely the career of this understanding until its gradual replacement by a different perception and a new set of attitudes toward parties. The rest of this chapter therefore concentrates on three kinds of public expressions which came forth continually during the first four decades of the nineteenth century and which reflected prevailing or at least important opinions about the state of politics generally and, often, about parties specifically: Election Sermons, governor's inaugurals, and Fourth of July orations, all of which were delivered every single year, though only two men each year gave the sermon and the inaugural.

**From Party Spirit to Party**

Election Sermons provide an excellent way to follow year by year, over an entire period, changing ideas of and attitudes toward party. When state officials and legislators gathered for the sermon, they expected a sort of "state of the state's morals" address, and clergymen since the sermon's origin had not hesitated to discuss secular affairs. Thus the annual sermons constitute a continual diagnosis of society and usually of polity, from a special perspective which imposes obvious limits on their utility.[20] Yet the sermons still can yield valuable information when interpreted in context.

Ministers were one of the groups least likely to be favorable to parties, and the occasion clearly demanded an emphasis on the common good. Indeed, governor's inaugurals and patriotic orations shared the same inherent hostility to anything factious. Moreover, since sermons can be observed over time and thus can be scrutinized for common modes of thought and distinct phases, the fact that the clergy formed an especially antipartisan group can be turned to advantage, in part because they stated antipartisan ideals over a longer period. More important, when the clergy or some of them began reflecting new attitudes and understandings regarding party, it was certain that something basic had changed.

The sermons can be grouped into three general periods from 1800 to 1844, the lines separating each period roughly paralleling those observed in the indicators of political activity in Chapter II. The most sharply defined years were those from 1801 to 1815, coinciding with the career of intense Federal-Republican rivalry.[21] The sermons then entered an "Era of Good Feelings" that lasted at least until 1827. The line between the second and third phases was less clear; a new attitude first appeared in 1828 but was not firmly established until 1832. Indeed, not until 1840 did a sermon imply a full acceptance of a two-party system. From 1840 through 1844 the question of political parties occupied the sermons to an unusual degree, and the ministers conducted a virtual running debate from one year to the next, novel in its length, tone, and substance.

Since most of the ministers chosen during the period 1801–1815 were Federalists, it is not surprising that these sermons expressed a decidedly antipartisan tone. The speakers assumed that the "party spirit" besetting the state and nation was an affliction dangerous to the Republic, and they tended to see the era as a *dark night of party*. Almost every sermon from 1801 through 1815 made some reference to the destructiveness of "party," "parties," or, especially, "party spirit."[22]

Perhaps the most vigorous strictures against "party spirit" came just after the bitterly divisive campaigns of 1811 and 1812, and during the three subsequent years of war which filled Federal New England with despair. In 1812, in a sermon notable for its low-key exhortations to restore unity, Edmund Foster nevertheless found the "party spirit" now raging "a merciless enemy; whom it will it kills, and whom it will it saves alive; or if it spares the man, it will be seen to murder his reputation. It not only robs us of justice, but does violence to nature herself. It is among us the dividing line between human perfection on the one hand, and total depravity on the other." In 1813 William Allen similarly called "unbalanced political zeal . . . an evil of wide extent" bearing "a most threatening aspect . . . a leprosy, which is felt from one extremity of the continent to the other." And the war closed as James Flint reviewed its lessons and found that the people had been taught at bitter cost "that 'party is the madness of the many for the gain of a few.' "[23]

To these preachers, "party spirit" was clearly an aberration in the body politic, not a system of political organization. Flint, for example, called "party spirit" an "indulgence" of passions, suggesting that "party spirit" was like sin or a condition of moral error, weakness, or evil. Others said that party was, indeed, "of short duration," or that rulers could check party spirit, "a national sin," by example as they might check other sins. When Aaron Bancroft (1802) referred to "the race of impiety and folly, of party and faction, of dissipation and vice, in which all Republicks have preceded us," he was not talking about party as a system of electoral competition or legislative management.[24]

Antipartisan values were so strong in this era that these sermons contain only the barest hint of the idea that parties might be a necessary evil. In 1809 the arch-Federalist David Osgood said that republican governments by their nature "almost necessarily engender parties and factions, divisions and contests." But he added quickly, "In these contests . . . men professing themselves republicans, lose sight of their principles in their blind, yet violent attachment to their respective parties. Enlisting under the banners of Caesar and Pompey, both sides fight most furiously for their republic. . . ." Osgood's thinking was rooted strongly in eighteenth-century ideals of unity, and he did not think of parties as permanent: since ancient times they had come and gone. Moreover, the implicit slur on Republicans revealed the ambiguity of Osgood's position: even as he condemned party zeal he acted the partisan.[25]

Osgood's sermon exhibited one of the central ironies of the antiparty epoch: the ministers most withering in their rejection of party were at the same time the most obviously partisan of all Election Day preachers from 1800 to 1844. This was above all a Federalist syndrome and a carry-over from the clergy's traditional role in the eighteenth century. The stronger the minister's Federalism, the stronger his denunciation of party and the more blatant his anti-Jeffersonian sentiments. Osgood's 1809 sermon was virtually an anti-Republican jeremiad, and Elijah Parrish's 1810 effort was even more unrestrained in its criticism of national commercial policy under Jefferson and Madison. Indeed, the latter so offended Republicans, and probably moderate Federalists, too, that the house of representatives refused to follow the normal custom of printing the Election Sermon–the first time this had happened in the long history of the sermons.[26]

All of this offers no paradox. The coexistence of clerical antiparty with high Federalism gives powerful evidence that these men rejected party politics and assumed that whatever party spirit existed was abnormal and temporary. The apparent contradiction was part and parcel of an ideology which rejected party as legitimate, which did not think at all in terms of two-party politics, and *which did not even have such a model in mind when it rejected parties.*

Beginning in 1816 the sermons immediately reflected the abating of partisanship that took hold with Monroe's administration. By 1818 a preacher for the first time did not mention party but dealt with "the prevailing neglect and open violation of the sabbath." And in 1819 Peter Eaton rejoiced that party prejudices had yielded "to the sway of better feelings."[27] Even during the hard-fought state elections of 1823 and 1824, the sermons continued to reflect "Good Feelings." The substitution of ministers chosen by Republicans for those selected by Federalists brought no change.[28] The sermons from 1816 to 1830 generally said less about politics and more about religion, yet they also addressed, as earlier discourses had not, secular issues of moral consequence, such as the condition of workers, the education of the poor, and slavery.

The first break in this pattern came in 1828 in the sermon of James Walker, a minister known as the "Unitarian Warrior," and constituted the first real sign of any implied acceptance of parties in the Election Sermons. Walker himself had battled only recently as a religious partisan in the Trinitarian-Unitarian controversy, had helped organize the American Unitarian Association, and later became a professor at Unitarian-dominated Harvard. His reference to parties was not unusual in the nation or state by 1828, but Walker departed from the earlier clerical consensus when he flatly declared "I am aware that parties are to be expected in a free country; and that they answer many useful and important ends, particularly by being a watch and check on one another, so as to prevent the party in power from abusing that power."[29] Walker's matter-of-fact statement, made in a brief and otherwise not at all unusual discussion of party and its dangers, indicated that outside of the sphere of Election Sermons attitudes to parties had been substantially changing.

Although the next sermon reverted to otherworldly concerns, the 1830 sermon of the famous Unitarian William Ellery Channing recalled the antipartyism of the early republic. The spirit of the times ("notoriously sectarian, and therefore hostile to liberty") caused men "to run into associations," said Channing, "to lose themselves in masses, to think and act in crowds, to act from the excitement of numbers, to sacrifice individuality, to identify themselves with parties and sects." Opinions should not be spread by means which would "enslave ourselves to party, or bring others into bondage. We must respect alike our own and others' minds."[30]

But the tide had turned, and in 1832 a further sign of party's growing acceptance came from Paul Dean, another veteran of sectarian struggles and a well-known religious liberal. "Among a free people there will necessarily be parties," said Dean, "from an honest difference of opinion on subjects of great national interest, and these parties while properly governed will be the watchful guardians of liberty; but when they become violent and lose sight of the public weal in the pursuit of party advancement, then the republic is in danger."[31]

The next year William Peabody in effect delivered a rebuttal to Dean's idea that parties could be good, but even in doing so he gave proof that attitudes had changed. Peabody said he could find it easier to believe "all that we hear of the benefits and blessings of party" if a party were no more than "an association naturally formed by sympathy among those who agree in opinion, and who unite, in order to spread their sentiments by free and fair discussion." But was not something more meant by party? "If . . . party may be an engine by which private judgment is prevented, and individual energy broken down, if the whole mass may receive an impulse from a single powerful hand, should not the free be ever on their guard . . . ?"[32]

Antiparty as he was, Peabody conceded that

> parties have always existed and always will exist in a free country. But must men therefore be slaves to them? Can they not answer every good purpose, without abridging freedom of individual thought and action . . . is it worth while, to surrender our heart and hand, mind and soul, to the

> dictation of party, when each must answer for himself to God? . . . Let our political parties consist of those who agree in desiring the good of the country, and simply differ as to the means. . . . Far different this from the party, which is an army in all but its arms.[33]

Peabody's sermon thus marked the onward march of the partisan ethos and a stage which could perhaps be called "party as necessary and potential evil." In the Federal era, no one had ever talked about "all that we hear of the benefits and blessings of party."

Peabody also showed clearly that antipartisan ideology had shifted its concern from society to the individual, as had so many other areas of thought. Channing and Peabody both articulated the moralist's objection to party's interfering between the individual conscience and God. As a combination of new fears and new perceptions, the party they feared differed from the "party spirit" which their Federalist predecessors had denounced.

The perception of "party" changed in the sermons of the 1830s within the context of a broader view that "the times" were changing too. Election sermons had always lamented change, and in the jeremiadical tradition their complaints about party or the times were nothing new.

Yet the sermons of the 1830s differed from those of 1801 to 1815 because of their relative lack of sensitivity to upheaval in politics and their greater awareness of turmoil in society. Though parties were not only forming again but entrenching themselves far more securely as organizations, the clergy said much less about politics or parties. Though the sermons shared much of the social conservatism of the dominant National Republican and Whig parties,[34] the preachers of the 1830s never boldly flew their partisan colors as had the early Federal antipartisans. They even neglected to mention the state's finally bringing the religious establishment, long in disarray, to an end in 1833. The ministers knew that "party animosity" was "rife,"[35] but they worried less about the political foundations of republican health and more about the dangers arising from social behavior. Society seemed to be breaking down, coming apart. They feared that deepening class divisions and fragmentation would enter all areas of life. Historians have often celebrated the "ferment" of the 1830s; these ministers worried about agitation, alienation, and centrifugal breakage. Party warfare was but part of the growing chaos.

Thirty years earlier, ministers had decried the "dark night of party"; now they spoke of the evil of party amid "dark days." Earlier, the great issues had seemed clearcut, and party rage over them too palpable to ignore; now they lamented the rage to get rich, social envy, class hatred, and a pervasive spirit of speculation and gambling. Prosperity itself was to blame, said Andrew Bigelow in 1836: "Every man is emulous to overtop his fellows." The very improvements of the age, said Dana in 1837, stimulated the "lust of wealth" and speculation which, "in a thousand forms, has become the very *mania* of the age." Alongside of this "ceaseless fluctuation" of social striving, the ministers also saw a disregard of all standards of authority and right. They witnessed increasingly *"a wonderful excitability of the public mind"* and a radical spirit which ignored authority, law, and morality.[36] Amid the preoccupation with social malaise, political parties as such received little attention in the last half of the 1830s.[37]

Still, it was only a matter of time until the acceptance of parties would register fully in an Election Sermon. In 1840, when it came, it touched off a debate that spanned half a decade. The discussion showed that antiparty still lived and, more important, that party meant something new, that a two party system was being regarded as an established way of political life, and that party organizations were now well on the road to being institutions.

John Codman, the Orthodox Congregational minister of Dorchester, probably did not intend to provoke any such reaction. His sermon "The Importance of Moderation in Civil Rulers" came just after the Democrats won a close election in November 1839, their first ever. While sharing the traditional negative view of party spirit,[38] Codman implied that he saw no reason for alarm in the transition of parties. Indeed, he celebrated a new moderation inherent in party politics. Even the occasion on which he spoke, he observed, no longer witnessed the "high seasoned political sermons" heard in earlier years. Urging the cultivation of forbearance "between the two great political parties, into which the inhabitants of the Commonwealth are, apparently, so equally divided," Codman rejoiced that "political party now, is widely different from what it was in former days,–that it has lost much of [its] asperity."[39]

Though Codman's acceptance of parties as something domesticated surely climaxed the trend of a dozen years, subsequent preachers of Election Sermons were not content to let the matter rest. Each took up the theme of parties at least to some degree and, in effect, debated with his predecessors. Both party and antiparty received a remarkably full airing from 1840 through 1844. Both the critique and the justification established that party was something different, that it had arrived, and that it thoroughly governed modes of politics. These ministers spoke far more of "parties" than of "party spirit," and some described parties as positive goods in terms that most political men probably found quite agreeable.

A year after hearing Codman's benign view of party, the state officials listened to David Damon resurrect the old demon of party spirit. While parties might inevitably arise, Damon would not endorse their "necessity" or "utility," and, hearkening back to eighteenth-century antipartisan views, he appropriately closed his remarks with the well-known warning against party spirit from Washington's "Farewell Address."[40] Yet the very attention Damon gave to party, amounting to several pages of his printed sermon, was unusual and testified to a new situation.

As Damon answered Codman, so in 1842 did Ezra S. Gannett reply to Damon in a sermon entitled "The Religion of Politics." Gannett went much further than Codman in accepting parties and in fact declared it "foolish and useless" to inveigh against parties as in themselves evil. Parties would exist, he said, in any government which permitted popular participation or even free discussion. Moreover, parties provided "thorough examination" of public measures and imposed "reciprocal vigilance" on the use of power. At the same time, Gannett admitted that parties ran to excess, and he even implied that they routinely acted not on principle but out of regard for office and their own interest. Self-preservation should not be a party's chief aim: "If a party cannot live without adopting what it condemns, let it perish." Gannett above all decried the idea that a man must go with a party even against his conscience, and on this point he was very much in harmony with the antipartisans who stressed the relation of the individual to God with which a party must not interfere.[41] Yet, on balance, Gannett's views reflected most of all the felt necessity to adjust to the inevitable existence of parties.

No mixed emphasis found its way into the next year's Election Sermon. In 1843 Samuel C. Jackson delivered perhaps the most antiparty discourse of the Whig era and of the entire period since 1800. Hostile comments to politics-as-usual studded the entire sermon, and few political men had probably ever heard anything quite like it. With only a token bow to party's utility, Jackson bore down heavily on the abuses of party. While owing something to older antipartisan thinking, Jackson's critique hit at what parties had become in the Whig-Democratic mode. Jackson devoted almost the entire second half of his discourse to the "extravagance and profligacy of party principles and party action." Even in his closing paragraphs, which in all other sermons sounded a congratulatory or hopeful note, Jackson hammered out his antiparty warnings. Partisans feared party more than God, he said, and party contests did not arise over honest differences of opinion. Worse, party obeyed its own, dangerous code of morals, pursued selfish ends by dishonest means, and disregarded patriotism and Christianity. "Instead of regarding all political power as a sacred trust from the Almighty," party seized power to perpetuate itself. "Like an unprincipled despot, it is swayed by prejudice and passion, acts without conscience, and legislates without God."[42] It was true of nearly all political movements, said Jackson, that "the reigning Deity is party." Their great goal, "however artfully concealed under professions of regard for 'the people,' is party emoluments and triumphs." He asked that moral men take action to bring about a revolution in politics to overthrow party: "Let them foil the machinations of evil men at those primary assemblies, where they concentrate their cabals to effect a nomination, relying on party machinery to secure an election."[43]

True to the pattern set in motion in 1840, the next sermon, by E. H. Chapin, returned to the defense of parties, and as Jackson had gone furthest in rejecting parties, so Chapin accepted parties with the most detailed rationale for their legitimacy yet pronounced in an Election Sermon. Though he was far from being consumed by the subject of parties as Jackson had been, his topic, "The Relation of the Individual to the Republic," caused him to skirt politics frequently and eventually led him directly to consider "party politics." Chapin observed, rebuking Jackson by implication, that the abuses of parties had generally been dwelled on excessively. But abuses should not hide the fact that "politics . . . are a noble public concern, involving the greatest questions, exercising the profoundest talent, and often securing the most vital good." Parties, too, had their uses: "They are legitimate and necessary organizations." They kept watch, even from selfishness, over government; they promoted discussion; and in their striving they achieved much for the common welfare.[44]

Chapin had said as much as any Election Day preacher ever had in favor of parties, but he went further. In defining what he meant by legitimate parties based on principle, he explained that though parties were rooted in individualism, they would have no influence without combining members in unity of action—and that this required compromise. "Some measure must be selected which represents the idea of the whole, and thus, uniting all, its success is rendered practicable." The interests of the individual were not sacrificed, but waived. Parties asked for "compromise not *of* principle but *for* principle."

Most men engaged in public life could no doubt readily agree with such a definition. But Chapin also drew the line at a familiar place: he could imagine parties' going too far, demanding that a man be false to his conscience, insisting that "the end justifies the means," making every question a party question, framing party laws, whining after office, and "tyrannizing over independent interests." At that point, party became illegitimate; an individual could by no means violate his moral sense, because then "it becomes a question between the individual and his God."[45] Extremes of party might thus require their dissolution. While few active party men gave much thought to the necessity of dissolving their parties, or their individual relation with it, most political leaders and professional politicians could have listened to Chapin's sermon and nodded in agreement. The historian need look no further for evidence that parties now had their defenders and proponents and that the idea of party itself had changed.

If Election Sermons can be expected to possess an antiparty tendency, governors' inaugurals also have limits as sources within which to find ideas and attitudes about parties. On such propitious occasions, governors naturally exuded confidence, satisfaction, and hope, while they counted blessings, urged harmony, and, not surprisingly, minimized discontents and divisions. They could be expected to say less about party spirit or parties than could the sermons, which could be relied on to find fault in the jeremiadical mode and thus to look for such cankers as party spirit and party. Yet the inaugurals are useful in part because of their limits, and also because they were given every year.

Though the governors said much less about parties than the preachers did, the inaugurals also can be divided into periods roughly similar to those by which the sermons can be arranged. Furthermore, they registered the same basic change in political culture as the sermons did. The inaugurals were in general antipartisan during the Federal-Republican era, most overtly political in the years 1808–1812, least expressive on politics during the 1820s, and, unlike the sermons, still quiet on the subject in the 1830s. But in 1844, finally, a Whig governor acknowledged that the new era had arrived when he not only accepted but also approved parties. By parties, furthermore, he meant something very different from what his predecessors had had in mind forty or thirty years before.

The inaugurals from 1802 through 1812 form the most coherent group in the entire period, those from 1808 through 1812 standing out as simultaneously the most aggressive against "party spirit" and the most blatantly partisan. As with the Election Sermons, nothing like them appears before or after; and as with the sermons, they meant, not that a two-party system existed, but just the opposite. The bitter controversy of those years intruded on a ritual speech that normally avoided direct confrontation with immediate political issues because governors believed that party spirit was threatening to destroy the Republic. Why did governors issue no similar warnings thirty years later? Partly because in 1808 such thoroughgoing and organized partisanship was very new, and partly because thirty years later "parties" had changed.

Even so before 1810 references to "party spirit" were few. Caleb Strong paused briefly in 1802 to denounce it but otherwise showed his antiparty sentiments by passing comments. In 1809 Christopher Gore echoed Strong's warnings against party and also his view of party not as an organization but as something rooted in the emotions, as a way of behaving, or as a moral condition.[46]

Then in 1810 Elbridge Gerry came into office calling for a union of parties. A year later he virtually declared war against the Federalists, a party war, but he did so, as described above, under an antipartisan banner.[47] Yet Gerry by his actions pushed partisan behavior to lengths it had not gone before. He flatly announced that he would no longer permit to stay in office any Federalists whose views he regarded as dangerous, and apparently went further than any other governor in removing opponents from office. Until then, governors had appointed their friends to office, but had done so as vacancies opened or because they had created new positions. After Gerry's defeat in 1812, Caleb Strong returned to office once again decrying party spirit. Strong also dwelled specifically on "official appointments" but maintained that state officers above all persons should not "elevate one portion of the community and depress another." In appointments, he said, "if we make it a rule to advance only our political friends, we shall become the heads of a party." If magistrates came to consider the power deputed to them as their property, and made "vacancies or appointments" for party purposes, then "political feuds would be endless and implacable;–the persons in office and their friends and retainers would employ every method to prevent any change in the Administration, while their rivals would be equally assiduous . . . to effect a change. From the frequency of our elections, there would scarcely be any interruption in these struggles, and the longer they should continue, the greater would be their violence."[48]

This was not idle talk: after reappointing the sheriffs, clerks, and others whom Gerry had replaced "for their opinions, and who wished to be restored," Strong said he intended "no other removals, unless sufficient cause is shown and proved, and the party accused is heard in his defense." Similarly, Worcester County's longtime Federal sheriff, Thomas W. Ward, dismissed by Gerry and reappointed by Strong, was expected by patronage seekers not to "pay so much attention to politics" and to eschew the hated "system of 1811."[49] Even the furious "party spirit" of 1810–1815 had its limits.

Strong's return began a decade of Federal ascendancy in the executive branch during which both Strong and his successor John Brooks said nothing of party spirit. Brooks's inaugurals, indeed, exuded the "internal tranquility" of the "Era of Good Feelings," and appropriately displayed the wordy formality of the eighteenth century.[50] Nothing was said about party until the Republican victory of 1823, when William Eustis made his inaugural a judgment on the Federalists' "disloyal course" during the 1812 war. This, too, was offered under an antiparty flag, but it disturbed Federalists nevertheless. The fact is that Eustis's intended audience for this address resided in Washington not Massachusetts and that its aim was to put Massachusetts "right" with her sister states and induce Congress and President Monroe to award the Commonwealth a long-sought payment of claims relating to the conflict with England.[51] The Federalists tried to stir their partisans in 1824 by making much of Eustis's inaugural, but to no avail. Meanwhile Eustis had conducted an otherwise conciliatory administration. Thereafter inaugurals began to deal with many new subjects thrust upon them by changing times: railroads (1829), imprisonment for debt (1832), banks and currency (1834), and many others, from care of the insane to the militia. But about parties and party spirit they said little.

As parties became entrenched, only the scholar-politician Edward Everett seemed to notice in January 1836, closing his inaugural with an old-time antiparty warning and recalling that the "Fathers of his Country" had pronounced "Party spirit . . . 'the worst foe of a free government.' "[52] But Everett's injunction was an anachronism; men no longer thought of party in the way the Federal-Republican generation had done.

In 1844, finally, another Whig governor, George N. Briggs, not only recognized the new order but did so in such a manner as to suggest that what was being recognized had been for some time a fait accompli. Briggs declared simply, "The people of all free governments will be divided into political parties." He stated their advantages with equal clarity and brevity: "The security of liberty is increased by such divisions. Differences of opinion upon measures best calculated to promote the public good, lead to discussion, and discussion leads to the discovery of truth."[53] Briggs then added two paragraphs of qualifications, but these consisted primarily of reminders to those of different parties about what they had in common. Remembering their underlying unities, however, served but to "modify the excess of political feelings" within a state divided into parties. Briggs did not assume or suggest that the subsidence of party spirit would lead to the dissolving of parties.

On the Fourth of July, towns throughout the Commonwealth celebrated the Declaration of Independence with festivities and "patriotic exercises" which usually included an oration delivered by different men every year. The speakers ranged from young lawyers just beginning political careers to established professionals and public men. The orations combined the historic, reflective, prophetic, and bombastic in about equal measures, and obviously encompassed much more diversity than did Election Sermons or governors' inaugurals. Nevertheless they shared a common form and can be examined over time for what they say about ideas of party.

The Fourth of July orations in fact tended to reveal much more about definitions of "party" while also reflecting much sooner an acceptance of the benefits of party competition. Not that all the orations of a certain time held uniform views of party, but these speeches do fit roughly into groupings reflecting dominant political trends, and several of them in each period provided exceptionally full articulation of prevailing meanings given to "party" in those periods.[54]

Historians have frequently noted that after 1800 partisan bitterness soon grew intense enough to cause Federalists and Republicans to hold separate Fourth of July celebrations. Without blinking that fact, it is important to look at what those partisan and patriotic orators meant by "party" and to recognize the antiparty assumptions which they shared, especially during the period when the orations, like Election Sermons and governors' inaugurals, were most obviously partisan.

The orators from 1800 to 1815 concerned themselves frequently with "party" and above all with "party spirit." Several made it clear that they saw "party spirit" not in terms of any manifest methods of political management but as a temporary condition which seized men and states. While preachers were calling it a sin, patriotic orators called it a "living serpent," or "that old serpent the Devil," or "this infernal spirit."[55] Metaphors of natural forces were as popular in these orations as in the sermons. One speaker said that party strife had been compared "to the winds, which purify the atmosphere, and to the agitated waves which prevent stagnation." But when these winds reached hurricane force, he added, they spread death and destruction.[56] And the Fourth of July orators explicitly declared that party spirit was temporary and could be cured by time, reason, or correct information. But whereas the Election Day preachers referred at times to Washington's farewell warning against party spirit, the Fourth of July orators far more often recalled the best-known sentence of Jefferson's first inaugural: "We are all Republicans, we are all Federalists."[57]

Although "Good Feelings" (1816–1824) put their stamp on Fourth of July speeches as quickly as on other public declamations, more positive attitudes toward party crept into the patriotic orations even before the Federal-Republican period came to an end.[58] The meaning of "party," however, had not seemed to change, and antiparty sentiments still gained more frequent expression. Even when, in the late 1820s, proparty ideas began to be aggressively propounded, it was "the spirit of party" which was held to be, within limits of course, "inseparable from, and . . . essential to Republican institutions."[59]

In the 1830s the acceptance of parties, implied or explicit, became frequent in Fourth of July orations, and unlike the Election Day preachers or governors, the orators spent little time agitating the negative side of the question, because, as one put it, in all free states and representative governments "parties must and will arise, by the very necessity of our nature."[60]

A full-blown rationale for parties came far earlier to the orations than to the sermons or inaugurals. In 1836 nothing less than a theoretical basis for a two-party system was a major theme in the Weymouth oration of Alexander H. Everett, brother of Edward, protégé of John Quincy Adams, but recently a convert to the Democrats, and, more important, a man whose career was becoming increasingly that of a professional politician. Everett did more than accept and approve. "The existence of free parties is a matter of course," he said, "if not of absolute necessity." Everett meant not only that opinions would differ and people would "form themselves into parties" but also that most governments were inherently constituted of "the elements of permanent political divisions, which, though more or less active at different times, are never entirely suppressed."[61] After tracing the history of parties in the United States, Everett made the more important point that parties rallied under two great principles—liberty and law. Both were essential to society "and neither can possibly exist in practice to the entire exclusion of the other. Liberty without law would be the subversion of society; law without liberty would efface the individual, and leave him no existence as a moral and intellectual agent." Thus the question as to which party was right could not be answered—

"both are in the right. Both profess and sustain principles in themselves correct, and essential to the public welfare."[62] Everett's argument went far beyond a mere listing of practical benefits deriving from party competition; instead, it formed a thoroughgoing philosophical basis for a two-party system.

Thus, in various public forums, parties had come to be accepted and justified by the late 1830s and 1840s. Degrees of acceptance existed, obviously, among such different groups as ministers and political men; but all were clearly adjusting to the *fact* of parties. No one seemed to be assuming that once "party spirit" had spent itself, the whole problem of party would go away. This much was evident and even acknowledged occasionally. A more subtle change went unremarked, but from the vantage point of a century and a half later appears just as significant—namely, that the terms "party" and "parties" no longer meant quite what they had meant a generation before, that the pictures of parties in men's minds had changed.

## V. Organization and Elections, 1800–1824

> Political parties provide leadership for the expression of discontent—or satisfaction—with the current state of affairs. These institutions of democracy consist in their essence of little groups of leaders and subleaders bound together at least by the ambition to control the machinery of government, and this party core ordinarily counts as its loyal followers a substantial number of voters. . . . The groupings called parties possess extraordinary durability and vitality. They persist over long periods and survive many a reverse. Moreover, in what is usually deemed a healthy party life, party leaders possess at least a rudimentary collective sense of responsibility for the party's welfare. In turn this sense of responsibility induces a degree of group discipline among the leaders who, although they may have their fraternal differences, unite to battle the enemy for control of the government.
>
> —V. O. Key, *Southern Politics*[1]

Federalists and Republicans contested elections in Massachusetts from just after 1800 through 1824, and at times engaged in activities quite different from the political modes of the eighteenth century. Although they departed from earlier political groupings, the Federalists and Republicans did not become party institutions of the kind that dominated political life in 1840. Early national partisans lacked, among other things, "a rudimentary collective sense of responsibility for the party's welfare," and the first parties' organizational life followed closely the course of events in national and international affairs.

When the embargo and similar measures injured New England commerce and when the Federal elite faced an unwanted war with England, passionate conviction and economic interest fueled efforts to spread "correct information" and get out the vote. At the height of national crisis in 1811–1812, state issues, brought forward principally by Republicans expressing local discontents, added even greater meaning to the power struggle. When the war ended, however, and national policy changed for the better in the view of the Federal leaders, emotion ebbed, and few took the trouble to sustain organized "exertions" in elections.

Still, Republicanism and Federalism remained alive after 1815. The national Republican ascendancy gave hope to that party that someday even Federal Massachusetts would come around, while Federal leaders, still frustrated by their lack of national influence, held on to power in Massachusetts as long as they could. After 1815, however, state elections became dull affairs and less partisan every year. Then in 1823 and 1824 the old parties waged two spirited contests for the governor's chair and in doing so rehashed the old issues of 1800–1815. But state and not national quarrels provided the main stimuli for electoral competition in 1823–1824, and domestic social quarrels powerfully affected the result. The parties thus resembled a dying patient enjoying a surge of color and life just before the end.[2]

### 1800: All Federalists, All Republicans

In the 1790s political acrimony spread throughout society, but not even the shadow of organized parties existed.[3] Partisanship flourished: Democratic-Republican clubs formed, Federalists wore black cockades, Republicans donned tricolored badges, and newspapers bristled with political invective. Though the nuclei of parties began to form at the leadership level, contests for the governorship remained a rivalry primarily between popular figures of the Revolutionary Center. Moreover, elite alignments remained in flux, the electorate unstable, and most potential voters uninvolved in state or federal elections.

Though voter participation rose dramatically in 1800, the state election, as described above, was not an organized party battle. Strong and Gerry were both put forward as candidates of the Revolutionary Center, and both aligned themselves with President Adams.[4] Although there was an outburst of partisan rhetoric in speeches and print, as voters were often called upon as "federalists" or "republicans," candidates were at the same time called many other names, including those of their opponents. "*All* call themselves Republicans," said one Federal paper in frustration, "and most say they are Federalists."[5] Naturally charges of name stealing flew back and forth, but this confusion was calculated.

Both sides, furthermore, tired to stigmatize their opponents as illegitimate. Federalists denounced Jacobins, the French party, antifederals, conspirators, demagogues, democrats, antis, disorganizers, a faction, and the evil-minded. Republicans cried out against monarchists, the junto, the Essex Junto, a faction, aristocrats, the order, dictators, high partisans, the arrogant, conspirators, and the tyrannical. Singly and together, these epithets implied that party competition was not normal.

In 1800 nomination methods were new and still evolving. Federalists used a caucus to nominate Strong—actually a *mixed caucus* consisting of many Federal state legislators joined by other Federal leaders. The Federalists described it as a "respectable convention" or "meeting" and claimed that they had no desire to dictate or control anyone's suffrage. The Republicans nevertheless attacked the meeting, calling it a "caucus" and an example of "party spirit," and Gerry supporters held that *"real* great men are always known and acknowledged" without need of such devices.[6] In 1800 even political leaders were not accustomed to party ways.

Other nominations displayed a lack of regularity. "Lists" of senators bearing various labels made their appearance, with little mention of their origins. Some lists named fewer candidates than others, and some Republican lists contained several nominees also on the Federal list.[7]

In May, soon after having elected a governor and state senators, the towns voted to choose representatives to the state legislature. Newspapers in the coastal towns portrayed the election as a struggle between two partisan groups and linked the outcome with the presidential contest between Adams and Jefferson. But no cohesive organizations appeared, and election-oriented activity occurred immediately before the elections.[8]

If the bid for re-election by the native son Adams had muddled politics in the spring, it also confused the fall congressional campaigns.[9] Various partisan names and epithets filled the papers, but there were still a striking number of appeals which avoided partisan terminology or which incorporated both "Republican" and "Federal." Some candidates were indeed highly partisan leaders, but in no district do the nominations and elections seem to have involved stable groups.[10]

Finally, the officers of the federal government employed in Massachusetts owed their positions to Washington and Adams, and many made no secret of their support of Adams. Some exerted their influence fully on his behalf. These officeholders included "customs officers along the entire Atlantic seaboard, postmasters in the interior towns, supervisors, inspectors, and collectors of internal revenue, federal judges, district attorneys, and marshalls."[11] That such men were partisans is beyond dispute, but it is difficult to see them as a "professional party" elite. They may surely be considered elements of the Federal party in 1800, provided that entity is understood to be a loosely associated group of like-minded men generally favoring Adams's election and Federal policies.

**Elections and Organization, 1801–1810**

> . . . if we mean to preserve the Commonwealth and New England, our organiz[ation] must be more complete and systematic; it must extend through every county and town, and an ample fund must be provided for the distribution of political truth.
>
> —Harrison Gray Otis, 1804[12]

In the early part of the decade after 1800, Federalists continued to mobilize support through quite traditional means. Officeholders, clergymen, and influential gentry exerted their influence—some openly, some tacitly—on behalf of Federal candidates. Just before the state election of 1801, for example, the Federalists established a newspaper to serve as the chief voice of Federalism, the Boston *New England Palladium.* Although Fisher Ames had called for such a paper for several years, it came into being principally as a creation of various Federal clergy. Both laymen and clergy provided financial support and written contributions. Jefferson may have exaggerated when he called it "the *clerical* paper," but from the outset free copies of the *Palladium* were sent to every minister in New England.[13] The paper did not realize the hopes of its founders, however, and no one paper served as central spokesman for either party, though the Boston *Columbia Centinel* was probably the most influential and widely read Federal paper.[14]

From 1800 through 1803 neither Federalists nor Republicans received much overall direction from any source. Governor Strong faced a weak opposition, and Federalists did not see the need to organize.[15] In 1804 that changed as the Republicans rallied behind James Sullivan, and both political interests became aware of the virtues of "organization." By 1804 both depended on mixed caucuses to make state nominations and to plan strategy for electoral competition. Overall direction thus emanated primarily from state legislators, and as organization grew throughout the decade, so did partisan consciousness within the legislature.

By 1805 both Republicans and Federalists had formed state central committees, and both worked closely with the state nominating "meetings" or mixed caucuses, and there was of course overlap between the two. Below the central committees were county committees, and under them town committees, or town chairmen or, in some cases, at least "some trusty Republican" (or Federalist) to carry out the directives of the state leaders. The town committees' main task was to get out the party's vote and to work for the election of the maximum number of state representatives.

Authority in both Federal and Republican ranks flowed from top to bottom.[16]

In 1808 Dr. Nathaniel Ames described the manner in which Norfolk County's Republican committees functioned: the county committees had to communicate with the central committee, and the town committees were "to watch over the Republican interest both in State & National Governments, especially as to elections and appointments–convey intelligence–confute false rumours–confirm the wavering in right principles–prevent delusion of weak brethren–& fight that most formidable enemy of civilized men, political ignorance."[17]

In 1806 the importance of control of the legislature received dramatic emphasis when a very close gubernatorial election needed to be decided by the legislature's rulings on valid and invalid ballots, and the struggle for the legislature became increasingly hard-fought. In 1810 the Republican Central Committee advised the town committees that "when the parties are nearly equal in numbers, it is generally good policy to be the attacking party and push for a Representative, this Conduct generally intimidates the opponents and ends in complete success or at least prevents them from sending."[18]

By the end of the decade both Federalists and Republicans possessed hierarchical organizations which aspired at least to reach into all towns in Massachusetts to mobilize voters, and the legislature, while not wholly given over to party, was the focus of an intensive struggle for power, especially as it affected election decisions, appointments and patronage, and particularly statements about national policy. Though no study of party-in-the-legislature exists for this period, all indications are that it increased from 1805 to 1810. At the same time, party cohesion among legislators continued to vary and did not extend to all issues.[19]

Federal reactions to Jefferson's embargo and commercial policies, furthermore, suggest the absence of institutionalized parties. Non-importation and embargo brought real distress to all parts of Massachusetts, to fishermen, shippers, and farmers. The economic woes, said Samuel Eliot Morison, rescued the Federal party "from the shadow of death," and revived party politics.[20] Yet Federal unhappiness with national policy led to actions not characteristic of normal party politics. Some Federal leaders began privately discussing the possibility of secession, and, as is well known, state rights sentiment grew increasingly aggressive from 1808 to 1815. The pervasiveness of these impulses indicates that organization was not directed toward limited goals within the framework of party politics.

Finally, while national issues stimulated organization in state politics, the presidential election of 1808 did not stir up electioneering.[21] The Federalists, like most of their brethren in other states, paid relatively little attention as the Republicans went about choosing a successor to Jefferson. While Republicans cheered for Madison, there was virtually no Federal presidential effort in 1808.

## Elections and Organization, 1811–1812

From 1810 through 1815 Massachusetts politics were filled with passion and partisan conflict. In four state elections from 1809 through 1812, the governorship changed hands three times, and it would be difficult to find a period in the state's history when ideological passion between contending parties burned more intensely. In 1811 and 1812 political activity and organization proliferated, and it seemed that a dam had broken, unloosing a flood of "party spirit" in greater force than ever before.

The Republican offensive of 1811–1812, described above, and the approaching war clearly drove partisanship to extremes. The Republican legislative majority, with Governor Gerry's approval, acted in such a partisan manner that the whole episode, not just the "gerrymander," became ensconced in political folklore. The Republican caucus functioned very much like a party-in-the-legislature, passing programmatic legislation, implementing by all accounts the most extensive "spoils" policy yet encountered in the state, and seeking to undermine both the legitimacy and the electoral strength of its rivals.

During these years party cohesion in the legislature probably rose to its highest levels. Both parties caucused frequently to discuss policy, patronage, and strategy. When Republicans controlled the legislature, one study has shown, they apportioned committee assignments in more partisan fashion than did the Federalists. Party lines probably held most firmly on national issues and on decisions directly affecting the fortunes of the parties, such as patronage or contested elections, or national policy. In 1812, for example, a vote on a resolution on recharter of the U.S. Bank was predicted to be "a party question and the vote in both branches, will be yea and nay, and show the political character of both branches."[22] A leading Federalist claimed, "Every law made this year has sprung from party views, their object being by bribes and persecution to continue themselves in power." The degree of distrust and animosity between the two legislative parties at this time was perhaps best revealed by a Federal reaction to a Republican suggestion in 1813 to reduce the size of the house by mutual compromise between the parties. One Federal leader called it an "unequal Bargain" and said he would not state all his objections to the plan: "It is sufficient that no confidence is to be placed in the promises or engagements of leading Democrats. They have neither honor nor conscience."[23]

Far more organization was present than in 1800, but this was not yet the convention system of 1840. In 1811–1812 both Federalists and Republicans still nominated their gubernatorial candidates in mixed caucuses in Boston. Then partisans in most of the state's counties called meetings or conventions "to nominate" the parties' choices. In effect these local meetings, while making nominations for state senators, *ratified* the earlier decision of state leaders.[24]

Later, Whig and Democratic local meetings would precede state conventions: in 1811–1812 they generally followed the state meeting. The county assemblages were also called in a variety of traditional, informal ways. In Berkshire County in 1811, for example, Republicans held a relatively "pure" convention of delegates from each town to nominate state senators. Yet this meeting was called initially by "inhabitants" of Lenox "with the advice of a number of respectable gentlemen of the adjacent towns." In Worcester County a Republican paper simply announced that the senate nominees "will consist of the same Gentlemen, who have hitherto been supported."[25] County conventions met at inns, taverns, churches, and other public places, and often in private residences. In 1812 Essex County Republicans began by calling on the towns to choose delegates to the county convention.[26] This method, most resembling the later convention system, seems to have been used infrequently. Rather, delegates were apparently recruited by party influentials, appointed, coopted, or self-selected. This elitist mode resulted naturally from the way political organization took form, radiating down and horizontally along lines of social, cultural, and economic influence.

Whatever the procedures, county meetings usually followed a script written by state leaders. On both sides the top leaders were merchants, lawyers, officeholders, or men who by wealth or position had time to devote to politics. They guided nominations and then directed efforts to get candidates elected. The state's representatives in Washington, predominantly Federalists, worked closely with the Federal inner circle and produced speeches, essays, letters in newspapers, broadsides, pamphlets, and circulars. The men in Washington had probably held state office and were well acquainted with state politics. The Republicans controlled the state government less and elected fewer men to Washington, so they relied more on federal officeholders appointed by Jefferson and Madison, such as the collector of the port of Boston, the federal marshal, and the Boston postmaster.[27]

What chiefly distinguished the partisan efforts of 1811–1812 from those of 1800, and from eighteenth-century factional politics, was above all their "exertions" to get out the vote. These differed from later Whig-Democratic campaigns in duration, geographic spread, explicit system, and consistency of partisan identification. But at times electoral appeals almost sounded post-Jacksonian: Federalists and Republicans spilled much ink in trying to persuade supporters of the importance of a single vote.[28] Boston and other large towns held caucuses and meetings during the month prior to elections, most of the meetings taking place only days before. These ranged from what were in effect large rallies to limited caucuses which laid meticulous plans for getting out the vote, appointed poll watchers and vote distributors, and lined up transportation to the polls for those needing it. Thus, in 1811 Boston Federalists deployed some dozen vote distributors in each of the town's twelve wards, sent schoolboys to distribute placards in the markets, and stationed what Republicans complained were "bully boys" at the polls.[29] Not all the large seaport towns possessed this degree of organization—nor did Boston Republicans, for that matter—but some larger coastal and inland towns approached it.[30]

Both Federalists and Republicans issued "addresses" in 1811 and 1812 which appeared in their newspapers across the state. These addresses were not called platforms or considered such, and in 1811 and 1812 they focused almost entirely on national issues, as they had for a number of years.[31] This was fitting becausc the power struggle within the state assumed large dimensions as a result of the division over national questions. Without the foreign-policy crisis, state questions would not have excited the same degree of political activity.

The April state election remained the touchstone of political strife, but elections both before and after were also highly partisan, which they had not been ten years earlier. Many of the "March meetings" to elect town officers produced nasty debates or tense maneuverings as partisans backed selectmen with reference to national and state issues. A Federal paper in Berkshire complained that in Washington's day everyone had assumed that "the people had penetration, to vote at least for Hog Constable" on their own, but that now a "caucus gentry" had erected "the *Banner of Party"* to dictate the choice of town officers.[32] By no means did party intrude into town affairs in all of the 300 towns of the state, and even in the larger towns compromises were often adopted by which coalitions or "union" slates would be formed. Yet such arrangements themselves testified to the strain which local traditions of consensus experienced under the impact of party competition.[33]

In 1800 electioneering had fallen off between the election of the governor and the May election of state representatives. In 1811 little slackening occurred. "There will be a great tug at our election for Representative," said one Federalist. "Both parties will make every possible exertion. The chance is about equal."[34] The election became particularly bitter as both parties saw state and national problems as interlocked, good and evil being unambiguously aligned in opposing camps all along the line.[35]

The Federal State Committee showed its concern for the 1811 representatives' election by sending a circular letter to Federal town committees urging on them an almost military organization. Federal grandees led by the merchant prince Thomas H. Perkins suggested that town committees adopt a mode "long beneficial" to the Federal cause in Boston: divide the town into school or surveyor's districts with each having a subcommittee; the later should assemble as many citizens as possible in their locale, especially the "wavering" and recent converts, and rouse them with spirited addresses and solemn resolutions; subcommittees should also collect lists of all ratable polls "and all the Federal and doubtful voters of their respective districts"; all should be persuaded to vote; and each town should heed its duty to send its full number of representatives.[36]

In 1812 Federalists in rural Worcester County were still following the plan of 1811. The North District Central Committee had written to town committees early in March calling on "the friends of the Constitution" to rally against the gerrymander. After Strong's election the committee congratulated the towns but exhorted them to do everything possible "to secure a *federal* house," to send a full complement from "all Federal towns," and to do "all you can to lessen, or prevent the Democrat representation."[37] It is difficult to know in how many towns such organizations came into being. In Dedham the Republicans prepared for the governor's election by convening at a local tavern a "caucus or consultation of Democrats pretty full from all parts of the town except South Parish [a Federal neighborhood], [to] appoint committees from each squad to hunt our Republican votes and to get their conveyance to poll–if lame or unable." And the next day the Federalists held a similar caucus.[38] There can be no doubt that efforts to mobilize the electorate were more extensive and differed not only in scale but in kind from those of even a few years before. Organization as such made some impact in creating more participation, but organization was clearly tied to the sense of crisis; when the latter relaxed, organization pretty much collapsed.

In 1812 the Federalists conducted what can be considered a campaign of "redemption" to defeat Gerry and the Republicans. Antipartisanship was perhaps their most potent weapon. They denounced the "gerrymander," along with other "party" measures. Two hundred and twenty-four Federal legislators, in protesting the "Districting Bill," identified themselves only as the "legislative minority." Newspapers condemned the Republicans for holding "democratic caucuses" in every county to decide on removals and replacements on grounds of party.[39] The Federalists' state address, thereafter echoed by county conventions, seldom mentioned the "Federal Party." While Republicans held meetings often named "Republican," Federalists more often clothed themselves in nonparty appellations. Federalists had been eclectic in this way in 1810–1811 and in 1812, as the "peace party" used nonparty labels to an even greater degree, preferring "True American Nominations" or "The Washington Ticket," or simply appropriated their rival's name, using the names "American Republican," "Washington Republican," or "True Republican." In 1812 it was rare to see the Strong-Phillips ticket headed simply "Federal nomination." Whenever possible, too, local protests against the national government's foreign policy convened as "town meetings."[40]

In 1811–1812 Federalists employed yet another means of mobilizing voters, the Washington Benevolent Societies. These fraternal organizations evolved into an important political arm of Federalism, raising money, holding colorful celebrations, and serving as battalions for maneuvering at town meetings. As David H. Fischer has observed, the societies combined mummery, benevolence, partisan enthusiasm, and filiopietism, while their chief purpose was to maximize the Federal vote. Fischer saw the societies as an important means by which the Federalists "acclimatized themselves to the society in which they lived," and noted that where Federal party organization was weak, the societies nominated candidates and supervised electioneering.[41]

Originating in New York City in 1808, the societies did not rise from the grass roots. They appeared first in Massachusetts's western counties, imported by Federal merchants and lawyers with close ties to New York. The societies did include all classes, and they represented a cross section of society. Indeed, one of their chief purposes was to bring poorer voters to the polls.[42] Perhaps bribery and "treating" were involved; above all the societies made funds available on election days with which younger or poorer voters could "prove" they were property holders of sufficient means. The societies became especially active in the larger towns, where they also helped finance partisan publications, and staged parades and orations filled with quasi-religious patriotism and thinly veiled Federalism. General citizen involvement ended after 1814, however; if the societies continued, they did so as in Boston as clubs of young gentlemen.[43] Mass participation in the societies thus declined more rapidly than did voter turnout in elections once the foreign-policy crisis ended.

Finally, although many towns saw their consensual traditions bend or even break under the strain of party strife, town affairs were not conducted permanently along party lines. Contested elections–especially ones involving town representatives–became more frequent in the years 1808–1811 than ever before, and party newspapers dwelled on cases of what they regarded as flagrantly partisan aggression by their opponents. In 1811 the townsmen of Rehoboth erupted into pushing, shoving, and brawling, so that they crushed a table and forced the presiding selectmen to duck for cover behind the pulpit of the meeting house in which they were assembled. While partisan feelings ran high, the Rehoboth men resembled the Guelphs and Ghibillines more than the Whigs and Democrats.[44] Yet, as already noted, many towns managed to preserve the appearance of harmony, and many the reality. Moreover, the high party spirit that blazed through many town meetings in this era disappeared after the climate of national crisis passed away in 1815–1816.

## Good Feelings

At the outset the War of 1812 hurt Republican candidates, and as it continued to grow in unpopularity in 1813 and 1814 fewer Republicans bothered to vote or they defected to the Federalists.[45] The latter, meanwhile, labored to shuck their partisan identity. Their legislative majority issued an address urging the people to organize "a *peace party* throughout your country, and let all party distinctions vanish." During the summer many town meetings assembled, especially in such Federal enclaves as the Connecticut River Valley, to adopt antiwar resolutions. Even the Federal clergy became reactivated, and once against Federalists mobilized traditional voices to air opposition to the war and to secure their hold on political power.[46]

Though the Federal party continued to have an infrastructure of committees during the war years, its reliance on nonpartisan devices tended to cause organizational structure to atrophy. Thus, the Republican organization grew weak from defeat amid the war's unpopularity, while Federal organization withered away in success.[47]

The Federalists had not wanted to create a party in any case. They had organized to keep control of the state and to maintain pressure for changes in national policy, the focus of which was now on ending the war. Soon they found themselves carried along by the great frustration with the war to the Hartford Convention in December 1814, a meeting of Federalists from Massachusetts, Connecticut, Rhode Island, two New Hampshire counties, and one Vermont county. The convention, as Banner has shown, originated as a plan of Federal hotspurs, but pragmatic moderates eventually controlled it and prevented it from taking any action. Instead the meeting issued a demand for seven constitutional amendments that reflected New England Federalism's unhappiness with southern Republican, and specifically Virginia Republican, domination of the federal government since 1800, and with embargoes and other Republican policies. The Hartford Convention had no impact on the course of the war, or on the peace, but it did act as a "safety-valve" for antiwar sentiment in New England.[48] While the convention can be appreciated as the handiwork of relatively pragmatic leaders—some dissidents remained at the "brink of secession"—the situation that produced it was not one of party politics.

Massachusetts became less competitive during the war, and large electoral majorities accompanied the official acts and statements of dissent and defiance of national authority. In the long run, the Hartford Convention helped to bring Federalism to an end, as will be seen below. But in the short run its effect on party politics was small.

The end of the war accelerated the decline of organized competitive politics. In Boston the pealing of peace bells brought the populace into the streets for a great holiday, "and even party spirit slept for that day, and Federalist and Democrat clasped each other's hands like ancient friends."[49] Partisanship did not disappear completely, but it continued almost as an anachronism that had outlived its purpose.

In Washington the crisis of the new nation was finally over, and the congressional parties faded even more rapidly than those in Massachusetts and many other states.[50] James Monroe's accession to the presidency in 1817 reflected the reaction against partisanship, and Monroe himself worked harder than any of his predecessors to make Jefferson's "We are all republicans, we are all Federalists" a reality. Even hard-core Federalists thought Monroe moderate and a man with whom they could do business. Many Massachusetts Federal leaders hoped fervently that this meant that Monroe would favor them with prestigious government appointments.[51]

In 1817 Monroe's goodwill visit to New England inspired Benjamin Russell, the crusty editor of the *Columbian Centinel* and a paragon of Federalism, to coin the term "Era of Good Feelings" to describe the abatement of party discord. Leading Federalists welcomed and courted Monroe, taking pains "to show all Party Spirit done away." Some Federalists grumbled, and the Republican minority kept a jealous eye because everyone knew that those seeking détente also hoped for national office.[52] In 1819 the Federal governor and legislature formally expressed approval of Monroe's administration, and more than the desire of influential Federalists for office was at stake. Massachusetts was getting nowhere in asking the federal government to pay the state for militia expenses incurred in the War of 1812, and Federal leaders feared that this issue might be used by the Republicans to oust them from control of the state house. Even if Monroe only tossed the Massachusetts men a patronage bone or two, the Federalists did not wish to give up place and power in Massachusetts.[53]

Thus Federalists would not and Republicans could not revive organization. The Republican condition may be inferred from a proposal made by Alexander H. Everett, a young Boston Republican, after the Republican defeat in the 1818 state election by approximately 10,000 votes. Despite this loss, Everett was encouraged by a recent healing of a division within Republican ranks between the legislative caucus and "the Bostonians."[54] The Republican house-senate caucus had appointed a "consulting committee" to survey political prospects. It concluded that the Republicans could "revolutionize" the state if they organized first for the fall congressional election, then for the 1819 spring contest. "There should be a central committee in Maine and one in Massachusetts and County Committees in each county who should be instructed to institute town committees in their towns—the Central and County Committees were accordingly appointed."[55] Perhaps this renewed spurt of organization helped the Republicans to do better in 1819, but as a plan virtually to reinvent Republican organization it indicated a drastic lack of continuity from the structures of 1811–1812.

In the "Era of Good Feelings" Republican and Federal legislators caucused frequently, and, because of much nonrepresentation and a smaller house, legislators' loyalties could be well known.[56] Yet even in the legislature party lines often blurred, and in state and federal elections, local bipartisan coalitions frequently elected candidates. The Boston

Federalists still deployed a system of caucusing and electioneering, but elections were quiet. William Eustis was the losing gubernatorial candidate in 1820, 1821, and 1822, as the Republicans barely exerted themselves on his behalf. Then suddenly the old fires of party spirit flared up again.

## The Election of 1823

By the 1820s party competition in most states had died or had faded to a shadow, but in 1823 and 1824 Massachusetts Federalists and Republicans staged electoral battles reminiscent of their classic campaigns before 1816. While echoes of the past filled political debates (some papers published documents and essays relating to controversies of the 1790s), new issues influenced the election. Indeed, Republican victories in 1823 and 1824 ended the Federal "Indian Summer," created a new political majority, vindicated Republican partisans and finally succeeded in stigmatizing Federalism with the Hartford Convention even while accelerating the amalgamation of parties. The Republicans won in 1823 primarily because of the weakness of parties and because they exploited Federal divisions with a centrist strategy.[57]

At the start of the election season, the Federal state committee urged its followers to "Take, once more, the good old *'Long Pull, Strong Pull,* and *Pull Altogether,'* " warning that their opponents had already "advertised" their " 'County Committees' to organize their opposition." Party organization indeed improved in 1823 over what it had been the past several years, but it did not reach the level of 1811–1812. Party lines still divided some towns during March meetings, but many had returned to old modes of consensus, or arranged compromise tickets, and even where parties appeared the old intensity was gone.[58]

While Republicans still used a mixed caucus to nominate their state ticket, the Federalists, anticipating later parties, held a convention which assembled two delegates from each congressional district. County meetings generally met as in the past, but they were lukewarm affairs, in which party lines were not sharply drawn. There appeared to be little follow-through from county meetings to towns. The general situation was best summed up by the Boston *Centinel* as it complained of a "multitude of candidates" in congressional races: "Some people used formerly to order such things better."[59]

In Boston the Federal leadership seems to have drawn itself into a tight little circle of congenial gentlemen known as the "club." These men had changed little in the past quarter century and still approached politics with an elitist contempt for "little people." In 1823 they deliberately nominated a gubernatorial candidate with enough liabilities to make him a high-risk gamble. Perhaps after having catered to "milk and water Federalists" for years, and with the parties less meaningful, they no longer feared defeat. In any case Harrison Gray Otis's candidacy aggravated a split within Federalism and made "Hartford" an issue, since he had been a leading delegate to the convention.[60]

Otis's major liability in 1823 was a reputation for religious liberalism and association with eastern Unitarianism and Harvard College. In 1821 Orthodox Congregationalists had opened Amherst College but could not grant degrees, because they lacked a legislative charter. In January 1823 both houses of the General Court almost unanimously rejected Amherst's petition on the grounds that it would injure Harvard and Williams colleges, and the Orthodox themselves were somewhat divided on the matter. But in the 1820s the Orthodox-Unitarian quarrel was raging and the Orthodox were losing churches to the Unitarians. Otis was a Unitarian and a member of the governing board of Harvard, which the Orthodox had lost to the Unitarians early in the century. In 1823 the outraged Orthodox vented their frustration on Otis and helped bring down the Federal party.[61]

Amherst's Orthodox friends aided the Republican campaign, joining in charges that Otis was "notorious for his profanity and disregard of the Sabbath," and also that he was "connected with a Boston and Harvard College aristocracy, who have . . . [had] the disposal of all the most important offices in the State . . . they are acquiring a religious as well as political control . . . dangerous to the civil and religious privileges of the great body of the Congregational, Baptist, Methodist, and Episcopal friends of true religion."[62] Federalists defended Otis as a Christian believer similar in his practices to recent governors, and a member of Boston's Brattle St. Church. But the Republicans exploited not only Orthodox anger, but also the dissenters' resentment of Unitarians. The Boston *Statesman* added class grievances, saying that Otis represented the aristocratic few who used sectarian zeal and party prejudice "to ride on the backs while they have picked the pockets and tied the hands of the middling classes of society."[63]

Other issues also worked against the Federalists in 1823, though it is difficult to gauge their impact. The tariff, at best a minor issue, was already dividing Federalists.[64] More weighty was the matter of militia claims from the 1812 war which the state had still not collected from

Washington. The Republicans clearly let it be understood that only after Massachusetts elected a Republican could it hope to receive the money.[65] Otis's identification with opposition to that war strengthened this argument and was itself a much debated issue.

Though many Federalists wished not to raise the ghost of Hartford, it inevitably entered the campaign. The "club" decided to reply to all charges against Otis concerning Hartford, not just for his sake but to justify their own opposition to the war. The Republicans welcomed the chance this gave them to continue denouncing the "partisans" who had prolonged the war by always vindicating England. Even after their victory, Republican orators refused to compromise on "the stand taken by Massachusetts during the late war"; the factious opposition which then sprang from "party madness . . . *never can be justified.*"[66]

Federalists returned the Republican charges that they were reviving party feeling, and counterattacked by warning voters that the "scenes of 1811" would be repeated if Republican partisans once again seized power. Both parties tried to portray themselves as patriots, and their opponents as disloyal; they thus manipulated many symbols and images to identify themselves with the Revolutionary Center.[67]

Whatever the impact of Hartford, the defection of orthodox Federalists definitely hurt Otis. This was especially clear in the Connecticut Valley, where the Orthodox had for years contributed to heavy Federal majorities. In the state returns Eustis raised his vote from 21,000 in 1822 to over 34,000, while Otis improved on Brooks's 1822 total by fewer than 2,000 (28,287 to 30,171). Otis's vote climbed somewhat in eight counties but fell in six: three of the latter were the Connecticut Valley counties of Franklin, Hampshire, and Hampden. Perhaps the symbol of the transition for western Massachusetts Federalism came before the election when the Springfield *Federalist and Journal* changed its name to the *Hampden Journal,* implying that the name "Federalist" had become a liability.[68]

In 1823 not only was electioneering much less extensive than in 1812, but neutralism was on the rise, and perhaps stronger than it had been in 1800. Newspapers, for example, once again printed the state tickets of both parties. The Nantucket *Inquirer* demonstrated its "determined political neutrality" by presenting the gubernatorial tickets in a novel way–side by side, facing each other. Other papers imitated the *Inquirer,* and most outside of Boston gave little attention to the gubernatorial election. In Salem, once a hotbed of partisanship, a paper appeared saying it would *exclude* politics from its pages.[69] Since the 1790s it had been difficult for a general paper to survive without becoming partisan. In 1823 the tide of party was running out.

Federal leaders like Daniel Webster were soon privately arguing that it would be best for Federalists not to compete as a party any longer. Webster's New Hampshire friend Jeremiah Mason said that since the dissolution of the Federal party in the United States he saw no benefit in "retaining its name and nominally supporting its principles in a single state." Worst of all, this had impeded the "amalgamation of parties" in other states. Some Republicans encouraged this drift by pointing to the Republican legislature's choosing Federalists for important state positions.[70] Yet despite actions from both sides tending to erase old party lines, "amalgamation" would be postponed for one more state election.

### 1824: The Last Storm Wind of Party

Though ignored by historians, the state election of 1824 marked a turning point in Massachusetts political history, finally bringing an era to an end. Federalists had always regarded Republican victories as aberrations, and many, including Republicans, thought the 1823 result just that. Federalist partisans thought they would patch up their differences and bring the state back to its true bearing.[71] Instead the 1824 election confirmed the Republican hold on the state and induced the Federalists to depart forever.

During the winter of 1823–1824 the legislature had been notably free of party action, and ancient chestnuts of "party declamation" now evoked laughter.[72] When the 1824 gubernatorial election ended, one editor assured his readers that all would soon return "to that smooth tranquility which prevailed before the late gust struck and swept with such potent energy all the 'independent electors' of the state."[73] The metaphor was apt: the election was like a storm wind bringing a last burst of party spirit through the state.

Though there had been more electioneering the year before, the state election was "the sharpest contest which has taken place between the two great parties for the last ten years." One observer saw "an earnestness . . . a solicitude about voting, which every individual felt in the election."[74] In fact, some 73,000 voted, almost 10,000 more than the year before, and the last time more men cast ballots was in 1817, when Maine was still part of Massachusetts. Yet the parties do not appear to have increased their organizational efforts in 1824, and "exertions," if anything, decreased. Thus the often posited correlation between organization and turnout did not operate at all in 1824.

The Federalists, wishing above all to prevent the Orthodox Congregationalists from defecting again, nominated Samuel Lathrop for governor, the son of an Orthodox minister of West Springfield, "on Connecticut River." The Boston Federalists made much of their candidate's associations with western Orthodoxy. They referred frequently to the *"Christian education"* he had received from "the *Reverend* Dr. Lathrop . . . that *distinguished divine."* Though one might have thought Dr. Lathrop the candidate, the younger Lathrop had served as state representative and senator, and was currently in Congress. But his name was his primary qualification. The Amherst-charter question was still alive, having been rejected again by the house after senate passage. While Federalists pointed out that the votes in the house came from no party or religious division, they still feared Orthodox reaction. Western Federalists were in fact sharply divided on the issue, and in Franklin County "friends of Amherst" had launched a splinter senatorial ticket to oppose the regular Federal nominees.[75]

Other issues from 1823 persisted. Otis was no longer a candidate, but the Federal state committee probably still preferred him and lacked enthusiasm for Lathrop. The Federal leaders also permitted Otis full access to the newspapers, and so once again "Otis" and "Hartford" were "continually before the public."[76] Eustis's inaugural attack on the state's behavior during the War of 1812 had enraged many Federalists, and it motivated some of the old leaders to make the 1824 contest a warmer fight, yet the county conventions seemed pale reflections of those of a dozen years before.[77]

Like the Federalists, Republicans were not straining every nerve and muscle to outorganize their opponents.[78] While some Republicans did begin to hold up higher standards of party conduct, political neutrality kept on growing. Despite intense electioneering in some quarters, organization and party spirit declined. An occasional Republican warned against "amalgamation," but it, too, was on the rise.[79]

The last election of the Federal-Republican era was thus a curious thing, full of contradictions, like the period itself. Voters turned out in considerable numbers once again, and many voted for governor along traditional lines.[80] Continuity may have been massive, yet the changes were enough to create a new majority. That "majority" itself, however, quickly became absorbed in a general convergence on the Center, the point to which the entire political culture had been straining since the start of competitive politics.

Even before this election, the likely candidacy of John Quincy Adams for the presidency had begun to undermine party lines. Adams's election completed their destruction and the "amalgamation" that Monroe and Federal office seekers had sought for the preceding eight years. The last time an Adams had been involved in a presidential election, the effect on parties had been similar. Then it had slowed the growth of party spirit, in 1824 it hastened its collapse.

Clearly the beginnings of a new political culture had appeared, but continuities with the past remained strong. Federalist-Republican organizational efforts and citizen participation arose within an antipartisan milieu which permitted parties of a sort to form, but not a two-party "system." The Federal and Republican groupings, far more than later parties, developed as creatures of circumstance and did not take root as full-grown party institutions.

The political organization deployed in this period should not be abstracted from its environment. Rather than being an independent force imposed upon political life, party-as-organization moved up and down as events dictated. Voter turnout and organization rose together, to be sure, and while the latter probably caused the former to increase, the career of both depended more on local and external causes of "political excitement."

Partisanship in the legislature seems to have been very high from 1807 to 1815, but quite weak from 1800 to 1806 and from 1816 to 1824. Voter turnout rose in 1823–1824, but organization and legislative parties lagged behind in relative decay. Political patronage, always highly susceptible to partisan influence, also varied in intensity through the period and apparently operated within some traditional inhibitions and restraints.[81]

The inner circles of both parties, but especially those of the Federalists, worked almost in the style of eighteenth-century English political clubs. Political relations sprang primarily from social and economic ties, and thus it was easy to keep most high-level politicking hidden from public view.

The relative secrecy which characterized political organization from 1800 to 1824 stands in marked contrast to the relative openness of the Whig-Democratic period. The Federal State Central Committee operated in secrecy until 1810, as the Federalists strove to keep its workings from becoming public knowledge. Although Republicans publicized their meetings to a greater extent, an intensive study of their efforts in Berkshire County found that while Republicans gave the appearance of openness "much of [their] operation was still hidden from view."[82] Secrecy was deemed necessary so that the actions of town committees would appear to have solely local, autonomous origins–expressions of popular sentiment must appear to come forth from an unprompted popular voice. Leaders labored especially to create the impression of spontaneity.

The parties did not take great pride, at least not publicly, in their "systems." With Whigs and Democrats the possession of an armylike discipline gradually became a subject of boasting, but earlier partisans treated the matter differently. When the Federal State Committee circular of 1811 fell into Republican hands, it soon appeared in Republican papers framed with charges of conspiracy, as the Republicans tried to turn the fact of Federal organization into political capital.[83] Obviously both parties respected the persisting antiparty climate.

The historian cannot help being impressed by the extraordinary efforts at mobilizing voters. Striking, too, are the public celebrations which, like those of a later day, provided drama, entertainment, and ritual to masses of people as participants and spectators. When in 1813 Boston's Washington Benevolent Society celebrated Washington's first inaugural (a date immediately preceding the election of the state representatives), it did so "with all the pomp and circumstance it could command,–a military escort, a procession, banners with appropriate devices, an oration, and . . . exercises in the Old South Church. One special feature . . . was a company of school-boy Federalists . . . two hundred and fifty, dressed uniformly in blue and white, with Washington's Farewell Address, in red morocco, hanging round their necks. . . ."[84]

Whig and Democratic public extravaganzas also included parades, music, religious exercises, dinners, banners, icons, uniforms, and orations—all pervaded by quasi-religious patriotism. But later celebrations were much different, often larger, of course, and accompanied by brass bands while the Washington societies were still in the age of fife and drum. In the Whig-Democratic parades, participants often wore uniforms, but masses also took part dressed in citizen's garb of Sunday best or in their everyday clothing. The later spectacles were exuberant, boisterous, and filled with social enthusiasm, whereas the earlier ones had tended to be somberly ritualistic and filiopietistic. But there was a more profound difference.

Whig and Democratic parades were unabashedly party celebrations: their symbols included both those belonging to the common national stock and those they made particularly their own. Daniel Webster or Henry Clay might be revered as a great American and as a great *Whig*. The Whig and Democratic parties themselves became for many people objects of reverence–something the Federal and Republican parties had not become. Because citizens in the early national years were not worshiping parties as such, auxiliaries like the Washington Benevolent Society served well as a beginning. A society orator in Berkshire County could thus say to his audience that they deserved the censure of their countrymen "should we suffer either personal, or party views to contaminate the fair objects of our associations."[85] Even if such expressions were pretense, the antiparty constraints which prompted them cannot be ignored. In the Whig-Democratic era, on the other hand, political celebrations flaunted their party purpose and nature.

## VI. Deference, Influence, and Balloting

The eighteenth century's deferential style of politics did not end suddenly. No single event or set of events marked its passing, and historians are hard pressed to decide which decade–from at least the 1780s to the 1820s–saw its utter demise.[1] While voters may be counted and organizations observed, face-to-face relations and the tacit assumptions often governing them are less easily seen or quantified. Historians have usually supposed that partisan competition and traditional influence were incompatible and that self-conscious elitism became dysfunctional in a more democratic environment. Neither of these things was necessarily so. Federalists and Republicans wielded "influence" and engaged in traditional role playing not out of nostalgia or idiosyncrasy, but often because it gave them power.

In a changing political and social milieu, deference and influence remained and adapted. The old and new existed side by side, or fused together. Was the glass half-full or half empty? Neither. As participation and organized competition grew, "influence" often provided the cement of organization.

Deference meant that men still deferred to their betters, to men of property and standing. Since the Revolution, of course, all men had stood on an equal footing as "citizens," a concept which militated against political hierarchy. The Revolution's ideology and social upheavals, as well as the struggles of nation making, had let loose powerful egalitarian impulses, and the rhetoric of politics had become grounded in popular sovereignty.[2] But political reality remained complex and changed unevenly. A "habit of subordination" continued while influence in politics reflected a man's standing in society. The 1780 Massachusetts constitution allowed only those citizens owning a "freehold of one thousand pounds value" to be governor, and for state senators it required a freehold of three hundred pounds or a personal estate of six hundred.[3] It is fairly well known that throughout the early republican years both in Massachusetts and elsewhere in the nation candidates for higher offices were drawn regularly from society's upper classes.[4]

Not so well appreciated, however, have been the "exertions" of "Gentlemen of respectability" before and especially during elections. Before elections prominent men made their positions known to peers, friends, dependents, and neighbors. While the polls were open, each party sent workers to distribute their "tickets," and in the larger towns in particular they often stationed influentials at the polls to survey the balloting. Their physical presence at the polls was of prime importance because voting was a social act, often if not usually open. The persistence of influence did not necessarily depend on citizens' at the polls observing one another or on their being observed by those taking an interest, but these were significant elements of a deferential-participant political culture.

American politics were never as deferential as English politics, but the former mother country's own experience in the nineteenth century is instructive.[5] Britain moved through very gradual stages toward the kind of wide popular suffrage of adult white males that prevailed, or nearly did, early in the United States. The period from 1832 to 1867, after the First Reform Bill, was perhaps the classic period of deferential politics. When the Second Reform Bill almost doubled the old electorate of nearly a million, the notables still dominated politics, including the constituency-oriented associations and clubs that grew outside of Parliament. Even after the changes of the late nineteenth century–the (Secret) Ballot Act of 1872, the Corrupt Practices Act of 1883, more expansion of the suffrage, to county householders, in 1884, all of which lessened the power of influence and purse–"the toughness of the old forms" can still be discerned even down to the First World War.[6]

During the 1870s and 1880s, mass party organizations came into being in Britain for the first time on a scale comparable to those foreshadowed in 1805–1815 and established by 1840 in the United States. Social movements had erupted in Britain from the 1830s on and had emphasized organization and constituency mobilization in the American mode. As the electorate kept widening (1832, 1867, 1884) and as methods of organization adapted, deferential styles persisted as party organization evolved slowly, and different kinds of politics hung together or formed an amalgam of old and new.[7]

The United States also had its "Deferential Participant" phase–briefer and less deferential than Britain's–but one in which mass participation grew rapidly, stimulated by elite conflict and encouraged by political authorities, even while the middling classes and rank-and-file voters still selected for office men from the upper strata, gentlemen of "respectability" and "influence."[8] This was a phase both deferential and democratic, traditional and modern, participatory and elitist.

### Deference in Massachusetts, 1790s–1820s

Most definitions of "deference" stress its constituting a network of beliefs and values concerning role expectations implicit in and regulating social interactions.[9] Its power lay in silence–in being a habit, largely unconscious and automatic. The historian thus must look at the hidden assumptions and tacit recognitions of social situations likely to reveal the continuance or rejection of deference. Surely deference was rejected by the laborer who, in a 1796 Dedham town meeting, rose to his feet after a carefully reasoned speech by Fisher Ames, a lawyer and prominent citizen, and said, "Mr. Moderator, my brother Ames' eloquence reminds me of nothing but the shining of a fire-fly which was just light enough to show its own significance." It was as surely acknowledged by members of the legislature in 1803 who, after turning down a petition from a majority of the inhabitants of the town of Kingston, gave as their reason the fact that "the Honorable Squire Sever is against it."[10]

Evidence may be found on both sides throughout the period, and sometimes the impressions one receives are double-edged. In 1800 during the official mourning of Washington's death in Boston, about 2,500 citizens marched to the Old South Meeting House, with notables leading the way. The "mechanic interest," bringing up the rear, found it must camp outside, and for days thereafter the artisans debated the fairness of the arrangements, some upholding their propriety and others complaining of mistreatment.[11] This incident is peculiarly representative of a transitional period, with evidence pointing both to deference's decline and to its persistence.

In 1827 in Berkshire County, during the annual cattle show, a procession marched to the church for an oration in an order reversing that of the Boston parade, by twos, with men separated from women, and the clergy and dignitaries to the rear. But when the head of the column reached the church, "a general halt took place, and a lane being formed . . . the two clergymen took off their hats, and advanced from the end of the line up the avenue formed by the double row of people." As the clergy passed, "about one in ten of those who were in line touched their hats." To the English traveler Basil Hall these proceedings appeared to be an "amusing though rather clumsy *compromise* which arises from wealth and station, and the nominal rights and privileges of that much talked of equality which belongs to a democracy." Over twenty years earlier in Berkshire, Catherine Sedgwick recalled, her father, Theodore, would glower when any "free-and-easy mechanic came to the *front* door, and upon one occasion I remember him turning off the 'east steps' (I am *sure* not kicking but the demonstration was unequivocal) a grown-up lad who kept his hat on after being told to take it off."[12] These incidents also point in two different directions–to a populace less tractable *and* to one with continuing habits of deference. Perhaps their greatest significance lies in what is most obvious: namely, the existence of clear social distinctions which continued to shape behavior even as formal and outward displays of deference weakened.

"Go into every village in New England," said John Adams in the late 1780s, "and you will find that the office of justice of peace, and even the place of representative, *which has ever depended only on the freest election of the people,* have generally descended, from generation to generation, in three or four families at most." Early in the next century, however, William Bentley complained of the destructive effects of political competition on the quality of officeholders. "To be accountable for the vices of a party, how heavy a tax upon influence! How can our best politicians answer? To quiet parties we must tolerate, and even promote those who have no claim to favor, not to say who have no desert but of contempt."[13] Bentley could not have put the case more starkly: "influence" waning before "party," and the Federal-Republican party wars had just begun.

Yet partisan competition and traditional influence were not necessarily incompatible. Sometimes the latter declined as the former increased, as Bentley suggested, but party and influence (or deference) did not invariably stand in inverse relation to one another.

Nor was it necessarily true that persisting elitism and influence were dysfunctional. Historians have often assumed that the Federalists' expectations of deference and their elitism turned them into political dinosaurs and that only as Federalists adapted to a more democratic environment did they raise their chances of political survival. In this view, Federal reliance on "influence" was anachronistic and a hindrance to effective responses to mass participation. This is part of the truth, in some places at some times. But reliance on "influence" hardly survived merely as a relic of the past and a source of weakness. Some dissonance appears in this view when it is recognized that many Republicans, who allegedly led the way in party organizing and in opening up politics, also shared the elitism and status consciousness of the Federalists.[14] That indeed was the case: many Republican and Federal leaders shared many assumptions about society and politics. Moreover, elitism and influence still were highly functional in electoral politics.

The Federal leaders' often observed liking for traditional dress and posturing was not simply an idiosyncratic, self-indulgent conservatism. It was rather an integral part of what their social roles required, and in keeping up "in the manner of life, the style of olden times," they perpetuated influence. Descriptions of Federalists offer a clue to their style by frequently emphasizing the "coldness," "frigidity," or "austerity" of their manners. This cloak of cold propriety would seem to have been particularly useful in creating or maintaining social distance in a transitional age. It seems especially appropriate for a new republic, and considering that many high Federalists had made fortunes only since the Revolution, their style strikes one as the bourgeois equivalent of aristocratic hauteur.

Christopher Gore represented one kind: rich, self-made, active in politics, and outfitted with the possessions and bearing of an English aristocrat, who mingled with the populace in city or country by riding through it, standing or seated in a glittering carriage behind outriders and liverymen. "When Governor Gore, in 1809, made a state visit to Newburyport, where he had once studied law, he came in a coach and four with outriders, uniformed aides, and a cavalry escort; and when the town fathers informed his ancient benefactress, Madam Atkins, that His Excellency would honor her with a call, the spokesman delivered his message on his knees at the good lady's feet."[15]

From modest beginnings, too, George Cabot emerged from the Revolution rich and ennobled: "there was nothing of an *arriviste* in his demeanor. He matured into a splendid figure of a gentleman, tall and straight as a grenadier, with alert penetrating blue eyes, ruddy complexion, and fine white hair queued neatly behind him."[16]

Among the powerful Federal justices was Theophilus Parsons, "considered by his contemporaries to be an impressive combination of frigidity and reason."[17] Even more forbidding, though he lived only until 1806, was Francis Dana, grandfather of Richard Henry Dana, and Parsons' predecessor as chief justice. Active in the Continental Congress, a signer of the Articles of Confederation, and a minister to Russia, Dana possessed "a prodigiously English look." On circuit the judge "travelled in the style of an English lord; in Cambridge he set himself apart by austere manners, by a fine mansion on top of Dana Hill, and by a spurious coat of arms. His costume was eccentric but imposing. He carried a gold-headed cane and a white fur muff, and over his embroidered waist-coat he wore a great cloak brought back from the court of Catherine the Great."[18]

Not all Federalists were cold, however, and not all cold Federalists were cold all of the time. Classically deference required that great men treat their clients and dependents with due recognition of their independence and dignity. Many occasions called for "affability" from the elite. "Only a great man," according to J. G. A. Pocock, "could have affable manners. It was a failure of *ton* to ascribe them to one not of superior station. . . ." Even so pure a Federalist as Fisher Ames, the Cassandra of his generation, could good-naturedly harangue voters in the streets of Dedham before an election. Ames's recent biographer has insisted that Ames's acute awareness of the common man's limitations "did not affect his amiable [or affable?] association with yeoman-farmer neighbors and other Dedham townspeople."[19]

Ames is well known to historians both for his eloquently gloomy assessments of the state of the nation after 1800 and for his efforts to adapt to mass participation. Though a dogged social and cultural conservative, Ames appreciated the power of organization and constantly urged his friends to be more systematic in their exertions. His leading project after 1800 was to create a central party newspaper for New England, and he hoped that the *Palladium* would become *"the* [London] Gazette of the party." At the same time, Ames proposed that this new "engine" be employed through "your clergy, your legislators, your good men." The recognition of the need to make and shape opinion constituted a change from what public men had assumed a short time ago.[20]

Yet a hierarchical view of public opinion was not simply discarded after 1800 in a rush to manipulate opinion systematically on a large scale. Political men still thought of exerting "influence" primarily by going through influential men.

The *Palladium* formed only the main prong of Fisher Ames's desired counteroffensive. He also exhorted his friends to secure state governments and courts for federalism: "Let the first men be persuaded to take places in the state assemblies. Let a system of conciliation and courting of the people–I mean such as are yet undecided–be pursued; let it be a system of proselytism." And pointing to an institution usually overlooked by historians but important to early republican politics, Ames said, "Let the popular and wealthy Federalists take commissions in the militia, and try to win the men."[21]

Militia companies offered an excellent opportunity to launch or assist a political career. Men of standing could court popularity without being obvious or losing stature. As officers in a military and thus a clearly hierarchic group, they could maintain distance while gaining reputations for affability.[22] It is doubtful that militia companies voted en bloc, and strict laws prevented any militia activities from taking place on election days. But it is clear that influence in the militia, like that in churches or voluntary associations, helped men in politics by providing communication networks across class and other lines of social differentiation. Militia elections could serve as trial runs and indicate a candidate's potential in standing for public office. And at the height of political competition after 1810, the militia's internal regulations became themselves subjects of political controversy.[23]

Although the militia, the Masonic fraternity, and other groups might be useful as vehicles for gaining popularity in politics,[24] Massachusetts political culture did not yet sanction candidates' openly "running" for office. Rather, nominees "stood" after being "put forward" by friends. Accusations that political opponents violated this norm testify to its continuing vitality. Candidates sometimes engaged in real or trumped-up controversies in the newspapers just before elections, thus gaining name recognition. These tactics themselves could elicit charges of a man's "coming forward in the public papers in his own favor." While it would take a separate study to determine the extent to which this convention was observed or flouted, there is evidence that the informal taboo against "running" lasted well into the 1820s. When Josiah Quincy, the epitome of the Federalist as self-conscious public servant, addressed a Federal caucus in Faneuil Hall in 1820 regarding the nominees for senator of Suffolk County, he claimed this was the first time in twenty years that he had addressed such a gathering, "he having always been a candidate for office of some kind, and it not being then the custom for candidates to address public meetings called to promote their own election." Though candidates for office might not compete openly, they nevertheless politicked privately and sometimes extensively with friends. William Eustis, for example, rode about quietly in a one-horse open wagon that became known as "his electioneering wagon, it was so often seen during the canvas at the gates of Esquire Seaver and his other political friends."[25]

Candidates who stood for office, like their English counterparts, also engaged in "treating" the voters—that is, buying them food, or usually drink, or supplying feed for their horses or other amenities, but especially drink. A Maine Republican complained in 1809 about "a want of Patriotic firmness among the common people" that Federalists induced:

"three traders with rum, can do more than Solomon with his wisdom." Again it is difficult to know the extent of these practices, but it is clear that drinking on election days was common and expected.[26]

In the 1820s, however, with the rise of temperance throughout Massachusetts, drinking and treating at elections must have declined. On March 3, 1828, for example, the town of Greenfield disapproved "of treating at elections" and declared "that persons elected to office be requested to abstain from this practice at this and all future meetings."[27] At the same time, towns and churches came down hard on the custom of drinking at funerals and other social occasions. Yet while the rites of burial became much drier across the state, the connection between politics and ardent spirits was not easily broken.

The emphasis above was on Federal perpetuation of influence, but it is worth repeating that Republicans also brought the habits and customs of the eighteenth century into fusion with modes of mass participation. At the very end of the period occurred an incident involving the Republican governor William Eustis which revealed much of the spirit of Federal-Republican political culture. It came after the final defeat of Federalism, and long after the democratizing influences of competition and organization had penetrated, so we are told, deep into political life. The story, told by Eustis's adjutant general (a Federalist), illustrated that while the former Revolutionary surgeon had a "high aristocratic bearing on all occasions," he could when necessary bend to be "friendly and familiar." One night while Eustis was at dinner with eighteen to twenty guests, two middling- or lower-class political friends of the governor burst in on the assembly. Brushing aside the servant at the door, they made their way determinedly into the dining room, avowing that the governor had promised to be ready to receive them always.

> Upon their entrance . . . the governor, desirous to impress them with the formality which was suited to the occasion, rose and took them familiarly by the hand, and said to Lord Stanley, "I introduce to your lordship two of my most worthy friends, Mr. Clough and Mr. Eaton. They have done me the honor of a call uninvited, no doubt with the object of paying their respects to my friends." Instead of being abashed as . . . would have . . . men of different habits, one of them broke out, "I am glad to have been introduced to your lordship, and to have been present on this occasion. The governor always expresses his willingness to see me on these great occasions, and I am very happy to have been present when your lordship was here."

After some further talk, Mrs. Eustis "got rid of" the two men by rising from the table and asking them to follow her, perhaps to the kitchen.[28]

**Influential Men at the Polls, 1790s–1820s**

In the Federal-Republican period, "campaigns" did not really exist, political leaders did not engage in extensive speech making, and parties held few political rallies. Most speeches and rallies occurred in large towns on the eve of elections. To these rallies came the party's "great men," its orators, cadres, and core voters, and especially those who would work at the polls or in the streets and countryside on election day.

Who a man was counted heavily on election day. Communities were still small and most people were known. Men most widely known and respected were essential to a partisan interest's viability.

Indeed, the informal activities of influential men just before and during elections probably formed the most important component of electoral competition.[29] For one thing, not much else was involved. Newspapers had only limited circulation, and it is perhaps too easy for later generations to fix on these surviving sources of past politics and to overestimate the degree to which electioneering depended on print.[30]

Influential men were important at the polls because voting was virtually open in most places. This aspect of political life was so revealing, indeed, that it will be treated extensively in a later section. Besides the openness of voting, the law required that a list of all eligible voters be displayed conspicuously throughout the town before election day so that all could know whether or not they were on the list. In closely balanced towns considerable efforts would be made to publicize these assessors' lists to insure that all of a party's eligible friends were on the lists.[31] Knowledge of *who* voted was thus readily accessible, and it was usually possible to know *how* men voted.

Open voting meant that influential men actually monitored the polls and engaged in surveillance. This gave incentive to friends, relatives, dependents, employees, and other members of influence networks, first, to appear at the polls and, second, to vote right.

Republicans tended to complain that Federalist "influence" often amounted to nothing less than "force." Levi Lincoln dramatically explained the Federal state victory of 1805 in these terms:

> By *force,* I mean an intolerant and oppressive violence towards laborers, tenants, mechanics, debtors, and other dependents: every species of influence, on every description of persons, has been practiced, and with a shameless effrontery. Individuals have been threatened, with a deprivation of employment, and an instant exaction of debt to the last farthing as a Consequence of withholding a federal vote, or rather of not giving one.

> Persons steeped in poverty, were enabled by federal art and management, not charity, to claim property . . . sufficient to qualify for voting. The chambers, and even the beds of the sick and dying, were forced to part with their possessors in the struggle.[32]

While the partisan Lincoln exaggerated, Federalists did, in part because of their social position and views, rely more than Republicans on throwing the weight of authority, property, and power behind their electoral efforts. To some extent this simply reflected the reality that Federal leaders' commanded more resources of "influence" than did Republicans.[33]

Federalists themselves provided ample testimony to the power of "influence" or wealth in elections by the arguments they gave *in favor* of a property qualification for voting. In the 1820 constitutional convention leading Federalists objected to a proposal to remove all property qualifications from voting, with the argument that this would only increase the power of wealth. For that reason, they said, the lifting of any property test was "anti-republican" because it greatly increased the number of voters of a kind "most liable to be improperly influenced or corrupted." Even in the country "a rich man in a populous town might command the votes of men without any property." Josiah Quincy stated bluntly that only the rich, not the poor, gained by such a measure. The rich man, "by the influence resulting from his property over the class of paupers, has a power of indemnifying himself a hundred fold." At present, said Quincy, the removal posed little danger, but that would change with the coming "establishment of a great manufacturing interest." There was nothing in the condition of our country, he maintained, to prevent workers from being "absolutely dependent upon their employers, here as they are everywhere else. The whole body of every manufacturing establishment, therefore, are dead voters, counted by the head, by the employer."[34] Quincy's vision referred to the future, but he and other Federalists had also testified to the role of influence in a nonindustrial setting.

A prominent merchant's economic power clearly contributed to his influence at the polls. In Boston the likes of Thomas H. Perkins, Stephen Higginson, and Harrison Gray Otis acted as vote distributors in the 1790s. In New Bedford in 1800 a Federal customs inspector stood by the selectmen and scrutinized every voter (according to Republicans). In Newburyport in 1804 "twenty-seven persuasive shipmasters" distributed ballots. In Salem in 1807 "the men of first name and property appeared in person to solicit votes at the pole [sic]."[35]

In 1806 the Federal State Central Committee sent a secret circular letter to Federal county committees which emphasized that electoral success depended on their rallying "the well-disposed citizens in the particular towns" and that they should get "valuable citizens . . . not only to attend the elections, but to be early at their posts, and to persevere until their objects are accomplished." The following year the committee urged the quarreling Federalists of Bristol County to patch up their differences and to elect their senators, because the balance of power in the legislature would be extremely close. The central committee called on "the exertions of every individual especially those of Influence . . . to promote the Election by all the means in their power. The least coldness or Indifference by Gentlemen of Respectability will advance the Democratic list. . . ." They asked further that "Gentlemen of Character and Weight in the County reflect on the Consequences of their exertions."[36]

Although "influence" was only one of many factors shaping the outcome of elections,[37] it nevertheless remained strong throughout the period because both Federalists and Republicans relied on it. In Salem the Reverend Bentley complained often that Federalists intimidated "the dependent citizens."[38] He observed, "We [Republicans] make a respectable figure in our numbers, but when we have any internal measures to pursue, wealth and rank tell us we have little independence." Yet two years later he attributed a Republican defeat in an 1810 congressional election to "the disappointed ambition of a few influential men [which] produced all the mischief,"[39] revealing that the Republican interest much resembled the Federal in its hierarchic structure.

The Federalists' tenacity in clinging to traditional holds over voters and the Republicans' willingness to criticize "influence," even while they were hardly strangers to its practical benefits, surfaced near the end of the era in a controversy in Boston. The town became incorporated as a city in 1822, a decision which engendered much debate. One major issue involved a proposal to establish decentralized polling places in wards instead of the traditional method of voting in Faneuil Hall. The Federal elite, which favored adoption of the city charter, wanted to continue having the voting for major offices in one place, though for years certain local officials had been elected by ward. Republicans tended to prefer ward elections for federal and state officials, because this would prevent "intrigues" and "the coaxing of mechanics." Journeymen, they said, often did not vote at the general town meeting, because they were unable to come the distance or for fear of offending their employers. Federalists replied publicly that the Faneuil Hall polling had been the "pride of the town" and the "wonder of strangers." Privately, Federalists conducted more candid discussions about the impact of the change on Federal influence.

Some Federalists accepted it and sought to assure worried friends that they need not fear that voters would lack guidance or be less inclined to vote. The Federal caucuses could continue to operate in wards, and "the tickets agreed on in the federal caucus may be, and probably will be voted for, by the same persons." Indeed, even more Federal votes might result, "because the old and infirm, and the indifferent, may go to the ward polls, who would not encounter the rough and tumble of an election meeting, held by all the Inhabitants."[40] Harrison Gray Otis, however, argued the reverse, and feared that the town would "be revolutionized to a certainty" if ward voting were adopted.[41] He urged that the traditional system be retained to save the city for Federalism:

> This depends upon the influence and example of the most respectable persons in the various walks and professions who have long been habituated to act together. The force of these persons is increased by the sympathy and enthusiasm of numbers, and by a feeling of shame or self reproach which attends the consciousness of a known dereliction of duty. The class which is *acted upon* by this example and influence realize a pride and pleasure in showing their colors upon a general review, which they cannot feel when trained in a gun house. The old leaders have learnt the art of giving a salutary impulse to the whole body when collected together. . . . It is easier to manage the town of B—— by a Lancastrian system of political discipline than to institute numerous schools. Practically, you know how languid is the attendance and interest taken in the ward meetings for assessors, board of health &c. by the right sort of people. . . .[42]

The "right sort" reluctantly bowed to the new ward system and continued efforts to overturn or modify its effects. More than a year later a Republican newspaper protested against "the aristocracy's" efforts to return to "the system of dictating and browbeating which had so long been practiced at Faneuil Hall." The gentry were now petitioning the legislature to allow ward meetings to be held out of the ward when no convenient place existed within. But, said the *Statesman,* there was no ward in the city without such a place, "whatever the Beacon-street gentry may aver to the contrary." They did not want meeting places located near mechanics' doors because then the artisans acted independently and "against an overbearing aristocracy. They wish to render it less convenient for mechanics to leave their work . . . [to vote]–they wish to have every vote put into the box at one place, where the rich, the proud, and the impudent, may take their stand and overawe those who may have more mind, more honesty, and more patriotism, but LESS MONEY!"[43] Though Otis and the *Statesman* obviously gave very different interpretations of the old way of balloting at Faneuil Hall, both testified clearly to the tenacity of deference and influence. Both suggested, if only because of their self-consciousness, that influence had waned by 1823. Yet the view of neither could be taken as evidence that traditional modes had passed entirely from the political scene.

### The Expansion of the Electorate

**Anecdote of the 1st of April [1811]**

> [The *"Chief"* or "Giant of the Law" came into Faneuil Hall] wrapt up in his usual habiliments of coats, surtouts, cloaks, bandannas, &c. marched up with great *dignity* to the Selectmen, and put in his vote. He then turned about and was marching out the same way.—"Sir, has your name been checked?" said one of the ward committee—*"That's your lookout, not mine,"* was the answer. This *broad hint* was received as a complete decision. . . . But what is the practice on the same floor as it respects *"common folks"?* The constable attending on the Selectmen, will frequently take a man by the sleeve, or the button of his coat, (not the *collar*) and ask him, "is your name checked?" If the answer is *no*—"you must get checked before you can vote," is the reply. The Selectmen receiving the votes will often draw in the box, and ask, "is your name checked?"—if the answer is no;—"you must be checked before you vote." But was all or any of this ceremony of sleeving, buttoning or drawing back observed with the *Giant of the Law?*—O no. . . .[44]

In the early nineteenth century the act of voting was hardly the antiseptically private procedure whose uniformity Americans take for granted. Not only did it vary from town to town, but, as this incident shows, individuals could be treated quite differently at any one place. This Faneuil Hall episode also reveals the discretionary power of local officials, especially of selectmen, in shaping the conduct and sometimes the outcome of elections. It is essential to recognize that the tremendous expansion of the electorate after 1800 must be seen in the context of local community practices and social relationships. Many new voters, probably most, decided on their own to take sides, drawn in by the highly charged issues of partisan competition.[45] Many other voters, perhaps as sincerely engaged in the great questions of the day, could cast ballots because local authorities and influential men in effect sponsored them as voters. Many poor or young men qualified as voters because selectmen loosened the rules or because wealthy partisans provided them with proofs of property.

Contemporaries disagreed about the effect of property requirements on lower-class and young voters. The 1780 constitution required that in order to vote in state elections male inhabitants twenty-one years of age must own a freehold estate of the annual value of three pounds or any estate of sixty pounds. In practice this meant that nonfreeholders usually came to the polls prepared to demonstrate ownership of sufficient personal property, which could consist of tools, livestock, household furniture, money, or even a note showing that someone owed a debt to the would-be voter. Federalists generally argued that "in this country, where the means of subsistence were so abundant, and the demand for labor so great, every man of sound body could acquire the necessary qualifications." Apprentices and the sons of poor farmers, they said, were encouraged by the property requirement "to lead a life of industry and economy." For most poor mechanics and laborers, even the "household furniture exempted by law from attachment" by creditors was nearly enough to give them the right to vote.[46]

Republicans tended to emphasize that the requirement excluded worthy men and that, worse, it was easily abused. At every election, said one delegate to the 1820 constitutional convention, questions are continually put to voters: "what property have you? have you the tools of your trade? Yes. What else? A pair of steers my father gave me. And if this was not enough, then, he said, a note, which is never intended to be paid, makes up the balance." Honest poor men who paid their debts often could not vote, said another Republican; nor could laboring men with no freehold or property to the amount of two hundred dollars, though they supported their families reputably with their daily earnings; nor could sailors who worked hard but spent too freely.[47]

Historians have held that the property requirement prevented very few adult males from voting, yet the number of those actually excluded from voting during the period 1800–1820 is difficult to determine.[48] Furthermore, the abundant testimony concerning illegal aid to voters suggests that even if an insignificant number could not vote, partisans nevertheless went to some trouble to make sure that all their potential voters would be able to satisfy the requirements on election day.

Federalists and Republicans repeatedly exhorted their adherents to check the assessors' lists to make sure their names were on them. An 1800 law required assessors and selectmen to post in public a list of all qualified voters for at least fourteen days before the April elections. The lists thus functioned as voter registration lists. In other states in the 1820s and 1830s, opponents of registration laws argued that they discriminated against the transient and poor.[49] In Massachusetts, it is likely that the lower classes were hindered in voting, and in any case those excluded constituted a significant group in the minds of rival partisans.

In the eighteenth century, cheating and confusion occasionally accompanied elections even in small towns.[50] After 1800, however, charges of fraud and bribery became common, and especially allegations that unqualified voters had been allowed to vote.[51] That illegalities took place is beyond doubt, though the extent of such actions will always be a matter of dispute for most periods of American history.[52] Both sides cheated at times, and, more important, men of property, influence, or authority on both sides led in efforts to maximize votes, legally or otherwise.

Amos Kendall described in his *Autobiography* how as a poor law student in 1813 he had been given money to take to the polls should he be questioned there about having enough property to vote. Those giving him the money to cast an illegal vote were Boston lawyers and, of course, men of standing. In Salem, Bentley described polling-place shenanigans in 1802, with an "alien Dutch man accepted & another refused. Both rejected at length. A Voucher for a man, whose family never lived in town. A Voucher for a Negro who had not one farthing of property, & the men were no less than a Derby, an Orne, & a Marston."[53] In 1820 even a political philosopher who condemned the "evil example" of election officers abusing their power by passing on voters' qualifications "under the influence of party feelings" added that doubtful cases should be resolved in favor of men's voting, "because it is more agreeable to the spirit of republican institutions to favour, than to restrain the rights of voting."[54]

Most selectmen apparently agreed, and their ability to control elections remained important throughout the period. Selectmen not only decided who could vote, but their general conduct could also affect the result. Unless they took a firm hand, there could be crowding, noise, and tumult. The polls might suddenly be opened or closed. The selectmen might insist on quiet, order, and discipline, or they might for political reasons be permissive and tacitly condone confusion. Therefore Federalists and Republicans continually reminded their cohorts of the necessity of voting at town meetings and urged that "'the greatest vigilance be exercized in the choice of town officers."[55] In 1809 a local Republican caucus met to decide how to cope with hostile selectmen: "the greatest thing we have to contend with is regulating the list–there being all federal Selectmen [who] are disposed to refuse republican votes and put in federal votes–however I was one of a Committee to meet with them and you may depend upon it we fought hard. . . ." "Where parties are so evenly balanced," said a Republican paper in 1817, "the majority may be determined either way by a few towns losing or gaining their town officers."[56]

As noted earlier, not all town elections became partisan. Political contention obviously became important in the larger towns and in some others at various times. After 1815, partisanship fell off here as in other political spheres. Town meetings and the selectman's post became depoliticized as consensual modes returned. In the 1830s, when party revived, local elections again became intensely contested in many towns.[57] By then there existed even fewer impediments to the re-expansion of the electorate, but selectmen could still have much impact on elections. At the same time, other traditional elements of political culture persisted, especially the character of voting as a social ritual and one that was usually open rather than secret.

## The Ballot

In 1820 the town of Ashburnham in Worcester County published a warrant calling for a meeting to vote on constitutional amendments: "All the voters to be seated and when called upon to vote then all that vote to rise and stand up with their heads uncovered until they are counted and then sit down in their seats again with their heads covered." This illustrated perhaps the most important aspect of elections in the early nineteenth century: voting was mostly open. Indeed, early statutes regulating voting probably encouraged open voting by their language.[58] It is impossible to determine exactly how much so, for election modes varied across Massachusetts, as they did throughout the United States, from the 1790s through the 1840s and after.

Election procedures did not move uniformly in one direction from open to closed, in accordance with the twentieth-century assumption that secret voting was inherently a better or freer way of voting. The very concept of complete freedom of choice in privacy was one that was still developing and establishing itself in the United States and Great Britain.[59] In Massachusetts, not only did election modes vary by locality in the period 1800–1850, but individual towns sometimes experimented with different methods, going back and forth from relatively closed to more open voting.

It was not the case, as many later observers have believed, that "the secret ballot was unknown."[60] Such blanket statements cannot possibly cover the variety of voting practices through time in Massachusetts, let alone the United States. And while the Jeffersonians and Democrats tended to agitate for a secret and thus protected ballot, the adoption of closed modes did not necessarily lead the electorate to move uniformly to their side in voting. Secrecy, Stein Rokkan has pointed out, could cut both ways. It might, as its advocates often intended, discourage bribery and protect workers and dependents from being intimidated. But the secret ballot could also allow the "deferential" lower classes to escape judgment from their peers if they voted for their betters. Secrecy thus reduced "the pressures toward conformity and solidarity within the working classes."[61] Many later assumptions which have governed views of voting and procedural "reforms" need to be discarded and the subject reopened.

The Ashburnham warrant's prescription for voting on constitutional referenda differed from Massachusetts voting procedures in one major way: all voting for federal and state offices was done by written ballots. In the eighteenth century the written ballot, in contrast to viva voce, seems generally to have been associated with a relatively secret ballot.[62] Both written and voice votes were common in the twenty-five years after the Revolution, and though by 1800 most states used paper ballots, practices differed widely. In 1792 Kentucky had adopted paper ballots, only to return in 1799 to viva voce voting, keeping it in most elections until 1891. For a long time thereafter in that state, extensive influence mongering and intimidation was also practiced, especially by sheriffs, the chief election officers, and by constables. In Connecticut, stand-up voting and habitual deferential practices lasted until the constitutional change of 1818. Elsewhere, written or printed ballots did not necessarily provide secrecy and even engendered charges that "slight of hand men" easily practiced fraud.[63] Though state courts in the decades before 1850 tried to preserve the secrecy of the ballot, voting remained virtually open in many states, and in several of them viva voce continued into the 1840s and 1850s.[64]

In Massachusetts, written ballots remained the rule in nonlocal elections from 1780 to 1830, and though some attempts were made to introduce printed ballots, Federalists and Republicans paid remarkably scant attention to the matter. A 1788 statute explicitly made it unlawful for any official presiding over state or federal elections to receive any vote unless "delivered in writing by the voter in person." Yet as early as 1794 John Adams condemned an "unwarrantable" and "indecent" attempt to influence an election "by sending agents with printed votes." In 1804 Federalists and Republicans apparently planned to make use of printed ballots in the fall presidential election, but about a month before the election the solicitor general gave an inconclusive opinion and "recommended adherence to the old custom as the safest course for the occasion." That sent the two parties scurrying to arrange for the writing of ballots with nineteen electors listed on each. In Salem Bentley observed: "the writing of Election Tickets [is] a serious concern to both parties, in which they are busy."[65]

Federalists and Republicans employed squads of scribblers to write ballots in quantity so that vote distributors could furnish supporters on election day "with WRITTEN VOTES, that is with votes *written with a pen.*"[66] In the 1820 constitutional convention the idea of printed ballots surfaced briefly and disappeared. So partisans continued to assemble pen men to write out ballots by the dozen. Even in voting for town moderator, as a children's primer said in 1829, "men write, on little pieces of paper, the name of the person they wish to have for moderator."[67]

Boston Republicans tended to urge the utility of printed votes, in part because they felt themselves at a disadvantage against the Federalists, who dominated the clerical classes of the capital and could more readily employ teams of writers. The Republican David Henshaw and the Boston *Statesman* faction, later the nucleus of the Jackson party, led the way in ballot innovation in the 1820s. In one election Henshaw provided voters with tickets "decorated and embellished with a fair type, and with a flaming ship and eagle."[68] After agitating for printed ballots in his newspaper, Henshaw challenged the constitutionality of the written-ballot requirement. In the May house election, Henshaw gave the election inspectors in Boston's Seventh Ward a printed vote for fifty-five persons, was refused, and then brought suit against the inspectors. Judge C. J. Parker heard the case and decided that "written" could, finally, mean "printed" and that surely the framers of the constitution intended that the words they used be adapted to the future.[69] Thus by 1831 political groups distributed printed ballots widely and probably tried to play even more tricks on opponents, since production of false tickets was much easier.[70] At the same time, tickets with various emblems and of different colors made it possible for voters "to show their colors" and for those interested to know how they voted.

Printed votes obviously helped to smooth the way for mass political parties to operate, yet the decision permitting them came at a time of political calm, and parties did not immediately spring up as a result of this change. Significantly, Henshaw, a political entrepreneur and later chief of the Democrats' office-holding faction, led the fight for this structural change. It is also striking that Federal-Republican political culture left printed ballots for a later politics to adopt.

Printed votes rapidly became the norm for most elections after 1830, but the eighteenth-century practice of open voting continued. Throughout the early national period, indeed, it was the case that, while practices varied, in general the more local the election, the more open the voting.

In elections for president, Congress, governor, or state representatives, which required written ballots, anything might happen from year to year, depending on local custom, the selectmen's preferences, and the ingenuity of partisans. In town meetings, voting was often viva voce, by a show of hands, standing and being counted, or standing and moving to opposite sides of the room.[71]

In Salem, during an 1811 town meeting that lasted three days, voters were virtually organized into phalanxes. The Federalists had formed a "Columbian Society" of almost 400 men who, according to Republicans, "signed an obligation, under a penalty," to go to the meeting and stay there until business was finished. This force assembled near the town hall, "and on the ringing of the bell, with unbroken ranks, and with the discipline of veterans, they have marched into Town-Hall, and filled more than half of it in less than 10 minutes." During the meetings balloting frequently proceeded by having everyone leave the hall and then return, those for one candidate coming in the east door, those for another in the west door. The Republicans protested that the polls should rather be kept open for long periods to permit balloting that did not require prolonged attendance. The results of various elections over the three days tend to substantiate the Republicans' claim that more men voted if they needed only to leave their work for brief periods. It did seem that workers and shopkeepers less able to take time off tended to vote Republican, and that Federal employers had taken unusual steps to let employees attend the meeting.[72]

In 1809 a Newburyport Republican had hoped that the returns for representative would be thrown out because "the principle adopted by the Selectmen [for receiving votes] was altogether illegal and unconstitutional and many Republicans and two federalists refused to vote under the restriction. . . ." The selectmen had insisted "that every Man should give his vote to the Selectmen who after examining of it, under the pretence of ascertaining whether there was not more than one vote, but in reality to deter those who were dependent, from voting according to their inclination, put the vote into the Box themselves. Every vote that was put into the Box was put in by the Selectmen, who by this maneuver had an opportunity of changing, if so disposed, every vote that was given." Yet this kind of protest against violation of "the principle of a free elective franchise" was not often heard during this period.[73]

The Republicans did tend to favor secret ballots. In his 1811 inaugural Governor Gerry told the legislature he would suggest to them revisions in the election laws "as well to prevent turbulent proceedings in our primary assemblies, as to ensure the right of ballot; which is a mode secret in its nature, for restraining an undue influence." The Republican majority agreed with him that the sanctity of elections could be violated by "fraud, unjust influence and partiality of officers concerned . . . or by open riot and 'turbulent proceedings . . .' or ungenerous influence of the wealthy over the poor, *by a too open ballot.*" Along with the set of election laws which the Republicans passed in 1811, they thus enacted provisions in order to try to gain privacy for voters. The law prohibited, under penalty of a fine and the closing of the polls, election officials from reading or examining, or permitting anyone else to examine, a voter's ballot without the consent of the voter. In 1812, however, the Federalists repealed this law, being more concerned, they said, about the possibility of fraud than about the protection of privacy.[74]

Most Federalists and Republicans paid homage to the proposition that "the actual exercise, and not the principle, of free and unbiased elections, is the essential means of supporting republicanism. . . ."[75] But somehow no strong sense arose that open voting contradicted that profession. Open voting remained an accepted norm, and the advent of printed ballots did not change the situation, and may have made voting even more visible. In 1831 Maine acknowledged this by requiring the use of ballots printed by the legislature and by specifically prescribing the color of the paper and the kind of ink and ordering that there be no distinguishing marks on any ballots.[76]

Harriet Martineau in her famous *Society in America* claimed that in American elections "a system of intimidation exercised by the rich over the poor" did not exist as it did in England. In the country no landlords cowed their tenants, and in the towns tradesmen did not depend on the patronage of the rich. "Though they vote by ballot, and any man who chooses it may vote secretly (and many do upon occasion), there is rarely any need of such protection." Martineau erred on several counts. Though not, to be sure, as powerful as in England, "influence" still operated at the polls in the United States. And voting practices in Massachusetts alone displayed far more variety than what an English ballot reformer later called "the optional right of secret voting."[77] Too much evidence shows that secrecy was frequently anything but optional.

Open voting was if anything a *local option* rather than an individual's choice throughout the Federal-Republican and Democratic-Whig periods—a decision made by selectmen, or a town majority, or sometimes de facto by partisan organizers. These conditions prevailed, at least, until the legislature intervened.

In 1839 the Whig-dominated legislature passed a law requiring that no vote be received at the ballot box unless presented "open and unfolded." The intent was to guard against fraud, but the real purpose, opponents charged, was to enable factory owners and managers to coerce workers to vote for the Whig party. Democrats became thereafter ardent proponents of a secret ballot, far more consistently than Republicans had ever been, and the issue hung on through the 1840s and beyond. The Democratic governor Marcus Morton, in his 1840 inaugural address, called for the elimination of any property or tax limits on voting and for the establishment of a secret ballot. The "laboring classes" and the "poorer portions of the community" needed to be protected from oppressive influences, he said, because men of wealth and extensive business advantages often controlled the suffrage of those dependent upon them for employment. "The secrecy of ballot," Morton said, "which should be inviolable, is frequently infringed."[78]

Though open voting now received far more criticism than earlier, Morton's call for a secret ballot, repeated in his 1843 inaugural, went unheeded, and no attempt was made to deal seriously with the issue until the early 1850s. The channels of influence and the character of the "dependent classes" had changed. Yet the continuities were impressive. Political party organization and all the "development" that made it possible had not acted as a democratic solvent of a practice which had long contradicted Republican principles.

The case of open voting reveals as clearly as anything else the inadequacies of any kind of linear progressive approach to political culture. It gives caution, too, regarding our notions of political development. In the politics of Massachusetts no trend or evolution from open voting to closed or secret voting occurred from the late eighteenth to the mid nineteenth century. Movement went in either direction.

Political life in the early national period is not understood primarily by looking ahead to a triumphant arrival of party organization and democracy. Political structures as they emerged were a synthesis of old and new. That partisan competition and traditional influence were not incompatible and that elitism and paternalism were not necessarily dysfunctional will be seen from a different angle in the next chapter, which examines the social bases of voting.

# VII. The Social Bases of Federalism and Republicanism, 1800–1824

> Precisely because of their ecology, the highlands tend to be culturally distinctive. . . . Protected by physical inaccessibility, dissident ideas and religions may flourish in highland regions: the Berbers of North Africa could remain Catholic in an Islamic setting, just as the Moors of the Aragon highlands could keep their faith in Muhammed while everywhere surrounded by Catholics.
>
> The inaccessibility of the highlands also means that these regions were among the last to be subject to the central authority of the state. Hence the hills tended to provide refuge not only for cultural dissidents but for outlaws and individualists of all kinds. Remoteness from the agencies of social control made the highlands a land of the free. . . . The Kurds and Druses in the Levant; the Skafiotes in Crete; the mountain villagers of Greece and Albania; the peoples of the Bruzzi, who remained independent from nearby Papal Rome; these are but a few historical examples of distinctive highland societies.
>
> –Michael Hechter[1]

The divergence between Center and Periphery which existed throughout the United States by 1800 existed in Massachusetts. Regions, communities, groups, and individuals constituting the Center of economic, cultural, and institutional life tended to vote Federal, while the Periphery leaned toward the Republicans. Other writers have hinted at this cleavage and have emphasized the eclectic diversity of the Republican coalition which drew together groups making "common cause against entrenched interests, usually Federalists, who thwarted the desires of newcomers and outsiders."[2]

The Center should not be construed as signifying only the urban or cosmopolitan, nor should the Periphery be taken to encompass all that was rural or local. Yet the Center-Periphery split resembled, and in some ways continued, the country-court or local-cosmopolitan divisions of the eighteenth century. Of course, political alignments had changed after the Revolution, and individuals and factions also shifted about in the 1790s.[3] Still, an overarching division kept emerging, pitting central networks of traditional authority against peripheral challengers, newcomers, dissenters, and outsiders who wished to be included in, protected from, or just let alone by the central establishment. "Energy in government" rallied the faithful of the Center, "anarchy" was their fear. "Economy" was the slogan of the Periphery, "consolidation" and "aristocracy" its bugaboos.

Religious dissent in particular had contributed much over several generations to shaping the state's political geography. To a considerable extent the geographic pattern reflected controversies between established religion and dissenters. Yet geography and religion formed only the most obvious correlates of Federalism and Republicanism. Less visible but often potent were networks of "influence" operating within towns, neighborhoods, or subcommunities, and sometimes between and among localities. Federal and Republican towns tended to possess different styles of elite governance, which in turn were related to a community's constituent groups and to patterns of social relations.

Thus it hardly has to be added that the Center was not entirely Federal or the Periphery totally Republican. No region of the state, no matter how disproportionately it favored one party, lacked a town or neighborhood that perversely stuck by the other political interest.

Thanks to the richness of the primary sources and existing scholarship a good deal is known about Massachusetts voting during the early national period. Moreover, modern historical accounts have presented complex descriptions of Federal and Republican constituencies and have appreciated the interplay of several variables. This chapter tries to build on earlier work, differing with it at points, while offering a perspective encompassing old and new research.

### Center and Periphery: Regions

From 1800 through 1824 Federalism received its strongest support from counties representing or allied with the Center. In 1805, for example, its banner counties were Hampshire (67.5 percent), Suffolk (67.4 percent), Worcester (58.7 percent), and Essex (57.1 percent). Suffolk and Essex meant Boston and the North Shore, and constituted the heartland of what Samuel Eliot Morison called "maritime Massachusetts." Boston delivered the greatest part of Suffolk's vote, and it was the largest town, central metropole, and ancient capital. Overwhelmingly Federal at the start, it stayed Federal to the end, though weakly so after the state had gone Republican. In Essex were the counting houses and mansions of the merchants and lawyers who gave Federalism so much of its leadership in the state and nation.

To the west of Boston, following the main line of travel to the interior and leaping over Republican-leaning Middlesex County, the Federal Center appropriated Worcester County, a broad band of farms, orchards, pastures, and forests, stretching from the northern to the southern border of the state. But Worcester's economy and geography do not fit readily into the Center-Periphery scheme.

The Federal Center–west was, rather, the Connecticut River Valley. Hampshire County, the heart of the valley in Massachusetts, led all counties in the Federal percentage of its vote during this period.[4] Connected by the river with Hartford, New York, and coastal and international commerce, the valley constituted an economic, social, and religious center in its own right. For generations before 1800 its wealthy merchants, prosperous farmers, and authoritarian clergy bore the popular name of "river gods." Allied by interest, marriage, and kinship, they formed as unitary an elite as any in the land, holding sway in the market, town meeting, and church, and wielding no small influence in the colony and state. In Hampshire, too, Congregational Orthodoxy reigned more securely–one might say more *purely*–than anywhere else in Massachusetts. The steadiness of all traditional authority in Hampshire contributed to the firmness with which it held the Federal banner aloft year after year.[5]

The Republican array of banner counties varied, but it consistently included regions clearly of the Periphery (Table VII.1). Aside from the counties immediately ringing Boston and constituting its periphery (Middlesex and Norfolk), the other sources of Republicanism were off the beaten track, isolate, and insular. Two Republican counties were in fact islands: Dukes (Martha's Vineyard) and Nantucket. Though their total votes were few (both were part of Dukes in 1805 and gave 402 Republican votes for governor), they symbolized the character of the Republican coalition.

Nantucket was an island archetype: "See what a real corner of the world it occupies," cried Melville's Ishmael, ". . . away off shore, more lonely than the Eddystone lighthouse. . . . Nantucket is no Illinois."[6]

**Table VII.1.** Republican Banner Counties, 1805, 1812, 1824

| *1805* | | *1812* | | *1824* | |
|---|---|---|---|---|---|
| 1. Dukes | 62.0[a] | 1. Nantucket | 67.1 | 1. Barnstable | 72.0 |
| 2. Middlesex | 59.3 | 2. Norfolk | 58.9 | 2. Nantucket | 68.4 |
| 3. Norfolk | 58.9 | 3. Middlesex | 58.0 | 3. Norfolk | 63.6 |
| 4. Berkshire | 56.6 | 4. Barnstable | 57.1 | 4. Berkshire | 59.7 |
| 5. Barnstable | 55.7 | 5. Berkshire | 54.1 | 5. Dukes | 59.3 |
| 6. Plymouth | 54.6 | 6. Dukes | 52.8 | 6. Plymouth | 58.0 |

a Republican percentage of vote for governor.

On Nantucket, said Morison, "aged shipmasters could be found who knew half the coral reefs of the South Sea, but had never set foot in the United States."[7] Barnstable County or Cape Cod was almost an island: "East twenty-five miles into the Atlantic, then north by west another score, pushes this frail spit of sand, ending in a skinny finger forever beckoning seaward the sons of Massachusetts. . . . Save for the great haven within its finger-tip, the Cape has no harbor fit for larger than fishing vessels; and Provincetown, in its ocean-walled isolation, could never become a center of commerce."[8]

Through 1820 the distant District of Maine far exceeded these enclaves in the number of votes it gave to Republicans. In 1805, after having previously voted Federal, Maine as a whole (a few of its counties remained Federal) moved into the Republican camp (56.4 percent) and remained firmly there: its 58.8 percent Republican margin in 1812 gave the Republicans a thumping 17,841 votes compared to 33,539 in all of Massachusetts proper. Maine, for all its size, could also be considered insular. Portland and the Maine ports "Down East" communicated with Boston more often and speedily by sea than over land. Outside of New England, Maine was thought to be a wild country, an image shared by not a few Massachusetts Federalists. Even in 1816 the author of a Maine gazeteer conceded that some people viewed the district "as a barren, frozen region, unfit for the support of man," while others saw it "as rich beyond all other parts of New England." Maine was neither; rather, it was a growing frontier, which exported raw materials, particularly lumber and fish, and whose largest import was people.[9] It was, above all with respect to Massachusetts central, a place apart.

So, too, was Berkshire County, which occupied the hills forming Massachusetts's western extremity. Indeed, Richard Birdsall, in his magnificent cultural history, which stressed the distinct regionalism of the area from 1761 to 1861, called it "A Place By Itself." Though not overwhelmingly Republican–Orthodoxy and Federalism maintained their own local strength–Berkshire managed to persist in the Republican column for most of the period. "Shut off from the Connecticut River and eastern Massachusetts by the Berkshire Barrier, and from the Dutch Hudson River settlements by the Taconic Mountains, the area indeed merited its Indian name *Housatonic* ('Beyond the Mountain Place')."[10]

Thus the islands, the hill country, and remote places usually supported the Republican challengers. The eastern counties of Norfolk, Middlesex, and Plymouth, which formed a kind of peripheral half-circle around Suffolk and Essex, fit loosely into the pattern. Plymouth, especially, had always possessed a heritage quite literally "separate" from the Center, having been founded in separatist Puritanism.[11] Nearby Bristol County was close to the disturbing religious influence emanating from Rhode Island. But many towns in these counties, as in most others throughout the state, were of almost identical geographic and socioeconomic character and yet of directly opposite politics.

A Center-Periphery division is suggested, too, in the voting patterns of the twenty largest towns (Appendix VII. Tables 1 and 2). In 1810 and 1820 Republican population centers tended to be insular or relatively isolated places. Both population and geography, however, as independent variables explain very little apart from historical and social circumstances. The Center-Periphery split can also be considered, for example, in relation to long-standing religious divisions.

## Center and Periphery: Religion

Isolation and distance easily breed self-sufficiency and a sense of independence. The disposition of the Periphery may be understood perhaps in part as the natural tendency of persons drawn to remote areas to be rebellious. More important, the Center-Periphery rift reflected in greater measure the singular religious history of the singularly religious people who had settled New England in the seventeenth and eighteenth centuries. The Puritans came to Massachusetts Bay, as has been said so often, not to practice freedom of religion but to practice their religion freely. They tolerated religious deviance to a point–once the point was reached, the deviants, disputants, or dissenters had to submit, be punished, or flee. Many fled, or simply moved on, some because they were more strict in their Puritanism and some because they thought otherwise and could not stay within the traces of Bay Orthodoxy.

By the late eighteenth century the Church of Massachusetts–quite lacking in denominational consciousness and only later called Congregational–had undergone many changes, and internal developments during the half century from 1780 to 1830 had important political consequences. Despite decentralization and the autonomy of local congregations, the key fact of religious and political life was that the state upheld an established church. Article III of the 1780 constitution provided that citizens must be taxed for the support of religious worship, which originally meant taxation for the support of the Puritan churches coeval with almost every town. After the Great Awakening theological schisms had divided churches, parishes, and towns. After the Revolution, dissension and disaffection had intensified and new sects, principally the Baptists and Methodists, had begun to proliferate. Disaffiliated Congregationalists, Baptists, Methodists, later the Universalists, and a few Quakers and Episcopalians who had been present early on, were known collectively as dissenters. They objected to paying religious taxes for a church not of their profession and continually sought to acquire legitimacy as churches themselves and hence exemption from paying taxes for the original church in their town. Not all inhabitants of the Periphery were dissenters, not all dissenters were Republicans, and many dissenters lived in the Center. But generally the Federal Center supported the state church and postured as the defender of religion and piety, while Peripheral religious groups opposed to the establishment or seeking its revision tended to gravitate toward Republicanism. The Republican Periphery, in short, had been settled heavily by dissenters.

Quakers in retreat from a "persecuting spirit" found refuge on Nantucket, thirty miles from the continent and one hundred from Boston. Baptists, Presbyterians, and others also found it a "safe retreat." Martha's Vineyard nourished some of the first Baptist churches in Massachusetts, and from 1780 on the church tax was a matter of controversy at Home's Hole. Cape Cod contained many mainstream churches, but its sand-dune retreats had also attracted Quakers at an early date, and by 1800 Baptists and Methodists were also well established.[12] In the Berkshires a similar situation prevailed, Orthodox churches being strong but at the same time confronting "A Great Deal of Dissent." Berkshire County's earliest settlers included Dutch from New York, Lutherans, Scotch-Irish, and Anglicans. After 1780, Rhode Island Baptists fed the growing numbers of non-Orthodox. Soon Berkshire became noted as the home of leading spokesmen for religious liberalism in the state.[13] In still more recently settled Maine both religious dissent and cultural variety prevailed. Paul Goodman asserted that dissent was stronger in Maine than anywhere else in the Commonwealth and that complaints over ministerial taxes were correspondingly loud.[14]

Thus the association of dissent with the Periphery is clear, but the full story of the relations between religion and party is far more complex. Indeed, the "full story" is probably unrecoverable, but enough is known to say that the division between dissenters and supporters of the original churches is only the starting point for understanding it.

### Religious Groups and Parties

From 1780 to 1800 much confusion existed regarding the legal status of dissenters, while the courts tended to treat them less tolerantly than earlier.

In 1800 the General Court tried to clarify matters by repealing all laws relating to religion and replacing them with a general statute; but it did not improve matters, and litigation and controversy continued. Federalist judges usually delivered conservative opinions and insisted that only incorporation gave new congregations immunity from taxation. They also made pronouncements from the bench about the necessity and virtues of the state's support of religion.[15] Dissenters continued their campaign in the courts and legislature and in their pulpits and journals. The original churches, themselves divided into differing doctrinal camps, were by no means uniformly reactionary or even agreed on the best means of preserving the system. These conditions made the state-church relation a source of turmoil for the first three decades of the nineteenth century.

Neither the Federalists nor the Republicans took formal positions as parties on religious laws, but their leading partisans were popularly identified with opposing positions. Federalists usually defended the establishment as received and more often wrapped their candidates and cause in an aura of Christian piety, while trying to stigmatize their opponents with deism, infidelity, irreligion, or immorality.[16] Republicans tended to associate themselves with "religious liberty" and "toleration," and protested vigorously against Federal priestcraft and oppression. To many dissenters "religious liberty" meant separation of church and state, but for Republican politicians "it meant primarily liberty from clerical support of Federalist policies. They wanted the Standing ministers to stop using their pulpits, pens, and prestige to attack the new Jeffersonian movement." Indeed, as William McLoughlin pointed out, the "Republican Party was born, flourished and died in Massachusetts without ever advocating Jefferson's position on disestablishment."[17] Yet Republicans made common cause with dissenters, as McLoughlin also observed, and pressed for measures which eased, while not removing, dissenters' grievances.

The first Republican to be elected governor, James Sullivan, probably owed his election to a surge of support from dissenters. Sullivan, however, made no efforts to advance their cause.[18] In 1807–1808, when Republican militants pushed forward a bill in the legislature to liberalize the tax-exemption rule, Federalists called it the "Infidel Bill," and it failed to pass a Republican house by a vote of 127 to 102. Republican newspapers blamed the Federalists for the bill's defeat, but their cohorts had given it only lukewarm support.[19]

After an 1810 supreme-court decision holding that no unincorporated churches or societies could be exempt from taxes, dissenters renewed their campaign for relief. In the 1811 elections, in an atmosphere in which Republican papers said much about religious "oppression" by Federal tyrants, dissenting support probably helped the Republicans to re-elect Gerry and to carry a clear-cut majority of the house. Gerry and the Republicans now got behind a bill which gave everyone the right to pay religious taxes to his own society, corporate or not. Assessments would still be collected by towns or parishes, but all denominations were now virtually on the same footing as far as ministerial support or certification was concerned. Though disestablishmentarians were not satisfied, the law was a boon to dissenters and came directly from Republicans.[20]

The Congregational clergy were nine-tenths or more Federal.[21] Before there was anything approaching a Federal party organization, there was a Federal establishment, and the clergy were in effect among the key mobilizers of local political support for the status quo.[22]

It did not follow that nine-tenths of the Congregational laymen voted Federal, though probably a majority did, including both Orthodox and Unitarian. In many towns and congregations where Federal ministers had long tenures and consensus was still deeply valued, it was hard to tell whether ministers led or reflected opinion. Many of the older generation did in fact command respect, affection, and deference. But many original churches also grew divided in political sentiments, and many parishioners found offensive the clergy's Federal politicking. In a strong *Federal* town in Worcester County, Westborough, a minister's harsh reproach of Jeffersonians led in 1807 to the town's dismissing him. In 1810, after a blistering politcial sermon from the Federal curmudgeon David Osgood, it was said that the Republicans intended to publish the sermon and sell copies for two cents each.[23] Thus the Federal clergy's open identification with Federalism was a two-edged sword: it could mobilize the faithful and obedient, but it could also create resentment and Republican voters.

Some Congregationalists did indeed vote Republican. Since Congregationalists made up about two-thirds of the population, the Republicans would never have won any elections without Congregational support.[24] After saying this, one must add that more precise statements about Congregational political loyalties, or those of other religious groups, are difficult to make.[25]

The basic difficulty begins with the absence of reliable information regarding the numbers of various church members, and especially of nonmembers who were adherents, affiliates, pew owners, financial backers, regular or occasional attenders, or still looser identifiers. It is exceedingly hard to estimate, except for a few towns, how many persons, let alone how many potential voters, considered themselves Baptists, Congregationalists, or whatever, including Nothingarians.

In 1808 Bentley recorded some unusual information about the town of Beverly, stating that the first society had 1,200 polls (males aged sixteen and over counted for tax purposes), a society petitioning for separation had 300, the upper parish had 100, and the Baptists 100.[26] In the state election Beverly voted 77 percent Federal and often went even more strongly Federal. Congregationalists there would appear to have been quite heavily Federal. More important, however, is the unfortunate absence of this kind of information for other places.

There exists enough evidence, however, showing that individual churches could be predominantly Republican or closely divided. Of Dedham's three parishes, said Fisher Ames, one was "decidedly federal," another steeped "in sin and Jacobinism," and "the old parish, where I live, is divided—the old half are Demos—the young chiefly Feds."[27] In Pittsfield the Federal members of Thomas Allen's church eventually became exasperated with their minister's uninhibited Republicanism, and withdrew to form a new church—the Union Congregational Parish (1809). The majority of those remaining in the First Church were Republicans.[28] In Reading, Middlesex County, the North and West parishes voted "nearly as a unit" Federal, and the South Parish was Republican. When the latter became South Reading in 1812, the old town's Republican percentage fell from 44 to 6, while South Reading cast a first vote that was 90 percent Republican.[29]

While Congregationalists were as a rule divided politically, the line between them did not follow the major rift within Congregationalism between Orthodox and Unitarians.[30] Both of these favored the Federalists while a minority of each formed an important element of the Republican coalition.

In the average and small towns, however, neither branch of Congregationalism seemed as important in signaling a Federal tone as did the appearance of consensus, relative religious homogeneity, and ministerial influence. Some of the most Federal parishes had escaped religious controversy and dissent, and tended to have pastors settled in them for long tenures. Some of these clergymen's active ministries spanned thirty or forty years. In Hampshire, Franklin, and Worcester counties, and in the eastern counties as well, these stable ministries and relatively consensual towns and parishes tended to produce heavy Federal majorities.[31]

For a long time religious dissenters in Massachusetts had chosen their own paths to heaven. In the 1620s or 1630s one William Blackstone, a nonconformist minister of the Episcopal church went into the virgin forest "because he would not joyne with the church." On quitting Winthrop's Boston, the hardy pioneer allegedly said, "I came from England because I did not like the Lord-Bishops, but I cannot join with you because I would not be under the Lord-Brethren."[32] After the Revolution the state's system of religious taxation infected many more with a dissenting spirit. The Baptists and Methodists grew also, as sects always have, in opposition to the formalism of a church, even, in this case, in reaction to the rather loosely associated congregations of the Puritans. Boston and Salem Federalists defended the establishment with appeals to the necessary relation of republican virtue and good morals, but the large towns were exempt from the parish system and instead raised taxes on pews. Country people thought this hypocritical, and they listened to Baptist "preachers" who were often "men who had rushed from the plow into the pulpit . . . with scarcely enough learning to read their texts, [and who] had commenced open war upon the whole educated ministry, declaiming strongly against 'dictionary larning,' [sic] 'Black coats,' 'fat salaries,' and 'hireling priests,' " and especially against the tax.[33]

Baptists also had learned and eloquent spokesmen, such as John Leland of Berkshire County and Heman Lincoln of Boston, both consistent advocates of disestablishment and ardent Jeffersonian Republicans. Baptists generally voted heavily Republican, and the ties between Baptist dissent and Republicanism were clearly stronger than those between Congregationalism and Federalism.[34] The Federalists sometimes tried to attract Baptists to their cause, inviting a prominent Baptist to deliver an Election Sermon, for example, and sometimes nominating Baptists for office.[35] But while individual clergy and wealthy Baptists occasionally were Federal, too many other circumstances pushed the rank and file into the Republican camp. Most Baptists were hardworking farmers or middle- to lower-middle-class town dwellers. Their sect was still new, growing in size, and looked down on as not respectable. Federalism was unmistakably the party of "respectability," and a natural repulsion between religious respectables and ardent sectarians powerfully enhanced Baptist support of the Federalists' opponents.[36]

The second major group of dissenters, the Methodists, resembled the Baptists in their piety, middling to lower social status, and Republican partisanship. A Methodist preacher of Pittsfield, an ardent Jeffersonian, recalled of his youth: "I wanted to be a Congregationalist and to be respectable, but I wanted the love and seriousness of the Methodists."[37] In Essex County the town of Lynn was an outpost of Republicanism and, not coincidentally, the first town in Massachusetts to embrace Methodism, after a visit in 1791 by the itinerant evangelist Jesse Lee. Over one hundred citizens, most of them already disaffected and not members of the church, withdrew from the parish to form a church. Methodism then grew rapidly, especially among the artisans engaged in shoe manufacturing. Lynn's Federalists were strongest among the merchants and traders who did business through Salem, and their leaders included the minister of the First Church, the preceptor of the Lynn Academy, and Quaker shoe merchants. But Methodists came from old families with extensive kindship ties, and included some shoe merchants, ship captains, a banker, and, of course, most of the town officers elected by the town's Republican majority.[38]

Generalizations about other non-Congregational groups are not easy to make, nor can they be lumped together simply as "dissenters." Episcopalians, for example, wanted the religious laws changed, but were generally urban, well off, quite respectable, and tied in to the Federal political elite.[39] Quakers perhaps cut a better figure as dissenters, but in towns like Lynn and New Bedford they were prospering in manufacturing, commerce, or shipping, and formed part of the respectable classes. Yet while most were probably Federal, some, as will be seen below, were Republicans.

There were other forms of religious experience in early national Massachusetts, some of which blossomed as sects and many others of which remained private. It was a time of questioning, when shrewd farmers who spent many hours under the sky in lonely contemplation wrought for themselves "a personal creed."[40] Many stayed in local churches, others took more exotic paths to salvation. Some assumed names that are misleading. It was well known, for example, that many Congregationalists angry at the compulsory tax declared themselves "Baptists" solely to avoid the tax. The Reverend Bentley, a Unitarian and Republican, believed that unpopular Calvinist preachers usually spawned "Baptists" and other defectors. Later on, many of these "dissenters" drifted back into Congregational churches.[41] This same process seems often to have created Republican voters.

Finally, what of the Nothingarians? Little is known of their numbers or social importance, if any. They were "individuals . . . who do nothing for the support of the gospel; who rarely, if ever, attend upon its institutions, and who would be heathen, were it not that christians live about them." Were the Nothingarians "legion," as some historians have suspected?[42] It is reasonable to guess that they had a Republican tendency, when they voted; it is also a fair guess that not many of them voted often.

**Maritime Massachusetts**

> Seaboard Massachusetts has never known such a thing as a social democracy; and in seaboard Massachusetts, as elsewhere, inequalities of wealth have made political democracy a sham. Few town meetings have been held near tidewater where the voice of shipowner, merchant, or master mariner did not carry more weight than that of fisherman, counting-room clerk, or common seaman. Society in seaboard New England was carefully stratified, and the Revolution brought little change save in personnel. The "quality" dressed differently from the poor and middle classes, lived in finer houses, expected and received deference, and "ran" their communities because they controlled the working capital of ships and goods. The only difference from old-world society lay in the facility in passing from one class to another.[43]

Morison's eloquent equation of "maritime Massachusetts" with Federalism has been qualified recently by the finding that Republicans made important inroads into the ranks of the seafaring elite. The merchants and captains who were Republican, though few, were important to the growth and maintenance of the Republican interest.[44] Not all of the seacoast, either, was Federal. There were pockets of Republicanism in the coastal towns that sent men down to the sea. Yet Morison conveyed the style of Federalism with an art few historians have mastered, and he also grasped the significance of the influence structure of local communities.

A town's authority, status, and class structure strongly influenced its political character. Towns with well-established and relatively unified leadership, where the original churches tended to be stable and vital, were likely to cast Federal majorities. In contrast, Republican communities (meaning towns or groups within towns) were less self-consciously hierarchical. Republican towns also tended to have experienced religious controversy or the growth of dissenting sects, and thus Republicanism often grew where leadership was fragmented and where authority was contested or uncertain.

The nerve center of maritime Massachusetts, Boston, was Federal. Its upper classes were predominantly so, and its middling and lower classes also cast many Federal votes.[45] "Influence" surely operated on many of the latter, if not through intimidation and bribery, as Republicans charged, then through a sense of dependence or an identity of interest.[46] Influence *in* Boston helped build Federal majorities there. *Boston influence* contributed to Federal vote counts around the state. Boston merchants had economic, kinship, and social ties from Cape Cod to the New York border; most merchants were Federal, and their influence radiated through these networks. So, too, did that of the professional and intellectual men of Boston, especially its orators of the bar and pulpit.[47]

Morison speculated that the pattern of division among maritime towns set smaller Republican ports against adjacent Federal centers of commerce.[48] While this pattern held in several cases, small seaports were not uniformly Republican, nor were the larger ports consistently Federal.

Essex County was almost synonymous with Federalism, yet Marblehead and Lynn were Republican, while Salem and Gloucester were sometimes Republican and at other times closely divided. In Beverly and Newburyport, however, Federal majorities were consistently large. The latter two represented as closely as possible, perhaps, the archetypal Federal maritime community.

Newburyport was the coastal head of a band of maritime industry running inland along the Merrimac River to Haverhill, since colonial days probably the greatest shipbuilding center in New England.[49] Newburyport itself was as purely maritime and nonagricultural as a port could become without weighing anchor. Occupying one square mile of land, it supported all manner of artisan crafts and shops; in 1810, even after the embargo, it sent some 160 vessels overseas to trade and over 50 more to fish. The fishing fleet alone carried crews totaling nearly 500 men. Its prosperity was reflected in its population growth from 4,837 in 1790 to 7,634 in 1810, and in the self-confidence of its upper class. (Morison judged its society to be "inferior to that of no other town on the continent,"[50] and that, to be sure, is how its gentry viewed itself.) Upper-class solidarity and stability was accompanied by relative homogeneity in religion. Some merchants and shipmasters were Republican, but "the most prominent" citizens were Federal. Republican leaders came more from the middling ranks of "those still working their way up from the quarterdeck to the countinghouse." Hence, the large artisan and middle-class groups probably divided somewhat evenly between the parties.[51]

Beverly, on the other side of Cape Ann, was even more Federal, and maybe even wealthier. Though a small port and partly farmland, it was the seat of rich merchants who had capital invested in ships that fished from Essex ports or traded from Boston. It boasted "many families of wealth and culture," including the Cabots, Lees, and Thorndikes, who sat in the highest Federal councils. Its social hierarchy was well marked and highly cohesive. Whether fishermen, artisans, or farmers, its citizens of all ranks were "distinguished for good order, sober manners, and sound morals." Its first parish was the largest in the state and perhaps the Union. Of

3,880 inhabitants in 1800, perhaps 2,000 to 3,000 belonged to the First Church, and no other congregation paid so large a public tax.[52] In 1803 this prosperous church hired a new minister, Abiel Abbott, sought also by the fashionable Brattle Street Church of Boston, and paid him what he would have been paid at Brattle Street. Abbott remained until his death in 1828. As a powerful orator and charming leader, he was much revered, and there were few public occasions at which he did not officiate. Abbott was "minister of the town, no less than of his parish." Beverly voted 92 percent Federal in 1800 and just under 85 percent in 1815.[53]

Republican Marblehead offered a striking contrast to Beverly not lost on contemporaries. Dr. Dwight found its fishermen "less industrious, economical, and moral" than those of Beverly or Salem, and its peninsula was "more rough, rocky, and unpleasant than any which I have seen." Morison described it as hardly three miles from Salem and as different as if it lay overseas, hilly and boulder-strewn, with a harbor open to fierce northeast gales. Its people had always been peculiar, according to Morison, originally "fisherfolk from Cornwall and the Channel Islands, who care[d] neither for Lord Bishop nor Lord Brethren. Their descendants retained a distinct dialect, and a jealous exclusiveness for over two centuries." Marbleheaders were not Puritans and did not mix or intermarry with the rest of New England–strangers might be greeted with what the fishermen called a "squalling," or a shower of stones. "Marblehead obeyed or not the laws of the Great and General Court, as suited her good pleasure; but as long as she 'made fish,' the Puritan magistrates did not interfere. Literally true was the Marbehead fisherman's reproof to an exhorting preacher: 'Our ancestors came here not for religion. Their main end was to catch fish.' "[54]

With one hundred fishing vessels and forty merchantmen in 1810, employing about 1,100 men, Marblehead did not lack wealth. Nor, with two Congregational churches and one Methodist and one Episcopal congregation, did it lack religion, though it had less than the Federal towns. But a spirit of independence ruled, and its gentry were far less secure than were Beverly's or even Salem's.[55] When the fishermen were in town, they came not shyly to the town meetings, nor did they hold their tongues. Few Marblehead fishermen became merchant sailors, one of the more exploited classes of seamen. "They make troublesome merchantmen," said Dr. Bentley. "But no men are equal to them in the things they know how to do from habit." One of their most ingrained habits was casting Republican ballots. During the embargo, while flags flew at half-mast and threats of defiance issued from the Federal ports, Marblehead men fiercely declared their support for the government, and made threats of their own against the disloyal. It was no coincidence, perhaps, that in 1811 when the Republicans in the state government went for the political jugular of the Federalists, a Marblehead native (Gerry) was governor and another (Joseph Story) Speaker of the house.[56]

Divided Salem *should* have been an impregnable Federal fortress: highly stratified, it possessed a wealthy elite more than willing to use its influence with the numerous dependents and poor people who filled the almshouse during hard times. But although Salem began Federal in 1800, it fell to the Republicans, returned to Federalism in 1812, and later gave slight majorities to the Republicans in 1823 and 1824. Unlike Beverly and Newburyport, Salem had serious divisions in its elite, which created a competitive politics, aided probably by somewhat more religious diversity.[57]

Most vitally, Salem's economic elite had split into two warring camps by 1800, led by the upstart Crowninshields on one side and the Federal Derby family on the other. The Crowninshields, outsiders of German ancestry, veered Republican for several reasons. In their rise to economic power in Salem, they found obstacles thrown in their way by old Federal families, who denied them both economic latitude and social recognition. Since the Crowninshields also rose by way of the risky French trade, their interests diverged from the English-oriented Federal elite. Yet when the Jefferson administration promoted policies at odds with Crowninshield interests (for example, in trying to close the Santo Domingo trade in 1804–1806), the Salem Republicans rejected that policy. In general, though, the Crowninshields backed Republican policy because they "believed that their real commercial interests demanded a firm national policy of restriction on American commerce." They supported nonimportation and the embargo because they saw these measures in the context of Britain's desire to retain commercial supremacy over the United States. The Crowninshields' nationalist reading of the struggle with Britain disposed some of them to war with Britain as early as 1806.[58]

The clan approached the struggle with the Federalists in Salem the same way, and fought the Federalists with their own weapons—publishing a newspaper, politicking in the militia and voluntary associations, mobilizing mechanics, artisans, seamen, laborers, and dependents. On patronage policy they were naturally militant, and urged Jefferson to sweep all Federalists out of office. In 1802 he removed the Federal collector of Salem, thus transferring another important source of influence to the Crowninshield-Republican side.[59] Victories in Salem, however, never seemed secure, and because of a divided elite neither political party won hegemony in this era.

The smaller ports of the North Shore, Morison to the contrary, had a Federal tendency. Perhaps the most important point, however, is that they were usually only small villages within towns having greater numbers of citizens engaged in nonmaritime occupations. The same condition held for the South Shore ports, beginning at Cohasset in Norfolk County and then going along the coast of Plymouth County. Most of these towns were also strongly Federal: only Hanover was lopsidedly Republican, Scituate was usually so, and Pembroke was until 1812. The largest was Plymouth, heavily engaged in farming and fishing, well ordered and moral, cohesive and Federal.

Below Cape Cod lay still another coast, from the ragged line of Buzzard's Bay southwest to Rhode Island. Its maritime star was New Bedford, with 5,600 inhabitants in 1810. Like Melville's Captain Ahab, the shipowners of New Bedford were of Quaker descent, and while there were two Congregational churches in 1800, Dr. Dwight found that "the great body of the inhabitants are Friends." Entrenched in meeting house and countinghouse, the Federalists also marshaled influence through the partisan activities of customshouse officials who, like the merchants they served, were staunchly Federal.[60]

In the town of Dartmouth, just west of New Bedford, the Friends had also accounted for most of the early settlers. And further down in Westport the farmers were "principally Quakers" and prospering by supplying daily produce to New Bedford. From 1800 through 1824 these towns were bastions of Federalism. Westport, perhaps the most uniformly Quaker, voted from 85 to 95 percent Federal: in 1813 when a peak of 339 voters went to the polls, 94.4 percent voted Federal (and against the Republican war).[61] The voting pattern of southern Bristol County is probably the best available evidence of Quaker communities in Massachusetts, both maritime and agricultural, voting Federal.[62]

On the whaling island of Nantucket, Quaker influence was still strong, but there Republicans prevailed. The place truly resembled "an ant-hill in the sea," with 6,800 persons in 1810, most of whom lived in a compact village of 1,800 houses. In 1811 its whaling fleet numbered twenty-four ships, one brig, three schooners, and three sloops, supplying fifteen to twenty spermaceti works that manufactured great quantities of candles for the United States, Europe, and the Middle East. Having 7,000 sheep, the islanders also exported wool, but the whalers gave Nantucket its character. Even during the War of 1812, with its fleet threatened with extinction, it still polled majorities for the Republicans.[63] Of course, Nantucket had experienced worse devastation in the Revolution, when it had lost 150 vessels and the English had seemed determined to sink the island itself. Memories of British cannonballs must have burned ever fresh in the islanders' minds and reinforced loyalty to the anti-British Jeffersonians. Nantucket Quakers were both less worldly and more democratic than those of New Bedford, but they also filled most positions of leadership. The old families–Coffins, Macys, Folgers, Garners, and others–included both Federalists and Republicans. After 1800, Methodists grew rapidly among the islanders and by 1820 claimed almost 300 members, and five years later over 400. They shared with the Quakers a hostility to the ancient theocratic tradition, as continued in the Federal-defended establishment.[64]

The other chief constituents of Martitime Massachusetts–Cape Cod and, to 1820, Maine–voted comfortably Republican, as noted earlier in this chapter. But there were pockets of Federalism in the maritime Periphery, and party differences there, too, can be traced to historic religious and cultural divisions and to patterns of influence emanating from both within and without communities (Appendix VII.A).

### Agricultural Massachusetts

Farmers did not vote as farmers, but as citizens of local communities and as constituents of networks of influence. Hence it is hardly surprising that agricultural Massachusetts voted both Federal and Republican, and could not be said to favor either party.

The overwhelming fact of agricultural life in New England at the opening of the nineteenth century was its uniformity. To be sure, towns differed; hill, valley, river, and coastal towns had quite different economies and characters. Except for some river towns and for those immediately adjoining commercial towns, however, most produced primarily for local consumption. Exports were important to economic life in all regions, but the average family farm did not focus its regimen on production for outside markets. The beginnings of industries existed in iron, shoes, and woolens and cottons, but manufacturing which produced articles for a wide market by persons wholly dependent on such work did not exist. Most of the adult population farmed for a living, and the handful of professionals in every village, a minister or two, a lawyer, and physician, also farmed in most cases. So did many men who ran taverns, sawmills, gristmills, tanneries, fulling mills, and the other "by-industries of agriculture."[65] In this unspecialized economy there existed a "union of manufactures and farming" in which people were "cultivators *and* artisans."[66]

Thus there is little reason to make much of "occupational" differences among voters. And while there were indeed rich and poor farmers, extreme differences did not exist between *most* towns. Throughout the state, towns of similar terrain, economy, and social structure differed widely in their politics. Federal and Republican majorities could be found in hill towns, and in lowland towns with commercial villages. In 1800 many towns were in fact quite lopsided in party vote, but as time passed became more closely contested.[67] The overall socioeconomic similarity of the two parties' supporters, however, did not change.[68]

A closer look at mountainous Berkshire County and the three counties of the Connecticut Valley confirms these observations. The entire region was characterized by a political polarity that cut across its considerable ecological variety.

In 1800 Berkshire's "simple agrarian economy," according to its leading historian, bestowed an "over-all similarity" on all its towns.[69] Politically, though, Berkshire's towns were polarized. From 1796 to 1816, for example, the average congressional vote in half the county's towns (fifteen) was 65 percent or more partisan. Even in the 1812 state election, four of the Federal and six of the Republican towns went over 70 percent.[70]

Political division in Berkshire went back at least to the Revolution, when even greater economic homogeneity had prevailed. Several streams of emigration had brought a diverse population and at least two broadly divergent religious traditions. Dissenters tended to settle in the northern tier, avoiding the older, more Calvinist towns in the south. This rough regional division was manifest in the 1780s and in the Federal-Republican era.[71] The alliance between dissent and Republicanism was particularly strong; that between Federalism and Congregationalism was a political fact but less consistently so; and Congregationalists, as was obviously true in Pittsfield, were sometimes Republicans.[72]

The leading Republican town of Berkshire, however, was the Baptist stronghold of Cheshire, where Rhode Islanders had first settled on a windswept hill they called New Providence. Cheshire was known for having more angles in its boundaries than any town in the state, because the town line ran along the summits of hills. Wits maintained that the lines had been drawn, rather, to leave out all Congregationalists and include all Baptists. The Rhode Islanders indeed found the hills attractive as a refuge from religious taxes.[73]

Like many Congregational towns, Baptist Cheshire was a close moral community keeping watch over the behavior of its numbers.[74] It enjoyed not only the seclusion of the hills but also the leadership of one of the most remarkable men of the day. To the church in 1792 came Elder John Leland, a pulpit orator of intelligence and humor and a veteran of the struggle for separation of church and state. In Virginia he had known Madison and Jefferson, and in Cheshire he was one of Massachusetts's best-known crusaders for religious liberalism. Leland did not want toleration; he wanted Article III and *all* religious laws eliminated, even those preserving the Sabbath. A strong-minded man, even one of great charm, when mixed with an independent and devout people can easily produce controversy. Consequently, Cheshire's religious record in these years is studded with disputes and schisms, healings and reconciliations, withdrawals and returns. But in politics Cheshire's Baptists functioned with a unanimity perhaps unparalleled even in New England.[75]

If the dissenters of Berkshire gave the western hills a Republican profile, the Orthodox of the river valley to the east gave the lowlands a decidedly Federal cast. In the Connecticut Valley the influence of Orthodox ministers was frequently powerful, their pastorates long. In many towns laymen who were leading churchmen also tended to be elected selectmen or representatives. In the lowlands, too, merchant influence was stronger, emanating from the market towns of Northampton and Springfield, both Federal. This was a "land of steady habits," Calvinist Orthodoxy, social hierarchy, and deference, where Federal majorities frequently reached near unanimity.[76]

Yet political polarization existed here as in Berkshire. In 1810 only nineteen of the valley's sixty-two towns cast gubernatorial votes ranging from 40 to 60 percent for either party. Thirty-eight towns went over 60 percent Federal and nine exceeded 60 percent Republican; the heaviest Republican majorities clustered in the south, in towns that became Hampden County in 1811.

Though Federal towns represented a cross section of valley life, whether small hill towns or prosperous river towns, they tended to possess well-established and relatively cohesive elites—usually an array of first families linked by wealth, marriage, kinships, and occupancy of many town offices. Dwight, for example, praised the people of Northampton for their "general love of order . . . a general submission to laws and magistrates, a general regularity of life, a general harmony and good neighborhood, a sober industry and frugality, a general hospitality and charity." Such towns as Northampton and its neighbor, Hadley, exported produce, and their prosperity suffered when hurt by embargoes and war. Their protests against

Republican national policy were as sincere and forceful as any emanating from Boston or Beverly.[77]

In Republican towns unitary elites tended not to be present; compared with federal towns, they contained fewer Congregationalists and more dissenters, had experienced more religious divisions, and kept ministers for briefer pastorates.[78] In Hampden County, particularly, Baptist and Methodist strength was far more in evidence than in the upper valley, and Hampden was the least Federal of the three river counties.[79]

Pelham was a typical hill town where social structure differed from the "patriarchal and hierarchical" communities of the lowland. Its core families "lacked the resources necessary to sustain family influence and power," and they could not produce "enough wealth or consensus to maintain a church continuously."[80] Pelham voted Republican. Earlier it had sympathized with the Shays rebels; indeed, it was Daniel Shays's home town. Pelham had been settled, significantly, in 1738 by a company of thirty-four Scotch-Irish families who included "families . . . who shall be such as were the inhabitants of the kingdom of Ireland or their descendants, being Protestants . . . and of the Presbyterian persuasion." Other pockets of Scotch-Irish settlement survived to a degree in western Massachusetts, and they, too, produced Republican votes.[81]

## Shifting Coalitions, 1823–1824

The voting patterns described above obviously did not remain unchanged for two decades. While many fluctuations in the social groups supporting parties are lost to the historian, several major trends did surface in 1823–1824. The Republicans emerged as the majority party because they managed to hold on to their most loyal supporters, especially Baptists and Methodists, and because the Federalists lost support at the Center, and especially among the Orthodox Congregationalists.

The Center's defection from Federalism was a necessary ingredient of the new Republican majority. When Maine left the state in 1820, Federal leaders believed that the departure of its Republican majorities would insure Massachusetts's remaining forever Federal. But the Republicans made up the loss at the Center: in 1823 eleven of the twenty largest towns of 1820 were at least slightly Republican (see Appendix VII.A, Table 3). The Republicans gained heavily, moreover, in old Center counties (Appendix VII, Table 4). Thus the Center-Periphery split that was observed earlier blurred considerably in the electoral changes of 1823–1824.

Until the early years of the century, the Orthodox Calvinists and Unitarians had coexisted in relative peace, and in some cases ministers of differing orientations had even served in the same church. When William Bentley, a Unitarian, was called to Salem's East Church as a junior pastor, his immediate superior was a Calvinist. In 1805, however, the Unitarians won control of Harvard, and from this point on the rivalry began to acquire sharp edges. At first a few Orthodox champions, led by the Reverend Jedediah Morse, took the lead in calling Unitarianism a heresy and sought to provoke Unitarians into doctrinal controversy. Orthodox ministers also began to refuse to exchange pulpits with Unitarians, though not commonly until after 1820. The Unitarians preferred to avoid public debate and disliked the very notion of explicit tests of orthodoxy. But it was only a matter of time before some of the "liberals" grew intolerant of militants like Morse.

After 1815, as politics cooled down, religious combat heated up. Morse attacked the Unitarians in his journal *The Panoplist,* and Unitarian spokesmen responded in pamphlets and sermons. Their counterattack soon went beyond rhetoric. In 1816 they established a divinity school at Harvard, in 1820 they held their own annual convention, in 1821 they set up a publishing society, and in 1825, with the formation of the American Unitarian Association, they recognized what was already fact–their existence as a separate denomination.[82]

Meanwhile the stakes in the dispute had been rising rapidly. In many local outbursts it appeared that when an Orthodox *church*–that is, the *members* in full communion, usually a minority in any town or precinct–came into conflict with the larger number of persons constituting the parish, or town, the church was usually outvoted by the Unitarian or simply anti- or non-Orthodox majority of the parish. When the church members then withdrew from the "worldly members of the parish," and the parties engaged in litigation over control of church property, the courts favored the parish majority over the church minority (although the latter usually made up a majority of the members and those vital to the actual life of the church). The courts had so ruled as early as 1811, and in 1820 they left no doubt of this construction in the famous Dedham decision. The supreme court decided against the church again, and from this point on the Orthodox lost many churches to the Unitarians. As the number of their "exiled churches" grew–to some one hundred by 1830–the Orthodox began to turn away from a religious establishment which favored the Unitarians and from a Federal party seemingly under Unitarian sway.[83]

In 1823 the political fallout from Orthodox disenchantment, as observed earlier, helped defeat Otis's gubernatorial bid.[84] In the traditional

Federal strongholds of Essex and the two upper Connecticut Valley counties, Otis's vote was far below the high levels once reached by Federalists (Appendix VII.A, Table 5). At the same time the Republicans remained strong among dissenting groups and probably did better among Congregationalists than they had done in the earlier years of the century (Appendix VII.A, Tables 6, 7, 8).

The religious establishment in Massachusetts came to an end formally in 1833, when the legislature and people constitutionally terminated it. The system of religious taxation itself informally ended in 1824 with another Republican-sponsored Religious Liberties Act. This further modification of the ministerial tax allayed the fears of dissenters, who had worried that the 1811 act would be repealed, and it benefited the Orthodox by removing the structure by which Unitarians had been capturing their churches. The law recognized religious societies of not fewer than ten members who separated from the regular parish: any ten voters could organize a church and thus avoid the tax for the support of the parish church; any person could leave one society and join another by certificate. This in effect opened the way for a multitude of unincorporated societies—an object which had been sought by dissenters for decades and which lately had become a necessity for the desperate Orthodox. Though the press gave the law little coverage, it was very significant. By 1830 an estimated nine-tenths of all the Commonwealth's parishes had become "poll parishes," and thus disestablishment was for all practical purposes accomplished.[85]

It was in part a matter of chance that the settlement of the religious question in Massachusetts politics coincided with the collapse of Federal-Republican politics, but the timing was more than fortuitous.[86] Neither the "settlement" of 1824 nor the amendment of 1833 ended religious antagonisms, or their expression in political life. But the withdrawal from the political arena of the leading religious-political question of half a century came just at the time when Federalists and Republicans, for a variety of reasons, decided to lay aside political party competition.

PART TWO

# Social Movements and the Formation of Mass Parties

## VIII. "Improvements" and Populism, 1820–1830

In the 1820s the citizens of Massachusetts became aware that their physical and social environment was changing rapidly. Travel and communication became faster, easier, and more regular than ever before. Certain industries, notably textile manufacture, began to move to large-scale production, and the image of industrial cities entered popular visions. While historians disagree about when "modern" values arrived, the important point here is that after 1815 the awareness of changing conditions of life became acute and pervasive. "Improvements" was the shibboleth of the age and referred most obviously to the tangible fruits of physical growth: new wharves, taller buildings, and a large central market in Boston; canals and turnpikes across the state; faster travel by stagecoach and sailing vessels; more newspapers; more post offices; new and larger textile factories; real-estate development; more bridges. Soon "improvements" meant railroads and also reforms affecting health, welfare, and morality.

For a long time, upper-class elites managed the construction of most "improvements," especially those public enterprises that entailed private risk and profit. They continued to do so, but in the 1820s, in the absence of political party competition, politics became an arena in which interest groups challenged elite control. As in many other states, a middle-class populism emerged in Massachusetts and upheld ideals of competition and equal opportunity. The "middling interest," for example, expressed the resentments and aspirations of middle-class businessmen and lower-middle-class shopkeepers and artisans who wanted their share of the direct benefits of "improvements." The Charles River Bridge controversy, similarly, marked in part the clash of entrepreneurial interest groups, one peripheral and rising, and another central and established. In the next decade, groups lower on the social scale and normally unorganized and without access to a public voice would mount populist protests more challenging in their critique of government and society. In the early 1830s, indeed, discontented groups rejected some of the central beliefs and dogmas held by most influentials concerning economic and political life.

The movements of the 1820s, though lacking the critical thrust of those soon to follow, involved new entrepreneurial groups playing on resentment against the "aristocratic few" and using transient local issues to elbow their way into economic activities dominated by the established elite. Though ostensibly on the defensive in the political arena, and several years away from creating a Whig party organization that would dominate state politics from 1835 to 1850, the central elites were not seriously impeded by political protests; in fact, they usually benefited from policies issuing from the state legislature, the courts, or local governments.

Though the new social movements emerged in a climate of apparent optimism, in the background loomed a growing negative reaction against the social costs and inequities of onrushing "improvements." A few men directed social change far more than did most of the populace. They decided to build factories and railroads, and their families and associates might easily share their satisfaction and optimism. The great majority of men and women, however, largely reacted to changes over which they had little or no control. Many adapted successfully, many found new opportunities, and many experienced dislocation and defeat. Even many of the new middle classes who enjoyed some success could be haunted by a thousand anxieties arising from "prosperity."[1] In any case, many sources fed a reservoir of latent hostility against the changes which had created new concentrations of power.

Many persons welcomed change, but many individuals felt a loss of mastery over their fate while others sensed that the community no longer guided them as it once had. The New England town in 1800 was not what it had been in 1750, but it retained some substance as a cohesive moral community. Traditions of consensus had survived even the fragmenting of religious community and the rise of quarrelsome sects.[2] In the 1820s, however, even with the subsiding of "party spirit" in politics if not in religion, it seemed to many that the traditional community was changing more perceptibly than ever.

The state's political leadership made no general attempt to guide social change. After some initial hesitancy, the state offered citizens reassurance through piecemeal and unrelated attempts to hasten improvements in industry and transportation. Established commercial and developing manufacturing groups benefited most from state action. But in both the state and the nation nothing like a planned, let alone equitable, approach to socioeconomic growth was attempted.[3] The efforts of particular groups to gain a share of, or redress or protection from, the new order gradually took the form of social movements.

### "Improvements": Communication and Manufacturing

Too often historical accounts tend to compartmentalize the social and economic changes of the early nineteenth century, in part simply because it is difficult to discuss all at once developments in transportation, technology, communications, manufacturing, and commerce. But these changes interacted with and stimulated one another, driving the whole forward, though not all communities were affected to the same degree, and different social groups were drawn into one or more processes of change at various times.

In 1800 the outstanding physical fact of life having relevance for political culture was the difficulty of travel and communication.[4] Newspapers and the mails had developed to a point making them indispensable for levels of political activity reached from 1800 to 1815, but the most vital communication was still face to face. Not the printed column but the "personal intercourse of men" provided immediacy of contact: "News then ran along the street, from mouth to mouth; the gossiping neighbor carried it; the post-rider brought it into the groups gathered at the village store." New forms of communication did not displace more traditional methods but provided greater opportunity for their exercise. Meanwhile, travel costs remained high and only the wealthy traveled much between cities and towns up to the 1840s.[5]

In the early part of the century, news moved more rapidly from Boston to New York and to Philadelphia than it did from Boston to Pittsfield. In 1806 Fisher Ames of Dedham complained that his region was "destitute of information, except by a slow creeping mail on horseback once a week." Ames lamented that too often "we sit in darkness; and instead of having the light of the newspapers . . . we often have to wait, as they do in Greenland, for the weather and the northern lights. The town stage is often stopped by rain or snow; the driver forgets to bring the newspapers, or loses them out of his box. . . . How much worse it is ten miles further from Boston, you may conceive. The darkness might be felt."[6]

The desire to improve such conditions existed well before any new technology for travel or communication; it had set off a wave of canal and turnpike building in the 1790s. But advances in transportation came largely from putting more men, horses, and stages on the roads–and, on the seaboard, from launching and putting into service many fast packets for regular sailings.[7]

Canal building revived in the 1820s, when New York's Erie Canal caught the popular fancy. As sections of Clinton's "Big Ditch" were brought into use after 1819, traffic rushed onto it and revenue tolls rose rapidly, aiding its completion. Cries naturally arose in other states for similar projects, and nowhere were they more filled with envy than in Massachusetts, where political leaders and merchants hungered for an east-west passage.[8]

In 1826, with the railroad almost a decade away, travelers who left Boston on Friday at 3:00 A.M. and arrived by the regular stage in New York on Monday in time for a late dinner congratulated themselves "upon living in the days of rapid communications." Not long before, the trip would have taken a week.[9] By 1829 thoughtful men were already pondering the implications of "the immense facility given to intercourse by modern improvements, by increased commerce and travelling, by the post-office, by the steam-boat, and especially by the press,–by newspapers, periodicals, tracts, and other publications."[10]

Improvements in transportation often received impetus from the desire of capitalists engaged in the growing manufacturing industry to acquire fast and regular access to markets. The factories in turn expanded partly because of better transport systems. In the mid-1830s this interdependence became clear when the mechanics in the machine shop of the Lowell factory complex turned to making railroad locomotives.[11]

Factories did not just grow like trees by the unaided operations of nature. They were the deliberate work of an enterprising segment of the established economic elite. The rise of manufacturing has sometimes been talked of in romantic terms suggesting that the old mercantile elite retreated before a rude invasion of manufacturers, bankers, and railroad builders. Frequently, too, the impression has been given that shipping and trade became unprofitable or simply declined because of the rise of new industry. In reality, commerce and shipping revived after 1815, grew, and coexisted quite prosperously for several decades with new industries. Aided by government protection, American shipbuilding yards expanded after 1817, and from 1830 to 1857 they enjoyed an extended boom.[12] Many merchant families retained their maritime interests while also putting money into manufacturing. A few merchants dramatically shifted all their capital from commerce to manufacturing, while some, conversely, refused to have anything to do with industry, but the merchant capitalists who spearheaded the movement to manufacturing kept their interests diversified and flexible. Most of them were Federalists, tied in securely to the old establishment. As Vera Shlakman put it, the "merchant princes of Boston" introduced the company town to New England.[13]

Both small- and large-scale manufacturing grew rapidly after the embargo and the War of 1812 had "raised a spirit of factory enterprize." The number of corporation charters granted by the Massachusetts legislature went from 15 in the period 1800–1809 to 133 in the next decade and 146 in the period 1820–1829.[14] The textile industry accounted for only a part of the total manufacturing labor force, but it was easily the most important branch of manufacturing. Furthermore, the new mills–huge "packing boxes," Lewis Mumford called them–cast a long shadow across the psyches of many workers and farmers who never set foot in them. They were the face of the Industrial Revolution, and their mass suggested the power of their owners.[15]

Yankee merchants initially feared textile manufacturing. Early experiments showed little profit, and the factory villages of England displayed to them a degraded humanity which they did not want to see in America. After 1807, economic and political conditions beckoned imaginative merchants like the Lowells and Appletons to invest in cotton textiles. The price of raw cotton was low, steady profits semed a certainty, and manufacturing appeared less vulnerable to political interference than did foreign trade. During the War of 1812, cotton mills sprang up throughout the countryside, and Francis C. Lowell and other capitalists built a new kind of mill at Waltham. After a postwar slump, business rebounded and the Waltham group, known as the Boston Associates, extended their mill system to Lowell, Chicopee, and Lawrence. Because profits were larger than expected, other Boston and Connecticut Valley merchants readily joined the Waltham-Lowell group. Besides wanting to make money and to prove their entrepreneurial prowess, the Boston Associates also acted out of a desire to preserve fortunes already made in commerce by creating an almost self-regulating world of factory towns which, like the world made by the God of the deists, would keep on running once set in motion.[16]

The new mills did seem to be a world unto themselves. Aided by capitalization far above what was usual, the Waltham-Lowell system brought together in one complex all elements of textile making from the raw material to the finished product. In 1813 the Boston Manufacturing

Company's capital of $300,000 "dwarfed" that of earlier concerns, but in 1828 the Appleton Company began with resources of $1,000,000. The mills were huge brick structures, five to six stories high instead of two or three, and sat parallel to rather than astride the rivers which drove their machines. The latter were power looms, newer and bigger than those used in older mills. In 1813 a large mill might contain 1,000 spindles; in the 1820s each company of the Associates operated several units of some 3,600 spindles each. By 1834 six Lowell companies ran nineteen mills with 110,000 spindles. As the factories grew, the concentrated economic power of the Boston Associates also grew, from textiles and textile machinery to railroads, insurance, and banking. The Associates controlled about 40 percent of Boston banking capital in 1848.[17]

The old mills had depended on their neighborhoods for a labor supply. In a daring attempt to prevent the growth of a "vicious" lower class of the English type, the Associates employed hundreds of respectable farmers' daughters to tend the machines and housed them in company boardinghouses under close moral supervision. Regarding the young women of the countryside as a ready-made class of "well educated and virtuous" laborers, as Nathan Appleton put it, the owners at first made conditions and wages decent enough to attract and keep the Yankee girls. Most of them came viewing mill work as temporary and were lured both by the chance of earning money and the excitement of social life amid so many other young women. In 1827 a traveler received a typical impression of the "mill girls" as "healthy and cheerful."[18]

That the factories of Jacksonian New England spawned so little political or social activism should not be surprising when it is realized that most factory operatives were either women or children, or poor transient families, and that most of them had roots elsewhere, especially the young women who traveled back and forth between the mills and their family's farm. In 1832 less than half of New England's factory workers were accounted for by the boardinghouse pattern. The other half worked in small mills of the "family" pattern, which was almost universal in Rhode Island and Connecticut and common in southern Massachusetts. Some single men and women formed part of this work force, but its core was families with every member over seven or eight years of age working in the mill. Many of these families were poor, transient, and frequently exploited. In 1832 it was reasonably estimated that at least two-fifths of those employed in factories were under sixteen years old. The common Jacksonian "factory workers" hardly possessed the wherewithal to develop a sense of themselves as workers with common interests, much less as political actors.[19]

In the 1820s skilled workers in several trades became threatened by centralizing and specializing trends, but the changes were not sudden. In the shoe industry, for example, which in 1837 employed 35,300 workers compared with 27,600 in textiles, a full-blown factory system arrived much later. But in the 1820s it was already apparent that the artisan class of shoemakers would be steadily undermined by the growth of the central shop. By 1840, in fact, regular apprenticeship for the process of making whole shoes had come to an end.[20]

Yet while the disruption of skilled trades proceeded only gradually in the 1820s, the agricultural population experienced dramatic change. By no means did all farmers meet the same fate, but as a group they were the most drastically affected. Their complaints that "rich mill owners" enjoyed too many privileges, especially that of damming their streams and depriving farms of riparian rights, were only symptomatic of the decline besetting many farmers by the 1820s.[21]

In central and western counties the agricultural hill towns declined in population and relative wealth from 1820 to 1830, and their inhabitants became increasingly older. Many lowland towns adapted to new markets, and some survived or prospered by turning to market gardening, orcharding, or dairying. Some with access to transport even grew crops for distant markets. But while the Connecticut Valley produced more wheat in 1840 than it did in 1800, overall wheat production fell sharply in Massachusetts and New England. Though towns near newly arisen manufacturing centers were particularly favored with markets, the persisting isolation of the state's interior can be seen in the fact that Boston received most of its firewood not from timber-rich Worcester County but from Maine via sailing vessels.[22] The dominant trends were suggested by the availability of female and male laborers from the country to tend the spindles and looms, by the ever swelling migration to the west, and by the sense of deprivation rampant in farming towns. In the 1830s Harriet Martineau said that she had met "no class in the United States so anxious about the means of living as the farmers of New England." Well might they be fearful, since, as Martineau observed, many were mortgaged to the "great Insurance Company at Boston," and "this Company will not wait a day for the Interest." In 1839 even an optimistic Whig leader described Massachusetts agriculture as "depressed as Nature seems to have doomed it to be at the best, by the hard and barren soil she has assigned it."[23]

It was not simply that manufacturing was displacing farming. Markets had been lost and trade patterns disrupted during the period 1807–1815. Factories and domestic production (shoes, palm-leaf hats) gave opportunities for supplementary income to farm families, just as fishing aided many coastal farmers. The peak time of labor supply for the Lowell mills was during the slackest time of work in the farm season. It was also true that farm life came to seem old-fashioned and distasteful to many. The work had always been back breaking and the hours endless at certain times of year. As much was in movement around them in the 1820s, and as many other people were apparently getting ahead by much less effort, many persons turned away from farming, or at least from the rocky soil of New England, partly because their former standard of living now seemed unacceptable by comparison with what was possible.[24]

While farmers experienced both real and relative deprivation, the absolute differences between classes widened considerably. There can be no doubt that the lower classes expanded after 1815 and were already becoming quite visible in the 1820s.[25] The town of Waltham, for example, was once a stable agricultural town. With the coming of the factories, the number of propertyless there rose rapidly. In 1822 of 475 male taxpayers, 48.6 percent had no taxable property, while the top 2 percent (9 persons) held 36.9 percent of all assets. By 1840 the number of propertyless had grown to 398, or 58.5 percent; in 1850 it was 698, or 62 percent.[26] Although the propertyless consisted mostly of newcomers to the town, that does not lessen the impact made on contemporaries by such new concentrations of the propertyless in one place. Moreover, class lines held firm in many ways as the upper classes created institutions exclusively for their own use or made existing institutions like Harvard College more costly and more difficult for the middle and lower classes to enter.[27]

The anxiety of the age can no doubt be exaggerated. The expanding economy created many jobs and opportunities to supplement family income as it simultaneously eliminated skilled crafts. Cotton mills were built so rapidly during the War of 1812 that masons and mechanics were in short supply. The textile industry also created numerous occupations for buying and selling, as did other industries. The great red fortresses at Waltham, Lowell, Chicopee, and Lawrence did not strike awe or fear into all those beholding them. Public leaders especially, as Carl Siracusa has shown, celebrated the advance of factories and machines and assiduously propagated the doctrine of a "harmony of interest" among all classes. Furthermore, the belief in America as the land of opportunity certainly grew quite powerful in this period, and given the expanding economy, chances for advancement up the class ladder were probably relatively better than during times of little or no growth.[28]

On the other hand, a number of concerns surfaced or intensified in the

1820s suggesting that "improvements" had a profoundly unsettling side. Suddenly the eternal poor, for example, were rediscovered as a "problem," both by those who wished to help them and by those who wished to punish them. Once regarded as inevitably part of any community and to be cared for within families or neighborhoods, the poor became in 1821 the subject of a legislative investigation. Similarly, prison reform became a public issue even before a prison mutiny shook the state in 1824. In the 1820s, too, temperance sentiment suddenly flourished amid a population hitherto given to free and regular use of ardent spirits.[29]

The "social ills" that overnight became objects of concern took on urgency in an environment of burgeoning factories, displaced or transient populations, and propertyless workers, who were now numerous *and* concentrated. Perhaps the reform most obviously stimulated by the growth of factories was the middle- and upper-class pressure group which formed to advance the cause of common schools and children's education. In 1830 a broadly based group of clergymen, educators, old Federalists, and merchants formed the American Institute of Instruction. These reformers worried about the growth of a vicious proletariat beyond the reach of traditional morality. They regarded the decentralized schools of the state as inadequate and favored a uniform system firmly grounded in religion and morality.[30]

The institute was as concerned about the rural as the urban poor, and, since factory villages tended to be spread through the countryside, its concern for country children was logical. Besides the growth of factories, these reformers also reacted to the approach of formal disestablishment, which was already a widespread reality in the 1820s.

In the next decade the Workingmen's party would take up the cause of factory children much differently. But in the 1820s concern for child laborers had already emerged as one part of a general awareness that the rapid social and economic changes brought costs as well as benefits and that the distribution of these among the citizenry was quite uneven.

## Social Movements: The Middling Interest

> –"a People opposed to a Party"–
>
> Measures and not men; the People and not a Cabal; the many and not the Few;–Public and not Party spirit are the leading maxims of the Middling Interest politics. We reject the names which serve to blind us to things. . . . The present party designations have become to us as obsolete, as they are, in truth, groundless and nugatory to ALL.
>
> –*Bostonian and Mechanics' Journal,* April 2, 1823

In the early 1820s a peculiar populism known as the Middling Interest emerged briefly in Boston and hastened the exit of Federal-Republican politics. The Middling Interest was a kind of restrained middle-class populism, but it anticipated social movements which flourished in the next several years. It also challenged the domination of Boston by a clique of high-toned Federalists, and released the resentment and aspirations of usually deferential middle- and lower-middle-class citizens.[31] Of course, Jeffersonian Republicans had made similar challenges and vented similar frustrations, but this time the protest came from within Federal ranks and from men who usually followed where T. H. Perkins, H. G. Otis, William Sullivan, and others had led. Though Republicans jumped on the bandwagon, the group was largely a Federal splinter group tired of the old slogans. For the most part it was a genuine grass-roots protest by the middling classes against "party" and against elite domination.[32]

Disagreement over Boston's change from town to city provided the immediate background for the emergence of the Middling Interest. During the winter of 1821–1822 a series of excited and tense town meetings which debated a new city charter served to create a volatile situation.

Until 1822, Boston town meetings were run most of the time by a Federal oligarchy which included many members of the middle classes who served in town offices. The elite did not always get its way, and it failed several times (1784, 1792, 1804, and 1815) to convince the citizens to adopt a city plan of government. The middle classes could wield, in effect, a veto on elite proposals, an informal rule of Boston politics which constituted a democratic element in the deferential-participant mix. Many citizens still distrusted any change in their habitual way of doing things, but evidence of the need for change could not be ignored. The population was growing rapidly, and the friendliness and cooperation of citizens had declined. Peace officers, for example, no longer dared to ask citizens for help in making arrests, and even fire wards found it difficult to organize bystanders into traditional bucket brigades.[33] But the most important stimuli for change came from abuses in the administration of justice and taxes. Many citizens wished to put aside an archaic county system over which Boston had little control, and a town committee had found recently that the tax laws were not enforced uniformly and that certain "opulent citizens" by various evasions did not pay their fair share.[34] In addition, the most popular reforms proposed by the city proponents called for abolishing the county court of sessions and replacing it with a municipal police court and for making the county treasurer the town treasurer. Voters approved these changes 4,557 to 257. The charter had tougher going.

The charter controversy was not a party matter. City advocates had always included leading Republicans on any planning committees, and Republicans, like Federalists, had been divided on the change. In general, town politics before and after 1822 remained far less influenced by party considerations than did state and national elections, and while Republican leaders led in calls for modification of the plan of 1821–1822, their support was gradually secured through several compromises.

Opposition to the town's becoming a city sprang from inertia and a vague attachment to traditional ways of doing things. Average and "middling" men feared that innovation would deprive them of their accustomed rights and liberties. This was not just negativism, and many in Boston besides opponents of the charter still clung to an ideal of their community that was no longer a reality. While the Middling Interest and those opposed to city incorporation were not necessarily the same groups, the doubts expressed by city opponents were vividly illustrated in the events of early 1822 which led to the Middling Interest revolt.[35]

After three days of intense but orderly debate in packed meetings at Faneuil Hall, the town insisted that the charter as well as several controversial items be submitted to a general vote. One of the latter was the provision to elect state and federal officers in wards and not at Faneuil Hall. This proposal had come from the floor and had been pressed by Republicans, who indicated that, without it, they would throw their weight against the charter. Republicans also received private assurances that they would be given a share of city councillors and aldermen each year. Though the Federal elite did not want ward elections, the measure and the charter both passed easily at the first balloting.[36]

The state legislature passed the new charter but left out ward voting. Bostonians had elected some city officials by ward since 1799, and the legislature's action outraged many of them and led to demands to resubmit the charter and ward voting to another referendum. Some moderate Federalists now warned that the legislature's action threatened acceptance of the charter. Both charter and ward voting again prevailed by healthy majorities, however, and support for ward elections had increased in the interim.[37]

The General Court had ignored the town's wishes on another matter which created an even greater storm of protest. During the past year a loose coalition of middle-class entrepreneurs and artisans had pushed for repeal of an 1803 law which prevented wooden buildings from being built over ten feet in height. The law had come into being after long and disastrous experience with fires, and specifically after major fires in 1787 and 1794 and lesser blazes in 1801 and 1802. Not only did tall wooden buildings burn easily, but the taller they were, the more they spread the conflagration by transmitting flying sparks. They also created difficulties and hazards for firemen attempting to pull them down. Fire from brick buildings, on the other hand, issued mainly from windows to the immediate vicinity. But many middle-class Bostonians now thought the 1803 law oppressive. Some artisans simply wished for larger homes built of cheaper materials, while some master carpenters (or contractors) and entrepreneurs wanted to develop row houses. They proposed a substitute for the 1803 law which would control the height of new buildings and would incorporate some safeguards. While those who wanted to keep the 1803 regulation were relatively quiet, the town's representatives in the legislature failed to get the 1803 law repealed, even though the town by vote clearly had expressed its wishes. The sense of betrayal felt by many, especially Federalists, was made more acute by the current debates over the city charter.[38]

All indications are that leading Federalists used their influence in the legislature to bury ward voting and the ten-footer repeal, not expecting serious reaction. In this they acted as generals who calculated without their army. Most of those supporting the ten-footer repeal were Federalists, and they not only carried their protest into city politics but also probably contributed to the Federalists' demise in the state in 1823 and 1824.

On March 7, 1822, the town voted 2,837 to 547 to revise the wooden-buildings law and to instruct its representatives to the legislature to press for its repeal. On March 11 a meeting of "citizens from all wards" ignored the traditional leadership and nominated a ticket of independent Federalists and Republicans for state senators to oppose any list put forward under the auspices of the Federal Central Committee. The organizers were men from the "middling" ranks while their candidates were drawn from the pool of substantial men typically prominent in the town's politics—men, in short, from the oligarchy just below the level of the "aristocrats." The March 11 meeting passed two resolutions which came to be the two main principles of the Middling Interest: (1) Government was for the common good and not for the profit or interest of "any one man, family, or class of men," and thus none had any special or "exclusive privileges distinct from those of the community"; and (2) history showed that all men were "in danger of being led by party names to act contrary to their own true interests—names which might have originally arisen from a difference of opinion with equally patriotic motives, but which are often kept up . . . long after that difference . . . has ceased among the great body of the people." The protesters soon came to call themselves the

Middling Interest, a name suggestive of both their social position and their desire to occupy a nonpartisan position in between Federalists and Republicans. "Party spirit," they said, was a device used by the overbearing few to control the many.[39]

The same themes dominated an anonymous pamphlet which could be regarded as the manifesto of this grass-roots political revolt, *An Exposition of the Principles and Views of the Middling Interest*. This brief tract located the origin of the movement clearly in the wooden-buildings and ward-voting issues, but it also defined the fundamental issue as nothing less than majority rule. The Middling Interest expected "from our constitutional agents some deference to the known will of the majority, and we deprecate the secret influence of a FEW." For several years now the truly patriotic men of both parties had grown dissatisfied "at the unnecessary excitement of the people, and the wanton violence of party spirit." Men of the Middling Interest supported good measures "without regard to any old party name."[40]

The Middling Interest's candidates for state senate did not win election but did get a respectable vote. As soon as the state election ended, the Middling Interest turned its attention to that for the new city government. The Federal elite planned to elect Otis, then serving as a United States senator, Boston's first mayor. The Middling Interest, however, decided to back Josiah Quincy, an arch-Federalist famous for his opposition to the War of 1812 and to all things Jeffersonian. Indeed, Quincy's extreme views had made him something of an embarrassment to the Federalists in the Era of Good Feelings, and in 1820 he had been rebuffed by the central committee, which dropped him from the state senatorial ticket. Moreover, Quincy had opposed incorporation in 1815 and 1821 before going along with it and helping to write the new charter, all of which made him an ideal candidate for the Middling Interest. He had also become a leading expert on poverty and other city problems, but more important was his availability and, in the words of his recent biographer, the Middling Interest's need for "a well-known figure, but one neither politically beholden to the Otises, Sullivans, Tudors, and Perkinses, nor terrified by the social consequences of crossing them." In early March a delegation of Boston Federalists led by a carpenter paid a visit to Quincy at home and invited him to stand for mayor.[41]

On April 4, at a large and unruly Federal caucus, the Otis forces beat back the Quincy men by a vote of 175 to 170. The Middling Interest denounced the result and withdrew, nominating Quincy the following night. Otis, ironically, had urged Federal leaders to give in on the wooden-buildings law "if you mean to prevent the triumph of the revolutionary movement manifested in the new city." He preferred negotiation and guessed that "the wooden project cannot be resisted for any length of time." Addressing a Federal caucus, Otis said he could recognize no such thing as a "Middling Interest," since any such class flowed naturally in and out of the monied interest. He saw, rather, a section of the Federal party leaving its friends–"with whom for many years they have kept sweet counsel together"–an outcome that could only aid Federal adversaries. Otis exclaimed that he wished every man of the Middling Interest might hear him ask, "Where are the tenants whom I have ejected, the Debtors I have sued, the labourers I have pinched, the embarrassed whose notes I have shaved, the poor whose faces I have ground?" Yet Otis's pleas for party loyalty seemed only to enrage the Middling Interest. The mayoral election, finally, was a standoff, with neither Otis nor Quincy elected, because a few Republicans refused to support either–though the Republican papers had backed Quincy and had even more enthusiastically made the cause of the Middling Interest their own. Several days after the election the regulars and the insurgents agreed in separate meetings on the popular Federalist John Phillips for mayor.[42]

In 1823 the Middling Interest gradually reunited with Federalism. In the city election the Federal candidate for mayor now became Josiah Quincy. The top brass still condemned Quincy for treachery the year before, but they needed him. Phillips had retired, and Otis, running for governor, wanted no feud with Quincy. At the ward level most Federalists and Middling Interest men rejoined forces.[43] Yet in the state election Otis, who should have been overwhelmingly popular in Boston, carried the city by one of the slimmest margins ever given to a Federal gubernatorial candidate (2,835 to 2,727), and not all of the regular Federal senate candidates won election. In May, however, the regulars and insurgents came together on a representatives' ticket and easily carried the election.[44] For all practical purposes, the Middling Interest had run its course, but in doing so it had contributed to a pronounced muting of partisan appeals.

The Middling Interest succeeded in two of its major goals: repeal of the wooden-buildings law, and ward voting.[45] The movement also helped change the climate of Boston so that the rights of the middling and artisan classes became openly discussed and more freely asserted. Newspapers now cried out boldly against imprisonment for debt as oppressive to the poor, and in July the *Bostonian and Mechanics' Journal* appeared to champion the rights of "mechanics," a term encompassing a variety of skilled craftsmen and small businessmen. The *Bostonian* even agitated for the rights of truckmen, laborers who carried heavy loads about the city on two-wheeled carts.[46]

The episode released powerful social tensions, not of poor against rich, but rather of middle- against upper-class men within the upper half or two-thirds of society.[47] The ten-footer and ward-voting issues tended to unite Federal mechanics, artisans, shopkeepers, and small businessmen with Republican lawyers, merchants, and carpenters, among others, in opposing the elite and their hard-core supporters. Middling Interest leaders included, as they themselves claimed, many "men of property and . . . business." There was a good deal of rhetoric about their conflict with "a MONIED ARISTOCRACY," and one anonymous circular spoke excitedly about a "contest between the DRONES and the WORKING BEES of the community."[48] But some Middling Interest spokesmen were, in fact, "no mean or middling sort of men." A few were rich. Even a crusty old Federalist like Christopher Gore described Middling Interest candidates as "probably as good, as those on the other List."[49]

The Middling Interest insurgency gave an early clue that the partisanship of the Federal-Republican era was on the way out. Many voters presumably had lost interest in the continuing debates over the 1807 embargo or the 1812 war. Besides heralding the dissolution of Federalism and of party lines, the Middling Interest showed the potential for channeling middle- and lower-middle-class resentments and aspirations into anti-elitist and antiparty politics.

As the town became a city, its middle classes thus asserted themselves through political action designed for no more radical purpose than to assert majority rule against an elite accustomed to lead by nods and gestures, by courtly speeches and partisan oratory. Economic interest joined with class resentment and frustration with party loyalties that had outlived their day. The Middling Interest revolt also came from men who normally had been deferential. Soon, other groups in the middling, and even lower ranks, would be asserting themselves and using some of the rhetoric of 1822–1823.

### Imprisonment for Debt

The Middling Interest movement was confined to Boston, but the middle and lower classes were restive in many places.[50] At about the time that the Middling Interest disrupted Boston's politics, imprisonment for debt came under attack through the state, which showed that the Middling Interest mentality was widespread.

The desire to abolish debtor's prison was not new, but in the early

1820s criticism of the system became more intense. This resulted in part from causes originating outside of Massachusetts, but the Middling Interest protest and the impulse to abolish imprisonment for debt had close affinities. In Boston, some of the ardent backers of the movement also joined in calls for reform of the debt laws. Soon voices all across the state were raised against debtor's prison. On July 4, 1824, Elder John Leland told a gathering of western Massachusetts Republicans that imprisonment for debt "now occupies the enquiring public." The rapid growth of this concern, though it never became an organized movement, showed that class resentments and inequities felt among the middle and lower classes extended well beyond Boston.[51]

Historians once thought the system of imprisonment for debt a cruel and unrelenting anachronism, brought down eventually by its own oppressiveness. Recent scholarship, however, has found the system to have been relatively mild.[52] If this was the case, then the new aggressiveness against the system did indeed owe much to the rising populist sensibility of the middle classes.

Although people did go to jail for debt in Massachusetts in the 1820s, there is some question as to how many, for how long, and under what conditions. Most were poor, but sometimes a person from the middle or upper classes went to jail. The architect Charles Bulfinch, Boston selectman and police superintendent, spent a month in jail after the failure of a real-estate-development scheme. "In jail," however, meant very different things in different places. Since the late eighteenth century, counties and towns had kept softening the system by extending the "limits" or the "liberty of the yard" to include a debtor's work place or even an entire village. In 1823 a Salem newspaper pointed to "absurd" disparities that existed between counties in debtors' liberties.[53] It was also true that *arrests* for debt were far more frequent than was imprisonment. That the latter could happen probably perpetuated the system. Reformers argued that the punishment made no sense because it deprived "honest debtors" of the means to pay. But the system could not have lasted so long if its chief return to creditors had been punishment. Rather, creditors could, through the mesne process, quickly bring debtors to the point of choosing between paying or going to jail. The effect of this, as one creditor put it succinctly, was that "Hundreds of executions are satisfied at the threshold of the gaol."[54]

While creditors thus enjoyed a good deal of power, sometimes arbitrary, perhaps the most offensive aspect of the debtor laws was that there were normally two sets of rules: one for the rich and one for everyone else.

The former set was called bankruptcy, and under it rich debtors seemed not to go to jail. The commercial classes themselves, as well as periodic economic crises, had educated the middling classes to this state of affairs.

Since the 1790s New England merchants had lobbied in Congress for a national bankruptcy bill which would protect creditors by providing full disclosure and equitable distribution of a bankrupt's property.[55] After each spell of commercial distress, agitation for such a bill revived. With the 1819 panic and depression, debates over bankruptcy renewed in Congress and in many states, some of which took action. At the same time, attention turned also to small debtors, and criticism of imprisonment for debt became more common than ever before. The issue now entered into much wider public discussion and was no longer debated primarily by political and economic elites.[56]

By 1820 the Society for the Relief of the Distressed and the *Debtor's Journal* were founded. In the next two years congressional bankruptcy debates received increasing attention in Republican newspapers, and when the Middling Interest emerged the imprisonment issue had already been taken up by many of those identified or allied with that movement.[57]

In early 1823, however, the legislature acted to bring more uniformity into the definition of jail limits, and in doing so it severely constricted them. It also passed an act regulating attachment of mesne process which gave further protection to creditors in overcoming delays in the transfer of property, but did nothing to placate reformers. Indeed, these acts served only to outrage critics of the debt laws and stimulated them to work harder to abolish the system.[58] But the agitation against it never became a full-fledged movement.

In the mid-1820s, Congress continued to debate bankruptcy and debt laws, and in Massachusetts criticism of imprisonment for debt continued. But in 1824 the legislature, this time dominated by the Republicans, once again disappointed those seeking abolition and simply passed another act regulating jails.[59] The defeat again goaded ardent critics of the system to lash out at the "professedly Democratic" legislature and to unleash a flood of antilawyer sentiment, which issued periodically in Massachusetts from radical republicans.[60]

The significance of what can at most be called this *flurry* of attention to imprisonment for debt lay in the revelation of a diffuse and unorganized, but widespread, sentiment responsive to an issue which illuminated legal and social inequities that were out of place in a republican society. The prevalence of this sentiment showed that the impulses underlying the

Middling Interest movement in Boston existed, if only latently, among many other citizens in other towns.

**Bridges and Railroads**

In 1824 Federalism's "Indian summer" in Massachusetts came to an end. John Quincy Adams's election to the presidency sealed the doom of Federal-Republican partisan competition and made "amalgamation" a reality. Most Federalists and Republicans thereafter formed a broad "union" coalition behind the national administration of Adams and the state regime of Levi Lincoln, Jr. Voting turnout and representation dwindled, and politics from 1825 to 1830 were quiet statewide, though various local squabbles boiled up from time to time.[61] Lincoln was re-elected governor throughout these years, of course, usually by large majorities in a much reduced electorate. His only opposition came from factional revolts which possessed interest-group and sectional bases, the most significant of which was the Free Bridge party. This movement represented in some ways an extension of Middling Interest politics. Once again middle-class groups, and a peripheral elite group, challenged the established economic and political elite, and to the populist contention that public policy should benefit the many and not the few it added the theme that open economic competition was essential to economic growth and to a republican society. The controversy was, however, essentially local, and the Free Bridge party a distinctly sectional phenomenon. Indeed, by the end of the decade sectionalism governed most responses to questions of internal improvements, which meant, by then, railroads.

The first challenge to "union" and Lincoln came in 1826 from old-line Federalists, who produced four different candidates, all with local followings. No electioneering took place, and Lincoln won handily though his vote total fell to 27,884. Samuel Hubbard, a prominent Federalist and corporation lawyer tied to the economic elite, attracted the most votes of Lincoln's opponents, 8,149; another 3,959 in all went to three different Federalists. Although a Bostonian, Hubbard received most of his votes in the old Federal stronghold of the Connecticut Valley, where he carried fifty towns. The legislature's shelving of some proposed river improvements in the valley perhaps contributed to this dissent, but a stronger source of unrest may have been Orthodox Congregational unhappiness with the Federal-Republican Unitarian elite and recent court decisions affecting religious affairs. Hubbard was in fact a prominent Orthodox layman, and thus a successor to Lathrop's political legacy. The vote for him predicted still greater Orthodox political independence in the future.[62]

A still greater portion of things to come was the 1827 Free Bridge party, another factional outburst of a decidedly local nature. This controversy sprang not from technological change but rather from the contagion of the "spirit of improvements" through the social-status hierarchy.

Its origins lay in Boston's geography and in the building of very ancient aids to travel–bridges. Boston was originally a peninsula, which for 150 years was joined to the mainland by a narrow neck of land. Thus the town was called, no doubt for other reasons as well, a "tight little island." In the 1780s, with the spirit of "improvements" already abroad, the first bridge had been chartered by the legislature and built across the Charles River to Charlestown. A project principally of Boston merchants and investors, the Charles River Bridge (1786) enjoyed popular support in Boston and Charlestown. The legislature set its toll rates and rules of maintenance, and the bridge immediately offered savings of considerable time and freight costs to Charlestown merchants and to farmers, millers, and other shippers of products from northern and eastern sections of Middlesex County. To its proprietors the bridge quickly paid handsome profits, and four other bridges soon ran out from Boston.[63]

Through the early 1820s all the bridges–West Boston (1793), South Boston (1805), Canal or Craigie's (1809), and Mill Dam (1821)–were ventures of the established commercial elite and, as it developed out of that group, of the merchant-manufacturing elite. These investors sought profits from tolls and, especially in the case of the South Boston Bridge, from real-estate speculation tied to the bridge's route. Extensive real-estate development changed the face of Boston and its waterfront during these years, both in connection with and apart from bridge building. Uriah Cotting was the leading promoter of the Broad Street Associates, who between 1805 and 1817 built India and Central wharves and the new customshouses.[64] Cotting shepherded the Mill Dam Bridge project, the last of this group of enterprises, which would cut off a huge tract of the Charles River known as the Back Bay. This bridge, unlike the others, was undertaken primarily as a means of developing new water-power sites along the approach to Boston. Cotting envisioned the creation of some eighty-one mills by the Mill Dam. It took seven years (1814–1821) to complete the system of dams and basins, and in the meanwhile Cotting sought broad public support and fought back against critics. In an 1818 prospectus he asked, "Is there a single person in Boston or the neighboring towns, who can spare eighty dollars, who would not wish to have it said hereafter that he had had a share in this great improvement? The question has been frequently asked, *How shall the citizens of Boston fill their empty stores?* The answer is easy,–ERECT THESE MILLS AND

LOWER THE PRICE OF BREAD."[65] Given this kind of public appeal on behalf of a bridge enterprise, it was not surprising that in the early 1820s new capitalists not closely tied to the entrenched economic elite should also seek to advance their fortunes by similar schemes.

In 1823 the Charlestown merchants John Skinner and Isaac Warren, representing some of Charlestown's most enterprising and wealthy interests, presented petitions to the summer session of the legislature asking permission to build a bridge over the Charles to compete with the Charles River Bridge. They proposed to collect tolls for no more than six years or until their expenses at 5 percent interest were recovered; thereafter the new bridge would be free. Their objectives have often been overlooked because of the important ramifications of the court case which resulted. The bridge promoters hoped to profit in several ways, most obviously by freeing themselves from paying tolls to send goods across the river. Charlestown merchants and many farmers of northeast Middlesex paid an enormous yearly sum in bridge tolls,[66] and some of the new bridge promoters were engaged in shipping beef, lumber, and other products into Boston. The Charlestown entrepreneurs also owned land in Charlestown and would benefit from the rise in real-estate values which a new bridge would bring, especially since land prices were considerably lower in Charlestown than in Boston.[67]

Though the legislature did not act on this petition, it soon received a similar one from a group of Boston entrepreneurs led by David Henshaw, who proposed a free bridge to South Boston which would also compete with an old bridge. Henshaw's brand of Republicanism, venomously anti-Federalist, and the source of his money, the not so respectable drug business, made him obnoxious to the Beacon Hill and State Street elite. Henshaw's paper, the *Statesman,* also railed against rich aristocrats, calling them "nabobs" and "Shylocks" and denouncing their secret economic power.[68] Not surprisingly, Henshaw's détente with the Lincoln administration had helped provoke the revolt of the old-line Federalists in 1826. His bridge group had the same objectives as the Tudors and Otises who had promoted the old South Boston Bridge—namely, to realize profits primarily through real-estate speculation and development in South Boston. The old bridge, moreover, had excited controversy from the beginning; it had failed at making money in any way and had become mainly a fashionable promenade with a pleasant view of the city.[69] It was, in short, vulnerable.

On March 15, 1824, a Boston city meeting voted overwhelmingly (2,847 to 779) in favor of a free bridge or dam to South Boston, to be built without expense to the city. In the mode of the Middling Interest, the Faneuil Hall meeting "instructed" the city government to petition the legislature to request that its senators and representatives support the petition. When the legislature dragged its feet, Henshaw mounted a newspaper and pamphlet campaign which expanded the egalitarian rhetoric of the Middling Interest to a denunciation of monopoly and a celebration of the benefits of competition: the privilege and profit of the few and the sacrifice of the interests of the many should not be perpetuated under the specious claim of the inviolability of chartered rights. "To gain the road to improvement you must open the door to competition, and shut it against monopoly, the latter destroys, whilst the former nourishes improvement."[70]

The old bridge's owners did not put up prolonged resistance. By 1826 the South Boston free bridge had won its charter.[71]

The Charlestown petitioners, however, would kill a goose that laid a golden egg. The owners of the goose, quite understandably, resisted furiously, and the controversy raged inside and outside the legislature. The petitioners criticized the operation of the old bridge while they frankly enumerated the economic benefits they expected from the new bridge, never hiding their desire to be free of the "heavy tolls." In 1826 a joint committee of the legislature rejected their arguments at every point, but that same year the legislature also approved the South Boston free bridge, without compensation to the old bridge, and the Charlestown group must have been heartened. In March 1827 the legislature voted to charter the Warren Bridge Corporation, fixing its terminus on the Charlestown side a mere 260 feet from the old bridge. The proprietors repeated their arguments, in which they were joined by a minority of the legislature, that this action endangered the security of all property and undermined basic property rights.[72]

To the aid of the old bridge at the eleventh hour came Governor Levi Lincoln, casting the first veto ever by a Massachusetts governor. Lincoln was no opponent of economic development but rather its energetic advocate. During these years he worked hard for a law to remove liability from individual stockholders in corporations, which became a major spur to private enterprise.[73] His siding with the old proprietors shows that the broad question of economic development was not at all the issue.

Lincoln's veto triggered a revolt of Republicans in Middlesex and Suffolk counties known as the Free Bridge party. The new bridge supporters met in caucuses in Middlesex and refused to renominate Lincoln for governor. In Charlestown and neighboring towns the insurgency was very broadly based and included former Federalists as well as many Republicans. In Boston support for the dissidents quickly came from some of those associated with the South Boston free bridge and even with the Middling Interest. But David Henshaw and the *Statesman* tried to straddle the fence, proclaiming support for the Free Bridge senate nominations and for Governor Lincoln. Henshaw accepted nominations to the senate from both the Lincoln Republicans and the Free Bridgers, but the latter finally forced his hand and thus ended Henshaw's brief alliance with the Lincoln administration.[74]

The Free Bridgers nominated William C. Jarvis, a Charlestown Republican, for governor. Even though Jarvis refused to accept the nomination, angry voters in Middlesex County cast their ballots for him anyway, and he carried the county with over 57 percent of the vote. Support for the Free Bridgers was confined mostly to Middlesex County, Boston, and their periphery (Table VIII.1).

Indeed, Jarvis's support was highly concentrated within Middlesex County. Almost all of the twenty-one towns he carried there were located within the radius of an arc running from north by northeast of Charlestown to slightly southwest by south, an area which most obviously stood to benefit from the free bridge.[75] Most of these towns had voted Republican in 1824 or earlier, but even a few formerly strongly Federal towns, such as Medford and Reading, cast almost unanimous votes for Jarvis.

Though clearly a local vote, involving a noncandidate who received only 20 percent of the state vote, the effort got results. While turnout in most counties in 1827 remained low, in Middlesex and Suffolk it rose to its highest levels of the period. The next year the legislature again chartered the new Warren Bridge, and Governor Lincoln, who relished his role as an all-popular consensus executive, did not oppose it.

The controversy marked a stage in the transition to two Republi-

**Table VIII.1.** Free Bridge Party Vote, Number and Percent, 1827

Gubernatorial Election

| *County* | *No.* | *(Within County)* % |
|---|---|---|
| Middlesex | 2,469 | 57.3 |
| Suffolk | 1,237 | 28.1 |
| Essex | 762 | 20.1 |
| Worcester | 669 | 11.5 |
| Norfolk | 235 | 9.0 |
| Other | 1,758 | — |
| State Total | 7,130 | — |

can factions–Adams men and Jacksonians–that would contest the 1828 presidential election and then would develop into the loosely organized National Republican and Jacksonian Republican parties. In the 1827 state-senate contest four tickets appeared in Boston, and in the May representatives election no fewer than five tickets eventually confronted the voters. Henshaw and several of his South Boston Bridge associates appeared as candidates on the Free Bridge ticket, but it came in fourth in the representatives election.[76] By July Henshaw was running for Congress on an antitariff program; he tried to cultivate free-trade merchants and artisans opposed to the manufacturing interest and got in line nationally with the Calhounites and others supporting Jackson. By then the "unionists" had formed a Suffolk Republican Administration Committee and were holding up Adams, Lincoln, and the defense of property rights as their standard.[77]

Despite the rhetoric about property rights, the Free Bridgers and the elite did not really differ on the basics of political economy. They certainly did not disagree on economic development: both favored it. The bridge conflicts simply but pointedly raised the question, Under whose auspices would development occur? That made the conflict anything but simple and required the arbitration of all the courts of the land. Depending on circumstances, both sides showed themselves willing to set aside traditional definitions of property which stood in the way of freeing *their* capital to maximize its potential.

The underlying consensus on development surfaced dramatically a short time later when railroad fever swept Boston. From 1827 to 1830 Boston's economic and political leaders, jealously watching the growth of New York City, became convinced that the key to Boston's prosperity lay in a railroad connection to the west which would link with the Erie Canal at Albany. Republicans of all kinds and factions joined in the enthusiasm and focused first on urging the legislature to build a state railroad, much as New York had built the Erie. In February 1829 the citizens voted 3,055 to 59 to authorize the city to purchase stock in such a road. But in the legislature all the peripheral regions of the state ganged up against Boston and other towns directly on such a line (Worcester, Springfield, Pittsfield) and refused to act. In 1830 both sides concentrated on sending representatives to the legislature, and the May elections aroused unusual interest. Boston closed ranks on this issue and sent delegations that were strongly prorailroad. But most of the seacoast, apart from Boston and many scattered central and western regions off the main line, again defeated state aid. The merchant-manufacturers wanting railroads for their inland factories decided to begin on their own with shorter lines. In 1830 and 1831 the legislature granted them charters for a line from Boston to Lowell and for another from Boston to Worcester. The charters showed that investors had learned well the lessons of the free bridges. The grants "paid lip service to public rights but actually put tremendous power into the hands of investors," giving them almost complete control over their property and routes and protecting them from possible competitors.[78] The views of the radical critics of "monopolies" regarding these charters are not known, but Henshaw and his friends were among the railroad boosters. Also unremarked were the views on property rights of the owners of the Middlesex Canal, alongside of which the legislature permitted the manufacturers to build the Lowell Railroad.[79]

The railroad question mobilized citizens to participate in politics just as the bridge controversy had. From 1828 to 1829 the house of representatives grew from 345 to 496 members, and the 1830 representative elections attracted much interest throughout the state. In Boston, the railroad debates in town meeting gave rise, as the ward voting, wooden buildings and bridge issues had done earlier, to a decidedly antideferential spirit.[80]

Just as the popular political battle over railroads drew to a close in 1830–1831, another issue was already gathering momentum. It would create a social and political movement that would remobilize voters to a much greater extent, and would have a profounder impact on political culture than the earlier, half-grown social movements had had. Antimasonry concerned itself with matters far less tangible than wooden buildings, bridges, railroads, or factories, and yet in many indirect ways it was related to these things, as well as to the process of secularization in religious life which had also advanced dramatically in the 1820s.

# IX. Antimasons and Masons

> In an age of transition, the divisions among the instructed nullify their authority, and the uninstructed lose faith in them. The multitude are without a guide; and society is exposed to all the errors and dangers which are to be expected when persons who have never studied any branch of knowledge comprehensively and as a whole attempt to judge for themselves on particular parts of it.
>
> . . . as in an age of transition the source of all improvement is the exercise of private judgement, no wonder that mankind should attach themselves to that, as to the ultimate refuge, the last and only resource of humanity.
>
> —John Stuart Mill, 1831[1]

After 1830, new social movements challenged the political establishment far more seriously than the diffuse or local agitations of the 1820s had done. The most successful of these was Antimasonry, which became both a genuine social movement and a political party organized at least as much as the top-heavy Republican factions of the early 1830s. The Antimasonic "crusade," as it has often been called, helped to generate far greater participation in politics than had been evident for some time. Masons organized no party but acted as a powerful pressure group within both factions of the now sundered Republican party, and especially in the inner circles of the dominant National Republicans. The Antimason-Mason struggle ranged, however, throughout society, in churches, newspapers, and voluntary associations, in the streets, and at the polls. Militant Masons in fact launched a countercrusade against Antimasonry, which only enlarged the struggle and probably prolonged opposition to Masonry. Both Antimasons and Masons brought an ideological passion to this contest that contributed significantly to reinvesting public questions with moral intensity.

The quarrel was essentially cultural and religious, between descendants of the Puritans who were very similar in socioeconomic status, and in many ideas and enthusiasms, but whose values clashed in fundamental ways. Antimasonry's growth owed much to the receptivity of many of the state's Orthodox Congregationalists to a movement highly distrustful of the political establishment. At the same time it united men of very different religious beliefs in demanding that the laws mean what they say and that republican society guarantee equality before the law. The movement also constituted a demand from a significant segment of the populace that government and politics be guided by principles of traditional morality. It was the first such movement to emerge in the United States and was an archetype of later movements, notably temperance and antislavery, providing inspiration and some personnel for those causes.

In the history of political culture, Antimasonry marks the emergence of a new kind of social movement—populist and widely based in the middle and lower-middle classes. In creating a political organization and in sustaining it over several elections, it defined a mode of action which would be repeated many times throughout the nineteenth century. It also anticipated and hastened the development of mass political parties.

In recent years Antimasonry has been rescued from an undeserved obscurity, and Antimasons are no longer being written off as fanatics or opportunists.[2] The western New York genesis of Antimasonry was not simply a trivial curiosity which originated in delusion or paranoia. Masonry has similarly become a subject of disinterested historical inquiry and can no longer be relegated to the role of a passive victim attacked by excited bigots. Masonry was in fact a popular and often powerful institution which had grown rapidly after 1815 and which had gained increasing acceptance and social prominence. One begins to understand Antimasonry by examining Masonry.

## Masonry to 1828

Masonry arrived in America in the eighteenth century as an offshoot of an English society of gentlemen, intellectuals, and scientists. It became in the colonies a secret fraternity of middle- and upper-class men, drawn mostly from the professions and commerce. While playing on fascination with secret rituals, code words, and signals, and on the appeal of grandiose titles for its officers and degrees, it showed an almost deist-rationalist emphasis on brotherhood and appealed increasingly to men wearied of clerical and lay arguments over theological dogmas. After 1800 it also provided men an excuse for indulging in purely male conviviality and legitimated an untraditional way of spending leisure time. It could also aid a young man in making his way in a new or old society.[3]

In the 1820s Masonry grew in popularity, and Masonic lodges spread from the major towns throughout the countryside. By 1827 there were 101 lodges in Massachusetts, with over 4,300 members, mostly from the urban, commercial, and professional classes. Though selection was by invitation or cooption, the fraternity gradually came to represent a cross section of the male population. In Massachusetts the "craft" included a few members of the upper class but did not penetrate as heavily into the ranks of prominent men as it did in Connecticut or New York. Masons were solidly middle class, however, and well entrenched in the middle echelons of government and in the clergy. In Boston several Masons had supported the "Middling Interest" or had taken the lead in the middle-class Mechanics' Association. Prominent printers like Benjamin Russell of Boston and Isaiah Thomas of Worcester were Masons; as businessmen, editors, and political leaders, they were men situated at the nodes of several networks of influence.[4]

Antimasons later protested that Masons controlled the government and press through their secret power, and while it is not likely that Masons acted as a political conspiracy before 1826, they did occupy many more positions of leadership in government and in publishing relative to their numbers than did the rest of the population. Masons were both Federalist and Republican (though in Massachusetts they may have leaned toward the Federalists), and later they could be found in the various factions of the 1820s. Masonic activity, like church activity, was a way of aiding a political career. As rising young politicians welcomed the opportunity to deliver Fourth of July orations, so they joined the Masons and gave Masonic orations to gain recognition.[5]

Masonry enjoyed public acceptance and prestige. From George Washington's funeral in 1799 to Lafayette's visit in 1825, Masons participated conspicuously in community rituals while holding many of their own celebrations in public view. Occasional murmuring might be heard about Masons' excessive drinking, but alcohol was consumed heavily by many other Americans until the 1820s. Masons often thrust themselves into a public role, particularly in the laying of cornerstones for churches and public buildings.[6] Their orators let few chances slip to point out their fraternity's goodness and social utility, but their very protestations signified that Masonry enjoyed an uneasy legitimacy, even as it attained an unparalleled prominence and acceptance.[7]

By 1826 even many clergymen were promoting Masonry's acceptance both by joining lodges and by delivering sermons that demonstrated Masonry's compatibility with Christianity and praised it as a vehicle of universal brotherhood. In 1826 a Vermont Masonic minister described the situation throughout New England when he observed that only a few years ago "unyielding prejudices . . . were existing in our religious community against this ancient order, and seldom did a professing Christian, and still more seldom did a minister of the Gospel, seek admittance into our lodges. But this prejudice has been chased away by the light of Masonry; and now many eminent Christians are . . . reforming our Lodges; and many, learned, pious, and laborious ministers of the Gospel are exerting themselves to extend . . . Masonry in the world."[8]

At times Masons revealed their uneasiness. They knew that secrecy gave them many advantages, but also that it would always arouse envy and fear because, as one said, "no man likes that another should be in possession of secrets to which he is a stranger." As a Masonic clergyman admitted at Holden in 1825, they were aware, too, of the greater danger that some people looked upon Free Masonry "with a jealous eye, because there are those who profess to be Masons, who . . . fear not God, nor regard man."[9] The frequent defenses of Masonry on religious grounds by themselves testify that a large part of the "religious community" must still have retained doubts about Masonry.

In the 1820s Orthodox ministers complained vehemently against the Unitarian clergy who insisted that doctrinal differences did not matter—the Orthodox regarded this as heresy or secularism. What could they think of Masons who propagated an even more eclectic and secular blend of latitudianarian "religion"? In 1826 a young Mason of Newburyport proclaimed that Masons were *"free,* because they soared above the prejudices of their contemporaries, and were free from the slavery of opinion, which palsied the minds of uninitiated men."[10] Even the non-Orthodox who happened to be "uninitiated" might have taken offense at such language.

Some Masons knew that a potential existed for a reaction. In a remarkably prophetic report of 1824, a Grand Lodge committee outlined the danger. The occasion was a proposal for an orphan asylum to be built by Masons. The committee doubted that the fraternity could afford it, and warned that even if funds could be had, there would be other dangers:

> The moment we depart from our present domestic policy and enlarge the circle of our concerns that moment we become an object of animadversion, jealousy and apprehension. . . . our sacred rule 'of conforming to the government under which we live' . . . would not shield us from the effects of envy and suspicion. The world knows that we are not exempt from the common frailties of human nature, that we are veiled in impenetrable secrecy; and that secrecy among so formidable a body is an engine of great power.

The Craft could keep the confidence of the community by staying quietly within its "Sanctum Sanctorum." To call excessive attention to "the growing numbers and increasing influence of our Order" might even create "a change in the public mind unfriendly to a continuance of our Charter."[11]

It was thus perhaps only a matter of time before events brought Masonry out of its domestic circle. The process began in the recently settled wheat country of western New York, when an unemployed stonemason, William Morgan, and a Batavia newspaper publisher, David Miller, hatched a plan to publish an exposé of Freemasonry, from motives of profit and personal revenge. In the late summer of 1826, Masons from several western counties went to extraordinary lengths to suppress publication of the book, engaging in arson, mobbing, and finally kidnapping and probably murder. Morgan disappeared forever, while Miller escaped from incarceration in a lodge and broadcast news of the Masons' vigilante actions in the service of a secret fraternity. Suddenly the community was aroused and demanded to know Morgan's whereabouts. As his fate remained unknown, public curiosity spread to Freemasonry itself. Citizens' committees sprang up to investigate as public officials at all levels took no action. Meanwhile, evidence accumulated that local authorities had cooperated with the Masons in their abduction of Morgan. In early 1827 a series of trials began throughout the region which lasted for four years and for all that time fanned the flames of Antimasonry by failing to produce satisfactory information or justice. The leading conspirators had disappeared, a few accomplices were let off with light sentences, and most were acquitted. Judges and juries seemed biased. A parade of Masonic witnesses went through witness stands refusing to testify. Masonic oaths seemed more binding than any other obligations. Meanwhile official Masonic bodies took no disciplinary action; on the contrary, they provided aid and sustenance to the vigilantes. By mid-1827 protest against Masonry had turned to politics and by 1828 it was sweeping Antimasons into office throughout western New York. For the next five or six years Antimasonry played a significant role in the politics of New York and several other northern states.[12]

### The Massachusetts Movement

Antimasonry began in Massachusetts with little help from those who shaped public opinion. News from New York about "Morgan" filtered in early by word of mouth and letters, but newspapers of all political types either ignored the "excitement" or tried to squelch it. In the spring of 1828, however, an Antimasonic weekly press appeared in Boston, the *Anti-Masonic Free Press,* and of course divulged fully the story of the "outrages" and trials. Some established papers wished merely to avoid controversy; many others seem to have been doing just what Antimasons later charged, namely, suppressing news unfavorable to Masonry.[13]

As a movement, Massachusetts Antimasonry emerged in 1829, springing not from some long-accumulating dislike of Masonry, but from the events in New York combining with latent distrust, suspicion, and envy.[14] As in New York, protest also grew from Masons' defiance, resistance, and harassment of their critics. In Massachusetts, Masonic vigilantism did not at all come close to the level of that in New York, but it was a factor in nourishing Antimasonry.

During the first half of 1829 some towns and churches gradually began to inquire into Masonry. The town of Lynn moved with exceptional speed: after listening to lectures from ex-Masons and a local Antimason, citizens at the town meeting voted on April 6 that they regarded Masonry "as a great moral evil" and its existence as "dangerous to all free government." Thereafter the Lynn town hall was available for any further "exhibitions" regarding Masonry.[15] In Boston, the advent of Antimasonry into public forums was not quite so smooth.

In August a group of Bostonians met in the city-council chambers, listened to a speech outlining Masonry's dangers by a young merchant, Amasa Walker, and announced the formation of a "Suffolk Committee" to investigate Freemasonry. Most of the men involved remained active in leading Massachusetts Antimasonry for the next few years, and though none came from the highest ranks of society, they were solid citizens. A few were well-to-do merchants, and some had served in the state legislature, as aldermen, or in lesser offices. But none stood out clearly as members of what John Quincy Adams called "the aristocracy" of Boston, and the lack of allies among the most prominent men of the city made the going tough for Antimasonry.[16]

On September 8, 1829, Antimasonry truly arrived when the Suffolk Committee staged a "great meeting" at Faneuil Hall, only to have it disrupted by Masons. They interrupted the Reverend Moses Thacher, an Orthodox minister from Wrentham and a seceded Mason, and when Samuel D. Greene of western New York and a former member of Morgan's lodge attempted to speak, they created a deafening uproar and shouted threats of violence. His Boston hosts prudently spirited Greene out of the city early the next morning, and soon thereafter signs appeared in the city bearing Greene's name and reading in part:

> Let his days be few, and let another take his office. Let his children be fatherless and his wife a widow.[17]

Most of Boston's elite seemed willing to tolerate such rowdyism, and in any case remained aloof from Antimasonry.

Outside of Boston, however, Antimasonry made converts among local notables throughout the Commonwealth, and at year's end an Antimasonic state convention gathered at Boston.[18] Delegates from eight counties met with the Suffolk Committee and other Bostonians from December 30, 1829, through January 1, 1830. It was very much a "movement" convention, exploring in detail the philosophical nature of Masonry as well as events in New York. Though many of the delegates had experience in local politics, this meeting was not overtly political. Its discussions were dominated by an inquiring spirit run rampant.[19]

Like Antimasons elsewhere, they began their address by quoting the Declaration of Independence and said that once again Americans faced a threat of tyrannical power. Masonry had erected a distinct government within the nation, one dispensing its own penalties and rewards. It had unlimited funds at its disposal and hence unrestricted power (*"Wealth is power"*). It used that power to subvert justice and defeat the law in punishing crime. Using insidious measures, it gained offices of public trust and thereby controlled seven-eighths of all offices. In New York, the Grand Lodge had aided and sheltered "perpetrators of *kidnapping* and *alleged murder*." Given the "indivisible" character of Freemasonry, Masons everywhere were responsible for these crimes; the convention therefore requested Massachusetts Masons to disfellowship those responsible for violence to Morgan and either to deny the truth of these "disclosures" or to renounce the system and its oaths.[20] Not only was all this rather moderate, given the hyperbole long ago reached in Antimasonic rhetoric in New York and even in New England, but the convention made no specific proposals for political action.

Denied access to most newspapers, Antimasons gradually established their own presses and claimed some half-dozen sympathetic to their cause.[21] Meanwhile, the movement continued to use traveling lecturers to spread the message, and Masons persisted in trying to disrupt all such gatherings, especially when Antimasons used a town's central meeting place and thus sought to cloak their proceedings with an "official" aura. When the Antimason Jacob Allen spoke at the Marlborough town hall, rowdy boys and men set off fireballs and accompanied the lecture "with the music of conch shells, tin horns, cow bells, and iron triangles," and later set fire to the woodpile of an Antimason. In August, the Boston Antimasons again tried to use Faneuil Hall, this time for a "debate" on Masonic oaths. Masons crowded in to hiss, shout, and stamp. When Mayor Otis was called to the scene, he could not restore order, and furthermore told the Antimasons he would not let the hall be used again under circumstances in which he could not keep the peace! Soon after, a similar tumult forced Antimasons to withdraw from the Springfield town hall to a nearby tavern.[22]

Antimasons nevertheless placed great faith in their fellow citizens' capacity to read and listen to information—which they termed "light"—about Masonry, and to reason for themselves. They tried also to be fair to Masons, though they approached them often as they would sinners whom they were asking to renounce their sins. At the same time, Antimasons were likely to believe the worst of Masonry, and in the heat of contesting for public sympathy with a determined foe, they often retailed wild rumors and unfounded charges. They claimed, for example, that Masons wanted to abolish the militia because they possessed an armory in Boston with firearms and weapons sufficient to arm two thousand men.[23]

While some Antimasons let their imaginations and tongues roam too freely, they were not responsible for introducing hyperbole or deception into public controversy. Excessive rhetoric had characterized political controversy for some time. Furthermore, Masons and their allies had engaged in deception and repression, both of which fed rumor mills and paranoia.

As elsewhere, the controversy escalated and pushed the Antimasons inexorably to political action. In Massachusetts, however, Antimasonry was slower to change into a political organization. Antimasons entered into politics in Bristol County as early as the fall of 1828, but until the first part of 1831 they essentially made up a faction of the National Republicans in Bristol, Norfolk, and Plymouth counties. In 1830, Antimasons elected several representatives and state senators, while at the same time supporting Governor Lincoln. They had been pleased to discover that Lincoln was not a Mason, and though he would not ally with them, he assured Antimasons that he kept his distance from Masonry. Supporters of Lincoln's Jacksonian Republican opponent Marcus Morton, meanwhile, openly courted Masons.[24]

Early in 1830 the Boston Antimasons had organized a "committee of one hundred" to spread information, but the city was largely hostile to Antimasonry.[25] Moreover, the state leaders generally were not pragmatic politicians interested in political power and patronage so much as they were reformers laboring in a cause. The Bostonians were not as inexperienced as an Antimasonic group in rural Worcester County who confessed themselves new to politics "like inexperienced children," but they were, as the *Free Press* said, "not generally political men."[26]

Yet a move to independent politics was perhaps inevitable, particularly given the course of Antimasonry elsewhere. Moreover, pragmatists were already urging that the press take "elevated grounds," that the party be made "respectable," and that "sight . . . not be lost of other great leading interests."[27] Planning with Antimasons in other states for the 1832 presidential election also pushed them farther down the road to independent action. In the spring of 1831, Antimasons nominated legislative candidates in Suffolk, Bristol, Norfolk, Plymouth, Worcester, Middlesex, and Franklin counties, while still supporting Lincoln and other National Republicans. The piggyback period soon ended, however, with growing Antimasonic strength and with a sharpening of the lines between them and the National Republicans. Masonic pressure in the ranks of the latter was increasing, and Antimasonic-National hostility was growing.[28]

In May the Antimasons' state convention showed how far the movement had come in a year and a half. The zeal of fact-finding and elucidating still had a firm grip on many delegates, but this convention simply took for granted the existence of the "Antimasonic party." It intended to keep adhering Masons out of public office, and urged citizens to use their franchise "to check and ultimately suppress this secret political domination."[29]

In the recent legislature, Antimasons had felt the weight of Masonic influence and come out of it burning with anger over the National Republicans' endorsement of Henry Clay, a Mason, for the presidency. On June 17 they held a "legislative caucus"–actually a mixed caucus of some legislators and other leaders totaling some two hundred–and protested that Masonry had controlled the Nationals' caucus and prevented Antimasons from being named to vacancies in the Senate. The insurgents no longer doubted that the Nationals, under Masonic influence, were making ruthless war on them. Antimasons now had no choice but to enter into state and presidential politics. As their brethren in other states had put it, Antimasory was *"necessarily* political."[30]

## Political Crusade and Countercrusade

Antimasons now took a tougher line with Levi Lincoln and asked him to take a position on Masonry–was it good or evil?[31] Lincoln described Masonry as "wholly unnecessary and useless" and susceptible to mischief, and its oaths as "unjustly reprehensible and offensive." But he also displayed some impatience with the questioners, saying he could not believe that many Massachusetts Masons did not love their country better than the society. In this "favored Commonwealth" of schools, Bibles, and religion, "I cannot distrust the fidelity of a numerous class of my Fellow-

Citizens, nor see elsewhere in the errors and crimes of a few misguided, deluded wretched men, evidence of the degradation and servitude of the Nation."[32] In September of 1831 this was no longer enough for the Antimasons.

In early October an Antimasonic state convention of seventy-five delegates from eight counties nominated Samuel Lathrop for governor, the last Federal nominee (1824) for that post. The choice of Lathrop had its shortcomings. He was not an active Antimason and had earlier endorsed Henry Clay. Furthermore, he committed himself as a candidate only after having criticized both Antimasons and Masons. But he was no Mason, and his Orthodox credentials were well known to "the religious community."[33] Like others drawn to Antimasonry, Lathrop had turned against the Unitarian-controlled religious establishment of the 1820s.

The 1831 fall state election thus developed into one of the most spirited contests in years. For the past four elections, opposition to Lincoln and the Nationals had come from Jacksonian Republican backers of Marcus Morton, an unreconstructed Jeffersonian and Jacksonian Republican who had refused nomination in 1828 and 1829. In 1830 Morton consented to run and more than doubled his vote, but in the spring election of 1831 he lost ground as Antimasonry was already taking effect:

| | *Lincoln* | *Morton* | *Lathrop* | *Scattering* | *Total* |
|---|---|---|---|---|---|
| 1828 | 27,981 | 4,423 | | 1,914 | 34,318 |
| 1829 | 25,217 | 6,864 | | 3,122 | 35,203 |
| 1830 | 30,908 | 14,440 | | 1,820 | 47,173 |
| 1831 Spring | 31,875 | 12,694 | | 4,326 | 48,895 |
| 1831 Fall | 28,804 | 10,975 | 13,357 | 279 | 53,415 |

In the fall of 1831 the scattering vote dropped to its lowest in years, and Lathrop vaulted into second place behind Lincoln.[34] Lathrop carried only two counties, the old Federal-Orthodox strongholds in the Connecticut Valley, but rolled up more votes in absolute numbers in three eastern counties. Indeed, well over half of Lathrop's total vote came from eastern Massachusetts:

| | |
|---|---|
| Eastern counties: | 7,925 |
| Worcester county: | 1,831 |
| Western counties: | 3,601 |

Antimasonry clearly appealed to all sections of the state.[35]

Loyalist Masons responded to Antimasonry in two major ways: (1) by going about their business as usual and (2) by waging a countercrusade.

While the fraternity went into decline, a significant number of Masons remained active and defended Masonry. With friends they counterattacked Antimasonry by trying to influence public opinion and by lobbying within the National Republican party. In December 1828, the Grand Lodge denied a request for a new local lodge because the "time is inauspicious . . . and. . . a greater evil would result therefrom to the Craft than any palpable good."[36] But in the next year, Masons came forth with their rhetorical guns blazing against Antimasonry, calling it an "excitement" of unprecedented violence and bigotry, a "night-wind of moral desolation and of death." Antimasons were "disappointed office-seekers and starving politicians [who] rode upon the whirlwind, directing the baleful contagion. Time serving parasites, and canting hypocrites, hitherto sunk in hopeless obscurity, crawling forth from their concealment, flocked to the standard of anarchy and joined in the general uproar . . . proclaiming 'Death to Freemasonry.' "[37] The Masons assumed many postures in their countercrusade: standing foursquare as champions of reason, tolerance, and order, or donning a mantle of piety, or claiming injury as victims of persecution. Most of all, they tried to crush Antimasonry by direct attacks on the personal reputations and "character" of Antimasons.[38]

In early 1828 Masons began publishing a monthly journal to defend Masonry, the Boston *Masonic Mirror;* by mid-1829 it was a weekly devoted wholly to excoriating Antimasonry. Its editor, Charles W. Moore, a man of middling background and passionately Masonic, was a leader in all phases of the countercrusade. He operated on the principle that "the spirit of persecution, ignorance and fanaticism, *can never be satisfied: it must be met and overcome."*[39] In retrospect one may wonder whether those Masons who counseled against such a course were wiser. At this stage Antimasonry was insignificant in Massachusetts: a year later it was well established as an organized movement.

As Antimasonry grew stronger, the defiance of militant Masons seemed to grow with it. In December 1829 the grand master delivered an address which, while making a few concessions to critics, was essentially an aggressive defense of Masonry's virtue and its determination to continue.[40] In 1830 the Grand Lodge decided to build a new lodge hall in Boston. On October 14 they laid the cornerstone with a procession, dinner, and much fanfare. Though some unknown vandals painted "Golgotha" on the unfinished walls, construction went forward speedily. Lodges in the countryside made contributions to the building's cost, estimated at over $40,000, and in 1831 past grand master Isaiah Thomas of Worcester died and left in his will $500 toward completion of the building while denouncing "the unjust and wicked excitement" against Freemasonry. By July 1831 John Quincy Adams noticed "a large body of mechanics" busily and nonchalantly engaged in finishing the hall, and in 1834 the Grand Lodge congratulated itself on having a "beautiful edifice" for a hall of its own.[41]

The climax of the Masonic countercrusade came in December 1831, when 1,200 of the brethren issued a "Declaration of the Freemasons of Boston and vicinity." For the most part, the declaration made a sweeping denial of all charges against Masonry, asserting that Masonic oaths required nothing incompatible with good citizenship and that Masonic obligations instead required strict obedience to the laws of God and man. And once again the Masons served notice, as auspiciously as possible, that they had no intention of giving up.[42]

The new Masonic hall, however, created problems for the Masons because their charter of incorporation allowed the Grand Lodge to hold real property not exceeding $20,000 in value. The Masons therefore petitioned the legislature for a modification of their charter, but the General Court turned them down by a large majority. Antimasons countered with a demand that the legislature investigate the Grand Lodge and determine what funds it held, how many members it had, and how much it spent on charity, but the legislature also rebuffed their requests.

After his break with the Antimasons, Governor Lincoln emerged as the rallying point for Masons. According to one observer, Lathrop's nomination "produced a good deal of feeling among [the Masons], and they are determined that Governor Lincoln shall suffer no harm."[43] The Masons also had most to gain by working with the National Republicans. Though they did not control that organization, they exercised much influence from within. However, in some localities the Nationals' organization was wholly converted to Antimasonry, while in others Antimasons and Nationals cooperated, as in Plymouth, where they together sent John Quincy Adams to Congress in 1830.[44] But gradually the lines between the Nationals and Antimasons became sharply drawn as Masons acquired more influence within National Republican inner circles.

In 1832 the legislature continued to put down the Antimasons. In choosing the Reverend Paul Dean, a Universalist of Boston, to deliver the Election Sermon, they could not have picked anyone more galling to Antimasons and more symbolic of Masonic defiance. Dean was a leading Masonic spokesman and a well-known religious liberal. He had recently exhorted Masons to cling to their institutions, and had implied that the Masons were defending "divine truth" and performing a sacred duty, just like "the holy prophets and martyrs of our Lord."[45] Dean's election sermon must have been completely satisfying to both National Republicans and Masons. Though he did not mention Antimasons directly, his remarks against "political fanaticism" and "party violence" were clearly directed against them. In addition, Dean scornfully denounced "agitations" for "innovation" in the militia and debt laws and also cast a stone at alleged champions of "workingmen," whom he characterized as "persons of confirmed habits of idleness." Dean thus stood staunchly for order and the status quo, and to Antimasons, Masonry seemed well shielded under the protection of the National Republican establishment.[46]

The Masons' success within National Republicanism came at a price to that party, especially in national politics. Andrew Jackson's presidency grew more offensive each year to the Nationals of New England, and in 1832 they wanted to present a united opposition. The Nationals' top leaders cared far more about electing Henry Clay and about enacting his "American System" of energetic government to promote national development than they cared about Masonry or Antimasonry. In the summer of 1832 their differences with Jackson reached a fever pitch as the president vetoed a bill for recharter of the Bank of the United States. Moderate Nationals and Antimasons hoped ardently for a union of anti-Jackson forces throughout the country. Daniel Webster, a National Republican kingpin and aspirant to the presidency, was not the least of those promoting compromise between Nationals and Antimasons. But the division would not only persist through 1832 but would escalate and continue for still another year.[47]

National Republicans and Antimasons both suffered from illusions. The former for too long believed that common ground on national issues would bring the Antimasons back to the fold. The Antimasons on their side operated as the inexperienced politicians they were. Since Henry Clay was a Mason and made absolutely no concession to Antimasonry, the Antimasons of various states—especially New York, Pennsylvania, and Massachusetts—met at Baltimore in September 1831 and, in the first such national nominating convention, nominated William Wirt, a prominent lawyer and former attorney general, for the presidency. Wirt's "Antimasonry" was belated and half-hearted, but he was the best available public man. Though hardly well known to later generations, his name was familiar to all political men of his day and probably to much of the voting public in 1830. His public stature, however, was the problem, not his visibility. His prestige did not at all rival Clay's, and yet the Suffolk Committee entertained hopes that Clay might be induced to withdraw in Wirt's favor, rather than face a likely defeat. Abner Phelps and his comrades entreated John Quincy Adams to join with Webster and Edward Everett to advise Clay to withdraw, and Adams bluntly revealed the facts of life: "I told him I should give Mr. Clay no such advice, nor did I believe that Mr. Webster or Mr. Everett would; but that, if we should, Mr. Clay would not take our advice. I believed, further, that Mr. Clay's party would not suffer him to withdraw, if he would."[48]

In September the Antimasons met in state convention in Worcester, with 319 members from eleven counties, and renominated Lathrop for governor and chose for lieutenant governor Timothy Fuller of Cambridge, a former Jeffersonian Republican and congressman (1817–1825).[49] Thus in 1832 Antimasons presented both presidential and state tickets and separate legislative tickets in most counties.

Voter turnout rose again, stimulated both by the heated controversies in state politics and by the dramatic presidential contest between Jackson and Clay. Indeed, some have attributed the additional turnout solely to presidential politics and the Bank controversy.[50] While the presidential struggle undoubtedly created additional interest and drove politicians to greater exertions, in Massachusetts the number of votes given for the three gubernatorial candidates was in every case greater than the average given for presidential electors:

| | *Nat. Rep* | *Dem. Rep.* | *Antimason* |
|---|---|---|---|
| 1831 Governor | 28,804 | 10,975 | 13,357 |
| 1832 Governor | 33,946 | 15,197 | 14,755 |
| 1832 President | 31,800 | 13,900 | 14,600 |

The Antimasons improved their total slightly over 1831, but both of the other parties gained more, and Lathrop's percentage was less than the year before. The relatively weaker showing resulted in part from Lathrop's never having been a solid candidate and also from Wirt's shortcomings. Lathrop's support, in any case, came from the same places that had backed him the year before. He again got his only majority in Hampshire County (51 percent), carried Bristol County with a plurality (48 percent), and won most of his votes in southeastern and central towns.[51]

On the national scene, Antimasons played the role of spoilers, and though it was difficult to prove that Clay might have won with their support, many Antimasons and National Republicans believed that was the case. Daniel Webster, viewing the disarray of Massachusetts's opposition to Jackson, urged again that Antimasons be conciliated with a seat on the governor's council. In exasperation he asked Lincoln, *"Cannot the thing be done?"* But despite efforts by Webster and his friends, notably Edward and Alexander Everett, the private and political war between Antimasons and Masons continued through 1833.[52]

The Antimasons concentrated their efforts on a petition campaign calling for a legislative investigation of the Grand Lodge, and by November 1833 had accumulated 6,000 signatures on a "memorial" to the legislature declaring the dangers of Masonry.[53] More important, the National Republicans refused to give offices to anyone tainted with Antimasonry and furthermore created a gerrymander of congressional districts designed to protect National Republican seats in regions of Antimasonic strength, especially in Bristol, Norfolk, and Plymouth counties.[54] Meanwhile, the national leaders continued to press for compromise. These more cosmopolitan men saw the controversy as a distraction, and even Masons among them seemed to take a broader view of state quarrels once they went to Washington.[55] In mid-1833 the focal point of compromise efforts was former president John Quincy Adams, who had been suggesting reconciliation to National Republicans and Antimasons for some two years.

Adams had become profoundly convinced that Masonry's flaunting of justice in New York constituted a grave danger to the Republic, and he had published several letters sharply critical of Masonry.[56] In 1831 he had discussed the possibility of an Antimasonic presidential nomination and had declined their invitation to stand for governor. Adams hoped to reunite the Antimasons and Nationals, but his comments on Masonry had been severe, and though he was willing to issue softer statements, he would not retract or equivocate. During 1833 both moderate Nationals and Antimasons besieged Adams with entreaties to be a joint candidate. He was extremely pleased, moreover, by his re-election to Congress by both National Republicans and Antimasons of the Plymouth district by an overwhelming vote.[57]

In September, Adams accepted the Antimasonic nomination in hopes that the Nationals would take him after some face-saving gestures. In ten days, however, Alexander Everett reported to him that the "Masonic faction in Boston are in complete combustion" and that National Republican newspapers were either denouncing the idea of fusion or were uncooperative. The Boston Nationals elected sixty-three delegates to their October convention, and, Adams observed, thirty-five of them were Freemasons. From Berkshire County came the distressing news that the Nationals were so incensed by the proposal of Adams that they were already putting forward a Clay Mason for governor. Everett told Adams that Daniel Webster, who had urged coalition throughout, "now saw great difficulties" in arranging a coalition, "and that it was astonishing to observe the supineness of all party action here, excepting among the Masons. He thought the Masonic power altogether unaccountable, considering in how low estimation it had been held before this controversy arose." The moderate Nationals still tried to persuade the National Republican convention to nominate someone acceptable to the Antimasons, such as Edward Everett, but after a long struggle they selected John Davis, a National Republican congressman from Worcester. They then asked Alexander Everett to prepare the state address. Everett confided to a friend that "I am desirous of giving it a temperate tone on the subject of Masonry but am a good deal embarrassed by the fiery zeal of my associates." Masons also pressured Everett to include anti-Adams comments in the address, but Everett's worst problem was yet to come. The Boston Masons opposed his being renominated to the state senate, and, after a bitter struggle in the city convention, the Nationals endorsed Everett by a bare majority of two.[58]

The party's state address of 1833 devoted but little space to Masonry and seemed to wish that Antimasonry would go away. The fears of that party, it said, were "exaggerated and extravagant." Free Masonry was not "of sufficient moment" to warrant all the attention. The National Republican party was neither Masonic nor Antimasonic, but it deplored fanaticism and believed that the Masonic fraternity gave no cause for political strife.[59]

The Democratic Republicans said even less about Antimasonry than did the Nationals. Boosted by Jackson's visit to the state in June, the Democrats concentrated on national politics and sought to capitalize on the growth of the president's popularity because of his opposition to nullification. The Democrats also stressed opposition to the Bank of the United States because of their desire to appeal to still another political organization that was breaking into Massachusetts politics–the Workingmen's party. The Workingmen were probably mostly defectors from National Republican ranks, and the Democrats saw these insurgents, unlike the Antimasons, as natural recruits, especially since the Workies talked in terms of opposition to economic aristocracy–a rhetoric with which the Democrats had long been familiar. Not all Democrats throughout the state were uniformly hostile to Antimasons, but the Democratic leadership continued to stand aloof from Antimasonry.[60]

In November, with no fewer than four political parties in the field, Antimasonry reached its greatest strength in Massachusetts. John Davis led the field with 25,149 votes but failed to secure a majority. Adams came in second, with 18,274; Morton third, with 15,493; and the Workingmen's candidate, Samuel C. Allen, fourth, with 3,459. Adams raised Lathrop's total vote by about 4,000 and garnered just under 30 percent of the vote, winning majorities in two counties and pluralities in three more. It seemed fairly clear from the returns of the preceding year that most Antimasonic and Workingmens' votes came from the Nationals or from new voters.

| | *Nat. Rep* | *Dem. Rep.* | *Antimason* | *Workingmen* | *Scattering* | *Total* |
|---|---|---|---|---|---|---|
| 1832 | 33,946 | 15,197 | 14,755 | | 327 | 64,225 |
| 1833 | 25,149 | 15,493 | 18,274 | 3,459 | 99 | 62,474 |

No politician needed to be told that opponents of the dominant party had accumulated 60 percent of the vote.[61]

At its 1833 peak, Antimasonry relied most heavily on votes from eastern Massachusetts, and not on those from the Connecticut Valley. The top five counties in *numbers* of Antimasonic votes were all eastern counties. And while the total Antimasonic votes in western Franklin and Hampshire were 654 fewer than in 1832, Adams improved on Lathrop's last run in three eastern counties–Middlesex, Norfolk, and Plymouth–by 3,219 votes.[62]

Antimasonry reached its electoral peak in 1833 because Adams's name headed the ticket, not because its organization was well developed. Some Antimasonic leaders did recommend that organization be attempted in every school district, but sustained politics was not the trademark of Antimasons, and their network was not much developed below the county level.[63] John Quincy Adams, moreover, was never one to encourage party organization, and in this case he had accepted the nomination hoping to reunite the anti-Jackson forces. It was thus no surprise that when the gubernatorial election resulted in no choice and a decision by the legislature was pending, Adams withdrew in favor of Davis. A few Antimasons strongly objected to this and preferred to try to coalesce with Morton's supporters, but Adams wanted no dealings with Jacksonians. Furthermore, the former president was already beginning to doubt whether much practical good could any longer come from "stubborn adherence to Anti-Masonry."[64]

Though Adams was beginning privately to retreat from Antimasonry, on January 1, 1834, he explained his withdrawal in a public address which was a scathing attack on Masonry. In this searching and detailed analysis of Masonry's political influence in the state and especially in the National Republican party, Adams revealed much of his thinking about Masonry, and his charges make it possible in retrospect to understand why many Antimasons remained determined to carry on the fight.[65]

The Masons, meanwhile, were issuing declarations of their own, the Grand Lodge having decided in December to surrender their charter. Masonic officials sent a memorial to the legislature asking that the lodge's act of incorporation of 1817 be repealed. Lest anyone construe this action as one of repentance, the Masons announced it in high-toned and combative language, claiming that the lodge was relinquishing "none of its Masonic attributes or prerogatives. These it claims to hold and exercise independently alike of popular will and legislative enactment–not of toleration; but of right."[66] This statement inflamed Antimasons and confirmed their suspicion that the lodge had given up its charter only to ward off legislative investigation. In 1833 the house of representatives had actually approved an inquiry, but the senate had blocked it. Now demands for an investigation reappeared, and Antimasonic petitions once more flooded the legislature, the number of signers rising to over 8,000.[67]

The Antimasons' petition campaign had three major aims: a full investigation of Masonry, the repeal of the Grand Lodge's charter, and a law forbidding extralegal or extrajudicial oaths. On all three objectives, Antimasons remained far from satisfied. The legislature finally appointed a joint committee to investigate Freemasonry, but the senate refused to grant the committee the routine power to send for persons and papers. Consequently no adhering Masons appeared before the committee, and most of those requested to come did not even reply. But a panel of legislators sympathetic to Antimasonry held hearings anyway and in March 1834 published a report of seventy-six pages, with fifty-four pages of appendices. The joint committee briefly defended Antimasons against charges of political opportunism and then unsparingly denounced Masonry, dwelling especially on its international and national activities as a secret combination. The report was, in short, virtually an Antimasonic tract, lacking the restraint of Adams's or William L. Stone's *Letters* but making some telling points against certain of Masonry's pretensions, particularly its claim to be a "charitable association."[68]

If the investigation fell short of what Antimasons wanted, so did the legislature's response to their chief demand for a law against Masonic oaths. The National Republicans themselves had introduced a bill against "unlawful oaths," but Masons had recently claimed that Masonic oaths were "neither lawful nor unlawful" but a "voluntary obligation," and a Pennsylvania court had supported that interpretation. Therefore, Antimasons wanted a law specifically directed against Masonic oaths.[69]

Meanwhile, the national leaders of the National Republicans, now becoming the "Whigs," wanted Antimasonic backing for resolutions condemning Jackson's economic policy, and in late February 1834 Webster and Everett again approached Adams in Washington and asked him to help. Adams replied angrily that he had already tried to persuade the Antimasons to rejoin the Nationals but that the latter had done nothing to conciliate them. Instead, "every possible thing had been done to fret and exasperate them: all their candidates for Senate had been swept off the board; not one Anti-Mason had been elected to the Council; a fraudulent law against unlawful oaths was now in concoction to baffle and deceive them; and just now the Senate had refused to grant to the joint investigating committee the power to send for persons and papers; and their aid was implored to pass National Republican resolutions in favor of the bank." Adams asserted that the Antimasons "would [instead] go over to Jacksonism."[70]

An Antimasonic-Jacksonian alliance indeed seemed to be in the making. In January legislators of both camps had combined on several votes (theirs numbered 250 to 260, compared to the Nationals' 300 to 350), and three Antimasonic senators had voted for Morton for governor. Morton and the Boston Jacksonians were for the first time exploring the possibility of coalition.[71] This led Daniel Webster and his associates to redouble their efforts to deflate Antimasonry. It meant, first of all, wringing concessions from the Masons and giving something of substance to the Antimasons. Webster again promised Adams that the Nationals intended to disentangle themselves "from the Masonic faction." All the Masons in Washington intended to recommend "total abandonment of the institution," and Webster himself saw no objection to a law against extrajudicial oaths. He also thought that one or two Antimasons ought to be placed on the governor's council. Adams thought that this was "just and conciliatory" and that such measures would bring the Antimasons to support Governor Davis the following fall.[72]

Webster and his friends hoped that Masons would be persuaded to give up their charters, and that the diehards would remain silent. At the same time, they showed some concern that Masons not appear to lose face. Congressman Rufus Choate, himself a Mason, told Governor Davis that the latter's "conversations with *masons* during the session will do everything. I have no doubt they will go as far as pride and manhood and principle will permit and beyond that I hope they will not be pushed."[73] Choate, an articulate champion of New England economic interests and a staunch ally of Webster's, had been elected to Congress with Masonic backing. In early 1834 he became one of the most tireless workers among Masons in order to gain their cooperation, and during the summer he visited Masonic lodges throughout Essex County. Meanwhile Governor Davis was cajoling the Masons of Worcester County to meet in convention and to declare their intention of giving up their lodge charters. Essex County's Masons soon followed suit, and in September the Masons of Hampshire, Franklin, and Hampden counties met at Springfield and said their charters also would be "surrendered and canceled." On these movements Daniel Webster bestowed his blessing and told Davis that he could not see how Antimasons could remain in opposition any longer.[74]

Some Antimasons, particularly those in Worcester County, began moving into Whig ranks, but diehards on both sides refused to bury the hatchet. Though they were becoming politically isolated, militant Masons controlled the Grand Lodge, refused to dissolve it, and in September condemned those Masons who were "surrendering" charters. Most newspapers, however, now ignored these militants. Among the Antimasons, Benjamin Hallett, editor of the Antimasonic *Advocate,* wanted to carry the Antimasons into the Jackson party. In October the Whig leader Edward Everett listed the causes leading to such a coalition: "the design of some of the [Antimasonic] leaders, the impracticability of many others, the fanaticism of some of the masons, the intrigues of the Jackson masons inside the lodges to keep up the Institution, and out of it to coax Antimasons, [together] with the inherent difficulty of bringing together parties, embittered by keen conflicts, threaten to produce a 'more perfect union' of Antimasonry and Jacksonism."[75]

In any case, most Antimasonic leaders could not accept Davis, and the legislative majority's hard line had already led them to conclude that "the whig party is the masonic party."[76] Thus, the Antimasons rallied for one more campaign and nominated Adams's friend John Bailey for governor, and George Odiorne, one of the movement's initiators and a benevolent reformer, for lieutenant governor. As a party, however, Antimasonry was probably less organized than it had been the year before.[77]

The 1833 election had marked the high point of protest in Massachusetts; the 1834 election signaled the coming domination of the Whig and Democratic parties. Bailey's total slipped below Lathrop's initial vote of 1831, and his percentage was down even more sharply. Morton added almost 4,000 votes to his total, but Davis improved by nearly 20,000 votes over 1833 and amassed a clear and stunning majority of just under 58 percent. The efforts at "conciliation" had borne fruit, but it was also true that national affairs were once again mobilizing the electorate on a scale not present for at least a decade.[78]

## Political Moralists and Populists

> For consider your call, brethren; not many of you were wise according to worldly standards, not many were powerful, not many were of noble birth; but God chose what is foolish in the world to shame the wise, God chose what is weak in the world to shame the strong, God chose what is low and despised in the world, even things that are not, to bring to nothing things that are, so that no human being might boast in the presence of God.
>
> –I Corinthians 1:26–29

As an independent movement, Antimasonry was finished, but it had left its mark on Massachusetts politics. Some recent interpretations of Antimasonry have held that its leaders tended to be a "displaced elite" frustrated by modern change while its voting public constituted an "alienated" mass of rootless men.[79] Such a view is wholly at odds with the character of Antimasonry and with the political and social context in which it flourished.

The state's Antimasonic leaders were in fact usually upwardly mobile, aspiring individualists, fully attuned to the spirit of "improvement," and, compared with Masons, more involved in nontraditional enterprises. Most had experienced improvement in their own condition and eagerly sought it for their fellow men as well. Several Antimasonic leaders promoted railroads as ardently as did any National or Democratic Republicans. Antimasons also extended their agitation for "improvement" to include *moral* as well as material reform.[80]

In its early stages Antimasonry depended heavily for leadership on men who were leaders in Orthodox churches and evangelical activity. In the early nineteenth century perhaps the only Boston church still clinging steadfastly to "the *old* paths" of Calvinist Orthodoxy was Old South.[81] Dr. Abner Phelps, an original member of the Suffolk Committee, was a leading member of Old South, and several other Antimasonic leaders were members or affiliates. In 1809, after a revival at Old South, the Park Street Church had come into being, deliberately founded as a center of "evangelical orthodoxy." Park Street waged war on Unitarianism and took the lead in launching a fleet of benevolent enterprises, including the American Board of Commissioners for Foreign Missions (1810), the American Education Society (1819), the Society for the Moral and Religious Instruction of the Poor (1816), and the Prison Discipline Society (1825). In 1823, in concert with other churches, it began a lecture series on the subject of slavery.[82] In 1826, with George Odiorne as moderator, a small group meeting in the Park Street Church vestry organized the American Temperance Society. Church members regarded it as their duty to prevent the spread of intemperance "by arraying public opinion against the use of ardent spirits," and to engage in the "regulating and enlightening of public opinion by the exhibition of truth and by example." This approach to public opinion not surprisingly resembled that taken by the Antimasonic movement in which Odiorne took a leading role. Odiorne was a small capitalist who had come to Boston at age thirty-six at the turn of the century. He had made money manufacturing and selling iron and nails, and had gone into banking by 1826. A founder of Park Street Church, otherwise known as "Brimstone Corner," Odiorne personified the Orthodox evangelical element in Antimasonry.[83]

Though there were several Unitarians in the Antimasonic state leadership, a Unitarian-Orthodox division often was the essence of Masonic-Antimasonic polarity. In Boston, for example, while leaders of Antimasonry came from Old South, from Park Street, and from the Reverend Lyman Beecher's Hanover Street Church (also an Orthodox offspring of a revival in 1823), Masons formed an important group in Boston's Twelfth Congregational Society. Founded in 1825 during the height of the Unitarian-Trinitarian controversy, the Twelfth was a Unitarian rallying point. Its leader, the Reverend Samuel Barrett, joined with such leading lights of Unitarianism as Channing, Parkman, and Palfrey in promoting "rational" benevolence and in contending against Orthodoxy. Barrett and several of the Twelfth's founders were also prominent Masons: the minister and laymen like Thomas Powers worked actively with diehard Masons through 1834–1835.[84]

Given the religious-political strife of the 1820s, it is hardly surprising that the Orthodox figured prominently in a rebllion against the Unitarian-dominated political regime. As the Orthodox lost control of the religious establishment, they fought back by launching revivals and reform crusades into a world in which, they believed, religion must take the offensive or traditional morality would decline beyond recall. The Orthodox also intensified their attacks on Unitarians and pointed out that most of the judges delivering decisions against them in the courts were themselves Unitarians. The Orthodox indeed went further, as in the Reverend Parsons Cooke's sermon "Unitarianism an Exclusive System, or The Bondage of the Churches that were Planted by the Pilgrims," and charged that a Unitarian conspiracy existed within the legislature and courts that was designed to make Unitarianism dominant. If these accusations sounded like those Antimasons would soon be making against Masonry, the Unitarian replies similarly rehearsed those which Masons would be giving to their critics.[85]

The association of Orthodoxy and Antimasonry was evident in Lathrop's nomination in 1831 and 1832, and in the opposition of Antimasonic publications to the religious establishment—a position now held by most Orthodox, including Lathrop. It seems clear that a good many Antimasonic votes came from Orthodox Congregationalists.[86] At the same time, Antimasonry was much more than a by-product of Orthodox frustration, and other denominations also provided Antimasonic votes. Antimasons themselves claimed broad support from "multitudes of Christians," while other observers placed their adherents among "the whole religious public."[87]

Members of the Quaker, Methodist, and Baptist churches also contributed to the Antimasonic cause. Quakers in Westport and New Bedford helped to make Bristol County an Antimasonic stronghold, while other Quakers gave leadership and money to the Antimasonic effort in Lynn. It is difficult to estimate the numbers involved. None of these groups were unanimously Antimasonic, and it is doubtful that a majority of the eligible Methodists or Baptists voted Antimasonic, otherwise Antimasons would have received more votes. In 1829 the New England Conference of Methodists passed resolutions attempting to neutralize Masonry and Antimasonry as issues, but individual Methodist and Baptist churches took stronger stands, resolving to disfellowship Masons. On the other hand, some Methodist and Baptist laymen and ministers had been Masons, and some of these men defended the fraternity while others became seceders and Antimasons. Overall, probably more Methodist and Baptist church members and affiliates supported Antimasonry than directly backed Masonry, while many of them remained neutral and for various reasons voted National Republican and Democratic-Republican.[88]

Antimasonic voters were, in any case, not very different from Masons or from other voters. The assertion by some social scientists that Antimasons were an unstable "mass" of poor and "alienated" men echoed the Masons who asserted that "Antimasonry like the cholera . . . prevails most among the lower classes."[89] But in Massachusetts there is no evidence at all to support that thesis. Logic alone rules out such a notion. The electorate of 1831 to 1834 was smaller than the pre-1825 or the post-1835 voting publics. Small, issue-oriented electorates have generally derived from stable, better-informed, and more-involved parts of communities. During "surge" elections, such as the presidential election of 1840, massive turnouts occur as new or habitual nonvoters go to the polls. These floating voters are not usually associated with the type of movements that flourished in the early 1830s.[90]

Political opponents often asserted that the Antimasons lacked principles and were utterly ruthless in pursuing the destruction of Masonry. Marcus Morton said that the Antimasons "do not pretend to act on political principles, and in this respect many of them are unquestionably *right.*" Yet John Quincy Adams exclaimed to the people of Massachusetts that "Political Antimasonry is founded upon a pure, precise, unequivocal principle of *morals*. . . . Moral principle is the vital breath of Antimasonry."[91] To men like Morton and Rufus Choate, politically experienced and astute, sensitized to the ways of professional politicians, and instrumentalist in their political modes, the Antimasonic moralizers did appear to lack principles. Most of the Antimasonic leaders did not recognize or acknowledge the rituals and implicit rules operative among public men. Most of them simply did not regard themselves as political men. The Antimasonic party, said an early state convention, "has no use for any office seeking, selfish, time serving politician. . . . [It requires] Men who will make no truce or compromise with any men–Clay men, Jackson men, Working men, Young men, or any other party, or set of men, while they *support adhering Freemasons, their aiders or abettors. . . .*" Later that year Abner Phelps made the point even more starkly:

> . . . Anti-Masonry will flourish on holy ground and no other. It is *"the tree of life–and its leaves are for the healing of the nations."* Once let it be defiled by the blasting influence of political intrigue–bargain and corruption, it must *wither*, and the nations can no more be healed of the curse of Masonry. For this reason it must be guarded by *"the pure spirits,"* who have hitherto shown themselves worthy . . . [and who] have the flaming sword of *truth* for its defense.[92]

This mentality remained influential in Massachusetts Antimasonry for most of its career through 1834. After that, Antimasonry became a shadow of its former self, a reduced faction within parties led by politicians looking for a deal. But the "pure spirits" dominated the active party far longer than they had in other states. In New York, for example, pragmatic politicians had quickly gained dominance of the political party. But in Massachusetts, for reasons given above, the movement men continued as prominent leaders for a much longer time.

Antimasonry was not the populism of the alienated or the reactionary; it was a middle-class moral populism. It did contain, as Charles Francis

Adams shrewdly discerned, "a strong secret cause, a tendency to the errors of radicalism, to the dislike of the established order of Society, by which talent does not always maintain the ascendency over wealth."[93] Antimasons, in other words, wanted government and society to purify their handling of equality of opportunity, just as they demanded, as an outgrowth of the New York "outrages," a strict application of equality before the law.

# X. The Workingmen's Movement and Party

> Education, religion, the currency, the bridges, the artificial channels of commerce, the rivers themselves, mechanic industry, and even agriculture, have . . . been in part subjected to capital, acting through corporations. And almost all this has been done in half a century! . . . It is the tendency of these measures, to degrade the many. The small farmer passes in the world for less than he did fifty years ago; the mechanic is not relatively what he once was. In the old times they were not called "the lower classes."
>
> —George Bancroft, Northampton, Oct. 24, 1834

> . . . now a few hundred men in Boston, Salem, & c. possess more property than all the farmers in the state. . . . Men with immense estates and men with no property are ten times more numerous than they were 40 or 50 years ago. Meanwhile the great middle class has been comparatively much diminished, and not a few of them live on mortgaged farms, and are borne down with debts. The condition of the people of this country has been approximating to that . . . of Europe. We have splendid cities and poor towns, palaces and poor-houses, luxury and want, the vices of high-life and low-life, superciliousness and servility, nabobs and paupers, Dives and Lazarus.
>
> —Sylvester Judd (editorial), Northampton *Hampshire Gazette,* Nov. 6, 1833

In certain periods social criticism appears to spread—especially in the eyes of defenders of the status quo—in contagious fashion, affecting group after group and bringing into the public arena voices that were hitherto silent, meek, or acquiescent. In the 1960s, for example, especially after the civil-rights movement had burst fully into the national consciousness, it seemed that every new season groups defining themselves as "minorities" or as oppressed came forward to make their presence known. Protesters quite different from one another sometimes expressed themselves in remarkably similar rhetoric. The force of example and imitation was evident, even among groups very hostile to one another. Manifest, too, was the common experience of rapid social and cultural change.

The social movements of the 1820s and 1830s bore a similar relation to one another. The Workingmen's movement of the 1830s differed greatly from Antimasonry; it generated the most radical criticism of its day of the northern economic and political system, sprang directly from socioeconomic change, and spoke directly to that change. Yet Antimasonry helped stimulate the growth of the Workingmen's protest, and anticipated the form of its critique. Likewise, the sectarian religious controversy which hastened disestablishment formed a part of the background of the Workingmen's movement in Massachusetts. Neither of these impulses fed directly into the Workingmen, however; American labor's first stirrings in this period probably owed more to English example. In 1815 the first ten-hour bill was introduced into Parliament, and precisely in 1830 there began popular agitation of "the great Ten Hours Movement" in Britain.[1]

In Massachusetts itself social criticism nevertheless clearly grew more radical from the early 1820s on, and a kind of spill-over effect came into being. A Workingmen's spokesman, for example, in protesting the opposition of judges to trade unions, charged that any judge well knew the power of professional unions, since he himself was a "member of a combination of lawyers, better organized and more strict and tyrannical in the enforcement of their rules, than even masonry itself."[2] But the argument being made here does not depend on the existence of such explicit analogies. Though the Workingmen's movement originated to some degree in hostility to Antimasonry, the latter still facilitated the Workingmen's appeal. In retrospect there clearly appears a progression of movements building on one another, carrying protest ever closer to the central dogmas of the culture.

The Orthodox Congregationalists came to believe that Unitarians exerted a sinister political influence by which they had cheated the true heirs of the Puritans out of their inheritance. The Antimasonic protesters also cried alarm at a particular conspiracy which controlled and perverted government, and they broadened their accusations to cover the normal and routine operations of politics. They emphasized, far more than the Orthodox, the need for the restoration of an uncorrupted republican polity, but sought no new structures for democracy.

The Workingmen's protest went deeper. Like the Antimasons, they saw the perversion of republican politics and condemned all political factions and parties as routinely unrepresentative. But their social criticism also engaged the economic organization of society since, as one spokesman put it, "so all-controlling are the social relations upon our political affairs."[3] As they viewed the development of merchant capitalism and manufacturing, they prophesied a continuing concentration of wealth and power in the hands of a "few," the "accumulators," the "non-producers," while the great mass of working people became steadily impoverished, degraded, and politically powerless. The Workingmen reacted directly to the suffering of artisans displaced by economic and technological change, to the growing factory population of women and children, to the widening of class distinctions, and to the loss by the laboring masses of true citizenship. They denounced, as few Americans dared, a privileged class of capitalists reaping an ever larger share of the fruits of everyone's labor, with the aid of legislation enacted by politicians of all factions and parties.

Historians have frequently clucked their tongues in dismay at the Workingmen because they have found their remedies inadequate to correct the ills exposed by their radical diagnoses. To some later observers, the measures advocated by the Workingmen have seemed mildly "reformist" and "naive," while others have faulted the Workingmen for being too optimistic.[4] In New England and Massachusetts the major thrust of the movement was toward the ten-hour day for ship and house carpenters, masons, caulkers, painters, and other artisans. This demand summarized skilled manual workers' concerns with wages, hours, conditions of work, and, indeed, with the very right of laborers to have a say in setting wages with employers. Focus on the "ten-hour day" really entailed what later would be called "collective bargaining." Since traditionally artisans, mechanics, and laborers had simply accepted a day of "sun to sun" with wages set by employers, this marked a basic change. The seriousness of its challenge to prevailing work practices may be gauged by the intensity with which the merchant capitalists of Boston rallied to crush it.

There was a Workingman's movement, which agitated to aid workers improve their lot and to publicize reforms in their interest, and there was a Workingmen's party, which engaged briefly in independent electoral politics. While the Workingmen's own ticket never received more than 6 percent of the total statewide vote, the Workingmen nonetheless clearly articulated concerns shared by many of those who never voted their ticket. Their presence in elections in 1833 and 1834, along with that of the Antimasons, formed part of the high tide of dissent from politics as usual, and represented the most extreme expression of distrust in political leaders of the major parties. All those who voted for the Workingmen certainly registered their lack of confidence in the National Republicans–Whigs and Jacksonian Democrats alike, and they quite possibly testified to a much broader, if latent, substratum of distrust.

As the Commonwealth's merchant capitalists looked anxiously to the booming port of New York as a pacesetter in material growth, so, too, did the middling classes and artisans of Boston receive notions and inspiration from the Empire State and its metropolis. In the late twenties,

Workingmen's movements emerged in Philadelphia and New York, and in 1829 New York City mechanics fielded a ticket of assembly nominations. By 1830 in Massachusetts both local conditions and cues from abroad had created a climate rife with apprehension over the relations of rich and poor and with sensitivity regarding the interests of workingmen in particular.[5] In 1830, indeed, a Workingmen's movement emerged in several towns and, though feeble and partially developed at first, displayed a pattern which would persist over the next five to six years.

**Shadows**

That pattern resembled Workingmen's activities elsewhere in alternating between organization for strikes and electoral activity. Both kinds of efforts were simply attempts to achieve concrete goals as well as to increase society's awareness of the needs of workingmen. There was nothing inconsistent in the two, but the political tendency often resulted from the influence of politicians and employers less willing to concede the legitimacy of strikes and more concerned about issues they could support (e.g., militia reform) and, of course, about workers' votes. Indeed, during the career of the Workingmen's movement various politicians fluttered like butterflies in and out of its front ranks, while the workers who were involved and a few of their radical spokesmen toiled arduously in pursuit of goals that affected their work and livelihood.

In 1830, artisans and journeymen met in several towns to agitate for shorter hours or higher wages and to advocate the general need of workingmen to share in the fruits of prosperity. In Lynn, journeymen cordwainers formed the Mutual Benefit Society and said they no longer wanted to be at the mercy of "the Bosses" who fixed the price of labor according to their own necessities; even the female domestic workers of Lynn whose low wages depressed those of the men attempted an ad hoc organization.[6] In Boston, after a strike by carpenters and masons had failed, mechanics and their spokesmen met at Julien Hall during August to announce a number of reforms desired by "Working Men": a liberal system of education; laws to provide for the more extensive diffusion of knowledge; an end to monopolies of any type; a reduction of lawyers' fees and simpler laws; instruction of representatives; the entire abolition of imprisonment for debt; the separation of all religious issues from politics; and reform of the militia system. Other measures advocated by Workingmen included equal taxation of property and an effective lien law for laborers on buildings.[7] In the December city elections and in the state representatives' election in May 1831, the "Working Men" seem to have had a rather shadowy existence as a faction within the National Republican party. Many of their candidates were in fact Nationals, and some were wealthy merchants or middle-class businessmen.[8] There is good reason to suspect, indeed, that the first stirrings of artisans and journeymen in Boston had been quickly diverted by "ruffle shirt radicals," sympathetic but moderate politicians, and also by employers and master mechanics whose basic interests differed drastically from those of their employees. These men could sincerely join with artisans on Middling Interest goals. By 1830, for example, the sentiment against imprisonment for debt had spread into the middle classes and had enlisted politicians of all parties.[9] But employers and merchant capitalists would not negotiate with artisans and journeymen on matters of hours and wages.

Politicians quickly appropriated the label "Working Men's" for a variety of purposes. In March, 1831, a self-advertised "Working Men's Convention" assembled at Northampton, and while it linked itself on some issues with artisans, it appeared to be primarily a faction of National Republicans. It called for reform of credit facilities and a check on the influence of "monied institutions" over "property." Its specific recommendations appealed most to farmers, not to mechanics, in calling for property-tax reform and lower interest rates on mortgages. The convention also demanded, as farmers of the periphery had for generations, a reduction of exorbitant state expenditures and of salaries of state officials. Meanwhile, the delegates, representing a dozen or so western towns, nominated a prominent National Republican for governor. Their nominee, "Squire" Henry Shaw of Lanesborough, was not only a successful lawyer, farmer, and sheep raiser but also an early promoter of woolen mills in Pittsfield. A friend of Henry Clay, Shaw had gained notoriety as a congressman by voting for the Missouri Compromise in 1810–1821, but he remained a power in local affairs as well as the "social magnate" of his town. Antimasons attributed his nomination to Masonic intrigue, while some Nationals believed the putative Workingmen's nomination to be "Jacksonism disguised." Yet Shaw remained in good standing with the National Republicans and the following year was a presidential elector on the Clay ticket.[10] Obviously Shaw had little in common with artisans who wanted an effective lien law or with labor agitators who would soon begin a campaign for a ten-hour workday. Yet Shaw and his backers also complained, sincerely or not, about the growth of concentrated capital and political power and about a sense of displacement and decline.

**Substance: The Ten-Hour Movement**

Whatever the meaning of the Northampton nomination, most political factions claiming the Workingmen's name bore little relation to the movement that sprang from the specific needs of artisans and journeymen. In late 1831 the latter revived and headed for a struggle over bread-and-butter issues. On December 6 at Providence, Rhode Island, a mechanics and workingmen's convention adopted an organizational form designed to strike out for worker bargaining power. Capitalists, merchants, and manufacturers, said the convention, could not keep on having the "absolute and unconditional right of stipulating the prices of labor, and making such deductions from the bills of their workmen, as may suit their own interest . . . [and] extend the hours of labor, at pleasure." With delegates present from Lowell, Springfield, New Bedford, and other places in New England, the convention resolved to make the ten-hour day its standard and called for another convention at Boston.[11] Thus in February 1832 was founded at Boston the New England Association of Farmers, Mechanics, and Other Workingmen. It required that no workers could be members unless they pledged themselves to work no longer than a ten-hour day without being paid a one-tenth daily wage for each extra hour, and also never to accept any arbitrary deduction from a bill by any employer. The association levied a tax on members to provide a fund for those who might be "distressed" because of adherence to its rules, a clear sign of preparation for strikes if necessary.[12]

This phase of the movement was radical in two ways: it was organizing to strike for the ten-hour day, and it took up the cause of the growing numbers of factory workers as its own, particularly that of the children. The association estimated that at least two-fifths of all factory workers in New England were under sixteen years of age. To appreciate what the association was up against in pressing for a ten-hour day for adult males, one has to consider the lack of concern for hundreds of children who worked much longer days. In 1825 a legislative committee found that in the incorporated factories of the state over 900 children worked, on the average, twelve to thirteen hours a day, and while recognizing that this left little time for "daily instruction," the legislators found no cause for alarm. In 1832 the Workingmen's association said that two-fifths of the factory workers under sixteen worked thirteen and a half to fourteen hours a day "factory time" and that, with the exception of the large mills at Lowell and Chicopee, they were given little or no time off for education.[13] ("Factory time," as the association and its official paper the Pawtucket *New England Artisan* pointed out, generally ran from twenty to thirty minutes behind "solar time" because of a strange maladjustment universally afflicting factory clocks and the watches of overseers throughout the region.) Factory owners, their agents, politicians, and most of the press, either defended the handling of factory children or criticized the Workingmen as sowers of discord.[14] Thus, the Workingmen's demand for "equal education," within the context of factory exploitation and the acquiescence of politicians, was hardly a naive expression of optimism or faith in education as a provender of social mobility. Rather, it constituted in effect a rare challenge to society's most powerful men on behalf of some of society's most vulnerable members.

Apart from simply calling attention to the matter of children's welfare, the association's basic point about factory workers was that they were no freer to exert any influence on their hours or wages than were the skilled and semiskilled workers from whose ranks the Workingmen came. A mule spinner could theoretically go to factory after factory and ask for $1.50 per day, but he would be told the same thing in every factory in New England: " '*we* give only one Dollar'; and his negotiation is at an end."[15]

The Workingmen decided to challenge the tradition of "sun to sun" by instructing its members in Boston to insist that, from March 20, 1832, on, they would work no more than a ten-hour day, while doing their best to provide employers with a reasonable day's work. Ship carpenters and caulkers of Boston and Charlestown took the lead in the agitation, and were soon joined by house carpenters, masons, painters, slaters, and other artisans. These workers of Boston were well aware of similar activities by artisans in other cities; in 1825, moreover, journeymen house carpenters had struck in Boston, seeking a ten-hour day as a means of gaining more leisure time and greater income. The journeymen carpenters had claimed then that they found it difficult to raise a family on their wages and that master builders in New York, Philadelphia, and Baltimore had already accepted a more liberal policy. In Boston, work for carpenters had expanded quickly in the 1820s, especially after the Middling Interest's assault on the ban on wooden buildings over ten feet high. No doubt the journeymen carpenters and others had supported the master builders and entrepreneurs of the Middling Interest. In 1825, however, the journeymen's strike revealed the limits of the Middling Interest's economic democracy. Master carpenters joined with the "capitalists" who cajoled and threatened the journeymen to retrace their steps to "the good old way," and who soon broke the strike.[16]

In early 1832 the climate of opinion grew somewhat more favorable to a shorter workday. Several established newspapers endorsed the proposal while auxiliary branches of the Workingmen's association formed in Boston and its vicinity.[17] Workers do not seem to have planned strikes for March 20; rather, they began negotiations with master mechanics and merchants, and many apparently reached settlements without leaving work. In Providence and Fall River, however, according to the *New England Artisan,* workers had been dismissed, while the cotton mill owners allegedly were making known their opposition. By May the situation in Boston had deteriorated, and the ship carpenters and caulkers of Boston and Charlestown met with many house carpenters and voted to "use every exertion to persuade their employers to allow their hands three hours instead of two, for their meals, during the hot months of summer, and also allow them to quit work on Saturdays at 6 o'clock P.M., commencing June 1st."[18]

While house carpenters and other artisans joined in, the heart of the strike was in the shipyards, in an industry experiencing a boom and among workers who had already organized a mutual-benefit association. The legislature had incorporated the Columbian Charitable Society of Shipwrights and Caulkers of Boston and Charlestown, in January 1823. Its purpose was to promote inventions, to provide loans of money, and to relieve the distresses of unfortunate mechanics and their families.[19] By the early 1830s, however, no able shipyard workers suffered from lack of work, as wooden shipbuilding was experiencing the beginning of an extended period of prosperity that would carry into the 1850s. In many small yards along the coast, work was seasonal, the work crews were generally small, and labor relations were easy and familiar. In the big yards, however, crews which had numbered eight to twenty-five men now were much larger, work was more specialized, and the size of ships was growing steadily. Apart from carpenters, shipbuilding employed "joiners, blockmakers, caulkers, blacksmiths, painters, riggers, besides the common laborers and teamsters, ropemakers," and many other "artists and mechanics."[20] The work was long and hard, especially when vessels needed to be repaired quickly. The shipyard workers' complaints, however, focused on the arbitrary control of employers over hours and wages. In good weather they worked from sun to sun, but rain, snow, or ice left them idle for long stretches. After working several hours on a given day, they said, rain might force a work stoppage, and they would be paid nothing because the bosses maintained, "we do not pay for hours." The workers also protested about the "arrogance" of "overbearing" merchants and forthrightly stated, "We were all born free and equal, and we do not ask to have our grievances redressed as a favor, but we demand it as a right."[21]

The merchants who owned the ships and the shipyards, and who included some capitalists who owned the new factories as well, would not negotiate with the artisans and journeymen. They issued a statement saying they would neither employ journeymen or artisans pledged to any "combination," *nor contract with any master mechanics* who employed any such agitators. A shorter work day, they said, would cause delays in repairs and shipowners would take vessels elsewhere for repairs. This would lead to unemployment, idleness, and intemperance among workers.

The strikers replied that they could work long hours on any emergency repair so long as they were fairly paid, and they bluntly pointed out, amid the silence of pulpits so ardent in temperance reform, that their employers habitually dispensed grog to workers to sustain physical exertions through brutally long days. After an exchange of statements in the newspapers between strikers and merchants, the master mechanics, who had no wish to stand against the merchants, came out foursquare against the strikers. So, too, did many clergymen, newspapers, lawyers, and judges, and the strikers succumbed. In July the merchants issued another statement—dubbed by militant Workingmen the "UKASE"—conceding that, because of the extreme heat and the presence of cholera, workers might take two hours off at noon, provided that they strictly adhered to a sun-to-sun day. The epitaph of the strike, however, was written in September when a demoralized Workingmen's association met and repealed the provision that allowed it to fellowship only with those workers adhering to the ten-hour standard.[22]

The Workingmen had challenged not only the merchant-capitalist control of the labor market but also the paternalist system of social and economic relations which allowed the capitalists to take advantage of "premodern" work customs, while behaving as industrial capitalists in other ways. If this challenge to paternalism had won a victory, its impact might have been far-reaching. According to the Workingmen, the merchant capitalists' opposition to the ten-hour day in Boston derived in part from their concern about the effect of such a reform in Lowell and other factory towns: "if hours are reduced here," the merchants allegedly reasoned, "our 'help' in the mills will hear of it, and it will make them uneasy."[23]

The ten-hour men knew that it was ultimately the power of the merchant manufacturers that had beaten them, and in the frustration of defeat they turned to more radical leaders who now denounced the factory owners more directly than anyone had before. The ten-hour men lashed back, in short, by raising the issue of the overworking and mistreatment of children and women in the huge textile factories.

In February the association had discussed the issue of child factory labor in a temperate fashion, having even remarked favorably on practices at Lowell and Chicopee. But in June and July one of the movement's organizers gave voice to the Workingmen's frustration in a sweeping denunciation of the cotton mills. Contrary to the paid propagandists and politicians who described the big factories as "palaces of the poor," Seth Luther saw them as unrepublican, oppressive, and on their way to resembling English factories. Cotton mills were places where "cruelties are practiced, excessive labor required, education neglected, and vice, as a matter of course, on the increase." Luther himself had sprung from the artisan class of Rhode Island, the son of a Revolutionary War veteran, and, almost alone among labor leaders, he not only had worked as a carpenter but had toiled as a common laborer in factories.[24] The emergence of such a spokesman–whose basic speech, repeatedly given throughout New England, was a compendium of specific incidences of worker mistreatment in factories–signified the radical perception of the Workingmen's movement as it suffered a major defeat. That the expression of it was somewhat distorted by rage, not solely Luther's, is understandable.

The Workingmen were not alone in nursing hard feelings in the wake of the strike. While relations between shipyard workers and bosses returned to normal, at least one strike ringleader was "proscribed" and could get no work. And roughly a year later, after a misunderstanding about hours that had inconvenienced workers, a haughty merchant stood before fifty men in a shipyard and blustered, *"You . . . will be in the House of Correction* in less than *two months."* There were also reports of merchants sending recruiters "down East" and elsewhere to hire scabs to replace workers they thought intractable.[25]

The movement met with mixed results elsewhere. In the big factory towns it made little headway, while in towns like Fall River and New Bedford, which had many small mills and many owner-employers close to the actual work, labor conditions improved. In New Bedford, particularly, the Workingmen's association was strong and successful, and shipyard workers there were among the best-paid such workers in the state.[26]

In early September 1832, the association held a second convention at Boston; while tacitly admitting the failure of the ten-hour campaign, it did not retreat from its belief in its desirability, or from its general concern for political and social justice. It called again for Workingmen's organizations throughout New England, for lyceums and institutes, abolition of imprisonment for debt, for a halt to the loss of individual farms to banks and insurance companies, for government protection of women and children in factories, for reform of the militia, for elimination of banking monopolies, and for a lien law for all mechanics to insure them suitable compensation for work performed. The convention heard Seth Luther provide a "mass of information" about conditions in factories, and it approved a report calling for "Co-operative Trading Associations," to try to escape from arbitrary treatment by company stores and other merchants. The president of this convention was Dr. Charles Douglas of New London, a veteran organizer, whom the convention decided to make editor of the *Artisan,* which it now proposed to move from Providence to Boston. The prominence of Douglas showed that the Workingmen remained wary of political parties and political movements generally. Douglas had told the convention that the aristocracy controlled "all the political parties of the day" and that the Workingmen must ignore all unprofitable divisions, whether over Masonry or tariffs.[27]

Throughout most of 1832 the chief Workingmen's spokesmen had deprecated political action. While the *Artisan* had joined Jacksonians in criticizing the Bank of the United States, the Workingmen who were associated with the ten-hour movement, as opposed to those who simply exploited the term "Workingman," attached no particular importance to the "Bank War." The *Artisan* asserted, indeed, that all the political contests of the past thirty years had not benefited the workingman, and another speaker at the September convention said that in relation to Workingmen's goals, the differences between Jackson and Clay dwindled into "utter insignificance."[28]

Yet when the ten-hour movement was stalled, the Workingmen moved almost inevitably into politics. Even in late 1832 Douglas himself recognized that unsatisfactory results as a pressure group suggested the need for independent candidacies.[29] In 1833, then, the Workingmen's association turned to politics as well as to a trades-union effort. The latter, they observed, had helped mechanics in New York and other cities to improve their lot. Both approaches represented a change to a more indirect and long-range strategy to achieve the goals set forth but not achieved in 1831–1832.

The association's convention of October 1833 said little about the ten-hour day, but it retained its concern with the condition of factory laborers, banks, imprisonment for debt, and the other controversial issues it had already raised. While recommending that local trades unions be formed, it also urged that the producing classes seek redress of their grievances at the ballot box.[30] The move to parties may have been inspired at least partly by the Antimasons' example and perhaps by Jackson's "Bank War," which had made political economy and corporations part of common political discourse. But the Workingmen did not accept the local Democrats' professions of friendship. The Jacksonians were not at all opposed to state banks, said the *Artisan,* and too many professed Democrats were "slaves of mammon."[31]

For governor the Workingmen nominated Samuel Clesson Allen, a onetime minister (1794–1798) and a former state legislator and congressman (1817–1829), who since leaving Congress had been speaking out on the dangers that economic change posed to political liberty. Allen had come to believe, he said in a public letter designed to win the Workingmen's approval, that society was divided into "producers" and "accumulators," that governments consistently represented the latter, that he could think of no government in which the laboring class had predominated, and that it was time for a change. At first glance, Allen seemed an unlikely choice: a Connecticut Valley Federalist whose youthful Orthodox preaching had been too pungent for his church and had caused him to leave religion and take up law. But many citizens in the western counties, both dissenters and Orthodox, possessed an acute awareness of the new power of associated capital, of a growing "aristocracy," a declining yeomanry, and a growing proletariat. Antimasonry had burned through the valley and helped bring to consciousness considerable discontent with the emerging social order and the elites who managed it. In accepting the Workingmen's endorsement, Allen observed that increasing social inequality was causing the United States to resemble Europe. Our ancestors who threw off a foreign yoke, said Allen, did not expect "that the method of extracting wealth from other men's labor, which prevailed under European institutions, would gain admittance here and obtain the sanction of the government they had instituted." By "government" Allen meant the state government, and he called for a change of its *"economical policy"* by the election of wise and efficient legislators who would reverse the widening inequality between classes. Thus the Workingmen put their ticket into a field already crowded with three others: National Republican, Antimasonic, and Democratic-Republican.[32]

Allen ran a poor fourth, receiving only 5.5 percent of all votes (3,459), and carrying only ten towns, six in the Connecticut Valley. In Boston he received 519 votes, a greater number than anywhere else, but only 9 percent of the total there. Since the Workingmen had organized in several wards and electioneered like other parties, the result was disappointing. Allen did carry nearby Charlestown, with 34 percent of 276 votes, and perhaps for the shipyard workers there a vote for Allen gave a particular satisfaction.[33]

The impact of Allen's candidacy extended beyond his vote total. The Nationals and Democrats did not ignore the Workingmen, as they did the Antimasons, but responded directly in several ways to undercut their appeal. The Democrats hailed the Workingmen as fellow laborers in the cause and sought to eliminate their ticket by embracing them to death.[34] The National Republicans reacted with both outrage and cajolery, the former excessive, the latter restrained. The Nationals directed their venom at Allen; the Boston *Atlas* called him a "priest turned demagogue" and said that it was a libel on the community to talk of producers and accumulators, since no such distinction existed. According to the *Atlas,*

> Our household "help," who deposit their earnings in the Savings Banks, are "accumulators," and therefore not of it. The factory girls at Lowell, would despise to be classed with this party. . . . Even the Irish laborers, on our railroads and on our streets are among the accumulators. There is no class in our community that would not . . . feel insulted when they are addressed as mere *asses in a mill.*

Otherwise, however, the Nationals claimed the Workingmen as their own and pointed out that their own party was made up of workingmen.[35]

The most powerful argument employed against Workingmen was, always and everywhere, the doctrine of the "harmony of interests." The National Republicans, Whigs, employers, merchants and even some Democrats universally asserted that there was no need for a workers' party because the manufacturer's interest was the same as the mechanic's.[36] Yet powerful as this doctrine or myth might be, it was obvious that more and more persons were beginning to see society in terms of conflict and that the vocabulary of the Workingmen served many in defining conflict.

In early 1834 the Boston Trades Union formed and managed to bring a degree of solidarity to the working classes of the city that had not been evident in recent strikes or elections. Meanwhile, the efforts of Democrats to absorb the Workingmen intensified, and a radical wing of the Democrats became quite vocal, while the independent political thrust of the Workingmen's association became even weaker.[37]

During a series of meetings from January to March, the association's organizers put their energies into forming the Boston Trades Union, consisting of sixteen different branches of artisans and mechanics. Each branch elected two or more delegates to a citywide union which formulated policy for the whole (one of the carpenter's delegates was Seth Luther). It was described as a "mutual benefit society," and its members paid dues to a general fund used to relieve those who were hurt in accidents, who were sick, or who for "other causes" might be "out of employ." On July 4 two thousand union backers staged their own patriotic celebration, complete with horse-drawn floats, banners, and a company of riflemen. Amid the fanfare, it was clear that the ten-hour movement's original spirit and goals lived on. They came through clearly in the oration of Frederick Robinson, a radical Democrat from Marblehead who had just steered the abolition of imprisonment for debt through the state legislature.[38]

Robinson delivered his speech outdoors at Fort Hill after twenty-two churches had refused the Workingmen the use of their buildings. Robinson was one of the few politicians who spoke directly to the reality of the workingmen's situation. Though he spoke of the conflict between the few and the many, of the power of the aristocracy and the evils of banks, as many Democratic politicians were doing, Robinson did so in a way that made clear that the ten-hour day, and the right to negotiate hours and pay, was still on the union's and the mechanics' minds. The right of the producer to fix the price of his own labor was unquestionable, said Robinson, but the attempt of the workingmen to exercise it had met the determined opposition of the aristocracy. Furthermore, that right was a "social right," because it was useless if exercised only by individuals, being effective only "in concert." But the aristocracy had everyone frightened against combinations of workers, and a Boston judge had recently "charged the grand jury to indict the workingmen, who attempt by unions to fix the price, or regulate the hours of labor." This, said Robinson, was hypocrisy. The judge and all lawyers were themselves members of a secret union called the bar; they and many other "upper professions" engaged continually in price-fixing. But they and the aristocracy did not want laborers to do so. For this reason, Robinson's recommendations for reform began with the judiciary and the unintelligibility of the laws. He would make judges elective, and after that he would deal with monopolies, especially banks; repeal all laws relating to religion; repeal the militia laws; and pass legislation making it a crime to overwork women and children in factories and providing for the relief of orphans and fatherless children.[39]

Other Democratic politicians also cozied up to the Workingmen during 1834—some of them, like Robinson, not only shared their rhetoric but dealt concretely with the issues on which they had staked their livelihood.

Some, like Abel Cushing, editor of the Boston *Reformer* (formerly the *Artisan*), and George Bancroft, himself a capitalist on the verge of joining the Democrats, now tried to channel the workers' movement into the political fight of President Jackson and his party against the Bank of the United States and its Whig defenders.[40] Old-line Jacksonians had attempted to co-opt the Workingmen from the beginning, of course, and the new brokers between the Workingmen and the Democrats were important as much for their impact on a reinvigorated Jackson party as for their effect on the Workingmen.

A small group representing the last gasp of the Workingmen's political venture assembled at Northampton to renominate Allen for governor. Charles Douglas came down from Boston to address them but did so after many of the "country members" had gone home.[41] The Democrats gave the declining Workingmen another push down by selecting their candidate for lieutenant governor to accompany Marcus Morton at the head of their state ticket. The unsurprising result, given the lack of a campaign by the Workingmen, not to mention the absence of support by any newspapers or prominent leaders, was the slippage of Allen's vote by some 850, to a mere 3.4 percent of the total.

As a political party the Workingmen disappeared. Some of their goals and much of their rhetoric would be taken up by Democrats, and that will be discussed in the next chapter. But agitation among workers by no means ceased; in 1834 and 1835, factory operatives, both men and women, and artisans and mechanics in many trades remained restless. Labor troubles continued throughout the country, in fact, until the panic of 1837.[42] In Boston, the ten-hour movement came to life for one more major upheaval during the 1830s.

Fourth of July oratory and Democratic tirades against banks notwithstanding, many mechanics of Boston still saw themselves as underpaid, overworked, and treated with overbearing arrogance by the capitalists and their "servants," the master mechanics. In May of 1835, angry carpenters, masons, stonecutters, and others gathered at Julien Hall, where the first meetings of Workingmen had taken place five years before, and proclaimed that it was their "Natural Right to dispose of our own time in such quantities as we deem and believe to be the most conducive to our own happiness, and the welfare of all those engaged in Manual Labor." The contest was between "Money and Labor: Capital, which can only be made productive of labor, is endeavoring to crush labor the only source of wealth." Once again the mechanics used the fierce pen of Seth Luther as the spearpoint of their protest:

> We contend that no man or body of men, have a right to require of us that we should toil as we hitherto have done under the old system of labor.
>
> We go further. No man or body of men who require such excessive labor can be friends to the country or the Rights of Man. We also say, that we have rights, and we have duties to perform as American Citizens . . . which forbid us to dispose of more than Ten Hours for a day's work.[43]

Again the strike fever mounted during the long days of summer, and in July journeymen carpenters marched through the wealthy wards of the city singing the "Marseillaise." But once more the strike was lost as the master mechanics and the merchant capitalists combined to defeat it.[44]

Indeed, the full weight of "respectable" society was against the ten-hour men, and even many who were otherwise critical of the establishment did not support the ten-hour agitators. Robert Rantoul, for example, who was just emerging as a Jacksonian reformer at odds with the established Whig elite, and whom some historians have viewed as a "radical," in 1834 opposed the ten-hour movement. Rantoul held to the evasive dogma that hours and wages must be settled by agreement between buyer and seller, without interference, as if "buyer" and "seller" stood on equal footing. Workmen could sell time for ten, twelve, fifteen, or more or less hours, said Rantoul, but "if we offer to contract to labor ten hours a day and nobody wants less than twelve, we must not wonder that nobody accepts our offer. . . . Still less can we complain if those who are willing to buy ten hours, refuse to give us the price of twelve."[45]

In late autumn Boston's master mechanics did move to improve work conditions slightly "for themselves and for those who labor for and with them." In November and December a committee of master mechanics met with representatives of over fifty different trades in each of the city's twelve wards and agreed to change the dinner hour from 1 P.M. to 12 noon. It was otherwise too long, especially in summer, they said, to go without nourishment; the body got exhausted, and weary men were apt to take stimulants, which only worsened the situation.[46] The master mechanics said nothing about the length of the working day; they spoke only of the starting time for the "dinner hour."

It should not be surprising that the master mechanics cast their lot decidedly with the merchant capitalists. As much as any group, they shared the values of the merchants, particularly the ideology of the "harmony of interests." All "classes"—a word they used often as a synonym for occupations—shared an underlying common interest. But classes were inevitably unequal, said a conservative Whig speaker to the semi-elite Massachusetts Charitable Mechanics Association in 1839.

> What are the honors of life? If they mean anything, they mean that he who wears them is better than his neighbor. . . . Distinction is the prize of life, and courted only because in its great lottery there are so many blanks. . . . Success cannot be universal and some must be disappointed. . . .
>
> It is impossible not to perceive in that management which throws mankind into distinct classes, the same beauty of design which marks every operation of the Supreme intelligence.[47]

## Radical Populists

Historians have noticed the wealth and status of many Workingmen's candidates for office and wondered to what degree these men were genuine labor leaders.[48] Regarding the political movements of 1830–1831, for example, such skepticism is quite justified. In this phase political leaders exploited and co-opted the nascent labor movement. This surely accounts for the powerful aversion to politics displayed by the Workingmen's association. The genuine movement always paralleled politics, even after the association decided to turn to the ballot after the 1832 failure of the ten-hour campaign. It depended most on thoughtful reformers like Charles Douglas, misfits like Seth Luther, and anonymous leaders from the rank and file of artisans and mechanics who were the true heroes of the workingmen.

Because of the ambivalent relation of the movement to politics, perhaps not too much importance should be placed on the number or location of votes given to the Workingmen's gubernatorial ticket in 1833 and 1834. Samuel C. Allen was hardly a man best calculated to bring out a Workingmen's vote among the skeptical and distrustful (and non-Orthodox) mechanics and artisans in manufacturing villages in eastern Massachusetts. As it was, while the only towns which Allen carried were in the west, where he often cut into Antimasonic strength in formerly Federal towns, the pattern of support for the Workingmen almost defies generalization.

In 1833 Allen received a bare plurality in Charlestown (34 percent) and attracted votes in several other towns with maritime industry: Fairhaven (41 percent), Yarmouth (41 percent), and Nantucket (38 percent). But in most other towns with maritime workers no significant vote was given for Allen. Similarly, throughout the state a few towns with factories or with numbers of skilled workers gave Allen pluralities or a large minority vote: Webster in Worcester County (43 percent in 1833), Northampton (49 percent in 1833), Hadley (36 percent in 1833), and Amherst (35 percent in 1833) in Hampshire County, Pawtucket (23 percent in 1833) in Bristol County, and Adams (9 percent in 1833) in Berkshire County. But many towns with similar economic structures did not respond at all to the Workingmen. There is also no way of knowing for sure, without lists of individual voters and their preferences, whether the Workingmen's votes came from nonfarmers or from farmers in country towns within which manufacturing villages had grown up. In many farming towns, however, there was no doubt about the source of Workingmen's votes. Such places as Windsor (23 percent) in Berkshire County and Ashfield (45 percent), Gill (49 percent in 1833, 70 percent in 1834, a most unusual increase), Leverett (45 percent in 1834), and Leyden (17 percent in 1834) in Franklin County were entirely farming communities. The Workingmen's association had appealed frequently to farmers for support and had often denounced insurance companies, banks, and mortgages, and protested the dispossessing of farmers' land.[49] Yet if all hard-pressed farmers had voted for the Workingmen, their vote would have been much larger.

The foremost Workingmen's town in the state was the tiny hill town of Monroe in Franklin County, with a population of 282 in 1840. Monroe was unusual in another respect—it was peopled almost entirely by a clan of Universalists, led by relatives of the famous Universalist clergyman Hosea Ballou. Ties may have existed between the Workingmen's vote and Universalism in other towns, especially in Charlestown and Middlesex County, but several places with Universalist churches gave no votes at all to the Workingmen. Yet this was an age in which religious and social radicalism often went hand in hand. In 1841 Hosea's cousin, Adin Ballou, a leader of a radical faction within Universalism, founded Hopedale, a Christian socialist community that was among the first of the utopian experiments of the antebellum period. Furthermore, Universalist preachers seemed rather conspicuous among the editors and leaders of the Workingmen. Although not all adherents of Universalism were favorable to the Workingmen, there existed a definite link between Universalist social reformism and the more militant Workingmen's agitation.[50]

Still, generalization about the Workingmen's vote remains difficult: some artisans and mechanics, perhaps a few factory workers, some farmers, and some Universalists. Given the support for the Boston Trades Union celebration of 1834—some 2,000 active backers were claimed—it seems reasonable to infer that support for the Workingmen's concrete goals ran far deeper than the vote for Allen indicated. Furthermore, given the pervasiveness of factories and the impact of changing work relations, together with the concerns of the genuine movement, it seems off the mark to argue that the Workingmen's protest was not an outgrowth of industrial conditions or to ascribe to it an "agrarian" character.[51]

In Hampshire County the leaders of the Workingmen's party were middle-class professionals and respectable farmers who were men of some substance in their communities, including state representatives, selectmen, and church deacons. The ten-hour demand did not seem to engage them, but they did share a profound disquiet over the rise of great inequalities among social groups. The factories, and all that their presence implied, alarmed them, and not least because of the threat of mistreatment of child labor.[52] In Northampton, which gave Allen 49 percent of its vote in 1833, the local "radicals"–as they were called by Sylvester Judd, editor of the *Hampshire Gazette* (1822–1834) and a sympathetic observer–worried a good deal about the increase of "aristocracy," that is, of social distinctions and exclusiveness, about the influence of "monied corporations," and about the economic and social changes they saw taking place in society generally. Like Douglas and the association, they worried about the direction of society. But they are not easily classified as "agrarians" or as "displaced artisans," though the Workingmen's appeal in Hampshire county did extend to skilled mechanics experiencing loss of jobs, income, or status.[53] The Hampshire farmers, editors, clergymen, and minor officeholders who shared the radical diagnosis of the Workingmen's association spoke from the viewpoint of citizens possessing enough education and independence to see that unhealthy social trends did exist.

Sylvester Judd provides unusual insight into the discontent of 1833–1834, though he was neither an Antimason nor a full-fledged Workingman, but in fact an old Federalist and Orthodox Congregationalist. While Judd published what was ostensibly the National Republican newspaper of Northampton, he became increasingly alienated from the Nationals and associated with "the spirit of Antimasonry and Workyism." Judd abhorred office seeking and party management and disliked the way politicians manufactured "crises" in order to get people involved in elections. Judd looked very critically on "the moral influence of factories" and believed they led their workers into many vices, not the least of which was intemperance. Judd shared Samuel Allen's analysis of social conditions but disagreed with the latter's opinion that better laws could solve the problem, which he saw rather as springing from a deep-seated change in the virtuous character of the people. In the 1833 election Judd, while giving Allen a favorable notice in the *Gazette,* though not an endorsement, cast his vote (as recorded in his journal) for the Antimasonic candidate, John Quincy Adams. Commenting later that there was "too much aristocracy and too much masonry" in National Republican ranks, Judd thought the Antimasons "as honest as any party."[54] Meanwhile, his lack of partisanship, his friendly relations with "radicals," and his obdurate independence infuriated the Nationals-Whigs. The Whigs in turn disgusted Judd because of their arrogance and because they whipped up a frenzy against the Workingmen by portraying them as "infidels." By the end of 1834, acrimonious differences with the Whig elite caused him to sell the paper and to try to withdraw from politics. The "radicals," however, now coalescing with George Bancroft into the Jacksonian Democratic party, tried to enlist him as a candidate. Though he occasionally wrote articles for a new paper and often advised Bancroft on speeches, Judd refused to wear "the collar" of any party. He saw "more of the spirit of democracy in the Jackson party than in the other; but neither has much regard for the public good, as to other considerations. The Whigs are aristocratic in theory and practice to some extent; the Jackson men are democratic in theory, but often are contrary in practice. There is no honesty in the electioneering politics of this country, and a great want of honesty in the measures of legislative bodies."[55] In 1835 Judd became involved in founding an antislavery society in Northampton before retiring almost completely from politics to a life of research and study. Unlike many Workingmen, Judd was not a religious radical, but regularly attended the Orthodox meeting house, shared Orthodox moralism regarding personal conduct, and was a staunch temperance man who felt complimented in town meeting by the opposition of the "rummie" vote.[56] Sylvester Judd hardly fits any mold, but his sympathy for both Antimasonry and Workyism shows that these movements of protest had much in common and that the upswelling of discontent, though coming from various sources, expressed a similar populist distrust of the political system and alarm at growing social inequalities.

If emphasis on the "agrarian" character of the Workingmen is not warranted, it is especially misleading to view the absorption by the Democrats of remnants of the Workingmen as if it represented a culmination or higher stage of the movement.[57] The adoption of Workingmen's rhetoric and some of their goals by several Democratic leaders, whatever their intentions or degree of sincerity, was neither the apotheosis nor the salvation of the movement. It was its burial.

The distrust of parties on the part of Workingmen had not disappeared.

As men like George Bancroft and Allen putatively "led" the Workingmen to the Democrats, men like Douglas and Luther disappeared. Most significantly, the Democrats either ignored or opposed the ten-hour program. The genuine Workingmen who went into the Democracy had nowhere else to go. But they harbored few illusions. Their belief that aristocracies controlled both the Whigs and the Democrats remained strong. In 1835 a Deerfield radical, George Dickinson, wrote to Bancroft that the farmers and mechanics of the country did not trust "any political combination formed in the mercantile community and especially in Boston." They well knew that David Henshaw and the *Statesman* faction did not wish to enter the vineyard "as *fellow laborers* but as *masters* only." But even Marcus Morton and all other Democratic leaders were suspected of not being *"immutably* opposed to *all* exclusive privileges."

> Are not many or all interested in banks, insurance companies and mammoth factories? Are not the affinities greater between the aristocracy of the democracy and the aristocracy of the Whigs, than between the aristocracy of the democracy and the great body of the people of that party? . . .
>
> The observation of every day tends . . . to convince me that the great reformation which the workingmen propose can only be effected by the Farmers and that portion of the class of mechanics who reside among them and in many cases are in part Farmers themselves. Among all classes there may be found some patriotic spirits who are with us.[58]

Thus Dickinson implied that only those workingmen who possessed *economic independence*—for example, mechanics who were "in part farmers themselves"—could support Workingmen's goals. In doing so, Dickinson laid bare the power of *influence* and the inhibiting effects of economic dependence and deference on the ten-hour drive and a labor movement generally.

The Workingmen's emphasis on education and their distrust of parties and politicians need to be seen in the same context, that is, in relation to economic dependence/independence, influence, and deference. The Workingmen were concerned not just with helping the deprived children of the factories, or their own progeny, but also with the need to develop "talent" and "merit" from *among* the ranks of the laboring classes.[59] On the face of it, this has often seemed to later observers to be merely an expression of faith in education and of the ultimate ability of American society to reward self-improvement. In fact, it sprang from a recognition that so long as laboring men kept depending on their social betters for political leadership, so long would they remain divided and at the mercy of politics-as-usual. The apparently moderate and conservative exhortations to workingmen to cultivate learning and to produce their own leaders were thus challenges to them to overcome the continuing and inhibiting influence of deference in political life.

George Bancroft, though at best a fellow traveler when compared with the likes of Luther or Douglas, understood this problem as well as they did, and he also perceived (as well he might) how "the popular influence" continually lost its indigenous and natural leaders to the upper classes: "The capital of the country controls many of the organs of public opinion; and the men of ability and enterprise, as they spring from the ranks of the people, are absorbed into the ranks of the open aristocracy."[60] Some historians and sociologists have praised this process as providing stability; the change minded have equated "stability" with the "status quo" and have lamented the siphoning off of populist leaders. To the Workingmen it meant the difference between representation and no voice, between fidelity to their needs and betrayal.[61]

In this and other ways the Workingmen tried to break the bonds of a hierarchical, status-conscious, and deferential society—bonds in which, they knew, they had helped to wrap themselves. There were other kinds of deference they also sought to escape, as exemplified by the practice of merchants who habitually paid mechanics less than the mechanics asked for the work they performed: "the bill is presented, not a word is spoken, the merchant takes his pen, and in silence makes such deductions as he likes, and orders his clerk to pay it. . . ."[62]

In the same way Workingmen recognized both the direct and indirect political power of creditors. In the typical country town or manufacturing village, said the *Artisan,* most of the people were in debt to local merchants or lawyers, who usually lived in elegant and imposing houses. Lawyers of both parties "always held in their hands, *quantum sufficit* of bills, notes, writs, and executions, in favor of their patrons against their debtors, to command obediance" at town meetings, caucuses, and elections.[63]

From everyday things to large social occasions, the Workingmen envisioned a fairer order of things. The splendid Fourth of July parade of 1834 was a great source of pride because "it was got up, *completed,* and *enjoyed* by the *Mechanics alone.* We say this not in the spirit of exclusion—but our mechanics, and our most useful men, have been so long shut out from public festivals, or admitted only to be set down at the tail of the feast. . . ." Workingmen were thus debased because of the irrational denigration of manual labor, because of "injustice in the distribution of property," and because of invidious class distinctions resulting therefrom.[64]

The Workingmen's movement was thus radical and populist in several ways. Its call for equal education was taken up quickly by politicians, and in retrospect it seems almost conservative. But the Workingmen were not muddleheaded reformers. They knew their own limitations, their lack of real support in the middle and upper classes, and their need for leadership.[65] Their initial focus on education arose from a specific concern for the plight of factory children, a class ignored by the established political leadership. Their diagnosis of educational and social inequality was more generally linked with their perception of their need for talented, able leaders who would at once have the social status (because of merit) to gain election to office and who would remain true to their interests. They quickly learned that men of that sort were difficult to find. The Workingmen, as distinguished from their fellow travelers on popular issues, were above all concerned to win some bargaining strength in the marketplace, and they wholly distrusted politicians and party politics. They also offered a dissident view of American society which challenged prevailing dogmas regarding the harmony of interests, equality of opportunity, and even political equality.

If the Workingmen's significance depended solely on the number of votes they received, they would not deserve the amount of attention given to them here. They were less significant than the Antimasons, for example, in the development of the major party coalitions, though the Workingmen, as will be seen shortly, had an impact on the rhetoric and appeals of the major parties comparable to that of the Antimasons. But the Workingmen warrant close study because, apart from the attractiveness of their republican ideals, their very existence revealed much about changing socioeconomic conditions and about the impact of material change on key elements of political culture.

# XI. The Factory and the Revival: The Emergence of Mass Parties, 1829–1844

> We all know that party management, the intrigues of party leaders render the right of suffrage in, perhaps, a majority of cases where it is worth having, a nullity. A few individuals of one party get together and make a nomination, a few individuals of another party make another nomination, and my boasted right of suffrage is dwindled down to a choice between these two nominations.
>
> —Orestes A. Brownson, July 4, 1834

In the second half of the 1830s, Massachusetts politics dramatically polarized into two mass parties, whose almost ritualized electoral warfare replaced the creative chaos of the early 1830s. The minor parties had dissolved, and the political factions tied to traditional networks grew into organizations harnessing the discipline of factories and the fervor of revivals. Both Whigs and Democrats practiced the politics of opposition as a way of creating political crusades and tapping hopes and fears of public salvation.

The Whigs replaced the National Republicans as the majority party and dominated the state much as the Federalists had before them. The opposition coalesced into the Democratic party which, after absorbing some Antimasons and a corporal's guard of Workingmen, reclaimed much of the old Jeffersonian coalition. But if the Whig-Democratic division recreated Federal-Republican alignments to a degree, these differed in vital ways from earlier parties. By the late 1830s the new parties possessed far more explicit organizations and surpassed the earlier parties in complexity, durability, and visibility. While ideology and belief still motivated leaders and voters, the Whig and Democratic parties came to exist not just to influence policy but also to reward partisans with office. The distribution of patronage at all levels of government, accordingly, became rather thoroughly tuned to partisan politics. Functioning in a milieu which was far less overtly antipartisan and in which communication facilities were many times multiplied, the mass parties, like the factories, had come to stay.

As institutions with a life of their own, the Whig and Democratic parties developed convention systems for making nominations and enunciating policy that outwardly were quite unlike Federal and Republican "conventions." The informality of earlier usages gave way to a highly regular series of conventions, which began in wards, towns, and counties and moved up through higher levels. For all its democratic appearance, however, inner circles of powerful men still exercised disproportionate power much as they had earlier—and much as generals and their lieutenants in an army, or the owners and managers of factories.

The convention system itself developed slowly, and both parties continued to use the mixed caucus as well as the "pure" convention even into the 1840s. Though blending old and new and though still oligarchical, the Whig-Democratic convention system ultimately was the expression of a different kind of politics.

In the realm of electoral mobilization differences of degree became a difference of kind. By 1839 it is proper to speak of "campaigning" as against the more limited "exertions" and "electioneering" of years past. Campaigns resulted from improved communication, a more professional class of politicians, and an audience receptivity without which the leaders' passionate politicking could not have existed. If the electoral parties were armies, then, they were the legions of the first crusades or of the early, hopeful French Revolution—armies, in short, energized by conviction, like the multitudes that flocked in and out of revivals. In form and spirit the new mass party organizations had something in common with both the factory and the revival.

### Jacksonian and National Republicans

> The Opposition party, like the party of the Administration, was exceedingly tardy about taking on any name other than Republican. The necessity of distinguishing between two Republican parties, caused the terms "Jackson men" and "Adams men," or "Adams-Clay men," to be commonly used. Jackson's followers were very seldom spoken of as Democrats. To distinguish the followers of Jackson from the National Republicans they were sometimes called Democratic Republicans. Both parties were loath to relinquish the good old name of Jefferson's party and the term *Republican* remained one to conjure with. The use of the simple term *Democratic* for Jackson's party, or *Democrats* for his followers, was neither common nor popular until after the birth of the Whig party in 1834. Jackson habitually called himself a Republican and spoke of his supporters as Republicans.[1]

Control of communications facilities and government patronage have been essential to sustaining political power probably since the beginning of organized society. In eighteenth-century colonial politics, newspapers and government offices certainly constituted key resources of political influence, and they became even more important in the early national period.

The "communications revolution" of the early nineteenth century together with population growth increased greatly the patronage available to the national and state governments. At the time, transportation and communications improvements created a physical environment that made possible mass participation in highly organized political parties. The political culture of 1840 depended at bottom on a flow of information that had simply not existed in 1800. As mail, newspapers, campaign documents, and people could move about more quickly and cheaply, information networks could be sustained which were vital to permanent party organizations. In Massachusetts it was appropriately symbolic that several short lines of railroads began operation in 1834–1835, just when the Whig and Democratic parties emerged as mass organizations.

Though the 1828 presidential election has often been hailed as crucial to party formation, it was significant less as an embryonic party contest and more because of the shift in patronage distribution that Jackson's victory caused.[2] The election did sort out two "Republican" factions, both of which thought of themselves as the true Republicans. The Adams Republicans enjoyed a commanding position in the state, cemented by Governor Levi Lincoln's ability to hold together old Republicans and old Federalists. The Jacksonian Republicans at this point were a small and mixed group of outsiders forming neither a party nor a movement. Adams won the state handily in a lopsided election that aroused little interest,[3] but Jackson's national victory led the following year to his bestowing the prize federal offices in the state on the *Statesman* faction of Republicans who had earlier supported William Crawford.

David Henshaw, principal owner of the *Statesman* and leader of that faction, became collector of the port of Boston, a position rich in patronage and influence. Nathaniel Greene, editor of the *Statesman,* became postmaster of Boston, and other Henshaw lieutenants received lesser offices. Henshaw was a classic political entrepreneur and outsider who was master of the politics of resentment. Rejected by the elite and scorning high society, he was a sort of rogue merchant prince, with an ego equal to that of the Federal grandees. He and his political-business associates were men of new money, small businessmen, lawyers without good family connections, or Republicans-by-trade.[4] The *Statesman* officeholders played a key role in the transition to the new politics. Primarily interested in patronage, they created a tight little organization through which they controlled the Jacksonian Republican party and carried it about as far as it could go in purely practical partisanship.

In 1828 Jackson's Massachusetts supporters included another small group that was centered in Boston and that published a newspaper, the *Jackson Republican,* renamed the *Bulletin.* Led by Theodore Lyman, Jr., a wealthy son of an East India merchant, the *Bulletin* faction consisted of old Federalists who hated Adams, free-trade merchants, and silk-stocking Jeffersonians as well as the now ubiquitous editors and office seekers. This high-minded coterie met frequently at Lyman's mansion to discuss politics, but they were no match for Henshaw and his hungry men.[5] The two groups barely cooperated with one another in 1828, and after the election Henshaw and Greene moved quickly to nail down the chief patronage jobs by "re-organizing" the Jacksonian Republican party and establishing a "central committee" whose main business was the supervision of all appointments in the state. Lyman's group drifted off, leaving the collector and his men in undisputed command, though Henshaw and his lieutenants were essentially officers with only a palace guard of an army.[6]

The Jacksonians can hardly be credited with having invented "the spoils system," which continued an impulse perhaps traceable to a time not far removed from the Garden of Eden. But under Presidents Monroe and Adams the use of patronage declined as a partisan weapon. Jackson, however, made one of his cronies postmaster general and raised that office to cabinet status, so that its occupant became the patronage chief in close touch with the president. Removals of postmasters during Jackson's first term were not as numerous as his opponents charged, but they did fall heavily in the Mid-Atlantic and New England states where Jackson had been weak politically. Moreover, the Jacksonians openly avowed a spoilsmen's ethic and justified rotation in office on the grounds of both common sense and democratic principles.[7]

In Massachusetts, removals in the state's post offices grew gradually, so that by 1832 some 120 offices had changed hands. In contrast, from 1824 to 1828 some 76 post offices received new postmasters. More telling, however, was what happened in the larger towns. In the state's ten most populous towns in 1832, seven of ten post offices changed hands from 1828 to 1832, whereas only one change had occurred in those places under Adams.[8] After President Jackson's re-election in 1832, "the Collector" in Boston notified Jacksonian leaders in central Massachusetts, "You can obtain any [post office] removal you wish and as many as you wish."[9]

Post offices were vital because besides giving jobs, salaries, and printing contracts to party men and newspapers, postmasters also controlled the flow of information. An 1825 law allowed them the postage-free exchange of newspapers, a practice which became a staple of political communication. It was common for a key partisan to be both postmaster and editor or publisher of a newspaper.[10]

In the customshouse itself Henshaw ruthlessly applied his typically Jacksonian view of office: "Is the man whom you recommend a democrat? Does he vote for Morton? That is the test." Enjoying a salary of $4,400 and perquisites of several hundred dollars more, Henshaw controlled fifty-three offices with salaries amounting to $75,000, along with fifteen or so other officers connected to the customs. Anticipating later party bosses, he even tried to get his employees to contribute a "tax" out of their own pockets to "the party."[11]

Otherwise, the Henshaw faction used very traditional methods to acquire influence: a state central committee, a hierarchical organization, subservient county chairmen, a political club (the Washington Society), and, above all, patronage. They did not really innovate but carried old-style partisan politics further than anyone else had before. Indeed, Henshaw's "generalship" of the Jacksonian Republicans bears some resemblance to the "caudillo" style of politics of Andrew Jackson in the White House.[12]

### Party Organization: Early Stages

During the early 1830s the organizations of the later parties slowly evolved, while the electorate was in disarray. Not until 1834–1835, at the earliest, did electoral coalitions line up behind the Whig majority and one principal opponent. Even then, political leaders and groups were still sorting themselves out and party organization was not yet mature. But the roots of the later convention system may be traced to the early 1830s, and especially to the impact of the Antimasons.

Beginning in New York State in early 1829, Antimasons began to use conventions whose delegates were elected by some standard principle of representation, and by September 1831 they held the first national nominating convention at Baltimore. Two months later the National Republicans held a similar convention, at which delegates from each state were equal in number to the state's electoral votes. In 1832 the Democrats also held a national convention, for which seven states used conventions to select delegates.[13] In Massachusetts, similarly, Antimasons made conventions fashionable and held a state nominating convention in May 1831.

The Jacksonian Republicans, who up to that point had held legislative caucuses or mixed caucuses, soon paid the Antimasons the compliment of imitation. Their "Republican State Convention," which met in Worcester in September, was in fact a nominating convention.[14]

At this point no party was well organized. Factionalism in local nominations, split-ticket voting, and ad hoc electioneering prevailed, especially under the very inclusive National Republican umbrella. Organization was so haphazard that a National leader in Northampton complained that a bundle of National Republican newspapers had been sent to a local Jackson man who "probably would not take the deepest interest" in their distribution.[15]

In 1832 the Antimasons again held a state nominating convention to choose candidates for state office, but the Democratic-Republicans reverted to a mixed caucus. 1833 was the year of the convention: Antimasons, Nationals, and Jacksonians all nominated their state tickets in conventions.[16] The Nationals' convention also appointed a state central committee and chairmen of county committees with responsibility to appoint town committees. Meanwhile, the Democratic caucus's call for a state convention reflected the discontent of non-Boston Jacksonians with the domination of Henshaw and his placemen over the Democratic party.[17]

Yet while the convention was now well known in Massachusetts, it by no means became the uniform mode of operation. Nor were parties very different from early republican parties, or much more organized. Electoral coalitions, too, were still in flux. As mass alignments stabilized in the next three years and as voter participation increased, party organization would develop with the forming of two great coalitions.

## The Politics of Opposition: Electoral Coalitions, 1834–1836

In the mid-1830s the Whig and Democratic electoral coalitions gradually came together. These were new parties, yet the alignments in some important ways revived Federal-Republican lines, and at least partly renewed a Center-Periphery division. The Whigs and Democrats also conducted oppositional politics in the earlier mode of Federalists and Republicans.

The Whigs, like the Federalists before them, called on citizens to resist the arbitrary power of the national government. Once again a president hostile to New England's interests (they said) was running amok and corrupting the Republic. Once again the appeal rang forth to recall the principles of the Revolution and to save the Constitution. This time, however, the Whigs avoided any taint of sectionalism: advocacy of an "American

System," a strong Unionist disposition, and their very name gave them a patriotic identity.[18] The Jacksonian Republicans and Democrats also formed their character as an opposition party and, like the Jeffersonian Republicans, directed their fire against an oppressive aristocracy *within* Massachusetts. The Jacksonians became a magnet for local dissidents and for many protesters against the ruling elite of merchant manufacturers, lawyers, and Unitarians. As the Nationals and Whigs consistently emphasized national affairs, the Jacksonians concentrated on state issues. Social movements and local issues had begun to reäctivate voters—by the mid-1830s national events further stimulated citizens and political men to engage in still more intense oppositional politics.

In the state elections of 1831 and 1832, the Nationals had stressed the critical state of the national government under Jackson's mismanagement to the exclusion of any local issues at all. Even in 1833, when they briefly addressed the Masonic question, the president's abuse of executive power claimed the lion's share of their attention. In the winter of 1833–1834, however, national policy engaged not only political leaders but also rank-and-file voters as it had not since the 1812 war. Another "war" now unfolded on the national scene, once again bringing economic injury to Massachusetts. This time it was a war between President Andrew Jackson and Nicholas Biddle, president of the Bank of the United States (B.U.S.), whose headquarters were at Philadelphia.[19]

The "Bank War" probably originated in a move by New Hampshire's Jacksonian politician-entrepreneurs, led by Isaac Hill, to take control of the B.U.S. branch at Portsmouth. Its president was Jeremiah Mason, former Federalist and ally of Daniel Webster. Hill and his associates wanted to apply the principle of rotation and have the Bank run by someone more favorable to their interests. The controversy drew in both Biddle and Jackson, and while Hill failed to get Mason removed, he did wring some concessions from Biddle. Soon after, in his December 1829 message to Congress, Jackson delivered an unexpected criticism against the B.U.S.[20]

Later the same month, the Boston *Statesman* opened fire on the Bank, and argued that Massachusetts could be benefited by having the public deposits transferred to state banks. In 1830 Henshaw published a pamphlet, *Remarks on the Bank of the United States,* taking issue with a congressional committee report defending the Bank. A banker himself, Henshaw was hardly against banks or even against a central bank. That same year he joined with other businessmen of various political hues in petitioning Congress to charter in Boston a bank capitalized at $50 million, constituted otherwise than the B.U.S., having branches in various cities and paying a yearly tax to the states in which it resided. Boston's Jacksonian politicos wanted to bring down the B.U.S. for reasons similar to those of their New Hampshire friends.[21]

In 1832, National Republican leaders in Congress decided to make the B.U.S. an issue and pushed through a bill rechartering the Bank. Jackson took up the challenge and vetoed the bill in July. Though winning reelection by a smaller percentage than he enjoyed in 1828, the president interpreted his victory as a mandate to destroy the Bank. In September 1833, after having dismissed two secretaries of the Treasury who would not obey his orders and after having overruled cautious advisers, Jackson began removing the government deposits from the Bank and putting them in selected state banks which were known as "pets," chosen on the basis of their directors' Jacksonian politics, friendships, or kin connections. Among the first seven "pets" were two in Boston, including Henshaw's Commonwealth Bank.[22]

During the winter of 1833–1834, Jackson's "removal" policy and Biddle's reaction, a contraction of credit, together with other causes visited a brief financial panic on Massachusetts. The Nationals seized on this to launch a campaign protesting Jackson's removal of the deposits and calling for the recharter of the B.U.S. or, at least, a restoration of financial stability.

A great fear of an economic standstill swept through Massachusetts as some merchants had no money or credit, workers no work, and farmers no markets. Bankers held meetings and sent Congress petitions telling of rampant "distress"; larger popular meetings later did the same. Webster thundered against Jackson in the Senate, the Massachusetts legislature passed ringing resolutions, hundreds attended meetings, and thousands signed petitions. In Boston a "nonpartisan" meeting declared that the scarcity and high price of money fell most severely on the middling classes, while retired capitalists actually benefited. Similar meetings took place in towns and villages across the state. Many petitions denied any great love for the B.U.S. but simply wanted some institution to provide credit and sound currency. Though the meetings all called themselves nonpartisan, the organizers, aside from a few Antimasons, tended to be prominent National Republicans and soon to be leaders of the Whig party.[23]

The petitions from many towns represented a triumph of mobilization and often forecast the strength of the Whigs in the fall election. The memorials had passed from door to door, to shops, wharfs, farms, and factories. In the end, several mammoth petitions went to Congress from Boston, Worcester County, and elsewhere. The atmosphere must often have resembled that of days of protest against the embargo. Furthermore, the number of signatures in a town frequently approximated the number of Whig voters who cast ballots in the November 1834 election.[24] Thus the "Bank War" agitation had a potent activating effect and stimulated a high turnout in November both among Jackson's opponents and his supporters.

The 1834 turnout was indeed spectacular, even though it came in a nonpresidential year. In 1836 the aggregate vote exceeded that of 1834 by less than a thousand. (See Appendix II.A, Tables 5, 6.) Both national and state issues more than organization produced this result. The Whigs gathered in 44,800 votes, almost 11,000 more than the Nationals had ever polled, while Morton with 19,255 received his largest total ever.

In the next two years both parties solidified their electoral coalitions. During 1834 the Nationals had held various celebrations to rechristen themselves "Whigs," and the aura of a new name and a fresh start probably helped to attract Antimasons and other dissidents. Many Antimasons joined them in opposing Jackson's removal of the deposits and signed the various petitions. In Lynn, for example, over 700 voters signed a pro-Bank memorial, and in November the votes stood as follows: Whigs 335, Democracts 337, Antimasons 473, and Workingmen 1. The Whig-Antimasonic merger obviously remained incomplete, and the Democrats, of course, now were courting the Antimasons. But the Whigs hoped to bring both the Antimasons and, where they still existed, the Workingmen into their fold.

The Whigs continued, however, the Nationals' rather ambivalent response to the worker's movement. Whig propagandists frequently denounced the Workingmen as Jacksonian demogogues, as office seekers, as impractical theorists like Bancroft, or as infidel radicals like Fanny Wright and Abner Kneeland.[25] The Whigs also appealed to workingmen by claiming to represent best their interests. To the farmers, the Whigs described the cosmopolitan lawyer John Davis as a "Furrow Turner" and "Huge Paws" just like them, and the wealthy printer-bookseller Samuel T. Armstrong they called "a Mechanic and Workingman."[26] Yet they also showed a remarkable willingness to discuss the basics of political economy and to engage issues raised by the Workingmen. Though they usually supported the status quo or mild reform, their forays into political economy showed that the Workingmen had at least raised questions about the fairness of the economic system. Ultimately, of course, the function of such an apparently accommodationist response was profoundly conservative, as it has continued to be throughout American history.

In 1835 the Whigs reached out boldly to appeal to the minor parties by nominating the scholar-politician Edward Everett for governor. Everett had become popular among Workingmen by embracing some of their goals and calling himself a "workingman," though he was firmly opposed to the ten-hour movement and took no position on an artisan's lien law.[27] More important, Everett had also gained a reputation of being critical of Masonry and solicitous of Antimasons, though he was never an Antimason. Daniel Webster, tireless in trying to promote Antimasonic-Whig concord, led a behind-the-scenes movement for Everett, arguing that the Whigs' national goals depended on healing the breach with the Antimasons.[28] Early in 1835 a Whig caucus nominated Everett and arranged to send incumbent governor John Davis to the Senate. The Masonic Whigs and their allies exploded in protest, though largely in private or within party circles. They criticized "the plot" arranged by a few leaders and the "party management" by which it was done, and called for a convention to make new nominations. But the Masons could no longer veto nominations, though they continued to hate Everett and harassed him during his years as governor.[29] Actually, the Everett nomination was a year too late to have maximal effect. Antimasons had urged the Whigs to nominate him the year before, and most of the dissidents had seemed ready to support Everett then.[30] Still, Everett's candidacy did bring over many Antimasonic holdouts and further defined the coalitional patterns of the emerging parties.

That many Antimasonic voters supported Everett may be inferred from a comparison of the Whig and Democratic votes for governor and for lieutenant governor. In 1835 the Whigs nominated George Hull, a Mason, to the second spot on their ticket. The remaining Antimasons, mostly politicians by now, held a convention and endorsed Everett but gave their backing to the Democratic candidate for lieutenant governor, William Foster.[31] Everett beat Morton by 37,555 to 25,227, but Hull won over Foster by only 32,953 to 30,683. Everett led Hull by 4,602 votes, while 1,901 votes for governor went to the former National Republican and Whig lieutenant governor Samuel Armstrong and were probably also from Antimasons. Foster received 6,456 votes more than Morton, who was much better known. Moreover, Foster's vote was not evenly distributed throughout the state; he ran furthest ahead of Morton in Suffolk, his home county, and in six counties that had been Antimasonic strongholds.[32]

The Whig electoral base of 1836–1840 resembled the Federalist base, far more than did that of the Adams Republicans or the Nationals. The town-level interyear correlations of the National Republican and Whig vote suggest this (Appendix II.A, Table 7), while the interyear correlation of the 1812 Federal presidential vote with the 1840 Whig vote was .539.[33] In similar fashion the Jacksonian Republicans reassembled some of the old Republican coalition.[34] By the late 1830s the Democratic vote was correlated as positively with early Republican votes as the Whig vote was with the Federal vote (1840 Democratic with 1812 Republican: .551). Of course, it is risky to generalize from correlations of elections almost thirty years apart, and the point is only that some continuity was present, but that it was important.

Like the Jeffersonian Republicans, the Jacksonians built their coalition by mobilizing discontent against the state government and its ruling "aristocracy."[35] If the Nationals wished to give direction and definite goals to the federal government, the Jacksonian Republicans seemed to complain, in the ancient manner of the Periphery, about the very existence of government. In actuality, most of their calls for reform fit in with the Jacksonian emphasis on states rights and local autonomy. This put them in harmony with Jackson supporters in other sections and also allowed them to exploit a diverse array of local grievances.[36]

The Jacksonian Republican appeal owed much to old Republican opposition to the Federal establishment. As its rhetoric was that of outsiders and challenging groups, it was not surprising that in the mid-1830s the Democratic-Republicans absorbed the rhetoric of the Workingmen, without necessarily adopting their major goals.

"Politics is the art of unification," and during 1834 the "Bank War" helped the Democrats unify the opponents of the Whigs. The Bank provided, as "King Andrew" did on the other side, a great and visible enemy against which to rally. Even Charles Douglas, formerly of the *Artisan,* was one of the speakers at a March 14 meeting at Faneuil Hall which supported Jackson and opposed recharter. Douglas was still not a party man, but other Workingmen and especially their fellow travelers joined the anti-Whig coalition. The chairman of the meeting was the elderly capitalist and independent state legislator William Foster, the Democratic nominee for lieutenant governor the next year.[37]

While many of the true labor organizers of the Workingmen's movement went on to other things, the public figures most prominently associated with political Workyism became Democrats. These men made careers out of translating the Workingmen's ideology into a Jacksonian Republican framework. In the winter of 1834–1835 the foremost spokesman of such a synthesis, George Bancroft, finally completed his migration to the Democrats. By 1835–1836 Samuel C. Allen and Theodore Sedgwick, another former Federalist and exponent of Workingmen's ideas, had also enlisted in the Morton–Van Buren camp. These mavericks rejected Whig economic doctrine and especially the paternalism of the powerful manufacturer-capitalists they saw dominating the Whig party.[38]

The fusion of some Workingmen with the Democrats should not be overemphasized. Even if all 3,500 or so who voted for Allen in 1833 had gone over to the Jacksonians—and it is highly unlikely that they did—they would have been outnumbered by former Antimasons, because while most Antimasons did end up as Whigs, a large minority of them became Democratic supporters. In 1835 and 1836 some Democratic leaders worked as hard as the Whigs in courting the Antimasons, and they continued to be sensitive to the former Antimasonic vote even after 1836.[39] Yet all the former Workingmen and former Antimasons together were perhaps less important to the Democrats than were new voters and citizens who had not voted for years and who became mobilized by the national crisis of the mid-1830s.

The "Bank War" provided a "great national question" which tended "to draw people out—to compel them to take sides" and to create two parties "as distinct as they were in 1804."[40] But the fight against the Bank did not by itself lift the Jacksonian party's oppositional politics to the intensity of a crusade. The infusion of Workingmen's rhetoric gave the Democrats a much more powerful set of slogans than did warmed-over Republicanism and "rotation in office." Indeed, Democratic-Republicanism of 1835 leveled at society a criticism virtually as searching as that of the Workingmen had been a short time before. In all this the influence of that new Democrat George Bancroft was quite evident.

In 1835 the Democratic-Republican indictment of the establishment went far beyond simply serving as a magnet for localist complaints or the centrifugal particularism of the Periphery. Rather, the controlling premise of all they diagnosed was Bancroft's axiom that dangerous inequalities of wealth and social condition had arisen and threatened the ability of politics to function by republican principles. Similarly, social and educational institutions were being undermined and made incapable of giving equal opportunity to all classes of citizens. The question now separating the two political parties was whether the people were capable of self-government or whether they were to be "subjected to the controlling influence of self appointed guardians." To be capable the people "should be in an equality in their social and political condition." All combinations of wealth or influence which by special laws amassed power for the few subverted the just equality of the people and necessarily caused government and laws to be unequal. The Democracy would, therefore, uniformly check and discourage all charters of incorporation. Money or stock corporations were aristocratic instruments that the rich used to steal the rights of the people and "to change our equal social condition," and thus imperceptibly to change government. Though Bancroft's positing of a clash between the party of wealth and that of the people has attracted more attention from historians, his view of society, as it informed Democratic-party statements in 1835, was far more subtle and unusual. Not often has a major party in the United States asserted, if only for a brief time, "that pure democracy inculcates equal rights–equal laws–equal means of education–and *equal means* of wealth also, as incidental to the other blessings."[41]

The specific issues discussed by the Democrats included many they had agitated for years: excessive state spending, legislative malapportionment, free bridges, and others. They ignored state banks and attacked the B.U.S., while their support for specific Workingmen's goals was much weaker than their rhetoric. They promised to improve public spending for the middling and lower classes but only hinted at a mechanic's lien law: "the independent mechanic will be protected against unequal competition." More vaguely still, they asserted that all men, including laborers, had a "universal right to leisure."[42] Several more years would pass before Massachusetts Democrats would endorse a ten-hour day.

Still, this was the high-water mark of Democratic social criticism. Of course, there existed great variety in the local and factional emphasis that the foregoing propositions received. If a Henshaw man had written the 1835 address, it would have been very different. In 1836 the Democrats reaffirmed their commitment to the principles and proposals of 1835 in general, without repeating specifics. Already their radical thrust seemed restrained and directed more to cruder assertions of the conflict of vested rights with the sovereignty of the people. Yet the Democrats' populist appeal of 1835–1836 coincided with a reform of the party's power structure. The latter, and specifically the demotion of the Boston officeholders, gave the Democrats a credibility that significantly aided their growth as an electoral coalition.

### Party Organization: Later Stages, 1834–1837

In 1835 the Democratic state legislators took control of the Jacksonian organization and moved simultaneously to make the party's decision-making structure geographically representative, to expand the party's electoral base, and, not least, to give themselves influence in the awarding of federal patronage. The Democrats' improved showing at the polls that year owed much to their becoming less identified with the customshouse faction and the "evil city."

Since 1829 Henshaw had dominated the "Suffolk Committee," controlled Jacksonian nominations and patronage, and had most county chairmen as his allies. In 1832 the Democratic legislators had become restive, but Henshaw had managed to delay any change in party structure for another two years. Finally, in 1835 the "country" Democrats, primarily legislators (none of whom were from Boston, since Boston elected no Jacksonian representatives), took matters into their own hands.[43]

In February the Democratic caucus (calling themselves "the Republican members" of the legislature) announced a new organization of the Jackson party and sent emissaries to Washington to seek the blessing of the Jackson administration. The caucus named a new state committee and recommended that county and town committees be formed to call meetings to nominate state representatives and to contest elections.[44]

The reformers claimed that under the new system counties and towns could conduct political operations "in their own way."[45] Though politics at the local level did not change very much, Henshaw's influence was much reduced and different factions became better represented in the party's leadership. The legislators generally distrusted "the influence and management of the Boston brethren," and many of their constituents shared that distrust.[46]

Even the ascendancy of "reform" leaders, however, did not immediately lead the Democrats to adopt a regular convention system. In March the caucus nominated Morton and Foster, and subsequent state and county conventions held that fall merely ratified the caucus decision.[47] Though Morton would have been the nominee under any system, Democratic procedures still did not differ much from Federal and Republican methods.

In 1836 Democrats held no state convention at all. The caucus again nominated the state ticket, and the state committee chose the slate of presidential electors. Even the party's "address" came not from a "convention" but from the executive committee of the state committee.[48]

During 1837, at last, the Democrats held a nominating convention according to regular principles. In March the mixed caucus called for a fall convention and for the organization of county committees where none existed. In late summer the county committees asked the towns to choose delegates (equal in number to the representatives to which they were entitled in the last legislature) to attend a convention at Worcester in September.[49] Then another round of county conventions followed and generally adhered to the same principle. Already, greater numbers of men participated in this expanded system of nominations and campaign preparation.[50]

Though 1837 may be taken as the point at which the convention system arrived among the Democrats, the party did not thereafter invariably use a pure delegate convention to make nominations. It did so in 1838, when 407 delegates elected from 141 towns actually balloted to nominate Morton for governor and Theodore Sedgwick for lieutenant governor, but in 1839 a March "legislative convention" or mixed caucus "recommended" the Morton-Sedgwick ticket and adopted formal resolutions for that year. A state convention in October, made up of 550 delegates from over 200 towns, functioned primarily as a rally and as a publicity event. In 1840 the script changed slightly and suggested that the legislators were consciously shifting the decision-making capacity to the pure convention. The "legislative convention" again recommended candidates but added "subject to the decision of the State Convention." At Springfield that September, as 500 delegates prepared to ballot, George Bancroft's motion that the nomination of the legislative convention be unanimously confirmed passed "without a dissenting voice." In the next two years, nominations were made at fall state conventions, though these affairs became huge mob scenes at which nominations typically emerged "by acclamation."[51] Thus, by the 1840s the Democrats possessed a nominating system very different in appearance from Federal-Republican practices, though one in which state legislators, federal officeholders, editors, and other top leaders still exercised much control.

The Whig "legislative convention" held on to its decision-making capacity even longer. Not until 1842 did the Whigs hold a delegate-nominating convention. Before then, mixed caucuses had nominated the Whig state ticket in the mode practiced by the dominant political group in Massachusetts for over forty years.

In 1835 the Whig caucus's nomination of Everett had aroused some talk of a convention, but this died out quickly.[52] In 1836 a mixed caucus again made the principal nominations while also creating a state central committee. The Whigs' September convention nominated presidential electors, but that choice was a foregone conclusion. The central committee did adopt, however, the principle of town representation for the state convention, and that mode came into general use for most Whig local conventions.[53] In 1837, similarly, a "Whig State Convention" was nothing more than a mixed caucus, and the fall county conventions *ratified,* as in the past, the state ticket. Meanwhile the size of county conventions grew as some counties now asked the towns to send delegates equal in number to *twice* the town's representatives in the legislature. While procedures still varied much from place to place, these gatherings inevitably became more impersonal and formal.[54]

For the next four years, the Whig party functioned in pretty much the same way, with key decisions coming from the mixed caucus. In 1842, finally, the "legislative convention" recommended a state convention to make nominations. In September 1843 the Whig party thus held its first "pure" nominating convention at Faneuil Hall. Though John Davis was expected to be the nominee for governor, in theory, at least, the nominee was unknown before the convention met. In 1843 and 1844 the Whig legislative conventions similarly did not make nominations but set the machinery in motion by which conventions were called in June.[55] Thus, the history of the Whig organization, even more than that of the Democratic, suggests the need to revise previous historical accounts which have described a pure convention system that swept aside older methods by the mid-1830s.

Earlier histories have not erred, however, in stressing the numbers of people drawn into the convention system. As noted above, local conventions had become quite large by 1837, and by 1840 state conventions had grown to great size. The Democrats went from an already unwieldy 500 in 1840 to some 2,000 to 2,500 in 1841, which they scaled down the next year to a mere 1,500 to 2,000 delegates! Whig conventions, while not so large, could hardly be thought of as aristocratic. In 1842 their central committee asked for three times the maximum allowed representation, and over 1,000 delegates appeared at Faneuil Hall. In June 1843 they gathered some 1600 at the Worcester town hall, and in 1844 some 1,000 delegates.[56] The parties wanted to show themselves to be open and democratic, and in the process gave hundreds of delegates a sense of participating in decisions, or at least in meaningful ritual. Hundreds must have come away feeling that the party was *theirs,* even if they recognized, as most probably did, that the inner core of leadership made most of the important decisions.

Each party's leadership functioned through a set of interlocking county and local oligarchies which varied considerably in their relative centralization and openness.[57] State leaders were not always able to manage things at the local level, and county conventions seem to have been subject to more "uncertainty."[58]

The candidates, resolutions, and addresses of state conventions, however, originated almost uniformly with small circles of party leaders. Marcus Morton in 1834 had worried that a convention as large as the legislature would be "too numerous, too expensive, and too uncertain," and thought that 100 or 120 delegates would make for a "very able and efficient convention."[59] Yet Democratic and Whig leaders soon discovered that a large extravaganza of unity and bombast could be managed *more* easily than a small convention.

The locus of power in the Whig party resembled the old Federal pattern: nationally oriented men–chiefly merchants, merchant-manufacturers, and lawyers–exercised much power in state politics through the legislative caucus, governorship and congressional delegations. The Democrats, like the Republicans earlier, relied more on federal offices, and Democratic politicians in Massachusetts who had strong ties with cabinet officials in Washington enjoyed considerable influence.[60]

When after 1835 Henshaw tried to resign the collectorship and to pass it on to his close friend John K. Simpson, the succession hung fire for many months, disrupting the party and bringing forth many aspirants to the post. Finally, Washington gave disposition of the position to Morton, who had remained neutral and who now surprised many by choosing George Bancroft of Springfield.[61] The fight had laid bare the factional elements within the Democratic coalition; it also showed how much importance Democrats attached to patronage and the customshouse. Of the latter, John K. Simpson said that its "influence on the politicks of this section of the country is considerable."[62] David Henshaw, whose own power now declined further, had made the collectorship into a command post whose influence could be transferred to a different occupant.

Bancroft had no intention of wielding less power, but his purposes were different. He acted in many respects as other leaders would have acted and appointed friends and allies to office, some of whom included former Workingmen and radicals. He also shrewdly made alliances with editors in various parts of the state and established his own Boston paper, the *Bay State Democrat,* in order to dislodge Henshaw's *Post* as the state's leading Democratic organ. The Henshaw faction had used chambers at the Commonwealth Bank for caucusing; Bancroft opened a "reading room" at the *Democrat* offices to serve as a meeting place for "country" legislators. Though Henshaw's cadres sought to undermine all these projects, the Morton-Bancroft alliance was now the axis on which the party turned.[63] Moreover, Bancroft wanted to make the Democratic party into a popular movement that would win elections. In the mid-1830s the Democrats and Whigs had absorbed and channeled insurgent social movements of protest. In the late 1830s, as their organizations became far more regular, they tried to become social movements themselves, and, for a time at least, they succeeded.

### The Revival and the Factory

In 1838 and 1839 the Democrats and Whigs escalated their campaigning and together whipped themselves into a frenzy of politicking. Already equal to if not beyond Federal-Republican organizations, the Whigs and Democrats in those years clearly surpassed their predecessors and, for better or worse, reached into many more areas of public life than ever before. As institutions now, the parties took on some of the attributes of the factory and the revival. Alternately described as machines and churches, they harnessed the power of permanent system and interchangeable parts as well as the energizing drive of religious commitment and fervor. Revivals came and went, of course; their enthusiasm could not be sustained for a long time. The factory machine, however, so long as it had hands to tend it, mechanics to fix it, and managers to direct it—and so long as it yielded a profit—had a life of its own and could just run on.

Amid the parties' efforts to transcend themselves, the persistence of traditional elements of campaigning should not go unnoticed. Candidates for governor, for example, did not overtly campaign for office. Marcus Morton sat on the state supreme court during the many seasons of his candidacies and professed that his office prohibited him from politicking. Whigs made a great show of "calling" candidates to the governor's post. Frequently they renominated incumbents, who did not openly campaign but who made use of such devices as tours of militia inspection. These allowed the governor and a uniformed staff to travel the state and to revel in pomp and fanfare, joining local dignitaries at dinners enlivened by the "flow of the grape." Political leaders seldom failed to appear at cattle shows or meetings of county agricultural societies. And as in the Federal-Republican era, aspiring politicians found militia activity highly useful to a public career.[64] Similarly, in 1843 the Whig State Central Committee echoed its Federalist counterpart of twenty years earlier by reminding town committeemen that "nothing effectual can be done without the cooperation of influential persons in every town."[65]

There was nothing particularly new about Collector Bancroft's dispatching of one of his officials to full-time campaign work. Nor did the Whigs, who eternally called the Democrats the "office-holding faction," lag behind the Democrats in this respect. Indeed, given their long control of the state government, they were far ahead. In 1839 in Bristol County, for example, where the Democrats made up nearly half the electorate, there were some eighty Whig officeholders, including the sheriff, seventeen of nineteen deputy sheriffs, a dozen court officials, thirty-seven of forty coroners, and the trigonometrical surveyor. And in the crucial area of newspapers, the Democrats counted, in the entire state, no more than twenty as against some fifty to sixty Whig papers, including all the major Boston dailies except one.[66]

Their newspapers gave the Whigs much influence on public opinion. So did the prestige of their famous leaders, especially their battery of lawyer-orators, led by "the God-like" Daniel Webster, their scholar-politicians, such as Edward Everett, and their public men of old family who were party organizers, such as Robert C. Winthrop. The Democrat Bancroft, himself a renegade from the cultured classes, knew that extraordinary efforts were needed against the might of the Whig press, the brilliance of their leaders, the learning of Harvard, and the eloquence of many Boston pulpits.

Bancroft, a man of many talents, represented a particular type of Democratic leader—the educator-politician. It was characteristic of this species and of Bancroft that he established, late in 1838, a lecture series in Boston whose purpose was to bring learned Democratic orators before popular audiences. While expounding the Democratic creed on the issues of the day, the speaker also demonstrated that the Democrats, too, possessed worthy leaders. During 1839 the Democrats formed "Bay State Associations" to promote lecturing and politicking on the Bancroft model. This "educational" twist caught on, tapping the ever present American urge to self-improvement, and the "associations" and lectures enjoyed much success. Bancroft did not confine himself to an austere pedagogical approach, but often enlivened campaign speeches by bringing along a brass band. The effectiveness of Democratic innovations may be judged by the various Whig responses: editorial denunciations, privately expressed fears, and, most of all, imitation.[67]

In the 1838 state election, Democrats had climbed to real electoral respectability, winning almost 42,000 of just under 94,000 votes cast. In 1839 they won their first state election ever, aided by their new look and by Whig internal divisions, especially over a controversial temperance law. Yet the Whigs did not lose for lack of organization, because the Democrats' showing in 1838 had prompted Whigs to "raise the steam" all the higher.

Their first taste of defeat hardly impeded the onward rush of Whig campaigning. Whig managers moved quickly to reunite their divided forces, and Whig cadres rebounded from the gubernatorial loss with a renewed spirit. In New Bedford, for example, following a brief spell of despondency, the Whigs regrouped: "They have held their meetings every night—

crowded enthusiastic meetings. They have organized a permanent Whig Association–and they have resolved to devote this week, the whole of it, to their one great object of returning . . . Whig representatives." This devotion came, it should be emphasized, after more than a month of intense activity preceding a gubernatorial election which they had just lost.[68]

In 1839–1840 the Massachusetts Whigs, like their brethren in other states, waged a virtually continuous campaign. On January 6 the Whig caucus listened to Daniel Webster's exhortations and then proceeded to organize the Whig party into a voter-mobilizing machine. The caucus set up committees to prepare and distribute votes, and to iron out intraparty policy differences, especially on the temperance issue. The February convention continued the work while proclaiming the need to develop a "thorough, systematic organization" long before the election, as Whigs did in other states and as their opponents now did in Massachusetts. The state committee planned to meet monthly and to consult with county committees. What was most vital, town committees would create lists of voters and would mark Whigs with an "R." and "Locofocos" with a "T." (for Tory) and "doubtful men" with an "X." Local committees should estimate how the doubtfuls would vote, and inform the state committee, by June 7, as to the numbers of young Whigs, new voters, and recent residents in their towns. They should check also for "illegal voters, such as aliens, transient men who have not gained a residence, minors, persons that have become paupers during the year, or may have families in other parts." Spurred by Bancroft's example, the Whigs also organized "Whig Associations" across the state, and especially in the larger towns, in order to diffuse Whig truth "by means of Lectures and Reading Rooms, and the distribution of Whig newspapers and periodicals."[69]

While the central committee did a good deal of planning, enthusiasm at the local level ran at fever pitch. Reports came in from various parts of the state that Whig men and women were throwing themselves into campaigning. Soon Whig leaders were estimating that their "great gathering" to be held in June would exceed 5,000.[70] Their estimates were in fact too low.

Some ten to twenty thousand people descended on Worcester, almost four months before the election.[71] Railroad trains from Boston deposited several bulging loads of delegates and spectators. From all parts of the central countryside came cavalcades of horsemen, wagons, and carriages. Several towns in southeastern Worcester County together sent 1,400 persons, their vehicles drawn by teams of six, four, and two horses, seventy teams from Sutton alone; the chief marshall said that when they began unharnessing in Worcester the rear of the column could not have left Millbury.[72] Banners and log cabins, "emblems of the sylvan life of the early settlers," were everywhere. General Harrison's profile and name were also ubiquitous, especially on a huge transparency depicting him with a plough "as the Cincinnatus of America." Farmers were clearly the mass of this Whig army, but Leicester Whigs also held aloft a banner proclaiming, "We need relief/We demand reform/No reduction of wages," and several other delegations stressed their identity as nonfarm workers. Accompanied by bands, a parade some two miles long marched to a field to ratify the formal convention's business and to hear speeches.[73]

That the great fever of 1840 rose again in Fourth of July celebrations, barbecues, orations, and parades by both Whigs and Democrats was hardly surprising. But its continuation into August was a striking departure from the usual political torpor during summer months. On the Whig side, anticipation of another "great meeting" in September helped keep excitement alive:

> The people are all astir. There never was anything like it. There is no gainsaying or assisting it, and all we have to do, is to join in, and help give it a good direction, to bring it to good practical result.
>
> I never addressed so large a meeting as at the dedication of the Log cabin at Lynn, nor one so animated and at the same time so orderly. There were 2500 to 3500 present. It was really an exciting occasion.[74]

The climax came in September when 50,000 persons, the Whigs claimed, gathered at Bunker Hill. Even if the figure were lowered by ten or twenty thousand, it would still be astounding. The parade there was four miles long and took two hours to pass any given point. One hundred and fifty truckmen in white frocks headed the procession, followed by over a thousand "well-mounted citizens," fifty barouches and carriages with Revolutionary soldiers and dignitaries, a large body of seamen and many others on foot, a printing press in full operation drawn by six horses, and numerous banners and bands, all marching through streets decked out with signs, pennants, and triumphal arches of evergreens and flowers. At Bunker Hill the throng listened to addresses by the governors of New Jersey and Connecticut and, of course, by Daniel Webster.[75]

On election day the returns registered the magnitude of popular attentiveness: over 127,000 cast ballots for governor and over 125,000 for president. The Whigs benefited most, their total vote rising over 20,000 to almost 71,000, while the losing Democrats gained 4,100 more than their previous year's record. Not even inclement weather bothered the voters: "How they turned out [in Salem], amidst torrents of rain—all—

the sick and the aged–men over 90 years of age. I am almost sorry it is over–it is such a splendid victory. There will never be such another."[76]

Indeed, there would not be. Not only because the Whig party would win, barely, only one more national victory, but also because there was something unique about 1840.

More of an explanation than "party competition" is needed to account for this phenomenal campaign, which was national in its impact. Besides organization, the citizenry were also moved by economic conditions: the years 1837 through 1840 were "hard times" for many Massachusetts farmers and artisans, and Whig promises of prosperity undoubtedly helped to mobilize the citizenry.[77] But economic hardship and party organization have been present at other times without creating quite the memorable political excitement of 1840.

So much has been said about the 1840 campaign as a climax of the new political culture, and of its *representative* character, that its specialness has been lost. Not that historians have failed to make the campaign familiar to most students of United States history. Or that they have lacked an appreciation of it as "a grand dramatic experience," which with "all its attendant pageantry and exaltation meant to Americans what religious festivals meant to the peoples of Catholic Europe."[78] But at the time many observers thought that "there was never anything like it before," and later, even at the end of the century, those who had experienced it also believed that "probably there will never be anything like it again." This judgment seems valid on several grounds, not the least of which was the sheer sustained intensity of political interest on the part of men and women alike. Indeed, while the participation of women has been remarked on often, it has escaped notice that women did not participate in later campaigns to the same degree.[79]

The 1840 campaign was made possible by a political innocence and trust that would never be greater. Political parties as mass movements had just been created, and they seemed, during the season of popular upwelling in 1839–1840, to be ready instruments of the will of the people. In the great mass gatherings, people "saw themselves" and in doing so both expressed and reinforced their belief that their actions, their taking part, and their votes could steer government and society in the right direction.[80] While the citizens' sense of efficacy remained relatively strong throughout the nineteenth century, especially when compared with recent levels, it was perhaps never livelier than in 1840.

The secular revivalism of 1840 was in part an expression of hope for worldly salvation. It sprang from newly arrived expectations that government, with the right leaders setting the proper course, could "redeem" society as a whole. No public opinion polls exist that verify this conclusion, but the 1840 turnout strongly suggests that people believed that "right representation" made a difference, that it mattered who was elected to office and which party's principles triumphed. These beliefs would then go through cycles of optimism and disillusion, as they continue to do in the present. But in 1839–1840 the distrust expressed by movements critical of the social order and of conventional political leadership was set aside or redirected; antiparty attitudes, except among a small minority, were overcome at least temporarily. Political parties emerged as electoral coalitions from social and political movements seeking to preserve, save, or reform the Republic, each of them armed with a galvanizing focus on an adversary. They practically duplicated the style and modes of religious revivals and, above all, tapped the wells of popular enthusiasm that animated revivalism. "Great" revivals, however, have come in intervals marked at least by generations, and political excitement on this scale would not appear again for at least another generation, and not until a new mass party, drawing again on social movements, grew up to replace the Whig party. In the meanwhile, the parties also imitated the factory and became to a degree self-sustaining. Their machines, like those on the Merrimack, could adjust to the rise and fall of energy flowing through; and they commanded a permanent loyalty not only from managers and cadre but also from many of the rank and file.

## XII. Whigs and Democrats: Ideology and Social Sources

> Again I saw all the oppressions that are practiced under the sun. And behold, the tears of the oppressed, and they had no one to comfort them! On the side of their oppressors there was power, and there was no one to comfort them.
>
> —Ecclesiastes 4:1

If the Whig and Democratic parties differed as organizations from Federal and Republican parties, they also differed in their sources of support at the polls. Yet though the Whig electoral coalition did not replicate the Federalist coalition, it resembled it; similarly the Democratic "army" constituted a rough reassemblage of the Jeffersonian Republican coalition. Indeed, the Whig-Democratic division expressed some conflicts reaching well back into the eighteenth century. As in the Federal-Republican era, a major line of separation was that between Center and Periphery. The Whigs even more than the Federalists wanted to use state power to foster economic growth and moral improvement, as well as to protect the weak and disabled and to guide the more dependent members of society. The Democrats spoke for those who for generations had distrusted and resisted centralizing power and who sought protection usually in the fullest retention of individual and local autonomy. The Democrats, like the Republicans before them, wanted fewer laws, less government, and the freest possible field in society for the benevolent operation of natural laws. They complained that special legislative laws always tended to enrich a few at the expense of the many. In contrast, the Whig governor Edward Everett exclaimed joyously that "the greatest single engine of moral power known to human affairs, is an organized, prosperous state."[1] To most Democrats, that idea was dangerously wrong, being contradicted by centuries of state oppression. Thus the Whigs continued to articulate the ideology of the Federal Center, while the Democrats expressed the beliefs of the Periphery, which roughly carried on Republican ideology.

The division between Center and Periphery may also be detected in the partisan array of regions in the 1830s and 1840s. While not as consistent as the regional alignment of 1810, the Center-Periphery cleavage still held to a significant degree. Furthermore, the religious and cultural character of the division not only persisted but was taking on new dimensions as religious and demographic changes brought into being a more heterogeneous population. As before, these patterns were rough and not always exactly symmetrical. Whigs had support in peripheral regions, and Democrats attracted voters of the Center. Yet the pattern generally gave shape to Massachusetts politics even as party forms and modes of operation changed significantly.

## Ideology and Belief

Ever since 1800 a cruel irony had cut through Massachusetts politics and wounded the pride of its most distinguished public men. The very men who favored an energetic federal government, or who would have, were the same ones who repeatedly found themselves in opposition to national administrations. In the early 1800s and in the 1830s, the party that advocated a strong, purposeful government campaigned in Massachusetts with appeals to their fellow citizens to help them save the country from its rulers. Federalists and then Whigs mounted crusades against an outside power whose original potential for good had been perverted by wrong-headed or corrupt men. Both these parties represented the dominant elites in Massachusetts, and in rallying their fellow citizens against Washington, almost as if it were a foreign power, they surely helped to maintain their local hegemony. Yet Federal and Whig opposition to the national government, or rather to particular administrations and their policies, was an irony of history resulting from the continental Periphery's control of the national government for most of the years from 1800 to 1840.

No longer, however, did sectionalism taint the Massachusetts Whigs as it had the Federalists. They were without peer the party of the Union, identified especially by their great orator Webster with defense of the Constitution and preservation of the Union as sacred and supreme goals.

While the party of the Center campaigned against Jefferson, Madison, Jackson, and Van Buren, the party of the Periphery within Massachusetts launched its crusades to mobilize voters against the state government at home. The symmetry of it was calculated to please the most compulsive of political philosophers. Both parties drew life from their claims to represent the people against tyranny and oppression; both formed themselves as oppositional crusades.

To read the state addresses (or what passed for such) of the major parties in Massachusetts after 1830 is to keep switching from one political world to another.[2] The Nationals and Whigs lived primarily in the realm of the nation and the Atlantic, while the Democrats dwelled in the state and its counties. The Whigs denounced tyranny in Washington; the Democrats declaimed against oppression from Boston.

The Whig desire to use government to promote material and moral improvement, frustrated on the national stage, received few checks in Massachusetts. As a result, state spending rose steadily throughout the 1830s. Even before it reached what seemed, by earlier standards, staggering proportions, the Jacksonian opposition made the cry "excessive expenditures" or "extravagance" its leading shibboleth. In 1831 the National Republicans reacted defensively, claiming that charges of excess were exaggerated.[3] In the late 1830s the Whigs responded more positively, citing the benefits that spending for their various programs bestowed.

The Whig desiderata differed little from those of the Nationals. The "high objects of general improvement and public good" of which Levi Lincoln boasted in 1832 were interchangeable with those on the Whig agenda several years later. Lincoln's "objects" included identifying the state's boundaries, improving roads to public lands, repairing the capitol, constructing a costly penitentiary, conducting geological and geographical surveys, giving "noble charity" for the Institution for the Lunatic, providing for the education of the destitute deaf and dumb, and encouraging agricultural societies and various industries.[4] The Nationals' and Whigs' ardent support of a national tariff was, of course, a matter of economic interest, and it was also entirely consistent with their whole approach to the role of the state in society.[5]

In 1839 the Whig party leader Robert C. Winthrop stood before the State Convention of Whig Young Men at Worcester and met the Democratic charge of extravagance head on. He asked,

> which one of all the manifold appropriations . . . would you desire to have revoked? Would you have the Statutes of Massachusetts decomposed again from that Convenient Code which now lies on the table of almost every citizen . . . ? Would you have the wretched maniac cast out from yonder blessed retreat and remanded again to his manacles and dungeon?—Would you leave the Territory of the State still exposed to be clipped and cheated . . . at the unfounded pretension of every neighboring power . . . for want of an authentic survey and an accurate Map . . . ? Or do you begrudge to the Agriculture of the Commonwealth the little encouragement and assistance it may receive from a few bounties on Wheat and on Silk, and from a scientific investigation of the kinds of crop and the modes of cultivation to which our soil may be least unadapted?[6]

The young men expressed themselves in favor of all these worthy undertakings, and also reaffirmed their support for state aid to internal

improvements—which included, since 1836–1837, the C
extending major financial aid by way of stock subscriptio
the Western Railroad.[7] Of course the Young Whigs pas
bearing on national policy. Indeed, these came first on the
port of labor and industry by a protective tariff; a well-regulated system of credit; condemnation of the "absurd, pernicious" financial policy of the president; business's need for paper in some form; rejection of President Van Buren's "Independent Treasury" as a dangerous accession of patronage and power to the executive; and exhortations to the government to use the public lands in the West to profit all the states. Throughout the 1830s, Whig conventions and orators consistently pointed to the aggrandizement of presidential power, which had been turned into an engine of party corruption through the spoils system—at the same time that they lamented the undermining of Congress's ability to create a coherent approach to national economic policy.[8]

Under Whig direction the Commonwealth extended toward the less fortunate members of society what Governor John Davis once called its "paternal sympathy."[9] That phrase, natural to a Whig, was anathema to Democrats. The latter wanted no paternal or benevolent state, or, rather, not trusting the state, they wanted less state, less government, fewer laws. This was the classic posture of the Periphery. As the Democratic governor Morton said in 1840, the "common objects" of legislation and expense were "few, and easily understood," while "too much legislation and too much government, are among those tendencies of the age against which it is our duty to guard."[10]

Some historians have stressed the change in the Democrats' program which occurred in the mid-1830s when they took up much of the Workingmen's protest.[11] In 1835 the Democratic appeal did become, as observed above, more radical. Yet the new emphasis on the inequities fostered by special laws for bankers, manufacturers, and the privileged wealthy not only continued the antiaristocratic thrust of old Republicanism but also blended in with the demands for less law and for local autonomy that various elements in the Periphery had voiced for generations.[12]

When in the early 1830s Jacksonian Democratic legislators led in demanding radical reform of the law profession, they were not acting in a historical vacuum. Some radicals demanded that every man be allowed to be his own lawyer, while other Democrats, and some Whigs, wanted fee schedules to be reduced and statute law codified. Protests from Workingmen, Democrats, and others succeeded in making the law and lawyers political issues in the 1830s. In the end, moderate Whigs joined in support-

.g codification and in taking regulation of the law profession out of the control of local bar associations and giving it to the state. This meant greater uniformity of standards for lawyers, but it did not open the professions as radicals had wished. The important point, however, is that similar protests had burst forth in Massachusetts in the early 1800s, and in the 1780s when rage against lawyers had accompanied the Shays rebellion and other protests from the Periphery.[13] In the 1830s Democrats wove their critique of lawyers into the fabric of their program for removing all the artificial devices by which the aristocratic wealthy profited at the expense of the many.

The Democratic thrust after 1835 toward social justice should not be minimized even if it was largely frustrated by Whig power, beset by internal divisions, and easily diverted. Even so radical a spirit as Thomas W. Dorr of Rhode Island, while finding the "Jackson party in Massachusetts" not living up to its own principles before then, found that he could approve the principles laid down in the 1835 state address.[14] Democratic criticism of privileged wealth appealed to all who believed that the rules of the marketplace were loaded and that equal economic opportunity was not a reality. In 1835–1836 Democratic leaders in the legislature battled with the Whig majority for such causes as removing tolls from the Charles River Bridge, investigating banks and corporations, abolishing capital punishment, granting civil liberties to atheists, and removing the last vestiges of imprisonment for debt.[15] Some of these were wholly or partly realized, but the Democrats never controlled the state long enough, nor were radical Democrats numerous enough, to enact much of their economic program. Still, the very existence of a critical minority helped to keep the Whig elite honest. The record of cooperation between the state and the Western Railroad, for example, was a good one and probably better because of Democratic watchfulness and criticism.[16] The Democrats at least offered, flawed at some of its roots though it may have been, an alternative.

Much has been made of Democratic disagreements over corporations and banks. Henshaw's faction was deeply involved, of course, in banking, insurance, real-estate speculation, and other enterprises. During the fight over the collector's job, rival Democrats attacked Henshaw as a greedy apologist for corporations. Henshaw in turn denounced "ultra antimonopolists" and argued that if corporations served the public good then they were beneficial, so long as the legislature could make or unmake them. In 1837, similarly, Henshaw defended banks while Democratic radicals called for government prohibition of "money-manufacturing" institutions, elimination of bank paper, and establishment of a currency of hard money supplemented by "treasury notes."[17] Although these intraparty divisions were important, Henshaw and his rivals were also alike in certain basic ways.

Henshaw's argument that corporations should enjoy privileges no more and no less than any individual, was in harmony with the tendency of Democratic thought to begin with the individual rather than with society. And even while defending corporations, Henshaw could lash out against the judiciary as a supporter of religious intolerance and economic privilege, and call for the popular election of judges.[18] No Whig would have made such a proposal.

It is proper to be skeptical of Henshaw's professions, and especially of the egalitarian rhetoric of his newspaper, the Boston *Post.* In the same breath that he had criticized lawyers and judges, Henshaw had undermined trade unions as "monopolies" comparable to "the Bar" or Doctors' associations. Yet most of the Democrats did not openly support trade unions, and none came forth at this point as champions of the ten-hour day.

Some of Henshaw's rivals, too, were entrepreneurs involved in corporations. Benjamin Hallett's *Advocate,* the radical paper which advocated "No Banks" and "Divorce of Bank and State," included among its financial backers, as the *Post* observed, the former Antimasons and bankers John D. Williams and George Odiorne. And George Bancroft, the very voice of Democratic-Workyism in Massachusetts, was himself interested in banks and western land speculation and frequently promoted the interests of his in-laws, the Dwights of Springfield, who were powerful allies of the Whig "Boston Associates." Too many radical Democrats, indeed, became mere partisan careerists after their early political labors had brought them into a lucrative government post.[19] But neither ambition nor hunger for office and profit among Democrats detracts from their expressing the cause of the underprivileged and exploited, and, in general, of the casualties of "improvement." Office seeking and the lack of any sense of a conflict between public and private interest existed in both parties, though perhaps more insatiably in the minority. The Democrats were also moved to a great extent by resentment at Whig wealth, power, and pretensions.[20] But if resentment was a source of concern for equity, and of distrust and watchfulness toward the powerful, then so be it.

The commonalities among Democratic factions were more important than every twist and turn of doctrine coming from the ever busy pens of Boston editors.[21] The electorate surely did not calibrate its responses to such almost theologically complex disputes. It is easier to imagine that the voters grasped the basic position of most Democrats toward corporations: they were not sacred things but often dangerous to the public good.

Similarly, the man behind whom the Democrats united year after year, and whom they twice elected governor in the period 1830–1843, reflected in his thought and policies the basic ideology of most Democrats. When in 1838 and 1839 the Democrats raised the cry "Everett and Extravagance" and the banner "Morton and Economy," they sounded a theme which had been a major part of the old Republican appeal to the Periphery. Morton himself had grown up steeped in Jeffersonian orthodoxy, and as far back as 1804, while delivering the Brown University commencement oration, had eulogized "economy" in public affairs and declaimed against "extravagance" with public money as inevitably creating privilege and inequality. He was a staunch backer of Jeffersonian and Madisonian foreign policy, and his long career perhaps owed much to his having his native Bristol County as his political home base–a traditional stronghold of dissenters and the Periphery.[22]

Morton adjusted easily to the radical currents surging into the Jackson party in the 1830s. As he wrote to George Bancroft in 1835, his sympathies had always been "altogether with the workingmen and poorer classes."

> I do not believe that the *strong* are in danger from the *weak* or the *rich* from the *poor*. The tendency is all the other way and must be resisted and counteracted. Wealth has an undue and dangerous influence that it should be the first duty of Government to guard against its encroachments. But the wealth of many managed by a few, is more alarmingly dangerous for it has not the same powerful restraint of self interest and individual responsibility to check its abuse.[23]

In his 1840 inaugural Morton made clear his strategy for protecting the weak and poor. He would reduce government and laws to a minimum and separate government from all economic activity, especially from its involvement with banks and corporations. Though Edward Everett and Webster thought Morton's speech quite "radical," it was by Locofoco Democratic standards fairly moderate.[24] He did not call for an exclusively metallic currency but did want banks to be restrained from manufacturing too much currency, and he wanted to withdraw the state's "guardianship" from their frequently irresponsible behavior. All corporations were dangerous, said Morton, and the state made too many of them: in the last five years the legislature had passed 900 acts, of which 700 were "special legislation." Morton recognized that government and business had become closely intermeshed in the last half century, and that *disentanglement* must proceed cautiously. He would, however, firmly call a halt to the process and reverse its direction.[25]

Morton's proposals for less government with regard to cultural and moral questions perhaps illustrated better his basic attitude toward government and society. His outright call for repeal of the temperance law of 1838–1839 is among the best known of these; it reflected his premise that government could not legislate morality. In the area of criminal law, he pushed this logic even further. Noting approvingly that the severity of punishments for crimes had been lessened—and that there were, in particular, fewer instances of capital punishment—he concluded that "crimes have diminished nearly in proportion to the amelioration of criminal law."[26] Less law and less punishment produced, in effect, less crime.

Morton's program reflected strongly the character of Democratic thought as an attempt to adapt eighteenth-century republicanism to the nineteenth century. His call for a constitutional amendment to correct the unrepublican situation by which the concentration of wealth in Boston allowed it to be overrepresented in the General Court, recalled the eighteenth-century country view of the metropolis as the encroaching Center.[27] At the same time, Morton's call for a secret ballot showed that he had adopted some of the Workingmen's perspective and that guarding against encroaching wealth and power was for him more than a geographic question.

Morton argued, much to the Whigs' dismay, that informal interference with the free exercise of the elective franchise by the laboring poor was now widespread. Men of wealth and business sometimes infringed on the sacred right of choice of the dependent classes, because the act of voting was usually not secret. Though the laborer should be truly independent, since he produced more than he consumed and actually created wealth, too often he was dependent on his employer and obeyed his will at the poll.[28]

Morton's view of public schools also displayed a sensitivity to the inequities and injustices flowing from disparities of wealth. He essentially praised the local district schools for socializing the young to democratic instincts by assembling children of all circumstances "before the pride of family or wealth, or other adventitious distinction has taken deep root in the young heart."[29] Many Democrats shared this sensitivity; few Whigs did, and no Whig leaders identified themselves with such views.

Whigs started from wholly different premises about the nature of society. They thought it destructive to talk of class divisions and inequities. In their usage, the term "class" normally referred to occupations or interest groups, or served as a synonym for "category" or "type." Indeed, by "labouring classes" Whigs most often meant practically every working male, whether employed or self-employed, mule spinner or factory owner.[30] All classes, they believed, shared a natural "harmony of interests." For this reason, above all, when energy in government promoted economic development, it could only lift up all classes together to prosperity. This premise of a "harmony of interests" was not only a key element of Whig thought but found a resonance in popular thinking as well. It was implicit, when not explicit, in the uninhibited Whig campaign appeals to "all classes," and it removed all self-consciousness of hypocrisy when well-to-do Whig lawyers and entrepreneurs presented themselves to the horny-handed electorate as fellow "workingmen."[31]

In reply to Bancroft's charge that new accumulations of money and power created obstacles to realizing the egalitarian promise of republican institutions, the Whigs flatly asserted that "there is no inequality here." The sun never shone, said the Boston *Courier,* "upon a land where all the blessings of equality . . . can be enjoyed in such perfection as in our New England. . . . Every avenue to distinction, every path to wealth is open to every citizen alike, and every citizen can make himself what he chooses to be." Whig orators like Webster, Davis, and Everett, themselves risen from modest beginnings, expressed this theme repeatedly. In 1838 Everett declared to a group of Boston merchants that he simply could not understand the prejudice against capital found in some quarters; he saw no basis for it in the United States. "Wealth, in this country, may be traced back to industry and frugality; the paths which lead to it are open to all; the laws which protect it are equal to all . . . the wheel of fortune is in constant revolution, and the poor, in one generation, furnish the rich of the next."[32] Clearly, Whigs and Democrats saw society quite differently. One party began from premises of class harmony and social mobility, and the other from perceptions of maldistribution and loaded dice in the pursuit of prosperity.

All Whigs and Democrats, of course, did not share all of these distinguishing ideological attributes to the same degree. Given the coalitional character of parties, the parties covered considerable diversity under their capacious ideological umbrellas. Any portrait of a party's belief system is an attempt to find common denominators of thought, but inevitably these cannot predict the positions of all of a party's constituents, or of all of its leaders.[33]

Democrats differed among themselves, as noted above, on the best policy to take in regulating corporations. In 1838–1839 the Whigs split over temperance legislation, and though the Democrats profited from the outcome of the temperance struggle, sentiment in their ranks was by no means uniformly opposed to any state action on the measure. After codification of the state's statutes had become a reality, both Whigs and Democrats claimed credit for the measure. Massachusetts Democrats, unlike their brethren in other parts of the country, soft-pedaled the topic of free trade, and Marcus Morton recognized both good and bad effects from tariffs, which he regarded, in any case, as inevitable. And these examples do not exhaust the issues on which minorities of varying size and composition, in both parties, sided with the opposition.[34]

Yet the central ideological tendencies of each party may be observed even in cases in which relatively high "breakage" occurred. In 1840, for example, the Whig-created state board of education was attacked by Democratic legislators, especially by those from small, commercially undeveloped, and agricultural towns. Whig "backbenchers" from western counties and small towns aided the Democratic assault on this central state agency, while at the same time prominent Democrats like Rantoul and Bancroft endorsed the board. In the end the Whig legislature defeated an attempt to abolish the board, as one-third of the Democratic legislators supported the board and nearly one-fifth of the Whigs voted against it. A recent study of this episode, based on an analysis of the roll-call vote, found that party loyalty was the most important determinant of a legislator's vote, followed by the degree of commerce and manufacturing in his constituency and by the latter's geographic location.[35] The authors of this study made the even more significant finding that the most "fundamental disagreement" between Whigs and Democrats "was over the proper role of state government in education."

> The Whigs argued that positive government intervention was a necessary and useful means of improving the quality of public schools. . . . The Democrats . . . felt that any increased state interference in local educational matters created the potential, if not the reality, of a centralized state school system that would dictate how children were to be educated. Furthermore, many Democrats felt that the board of education and the normal schools were unnecessary state expenses at a time when the state needed to retrench its expenditures.[36]

Thus, the legislative division over the state board of education expressed in its main tendencies the ancient conflict between Center and Periphery. It was precisely the kind of issue which had always divided cultural, religious, geographic, economic, and status groups, and it also created alignments which had appeared on similar issues at least as early as the 1780s.

### Social Change and Party Loyalty, 1836–1844

In 1840 Massachusetts's population differed greatly from what it had been in 1800 in size, geographical distribution, and work patterns. Changes in life-style and especially in religious-group associations had been enormous. Yet the main lines of political division still roughly followed Federal-Republican patterns.

From 1800 to 1820 the population remained largely agricultural and partly maritime and grew very slowly. During the Federal era, in fact, many farm families left the state in search of a better living; then from 1820 to 1840 the Commonwealth's population increased by 40 percent to nearly 740,000. Now many natives and newcomers stayed behind because they could find work, not in the saturated agricultural sector, but in manufacturing, commerce, and even in reinvigorated maritime industries.[37]

Despite the changes in social life, political contests can still be understood to a degree as battles fought between a coalition of the Center and another of the Periphery. Like the Federalists before them, the Whigs commanded heavy majorities in the ancient coastal Core of Suffolk-Essex, the upper Connecticut Valley, and rural Worcester County. But they had also broken off two earlier redoubts of Jeffersonianism–Nantucket and Cape Cod, both maritime and both strongly Whig during the period 1836–1844. The Democrats' strength otherwise remained concentrated in peripheral counties which had earlier voted Republican. The leading Democratic county was Bristol, once part of Rhode Island, still a hive of religious diversity and dissent, and testimony that ancient religious rivalries still helped shape the Center-Periphery division, though obviously not to the same degree or in the same way as earlier.[38]

The Whigs also won in most of the major population centers. In 1840

**Table XII.1.** Strongest and Weakest Whig Counties, Presidential Election of 1840

| *County* | *Whig %* | *County* | *Whig %* |
|---|---|---|---|
| Hampshire | 69.6 | Bristol | 49.7 Dem. pl. |
| Nantucket | 67.6 | Hampden | 50.1 Whig |
| Barnstable | 62.9 | Berkshire | 50.5 " |
| Suffolk | 62.7 | Middlesex | 52.3 |
| Worcester | 62.4 | Dukes | 53.2 |
| Franklin | 61.2 | Plymouth | 55.3 |
| Essex | 57.9 | Norfolk | 55.5 |

they carried eleven of the thirteen largest cities and towns and, more to the point, exceeded the party's state percntage of 57.1 in eight of the thirteen (Appendix XII.A, Table 1). The Whigs carried Boston, of course, and seven towns contiguous to the metropolis (Appendix XII.A, Table 2). All of these towns except Charlestown, earlier a Free Bridge and Jeffersonian fortress, were more Whig than the rest of the state–indeed, all voted at least 60 percent Whig. On the other hand, the sixteen peripheral towns within ten miles of Boston, and outside the capital's immediate orbit, included only four with better-than-average Whig percentages (Appendix XII.A, Table 3).

Even more striking was the similarity of the relative strengths of the Federal-Republican and Whig-Democratic parties during their formative years. Despite the passage of three to four decades and the upheavals that they brought, the proportion of voters supporting the major parties remained remarkably similar. *Whereas the Republican mean percentage in state elections from 1805 through 1815* (in Massachusetts proper, excluding Maine) *was 44.7, the Democratic mean from 1836 through 1844 was 44.1.*[39]

The Whig and Democratic parties did not simply reconstitute, respectively, the Federal and Jeffersonian parties. Nevertheless, vestiges of Federal-Republican divisions persisted, and the Whig and Democratic coalitions can be explained broadly as created by change *and* continuity. Networks of influence, old and new, underlay partisan loyalties. So did cultural and religious divisions, some of which reached back several generations, while others had arisen only recently in the rapidly changing world of the early nineteenth century.

Some men lived to be Federalists and Whigs; others went as naturally from Republicanism to Democracy. But although many other men crossed these paths, the identification of masses of voters with Whigs and Democrats was qualitatively different from what had gone before. In the late 1830s, parties demanded more and party loyalty ran deeper. "Passionate conviction" in the public arena was, in a sense, finally democratized.

Once party loyalties had formed in the late 1830s, they possessed enormous staying power. Families served as primary agents of socialization into politics, and sons usually followed their fathers. As one who grew up in the 1830s put it, "politics was with the boy as with the father." It was natural for sons in politics to be "chips off the old block." And the 1840 campaign drew into politics not only women but entire families, especially the boys: "As the old cock crows, the young un' larns." For the great majority, party loyalty was a high virtue, and changeability in politics suspect. In 1852 at a man's graveside the minister paid tribute to his partisan fidelity: "He never crossed the line."[40]

The continuity of party loyalty through the middle of the nineteenth century is a point well established by contemporary historical scholarship. The Whig party was doomed to collapse in the 1850s, of course, wracked by social movements that rebelled in part against political party organizations *as such.* But the habit of partisanship ingrained by the Whigs and Democrats was not ephemeral. Though some voters changed parties and though party realignments took place in the 1850s, party loyalties soon reasserted themselves. In the northern United States, particularly, the post–Civil War Democratic party represented a massive continuation of the Jacksonian party, while the Republican party largely preserved antebellum Whiggery.

### Social Change and Party Division: Massachusetts

A recent study of the social bases of Massachusetts's Whig and Democratic parties found that the Whigs' "strongest following was in the large cities, the fishing towns, and in towns with only Congregationalist churches. . . . The party ran less well in, though it usually carried, the nonindustrial towns, the boot and shoe towns, and those in which Baptists, Methodists, Universalists, and Quakers were numerous." The Whigs usually lost towns which were dominated by dissenting churches and which lacked Congregational churches. "The Democrats' best showing was in the agricultural towns least touched by industrial and commercial development, and in towns where dissenters were prominent, especially Baptists."[41] These statements, resting on a careful examination of township-level data, convey some of the central tendencies of the parties as well as the Whig party's broad base. A problem arises, however, in using data aggregated by towns, because they often fail to impart accurate information about subcommunities *within* towns. More basically, there is some question as to whether one may speak at all of, for example, "fishing towns" or "boot and shoe towns."

What kind of town was Quincy, famous as the seat of two presidents? In the elder Adams's day it had been a quiet farming community, but from 1820 to 1840 its population had risen by 115 percent, to nearly 3,300. Besides its ancient farms, it boasted a small fishery of ten vessels with 100 "hands." The town was now also known for its granite quarries, which employed over 500 laborers. Another 20 men worked at various crafts, while 163 "males" (many no doubt under twenty-one) made boots and shoes.[42] Did the young quarry hands, shoemakers, and fishing crews, whose labor was often seasonal and whose residence was probably elsewhere, constitute a considerable part of the electorate?

The town of Marblehead possessed, according to Harriet Martineau, a distinct character: "the people are noisy, restless, high-spirited, and democratic." Marblehead was a fishing town, with fifty-five vessels and 500 hands, but in the cold months the fishermen made boots and shoes, most of them working for the small capitalists of Lynn. Thus, it was also a boot and shoe town. Yet the face of rock-bound Marblehead was set to the sea, and if any place can be called a fishing town, Marblehead surely can be.[43]

Many towns, however, simply defy classification, even some that were quite small. Take Manchester, for example, an Essex County town of 1,346 souls. Five hands worked at shipbuilding, and fourteen small vessels engaged 65 hands fishing for cod and mackerel. Twelve small furniture factories gave work to another 120 hands, not counting a variety of individual craftsmen. A substantial part of the population, in addition, still earned its living principally from agriculture.[44]

The pervasive nature of socioeconomic change simply does not permit the historian to separate communities into exclusive types. Historians have too often depicted the coming of factories, railroads, and population concentration as if these things wholly displaced whatever had gone before. Some writers have left the impression that with the creation of Lowell, the transition from "wharf to waterfall" was well advanced. But Massachusetts, even after the separation of the Maine coast in 1820, remained the leading shipping state until 1843, and the clipper-ship era still lay ahead. While many small ports declined, Boston's maritime enterprise boomed; still other ports specializing in whaling or fishing expanded their fleets in the 1830s and 1840s.[45]

When some coastal towns turned to manufacturing, they joined a great many towns, large and small, which had waterpower sites and into which manufacturing entered. Lowell, Waltham, and Chicopee were awe inspiring as over-night wonders and for their size, but they were exceptions. In 1837 some 282 cotton mills employed almost 5,000 males in hamlets, villages, and towns scattered through eleven counties. The mills of Middlesex County, of course, were the largest, employing 1,054 males as well as 6,435 females of the 14,757 females in cotton mills statewide. But there were 74 mills in Worcester County, 57 in Bristol, 32 in Norfolk, 31 in Berkshire, 20 in Hampden, even 2 small ones on Cape Cod. The 192 woolen mills in the state, employing 3,612 males and 3,485 females, were even more dispersed. Few towns can therefore be typed as purely manufacturing towns, whatever the industry.[46]

This does not mean that manufacturers or mill workers never possessed distinct political interests, but it does mean that given the form in which election returns are usually available–namely, by town–and given the mixed socioeconomic character of many towns, it is difficult to generalize about most voters engaged in manufacturing occupations.

The gradual character of change creates problems in the simple process of classifying workers. In 1837 more "males" (23,702) worked in shoemaking than in cotton and woolen production. Yet the proportion of the electorate which they constituted in most towns is almost impossible to determine. Many were under twenty-one years of age, and central shop factories could be found only to some degree in just a few shoe centers (Lynn, Randolph, Haverhill, Danvers, Salem, Stoughton, and Grafton). But these were not comparable in size, capitalization, or organization to the factories of Lowell or to those which emerged later in the shoe industry. Most boots and shoes were made by a putting-out system, usually on a piecework basis, and many or most adult males who were shoemakers in winter worked at other jobs in warmer seasons. "Outwork" was in fact an enormously important part of the economy, and not confined to the making of boots and shoes. The palm-leaf hat industry, for example, functioned almost entirely as an adjunct to other activities: yet in 1837 some 2 million palm-leaf hats were made, by hand, in Worcester County alone, and about 3.3 million in the state.[47]

Work rhythms were highly seasonal in every industry, from shipyards to iron forges.[48] Even at Lowell the labor supply, male and female, dwindled during months of peak agricultural activity, and the mill managers themselves sought to adjust employment up and down with the rise and fall of the level and motive force of the Merrimack River. Thus a good many workers shuttled back and forth between jobs and towns.

Given the difficulty of merely classifying towns according to socioeconomic type, any conclusions about social-group voting behavior based on such data should be treated as hypotheses. My own attempt at classifying nonagricultural towns uncovered no definite political tendencies; multiple regression analysis of all the state's towns, using economic data from the 1840 federal census, also proved inconclusive.[49]

In the early industrial period, few Massachusetts towns still had a uniform social character. Only a minority continued to possess the cohesiveness that had once made for so many one-party or heavily partisan towns.

Within civil boundaries, party competition flourished, in part because social-group diversity had grown. The available ecological data do not reveal the relevant subcommunities of religion, work, culture, and interest. Yet there is abundant evidence of other sorts—both direct and indirect—that such subcommunities existed and that within them, often, political loyalties pitched heavily toward the Democrats or Whigs. In some cases these tendencies followed those of the Federal-Republican era; in others they did not.

### "Influence" and Voters

> . . . *State Street* you know, governs Boston, and Boston Massachusetts, and Mass. all New England, and more too.[50]

Perhaps all that needs to be known to explain voting behavior in this period is that most of Boston's, and hence the state's, elite, its rich and powerful men, were Whigs.[51] These men enjoyed great economic, social, and intellectual influence throughout the state, directly through their many enterprises, their kin, associates, managers, agents, factotums, and lackeys. At the center of the elite stood the "Boston Associates" who owned the big mills and whose influence radiated through many small, independent factory owners who were financially tied to the magnates, or who appreciated the efforts of Appleton, Lawrence, Webster, and others to secure tariffs protecting mills large and small. The political power of these men was great, they loomed large in the higher councils of the Whig party, and they enjoyed the patronage of the federal and state governments. The side effects of that patronage and of their prosperity extended to many other merchants, professionals, clerical workers, shopkeepers, artisans, and laborers—even to many independent farmers and fishermen.[52] To know the reality of this influence is to understand much, but not all.

If influence elicited deference, it also begat resentment. And there existed competing networks of influence, some of which had always set themselves against potentially domineering outsiders. Whig votes also came forth independently of influence, and were cast by many in as defiant a spirit of self-assertion as those cast by upstart Democrats. In addition, religion, culture, and place often formed the bases of subcommunities whose common values and political loyalties cut across lines of class and occupation.

Still, the power of the Whig merchant-manufacturers was a political force not to be denied. Democrats believed that "Boston influence" created an "immense disproportion in the means of influence between the two parties." Even Marcus Morton, who prided himself on knowing the reach of Whig "talents, their wealth, their discipline and their innumerable means of influence," chided himself for underestimating "their power to call forth, at their bidding, on all occasions, their whole *rank and file, volunteers,* conscripts and mercenaries." In 1837 he claimed that Whig majorities were largest in "towns of banks and other corporations." The belief that every man "who employs hired laborers will exercise a certain degree of influence over their votes" was certainly widespread.[53]

Such thinking no doubt received encouragement from the practice of small-factory owners like Jacob Dunnell of Pawtucket, Rhode Island, just across the southeastern Massachusetts border. According to a journalist who worked as a young man at the Franklin Print Works, "Jake" was an ardent Whig and on election days rounded up his employees in the counting room and marched them to the polls. "On arriving at the voting place Dunnell put a ballot into each man's hand, stationing himself at the polls for them to pass in review before him and place their ballots. One of his oldest and best employees was discharged by him for standing by his principles and voting the 'loco-foco' ticket. . . ."[54]

It is difficult to know how common this sort of thing was. The Workingmen and later the Democrats often charged that factory owners coerced their "operatives" to vote National Republican and Whig, but such complaints were not as frequent as they might have been if "Jake" Dunnell had been a representative type, and such charges were rarely specific.[55] Of course, Democrats throughout the state also owned small factories, or were merchants or lawyers to whom small farmers and artisans were indebted. Even in maritime Massachusetts, now more heavily Whig than it had been Federal, there were some Democratic shipyard owners, captains, and merchants who also employed considerable numbers of men.

More important than overt coercion was the reality that the typical small industry—and especially the successful one—often functioned on the basis of a strong community feeling. Certain families might be associated with a firm over several generations, and staunch loyalties and a sense of identity of interest could easily spill over into politics or, perhaps, permit considerable tolerance of divergent party preferences.[56]

The factories of Lowell, Waltham, Chicopee, and Lawrence were very different—yet the operation of "influence" there, and of the resistance to it, was complex. There was nothing subtle, however, about the paternalism, elitism, and Whiggery of the capitalists who built and ran the mills.

At Lowell, as in many factories, a highly patriarchal and hierarchical system prevailed, with laborers spending twelve to thirteen or more hours per day at work, living in company housing, and having what social life they had closely watched by the managers.[57] The first resident agent was Kirk Boott, a former soldier who had campaigned with the Duke of Wellington and an upper-class businessman who was as august a personage as any of the absent lords of State Street and Beacon Hill. The establishment of this man in an imposing mansion on company land as the symbol of authority at Lowell tells much about the social views of its owners. Boott's high-handedness, and reactions to it, became the stuff of early Lowell legends. Boott not only built an Episcopal church, named it after his wife, and taxed workers to support it; he also dismissed a foreman bold enough to promote a Universalist church *and* to vote for Jackson. Boott's church tax, however, raised a storm of protest and encouraged the rapid founding of new churches. On one Fourth of July, Boott raised both the American and the English flags on the pole at his residence, with the latter on top. When he refused an angry crowd's demand to reverse the flag's positions, men and boys swarmed into his yard and did it for him.[58] Obviously, many of the citizens of the town springing up around the mills refused to accept the authority of Boott and his successors, and some 40 percent of the voters rejected Whiggery in the 1830s. Later on, with defections from the Whigs to the Liberty and Free Soil parties, elections became quite closely contested.

One such election, in 1851, gave rise to charges of Whig intimidation of factory workers. These accusations were repeated throughout the state and have endured in the traditional view that within the mills Whig votes were uniformly produced by coercion whenever the will to vote Whig was absent. But in the 1830s employer-worker relations tended to be good, and though class lines were distinct, many workers identified their interests with their Whig employers'. In 1840 even some of the mill girls, like women elsewhere, named their sunbonnets "log-cabins" and went to rallies and meetings for Harrison.[59]

In the 1840s, though, as is well known, the owners' concern for their employees deteriorated, the work force itself began to change in character, and a much harsher work environment developed.[60] The political incidents of the early 1850s represented one logical culmination of these changes.

In fact, testimony before a special legislative committee investigating political coercion at Lowell tended to reveal that overt political pressure had not been common earlier. In 1851, however, in a hotly contested election requiring two ballotings, and with the balance of power in the legislature hanging on the outcome in Lowell, the agent (Linus Child) and overseers of the Boott Mill (named for the first agent, who had died in 1837) had made statements about not wanting to employ workers who voted for the Democrats and their "Ten Hour Ticket." At the Lawrence Company an overseer elected as a Democrat to the legislature had been dismissed, though Whigs so elected earlier had never been discharged. Witnesses also testified that many overseers changed their politics or became active politicians about the time of their promotion (obviously, some had previously been Democrats) and that overseers who worked on Whig committees usually received full pay while politicking on company time. Most of all, after the second election in November 1851 and just before the city election, the Whig Union Club was formed at the Lowell Corporation to advance the Whig party and to find out who "in the yard" were Whigs. Several Democrats said they had signed the club constitution and had believed they needed to do so to keep their jobs. The legislative committee thus concluded that while some overseers were not Whigs, and while in some of the units at Lowell large numbers of men opposed to the Whigs were kept on their jobs, nevertheless substance existed to the charges that *some* men had been threatened, that some had been denied work, and that some had been induced to vote for the Whigs for fear of losing employment.[61] More impressive still was the story the committee told between the lines as it piled up evidence of what might be called the implicit, informal, or "natural" coercive power of the factory and its owners.

One small detail of testimony spoke volumes about deference and politics at Lowell and elsewhere. What the Boott agent Linus Child had or had not said was the subject of much discussion by diverse witnesses, men from within the mill (overseers, machinists, operatives), and men from outside the mill (lawyers, small merchants, politicians). The in-house men referred to the agent as "the 'Squire" or " 'Squire Child," while the town men spoke of him simply as "Mr. Child."[62]

If the mills could powerfully nurture deference, the careers of Democratic politicians like Benjamin Butler or Nathaniel Banks (the former "Bobbin Boy") indicated that the factories could also breed resentment and Democrats. The flamboyant and opportunistic Butler was typical of several Democratic leaders in having served an apprenticeship as a lowly factory hand at Waltham. Goaded in part by his Scotch-Irish and Jeffersonian ancestry, the poor, handsome, ambitious, and status-conscious Butler clashed with Waltham's paternalism and grew to detest (and envy) the wealth, power, and pretensions of its managers and owners. Other men with similar reactions moved on to become not politicos but small-factory owners (and Democrats) themselves.[63]

If resentment and resistance could develop at Lowell and Waltham, it is not surprising that in the booming manufacturing town of Fall River a variety of conditions combined to reduce the Whig vote and even, in the early 1840s, to give the Democrats a slight majority or plurality.[64] One might have expected Fall River to vote strongly Whig, completely devoted as it was to textile manufacturing, shipbuilding, shipping, and fishing. Yet Fall River's industry had arisen only recently, financed by local capital, and its varied enterprises were highly decentralized. In the 1820s and 1830s, owner-worker relations were generally good, but in 1841 "a number of Operatives and others" formed the Association of Industry. They presented textile-mill owners with three demands: a shorter (ten-hour) workday, lyceums and lectures for workers, and obedience by owners and parents to an 1836 state law requiring children under fifteen to attend school at least three months of the year. In addition, Fall River lay just across Mount Hope Bay from Rhode Island, and its religious groups were diverse and numerous. In 1840 it possessed at least ten different congregations, including Methodists, Baptists, Catholics, and Universalists. Perhaps as pure a young manufacturing town as one could find in Massachusetts, Fall River contained many social ingredients for a closely competitive politics. The Whigs certainly did not take the votes of Fall River factory workers for granted; in 1840 they waited until evening, when the shops had emptied, to deliver campaign speeches.[65]

There were at least two kinds of male factory workers eligible to vote—the unskilled and semiskilled "operatives," and the skilled mechanics, at least some of whom were middle or lower-middle class. A number of the latter were English and Scotch immigrants who tended to identify with the managers and with the British-American aura of Whiggery. In the mid-1830s, for example, there were some 300 skilled workers in the machine shops at Lowell, who lived in housing set apart from the workers' dormitories and also from the managers' homes.[66] Unfortunately, information is lacking with which to make reliable estimates.

Too rare is the information contained in an 1844 explanation of the Dudley (Worcester County) Whig chairman as to why the Whig vote had declined in his town: from the loss of Whigs to the "Abolitionists," he said, and from "the failure of the Duley Manufacturing Company, where a few years ago every voter but one or two (say from 20 to 25 voters) were Whigs. Since the suspension of business in that village, the tenements have rented low, and consequently many of them to our political opponents."[67]

Another rare glimpse of factory workers' political preferences in one town survives in the report of the Whig chairman of Lancaster in 1844, which listed the town's thirteen school districts and estimated the number of voters in four categories:

| *No.* | | *Whig* | *Democratic* | *Abolitionist* | *Doubtful* |
|---|---|---|---|---|---|
| 1 | Almshouse | 3 | 12 | 1 | 1 |
| 2 | Sodi Sanderson | 4 | 10 | | |
| 3 | Oliver Hahnam | 10 | 9 | 1 | 3 |
| 4 | Ballard Hill | 20 | 14 | | 3 |
| 5 | North Village | 23 | 7 | | 4 |
| 6 | E. side of Neck | 23 | 1 | 3 | 5 |
| 7 | George Hill | 21 | 2 | 1 | |
| 8 | Old Common | 7 | 4 | | |
| 9 | Deer Horn | 14 | 5 | 2 | |
| 10 | *Factory* | 43 | 10 | 16 | 4 |
| 11 | South Woods | 5 | 13 | 2 | 5 |
| 12 | New Boston | 45 | 7 | 2 | 2 |
| 13 | Center | 32 | 7 | 7 | 3 |
| | Total | 253 | 101 | 35 | 31 |

The largest number of voters were in No. 10, the "Factory" district, which would soon become the industrial town of Clinton. It voted strongly Whig and had the most Liberty party voters, suggesting a high degree of independence among its factory workers. "New Boston" also contained mills and also was strongly Whig. The "Center" and "North Village" districts were probably the two most commercial areas–the latter was on the road to Boston and consisted of a cluster of taverns and artisans servicing travelers and stages; both voted Whig, and the "Center" district also contained seven "Abolitionists." Districts 1 to 4 were in the north part of town, generally agricultural and sparsely populated by small farmers, and were far more Democratic than was the rest of Lancaster. Indeed, the only Democratic district in the lower half was No. 11, "South Woods," a rural district populated in part by Baptists and Universalists. The major church in the "Factory" district in 1844 was Orthodox, with fifty-one members.[68]

Thus it seems evident, whenever it is possible to look inside towns at neighborhoods, local networks, and subcommunities, that more than "influence" and economic interest are needed to explain partisan loyalties. Networks of influence and interest were in fact frequently crosscut by religious and cultural divisions.

### Religion and Party Division

> In contrast to class, status is necessarily a matter of consciousness since it is dependent on beliefs; and status groups can be defined as communities held together by common values. They are in fact membership reference groups fulfilling normative functions for their members. Whereas class politics—or, to adopt an American term, "cultural politics"—are not. Their modes are conditioned by the general ideological influences prevalent in society. In Victorian England the clash of life styles was most distinctively characterized by religious and quasi-religious differences. Despite the evidence of secularization, it was these rather than class divisions which did most to mould political consciousness.[69]

As the new party of the Center, Whiggery quite naturally appealed to the state's original Congregational majority, though that population was much reduced by defections and divided internally between Unitarians and Orthodox.[70] The minority of Congregationalists who were Democrats formed an even more important group in the opposition than they had done in the Federal period, and individual Unitarians and Trinitarians were often Democratic leaders. But it is hardly surprising that most Congregationalists throughout the era of party formation (1800–1840), despite various internecine feuds, usually aligned themselves with the parties which grew almost organically from the core culture of Massachusetts Bay. Henry Cabot Lodge once called the Federalists "the Puritan party," and he might have said the same of the Whigs. The Federal and Whig parties both expressed the ancient Puritan concern for society as a corporate whole; both attempted to use the government to provide for society's moral and material development. However fraught with inconsistency these attempts might be, they nevertheless contrasted with the Jeffersonian Republican and Democratic defense of individual rights, libertarian values, localism, and weak government.

The minority party was still the party of dissent, but in 1840 religious differentiation was many times what it had been, religious group relations were very complex, and political-religious tendencies were far less predictable. Some of the traditional kinds of religious antagonisms, however, still undergirded the Center-Periphery division. There persisted a significant overlap of militant sectarianism, lower social status, and anti-Whig politics.

An embarrassing fact of life for historians of nineteenth-century politics is that while they have discovered that religion counted for very much in politics, it is almost impossible to measure precisely religious affiliation among the electorate.[71] The religious identifications of individual voters are exceedingly difficult to come by, and available data relating to civil units or denominations usually permit only the grossest kinds of estimates about the proportions of various groups in towns or counties. Historians have made do with estimates based on the number of church seats recorded in the 1850 census, with information from random local sources, or simply with the number of churches known to be in individual towns.[72] Researchers working with lists of individual voters normally find it much easier to discover the occupations or relative wealth of individuals.

For the historian wishing to ascertain the religious character of the electorate in Massachusetts in 1840, the basic facts are these: the number and kinds of churches in a town can usually be determined; unorganized religious societies are more difficult to find and are often omitted from official sources; some denominations' counts of their members and churches are available (these records sometimes contain minor errors, but a more serious problem is that different denominations used different criteria of membership and that only some made discriminations as to the sex of the members and none as to age); and, finally, except in rare cases it is almost impossible to reckon the number of adult males of each denomination who were not members or "communicants" but who were in the much larger group of affiliates, regular Sunday attenders, or otherwise identifiers with particular churches. It is, in short, nearly impossible using town data to calculate accurately, for an entire county or several sample counties, say, the percentages of each denomination represented in the electorate (see Appendix XII.B). Given the "softness," indeed the simple absence, of data, it is not feasible to include an inevitably artificial religious variable in statistical analysis, particularly in multiple regression.[73]

It is essential, on the other hand, to recognize that, while most adult males were not "members" or "communicants," religion nevertheless was of great social and political importance in antebellum Massachusetts.[74] The political relevance of religion is especially apparent in local sources, township histories, church annals, and the biographies of average citizens. The central tendencies of these myriad clues may be grasped in the way certain denominations functioned as social reference groups and thereby influenced the way religious groups aligned with political parties.

Unitarianism, for example, was politically significant and broadly symbolic because it was the religion of the Whig establishment's inner circles. Unitarianism was prevalent among Boston's upper classes and the elite who set the tone of fashionable society. Leading intellectuals also tended to be Unitarian. The philosophers of Harvard stressed the same themes of "moral paternalism" and the harmony of economic interest that were found in Whig ideology, and while too secular for Orthodox tastes, the Unitarians retained the "old Puritan sense of corporate moral responsibility." Though most Unitarian congregations could be found in eastern Massachusetts, some were scattered through central and western counties, usually in towns exhibiting middle-class and urban values. Unitarians were thus almost always impeccably respectable and usually Whig.[75] But, more important, they were associated with wealth, power, and secularism. In the 1830s and 1840s many Orthodox and other citizens continued to distrust the Unitarians as a powerful, exclusive, and domineering elite.[76]

The Orthodox Congregationalists obviously no longer possessed the power they had once enjoyed, but they were still an important reference group, especially in central and western counties. Their stubborn adherence to rigid moralism gave them a sense of being an embattled minority struggling to preserve the true Puritan past. As one aggressive Orthodox leader said of his ministry in antebellum Lynn, where Methodism was particularly strong, "Mine heritage is unto me as a speckled bird; the birds round about me are against her." On the other hand, Orthodox militancy and evangelicalism irritated and embarrassed Unitarians. The Orthodox held frequent revivals and agitated against drinking, dancing, vulgar popular amusements, travel on Sunday, and all forms of idleness and immorality as they defined them. Though the Whig party included many rich and poor men who rejected puritanical standards and embraced permissive or hedonistic life-styles, most Orthodox backed the Whig party as the lesser of two evils. In certain localities Whiggery well reflected Orthodox concern for moral issues and benevolent reform.[77]

In Worcester County and in the Connecticut Valley, time seemed to have left untouched the alliance between Orthodoxy and the Center party. In many towns the ministers, respectable farmers, merchants, and political leaders frequently were Orthodox and Whig, and if not Whig then at least not Democratic. State representatives and other officials all seemed to be deacons in the First Church.[78]

As the relations of Congregationalists to one another and to parties had changed, though, so the social position and politics of "dissenters" had grown more complex. The earlier pattern of overwhelming Baptist and Methodist support for the party of the Periphery had not survived. A significant minority of Baptists, in particular, had become Whigs, according to William G. McLoughlin.[79] Yet in 1840 the leading Democratic town in the state was Baptist Cheshire in Berkshire County, and the Baptists formed an important pressure group within the Democratic party. Isaac

Davis of Worcester, a Baptist leader, was a key Democrat in state councils and eventually would be nominated for governor. During the 1839–1840 struggle over the creation of the state board of education, Baptist leaders complained to Davis that Horace Mann, the Whig promoter of the board, did not have any regard for Baptist interests (though Mann was a graduate of Baptist Brown University):

> The interests of education in this country are in other hands than the Baptists. . . . If Horace Mann obtains complete control of the educational concern in Massachusetts Dr. Wayland [President of Brown] may whistle for students as the sailors do for a breeze in a calm. . . . We must take care of ourselves. For myself, I have no idea of bowing down to the Unitarians. . . .[80]

Yet Baptists were no longer the "outsiders" they had been in most communities. The Universalists, rather, were now the classic sectarian radicals in the forefront of anticlericalism and controversy, creating a stir by denying hell and damnation and promulgating universal salvation. They challenged both the social snobbery of the Unitarians and the evangelical meddling of the Trinitarians and often criticized the Baptists for joining in "evangelical demogoguery" with the Orthodox. They had experienced much harassment under the old order, and up to 1833 no sect had called more consistently for an end to the establishment. Their 20 churches in 1820 grew to over 140 in 1840, most of them in eastern Massachusetts and almost none in the Connecticut Valley.[81] Universalism "sought 'the common people' . . . cared little for social distinctions . . . for ecclesiastical precedents or establishments; for the prestige given to churches by educational institutions, or wealth . . . it would make its appeals to the masses." The Universalists were as natural allies for the anticlerical Democrats as the Baptists had been for the Jeffersonians thirty years earlier.[82]

The Universalist preacher Abner Kneeland had come to Boston in the early 1830s, helped found a group called the First Society of Inquirers, and began to publish a journal, the *Boston Investigator,* whose rank rationalism and pantheism brought a flush to the faces of many pious Bostonians. After publishing editorials expressing his disbelief in the God of the Unitarians and Trinitarians, Kneeland was indicted for blasphemy and tried before a Federal-Whig judge in January 1834. By November 1835 he had been tried four times and Democrats had provided lawyers for his defense and were championing his cause in public writings. David Henshaw proclaimed it a disgrace to the age that the courts were sustaining a criminal prosecution "for a matter of mere speculative theology." When the supreme judicial court affirmed his conviction, Marcus Morton dissented, holding that for his private opinions and practices a man "is answerable to his God alone." Although many Unitarian Whigs privately opposed Kneeland's conviction, the state's attorney general supported it and the governor's council refused a petition for a pardon. The Boston Democrats squeezed the case for all the antipatrician, anti-Unitarian, and anti-Whig capital it afforded them, but the Orthodox evangelicals seem to have been the most punitive toward Kneeland.[83]

While some Universalists might be found who voted Whig, or later Liberty party, most Universalist enclaves voted decisively Democratic. Universalism was strong in the peripheral eastern counties, particularly Bristol and Middlesex, which produced many Democratic votes, and several of the stronger Democratic towns in the east were centers of Universalism and dissent.[84] The two most Democratic towns in the upper Connecticut Valley, Monroe (85 percent) and Erving (71 percent) in Franklin County, were both tiny hill towns with populations of 254 and 309, respectively, and both were hives of Universalism.[85]

That Unitarianism and Universalism stood at opposite political poles is confirmed by lists of individual voters which happen to be available for three towns in 1840.[86] Since the lists are all from the same county, they are not representative of the rest of the state, but what they reveal fits with the above generalizations. These data also show the importance of local context in setting party alignments.

When the Whig State Central Committee sent forth the order in the 1840 campaign for the town committees to assemble lists of voters and their party preference, they met with an apparently enthusiastic response from Worcester County. Two such lists, at any rate, have survived for the Worcester towns of Northborough and Harvard. Coincidentally, a partial list of taxpayers for the town of Sutton, indicating party preferences, has also surfaced. The Sutton list contains 121 names, amounting to just one-fourth of those voting in the 1840 gubernatorial election; the Harvard and Northborough lists contain almost all the voters in those towns:

| | *Harvard* | *Northborough* | *Sutton* |
|---|---|---|---|
| Number on list | 295 | 243 | 121 |
| Total vote 1840(G) | 302 | 235 | 469 |
| Whig vote | 159 | 187 | 209 |
| Whigs listed | 142 | 174 | 35 |
| Democratic vote | 139 | 48 | 260 |
| Democrats listed | 122 | 37 | 67 |
| Doubtful listed | 31 | 24 | 17 |
| Other votes | 5 | — | — |
| Populations 1840 | 1,571 | 1,224 | 2,370 |

The kind of information available for these individual voters varied. Some measure of relative wealth as indicated by tax lists was most common, while their religious affiliations proved difficult to ascertain. In Harvard, for example, tax-assessment information was found for 248 of the 295 men listed, while religion was found for 116. Yet informed guesses can be made on the basis of family names, and in every town definite patterns appeared in the religious data, usually along predictable lines.

Harvard was a typically small agricultural town, famous as a site of some highly untypical social experimentation. Later in the 1840s the Alcotts and others would try to establish the utopian community of "Fruitlands" there, and meanwhile in 1840 a community of 150 to 200 Shakers had been thriving for some time. But these subcommunities did not really intersect with town life, except when intolerant mobs harassed the Shakers. In 1840 the Whig party chairman reported that there were "26 [eligible] voters among the Shakers who do not vote in elections." Thus Harvard's electorate was basically like that found in many of the state's small towns.[87]

There were no extremes of wealth in Harvard, or, rather, there were relatively few rich men. Most voters were middling or lower-middling farmers, and there was a contingent of village artisans and others who worked in small industries. The population was almost entirely native-born. The original church had divided in the 1820s, as in so many towns, when the Orthodox or Trinitarians withdrew from the town's first Congregational church, which had become predominantly Unitarian. By 1840, too, there were also Baptist, Methodist, and Universalist congregations. Diverse in religion, Harvard was closely divided in its party voting, usually giving a Democratic vote in these years, but by a very slight majority.

Whigs and Democrats of Harvard differed little in age, occupation, and relative wealth. Whigs ranked slightly higher, perhaps, on the tax-assessment rolls, but by very little.

Harvard Whigs and Democrats Ranked by Tax Assessment:

| | *Whigs* | | *Dems.* | |
|---|---|---|---|---|
| | *No.* | *%*[a] | *No.* | *%*[a] |
| $ 1– 4.99 | 57 | 43 | 50 | 44 |
| 5– 9.99 | 35 | 26 | 28 | 25 |
| 10–14.99 | 17 | 13 | 25 | 22 |
| 15–19.99 | 16 | 12 | 5 | 4 |
| 20–24.99 | 5 | 4 | 3 | 3 |
| 25–29.99 | 2 | 2 | 2 | 2 |
| 30–34.99 | 1 | 1 | | |
| 35–39.99 | | | 1 | 1 |
| 50–54.99 | 1 | 1 | | |

[a] Percentages are rounded off.

Slightly more Whigs engaged in nonagricultural occupations (30 percent to 24 percent), and among those listed by name as proprietors of manufacturing establishments in the 1833 *Report on Manufactures,* Whigs clearly outnumbered Democrats.[88] But the sharpest differences appeared in the religious affiliations of the two groups. Definite identifications for some denominations are not numerous enough to be significant alone, but Orthodox-Whig and Universalist-Democratic associations are abundantly apparent:

| | *Whigs* | *Democrats* | *Doubtful* |
|---|---|---|---|
| Orthodox | 35 | 17 | 10 |
| Unitarian | 3 | — | — |
| Methodist | 3 | 2 | — |
| Baptist | 5 | — | — |
| Universalist | 7 | 31 | 3 |
| Total | 53 | 50 | 13 |

The ministers of the Orthodox, Unitarian, and Baptist churches were all Whigs, and chances are that most of those active in the Unitarian congregation–the town's original church–were Whigs and that some were Democrats. The Baptists, despite what is shown above, were probably split between the parties, but, like the Unitarians, they also had a decided Whig tendency.[89]

The political ecology of Northborough, on the other hand, was quite different. This preponderantly Whig town possessed all the hallmarks of urban values and middle-class moralism, religion, and respectability which tended to accompany Whig majorities. Democrats made up a small minority and were decidedly a poorer, lower-status group. Fewer of the Democrats had been born in Northborough (22 percent as opposed to 39 percent), and fewer of them lived there in 1850. Whigs dominated the town's political and economic leadership, including the owners of a small cotton mill and of a comb-manufacturing business. The president of the Whig Association was Captain Cyrus Gale, proprietor of a general store, landowner, and entrepreneur, who was on his way to becoming the town's most influential citizen. Nine other officers of the Whig Association were either wealthy farmers, manufacturers, or artisans, and most of them were Orthodox Congregationalists, or connected with the First Church. These men and the town were already strongly committed to temperance and would become increasingly antisouthern and hostile to slavery during the 1840s.[90]

Respectability, moralism, and Whiggery thus formed a powerful trinity in Northborough, and the religious identifications of voters reflected the fact:

| | Whigs | Democrats | Doubtful |
|---|---|---|---|
| Orthodox | 19 | — | — |
| Unitarian | 26 | 3 | — |
| Baptist | 11 | 10 | 2 |

Though preponderantly Congregational, Whigs garnered support in all of the town's major religious groups and in all economic groups. The Democrats and "Doubtfuls" did not rise much above the lower-middle-class level and also tended to be younger. While majorities of all three were *not* born in Northborough, this was true of 61 percent of the Whigs but of 78 percent of the Democrats and 79 percent of the "Doubtfuls." Although slightly more Democrats than Whigs worked in manufacturing, most of these Democrats were probably factory operatives. The Northborough Whigs definitely constituted the in-group in this "proud," prosperous town, while Democrats were a low-status minority of outsiders.

The town of Sutton provided still another pattern of political ecology. This was a solidly, though not overwhelmingly, Democratic town located in southeastern Worcester County's cluster of Democratic towns near the Rhode Island border. As in Harvard, Whigs and Democrats were much more alike than different in relative wealth, occupation, and general condition. A few more of the Democrats did tend to cluster in the lower ranges of wealth and occupation, and at least seven Democratic voters, but only two Whigs, appear to have been propertyless factory hands.[91]

Yet Democrats were also well represented in the town's elite, and included the wealthy lawyer Jonas L. Sibley, whose father had been a state legislator and congressman for many years, and whom President Jackson had appointed U.S. marshal of Boston. Most of the Congregationalists on the list were Whigs (sixteen of twenty-one), and so was the Baptist minister. But many of the family names associated with the town's Baptist church were Democrats, and Baptist families were among the most venerable and prestigious in town.[92]

Thus, these findings tend to confirm patterns already observed in the aggregate data. Many more such lists of individual voters could be wished for and would no doubt reveal other variations arising from local context and historical circumstance. Yet the strength of religious, status, and economic group divisions in separating Whigs and Democrats seems well established by both aggregate and individual data.

### Whig Hegemony: Respectability and Morality

In the heyday of Whig-Democratic politics, the most important political dynamics still centered on the symbolic relations between native Protestant religious and status groups. Non-Protestant and nonnative groups had not yet made a significant impact on political alignments, though they were present, to be sure, and were voting in small numbers. The Democrats commanded the almost total loyalty of the Catholic Irish immigrants who were just beginning to be a political factor in Boston, Worcester, Lowell, and elsewhere. Indeed, some Irish Catholics had been casting votes for General Jackson as early as 1828 in Boston, and while they already aroused deep-seated nativist fear and animosity, in the 1830s and 1840s they were not yet a critical reference group in the state's politics.[93] In the early 1850s a new assertiveness on the part of the Irish Catholics would become enormously important in the breakup of the Whigs and the formation of the Know-Nothing and Republican parties, as would national events. But before then the most politically significant social divisions were among native Protestants–divisions which tended to cut through individual churches, regions, classes, and occupations.

In the late 1830s and 1840s, Whig dominance of Massachusetts rested on an alliance of respectability and morality. After 1840 the minority of highly religious and moral men who gravitated toward antislavery would take some of the strength of "morality" away from Whiggery, but not until the Free Soilers and Democrats agreed to a coalition in 1850 would the Whigs lose the state. Yet the alliance of respectability and morality was always uneasy, and the loyalty of "moral" Whigs always uncertain. Indeed, in the late 1830s the alliance had faltered and caused the defeat of a Whig governor in an episode which revealed much in its broad outline and resolution concerning the Whig coalition.

A powerful temperance movement had emerged in the 1820s, drawing heavily on evangelical religion in the same way that Antimasonry and antislavery would. Not all evangelicals participated in or supported these movements, but most of their active leaders were pious Christians devoted to improving society's morals, and many of the same men turned up in temperance, antislavery, and Antimasonic circles.

The extensive consumption of alcohol was a reality in the 1820s. It prevailed in all classes of society and on all manner of occasions. Drinking was common not only at funerals, weddings, birthdays, militia musters, elections, barn raisings, and public celebrations, but even at church raisings and ministers' ordinations. It was traditional, also, for employers to provide strong drink at sites were men labored hard throughout the day with their hands or backs, whether Irish "navies" digging a canal or Yankee carpenters and caulkers in shipyards. Indeed, one historian recently estimated that in the period 1790–1830 Americans consumed more alcohol "than ever before or since."[94]

As the temperance movement became more aggressive, the antitemperance reaction grew apace. By the 1830s controversy had become acrimonious, sometimes violent; inevitably it entered politics, focusing at first on the election of selectmen, then on that of county commissioners (made elective in 1835, partly because of the temperance issue). In a number of towns and counties the temperance forces won "no license" rulings, which removed the sanction of local government from drink selling but did not stop selling or drinking.[95]

By 1837–1838 the temperance army had turned its attention fully to the legislature and to elections of state representative. Fervor at town meetings, a flood of tracts, and an avalanche of petitions to the legislature won passage of the "fifteen-gallon law," which banned the retail sale of ardent spirits in any quantity less than fifteen gallons. Opponents denounced it on many grounds, including that of class bias: the Beacon Hill and Chestnut Street gentry would have no difficulty keeping their wine cellars well stocked, while the poor laborer and farmer would have to do without any of the comforts of the grape or grain. Yet the issue divided class and status groups, and opponents included wealthy lawyers and merchants besides those distillers, grocers, and others who profited from the trade. Churches were also divided, but prominent Unitarians and anti-evangelicals were especially active among opponents, and Orthodox leaders and evangelicals conspicuous among prohibitionists.[96]

The 1838 "spirit law" would not go into effect until the next year, so the next legislative elections became in many places a struggle between "temperance" forces and "liberals" or "wets." The contest was fought mainly within Whig ranks, but the Democrats did not sit by idly; they threw their weight onto the scale to defeat any efforts at compromise, and were pleased to see the bill pass and the responsibility for it fall on Whig shoulders. Governor Edward Everett, with many misgivings and expecting the worst, gloomily signed it. His pessimism was warranted: in November he lost the executive's chair to Marcus Morton, elected by a majority of one out of the total vote cast.[97]

A number of unpopular acts of the legislature and a surging Democratic party contributed to Everett's defeat. But among Whig politicos it rapidly became accepted as gospel that the temperance law had caused their party's defeat. Many Whig town chairmen of Worcester County, for example, identified the temperance law as the issue most injurious to the Whigs in 1839. Yet their estimates of how many votes this cost them through nonvoting or defections were remarkably low.[98] To be sure, in a close election a switch of 1 percent is enough, and 5 percent may be considered large. It seems possible, too, that Whig party leaders focused blame on the fifteen-gallon law as a justification for removing the drinking question from politics. In any event, the fifteen-gallon law was soon abrogated by a new Whig legislature and a Democratic governor, and the Orthodox and evangelicals decided they would rather do without a state temperance law than live with a Democrat in the governor's chair.[99]

In the gubernatorial election of 1840 the Whigs swept back into state power, electing "Honest John" Davis once more as governor, then re-electing him in a low turnout the next year. In 1842 the Liberty party began to draw off voters from both major parties, but especially from the Whigs. Both parties were also racked by internal quarrels over patronage and personalities; out of the crosscurrents at work Marcus Morton managed to win a plurality that year, and the legislature, in which the antislavery men held the balance of power, elected him governor once again. The views of Morton with respect to religious toleration and moral coercion were well known. Elected lieutenant governor with him was Dr. Henry H. Childs of Pittsfield, one of those eternal Berkshire campaigners for religious liberalism who had opposed the religious establishment back in the constitutional convention of 1820. Though himself a Congregationalist, Childs was a typical anticlerical representative of the ancient Berkshire Periphery.[100]

During Morton's second term as governor, the Whigs and Democrats squared off against one another in the legislature and engaged in bruising two-party combat. In 1843 the number of roll-call votes reached an all-time high as Democrats, in control of the senate but with an uncertain house, seized the first opportunity they had ever had to enact some of their program. In the meanwhile, factional infighting plagued both major parties; David Henshaw again arose to trouble the Democrats, and the Whigs disagreed over national policy, especially over Daniel Webster and his electability to the presidency. On the state level, however, the Whig grandees patched up their differences and united behind a compromise candidate for governor, the western Massachusetts congressman George Nixon Briggs.

Historians have tended to ignore Briggs, and Ralph Waldo Emerson found him unfit to lead: "An excellent middle man; he looks well when speaking, and seems always just ready to say something good, but never said anything; he is an orateur manqué." Despite the fact that Briggs was elected for eight terms from 1843 to 1850, during a time when the Democrats were strong nationally and the Whigs were buffeted within by different factions and weakened by defections to the Liberty party, historians too seem to have written off Briggs as an amiable figurehead. Yet Briggs's importance lay precisely in what he symbolized, and in the fact that his personal style, deportment, and values suited the Whig coalition very well. His election also marked the coming of age of the Whig/Center party in the era of mass political parties.[101]

Briggs was the first "dissenter" ever elevated to the chief executive's chair by the party of the Center or, for that matter, by any party. His father was a Baptist "mechanic" and his mother a Quaker who raised him in western Massachusetts and northern New England in humble circumstances. As a youth Briggs was apprenticed to a Quaker hatter for three years, and the influence of his mother and the hatter stayed with him throughout his life, disposing him to a simplicity of dress and lack of social pretension. Briggs himself, as was common knowledge at the time, was an ardent Baptist and a founder of the church in Lanesboro, Berkshire County, which he made his home. Though zealous for religion, Briggs was able to gain the trust and friendship of pious men in other churches, and of a political man like Henry Shaw, the prominent National Republican who made Briggs his protégé. Thus, if a minority of the Baptists had already gone over to the Whigs, Brigg's candidacies probably confirmed these political conversions and perhaps encouraged others.[102]

The party of "religion" might lack a state temperance law, but they had Briggs in the chief executive's chair. When in 1844 he took up residence in Boston, Briggs went straight to the Marlboro Hotel, the one "fashionable" hotel in the city distinguished by its strict adherence to temperance and by the piety of its guests. Friends loved to tell about the time when Briggs had been asked, long before, whether he was a "teetotaller," and about his cheerful answer "I should say I was." Religious journals frequently praised this man who habitually wore a black stock without a collar and who in Washington on state occasions wore homespun. He was, they said, the model of a Christian citizen.[103]

At the same time Briggs was soundly orthodox in matters of political economy. As a National Republican and a Whig, he loyally supported the tariff and a national bank, and was moderate on matters touching the sensibilities of the South, not to mention those of Massachusetts textile manufacturers. But Briggs was very unlike the Whig leaders who had preceded him in the governor's chair—the intellectual Everett, the bourgeois lawyer Davis, or, before that, the "old school" Lincoln, all of whom had ties to the upper class and who were patricians or self-made gentry themselves. More than his Whig predecessors or his Democratic rivals, more indeed, than any man who was president during this era, Briggs was also a Common Man.[104]

Briggs lost few opportunities to reminisce about his and his father's backgrounds as "humble mechanics." His articulation of the central Whig doctrine of the "harmony of interests" might be clumsy and might ring somewhat hollow now, as when he told the Massachusetts Mechanics Association that he would not "unjustly elevate the mechanic at the expense of his brethren in the community. To talk of mechanics as a class and to undertake to give them the preference to, and set them above, all other classes, he knew his intelligent hearers would regard as an insult. . . . There was no test class in our community. It was false to pretend that one existed."[105] But Briggs needed no eloquence (most of his contemporaries and associates thought him an excellent extemporaneous speaker) when his person would suffice. He himself testified to the harmony" and to the rewards possible for a life, however humble in origins, of religion, perseverance, and sobriety.

**PART THREE**

# Conclusion: *Parties, Policy and Democracy*

## XIII. Parties and Policy: The Party Ethos: Parties as Institutions

When in 1811 a Federal Central Committee circular had fallen into Republican hands, opposition newspapers had pounced on the document and published it throughout the state, accompanied by charges of conspiracy, party despotism, secret cabal, and the like. When in 1841 a Whig State Committee circular came into Democratic hands, a Whig county committeeman reassured a worried friend that it contained nothing but directions for the "usual form of party organization," and since all of its recommendations were "honorable and open" its possession by their opponents, while undesirable, could do the Whigs no harm.[1] The two incidents reveal much about the changed milieu in which parties operated, as does the structure and outward operation of the convention system, whatever its inner workings and centers of power. In an environment far more receptive to fixed organization, the new mass parties blended together old and new political forms, as they evolved gradually into institutions distinct from the impermanent and furtive Federal and Republican parties.

The most obvious difference between the earlier and later periods is reflected in the contrast between what the Federalists and Republicans called "exertions," in reference to ad hoc efforts to influence elections, and what might accurately be termed the "campaigning" engaged in by Whigs and Democrats. The latter threw themselves into sustained pre-election activities that lasted for weeks and even months and that brought some of them to the point of exhaustion.

Men of talent, reputation, and eloquence came into great demand in that oratorical age, and it is difficult to imagine Federal patricians campaigning in the manner of the New Bedford Whig John H. Clifford, a court judge who was himself a cultured and learned man. After the 1839 election, nevertheless, Clifford said he had never worked harder in his life: *"Every night,* save Sundays, I speak literally, for three weeks previous to the election . . . I devoted myself to meetings of the committee and meetings of the party." In 1840 Clifford labored even harder, giving speeches constantly in the weeks before the election, "driving about from Dan to Beersheba 'sleeping in unaccustomed beds,' and making speeches of unreasonable length, breaking up ordinary habits, keeping the system alternately excited and chilled, taking a succession of colds, and using desperate remedies to fight them off." Another Whig leader spoke so frequently that by October 3 his health had "broken down" and he was "under the physician's hands."[2]

Amasa Walker, on the Democratic side, could well sympathize. After making a maiden impromptu speech at a Democratic convention at Springfield, he received some seventy-five to a hundred invitations to speak on the subject of a national bank and he spoke in so many places that he "brought on a severe bronchial attack which lasted for many months." Clifford's good friend Robert Winthrop was also going at a furious pace: in mid-October he went into Worcester County and made "two speeches of two hours each, one at Dudley, and the other at Southbridge."[3]

Democrats like Bancroft, Rantoul, and Hallett were also in great demand. Observing the "zealous exertions" of political leaders in 1838, Bancroft's *Bay State Democrat* had exhorted young men to give more of their time and means to politics: "THEY MUST MAKE A BUSINESS OF POLITICS." And the next year, glimpsing victory for the first time, the *Democrat* cried out for "AGITATION-ACTION." "AGITATION is what is wanted . . . to secure the democratic cause. Agitation by the press—agitation by Lectures and addresses—agitation by the people at home, and abroad, *among the people,* in conversation in the villages, in the fields and by the road side."[4]

This frenzied activity was part of the new mode of politics, of a changed political culture. The political leaders were generals and lieutenants mustering battalions to march on the ballot boxes. They were revivalists and itinerants preaching the threat of the devil adversary and the hope of salvation in the party's victory.

Though less conspicuously, money as a fuel for campaigns moved up a long notch in its steady rise throughout the history of American politics. It had always been important—it took money to set up printing presses and to pay editors or printers. The 1840 campaign, however, marked a new high in efforts devoted to party fund raising per se and in expenditures. Earlier raising and spending of funds had been sporadic and informal.

Now funds were raised for "the Whig Party" of Worcester or Salem or wherever, and a standing official of the party handled accounts. Furthermore, a campaign like the "Log Cabin" extravaganza, with its parades and profusion of paraphernalia, meant the sprouting of a great range of opportunities and jobs for artisans, merchants, provisioners, and service men. As a presidential primary today means treasure pouring into a state for a time, so the holding of a convention in a town meant employment and profit for many of its citizens. Increasingly, "the party" was the raiser and dispenser of money for campaign purposes.[5]

In making nominations, Whigs and Democrats used party loyalty more explicitly as a criterion than Federalists and Republicans had done before them. Parties and factions of all kinds, of whatever degree of institutionalization, are always pulled in at least two contrary directions: toward nominating moderates of the Center and toward choosing loyalists conspicuous for their party views or actions. Federalists and Republicans experienced this kind of internal struggle, of course, but they conceived of it more as a choice between moderate or extreme "principles," and more or less "consistency" of action on those principles, views, or doctrines. Whigs and Democrats spoke explicitly about loyalty to the party and emphasized it as a virtue—at least, they did so in private communications.[6] Party loyalty was not yet celebrated publicly as a qualification for office to the degree that it would be later in the century.

In discussions of patronage, however, which party leaders usually held privately, party loyalty and "service" to the party were now invoked explicitly and frequently. Aspirants to office and their supporters would offer as evidence of qualification service as a delegate to party conventions or as a chairman of a town or county party committee.[7] Again, however, office seekers did not always stress party criteria, or they did so indirectly; some intimated that they did not think it proper to do so, though they usually assumed that their fidelity was in fact known. More important, while still exercising some restraint in the apportioning of state offices, Whigs and Democrats brought a spoils-system mentality most uninhibitedly to federal offices, such as the profitable and powerful customshouses and large post offices.[8]

In the state legislature, too, parties appear to have been well developed and taken for granted by the late 1830s. Earlier, Antimasons and localism had seemed to make for considerable confusion, or at least unpredictability, in the legislature's behavior. But from 1834 to 1837 the consolidation of a coherent Democratic minority did much to advance the acceptance of party competition as a normal way of doing business.

Democratic voting solidarity apparently rose during the decade. In 1835 the Democratic press and many conventions repeatedly sang the praises of "the Spartan band" of Democratic legislators who opposed Whig attempts to create more "monied corporations" and more privileges for the commercial aristocracy. Yet the following year the Whig Speaker of the house reported privately to a colleague that in the session just past "scarcely any questions [were] decided by party votes."[9] Whatever truth may be attributed to this remark, it is certain that by 1837 the Democratic minority had grown and that party considerations influenced much, perhaps most, of the legislature's activity. In 1839 a Whig speaker could complain of the completely partisan behavior of a united Democratic bloc of 170 acting as a unit "throwing their weight alternately into either scale which would embarass us most . . . always at their post, always united, and making a party affair of everything that was proposed."[10]

Even more significant was the same Whig Speaker's defense of his actions in the 1839 legislature in regard to appointments to committees and chairmanships. Stung by charges in Democratic newspapers that he had packed the house standing committees wholly with Whigs, Robert C. Winthrop defended himself in detail against the "unfair" accusations. The Committee on Public Lands, for example, contained not three Whigs but "1 Tory to 2 Whigs—(*precisely the proportion* . . . which they claim as their right)"; County Estimates had not five Whigs, as charged, but one Tory "and 1 gentleman of an amphibious character, who could perhaps fairly be entered 'neither party.' " The point was that all down the line Winthrop had followed a rule of trying to let, when possible, the standing and special committees reflect the general proportions of party in the house —in this case the Democrats being one-third of the whole. Thus he gave them as close to one-third without giving them more in whole numbers— this generally came to 1 to 2, 2 to 5, or 4 to 10, since committees normally consisted of three, seven, or fourteen members.

Winthrop said that to 350 places on special committees he had named at least "80 Tories," nearly one-fourth of the whole, and had appointed 10 Tory chairmen (he named each one) to special committees "(hear it not *ye palace* Whigs)." If Whigs had somewhat more than their share of appointments, it was due in part to their predominance and to his "greater familiarity with the persons and personal character of the Whigs." Winthrop noted that "there were an unusual number of *new* members in the House this year. Out of 530 or 540 probably not more than 120 ever were in the legislature before." He could easily guess the "political complexion" of members coming from large towns. "But what could anybody know, during the first ten days of a session, of the exact party character of the 250 little towns which make up the rest of the Commonwealth."[11] Thus, while the Democrats had garnered only one-seventh of the 131 places on standing committees, he believed his Whig predecessor had not allowed very much more—"so far as my knowledge of party men and party names allows me to judge."[12]

Winthrop's defense revealed the growing importance of party as a framework for legislative business, but its most important aspect was probably that it was written at all. It was significant that the Democrats' charges of partiality hurt his sensibilities. Though he believed the charges politically inspired, Winthrop nevertheless was agitated by the Democrats' claiming that he had not abided by two-party norms. His reaction could happen only in a situation of role expectations in which the majority party's leaders had certain responsibilities toward the minority party.

Whereas Federalists and Republicans had been deadly serious about their political differences—literally so in the murder of young Austin by Thomas Selfridge in 1806—Whig and Democratic leaders treated politics as more of a game. To be sure, there were real stakes, and party loyalties created a good deal of animosity and conflict that carried over into other areas of life, but extensive ties between Whigs and Democrats existed in business and voluntary associations.

By the late 1830s and early 1840s political competition had itself become a kind of bond, or rather the parties' conflict had brought them into an almost symbiotic relationship. The parties drew energy and motive force from one another. This resulted in large measure from the narrowing of the popular vote separating them. After having lost to the Democrats for the first time in 1839, the Whigs roared back in the year of the "log cabin." Yet the Democrats' total in 1840 was also their greatest ever, hardly cause for them to fade away, and the following year the Whig majority over the Democrats slipped to just over 4,000 votes. Then in 1842 the Democrats scored another of their rare victories, by a tiny margin, only to lose to the Whigs again the next year. Because the Liberty vote was climbing (to almost 9,000 in 1843), however, the 1843 election was also very close. Marcus Morton's victory in 1842 set the stage for a tremendous intensification of party warfare during his governorship in 1843, which was especially manifest in the legislature (see Chapter II, Figure 5). Though factional fights within both parties also arose during this period and affected policy and patronage decisions, at the mass level intraparty conflict was far less important than the dialectic between the two major parties.

After 1840 it was easy for Whigs, left to themselves, to become dispirited, what with Harrison's death, troubles with Tyler, and internecine feuding, and these disillusioning events had come very soon after the upswelling of hope and the great victory. In 1841 the New Bedford Whigs had organized but were not showing much spirit; they had just called off a big meeting and were expecting the worst in the fall election. Then the Democratic chief "Bob Rantoul" came to town and gave a speech to the Democrats. "It operated upon the Whigs like a shock of Galvanism upon a dead body." Immediately sixty or seventy of the "old guard" called a meeting, and organization went forward with some of the "old Tippecanoe spirit at fever heat."[13]

In the summer of 1844 a Whig town committee chairman in a central Massachusetts agricultural town told a similar story. Earlier in the year he had decided "to 'abandon the ship' (so far as this town is concerned). But I have recently changed my mind, and became determined to give battle in 'fine style.'—The combined forces of abolition together with locofocoism are acting vigorously in this place and, for the purpose of meeting these forces, I want from fifty to a hundred of the N.Y. Tribune." The more he thought about the approaching election and the more he feared that the election of the governor and other Whigs was in doubt, that there would probably be vacancies in the senate, "and that the vote of every Whig that can possibly be elected may be wanted, yea *absolutely* needed to save us from a 'one vote overthrow' I could remain silent no longer."[14]

Clearly then, parties stimulated one another to greater exertions in campaigning. Whigs and Democrats watched each another with eagle eye, whether in saltwater ports or high hill towns, and reacted to actions by their opponents. They assumed that the opposition was there to stay; they did not expect it to go away after being beaten once or several times; and they did not expect ultimately to triumph in one big party, in a restoration of unity and harmony.

Surveying the defeated Democracy in 1840, Marcus Morton admitted, "We have met a Waterloo defeat." Then he added, "But though routed horse foot and draggoons, we have a standing army of 55,000 tried men, well disciplined and thoroughly united in a good cause."[15]

## Massachusetts in the Nation

A new kind of politics existed, clearly, and the change was evident to contemporaries, as it has been since. Yet a major theme of this study is that the new "machines" of mass-party politics retained much that was old.[16] Institutions usually grow in just such a way, not from nothing but out of existing customs and networks. Furthermore, in Massachusetts, and in other states, the machines were incomplete, and key elements of their national organizational apparatus would come into being later on in the 1840s.[17]

In the Federal-Republican period, Massachusetts went further than most other states in developing electoral organizations. Partisan consciousness rose to fever pitch during the years from 1805 to 1815, but it did not yet have a lasting effect on political life. In New York, for example, partisanship early imprinted itself on patronage practices, so that "New York politics" became a synonym for the systematic rewarding of friends and punishing of enemies. New York's electoral coalitions, on the other hand, and its factions generally, were less well developed than those of Massachusetts before the 1820s.[18] But the Bay State's early republican parties nevertheless did not become institutions.

In the Whig-Democratic era, political men created full-fledged parties in Massachusetts, as they did in most states of the Union. The new organizations first appeared during the years 1834–1839. President Jackson's removal of the Bank deposits in the winter of 1833–1834 led the anti-administration forces to coalesce under the name of Whigs. That name represented the opposition's attempt to proclaim its kinship with the Whigs of the American Revolution who had also stood against executive usurpation. In the South, many Whigs presented themselves also as defenders of states' rights (and slavery), while in New York, Massachusetts, and other northern states, leading Whigs often opposed states' rights. But in both the North and the South Whigs came together in 1834 under a common banner of resistance to "arbitrary" and "tyrannical" executive power.[19]

Across the nation in the years 1834–1840, both Whig and Democratic parties developed in the states at different rates and were at any given moment at various stages of completion.[20] General histories sometimes have ignored this fact, and in doing so have been led to minimize the social and ideological differences between the two major parties. If the parties are scrutinized for programmatic content during their formative years, they may more easily be seen to lack coherent belief systems. Of course, pragmatism always tempered principle, but the point is simply that a *developmental* view of what parties said and did gives a fairer picture of their differing ideologies or belief systems.

By 1839–1840 the politics of Massachusetts shared in the extraordinary degree of political excitement and participation that animated the entire nation. Voter turnout in Massachusetts, however, tended to be lower than in other states; indeed it was lower in New England generally. This condition has been attributed to the lack of a competitive balance between parties in New England and to the reluctance of the region's citizens to accept the new parties.[21] But in Massachusetts, despite the Whigs' dominance, both parties were well organized and the Democrats were always a threat. Although voter-turnout rates ranked among the lowest in the nation, Massachusetts's citizens did not lag in other forms of participation. The continuing attention of parties to ward, small-town, and school-district organization makes the relatively low turnout rates even more anomalous.

Historians have posited an almost axiomatic relationship between competition and organization on the one hand and voter turnout on the other. The case of Massachusetts indicates that organization may be intense and a competitive opposition present but that turnout may still be relatively low. It suggests also the need for comparative analysis of regional and state political cultures.

That Massachusetts was the state farthest along the road to industrialism may have depressed voter turnout, perhaps because of the transience of many laborers and the enforcement of residency requirements. Massachusetts was not, however, "industrialized," and the party system did not arise as a consequence of urbanization or industrialization. The new parties did owe much, as indicated earlier, to changes in communication, and the entrepreneurial spirit of "improvements" impressed itself on the new politics as well as on nascent industrialism. Before factories and machines were widespread, they became a powerful metaphor affecting social and political life.

In the 1820s and 1830s, for example, the new temperance societies were spoken of as "moral machines." Whereas the first such societies, of the period 1800–1820, had been elite associations which proffered reform through the personal prestige and influence of their leaders, the later organizations reached out more impersonally to a broad public through "paid, full-time organizers, a network of voluntary organizations, systematic financing, and the printed word as the basis of temperance propaganda rather than the spoken word from the lips of local notables."[22] The contrast between the Federal-Republican and Whig-Democratic parties was similar.

The new parties did not arise with industrialism, nor were they offspring or correlates of "modernization" in any simple sense. The Idea of Progress, or corollaries of it, has for too long influenced historical views of party development. Even the word "development" often has progressive connotations, and has frequently served, if unconsciously, to boot-leg in implicit value judgments.

To say that by the 1840s political parties had *developed* into what was in basic outline their modern form is to suggest that since that time not much new has been added to the nature of political parties, and that no radical changes in their structure, purpose, or methods have occurred. This statement does not imply that the parties of the 1840s had left behind all that was traditional and had replaced it with rational efficiency. Much less does it claim that politics had become purged of all that was elitist, oligarchic, and undemocratic. The continuation of traditional modes of conducting political business is becoming better appreciated, as is indicated, for example, by a recent study of the process of selecting federal judges during the antebellum period. "In the midst of this supposedly modern mass two-party system," Kermit Hall concluded, "significant vestiges of a traditional political order existed." The importance of traditional personal connections, consanguineal and affinal, in the selection of judges for lower federal courts revealed a "contradictory and contentious . . . transitional two-party system. . . . the political culture of the era moved gradually, incrementally, unevenly, and incompletely toward political modernity."[23]

Within the regions of the country and within individual states, the party system*s* of the 1840s varied in their mix of contradictions and contentions. Massachusetts differed from neighboring Rhode Island, where the rather fundamental issue of suffrage led to armed violence in the 1840s. Both these still largely Yankee states differed from the ethnically heterogeneous Middle Atlantic States, while within the southern and western regions further variations of political culture could be found.

In the South and West, for example, the practice of having candidates for office appeal to voters on their own behalf was well established early in the century. In Massachusetts and other northern states, inhibitions against "self-electioneering" lingered into the 1830s. Early in that decade, for example, the Newburyport *Advertiser* spoke directly to the matter: "New Englanders hold no fellowship with 'stump orators,' and a self-nominated candidate for any office in the gift of the people is sure to be met with scorn and contempt however great may be his abilities or acquirements."[24]

In other sections, too, "new men" rose to prominence as leaders of the new parties. The new breed of professional politician tended to come from humbler backgrounds and to use politics as a career leading to upward social mobility.[25] There is much truth to this generalization for the United States as a whole—and certainly some for Massachusetts, as well—yet in the

Bay State men of old families or men raised in the households of prominent Federalists or Republicans also participated in creating the new parties.

The professional was *one type* of leader found in the Whig and Democratic parties of Massachusetts. Even the throng of hungry office and sinecure seekers infesting the middle and lower levels of both parties included men who pursued occupations or sought to advance their fortunes—or even to do good—in ways far removed from politics. Among the chiefs of both parties were men well adapted to the new politics but difficult to pigeonhole as professionals.

The Whig organization contained blue bloods like Winthrop and Chapman who were comfortable as party leaders and who attended to the details of committees, conventions, patronage, and campaigning. While they might have been outnumbered by "new men," the latter did not always rise simply as politicians. Edward Everett, for example, was a self-made man who advanced not just by politics but first of all by virtue of his talents as a scholar, minister, and man of letters—by dint, in short, of his acquiring "talents" traditionally associated with public leadership. Even Everett's friend George Bancroft personified less the professional and more the scholar-educator type. Politics was simply one of the chief ways in which Bancroft sought to make his mark on the world, and to make his fortune.

Other types can be found in both parties. Among the Whigs were Brahmin public men, such as Robert C. Winthrop; Christian merchants, such as the Lawrences and Appletons; and, of course, the lawyer-orators, such as Choate and Webster, though "the Godlike" no doubt belongs in a class by himself. The Democratic minority presented less variety, and certainly more Democrats-by-trade; or it may be that the Whigs' dominance of elective office gave them both greater historical familiarity and greater latitude to develop self-transcending identities. Still, the Democrats managed the scholar-educator Bancroft, the Old Republican public servant Marcus Morton (a type in short supply), and the reformer-politician Robert Rantoul, Jr., who seems to have shared the hunger for lucrative appointive office so characteristic of the Halletts, Butlers, Banks, and all their lesser-known cousins.

Massachusetts Whiggery especially was directed at its core by a Brahmin elite of merchant-manufacturers and their lawyer-politician allies. The Whig Party, it is not farfetched to say, was the instrument of this elite. Not until the late 1840s did the party begin to become something of a sorcerer's apprentice—but this change sprang primarily from a new generation of young rebels, most of whom left the party. The organization remained a bastion of defense against dissidents within and without and served its purpose until it was struck down in the mid-1850s in an upheaval during which the Brahmin elite temporarily lost much control over politics. Until then, Boston's "aristocracy" played a role in political affairs that was anything but retiring. Indeed, compared with elites in other cities, they were conspicuous for their power and for their place in the forefront of public life.[26]

If the adaptability of the highest social classes to party politics revealed much of the persistence of tradition, the behavior of some of the lowest classes showed that political modes associated with an older political culture might revive and grow more prevalent in the new milieu. There is a well-known apocryphal story which expresses the spirit of the crassly pragmatic politics of the late nineteenth century. Two ward bosses are contemplating a group of voters. One inquires whether they are for Bryan or for McKinley. The other answers, "Well, some's for Bryan and some's for McKinley, but they's all for sale."

Corruption in politics, and specifically bribery of voters, may be assumed to be almost always present, though varying in kind and degree. In England, for example, "the purse" persisted as a factor in elections at least until the introduction of the secret ballot in 1872. Recent studies have shown that bribery of voters in English elections often did not so much change as confirm votes and that it probably rewarded many dependents who would no doubt have voted anyway in the manner the bribers desired, but it was nevertheless still true that by the late nineteenth century vote buying in England had decreased markedly. Ironically, in the United States the movement may have been in the other direction, as bribery–perhaps much of it "confirming"–increased in the second half of the century. In the case of Massachusetts, at any rate, there are many signs pointing to the existence of bribery in elections in the early 1850s, whereas the partisan charges of ten, twenty, or forty years before seem to lack substance. I have found nothing in the earlier period which remotely resembles the 1850 letter of the Whig State Central Committee chairman to the Sterling town chairman exhorting the latter to attend to those potential Whig voters who would not go to the polls because of the distance involved or "because of the expense of getting a conveyance."

> These two classes must be overcome by money, that is, you must see that a conveyance is provided for those who need one. Let it be done as cheap as you can. And to the other class, you must pay 25 cts, 37 1/2, 50 cts & up to a dollar, so as to be sure of getting them all out. You can in this way get

> out every voter. You will see how much money will probably be wanted, and what you can raise in your town, and the rest must be obtained elsewhere.[27]

This may be taken as a reflection of the increasing penetration of politics by a market economy, or may be seen as another flag of caution against applying a progressive view of political development to the history of political parties in the nineteenth century.

### Policy

What difference did the existence of mass political parties engaged in competitive electoral politics make in the policies enacted by state and local governments? Historians have commented most often on the contrasts–or lack thereof–between Whigs and Democrats, and the consequences that flowed from one or the other party's being in control of a particular policy. The question may be sharpened by asking whether policy would have been different if party institutions had not developed. If one attempts to discover this for one state, it would seem to possess the properties of a counterfactual hypothesis. Otherwise one would be compelled to address it by comparing states having highly developed party competition with states lacking well-organized parties or competition. Such a study has not been done for the American states in the 1830s and 1840s. But an investigation of the relation between interparty competition and "policy outputs," as they are called, of the American states from 1914 to 1963 found no such relation. Instead, "wealthy, urbanized, and ethnically diversified states tend[ed] to be more liberal in their public policies, regardless of the level of party competition." Furthermore, seasoned observers of the antebellum period who have expressed themselves on this matter tend to think that the presence or absence of party competition in the 1830s and 1840s did not make "any difference" in the kinds of policies that states created.[28]

On the question of whether it made a difference whether Whigs or Democrats were elected, many historical studies are available, along with a marked divergence of interpretation. Edward Pessen has presented the most comprehensive and trenchant arguments on the negative side. Surveying Whig and Democratic programs and policies throughout the states, he found few real differences in practice between the parties, and stressed overall "the sham nature of the era's party battles." Another student of the subject has conceded that "in the Jackson period" the parties took different approaches to the public promotion of economic development, but that by the late 1840s "the Democrats were succumbing to the lure of public promotional ventures, particularly railroads, and thereafter distribution ceased to divide the parties so starkly."[29] On the other hand, a number of writers have insisted not only that Whigs and Democrats possessed different ideas about society and government but that despite the entrepreneurial character of leadership in both parties, significant differences of policy existed.[30]

About Massachusetts the historians also have disagreed. Arthur B. Darling's 1925 study of Massachusetts politics from 1828 to 1848 and Arthur M. Schlesinger, Jr.'s *The Age of Jackson* (1945) portrayed the Democrats as a liberal, or radical, anti-business party advancing the interests of workingmen and oppressed classes. In contrast, Oscar Handlin and Mary Flug Handlin, in their still highly regarded study of the state government's role in the economy from 1774 to 1861, asserted that party competition itself contributed to instability and that Whig and Democratic party preferences made little difference in practical affairs.

The Handlins made an even more important point, one bearing *indirectly* on the question. According to them, the key changes in state policy making were well underway during the 1820s, and thus the state's course was firmly set *before* mass parties developed and in any case quite independently of interparty competition. The desire for "improvements" began to grow during the Federal-Republican era and rose greatly during the transition period of the late 1820s and early 1830s. By then the state government and courts of law already had displayed an eager willingness to assist well-organized and well-financed private groups in bringing about development. The legislature and the courts showed great solicitude in minimizing the risks and costs for the entrepreneurs, while giving short shrift to any people injured by the rush of technical improvement and economic growth. Governor Lincoln's successful effort in the years 1826–1830 to gain immunity from full liability for corporation shareholders, for example, was a tremendous aid to entrepreneurs achieved before party development, and the principle was seldom challenged in later years.[31] The Workingmen's movement went largely unheeded in its attempts to call attention to the consequences of growing imbalances in economic resources and power, to the less fortunate members of society whose lives were not improved, and to the incompatibility of growth (as encouraged by the state) with republican ideals.[32]

The irrelevance of political parties to the allocation of wealth and resources is a conclusion which can also be drawn from recent histories of American law during the early Republic; they make this point even less directly than do studies of state governments, but perhaps more forcefully.

William Nelson and Morton Horowitz, in separate studies, left no doubt that during the period from the 1780s to the 1820s a new, instrumental conception of common law emerged which judges and lawyers used to promote economic development. In the eighteenth century the common law had been regarded as consisting of fixed, unchangeable rules, whose purpose was to promote stability and unity. But in the early nineteenth century, judges interpreted common law to promote growth, competition, and efficiency; corporate rights were detached from serving the common welfare and put primarily in the service of private profit, and they were thus used to build great wealth and control over resources.[33]

Some of the changes described by Horowitz continued to evolve during the 1840s and 1850s, but in others the course of policy seems again to have been set well before the formation of mass parties. In addition, both Nelson and Horowitz stated boldly that the law came to serve the interests of those who were winning the most control over resources, allowing the powerful to acquire even more. According to Nelson, "the law came to be a tool by which those interest groups that had emerged victorious in the competition for control of law-making institutions could seize most of society's wealth for themselves and enforce their seizure upon the losers." Horowitz asserted, "During the eighty years after the American Revolution, a major transformation of the legal system took place, which reflected a variety of aspects of social struggle. That the conflict was turned into legal channels (and thus rendered somewhat mysterious) should not obscure the fact that it took place and that it enabled emergent entrepreneurial and commercial groups to win a disproportionate share of wealth and power in American society."[34]

There is some ambiguity here, since it is not clear whether the law was put to use by "emergent" groups in such a way that the rules were fixed to enable them to win, or, whether, having already gained wealth (for example, under the old rules as merchants), the rich (now as manufacturing entrepreneurs, for example) then changed the law to gain even greater wealth and power.

However this point is resolved, the implication for political parties seems clear. In large measure the question "who gets what?" was not decided in competitive politics, and the decision certainly did not depend on whether parties developed, though the dominance of the Whigs later on may have made some difference. Though Nelson and Horowitz departed from the Handlins' interpretation in several major ways, the end result of their studies did not differ much from the Handlins' assertion that "the merchants found a ready tool for control [of society] in the swiftly changing party system."[35]

The question whether it made any difference that Whigs rather than Democrats ruled in Massachusetts nevertheless deserves attention, if only because it mattered a great deal to many contemporaries. One cannot dismiss the problem by asserting that merchants controlled the Democratic Party—they did not. David Henshaw and his entrepreneurial, officeholding faction, it is true, possessed inordinate influence in the Jacksonian Republican and Democratic Republican faction and party from 1829 to 1835. But from the mid-1830s on, and especially after Henshaw's fall from grace, other elements came to have an influence in a much broader and differently organized Democratic party. The merchant-manufacturing elite which sat at the center of power in Whiggery rejected totally the policies proposed by the state Democratic party under the influence of Bancroft and Morton. Morton's inaugurals of 1840 and 1843 called for a reversal of state largesse to corporations and pointed to unrepublican practices, inequities, and the needs of those hurt by "improvements." Morton not only called attention to inequities in the tax laws, arguing that the owners of real estate, the "agricultural interest," and the "poorer classes" bore a disproportionate share of taxes as against owners of personal property, corporate stocks, money at interest, and the "wealthier classes"; he also proposed that the members of "joint-stock companies" be made personally liable for debts.[36]

The Democrats, of course, never had power sufficient to put their professions to the test. It may also be objected that the sincerity of some Democrats left much to be desired. It was indeed true that "those who condemned the chartered company in the abstract often yielded in practice to its temptations. Rantoul hoped to make the Democratic organization the instrument of the disaffected, but the members of that party showed a distressing inclination to vote for new grants when their interests dictated, even grants for banks, the most reviled of institutions."[37] Even Rantoul, according to his recent biographer, compromised when necessary for the sake of party unity and, perhaps, of his career. In 1837, as he prepared to give a speech in Worcester criticizing banking practices and proposing reforms, he checked first with Democratic leaders to make sure he would not offend any local Democrats: "when he learned that all the leaders were connected with banks as stockholders or officers, he promised that he would qualify his remarks so as not to give offense." After all, he said, the important thing was to bring the matter under the control of the legislature.[38] It should be added that the next year Rantoul fought hard in the legislature for banking regulations and even tried to get legislators who were bankers barred from voting on the matter and, failing that, from serving on the special committee to handle bank affairs.

The Whigs retorted that a majority of the legislature might be excluded by such a test. "It cannot be disguised," Rantoul said, "the great banking interest is here, fighting hard and desperately for that which it has in its pockets, and that which it hopes to put in its pockets." The Whig house Speaker Winthrop ruled that bank stockholders could vote, and the house upheld him by a vote of 337 to 97; Rantoul's proposal that bank directors should be excluded also fell, 136 to 300, gaining just over one-fourth of the votes of the house. Little wonder that later that year, in a fourth of July oration delivered in Berkshire County, Rantoul sounded as radical as a Workingman when he analyzed the way in which wealth enlisted talent in its service and together regulated "the standard of opinion and fix the fashion":

> The instruments of the moneyed cabal, knowing how odious their principles are to the people, seldom make a full avowal of their creed, but content themselves with steadily acting up to it, as often as they dare, giving way to the pressure from without whenever [necessary]. . . . From these causes, the real interests at the bottom of most of our political disputes are seldom mentioned in public discussion.[39]

Rantoul's role as leading defense counsel in *Commonwealth* v. *Hunt* should also be mentioned in his, and the Democrats', defense. This famous case, decided before the supreme judicial court in 1841, struck down an attempt to illegalize trade unions as "conspiracies." At issue, significantly, was overtime pay as it related to a shoemakers' union and its arrangements with an employer for a ten-hour day. Though the quest of other artisans and factory workers for a ten-hour day revived in the 1840s and encountered stiff resistance, this case suggests that the movement of the 1830s had not been without successes and that the aid of prominent Democrats (despite the hostility of others) helped workingmen in their quest for bargaining power and better hours and pay.[40]

In the 1840s, however, as the Whig and Democratic parties became more and more ends in themselves, and increasingly controlled by professional politicians seeking office or prestige, they settled more firmly into a game of politics governed almost wholly by a practical, marketplace calculus. Both idealism and discontent turned in like measure away from the major parties into the Liberty and Free Soil parties or into other social movements. By the 1850s, frustration and discontent were boiling up in several major movements that paralleled and interpenetrated one another, the most powerful of which was the nativist Know-Nothing movement. Know-Nothingism sprang from many sources—antipartyism and distrust of party politics were clearly major ones.

# XIV. Parties and Democracy

> One great blemish in the popular mind of America, and the prolific parent of an innumerable brood of evils, is Universal Distrust. Yet, the American citizen plumes himself upon this spirit, even when he is sufficiently dispassionate to perceive the ruin it works; and will often adduce it, in spite of his own reason, as an instance of the great sagacity and acuteness of the people, and their superior shrewdness and independence.
>
> "You carry," says the stranger, "this jealousy and distrust into every transaction of public life. By repelling worthy men from your legislative assemblies, it had bred up a class of candidates for your suffrage, who, in their every act, disgrace your institutions and your people's choice. It has rendered you so fickle, and so given to change, that your inconstancy has passed into a proverb. . . . Any man who attains a high place among you . . . may date his downfall from that moment; for any printed lie that any notorious villain pens . . . appeals at once to your distrust, and is believed. . . . Is this well, think you, or likely to elevate the character of the governors or the governed among you?"
>
> The answer is invariably the same: "There's freedom of opinion here, you know. Every man thinks for himself, and we are not to be easily overreached. That's how our people come to be suspicious."
>
> –Charles Dickens, *American Notes* (1842)

> Every government is an aristocracy in fact. The despotism of Genghis Khan was an aristocracy. The government of the most popular French convention was an aristocracy. The most democratical canton in Switzerland was an aristocracy. The most leveling town meeting in New England is an aristocracy. The empire of Napoleon is an aristocracy. The government of Great Britain is an aristocracy. But as they, the Aristocrats, are always ambitious and avaricious, the rivalries among them split them into factions and tear the people to pieces. The great secret of liberty is to find means to limit their power and control their passions. Rome and Britain have done it best. Perhaps we shall do it better than either. God knows.
>
> –John Adams, 1810[1]

How democratic were the new political parties? The difficulty of answering this question, inherent in the task of defining "democratic" and in its raising a host of other questions, has not prevented political philosophers and historians from delivering many and contending answers. Some time ago Mosei Ostrogorski asserted that parties developed from "unhealthy politico-social conditions." Among recent historians, Edward Pessen has made the most unequivocal criticisms of parties, characterizing party politicians as little better than high-priced snake-oil salesmen, manipulating "blue smoke and mirrors" (to borrow a phrase of Jimmy Breslin's) while gathering in patronage, profit, and prestige. "The great major parties," said Pessen recently, "were in a large sense great hoaxes." Richard P. McCormick perhaps reflected the caution of many other historians in being certain only that the "style" of mass parties was more "egalitarian," while the apparently democratic structure of parties was merely a "cosmetic" cover for oligarchy.[2] In contrast, many other scholars, and most political scientists, have tended to celebrate parties as democratic. Since World War II and the Cold War, the celebrants have virtually equated the "two-party system" with "Western democracy."[3]

Ever since this question was first raised—and it has been posed in one form or another at least since parties began—it has been answered according to two different sets of criteria, one external and one internal. Those using the external have insisted on comparing American parties, or American society generally, with those of the "old" world, to England, continental Europe, or more distant places. In the world of politics and business, this line of reasoning has been used most often by those satisfied with things as they are. Those taking internal standards of evaluation have held that American institutions should be assessed according to American ideals, by our own professions and historic values. This approach has often characterized critics of the status quo who are distrustful of power. Neither all defenders of the established order nor all challengers of it have limited themselves entirely to just one kind of criterion, but these have been the central tendencies.

Many Whig leaders, for example, took great pride in the existing social, economic, and political order, and their speeches were laced with favorable comparisons of America, and Massachusetts in particular, with the rest of the world. Massachusetts possessed, said Governor Everett in 1836, "a degree of prosperity seldom equalled and never surpassed among men." Robert Winthrop similarly asked the 1839 Whig convention, "Whose stock stands highest on the Foreign Exchange? What State is termed 'the pattern State' by the intelligent English tourist? What State is selected as an example by the philosophical Frenchman who would depict to the world a true American Democracy?"[4]

However true these comparisons were in actuality, there were many other American citizens who took much more critical views of American society and of its vaunted political institutions. Occasionally such dissent was heard from a prestigious forum, as in 1843 when the Democratic governor Marcus Morton began his inaugural address by observing that while the country was blessed with natural abundance, shortsighted selfishness had operated to oppress part of the community and "to mar the harmony and happiness of the whole." Where Whigs saw prosperity, Morton saw "gross inequality of social condition, which is not only inconsistent with the principles of human brotherhood, but subversive of those equal political rights which are the basis of our civil institutions."[5] More often, however, this kind of critical view came not from spokesmen of the major parties but from dissenters associated with populist movements which had usually arisen in opposition to the parties.

In the early 1830s this kind of dissent had flourished in Massachusetts. Antimasons and Workingmen had called into question the fairness and justice of the existing political and economic order, and had expressed profound distrust with the normal operations of government and political men. Their point of departure was a vision of what *should* be according to the American republican ideals and beliefs into which they had been socialized. They came to perceive a contradiction between what ought to be and what actually was.[6] Less tolerant of this contradiction than most men experienced in politics, they were neither alienated nor extremist. Nor were they reassured or comforted by observations about how much worse the state of affairs was in England or elsewhere.

Thus in considering the question of how democratic the new political parties were, it will be useful to examine the antiparty populist movements which challenged the parties to live up to their own professions. It will also be illuminating to cast a brief look ahead to the 1850s, when a populist upheaval springing from many sources came together in a powerful antiparty movement which shattered seemingly unbreakable party loyalties in one of the major party realignments of American history.

An evaluation of American political parties based on external comparisons can hardly fail to cast them in a favorable light. In general, the United States led all nations in developing representative government and in extending the vote to large numbers of citizens. The parties, however, did not create these conditions so much as they arose from them. Still, competition contributed to motivating citizens to vote and to take an interest in public affairs, and parties were certainly, by the 1840s, the centerpiece of the democratic culture of the day, for better or for worse.

If, moreover, antebellum parties are compared to those of the twentieth century—indeed, if the political cultures of the two eras are observed whole—the relative lack of alienation from public life and politics in the nineteenth century is quite clear. The higher rates of participation in voting, campaigning, and other political activities are well known.

Turnover in the legislature, for example, tended to be higher in the nineteenth than in the twentieth century—and higher than it had been before 1820 (see Figure 6). Political parties did not create this situation, apparently, but low incumbency remained the rule after parties organized and greater numbers of men served as state representatives. This situation was healthier than that in the twentieth century because more elements of society were kept closer to government.

If one compares simply the eligible electorates, then the nineteenth-century electorate of most adult white males resembled a citizenry far more than does its present counterpart. That women could not vote was not a source of concern before the Civil War, and nonwhites had a better chance of voting in Massachusetts than perhaps in any other state. At least until about 1900, the voters possessed a much greater "sense of efficacy," that is, the belief and feeling that they could by their participation make a difference, that they could have an impact on policy and on their lives.[7] Antebellum politics was thus in many respects democratic in character—as were the new parties which flourished in it.

If the parties are assessed by their own professions, however, by the ideals which they claimed guided them and which were shared by most citizens, then certain contradictions and shortcomings must be observed. Decision making in the parties was centralized and oligarchic, not open or democratic. This feature of the new parties is well known and needs no elaboration. Furthermore, the parties spoke as if their ideal voter were a rational being following the dictates of reason and conscience, but both tolerated and to some extent perpetuated a high degree of interference with the individual's act of voting.

The politicians' part in rendering the ballot less than free fit into a larger pattern of managing opinion and of manipulating voters' ignorance and fear. In the 1830s it was a well-established fact that partisan newspapers felt little or no responsibility to the truth and that people expected partisan publications to be filled with distortion or outright lying.[8] Editors' and publishers' attitudes varied, of course, and perhaps not all were as cynical as David Henshaw's staff at the Boston *Statesman*. One dropout from that faction later disclosed that the *Statesman* cronies would sit about every few days and " 'crack our sides' over statements in the Post and Statesman so notoriously false, that the very audacity with which they were published was supremely ridiculous." In 1839 Bancroft's newspaper, the higher-minded *Bay State Democrat,* admitted that it was a matter of common remark "among all classes" that with few exceptions "the press is giving to lying."[9]

Historians have sometimes treated newspapers as if they reflected public opinion, and while at times this must have been so, editors and politicians often worked deliberately to *create* opinion. Usually newspapers did not reflect public opinion so much as they reflected the determined efforts of inner circles within parties to shape and direct opinion.[10]

In viewing politicians' interaction with the public, it needs to be added that campaign stump speeches and the like were pitched generally at a much lower level than was all the printed bombast that parties hurled at one another. In one particularly unrestrained speech, Robert Rantoul charged that the Whigs would mortgage farmers' lands to pay debts incurred by state grants to railroads; that the Whig candidate and former general William H. Harrison wanted to create a standing army out of the militia, with military courses to be given in the common schools every summer; and that the Whigs would encourage the British to unleash 60,000 Indians on the frontier and to send out the English navy to destroy American shipping. The Whigs, for their part, matched this bunkum with talk that Van Buren used gold spoons in the White House, and charges that during the Seminole War the navy had bought wood in New Orleans at twenty-four dollars a cord and transported it to Florida. Who, asked one Whig speaker, " 'is Martin Van Bulen? Martin Van Bulen! [sic] He is the man who bought the wood in New Orleans, paid twenty-four dollars a cord for it, carried it round to Florida, and had to cut down the trees to land it.' A fellow in the crowd cried out, 'Carrying coals to Newcastle.' 'Yes,' said the speaker, 'them coals he carried to Newcastle. I don't know so much about the coals, but about the wood I've got the documents!" There is much evidence–and one suspects much more that is by its nature unrecoverable–that the general public was "disposed to accept every wild statement" and that "the average intelligence" was low–"intelligent" often having the meaning, as probably here, of *possessing information.*[11]

Not that the Massachusetts voter was less "intelligent" than voters elsewhere, or more susceptible to bunkum. This condition prevailed to varying degrees throughout the states. It may indeed have been worse in other quarters. While concluding that Alabama's political culture was essentially democratic, a recent history of that state before the Civil War observed "the fatal subservience of the Alabama political system to the demagogic appeal." Though, according to this study, "Alabamians governed themselves," the "fundamental business of Alabama politics . . . was the manipulation of the dread of manipulation."[12]

One might conclude not only that the parties were hoaxes but also that the voters got the parties and government they deserved. Perhaps adult white male suffrage led inevitably in this direction. Yet a softer view is suggested by Neil Harris's superb biography of P. T. Barnum, a man who knew something about hoaxes, who grew up in the early national period, and who had great kinship with politicians. Barnum was a great showman, of course, and one of the great deceivers of the nineteenth century. He was also an exposer who appealed to his audience partly by evoking certain shared assumptions about the nature of reality and illusion.[13] Harris showed that it is far too simplistic to think of Barnum as a mere confidence man; it would be as much of an error to see parties as false to the core.

Political leaders, especially those at the top, often considered voters ignorant and credulous, but they also devoted much effort to informing them and appealing to them with "intelligence" and argument. Local cadres, probably because they were less removed from and less condescending toward the average voter, seemed genuinely to believe that political literature and well-informed speakers could influence the electorate.[14]

Both local and state leaders preferred to focus on "great national questions" such as the tariff, a national bank, the subtreasury, and the currency. Sectional issues also engaged them, and Clay's slaveholding greatly worried Whig leaders trying to prevent defections to the Liberty party.[15] The party leaders tried to avoid slavery or slavery-related issues; they similarly eschewed, or equivocated on, other moral issues, such as temperance. They avoided slavery because they believed that the very existence of national parties depended on removing slavery from politics; they avoided temperance because it had the capacity to arouse normally nonpolitical citizens (on both sides) and to cut unpredictably across party lines; and they avoided a frank and open discussion of a good many economic and social matters directly affecting the lives of Massachusetts citizens because they were content with the status quo or shared the viewpoint of those elites who benefited most from the political economy of the emerging order.

In the early 1830s, and in the mid-1850s, populist movements arose to force politicians to confront such issues. The Antimasons and Workingmen both entered politics at a time when political parties were not yet well organized, and hence found the going somewhat easier than the antislavery protest was to find it a short time later. The abolitionist contended with new or transformed parties that were gathering organizational momentum and great electoral appeal. Moreover, party and community elites, still smarting from the Antimasonic-Masonic controversy, had learned from that episode and reacted much more harshly to agitation of slavery.

Antimasonry's legacy to antislavery in personnel and methods is well known.[16] Some Antimasons were even actively sympathetic to the fledgling abolition movement during the years they were pursuing Masonry's destruction–antislavery was simply one of the many evangelical causes of moral reform which they propagated.[17] Less apparent has been the Antimasonic-Masonic controversy's effect on anti-abolition and repression. If evangelical reformers drew lessons from the Antimasonic experience, so did party politicians and community leaders interested above all in stability.

The early 1830s were heady years for protesters and dissenters of all kinds. William Lloyd Garrison attended the 1832 state Antimasonic convention at Worcester as a delegate from Suffolk County and praised his fellow Antimasons as a "substantial, sober . . . intelligent body of men," who were

> the last to be suspected of sinister motives, or seeking popular preferment —the last to abandon the ground of principle and equality. I feel proud being admitted to a seat with them. . . . I go for the immediate, unconditional and total abolition of Free-Masonry. Pillar after pillar is falling—the mighty Babel begins to shake and, ere long, it will be broken into fragments by the American people, and scattered to the winds of heaven.[18]

During the convention, Garrison took time to deliver a speech on slavery at the town hall, which he described as "well filled with ladies and gentlemen, although notice of the meeting was a limited one." To Garrison the moment seemed filled with opportunities, and there existed for a time a much greater willingness to debate the slavery question, in newspapers and public places, than had existed initially in reference to the New York "outrages." In 1832, 1833, and 1834, there seemed to be some fluidity and openness toward the question, though the climate of opinion was changing.[19]

By the end of 1835 Garrison had been pushed roughly through the streets of Boston with a rope around his neck by a "broadcloth mob" which included many "gentlemen of property and influence." That same year the Methodist preacher and abolitionist Orange Scott started to give a speech at the Worcester town hall, where Garrison had spoken three years before. Rowdies stood near the back and hissed, stamped, and shouted; before long, Levi Lincoln, Jr., son of the ex-governor, with the "stout Irishman" Patrick Doyle at his side, strode into the hall and to the lectern and deliberately took away Scott's notes. Doyle then seized Scott to drag him off, but cries from the audience stopped him, though the meeting ended abruptly. Ten days later at Faneuil Hall a nonpartisan group of community leaders presided over by Mayor Theodore Lyman and such men as the textile magnates Amos Lawrence and Patrick T. Jackson, the merchant Henry Lee, and the rich lawyer Richard Fletcher issued a protest against the "reckless few" who were threatening the Constitution and Union by agitating slavery and thereby perhaps scattering "firebrands, arrows, and death" among their southern brethren. In his January 1836 inaugural, Governor Everett appealed to the patriotism of his fellow citizens to abstain from discussing slavery, which would only exasperate slaveholders, make more oppressive the condition of the slave, and perhaps lead to the breakup of the Union.[20] Most of the state's political and economic leaders clearly desired a quick and total end to "agitation" of slavery.

For economic and other reasons, they did not want slavery to rise from the agenda of church lectures, lyceum and town hall debates, and the like, to demand attention from political leaders. They feared, as Harriet Martineau recognized, that the slavery question would, like Masonry, become a charged and divisive political issue with far more than local consequences.

The mid-1830s were years of increasing mob violence throughout the country, and religious and ethnic hatreds had already resulted in Boston in the burning of a convent in Charlestown in 1834 by an anti-Catholic mob. Boston's prominent citizens presented a united front in denouncing this ugly episode as an act casting shame on the entire community. Leaders of all factions joined in rejecting it root and branch.[21] A short time later, though, some public leaders were not only failing to denounce violence aimed against abolitionists but were, at the least, implicitly manipulating a threat of violence to suppress agitation of slavery.

The Antimasonic analogy probably stiffened the attitudes of notables and party leaders, leading them in Boston and elsewhere to warn abolitionists that if they held more meetings they would be fair game for mobs. That at least was Martineau's interpretation of the 1835 Faneuil Hall anti-abolitionist meeting of notables: "It is an invariable fact, and recognized as such, that meetings held to supply the deficiency of gag laws are the prelude to the violence which supplies the deficiency of executioners under such laws. Every meeting held to denounce opinion is followed by a mob. This was so well understood in the present case that the abolitionists were warned that if they met again publicly, they would be answerable for the disorders that might ensue."[22]

Though the abolitionists have received far more favorable attention from historians in the past twenty years than they had earlier, these crusaders are still controversial. At one time they were widely seen as misguided idealists who were "really" reacting to growing social inequality (and to their own status displacement) *in the North* and venting their frustration and aggression on southern slavery. This displacement thesis, though countered by other, more positive interpretations, will probably never fade completely. As a corollary to it, historians have frequently commented that the abolitionists ignored problems in their own communities, particularly the hardships endured by many of the lower classes during economic change. In the 1830s, too, Workingmen, while not paying much attention to slavery or its opponents, occasionally hinted that they found incongruous the abolitionists' concern for southern slaves and their lack of interest in women and children in New England factories. Yet if the abolitionists gave too little attention to factory laborers and the struggle for a ten-hour day, they did not attempt to keep that issue from being discussed. The party managers worked to keep both the hours of labor and slavery off the political agenda.[23]

The Whigs' ability to muster majorities in the cities and large towns of the Commonwealth, combined with a general-ticket system of at-large election of state representatives in Boston and other urban places, gave the Whigs control of the legislature throughout the 1840s. Even though the apportionment system technically gave the state's small towns overrepresentation, many such towns did not send representatives every year, by law and by choice. The large blocs of delegates from the cities gave the Whigs all the advantage they needed, especially since state senators had to be elected by majorities and, failing that, by the legislature. The Whigs always elected a bloc of senators, and a number of senate seats usually remained vacant for lack of majorities, especially where the Liberty or Free Soil parties cut heavily into the two-party vote. The Whigs would then fill all the vacant seats with their men, thus giving them a majority in the senate wholly unrepresentative of their relative numbers at the polls. Throughout the 1840s this virtual gerrymander—indeed the system probably operated more effectively than a real gerrymander—along with other conditions allowed the Whigs to exercise great control over the public agenda, and caused a prolonged "bottling up" of demands for change, both among Democrats and among dissident Whigs, many of whom had gone into the Free Soil party by the late 1840s.

Various aspects of the Whigs' dominance of Massachusetts in the 1840s have been examined extensively by scholars, especially the intra-party factional fighting between the conservative ("cotton") and antisouthern/antislavery ("conscience") Whigs.[24] The latter finally broke with the party, and though they detested the Democrats, most of whom they thought of as contemptible spoilsmen, in 1850 their desire to influence policy and to strike back at the Whigs led them to enter into a coalition with the Democrats.

The "Coalition" proved a success at the polls and for two years (1851–1852) the Democrats and Free Soilers divided state offices between them and managed to pass some of the legislation desired by each. Not enough, however, to suit those elements calling for reform of the electoral rules by which the Whigs controlled the state's politics. In 1852 the Whigs regained the state government in the fall election and the national Democratic party's return to the presidency strengthened those Democrats (the "Hunker" faction) opposed to cooperation with Free Soilers, and so the Coalition fell apart. At the same time, reform of the state's election laws remained on the agenda as the Coalition's ongoing campaign to revise the state's constitution bore fruit in the narrow passage of a referendum calling for election of delegates to a constitutional convention.

Returning to power in early 1853, the Whigs set about undoing as much of the Coalition program as possible. Their hard-line partisanship begot a reaction, however, and Democrats and Free Soilers, former Coalitionists, won heavily in the election of delegates to the constitutional convention. The proposed constitution of 1853, therefore, was very much a Coalition project, containing changes in government operation and in political economy advocated by opposition parties during the last two decades. It also knocked away the stanchions of Whig hegemony, and then erred in biasing the apportionment and electoral system too much in favor of rural areas and out-parties, much as the Republican opposition had tried to write the rules in its favor in 1811–1812. The result, at least at first, was the same–a boomerang.

A united Whiggery rallied all its forces against the new constitution, joined by a few Democrats and Free Soilers who found it unfair. With the popular vote generally following party lines, the constitution lost by a narrow margin.[25]

Yet in their zeal to put down the constitution, Whig leaders enlisted rather strange bedfellows. The Irish Catholics had arrived recently on the political stage as a force aided as much by cohesion as by numbers. While normally Democrats, the Irish disliked all forms of antislavery and balked at coalition with Free Soilers. They found much to object to in the new constitution and thus joined the vociferous opposition to it. Their bloc in Boston contributed to a heavy majority in Suffolk County that rejected the document.

Elsewhere in the United States, nativist and anti-Catholic movements were just gathering strength, having surged through England and Europe, and were about to erupt into politics. Catholic Irish political assertiveness helped stimulate such an outbreak in Massachusetts. At the same time, other protest and reform movements were already running into politics or poised to do so. In 1854 the antislavery movement would gain a new lease on life from the release of a powerful wave of antisouthernism throughout the North. But before that the events of 1853 had already had a devastating impact on party lines and Whig hegemony. Perhaps more than anything else, the Irish-Whig alliance made the constitution's defeat "the last victory of the conservative Federalist-Whigs who had governed the state for so long, and the end of an era."[26]

What followed was a populist revolt of unprecedented proportions, a movement whose lowest common denominator was nominally nativism and anti-Catholicism, but which included temperance, antislavery, and other dissident elements gathered into one great rejection of party politicians and the established party organizations. This grass-roots upheaval had already decided local elections in late 1853 when early the next year an electorate in motion absorbed another shock in the repeal of the Missouri Compromise and the passage of the Kansas-Nebraska Bill.[27] During 1854 a host of impulses and movements came together, bypassing the old parties and even the new anti-Nebraska party, leaving their most prestigious leaders high and dry, and bringing to power a grass roots, secret movement of middling and very average men—a movement known as Know-Nothingism.

One element of this upheaval was the temperance movement, which had been gaining momentum once again since the 1851 passage of a stiff prohibitory law in nearby Maine. Temperance had always cut across party lines, and both Whig and Democratic politicians had therefore tried to keep it out of politics.[28] Not only had their ability to do so gradually weakened from 1851 to 1854, but temperance advocates shrewdly seized the opportunity to associate pro-drink sentiment with Irish Catholics, and much of the prohibitory movement's success in 1854–1855 derived from the potency of this temporary association.[29]

Thus the sources of mid-fifties populism were complex, sometimes conflicting with one another and sometimes complementary. In any case, it has been clear for a long time that "Know Nothingism was the successor of the coalition," precipitated most immediately by outrage at the " 'Catholic and Cotton' entente" which had struck down the constitution of 1853.[30]

Know-Nothingism burst the dam against change erected by party politics, and released a flood of reforms. In the 1854 fall election, former Democrats, Whigs, and Free Soilers ignored the regular party nominees and voted instead for men whose nominations had not been made public. Two out of every three votes cast for governor, over 80,000, went to Henry Gardner of Boston, a result entirely unexpected by the state's leaders. The senate was entirely Know-Nothing. The house, numbering 380 to 390 or so, was almost completely Know-Nothing, the number of non–Know-Nothings being reported variously as from 1 or 3 to a maximum of 8. An unusually high number of the legislators were new to the General Court, even during an era when turnover was high and legislators tended to lack experience. Some 89 percent of the men in the 1855 legislature (elected in 1854) were first-termers (another 3 percent had one year's experience). This figure was 16 percent higher than that for any other legislature from 1848 through 1862 and 26 percent above the mean in a distribution with a standard deviation of 9.15. This legislature and the next either enacted or set in motion legislation that made the mid-1850s a watershed of policy making in general and democratization in particular. Oscar Handlin, for one, judged the Know-Nothing regime "progressive and fruitful."[31]

The Know-Nothing legislatures established the first board of insurance commissioners, with power to visit companies, inspect books, and examine officers; made county, city, and town officials who embezzled liable to punishment for larceny; required vaccination for all public school children; withdrew state support from all sectarian schools; gave strong support to the public school system; made it easier for rural children to go to school by making it possible, if they lived remote from a school in their town, for them to attend public school in an adjoining town; abolished imprisonment for debt, long desired by small debtors, and overhauled the system of bankruptcy, long desired by creditors; exempted $800 of a homestead, rather than $500 as previously, from execution for a man's debts, and extended the protection to his family; gave mechanics an improved lien law entitling an unpaid worker to put a lien on buildings and land for which he had furnished labor or materials; permitted married women to hold property separately from their husbands and exempted them from their husband's debts; provided for a decennial state census in between federal censuses and took one in 1855; created a state reform school for girls; empowered juries in criminal cases to interpret law as well as facts; prohibited factories from employing any child under fifteen who did not attend school at least eleven weeks a year; and tried to tighten the Maine liquor law passed in 1852.[32]

The Know-Nothings also reacted sharply to southern aggressiveness: electing Henry Wilson, a former Free Soiler known for his antisouthernism (and his ties to middling, working men), to the United States Senate; passing resolutions deploring the border ruffianism of proslavery Missourians in Kansas and requesting Congress to repeal the Fugitive Slave Act and restore the Missouri Compromise; granting the New England Emigrant Aid Society a new charter and calling on citizens to send aid to Kansas; and, over the governor's veto, enacting a personal-liberty law which killed the Fugitive Slave Act in Massachusetts. Motivated in part perhaps by defiance toward southerners, and in part by a punitive disposition toward Irish Catholic defenders of slavery, the Know-Nothings passed a law desegregating all public schools, a measure aimed chiefly at Boston, where blacks and white abolitionists had been trying to get black children out of a separate and inferior black school and into schools close to their neighborhoods. The law also forbade the exclusion of any children from public schools on religious grounds.[33]

Making no attempt to disguise their intention of limiting the influence of Catholics and foreigners in public affairs, the Know-Nothings debated a great many nativist measures. Though the most extreme of these were not passed, Governor Gardner and the legislature responded to this part of the impulse which had brought them into office: they disbanded Irish militia companies (which had provided escort for the rendition of fugitive slaves); dismissed foreigners in the police force and in state agencies; deported summarily several hundred alien paupers (Gardner claimed the state thereby saved $100,000 for that year); removed "foreign" symbols and influences from the state house and schools in petty ways; and sent the notorious and ultimately ridiculous Hiss Nunnery Committee off to investigate Catholic convents and schools. In 1857 one of their nativist constitutional amendments finally succeeded, with Republican help; it made the ability to read the state constitution in English and to write one's name necessary to vote—hardly a Draconian requirement, whatever the motives behind it. In 1859, however, the Republicans, now completely in control of the state, went much further and required foreigners to wait two additional years after naturalization before voting.[34]

The Know-Nothings simultaneously settled a number of long-standing problems of representative government, in the process showing more respect for democratic principles than Whig or Democratic party politicians ever displayed. They amended the constitution to permit a plurality to elect the governor and all state officers; to make the executive council smaller and elective; to equalize senate districts and house districts and put apportionment on a fair basis; to make the offices of the secretary of state, state treasurer, auditor, and attorney general elective; and to do the same for the offices of, among others, sheriffs, probate registers, clerks of the courts, and district attorneys, up to then appointed by the governor.[35]

The Know-Nothings thus present the ironic spectacle of a populist movement which was charged with an animus against foreigners and Catholics but which brought to fruition perhaps the most sweeping single impulse of democratization and utilitarian reform in the history of Massachusetts. The Know-Nothings sought the greatest good for the greatest number–of the native population, men, women, children, and nonwhites. Their illiberal actions become less significant beside their concrete achievements, their wide-ranging sensitivity to inequity and injustice, and their relatively immense lack of attentiveness or deference to the always understood wishes of political and economic elites.

The established party presses excoriated the legislatures and administrations of 1855–1856. The private papers and memoirs of prominent politicians are filled with hostile and unfavorable comments about the Know-Nothings and their actions. Historians, not surprisingly, have more often than not echoed the negative attitudes of the men who were swept aside in the populist revolt of 1854, and have usually minimized the impact of the Know-Nothings and their contribution to the Republican party which emerged in its place after 1856. It has been more attractive to stress the significance of antislavery (or antisouthernism) in the genesis of the new party which elected Abraham Lincoln president.[36] Yet the simultaneous flowering of populist, democratic, nativist, and moralist movements in the mid-1850s was unusual perhaps only for its size and success in American politics.

The alliance of anti-Catholicism and reform was typical of Anglo-Protestant culture. Given the frequent conservatism of the Roman church in opposing nationalism and liberalism in nineteenth-century Europe, given the perception of "Popery" among liberals in the Anglo-American world, and given the conservative ideology of Boston's Catholics and their support of the national Democratic party and its prosouthern policies, the temporary alliance of anti-Catholicism and democratization was hardly accidental.[37]

The Know-Nothings in several important ways also succeeded the Democratic–Free Soil Coalition, despite the fact that many former Whig voters also contributed to the populist victories of 1854–1855. The Coalition legislatures of 1851–1852 anticipated those of 1855–1856 by passing laws, for example, permitting pluralities to carry federal elections, changing the charter and governance of elite, Unitarian Harvard College, and aiding laborers, mechanics, and builders with lien laws. Indeed, in the area of economic reform there was an almost steady flow of legislation from 1851 through 1856 and beyond, beginning with general incorporation laws for manufacturing companies, which continued from Coalition to Know-Nothing and then Republican legislatures.[38]

The Know-Nothings, moreover, expressed a good deal of the era's popular fear of "monopolies" or chartered corporations. Railroads bore the brunt of the criticism, and the legislature turned down requests for more state credit to railroads. Criticism of the railroads was perhaps never stronger before the Civil War, though its practical effects were limited. The Know-Nothings did take the first steps, however, to force railroads (and ferry boats) to be more attentive to the safety of their passengers and employees. A law requiring trains to stop at crossings where other trains passed proved impractical, but it was the first check administered to an enterprise otherwise given a free hand by legislatures and courts.[39]

Thus Know-Nothingism was far more than just an outburst of nativism and anti-Catholicism, though it was that too. Its roots can be traced to the Coalition, to dissident Whigs, and even to the Workingmen of the 1830s. Even more significantly, its voting support in 1854 came in nearly equal amounts from former Whigs, former Democrats, and former Free Soilers, indicating the staggering antiparty dimensions of this smashing of the political logjam.[40]

Before it entered party politics, Know-Nothingism had been a secret brotherhood of "lodges" originating in the "Order of the Star Spangled Banner" and caught on as a lower-middle- and working-class organization designed to influence local affairs by bypassing the party, factory, and yard bosses. Know-Nothingism's secrecy thus differed from that of Masonry by being at least implicitly anti-elite. The importance of secrecy in effecting the populist revolt cannot be overemphasized, particularly in view of the part played by demands for the secret ballot and the ten-hour day in mobilizing support first for the Coalition and then for Know-Nothingism. Ironically, neither was enacted, yet both fed the growing anger against the Whig cotton magnates and their lawyer-politician colleagues.

How the secret ballot and the ten-hour day came to be linked and to be unrealized goals of the 1850s upheaval is a story of great complexity, which has not yet been told. Only its main outlines can be sketched here; they reveal both the radical potential as well as the limits of the antiparty populism of the 1850s.

Since the defeat of the Workingmen in the 1830s, state regulation of labor had remained on the periphery of politics, never gaining support from the major parties. Some effort to limit the hours and to provide for the schooling of children in factories had been made in 1836 and 1842,[41] but the workday for most employees remained longer than ten hours. In Lowell in 1845, according to a champion of the factories, hours in the mills ranged from a peak of 13.31 in April to a low of 11.24 in December–January. Ten or eleven hours were becoming the standard in some small shops, especially for skilled workers, but it is difficult to determine how prevalent the ten-hour day was in 1850 throughout Massachusetts.[42]

The ten-hour movement revived in the 1840s among mechanics in Fall River, the women operatives of Lowell, and skilled workers and mill hands in other towns, and it briefly received some distracting support from a few transcendentalists and middle-class utopians. A steady stream of petitions for a ten-hour day flowed from the mills to the legislature after 1842, some of them echoing the Workies' demands of the 1830s in asking for lyceums and lectures, enforcement of existing child-labor laws, and tax reform. In 1845 the legislature began to conduct hearings, at least, on the matter, but delivered reports arguing strongly against the ten-hour day. Though the movement was heartened by England's enactment of a ten-hour law in 1847, abetted by the 1849 report of a Lowell physician to the American Medical Association asserting that factory conditions were unhealthy, and finally validated by an 1850 minority report in the legislature in favor of ten hours, the measure still lacked any significant support among regular party politicians.[43]

Individual Democrats occasionally advocated a ten-hour law, but most ignored it. Even Lowell's Democratic newspaper, for example, while printing many articles critical of factories, seldom mentioned long hours, speed-ups, or the other topics of central concern to the ten-hour agitation. The Democratic state convention mentioned it once, in 1850, and supported a ten-hour law in the abstract and in the kind of language uniformly used by its opponents. When in 1852 a freshman Free Soil legislator gave the first speech in the legislature itself in favor of "short hours," the effort, he recalled, "was received with great derision. The House, usually very courteous and orderly, seemed unwilling to hear me through. One worthy old farmer got up in his seat and said: 'Isn't the young man from Worcester going to let me get up in the morning and milk my caows [sic]."[44] Meanwhile, ten-hour agitators were holding state conventions and meetings in all the major mill towns, and were bringing unity and effective legal language to a renewed barrage of ten-hour petitions.[45] While politicians laughed, the ten-hour workers were increasingly benefiting from the growing unpopularity of the mill managers and owners. The latter's highhandedness in trying to influence elections in Lowell, in fact, fed sentiment for both a secret ballot and the ten-hour day and probably contributed as well to the many springs of Know-Nothingism.

Events in Lowell in 1851 dramatically illustrated the relation between the ten-hour day, the secret ballot, and Whig political hegemony in Massachusetts. Ten-hour sentiment was perhaps as strong in Lowell as anywhere in the state, and so, too, was the opposition to it in the mill management and among loyalist foremen and workers. After the Coalition had managed to elect most of its slate of state representatives, Whigs were able to get the election voided on technicalities, and another became necessary. Once the other state returns were in, the balance of power in the legislature could be seen to hang on the Lowell outcome; and because the Coalition ticket was nominally for a ten-hour law, the contest became fierce.[46] Mill agents and foremen brought heavy pressure to bear on workers to vote Whig, and in doing so they stimulated a statewide outcry against interference in elections.

The Coalition legislature of 1852 accordingly passed a secret-ballot bill requiring that all ballots be deposited by voters in unmarked envelopes of uniform size and color and provided by the state. In 1853 the Coalitionists also made the secret ballot part of their proposed constitution and drew attention to it as one important reason for the voters to approve the constitution.

When the Whigs returned to power in early 1853, they nullified the measure by permitting voters to have the choice of using a sealed envelope or no envelope. They even applied the option to the March 7 election of delegates to the constitutional convention, which the people had in a referendum directed should be by secret ballot. This brazen act may have contributed to the Whigs' failure to elect many delegates and must have fed the silent growth of the Know-Nothing lodges. When the 1853 constitution went down to defeat, the secret ballot went with it.[47]

The Know-Nothings debated a secret ballot, but it failed to pass when the president broke a tie in the senate with a vote against it.[48] Perhaps the need for it, and the desire, had been exaggerated. The 1854 election demonstrated, certainly, that the ballot was free enough for a determined and organized mass of voters to bypass the factory and party bosses. At the same time, the extraordinary circumstances and proceedings which prompted that revolt should perhaps have created an imperative for a secret ballot.

The ten-hour question, even more than the ballot, defined the limits of nativist populism in the 1850s, though the legislature of 1855 considered the measure far more seriously than did any others of the mid-nineteenth century, debating it extensively and voting on it in the house and senate. Ten-hour feeling had provided strong backing for the Democratic–Free Soil Coalition, and probably contributed even greater support to the Know-Nothing coalition. How much, is difficult to say, but ten-hour sentiment was certainly stronger in the American Republican party (the Know-Nothings' formal name) than in any other party of the era save the Workingmen of the 1830s.

Just as some Know-Nothings supported temperance while others opposed prohibition, so Know-Nothings divided on the ten-hour law. The Boston *Daily Bee,* a leading nativist paper which described itself as a "Friend to the Worker," opened its columns to both proponents and opponents of the measure but also persistently advocated higher wages and better working conditions for workers.[49]

In contrast, the nativist Worcester *Daily Transcript* denounced any state regulation of working hours, criticizing the proposed law as unconstitutional and as discriminating against corporations since it would affect only those manufacturing corporations chartered by the state (which, of course, was its chief object). According to the *Transcript,* the ten-hour law struck "at the very root of the principle of Free Labor." Times were hard, and manufacturing corporations were already "distressed" and were practically being run just to employ workers. If hours were reduced, wages would need to be lowered. Pieceworkers such as weavers would be especially injured by the law, which was "a gross interference with personal rights." If Massachusetts were South Carolina and the operatives were slaves, the *Transcript* could approve of "legislative interference," but this measure insulted the intelligence and manhood of free workers. The hours of labor were the subject of mutual contract: "the proudest boast of Massachusetts is, that her labor is *free!*"[50]

While the issue was debated passionately in the legislature, workers again sent in petitions asking for such a law. Several large petitions from operatives *opposed* to it also came in, while a few, some seeking to effect a compromise and some perhaps to obfuscate, proposed an eleven-hour standard for the mills. In September 1852, in fact, the machine shops of Lowell, Lawrence, Manchester (N.H.), Biddeford (Maine), and Holyoke had reduced their hours to eleven, and in September 1853 the big mills in Massachusetts had voluntarily reduced hours for operatives to eleven. Along with the counterpetitions, this action by the managers must have reduced some of the momentum the ten-hour movement had built. Regarding the minority of workers against the law, however, the Free Soiler William S. Robinson had already observed in his 1852 minority report that it was not surprising that "among a class of people whose wages are at present none too high, there should be great hesitancy about asking for legislation, which they are told [by mill agents, etc.] may take from them a portion of their slender pittance."[51]

The ten-hour question, like temperance and antislavery, overlapped to a degree with the reaction against foreigners, especially Irish Catholics. The latter were associated in the native evangelical mind with rum, pauperism, prosouthern Democrats, anti-abolition, illegal voting, crime, and a host of other "problems." Irish Catholics were especially part of the "labor problem." Though the Irish were not all unskilled workers, they did begin to enter the mills increasingly in the late forties as the native population left because of deteriorating working conditions and management intransigence. In 1850, for example, one-third of the work force in the Hamilton Company mill at Lowell was Irish. In 1852 workers at the Salisbury Manufacturing Company at Amesbury went on strike against a reduction in their time for eating, and began to agitate for a ten-hour day. Eventually that strike was broken, and most of the native workers were replaced by recent immigrants.[52]

The workers of Salisbury and other ten-hour proponents argued that better working conditions and wages were necessary to keep the native American workmen in the factories. They saw that more manageable foreign laborers were replacing natives, and they predicted that the populations of the factory towns would in a few years replicate the sad condition of those of England.[53]

Yet neither the ten-hour men nor the Know-Nothings extensively exploited antiforeign and anti-Irish feelings in support of labor legislation. It may have been a situation so well understood that no elaboration was necessary. Moreover, the mill owners and their allies also resorted to nativist appeals. Some textile magnates (notably Amos A. Lawrence) kept their lines open to the nativists and argued that if the ten-hour limit passed, corporations would lower their wages and native workers would leave

Massachusetts factories and go to neighboring states like New Hampshire "where," in the words of the *Transcript, "labor is free,"* and foreigners would take their places. Ironically the Lawrences owned a New Hampshire mill which already employed mostly Irish immigrants.[54]

The ten-hour law made its way through the legislature in March and April of 1855. Opponents in the house tried to kill it with amendments, but it emerged fairly intact, only to lose in the senate by a large margin.[55] The history of this bill, only sketched here, is surely worth historical study, as is the claim of a well-informed historian of Lowell that "the corporation managers adopted the policy of Walpole and killed the Bill by secretly buying up some of the most influential of its advocates." Perhaps "pockets lined with gold" did make a difference.[56]

The Know-Nothings' failure to pass a ten-hour law suggests that no party or popular movement, no combination of classes and interest groups capable of electing a legislative majority, could have gained a law stipulating that the interests of factory workers merited the same protection accorded to entrepreneurs and other groups. The native workers were already fleeing Lowell and the other textile mills: the Lawrences and Appletons consistently responded to serious labor agitation with dismissal and then hiring of the cheapest and most pliant labor available, native or foreign.[57] After 1856, in addition, workers' gains of the period 1853–1855 appear to have been wiped out as the hourly rate paid to workers fell more rapidly than did daily or annual earnings.[58]

After 1856, of course, the sectional crisis over the extension of slavery caused the new Republican party to become the successor to the Whigs as the state's majority party, and the Know-Nothing movement gradually dissolved. When the ten-hour movement revived after the Civil War, individual Republicans, particularly former Free Soilers and Know-Nothings like N. P. Banks and Henry Wilson, were sympathetic to workers' interests, but the Republican party as a whole shunted aside renewed requests for regulation of factory hours.[59]

The willingness of the Know-Nothing legislatures to consider and to *enact* legislation, whatever their shortcomings in wrong action or in failure to act, differed dramatically from the kind of "politics as usual" attitude of party leaders which had ruled Whiggery, part of the Democracy, and the state for much of the past two decades. The latter was expressed perfectly in 1836 by Winthrop's predecessor as house Speaker, Julius Rockwell, a precocious western Massachusetts politician admired for his supreme "tact." Rockwell's confidential letter regarding the career of the 1836 legislature deserves to be quoted at length as a classic description of how many legislatures have operated and as a candid revelation of a standpat manager's point of view. At the beginning of every session, he said,

> a thousand movements are made, which never come to maturity. Many votes are taken early in a session, which seem to indicate a disposition, to change and innovation, which those who have experience here, know, indicate no such settled purpose. This was the case this year. I believe that less, by about 100, than half the members this year, were last year's members. Apprehension was expressed by some persons, that this legislature would assume a character bordering upon revolutionary. I have never for a moment entertained such an apprehension. . . . it was entirely unfounded. His Excellency's speech, touched . . . upon several topics which have been made the hobbies of the advocates of political changes. Now, mark the result. The stand taken in the Revised Statutes, respecting gaol limits, is preserved by a large vote in the popular branch. The prospect of Codifying the Common Law, reduced to a Commission to report upon *its expediency*. The Abolition of Capital punishment, (not yet definitely acted on) but unpromising. The sentence about monopoly construed into a theoretical truism, commented on, by a clear disposition in the legislature, to pursue the settled policy of the Commonwealth in granting, in all reasonable cases, the *facility* of corporations. The "root of bitterness," withering in the ground, rather than being painfully extracted, & c. & c. A vote taken today is as good an indication perhaps as any of the state of parties. A committee had reported against a project of making the office of sheriff elective—Mr. Rantoul made a motion to recommit (?) it, with instructions to report an Amendment to the Constitution, and the motion was rejected, by a vote of 242 to 125. In the Senate they have long discussions about corporations & c., but they have a clear Whig majority of four, when they are all in. In the House we have had scarcely any question decided by party votes, except the one, just mentioned, today. I apprehend they cannot make any questions about corporations party questions, with advantage to themselves, inasmuch as a good many Jackson men, in the House will go strong for the proper policy in that respect. Some of their leaders mean to make the subject of Mr. Clay's Land Bill a party question—it is to be hoped they will. Their own party would be divided upon it.[60]

There is something timeless about this statement. It is not impossible to imagine something like it being written in Massachusetts, or some other state, in 1736, or 1936.

In the final analysis the populist movements which challenged the status quo and which tensely coexisted or conflicted with mass organized parties were essential to the democratic health of the political culture. The populist upheavals of the early 1830s and especially those of the 1850s were democratic moments, the first set constituting a countertrend to parties as they developed and the second an antiparty insurgency rising up against, setting aside, or bypassing party politics.[61] These movements had their unattractive and undesirable aspects, as have most populist movements in this country. In the twentieth century, indeed, nativist populism in particular has often been quite ugly and possessed of few redeeming features. In the nineteenth century, antiparty populism did much to reinvigorate and sustain democracy, more than did organized mass political parties. Yet democracy is a thing of degrees, and it is too simple to conclude that parties were not at all democratic. This book has aimed to get beyond both the celebratory tradition which equates mass-party competition and democracy, and the condemnatory skepticism which sees primarily the selfishness of parties.

The celebratory tradition has surely been the stronger, however, and with it has prevailed a tendency to dismiss populist movements such as the Antimasons, Workingmen, Know-Nothings, and, to be sure, late-nineteenth-century populism as "alienated" or "extremist." Celebrants also imply (or assert) that political elites have defended political stability and democratic principles against impractical populist moralizers. Because of their education, their experience, or their general political character, elites, it is held, are more tolerant, pluralist, and pragmatic than are aroused publics. Some political scientists deny that this theory yields a valid description of recent politics, and the history of parties and social movements in the United States and England in the beginning and the middle of the nineteenth century suggests that not elites but average citizens temporarily mobilized into movements of protest and reform contributed mightily to the vitality of representative government.[62] "Mass publics" were hardly present, in any case, in nineteenth-century America, but many average citizens did possess a sense of efficacy; and when they grew, for various reasons at various times, highly distrustful of elites, they organized and became actively political.[63]

We no longer live in a world in which either "external" or "internal" criteria alone can be used to evaluate American institutions. Not only has the American sense of exceptionalism, uniqueness, and moral superiority to the Old World declined, it has been tempered and made more mature in recent decades. Americans now know that in some other nations workers are paid higher wages, that health care costs less and is better, that democratic institutions work well, and that many foreign products, especially high-technology items, outdo ours in world markets. Obviously, we have much to learn from others (as they have learned from the United States), and though a nation cannot simply copy the methods of another, it can try to adapt them to its own cultural patterns.

In the first instance, however, American political parties of the early nineteenth century must be assessed by values and ideals which matured on native grounds for over two centuries, and whose seedtime reached back another century and a half. Many Antimasons, Workingmen, Libertyites, Free Soilers, and Know-Nothings, though diverse and surely flawed, also judged American politics and society first according to internal criteria. Far more than Whigs or Democrats, the populist challenging groups appealed to the American Revolution as a source of inspiration and ideals. The Declaration of Independence had invoked universal truths, and in doing so had created a sufficient standard of ideals to which Americans could, and did, continually refer. The Declaration and Constitution were nation-creating actions and profound shapers of popular identity and aspirations within a particular and limited context of early republican (not necessarily "democratic") idealism. At the same time, they held up goals of justice and equity which permitted continual reinterpretation and expansion in a democratic direction, thereby conferring greater legitimacy on what has been called here the internal scale of cultural self-evaluation. The diverse sources of this tradition reach back further still. One might begin at least as early as the mid-ocean covenant of community intent composed aboard the *Arabella:* how can a people be as a "city upon a hill," a beacon light of example, unless it guides itself not by the standards of other nations, congratulates itself not on the failures and imperfections of distant civilizations, and justifies itself not by the oppression wrought by whatever despotisms happen to exist elsewhere, but adheres faithfully to ideals it has saved and carried from generation to generation, especially at those self-defining moments of crisis when a Winthrop, a Jefferson, or a Lincoln, or men and women whose names are not known to us, uttered a people's best and most deeply cherished hopes?

# Appendix I. A Note on Sources of Election Returns and Demographic Data

The basic file of election returns for this study consisted of township returns located at the Massachusetts State Archives at the State House, Boston. I collected returns for all Massachusetts (excluding Maine) counties and towns for

Governor's elections 1800–1844 (annual) and

Presidential elections 1824–1844.

In addition to my own file at Clark University, these data are also available in machine-readable form at the Inter-University Consortium for Political Research, Historical Archives, Ann Arbor. At the very beginning of this study, county-level returns and demographic data (1824–1860) were available at the consortium.

Most of the information about the Massachusetts legislature came from the annual *Journal of the House of Representatives,* and also from Ephraim M. Wright, ed., *Tabular View of Representation in the Commonwealth of Massachusetts, from 1780 to 1853* (Boston, 1854).

Information most useful for the economic character of towns was found in the following:

Massachusetts Tax Valuation, 1801, Massachusetts State Archives.

John B. Bigelow, *Statistical Tables: Exhibiting the Condition and Products of Certain Branches of Industry in Massachusetts . . . 1837* (Boston, 1838). Enumeration of various mills, factories, tan-yards, etc., with numbers of males, females, or "hands" variously given.

Louis McLane, *Report of the Secretary of the Treasury, 1832: Documents Relative to the Manufactures in the United States* (Washington, 1833), 1 (22nd Cong., 1st sess., *House Executive Documents,* no. 308). Provided the average number of males over sixteen working for each establishment, average number of boys under sixteen, and average number of women and girls, and often listed the name of owners.

Worcester County Papers, MWA. Principally for Worcester County, a great variety of information, aggregated by town, pertaining to agriculture, buildings, etc., collected for tax purposes.

*The Massachusetts Register* provided an annual list of the churches in each town, but this usually needed to be supplemented by county and town histories, which sometimes provided information about the relative strengths of denominations in each town. Otherwise, the latter could be estimated, quite roughly at best, for some places and some times from different kinds of information provided in official church sources.

The most useful were the following:

*Congregationalists:* Number of male and female communicants per church (no information about age) in "Abstracts of Statistical Reports," published in *Minutes of the General Association of Massachusetts, 1831–1840* (Boston, 1841). Information for earlier years was also available in the same source at the Congregational Library, Boston.

*Baptists:* Total number of members per church, not discriminated by sex or age. *Minutes* of various regional associations published between 1820 and 1840 were available at the State Library or at the Andover-Newton Theological School, Newton–including Worcester, 1820, 1835, 1840; Boston, 1830, 1835, 1840; Salem, 1830, 1835, 1840; Berkshire, 1835; Sturbridge, 1835, 1840; Westfield, 1831, 1836; Barnstable, 1843; Wendell, 1830, 1835, 1840.

*Episcopalians:* Number of communicants per church. *Journal of the Proceedings of the Annual Convention of the Protestant Episcopal Church, Massachusetts, Trinity Church, Boston, June 16, 17, 1830* (Cambridge, Mass., 1830). Episcopal Library, Boston.

*Methodists:* Total members per church (1840, 1847). Minutes of the New England Conference of the Methodist Episcopal Church, Vol. II . . . From 1822 to 1844, typescript of manuscript, New England Methodist Historical Society, Boston University Theological Library; and *Minutes of the New England Annual Conference of the Methodist Episcopal Church Held in the Lynn Common Church, April 28, 1847* (Boston, 1847). The total number of members per church in the Boston district for 1830 is also available, *Minutes . . . 1830.*

Two other sources, though they provide no numbers, were extremely helpful in identifying the presence or absence of Unitarian Churches, and of churches of all denominations:

Harold Field Worthley, ed., *An Inventory of the Records of the Par-*

*ticular (Congregational) Churches of Massachusetts Gathered 1620–1805* (Cambridge, Mass., 1970). The Proceedings of the Unitarian Historical Society, vol. 16, Parts 1 and 2, 1966–1969.

Carol D. Wright, *Report on the Custody and Condition of the Public Records of Parishes, Towns and Counties* (Boston, 1889), which contains tables of existing and extinct churches by county and town.

# Appendix II. The Contours of Massachusetts Elections, 1800–1848

**Table 1.** Party Vote, Percentage, and Total Vote in Governors' Elections 1800–1819

| *Year* | *Federal* | *Republican* | *Scattering* | *Total* |
|---|---|---|---|---|
| 1800 | 19,630 (50.3)[a] | 17,019 (43.6) | 391 (1.0) | 39,059[b] |
| 1801 | 25,452 (55.6) | 20,184 (44.1) | 180 (.3) | 45,816 |
| 1802 | 29,983 (60.5) | 19,443 (39.2) | 157 (.3) | 49,583 |
| 1803 | 29,199 (67.3) | 13,910 (32.0) | 300 (.7) | 43,409 |
| 1804 | 29,993 (55.1) | 24,006 (44.0) | 500 (.9) | 54,499 |
| 1805 | 35,204 (51.0) | 33,518 (48.6) | 264 (.4) | 68,986 |
| 1806 | 37,740 (50.2) | 37,109 (49.3) | 367 (.5) | 75,216 |
| 1807 | 39,234 (48.1) | 41,954 (51.5) | 328 (.4) | 81,516 |
| 1808 | 39,643 (48.9) | 41,193 (50.8) | 311 (.4) | 81,147 |
| 1809 | 47,916 (51.3) | 45,118 (48.3) | 288 (.3) | 93,322 |
| 1810 | 44,079 (48.5) | 46,541 (51.2) | 193 (.2) | 90,813 |
| 1811 | 40,142 (47.8) | 43,328 (51.6) | 447 (.5) | 83,917 |
| 1812 | 52,696 (50.6) | 51,326 (49.3) | 134 (.1) | 104,156 |
| 1813 | 56,754 (56.6) | 42,789 (42.7) | 680 (.7) | 100,223 |
| 1814 | 56,510 (54.8) | 46,502 (45.1) | 151 (.1) | 103,163 |
| 1815 | 51,099 (53.2) | 44,505 (46.4) | 359 (.4) | 95,963 |
| 1816 | 49,527 (51.1) | 47,321 (48.8) | 122 (.1) | 96,970 |
| 1817 | 46,610 (54.6) | 38,129 (45.1) | 207 (.2) | 84,496 |
| 1818 | 39,538 (55.7) | 30,041 (42.4) | 1,348 (1.9) | 70,927 |
| 1819 | 42,875 (53.7) | 35,271 (44.2) | 1,739 (2.2) | 79,885 |

[a] A second Federalist candidate got 2,019 (5.2) in 1800.
[b] Totals through 1815 are taken from Banner, *Hartford Convention;* others from manuscript returns in Mass. State Archives.

**Table 2.** Percentage Difference Between Federalists and Republicans 1800–1826

| | | | |
|---|---|---|---|
| 1800 | 11.8 | 1813 | 13.9 |
| 1801 | 11.5 | 1814 | 9.7 |
| 1802 | 21.3 | 1815 | 6.8 |
| 1803 | 35.3 | 1816 | 2.3 |
| 1804 | 11.1 | 1817 | 9.5 |
| 1805 | 2.4 | 1818 | 13.3 |
| 1806 | .9 | 1819 | 9.5 |
| 1807 | 3.4 | 1820 | 17.2 |
| 1808 | 1.9 | 1821 | 17.0 |
| 1809 | 3.0 | 1822 | 14.6 |
| 1810 | 2.7 | 1823 | 6.5 |
| 1811 | 3.8 | 1824 | 6.1 |
| 1812 | 1.3 | 1825 | — |
| | | 1826 | 49.3 |

**Table 3.** Party Vote, Percentage, and Total Vote in Governors' Elections, 1800–1826: Excluding Maine—Massachusetts Counties Only

| *Year* | *Federal* | *Republican* | *Scattering* | *Total* |
|---|---|---|---|---|
| 1800 | 15,747 (50.8)[a] | 13,908 (44.9) | 260 (.8) | 31,001 |
| 1801 | 20,144 (55.0) | 16,387 (44.7) | 112 (.3) | 36,643 |
| 1802 | 23,447 (58.8) | 16,281 (40.9) | 115 (.3) | 39,843 |
| 1803 | 23,244 (65.6) | 11,910 (33.6) | 260 (.7) | 35,414 |
| 1804 | 23,281 (56.6) | 17,638 (42.9) | 205 (.5) | 41,124 |
| 1805 | 28,003 (53.5) | 24,140 (46.1) | 227 (.4) | 52,370 |
| 1806 | 29,969 (53.5) | 25,709 (45.9) | 298 (.5)[b] | 55,976 |
| 1807 | 31,214 (51.1) | 29,630 (48.5) | 235 (.4) | 61,079 |
| 1808 | 30,660 (51.4) | 28,785 (48.3) | 211 (.4) | 59,656 |
| 1809 | 36,087 (52.8) | 32,022 (46.9) | 222 (.3) | 68,331 |
| 1810 | 33,748 (50.7) | 32,652 (40.1) | 118 (.2) | 66,518 |
| 1811 | 31,710 (50.7) | 30,479 (48.7) | 390 (.6) | 62,579 |
| 1812 | 40,256 (54.5) | 33,485 (45.4) | 71 (.1) | 73,812 |
| 1813 | 43,019 (60.4) | 27,984 (39.3) | 177 (.2) | 71,180 |
| 1814 | 42,743 (58.9) | 29,753 (41.0) | 107 (.1) | 72,603 |
| 1815 | 38,999 (57.9) | 28,162 (41.9) | 103 (.2) | 67,264 |
| 1816 | 37,985 (55.4) | 30,545 (44.5) | 84 (.1) | 68,614 |
| 1817 | 35,414 (58.8) | 24,723 (41.0) | 139 (.2) | 60,276 |
| 1818 | 30,530 (60.8) | 18,627 (37.1) | 1,037[c] (2.1) | 50,194 |
| 1819 | 33,798 (57.0) | 24,273 (40.9) | 1,206 (2.0) | 59,277 |
| 1820 | 31,072 (58.3) | 21,927 (41.1) | 298 (.6) | 53,297 |
| 1821 | 28,608 (58.3) | 20,268 (41.3) | 210 (.4) | 49,086 |
| 1822 | 28,487 (57.1) | 21,177 (42.5) | 185 (.4) | 49,849 |
| 1823 | 30,171 (46.2) | 34,402 (52.7) | 757 (1.2) | 65,330 |
| 1824 | 34,210 (46.8) | 38,650 (52.9) | 191 (.3) | 73,051 |
| 1825 | | 35,221 (94.1) | 2,205 (5.9) | 37,426 |
| 1826 | 8,149 (20.4) | 27,884 (69.7) | 3,959 (9.9) | 39,992 |

a A second Federalist candidate got 1,086 (3.5) in 1800.
b 106 of these were intended for Republican candidate.
c Most of these were intended for Republican candidate.

**Table 4.** Percentage Difference Between Federalists and Republicans 1800–1824–Excluding Maine 1800–1826

| | | | |
|---|---|---|---|
| 1800 | 5.9 | 1816 | 10.9 |
| 1801 | 10.3 | 1817 | 17.8 |
| 1802 | 17.9 | 1818 | 23.7 |
| 1803 | 32.0 | 1819 | 16.1 |
| 1804 | 13.7 | 1820 | 17.2 |
| 1805 | 7.4 | 1821 | 17.0 |
| 1806 | 7.6 | 1822 | 14.6 |
| 1807 | 2.6 | 1823 | 6.5 |
| 1808 | 3.1 | 1824 | 6.1 |
| 1809 | 5.9 | 1825 | — |
| 1810 | 1.6 | 1826 | 49.3 |
| 1811 | 2.0 | | |
| 1812 | 9.1 | | |
| 1813 | 21.1 | | |
| 1814 | 17.9 | | |
| 1815 | 16.0 | | |

**Table 5.** Party Vote in Governors' Elections, 1827–1848

| | *Nat. Rep.-Whig* | *Jack. Rep. Dem.* | *Antimason Liberty Free Soil* | *Other* | *Scattering* |
|---|---|---|---|---|---|
| 1827 | 29,029 (74.2) | | | 7,130 (18.2)[a] | 2,960 (7.5) |
| 1828 | 27,981 (81.5) | 4,423 (12.9) | | | 1,914 (5.6) |
| 1829 | 25,217 (71.6) | 6,864 (19.5) | | | 3,122 (8.9) |
| 1830 | 30,908 (65.5) | 14,440 (30.6) | | | 1,825 (3.9) |
| 1831S | 31,875 (65.2) | 12,694 (26.0) | | | 4,326 (8.8) |
| 1831F | 28,804 (53.9) | 10,975 (20.5) | 13,357 (25.0)[b] | | 279 (.5) |
| 1832 | 33,946 (52.9) | 15,197 (23.7) | 14,755 (23.0) | | 327 (.5) |
| 1833 | 25,149 (40.3) | 15,493 (24.8) | 18,274 (29.3) | 3,459 (5.5)[c] | 99 (.2) |
| 1834 | 44,802 (57.7)[d] | 19,255 (24.8) | 10,795 (13.9) | 2,602 (3.4) | 171 (.2) |
| 1835 | 37,555 (57.9) | 25,227 (38.9) | | 1,901 (2.9)[e] | 220 (.3) |
| 1836 | 42,160 (53.8) | 35,992 (45.9) | | | 237 (.3) |
| 1837 | 50,656 (60.3) | 33,089 (39.4) | | | 286 (.3) |
| 1838 | 51,642 (54.9) | 41,795 (44.5) | | | 504 (.5) |
| 1839 | 50,725 (49.7) | 51,034 (50.0) | | | 307 (.3) |
| 1840 | 70,884 (55.7) | 55,169 (43.3) | 1,081 (.8)[f] | | 181 (.1) |
| 1841 | 55,974 (50.4) | 51,367 (46.3) | 3,488 (3.1) | | 233 (.2) |
| 1842 | 54,939 (46.6) | 56,491 (47.9) | 6,382 (5.4) | | 180 (.2) |
| 1843 | 57,899 (47.7) | 54,242 (44.7) | 8,901 (7.3) | | 246 (.2) |
| 1844 | 69,570 (51.8) | 54,714 (40.8) | 9,635 (7.2) | | 306 (.2) |
| 1845 | 51,638 (48.8) | 37,427 (35.3) | 8,316 (7.9) | 8,089 (7.6)[g] | 454 (.4) |
| 1846 | 54,831 (53.8) | 33,199 (32.6) | 9,997 (9.8) | 3,423 (3.4) | 484 (.5) |
| 1847 | 53,742 (51.0) | 39,398 (37.4) | 9,193 (8.7) | 2,876 (2.7) | 234 (.2) |
| 1848 | 61,640 (49.7) | 25,323 (20.4) | 36,011 (29.0)[h] | | 1,081 (.9) |

a Free Bridge
b Antimasonic
c Workingmen
d Whig
e Independent
f Liberty
g Native American
h Free Soil

**Table 6.** Percentage Difference Between Major Parties in Governors' Elections, 1827–1848,[a] and Total Vote

| | | | | | |
|---|---|---|---|---|---|
| 1827 | 56.0 | 39,119 | 1838 | 10.4 | 93,941 |
| 1828 | 68.6 | 34,318 | 1839 | .3 | 102,066 |
| 1829 | 52.1 | 35,203 | 1840 | 12.4 | 127,315 |
| 1830 | 34.9 | 47,173 | 1841 | 4.1 | 111,062 |
| 1831S | 28.9 | 48,895 | 1842 | 1.2 | 117,992 |
| 1831F | 33.4 | 53,415 | 1843 | 3.0 | 121,288 |
| 1832 | 29.2 | 64,225 | 1844 | 11.0 | 134,225 |
| 1833 | 15.8 | 62,474 | 1845 | 13.5 | 105,924 |
| 1834 | 32.9 | 77,625 | 1846 | 21.2 | 101,934 |
| 1835 | 19.0 | 64,903 | 1847 | 13.6 | 105,443 |
| 1836 | 7.9 | 78,389 | 1848 | 20.7 | 124,055 |
| 1837 | 20.9 | 84,031 | | | |

a Minor party votes not included in calculations.

**Table 7.** Massachusetts Townships Gubernatorial Vote, Interyear Correlations, 1800–1844

| *Federalist / Adams Republican / National Republican / Whig* | | *Republican / Jacksonian Republican / Jacksonian Democrat / Democrat* | |
|---|---|---|---|
| 1800/01F | .817 | 1800R/01R | .824 |
| 1801/02 | .907 | | .907 |
| 1802/03 | .835 | | .831 |
| 1803/04 | .807 | | .793 |
| 1804/05 | .897 | | .884 |
| 1805/06 | .958 | | .948 |
| 1806/07 | .917 | | .915 |
| 1807/08 | .947 | | .944 |
| 1808/09 | .952 | | .953 |
| 1809–10 | .973 | | .974 |
| 1810/11 | .973 | | .974 |
| 1811/12 | .964 | | .963 |
| 1812/13 | .960 | | .953 |
| 1813/14 | .973 | | .964 |
| 1814/15 | .966 | | .966 |
| 1815/16 | .974 | | .974 |
| 1816/17 | .976 | | .975 |
| 1817/18 | .955 | | .953 |
| 1818/19 | .956 | | .954 |
| 1819/20 | .950 | | .944 |
| 1820/21 | .939 | | .932 |
| 1821/22 | .960 | | .955 |
| 1822/23 | .852 | | .851 |
| 1823/24 | .908 | | .928 |
| 1826AR/27AR | .100 | | |
| 1827AR/28AR | .207 | | |
| 1828AR/29NR | .543 | 1828JR/29JR | .631 |
| 1829NR/30NR | .546 | 1829JR/30JR | .610 |
| 1830NR/31NR (Sp) | .645 | 1830JR/31JD | .737 |
| Sp1831NR/F31NR | .546 | 1831JD/32JD | .844 |
| F1831NR/32NR | .741 | 1831JD/32JD | .834 |
| 1832NR/33NR | .064 | 1832JD/33D | .864 |
| 1833NR/34W | .090 | 1833D/34D | .847 |
| 1834W/35W | .581 | 1834/35 | .714 |
| 1935/36 | .727 | 1835/36 | .756 |
| 1836/37 | .873 | 1836/37 | .870 |
| 1837/38 | .882 | 1837/38 | .874 |
| 1838/39 | .891 | 1838/39 | .895 |
| 1839/40 | .892 | 1839/40 | .893 |
| 1840/41 | .946 | 1840/41 | .964 |
| 1941/42 | .862 | 1841/42 | .911 |
| 1842/43 | .886 | 1842/43 | .902 |
| 1843/44 | .935 | 1843/44 | .949 |

**Table 8.** Massachusetts Townships Presidential Vote, Interyear Correlations, 1824–1844

| *Adams Republican National Republican Whig* | | *Jacksonian Republican Jacksonian Democrat Democrat* | |
|---|---|---|---|
| 1824AR/1828AR | .223 | | |
| 1828AR/32NR | .280 | 1828JR/32JD | .723 |
| 1832NR/36W | .516 | 1832JD/36D | .483 |
| 1836W/40W | .821 | 1836D/40D | .815 |
| 1840W/44W | .856 | 1840D/44D | .888 |

**Table 9.** Actual Legislative Turnover: Number of Different Men Serving as State Representatives in Selected Counties, 1800–1803, 1809–1812, 1835–1838

| | *1800–1803* | | *1809–1812* | | *1835–1838* | |
|---|---|---|---|---|---|---|
| *County* | *No.* | *%* | *No.* | *%* | *No.* | *%* |
| Worcester | 138/74 | *53* | 271/126 | *45* | 316/228 | *72* |
| Berkshire | 69/31 | *42* | 146/87 | *59* | 147/119 | *80* |
| Hampshire | 56/23 | *41* | 94/47 | *50* | 107/84 | *78* |
| Plymouth | 45/19 | *42* | 118/58 | *49* | 153/85 | *55* |
| Barnstable | 69/31 | *42* | 71/39 | *55* | 147/119 | *80* |

**Table 10.** Standard Deviations of Federalist and Republican Percentages, 1800–1824, and Democratic and Anti-Democratic Percentages, 1828–1844

| | *Fed.* | *Rep.* | | NR-Wg | JR-Dem |
|---|---|---|---|---|---|
| 1800 | 32.66 | 33.92 | 1828 | 21.05 | 19.08 |
| 1801 | 30.23 | 30.20 | 1829 | 28.68 | 23.44 |
| 1802 | 27.57 | 27.61 | 1830 | 25.71 | 23.98 |
| 1803 | 25.41 | 25.24 | 1831 | 28.81 | 24.23 |
| 1804 | 25.70 | 25.85 | 1831F | 22.44 | 21.16 |
| 1805 | 22.69 | 22.96 | 1832 | 21.47 | 19.47 |
| 1806 | 22.35 | 22.26 | 1833 | 14.05 | 19.57 |
| 1807 | 21.57 | 21.41 | 1834 | 21.60 | 19.14 |
| 1808 | 22.44 | 22.30 | 1835 | 19.37 | 19.23 |
| 1809 | 22.05 | 22.02 | 1836 | 18.63 | 18.61 |
| 1810 | 21.83 | 21.81 | 1837 | 17.81 | 17.95 |
| 1811 | 21.87 | 21.85 | 1838 | 15.89 | 15.96 |
| 1812 | 21.30 | 21.31 | 1839 | 14.24 | 14.31 |
| 1813 | 22.11 | 21.98 | 1840 | 14.57 | 14.71 |
| 1814 | 21.36 | 21.31 | 1841 | 14.49 | 14.72 |
| 1815 | 21.75 | 21.71 | 1842 | 13.92 | 14.66 |
| 1816 | 21.93 | 21.88 | 1843 | 14.08 | 14.92 |
| 1817 | 22.23 | 22.21 | 1844 | 13.95 | 14.60 |
| 1818 | 22.48 | 22.44 | | | |
| 1819 | 22.11 | 22.16 | | | |
| 1820 | 22.57 | 22.18 | | | |
| 1821 | 21.62 | 21.85 | | | |
| 1822 | 22.01 | 22.08 | | | |
| 1823 | 21.82 | 21.87 | | | |
| 1824 | 20.66 | 20.59 | | | |

# Appendix VII. Maritime Massachusetts

A useful source for identifying small ports in the Federal period is the state tax-valuation manuscript of 1801, at the Massachusetts State Archives, which gave the "tons of vessels" for every town. Though misleading in some respects, because some ports were still recovering from the Revolution and would grow more prosperous after 1801, the valuation list's targeting of almost fifty towns with vessel tonnage, one-sixth of all the towns, excluding those in Maine, gave an excellent sense of how much "maritime industries" pervaded the coast in a nonspecialized economy, ranging from Boston with 74,530 tons to Marshfield with 177, Malden with 37, and Orleans with 23.

Most of the small ports on the north and south shores were parts of towns in which other economic activities, chiefly farming, supported most of the population. Whether the presence of maritime enterprise by itself contributed to Federal majorities is difficult to say. Most of the *towns* voted Federal, some did not. Their partisan loyalty appeared to be related to the several conditions that affected political preferences throughout the state: the religious composition of the town, its authority and influence structure, and so on.

If most of the voters in these towns were farmers, the citizens of Cape Cod presented a special case. On the Cape, which was truly a part of Maritime Massachusetts, the inhabitants cultivated the sea and shore as intensively as farmers fifty miles inland used the varied resources of the land. Cope Codders engaged not only in fishing and the coasting trade but also in boat and ship building, and some whaling, and they harvested shellfish from the water and shore as well as tons of salt from sea water. Any agriculture that could be managed was serendipitous.

*Small Ports Tons of Vessels 1801*

| | |
|---|---|
| *Essex County* | |
| Haverhill | 712 |
| Manchester | 593 |
| Ipswich | 846 |
| Salisbury | 445 |
| Danvers | 525 |
| Newbury | 239 |
| Lynn | 189 |
| Amesbury | 365 |
| Bradford | 30 |
| *Suffolk County* | |
| Chelsea | 108 |
| *Middlesex County* | |
| Charlestown | 372 |
| Watertown | 3,200 |
| Medford | 142 |
| Malden | 37 |
| *Norfolk County* | |
| Hingham | 1,140 |
| Hull | 625 |
| *Plymouth County* | |
| Plymouth | 3,411 |
| Duxbury | 2,163 |
| Rochester | 900 |
| Scituate | 639 |
| Wareham | 645 |
| Kingston | 576 |
| Pembroke | 257 |
| Marshfield | 177 |
| Hanover | 30 |
| *Bristol County* | |
| New Bedford | 7,472 |
| Westport | 695 |
| Dighton | 308 |

The eastern Cape, consisting of the elbow which bent at Chatham and then continued north through Orleans to Provincetown, was its most purely maritime part. Beyond Orleans the Cape became inhospitable to agriculture or pasturing, and its folk engaged almost entirely in fishing, coasting, or sea-related work. The sand dunes of Truro and Provincetown perhaps surpassed any other place in New England in the degree to which it was nonagricultural.[1] The eastern Cape was generally Republican, though except for Orleans not overwhelmingly so.

The west Cape supported some agriculture and more numerous populations. Though consisting of very similar towns, it was much more divided in partisanship than was the eastern Cape. In the west, Sandwich, Falmouth, and Barnstable were all solidly Republican. They were the Cape's most populous towns in 1810, and Barnstable and Sandwich were probably the two most prosperous.

*West Cape Republican Percentage and Total Vote, 1812*

| | | |
|---|---|---|
| Sandwich | 66.6 | (302) |
| Falmouth | 88.3 | (266) |
| Barnstable | 78.8 | (405) |
| Yarmouth | 14.8 | (229) |
| Dennis | 17.5 | (154) |
| Brewster | 14.3 | (126) |
| Harwich | 75.4 | (130) |

Federal Yarmouth, known as a "shipmasters' town," resembled Barnstable and Sandwich, with shipbuilding, fishing, and farming its major interests. Federal Dennis had been part of Yarmouth and in addition to fishing and shipbuilding took the lead in building saltworks. While these were thriving towns, Dr. Dwight, never prejudiced against Federal towns, found Republican Barnstable to be more impressive in showing marks of wealth and taste. Staunchly Republican Falmouth was, according to Bidwell, the "most maritime" of the Cape towns.[2]

The Republican cast of the Cape had much to do with the presence of religious dissenters in this peripheral region. In the town of Barnstable, controversy over religious taxation dated back to at least the 1770s, when a Baptist society had first formed—by 1809 it had acquired two Baptist churches. At Yarmouth, by contrast, not until 1819 did a tiny group of Methodists set themselves apart, with Baptists following in 1824. Even on the Cape, Congregationalists were in a majority, so there must have been many Congregationalists there who also voted Republican.[3]

Sometimes the line between Republican dissenters and Federal Congregationalists could be sharply drawn. The town of Harwich, like its sister towns, made its living from both land and sea. Since the middle of the eighteenth century, two separate churches and a Baptist church competed with the standing church for dominance in the parish. From the 1760s to the 1790s the Baptists' tax status was uncertain, until they gained incorporation and exemption in 1798. In 1809 a Methodist church formed and dissenters were strong enough to force the Congregational church to go to a voluntary system for financial support, and by 1819 that church had dissolved. Meanwhile in 1803 the Federal legislature, desirous of creating a Federal town in unfriendly Barnstable County, had taken the northern half of Harwich and made it into the town of Brewster, named after Elder William Brewster of the *Mayflower,* who had many descendents in that neighborhood. In 1803 Brewster was a settlement of prosperous farm buildings, saltworks, and two fishing vessels. More important, it was also the seat of the old North Parish, which had had only two ministers from 1755 to 1831. Brewster thus well represented the traditional church and a settled ministry, while Harwich had experienced many of the kinds of turmoil and change that transformed the established church in the early national period.[4] In 1812 Harwich voted 75 percent Republican while Brewster voted 85 percent Federal.

**Table 1.** Massachusetts Population Centers, 1810, and Party Percentages

| *Town* | *Population* | *Federalist* | *Republican* |
|---|---|---|---|
| Boston | 33,250 | 58.2% | |
| Salem | 12,618 | | 55.7% |
| Newburyport | 7,634 | 69.7% | |
| Nantucket | 6,807 | | 78.5% |
| Gloucester | 5,943 | 55.0% | |
| Marblehead | 5,900 | | 89.9% |
| New Bedford | 5,651 | 63.6% | |
| Newbury | 5,176 | 63.3% | |
| Bridgewater | 5,157 | 50.8% | |
| Charlestown | 4,954 | | 64.4% |
| Rehoboth | 4,866 | | 54.0% |
| Beverly | 4,608 | 73.3% | |
| Middleboro | 4,400 | | 69.6% |
| Plymouth | 4,228 | 63.0% | |
| Lynn | 4,087 | | 61.7% |
| Taunton | 3,907 | 50.6% | |
| Roxbury | 3,669 | | 75.3% |
| Barnstable | 3,646 | | 85.3% |
| Ipswich | 3,569 | 66.7% | |
| Dartmouth | 3,217 | 72.6% | |

An analysis of population and party vote based on computation of correlation coefficients for all towns in 1810, and for all towns except Boston, Salem, and Nantucket, indicated very little correlation between size of town and partisan vote.

**Table 2.** Massachusetts Population Centers, 1820, and Party Percentages

| *Town* | *Population* | *Federalist* | *Republican* |
|---|---|---|---|
| Boston | 43,298 | 67.6% | |
| Salem | 12,731 | 81.5% | |
| Nantucket | 7,266 | | 59.1% |
| Newburyport | 6,852 | 69.3% | |
| Charlestown | 6,591 | | 55.7% |
| Gloucester | 6,384 | | 54.2% |
| Bridgewater | 5,670 | 65.4% | |
| Marblehead | 5,630 | | 75.1% |
| Middleboro | 4,687 | | 57.3% |
| Taunton | 4,520 | 68.9% | |
| Lynn | 4,515 | 55.1% | |
| Plymouth | 4,348 | 66.3% | |
| Beverly | 4,283 | 95.0% | |
| Worcester | 4,172 | | 59.2% |
| Roxbury | 4,135 | | 60.2% |
| New Bedford | 3,947 | 92.2% | |
| Springfield | 3,914 | 57.5% | |
| Barnstable | 3,824 | | 66.1% |
| Dorchester | 3,684 | 54.1% | |
| Newbury | 3,671 | 69.3% | |

**Table 3.** 1823 Party Vote of 1820 Population Centers

| *Town* | *Federalist* | *Republican* |
|---|---|---|
| Boston | 50.4% | |
| Salem | | 52.6% |
| Nantucket | | 51.1% |
| Newburyport | 55.4% | |
| Charlestown | | 67.2% |
| Gloucester | | 58.6% |
| Bridgewater | 61.2% | |
| Marblehead | | 91.2% |
| Middleboro | | 64.6% |
| Taunton | 59.5% | |
| Lynn | | 69.4% |
| Plymouth | 55.7% | |
| Beverly | 67.8% | |
| Worcester | | 59.0% |
| Roxbury | | 74.9% |
| New Bedford | 73.4% | |
| Springfield | | 58.0% |
| Barnstable | | 80.9% |
| Dorchester | 54.1% | |
| Newburyport | 69.3% | |

**Table 4.** Republican Gain in Massachusetts Counties 1812 to 1824, Ranked by Whole Number of Votes

| *County* | *1812* | *1824 (%)* | *Votes ±* |
|---|---|---|---|
| Suffolk | 1,884 | 3,121 (47.8) | +1,237 |
| Essex | 4,321 | 5,350 (53.2) | +1,029 |
| Worcester | 4,334 | 5,206 (44.8) | + 872 |
| Middlesex | 5,153 | 5,881 (63.6) | + 728 |
| Norfolk | 3,028 | 3,468 (63.6) | + 440 |
| Bristol | 2,463 | 2,824 (50.7) | + 361 |
| Plymouth | 2,805 | 3,155 (58.0) | + 350 |
| Hampshire | 1,068 | 1,397 (32.9) | + 329 |
| Hampden | 1,957 | 2,086 (55.6) | + 129 |
| Franklin | 1,571 | 1,670 (41.4) | + 99 |
| Barnstable | 1,278 | 1,233 (72.0) | − 45 |
| Dukes | 209 | 144 (59.3) | − 65 |
| Berkshire | 2,932 | 2,862 (59.7) | − 70 |
| Nantucket | 482 | 253 (68.4) | − 229 |

**Table 5.** Federal Loss of Votes in 1823 Election Compared with 1812 Election, by County

| *County* | *No.* | *Percent of 1812* |
|---|---|---|
| Essex | −2,131 | 34 |
| Suffolk | −1,001 | 26 |
| Franklin | − 955 | 34 |
| Bristol | − 896 | 29 |
| Worcester | − 884 | 14 |
| Hampshire | − 877 | 26 |
| Hampden | − 760 | 40 |
| Middlesex | − 707 | 19 |
| Norfolk | − 536 | 25 |
| Berkshire | − 531 | 21 |
| Plymouth | − 439 | 16 |
| Barnstable | − 434 | 46 |
| Dukes | − 101 | 55 |
| Nantucket | (+ 69) | (+29) |

**Table 6.** Congregational and Non-Congregational Churches in Federal and Republican Towns (75 Percent or more), 1800, 1811, 1823

| | *FEDERAL* | | *REPUBLICAN* | |
|---|---|---|---|---|
| | *Cong.* | *Non-Cong.* | *Cong.* | *Non-Cong.* |
| *1800* | 96 | 45 | 53 | 25 |
| *1811* | 45 | 7 | 34 | 34 |
| *1823* | 34 | 8 | 50 | 39 |

**Table 7.** Churches of Major Denominations in Federal and Republican Towns (75 percent or more), by Denomination, 1811

| | *Cong.* | *Bap.* | *Meth.* | *Pres.* | *Univ.* | *Epis.* | *Frds.* |
|---|---|---|---|---|---|---|---|
| *Federal* | | | | | | | |
| No. | 45 | 6 | 1 | | | | |
| % | 87 | 12 | 2 | | | | |
| *Republican* | | | | | | | |
| No. | 34 | 23 | 7 | | | 2 | 2 |
| % | 50 | 34 | 10 | | | 3 | 3 |

**Table 8.** Churches of Major Denominations in Federal and Republican Towns (75 percent or more), by Denomination, 1823

| | *Cong.* | *Bap.* | *Meth.* | *Pres.* | *Univ.* | *Epis.* | *Frds.* |
|---|---|---|---|---|---|---|---|
| *Federal* | | | | | | | |
| No. | 34 | 5 | 1 | 1 | 1 | 0 | 0 |
| % | 81 | 12 | 2 | 2 | 2 | | |
| *Republican* | | | | | | | |
| No. | 50 | 25 | 9 | 1 | 1 | 3 | |
| % | 56 | 28 | 10 | 1 | 1 | 3 | |

# Appendix XI. Party Organization in Worcester County, 1840–1844

The Whigs' extraordinary efforts at party organization in 1840 make it possible to examine in detail the state of Whig organization in the towns of Worcester County. The state central committee sent a list of questions to all county chairmen who then passed them on to town committeemen. The central committee wanted to know such basic information as the town's population, its vote in the last state and town elections, the names and politics of the selectmen, town clerk, postmaster, and the like. The committee asked what issues had been important in the last election, what organization had existed previously, and "What organization of the whig party have you now?"[1] The replies provide unusually good information about one party's organization at the local level.

In town affairs a very mixed situation prevailed with respect to party politics. Perhaps it should be noted first that Worcester, the shire town, population center of central Massachusetts, bustling canal teminus, and railroad town, was not representative of the county's fifty-three other towns. Worcester possessed both a Whig and Democratic newspaper, not to mention many professional men of the type who took the greatest interest in politics. By the late 1830s, party lines had entered into elections at all levels and the Whigs particularly had fielded an elaborate array of committees in all of the town's twelve school districts.[2] Politics in Worcester, in short, had an urban flavor and resembled more the politics of Salem or Pittsfield than that of many of Worcester County's towns.

To be sure, Whigs and Democrats could be found in every town, and before the Liberty party made inroads virtually all the ballots cast in state and federal elections were for one of the two parties. The politics of every town's leading men accordingly were known, and the Whig town chairmen readily supplied the party identities of town officers. In Ashburnham, for example, the case with the selectmen was watertight. "You may shoot them if they are not Whigs, and they were elected by a strictly party vote." In Hardwick four of five selectmen were "Loco," but two of three assessors were Whigs. Several postmasters were identified as "Loco Foco–*of course,*" probably in reference to the Democrats having had the federal appointive power for so long. The Sutton town clerk was a Whig but unhappy with the liquor law, and so he was thought to have voted for Morton in 1839, "which induced the other party to put him in [as] town clerk." Yet while party considerations did influence voting for town officers in some towns, and while an official's party affiliation was usually known, in most towns party did not determine local outcomes.

The central committee had asked directly whether town elections were conducted on party lines, and of the forty-six towns replying to this question, only thirteen reported that party lines clearly prevailed.[3] In ten towns the situation was mixed or unclear–party probably ruled in three of these, while in five the local officials belonging to the dominant party were elected with no opposition. In twenty-three other towns from which replies came, however, town elections proceeded without reference to party or "political considerations." In Northborough the March elections were "not in the least affected by party considerations"; in Brookfield they went on "without reference to politics"; Hardwick reported "several important ballotings," but none constituted a "test of party strength. Our Town Offices have never been elected by party votes." The Lunenberg chairman explained that the party test came "at the choice of county com'r; in choice of other officers local rather than political feelings prevailed"; in Grafton the "election for Municipal officers turned upon the question of temperance"; and in North Brookfield "Politicks was not called in question."

More revealing, perhaps, were answers directly concerning past and present states of party organization. The forty-six replies to the question about organization "heretofore" clearly indicated that the towns rarely had permanent committees, and that if they did the committees became activated only shortly before elections. Almost every town now had a town committee, a Whig Association, or some kind of organization, but twenty-three had possessed none before 1840. Nine towns appear to have had some organization, while only six claimed to have had a strong organization previously. Eight others stressed that they got organized just before each election and that those taking the lead varied each year. Some towns in which Whigs had yearly formed committees on an ad hoc basis actually put forth quite respectable efforts. Lancaster, Hubbardston, and

Sturbridge, for example, got up committees in every school district before each election, so perhaps a dozen towns had possessed fairly good Whig organization before 1840. But for the great majority, the system and zeal of 1840 were exceptional.

The evidence thus testifies to the long-standing difficulty that political parties have experienced in penetrating local elections in small-town America. At the same time the powerful impact of 1840 on the usual norms of community nonpartisanship is also quite apparent.

In 1844 party mechanism again came into play, but not to the same extent or in the same way as in 1840. Enthusiasm still popped up, but the great revival spirit was gone. For one thing, few towns bothered to organize in the spring as they had in 1840. In late July, Athol found "at present no excitement"; in August, Oakham's chairman reported that it was not as organized as previously and that there was "little animation in either party." The Dudley committeeman wrote that he had been too busy "haying" to rouse the Whigs but that he was still confident they would do well. Several chairmen reported that the "abolitionists" presence was having an unsettling effect on the Whigs, and this theme grew stronger during the fall. Whereas in 1840 a buoyant spirit had kept Whig cadres engaged and optimistic from spring to fall, now even in early November some Whigs complained of lack of organization or low spirits. Sutton, for example, possessed a large Whig town committee and vigilant subcommittees in each school district, but the Whig chairman expected a lower turnout and an increase in the Liberty-party vote; besides, Sutton was a strong Locofoco town and there was "want of life, courage and unity" among Whigs.[4]

On the other hand, Whig organization did not start from scratch in 1844; much of it had remained in place since 1840, and many of the same men were acting as local leaders. Furthermore, the practice of drawing up systematic lists of voters seemed well established.[5] Though the Whigs started later, their hopes darkened by the shadow cast by defections to the antislavery cause, the party's institutional vitality carried it forward as a campaign organization in this and succeeding elections until its collapse and displacement by the Know-Nothing and Republican parties in the 1850s.

# Appendix XII.A.

**Table 1.** Whig Vote in 1839 and 1840, in the Thirteen Most Populous Places

| | Whig Percentage 1839 Gov. | Whig Percentage 1840 Pres. |
|---|---|---|
| Boston | 56.8+ | 62.8+ |
| Lowell | 55.8+ | 62.0+ |
| Salem | 67.3+ | 70.7+ |
| New Bedford | 52.3+ | 53.3 |
| Charlestown | 41.2 | 48.0 |
| Springfield | 48.9 | 56.6 |
| Lynn | 43.5 | 48.8 |
| Roxbury | 51.5+ | 62.5+ |
| Nantucket | 66.0+ | 67.6+ |
| Cambridge | 58.7+ | 63.2+ |
| Taunton | 45.5 | 53.5 |
| Worcester | 60.2+ | 69.6+ |
| Newburyport | 53.6+ | 65.9+ |
| *State Percentage* | 49.7 | 57.1 |
| Number Over | 9 | 8 |

**Table 2.** Whig Vote in 1840 in Boston and Seven Contiguous Towns

| | |
|---|---|
| Boston | 62.8 |
| Chelsea | 60.2 |
| Charlestown | 48.0 |
| Cambridge | 63.2 |
| Brighton | 62.8 |
| Brookline | 69.1 |
| Roxbury | 62.5 |
| Dorchester | 62.6 |

**Table 3.** Whig Vote in 1840, in Sixteen Towns Not Contiguous to and within Ten Miles of Boston

| *Place* | *Population* | % |
|---|---|---|
| Lynn | 9,367 | 48.9 |
| Saugus | 1,098 | 33.1 |
| S. Reading | 1,517 | 60.2 |
| Stoneham | 1,017 | 43.4 |
| Malden | 2,514 | 47.3 |
| Medford | 2,478 | 46.7 |
| Woburn | 2,993 | 33.7 |
| W. Cambridge | 1,363 | 45.6 |
| Lexington | 1,642 | 48.0 |
| Waltham | 2,504 | 53.2 |
| Watertown | 1,810 | 57.1 |
| Newton | 3,351 | 64.5 |
| Dedham | 3,290 | 57.7 |
| Milton | 1,822 | 49.1 |
| Quincy | 3,486 | 49.3 |
| Hull | 231 | 65.7 |

## Appendix XII.B. Religious Data and Political Parties

In Massachusetts religious diversity and alienation from institutions were greater in 1840 than ever before. But a commanding if not overwhelming majority of the population remained somehow involved or identified with churches or sects. The low incidence of membership for adult males does not accurately reflect overall male participation in religious life. Membership usually implied "full communion" and acceptance of a set of standards and identification with an inner circle of the church which most men, for a variety of reasons, chose to avoid. But they did not necessarily absent themselves from the life of the *congregation,* or disassociate themselves from the beliefs of their denomination.

Many town and county histories tell of local notables who, while never becoming members of or "uniting" with a church, nevertheless supported it with their time or money. A nonmember might be a choir leader, the donor of the church organ or bell, a lifelong regular attendant, a tireless defender of a church's legal rights, a member of the building committee, or a man who had given more money to the church than had anyone else in town. The "Natick Cobbler," Henry Wilson, was a regular churchgoer, a heavy financial backer, and a close friend of the minister–but never a communicant of Natick's Second Church.[1] In 1821 the original Puritan church of Bedford, a small Middlesex County town, counted 105 members from among the 650 or so souls who inhabited the place. Of the 105 members, 66 were women and 39 were men. Of course, not all of the men were necessarily of voting age. Indeed, only 29 of all members, mostly males, were taxpayers, while in Bedford as a whole there were 155 polls or taxed persons. Since the potential electorate numbered perhaps 100 to 110, the proportion of voters who were church members was certainly under 30 percent, and perhaps closer to one-fourth or one-fifth. In 1817, however, *56 men* had bought the 71 pews in the new meeting house just completed that year, suggesting that the number of male heads of families in Bedford who took part in church life was undoubtedly half, and perhaps a substantial majority, of the voters.[2]

Bedford was not even typical of Middlesex, let alone Massachusetts. Indeed, given the variety of experiences that characterized New England towns in this period, it is difficult to know what was typical. In some towns, for example, once rival religious societies or churches formed, then denominational lines became quite rigid, and religious identities filled with passionate differentiation. In other towns, or even after the lapse of some years in the case just described, denominational boundaries were relatively loose, varying with the shifting sands of local disputes and personalities. In all parts of rural Massachusetts, different sects often availed themselves of the same minister, or sometimes worshiped together. Historians have duly noted the galloping division and subdivision of parishes in the period from the Revolution to the 1830s, but reunions, mergers, and cooperation have attracted less attention. The Orthodox-Unitarian dispute has impressed a profile of polarization on the history of the Congregational church before and after disestablishment, but there were in many towns moderates who managed to prevent or delay separation, or who fought losing battles, but who in any case have been largely forgotten.[3]

By 1840 "the disorganized condition of most parishes in New England" was well known and much remarked upon. In 1833 a Northborough minister typically recalled with sadness a time (1816) when the whole population of the town had welcomed him as a new minister, when all the town's children had assembled for religious instruction, when neighboring churches had been friendly, and when most communities except the larger towns had been the same way. The Reverend Fiske of New Braintree was surely an exception when he could in 1846 claim, despite the existence of a minority of dissenters in his town, to have attended *every* funeral and to have been in every household at some time during his fifty-year pastorate.[4]

In the larger towns not only had sectarian division long been common but the numbers of unchurched had prompted deep concern among pious folk. In 1818 the Salem Society for the Moral and Religious Instruction of the Poor had formed because benevolent leaders had become alarmed at the existence of "several hundred families of poor people in the town unconnected with any religious society."[5] If Salem was so afflicted, what was the condition of Boston? And what was the state of religion in such places as Lowell and other factory towns?[6] Was religion in the larger towns far less important than in the country, and, if so, was it less important among voters?

The case of the booming manufacturing town of Fall River in 1840 warns against assuming that lack of religious affiliation was widespread in all such places. The information available in this case, compiled in a "historical sermon," indicates the kind of data that historians minimally require in order to be able effectively to measure religious affiliations in communities. In this rapidly industrializing town of 6,738, there were 3,288 white males, 1,603 taxable polls, and 1,113 legal voters. On Sundays eleven different religious congregations gathered to worship in Fall River, and eight of these counted 1,875 members or communicants. More important, the number of families "nominally connected" with some congregation was 1,110, or just about equal to the number of eligible voters. However, of these 1,110 families "many (it is believed not less than 200 families) rarely, if ever, attend public worship."[7] Thus, a conservative estimate would be that at least 75 percent of Fall River's voters were affiliated with churches or attended worship on Sundays.

Some Massachusetts church membership records are available for the period 1830–1850, the Congregational being the most complete, followed, in declining order of utility, by the Baptist, Episcopal, and Methodist. These records are not always easy to match, for they differ in the years available, in the units reported on, in the definitions of members, or in the differentiation between men and women. It is possible that these records can be combined with other sources, notably with county and town histories, to generate estimates of the numbers of men affiliated with churches. I attempted to create such data for Worcester County's fifty-six towns in 1840, making use of sources mentioned in Appendix I, a manuscript list of churches of the county, apparently for 1840, and other information regarding voluntary associations and churches.[8] The manuscript list, the *Massachusetts Register,* and local histories, unfortunately, did not always agree. Worse, enough information to make rather gross estimating unnecessary was seldom available. The recovery of systematic religious information regarding antebellum electorates is, in short, a subject worthy of dissertations, books, and funded team research.

# NOTES

## I. Party Mobilization in the 19th Century

1. John Stuart Mill, *The Spirit of the Age,* ed. Frederick A. von Hayek (Chicago, 1942; first ed., 1831), p. 5; Louis Wirth, pref. to Karl Mannheim, *Ideology and Utopia. An Introduction to the Sociology of Knowledge* (New York, 1936), pp. xxii–xxiii. For other definitions of political culture, adapted here in part, see J. P. Nettl, *Political Mobilization: A Sociological Analysis of Methods and Concepts* (New York, 1967); Harry Eckstein, "A Perspective on Comparative Politics, Past and Present," in Eckstein and David E. Apter, eds., *Comparative Politics: A Reader* (New York, 1963), p. 26; Donald A. Devine, *The Political Culture of the United States: The Influence of Member Values on Regime Maintenance* (Boston, 1972).

2. Charles Grier Sellers, Jr., "Andrew Jackson versus the Historians," *Mississippi Valley Historical Review,* 44 (1958), 615–34; Ronald P. Formisano, "Toward a Reorientation of Jacksonian Politics: A Review of the Literature, 1959–1975," *Journal of American History,* 63 (1976), 42–65; Edward Pessen, *Jacksonian America: Society, Personality, and Politics* (Homewood, Ill.; 1978), pp. 329–67. For introductions to the historiography, see John Higham, with Leonard Krieger and Felix Gilbert, *History* (Englewood Cliffs, N.J., 1965); and Bernard Sternsher, *Consensus, Conflict, and American Historians* (Bloomington, Ind., 1975).

3. For a longer version of this argument, see Ronald P. Formisano, "Deferential-Participant Politics: The Early Republic's Political Culture, 1789–1840," *American Political Science Review,* 68 (1974), 473–87.

4. In a different context Thomas Bender has inquired, "Why cannot gemeinschaft and gesellschaft simultaneously shape social life? Why must we assume that there is a single direction of change in a single social process?" *Community and Social Change in America* (New Brunswick, N.J., 1978), p. 31. Similarly W. J. Rorabaugh has argued that patterns of whiskey consumption from 1790 to 1840 illustrated that Americans were content with traditional society *and* that at the same time the surplus of spiritous liquors helped unleash powerful influences for change: *The Alcoholic Republic: An American Tradition* (New York, 1979), pp. 87–89. Richard D. Brown has attempted to use the concept of modernization to describe social change without assuming that change is better or that the beginning and end are dichotomous: *Modernization: The Transformation of American Life, 1600–1865* (New York, 1976), pp. 8, 19.

5. Lars Sväsand, "The Emergence of Organized Parties: Dimensions, Sequences,

Forces" (Paper delivered at the Edinburgh International Political Science Association Congress, Aug. 16–21, 1976; mimeographed copy, Institute of Sociology, University of Bergen); H. J. Hanham, *Elections and Party Management: Politics in the Time of Gladstone and Disraeli* (London, 1959), pp. 93, 100–103, 109–11; Samuel H. Beer, "Great Britain: From Governing Elite to Organized Mass Parties," in Sigmund Neumann, ed., *Modern Political Parties: Approaches to Comparative Politics* (Chicago, 1956); Bo Särlvik, "Sweden: The Social Bases of the Parties in a Developmental Perspective," in Richard Rose, ed., *Electoral Behavior: A Comparative Handbook* (New York, 1974), pp. 374–75; P. Loveday and A. W. Martin *Parliament Factions and Parties: The First Thirty Years of Responsible Government in New South Wales, 1856–1889* (London, 1966), pp. 121–48.

6. Lewis O. Saum argued recently that "common people" during the period 1830–1860 thought far more about religion than about politics, and far less about politics generally than political historians seem to think: *The Popular Mood of Pre-Civil War America* (Westport, Conn., 1980), pp. 3–54, 143–74.

7. Lars Sväsand, "The Political Behavior of Social Movements: Scandinavia in the Era of Democratization" (Paper prepared for ECPR Workshop on Social and Political Movements in Western Europe, Berlin, 28 Mar.–2 Apr., 1977; mimeographed copy, Institute of Sociology, University of Bergen); Hanham, *Elections and Party Management,* pp. 117–24; John Vincent, *The Formation of the Liberal Party, 1857–1868* (London, 1966); Särlvik, "Sweden," p. 378; Loveday and Martin, *Parliament Factions and Parties,* p. 139; Arend Lijphart, *The Politics of Accommodation: Pluralism and Democracy in the Netherlands* (Berkeley, 1975), pp. 16–36.

8. Seymour Martin Lipset and Stein Rokkan, eds., *Party Systems and Voter Alignments: Cross-National Perspectives* (New York, 1967), pp. 14, 18–19.

9. Henry Valen and Daniel Katz, *Political Parties in Norway: A Community Study* (Oslo, 1964), pp. 13–24; Henry Valen and Stein Rokkan, "Norway: Conflict Structure and Mass Politics in a European Periphery," in Rose, ed., *Electoral Behavior,* pp. 317–21. Regarding Center-Periphery divisions elsewhere, see Sväsand, "Emergence of Organized Parties," pp. 8–9; Keith Hill, "Belgium: Political Change in a Segmented Society," in Rose, ed., *Electoral Behavior,* pp. 31–33; Särlvik, "Sweden," pp. 374–78; David J. Meyers, "Urban Voting, Structural Cleavages, and Party System Evolution," *Comparative Politics,* 8 (1975), 119–51; and T. J. Nossiter, *Influence, Opinion and Political Idioms in Reformed England: Case Studies from the North-east, 1832–74* (Sussex, 1975). Regarding northeast England's role as "Liberal Citadel" and Periphery, Nossiter states the Northeast was "isolated from the rest of the country; it diverged from the national pattern in both the structure of land-ownership and the nature of agriculture; its main industry was coal mining, in which the landed magnates were themselves deeply involved, and it was one of the leading nonconformist areas of England" (p. 2).

10. Michael Hechter, *Internal Colonialism: The Celtic Fringe in British National Development, 1536–1966* (Berkeley and Los Angeles, 1975), p. 18.

11. Regarding the "mobilization of the periphery," several works by Stein Rokkan are relevant, including Stein Rokkan et al., *Citizens, Elections, Parties: Approaches to the Comparative Study of the Processes of Development* (New York, 1970), pp. 181–225. For a similar situation, see Tom Garvin, "Political Cleavages, Party Politics and Urbanization in Ireland: The Case of the Periphery-Dominated Centre," *European Journal of Political Research,* 2 (1974), 307–27.

12. The classic and ironic account of this is Henry Adams, *History of the United States of America during the Administrations of Thomas Jefferson and of James Madison,* 9 vols. (New York, 1889–1891).

13. Since the American Revolution, two meanings of "liberty" had struggled for su-

premacy in the new nation. One view stressed liberty as self-government, and was not far removed from John Winthrop's seventeenth-century definition of "liberty" as the freedom to obey God. The other meaning of "liberty" sprang forth almost naturally in a land of vast, untamed spaces: the liberty of individuals to enjoy what rights they could, the liberty of individual autonomy. Men were not exclusively committed to one of these versions of liberty, and the Constitution of 1787 was in some ways a compromise between them; a large portion of those preferring liberty as autonomy remained unconvinced as to a new central government's necessity and deeply fearful of the dangers it posed to liberty. Ronald M. Peters, Jr., *The Massachusetts Constitution of 1780: A Social Compact* (Amherst, 1978), p. 1; Edmund Morgan, *The Puritan Dilemma: The Story of John Winthrop* (Boston, 1958); and among several relevant studies of Federalist ideology, especially, Linda K. Kerber, *Federalists in Dissent: Imagery and Ideology in Jeffersonian America* (Ithaca, 1970).

14. Josiah Quincy, *An Answer to the Question, Why Are You a Federalist and Why Shall You Vote for Gov. Strong* (Boston, 1805); Lovell Walker, Templeton, 1812, to Abijah Bigelow, A. Bigelow MSS, American Antiquarian Society (hereafter MWA); John Leland, "An Oration, Delivered at Cheshire, July 5, 1802, on the Celebration of Independence," in L. F. Greene, ed., *The Writings of the Late Elder John Leland* (New York, 1845), pp. 262, 266. In 1810 a Federalist congressman charged that Jefferson had betrayed the "promises of reform and economy on the faith of which Mr. Jefferson came into power." Volm Stanley, May 10, 1810, in Noble E. Cunningham, Jr., ed., *Circular Letters of Congressmen to their Constituents, 1789–1824* (Chapel Hill, 1978), II, 725.

15. The first quotation is from Thomas Coffin Amory, *Life of James Sullivan: With Selections from His Writing* (Boston, 1859), II, 126; the second from Alexander H. Everett, *A Defense of the Character and Principles of Mr. Jefferson: Being an Address Delivered at Weymouth . . . on the 4th of July, 1836* (Boston, 1836), pp. 27–28.

16. Kerber, *Federalists in Dissent,* p. 178; Commonwealth of Massachusetts, *Resolves of the General Court, 1804,* p. 13; Boston *Repertory,* Dec. 18, 1804, quoted in Richard E. Ellis, *The Jeffersonian Crisis: Courts and Politics in the Young Republic* (New York, 1971), p. 205.

17. Robert E. Lane, *Political Ideology: Why the American Common Man Believes What He Does* (New York, 1962), p. 344; see also Werner Stark, *The Fundamental Forms of Social Thought* (London, 1962); and Pitirim A. Sorokin, *Social and Cultural Dynamics: Fluctuation of Social Relationships, War, and Revolution* III (New York, 1937), 132–60.

18. Thus, said a Federal organ in criticizing Madison's commercial policies, the "sacrifice of the interest and property of merchants, will be felt throughout the community." Boston *Repertory,* Mar. 12, 1811. For an excellent appreciation of this aspect of Federalist thought, see David Hackett Fischer, *The Revolution in American Conservatism: The Federalist Party in the Era of Jeffersonian Democracy* (New York, 1965).

19. Leonard W. Levy, *Jefferson and Civil Liberties: The Darker Side* (Cambridge, Mass., 1963); Richard Hofstadter, *The Idea of a Party System: The Rise of Legitimate Opposition in the United States, 1780–1840* (Berkeley, 1969); Daniel Sisson, *The American Revolution of 1800* (New York, 1974). For an analysis of John Quincy Adams as a "nonpartisan politician," see Daniel Walker Howe, *The Political Culture of the American Whigs* (Chicago, 1979), pp. 43–68.

20. Ronald P. Formisano, "Federalists and Republicans: Parties, Yes—System, No," in Paul Kleppner, et al., *The Evolution of American Electoral Systems* (Westport, Conn., 1981), pp. 33–76.

21. In a letter of 21 Jan. 1800, George Cabot remarked that though a certain con-

gressman possessed "great talents and I believe great virtues," he feared he was "not yet a politician, and has much to learn on the subject of practicable theories of free government." Henry Cabot Lodge noted that "By 'politician' Mr. Cabot meant one versed in public policy and the practical arts of statecraft and government." *The Life and Letters of George Cabot* (Boston, 1877), I, 269.

22. William A. Robinson, *Jeffersonian Democracy in New England* (New Haven, 1916), p. 3.

23. The quotation is from George Barstow, *The History of New Hampshire* (Concord, N.H., 1842), p. 302; Hobart Pillsbury, *New Hampshire: A History* (New York, 1927), II, 352–53.

24. Barstow, *History of New Hampshire,* pp. 349–52; Pillsbury, *New Hampshire,* II, 334–35; Sue Taishoff, "New Hampshire State Politics and the Concept of a Party System," *Historical New Hampshire,* 31 (1976), 33–38; Lawrence Shaw Mayo, *John Langdon of New Hampshire* (Concord, N.H., 1937), passim, esp. pp. 280–84; Mark D. Kaplanoff, "From Colony to State: New Hampshire, 1800–1815" (Unpublished manuscript, Cambridge University, England, 1974), pp. 177–78. Before Langdon, the Republicans first tried Judge Timothy Walker, a moderate Federalist. In the 1780s New Hampshire's first "president" was John Sullivan, a veteran military commander. Jeremiah Smith, a Federalist judge who served briefly in between Langdon's two stints, had been wounded at age seventeen at the battle of Bennington. Pillsbury, *New Hampshire* II, 336, 366. In 1818 Isaac Hill, editor of a Concord Republican paper, urged that only Revolutionary War veterans should serve as presidential electors. Donald B. Cole, *Jacksonian Democracy in New Hampshire, 1800–1851* (Cambridge, Mass., 1970), pp. 4, 44–45.

Across the Connecticut River in Vermont, Isaac Tickenor was from 1797 through 1807 a popular Federalist governor, whose centrist politics resembled that of other governors discussed here. See *DAB,* XVIII, 523; Edward Brynn, "Patterns of Dissent: Vermont's Opposition to the War of 1812," *Vermont History,* 40 (1972), 21.

25. The quotation is from Patrick T. Conley, *Democracy in Decline: Rhode Island Constitutional Development, 1776–1841* (Providence, 1977), p. 174; see also pp. 175, 178–79. On Fenner's career, see *DAB,* VI, 322–23; Irwin H. Polishook, *Rhode Island and the Union, 1774–1795* (Evanston, Ill., 1969), pp. 225–26, 234. On the political situation, see Clarence S. Brigham, *History of the State of Rhode Island and Providence Plantations* (n.p., 1902) pp. 282–301; Samuel H. Allen, "The Federal Ascendancy of 1812," *Narragansett Historical Register,* 8 (1889), 381–94. On William Jones, see Brigham, *Rhode Island,* 295; *DAB,* XI, 204–5.

26. *DAB,* IV, 226–28; Howard Lee McBain, *Dewitt Clinton and the Origin of the Spoils System in New York* (New York, 1907), pp. 24–50, 97–125; E. Wilder Spaulding, *His Excellency George Clinton: Critic of the Constitution* (New York, 1938), pp. 215, 217, 249–58.

27. The quotation is from Kenneth R. Rossman, *Thomas Mifflin and the Politics of the American Revolution* (Chapel Hill, 1952), p. 215; on Mifflin's maneuvering, see ibid., pp. 204–6; William G. Armor, *Lives of the Governors of Pennsylvania* (Philadelphia, 1872), pp. 272–88; Harry Marlin Tinkcom, *The Republicans and Federalists in Pennsylvania, 1790–1801: A Study in National Stimulus and Local Response* (Harrisburg, 1950), pp. 37–38, 40, 91–112, 135–37, 219–20.

28. Ibid., p. 226.

29. The last quotation is from ibid., p. 224; see also pp. 225–27; Armor, *Governors of Pennsylvania,* pp. 302–5; John M. Coleman, *Thomas McKean: Forgotten Leader of the Revolution* (Rockaway, N.J., 1975), pp. xii–xiii, 5, 12–15; Sanford W. Higginbotham, *The Keystone in the Democratic Arch: Pennsylvania Politics, 1800–1816* (Harrisburg, 1952), pp. 25, 36–38, 46–49, 74–75, 99–100, 103–4. Simon Snyder won

election in 1808 and re-election in 1817 and was the first governor descended from the state's German population. The next governors were Scotch-Irish and then German again.

30. John A. Munroe, *Federalist Delaware, 1775–1815* (New Brunswick, N.J., 1954), pp. 208–11, 232; David P. Peltier, "Party Development and Voter Participation in Delaware, 1792–1811," *Delaware History*, 14 (1970), 91–95.

31. None of the works cited here give this particular interpretation, though several are compatible with it. The best overall discussion of Federal and Republican strength in 1800 is Fischer, *Revolution in American Conservatism*, pp. 203–4; see also Robert Kelley, *The Cultural Pattern in American Politics: The First Century* (New York, 1979), pp. 109–40; Brigham, *Rhode Island*, pp. 272–334; Kaplanoff, "New Hampshire," pp. 54, 88–89, 96; Arthur Irving Bernstein, "The Rise of the Democratic-Republican Party in New York City, 1789–1800" (Ph.D. diss., Columbia University, 1964), pp. 255, 258; Alfred F. Young, *The Democratic Republicans of New York: The Origins, 1763–1797* (Chapel Hill, 1967), pp. 468–95; William Bruce Wheeler, "The Baltimore Jeffersonians, 1788–1800: A Profile of Inter-Factional Conflict," *Maryland Historical Magazine*, 66 (1971), 164–65; James H. Broussard, *The Southern Federalists, 1800–1816* (Baton Rouge, 1978), pp. 375–80.

32. Kaplanoff, "New Hampshire," pp. 139–50; Rudolph J. Pasler and Margaret C. Pasler, "Federalist Tenacity in Burlington County, 1810–1824," *New Jersey History*, 87 (1969), 197–200; Walter R. Fee, *The Transition from Aristocracy to Democracy in New Jersey, 1789–1829* (Somerville, N.J., 1933), pp. 135, 158, 160–61; James H. Broussard, "The North Carolina Federalists, 1800–1816," *North Carolina Historical Review*, 55 (1978), 20–21.

33. Munroe, *Federalist Delaware*, pp. 239–55, quotation on p. 261. Republicans frequently accused the Federalists in good peripheral fashion of "taxation and Extravigance [sic]." Ibid., p. 211.

34. Emerson is quoted in William R. Brock, *Parties and Political Conscience: American Dilemmas, 1840–1850* (Millwood, N.Y., 1979), p. 34. Thomas Bender, aware that change is not sequential, or uniform, or total, and conscious of the claims made for so many eras as key times of transition, nevertheless chooses the 1820s as a time when community began to be separated from place, when a dichotomy most rapidly developed between the communal, traditional, folk, and organic on one hand and the noncommunal, modern, urban, and mechanical on the other. *Community and Social Change*, pp. 15–23.

35. Allan R. Pred, *Urban Growth and the Circulation of Information: The United States System of Cities, 1790–1840* (Cambridge, Mass., 1973), pp. 20–22, 73, 78; George Rogers Taylor, *The Transportation Revolution, 1815–1860* (New York, 1951); Edward G. Daniel, "United States Postal Service and Postal Policy, 1789–1860," (Ph.D. diss., Harvard University, 1941), pp. 27–28, 64–66, 69, 595–96. See also William Charvat, *The Profession of Authorship in America, 1800–1870*, ed. Matthew J. Bruccoli (Columbus, Ohio, 1968), p. 37.

36. Wesley Everett Rich, *The History of the United States Post Office to the Year 1829* (Cambridge, Mass., 1924), pp. 108, 127–31, 146–47. The best study of the politicizing of the post office is Dorothy Ganfield Fowler, *The Cabinet Politician: The Postmasters General, 1829–1909* (New York, 1943), pp. 3–20. Although Jackson removed only a small percentage of the 8,000 postmasters for political reasons, those chosen represented "almost all the post masterships worth bothering about." Gerald Cullinan, *The United States Postal Service* (New York, 1973), pp. 54–56.

37. Daniel, "Postal Service," pp. 96, 99; Fowler, *Cabinet Politician*, pp. 19–20, 31–35. Van Buren's "first concerns when appointed to Jackson's Cabinet were for proper dispensation of patronage, to strengthen state machines." James C. Curtis, "In

the Shadow of Old Hickory" (Paper delivered at the Conference on the Times and Life of Martin Van Buren, State University College, New Palz, N.Y., Mar. 11–13, 1976).

38. John Barton Derby, *Political Reminiscences* (Boston, 1835), is the best source on the Boston customshouse; Malcolm J. Rohrbough, *The Land Office Business: The Settlement and Administration of American Public Lands, 1789–1837* (New York, 1968); Ronald N. Satz, *American Indian Policy in the Jacksonian Era* (Lincoln, Neb., 1975); Cole, *Jacksonian Democracy in New Hampshire*, pp. 102–28.

39. The 1824 campaign implicitly involved a contest between Center and Periphery. See Charles S. Sydnor, "The One-Party Period in American History," *American Historical Review*, 51 (1946), 439–51.

40. The Disraeli quotation is from Robert Blake, *The Conservative Party from Peel to Churchill* (London, 1970), p. 3. The choice of the name "Whig" was "natural," according to Daniel Walker Howe, for a party composed predominantly of British Americans whose leaders tended to see American history as an extension of British history. *Political Culture of the American Whigs*, p. 88. As late as 1853 in Massachusetts a Whig governor appeared before the legislature to give his inaugural address attired in "black pants, buff casimere vest and blue dress coat—the Fox colors of the Whigs of old times." Boston *Atlas*, Jan. 15, 1853.

41. William G. Shade, "Political Pluralism and Party Development: The Creation of a Modern Party System, 1815–1852," in Kleppner et al., *American Electoral Systems*, pp. 77–111.

42. According to Frederick Jackson Turner, "the rough, the poorer lands, the illiterate counties were for the most part Democratic . . . while the fertile basins . . . were Whig. The Whigs tended to be strong in the areas of the greater rivers and commercial centers and routes, and in the counties with the better record in . . . illiteracy." *Frontier and Section: Essays* (Englewood Cliffs, N.J., 1961), pp. 132–33; Kelley, *Cultural Pattern*, pp. 146–79; J. Mills Thornton III, *Politics and Power in a Slave Society: Alabama, 1800–1860* (Baton Rouge, 1978), pp. 40–41.

43. Hechter, *Internal Colonialism*, pp. 15–16. Some kind of Center/Core versus Periphery cleavage characterized Massachusetts politics at least from the 1780s through the 1880s, as can be inferred from Van Beck Hall, *Politics without Parties: Massachusetts, 1780–1791* (Pittsburgh, 1972); Jackson Turner Main, *Political Parties before the Constitution* (Chapel Hill, 1973), pp. 83–119; Samuel Eliot Morison, *The Maritime History of Massachusetts, 1783–1860* (Boston, 1921), pp. 39–40; Geoffrey Blodgett, *The Gentle Reformers: Massachusetts Democrats in the Cleveland Era* (Cambridge, Mass., 1966), pp. 11–12.

44. Charles Grier Sellers, Jr., "The Equilibrium Cycle in Two-Party Politics," *Public Opinion Quarterly*, 29 (1965), 33; Formisano, "Federalists and Republicans."

45. Representative of this point of view are Paul Goodman, "The First American Party System," in William Nisbet Chambers and Walter Dean Burham, eds., *The American Party Systems: Stages of Political Development* (New York, 1967), pp. 56–89; and William N. Chambers and Philip C. Davis, "Party, Competition, and Mass Participation: The Case of the Democratizing Party System, 1824–1852," in Joel H. Silbey, Allan G. Bogue, and William H. Flanigan, eds., *The History of American Electoral Behavior* (Princeton, 1978), pp. 174–97.

46. For a trenchant general discussion of the "political stratum," see Robert A. Dahl, *Who Governs? Democracy and Power in an American City* (New Haven, 1961), pp. 90–95, 276–81.

47. Indeed, by the 1840s some of the features of a secular political culture were present to a greater degree than ever before. A secular political culture engenders many roles which involve rational calculation, bargaining, and experimentation. "The politi-

cal system is saturated with the atmosphere of the market. Groups of electors come to the political market with votes to sell in exchange for policies [and sometimes, perhaps, to sell for money]. Holders of office in the formal-legal role structures tend to be viewed as agents and instrumentalities, or as brokers occupying points in the bargaining process . . . policies offered by candidates are viewed as hypotheses." The political culture thus "takes on some of the atmosphere of a game. A game is a good game when the outcome is in doubt and the stakes are not too high. . . ." Gabriel Almond, "Comparative Political Systems," *Journal of Politics,* 18 (1956), 398–99. A particularly pertinent demonstration of the secularization of religious and public life during this period may be found in Richard D. Birdsall, *Berkshire County: A Cultural History* (New Haven, 1959), esp. pp. 14–15, 69, 125–26.

## II. The Contours of Political Change in Massachusetts, 1790s–1840s

1. Robert Zemsky, *Merchants, Farmers, and River Gods: An Essay on Eighteenth-Century American Politics* (Boston, 1971), pp. 2–3, 7–8, 234.

2. Quoted in Stephen E. Patterson, *Political Parties in Revolutionary Massachusetts* (Madison, Wisc., 1973), p. 221.

3. J. R. Pole, *Political Representation in England and the Origins of the American Republic* (New York, 1966), p. 44. See also Dirk Hoerder, *Society and Government, 1760–1780: The Power Structure in Massachusetts Townships* (Berlin, 1972).

4. Pole, *Political Representation,* pp. 44–45, 46.

5. This statement is based on an examination of numerous township histories and lists of town and church officials. For a similar view, see Benjamin W. Labaree, *Partiots and Partisans: The Merchants of Newburyport, 1764–1815* (Cambridge, Mass, 1962), pp. 14–15; Robert J. Taylor, *Western Massachusetts in the Revolution* (Providence, 1954), p. 33; Zemsky, *Merchants, Farmers, and River Gods,* pp. 287–300; Kevin Joseph MacWade, "Worcester County, 1750–1774: A Study of a Provincial Patronage Elite" (Ph.D. diss., Boston University, 1974); Robert A. Gross, *The Minutemen and Their World* (New York, 1976), pp. 11–15, 22–23, 157–58.

6. James A. Henretta has observed that community values of uniformity and consensus probably were articulated most often in times of stress and conflict when, for example, an issue "threatened the internal cohesion of the community." "The Morphology of New England Society in the Colonial Period," *Journal of Interdisciplinary History,* 2 (1971), 395.

7. Michael Zuckerman, *Peaceable Kingdoms: New England Towns in the Eighteenth Century* (New York, 1970), p. 30, note. Zemsky, *Merchants, Farmers, and River Gods, pp.* 234, 236–37, 252; Pole, *Political Representation,* p. 72.

8. Useful in thinking about this problem are James S. Young, *The Washington Community, 1800–1828* (New York, 1966); and Nelson W. Polsby, "The Institutionalization of the U.S. House of Representatives," *American Political Science Review,* 62 (1968), 144–68.

9. Zemsky, *Merchants, Farmers, and River Gods,* pp. 22, 100–101, 158; Zuckerman, *Peaceable Kingdóms,* pp. 209–11; Richard D. Brown found party politics "as we understand them . . . no more characteristic of the General Court than the towns." *Revolutionary Politics in Massachusetts: The Boston Committee of Correspondence and the Towns, 1772–1774* (Cambridge, Mass., 1970), pp. 6–7.

10. Zemsky, *Merchants, Farmers, and River Gods,* pp. 39–42. Thus the question of whether or not a large majority of adult males could vote is superseded by (1) the low numbers actually voting and (2) their consistently electing their social betters. For an overview, see J. R. Pole, "Historians and the Problem of Early American Democracy," *American Historical Review,* 57 (1962), 626–46.

11. Patterson, *Political Parties,* pp. 34, 35.

12. Zemsky, *Merchants, Farmers, and River Gods,* pp. 244–45.

13. H. N. Fieldhouse, "Bolingbroke and the Idea of Non-Party Government," *History,* n.s. 23 (1938–39), 44, 50; Caroline Robbins, *The Eighteenth-Century Commonwealthman: Studies in the Transmission, Development and Circumstance of English Liberal Thought from the Restoration of Charles II until the War with the Thirteen Colonies* (Cambridge, Mass., 1961); T. J. Nossiter, *Influence, Opinion and Political Idioms in Reformed England: Case Studies from the North-east, 1832–74* (Sussex, 1975).

14. Ellen E. Brennan, *Plural Office-Holding in Massachusetts, 1760–1780: Its Relation to the "Separation" of Departments of Government* (Chapel Hill, 1945), pp. 20–22; Bernard Bailyn, *The Origins of American Politics* (New York, 1968).

15. Brennan, *Plural Office-Holding,* pp. 105–35, Adams is quoted on p. 113.

16. Gordon S. Wood, *The Creation of the American Republic, 1776–1787* (Chapel Hill, 1969), p. 146.

17. Bernard Bailyn, *The Ordeal of Thomas Hutchinson* (Cambridge, Mass., 1974), pp. 176, 177–78, 183–84.

18. Ibid., p. 180. During the 1760s and 1770s the laboring people of Boston were very active in defying the British, and social tensions ran high, but the lower ranks "made virtually no demands for an enlargement of their role in the political process," and after 1765 challenges to gentry control actually receded. Gary B. Nash, *The Urban Crucible: Social Change, Political Consciousness, and the Origins of the American Revolution* (Cambirdge, Mass., 1979), pp. 351, 359–60.

19. J. G. A. Pocock, "Virtue and Commerce in the Eighteenth Century," *Journal of Interdisciplinary History,* 3 (1972), 119–34; on the court and country ideologies' relation to modernity, esp. 128–30; see also idem, *The Machiavellian Moment: Florentine Political Thought and the Atlantic Republican Tradition* (Princeton, 1975), pp. 526–29; Zemsky, *Merchants, Farmers, and River Gods,* pp. 260–65.

20. Benjamin W. Labaree, *Patriots and Partisans,* p. 155. Pole, *Political Representation,* pp. 190, 194, 199, 200. Page Smith described the constitution as "a classic document of the conservative stamp." *John Adams* (Garden City, N.Y., 1962), I, 444. See also Oscar Handlin and Mary Flug Handlin, *Commonwealth: A Study of the Role of Government in the American Economy: Massachusetts, 1774–1861* (Cambridge, Mass., 1969; first ed. 1947), pp. 24–31; and Ronald M. Peters, Jr., *The Massachusetts Constitution of 1780: A Social Compact* (Amherst, 1978), p. 193.

21. Wood, *Creation of the American Republic,* pp. 218–20.

22. Van Beck Hall, *Politics without Parties: Massachusetts, 1780–1791* (Pittsburgh, 1972); for the period before the 1770s, see Zemsky, *Merchants, Farmers, and River Gods,* pp. 22, 227, 281, 282, 333. For a contrary view of the 1770s, see Patterson, *Political Parties.* For a recent statement by Oscar Handlin of the view argued here, see *Truth in History* (Cambridge, Mass., 1979), pp. 353–67.

23. Hall, *Politics without Parties,* p. 122. Jackson Turner Main used the word "party" to describe preconstitutional legislative blocs in state assemblies, but he recognized that "party" was used loosely and interchangeably with "faction" and that when we encounter it in the eighteenth century, "we must divest it of recent accretions." *Political Parties before the Constitution* (Chapel Hill, 1973), p. xviii.

24. Hall, *Politics without Parties,* pp. 90–92.

25. Zuckerman, *Peaceable Kingdoms,* p. 29.

26. See Figure 3, based on *Senate Documents,* no. 56; Handlin and Handlin, *Commonwealth,* p. 250.

27. Hall, *Politics without Parties,* p. 92; Richard D. Brown, "The Emergence of

Urban Society in Rural Massachusetts, 1760–1820," *Journal of American History,* 61 (1974), 36–37.

28. Fisher, Ames, 22 Aug. 1796, to Timothy Dwight, in Seth Ames, ed., *Works of Fisher Ames* (Boston, 1854), I, 198; Boston *Gazette,* Apr. 13, 1801.

29. Hall, *Politics without Parties,* p. xvii and passim.

30. Ibid., pp. 173–89; Anson Ely Morse, *The Federalist Party in Massachusetts to the Year 1800* (Princeton, 1909), pp. 21–22.

31. Quoted in Paul Goodman, *The Democratic-Republicans of Massachusetts: Politics in a Young Republic* (Cambridge, Mass., 1964), pp. 10, 25.

32. Quoted in Patterson, *Political Parties,* p. 58.

33. Henry Cabot Lodge, *Boston* (London, 1891), pp. 176–77.

34. Herbert S. Allan, *John Hancock: Patriot in Purple* (New York, 1948), p. 295; for more details on Hancock's "display," see Lorenzo Sears, *John Hancock: The Picturesque Patriot* (Boston, 1913), pp. 272–76, 284–85.

35. Morse, *Federalist Party,* p. 21, n. 34. Hancock's sometime foe Elbridge Gerry viewed him as a specimen of the old "Political Idolatry." George Athan Billias, *Elbridge Gerry: Founding Father and Republican Statesman* (New York, 1976), p. 103. Calling Hancock "America's first modern politician" would thus seem to be off the mark. William M. Fowler, Jr., *The Baron of Beacon Hill: A Biography of John Hancock* (Boston, 1980), p. 280.

36. Richard P. McCormick, "New Perspectives on Jacksonian Politics," *American Historical Review,* 65 (1960), 288–301; J. R. Pole, "Suffrage and Representation in Massachusetts: A Statistical Note," *William and Mary Quarterly,* 14 (1957), 560–92; James M. Banner, Jr., *To the Hartford Convention: The Federalists and the Origins of Party Politics in Massachusetts, 1789–1815* (New York, 1970), pp. 359–61; Walter Dean Burnham, "The Changing Shape of the American Political Universe," *American Political Science Review,* 59 (1965), 7–28. The low rates of voting in the 1820s also resulted from what in 1829 Governor Lincoln called the "great remissness" of some local officials in sending election returns fully and promptly to the state. Of course such a situation itself reinforces the impression of apathy. *Resolves of the General Court, May, 1829–June, 1831* (Boston, 1831), p. 90.

37. Richard P. McCormick attributed New England's low turnout rates generally to the reality that parties tended to be less evenly balanced there than in other sections and perhaps to the facts that New England never entirely accommodated itself to parties and that the major parties and their candidates had less appeal "in terms of the issues and concerns that mattered to the region." *The Second American Party System: Party Formation in the Jacksonian Era* (Chapel Hill, 1966), p. 98. In Massachusetts, however, the Whigs and Democrats were very closely balanced in 1839–1840, and by then party organizations were well developed (see Chapter XI).

38. Samuel Eliot Morison, "Vote of Massachusetts on Summoning a Constitutional Convention, 1776–1916," *Massachusetts Historical Society Proceedings,* 50 (1917), 241–49; Susan Kurland, "A Political Progress: Processes of Democratization in Concord, Massachusetts, 1750–1850" (Honor's thesis, Brandeis University, 1973).

39. William Bentley, *The Diary of William Bentley,* III (Salem, Mass., 1911), 517.

40. Charles F. Gettemy, *An Historical Survey of Census Taking in Massachusetts* (Boston, 1919), pp. 35–40; Albert Bushnell Hart, ed., *Commonwealth History of Massachusetts,* IV (New York, 1930), 15–17; Samuel Shapiro, "The Conservative Dilemma: The Massachusetts Constitutional Convention of 1853," *New England Quarterly,* 33 (1960), 207–24.

41. Ezra S. Stearns, *History of Ashburnham* (Ashburnham, Mass., 1887), p. 221; Benjamin Hobart, *History of the Town of Abington, Plymouth County, Massachu-*

*setts, from Its Settlement* (Boston, 1866), p. 179. In Figure 3 the percentages are based on data for the first session only of each legislature, though the General Court normally held two sessions through 1830; after 1809 only three years had more than two sessions (three in 1812, 1814, and 1820); after 1830 the legislature held only one session each year, and in only three years during the period 1831–1853 did it hold extra sessions, all of which are not included in these calculations.

42. The quoted phrase is from Nathaniel Cogswell, Newburyport, 11 Apr. 1809, to William King, Bath, box 8, King Correspondence, Maine Historical Society; Boston *Constitutional Telegraph,* Sept. 6, 1800; Bentley, *Diary,* III, 358; Northampton *Hampshire Gazette,* May 22, 1811; Springfield *Hampden Gazette,* May 23, 1811; Charles Warren, ed., *Jacobin and Junto: or Early American Politics as Viewed in the Diary of Dr. Nathaniel Ames, 1758–1822* (New York, 1968), p. 243.

43. The quotation is from Salem *Essex Register,* Feb. 16, 1811; Boston *Columbian Centinel,* Mar. 2, 27, Apr. 11, 1811; New-Bedford *Old Colony Gazette,* Mar. 15, 1811; Boston *Independent Chronicle,* Mar. 28, 1811; Boston *Patriot,* Mar. 13, May 1, 15, 1811.

44. *Centinel,* Feb. 6, 1811; Newburyport *Herald,* Feb. 15, 1811; Commonwealth of Massachusetts, *Reports of Contested Elections of the House of Representatives* (Boston, 1812), pp. 25–31.

45. Hart, ed., *Commonwealth History,* III, 203–4. For a Maine Republican's complaint that the hesitations of small, poor towns in sending representatives hurt the Republicans, see E[dward] Jones, Union, 8 Feb. 1810, to William King, Bath, King Correspondence. Hart, ed., *Commonwealth History,* IV, 15; *Official Report of the Debates and Proceedings in the State Convention, Assembled May 4th, 1853* (Boston, 1853), p. 626. Nathan Hale and Octavius Pickering, eds., *Journal of Debates and Proceedings in the Convention of Delegates, Chosen to Revise the Constitution of Massachusetts* (*1820–1821*) (Boston, 1821), p. 282. For the failure of this law in the Senate in 1824, see Worcester *Massachusetts Yeoman,* Feb. 25, 1824. Governor John Davis reviewed the history of the subject from 1825 in an address of Jan. 5, 1842, *Acts and Resolves, 1842,* p. 607.

46. Harry A. Cushing, *History of the Transition from Provincial to Commonwealth Government in Massachusetts* (New York, 1896), pp. 237–40 discuss 1779–1780; the quotation is from *Report of Debates in the State Convention, 1853,* p. 518.

47. Banner, *Hartford Convention;* Goodman, *Democratic-Republicans;* David Hackett Fischer, *The Revolution in American Conservatism: The Federalist Party in the Era of Jeffersonian Democracy* (New York, 1965). Lars G. Sväsand has tried to develop a quantitative approach to organization in Norway: "Regional Variations in the Process of Party Formation in Norway" (Paper prepared for the ECPR Workshop on Regional Variations in Europe, Strasbourg, France, 28 Mar.–2 Apr. 1974; mimeographed copy in Institute of Sociology, University of Bergen).

48. For the most coherent and insistent case that a strong relationship existed between party organization and increases in both turnout and competition from 1824 to 1852, see William N. Chambers and Phillip C. Davis, "Party, Competition, and Mass Participation: The Case of the Democratizing Party System, 1824–1852," in Joel H. Silbey, Allan G. Bogue, and William H. Flanigan, *The History of American Electoral Behavior,* eds. (Princeton, 1978), pp. 174–97. On the other hand, the close relationship usually posited between competition and trunout, though bordering "upon the status of a law," has been questioned. Virginia Gray, "A Note on Competition and Turnout in the American States," *Journal of Politics,* 38 (1976), 153–58.

49. Historians and social scientists have persisted in pursuing this path of inference from aggregate units to individuals despite the well-known "ecological fallacy."

50. From among the useful studies of roll-call voting in legislatures in recent years

by historians, see Herbert Ershkowitz and William G. Shade, "Consensus or Conflict? Political Behavior in the State Legislature during the Jacksonian Era," *Journal of American History,* 58 (1971), 591–621.

51. Banner, *Hartford Convention,* p. 292.

52. "What kind of reality is competition, and how is it divisible? If a system is fully competitive when leading competitors are persistently of nearly equal strength, when, for example, is the system 'half competitive'?" Paul Davis, *Party Strength in the United States, 1872–1970* (Charlottesville, 1972), pp. 13–14.

53. Anthony Downs, in his celebrated book *An Economic Theory of Democracy* (New York, 1957), p. 115, explained phenomena similar to this as a result of parties in a two-party system deliberately "moving closer to one another and resembling one another in their platforms, in contrast to parties in a multiparty system which try to remain as ideologically distinct from each other as possible." The problem with applying this theory to the Whigs and Democrats is that although Federalists and Republicans were probably more distinct ideologically than were the Whigs and Democrats, the latter did see themselves as posing quite different alternatives, and, more important, the electorate most certainly was convinced that the parties "stood for" quite different things.

## III. The Politics of the Revolutionary Center

1. Carolyn Sue Weddington, "The Image of the American Revolution in the United States, 1815–1860" (Ph.D. diss., Louisiana State University, 1972), pp. v, 4, 31, 36, 44–45. For a provocative and wide-ranging discussion of this subject, see Michael Kammen, *A Season of Youth: The American Revolution and the Historical Imagination* (New York, 1978). Kammen refers often to the early national period; see esp. pp. 15–21, 37–49.

2. William Manning, *The Key of Liberty: Shewing the Causes Why a Free Government Has Always Failed, and a Remedy against It,* ed. Samuel Eliot Morison (Billerica, Mass.; 1922), pp. 19–20.

3. Alden Bradford, *History of Massachusetts,* III (Boston, 1829), x.

4. Geoffrey Blodgett, *The Gentle Reformers: Massachusetts Democrats in the Cleveland Era* (Cambridge, Mass., 1966), p. 13.

5. Other historians have noted the centrist tendencies of one party or both: notably Paul Goodman, *The Democratic-Republicans of Massachusetts: Politics in a Young Republic* (Cambridge, Mass., 1964), passim; Oscar Handlin and Mary Flug Handlin, *Commonwealth: A Study of the Role of Government in the American Economy: Massachusetts, 1774–1861* (Cambridge, Mass., 1969; first ed. 1947), p. 56.

6. Boston *Constitutional Telegraph,* Feb. 26, 1800. The politics of the Revolutionary Center can be seen in part as an outgrowth of the process of consolidating a revolution, one discussed in Cynthia H. Enloe, *Ethnic Conflict and Political Development* (Boston, 1973), pp. 249–50. This perspective in part informs Richard Buel, Jr., *Securing the Revolution: Ideology in American Politics, 1789–1815* (Ithaca, 1972).

7. John Allyn, *A Sermon Preached on the Day of General Election, May 29, 1805 . . .* (Boston, 1805), p. 33.

8. Josiah Quincy, *Figures of the Past: From the Leaves of Old Journals* (Boston, 1884), p. 295, on the talk of the past; on Lafayette's visit, see ibid., pp. 130–31, 135, 142, 147–48; Weddington, "Image of the American Revolution," p. 5. Historians have observed that in the 1820s and 1830s there came an outpouring of reminiscences about the Revolutionary period: Jesse Lemisch, "The American Revolutionary Bicentennial and the Papers of Great White Men," *American Historical Association Newsletter,* 9 (1971), p. 16.

9. Thomas Wentworth Higginson, *Old Cambridge* (New York, 1899), pp. 20–22. As a youth Benjamin F. Butler heard many tales of the Revolution and learned "that the highest achievement in life was to get behind a stone wall and shoot a Britisher." *Butler's Book* (Boston, 1892), pp. 47–48; George F. Hoar's memories were similar: *Autobiography of Seventy Years* (New York: 1903), I, 49–50.

10. Marcus Morton, 22 Mar. 1829, to S. D. Ingham, Morton Letterbooks, MHi; J. H. Clifford, New Bedford, 21 Sept. 1836, to Robert C. Winthrop, Winthrop Papers, MHi; see also Festus Currier, *Reminiscences and Observations of the Nineteenth Century* (Fitchburg, 1902). In the case of Benjamin Lincoln, federal collector of the port of Boston, several considerations prevented President Jefferson from removing Lincoln, including his record as a Revolutionary hero: Benjamin Lincoln Papers, reel 11, MHi; Carl E. Prince, *The Federalists and the Origins of the U.S. Civil Service* (New York, 1977), pp. 22, 27–29.

11. William H. Prescott, Pepperell, 17 June 1835, to George Bancroft, Bancroft Papers, MHi.

12. Benjamin Hobart, *An Oration, Pronounced July 4, 1805, at Abington . . .* (Boston, 1805), p. 15; Charles Warren, ed., *Jacobin and Junto: or Early American Politics As Viewed in the Diary of Dr. Nathaniel Ames, 1758–1822* (New York, 1968), p. 81, regarding cockades; the first quotation is from the New Bedford *Old Colony Gazette*, Feb. 8, 15, 1811, two essays entitled "For What Was the Revolution Accomplished?" Other examples: "To All People," by Hawley, [1808] Broadside Collection, MWA, and "National Honor, and Permanent Peace–Or a Glorious Struggle For Independence." Ibid.

13. Linda K. Kerber, *Federalists in Dissent: Imagery and Ideology in Jeffersonian America* (Ithaca, 1970), p. 7. Salem *Essex Register*, Mar. 27, 1811; Boston *Patriot*, Mar. 30, 1811, "To the Republicans of Massachusetts"; Boston *Columbian Centinel*, Feb. 26, 1800; Boston *Gazette*, Apr. 3, 1823. And esp. John Adams, 25 Feb. 1808, to Benjamin Rush, in John A. Schutz and Douglass Adair, eds., *The Spur of Fame: Dialogues of John Adams and Benjamin Rush, 1805–1813* (San Marino, Calif., 1966), p. 104. In a related discussion, Peter Karsten has emphasized that the "patriot-heroes" of England and America in the eighteenth- and early nineteenth-centuries were antistatist. *Patriot-Heroes in England and America: Political Symbolism and Changing Values over Three Centuries* (Madison, Wis., 1978), pp. 11–12.

14. Francis Blake, *An Oration Pronounced at Worcester (Mass.) on . . . July 4, 1812* (Worcester, 1812), p. 5.

15. See, e.g., Worcester *Massachusetts Spy*, Mar. 27, 1811.

16. The appeal to the Revolution and to moderate centrists in 1800 is evident in Anson Ely Morse, *The Federalist Party in Massachusetts to the Year 1800* (Princeton, 1909), pp. 179–80, 184–85; Goodman, *Democratic-Republicans*, p. 128; George Athan Billias, *Elbridge Gerry: Founding Father and Republican Statesman* (New York, 1976), pp. 302–3. An appeal for Gill is in Boston *Columbian Centinel*, Feb. 26, 1800.

17. On Strong, see *Centinel*, Jan. 4, 1800; Worcester *Independent Gazette*, Mar. 18, 1800. On Gerry, see Boston *Independent Chronicle*, Mar. 20, 1800, which opened its columns to supporters of both Strong and Gerry. In this year Adams's supporters also worked hard to remind voters of Adams's Revolutionary services. Nobel E. Cunningham, Jr., "Election of 1800," in Arthur M. Schlesinger, Jr., and Fred L. Israel, eds., *History of American Presidential Elections: 1789–1968* (New York, 1971), I, 116.

18. *DAB*, XVIII, 145; Edwin Rozwenc also emphasized Strong's moderation: "Last of the River Gods," *The Northampton Book: Chapters from 300 Years in the Life of a New England Town, 1654–1954* (Northampton, 1954), pp. 56–74.

19. G. Cabot, 14 Feb. 1804, to T. Pickering, in Henry Cabot Lodge, ed., *Life and Letters of George Cabot* (Boston, 1877), p. 343, italics mine; see also G. Cabot, 17 Mar. 1804, in ibid., p. 345. In 1801 Strong had opposed those Federalists who had supported Vice-President Aaron Burr's attempt to displace Jefferson as president. Richard E. Welch, Jr., *Theodore Sedgwick, Federalist: A Political Portrait* (Middletown, Conn., 1965), pp. 224–25.

20. Alden Bradford, *Biography of the Hon. Caleb Strong* (Boston, 1820), pp. 9–10, 11.

21. Josiah Quincy, *An Answer to the Question, Why Are You a Federalist and Why Shall You Vote for Gov. Strong* (Boston, 1805), pp. 20–21. This did not mean that Strong had no sense of what was "correct," for he paid careful attention to such matters as dress. His reprimand in 1803 to his college-going son was revealing. The last time he visited, said the father, "I thought your dress was hardly elegant enough." Even a scholar must "have somewhat the appearance of a gentleman. . . . The coats that are cut straight down before may perhaps be called buckish, but, so far as I have observed, they are not worn by genteel people." C. Strong, 5 Mar. 1805, to Lewis Strong, quoted in Henry Cabot Lodge, *Studies in History* (Boston, 1884), pp. 259–60; For Lodge's biographical sketch of Strong, see pp. 224–62.

22. *Resolves, 1815–1819,* p. 217; Charles Brooks and James M. Usher, *History of the Town of Medford, Middlesex County, Massachusetts, 1630 to 1855* (Boston, 1886), pp. 129–32, 134, 135–36. Samuel Eliot Morison described Brooks as follows: "Dignified though democratic, interested in people and helpful in their troubles, a useful townsman and faithful member of the First Church (changing with it from Calvinism to Unitarianism), Brooks appeared to be the ideal republican soldier and citizen, the sort of man every one loved, and delighted to honor." *DAB,* III, 80. Partisan feelings had not subsided completely, and some Republicans thought Brooks implicated in the Strong administration's obstructionism. John Quincy Adams, a supporter of the war, nevertheless observed that while Brooks did not openly criticize the Federalists' conduct during the war, his silence on the matter on taking office was censure enough. "Nor can I forget," said Adams, "that in that very war, he had a son, who died in the Cause of his Country." John Quincy Adams, 23 Nov. 1817, to Alexander H. Everett, in Andrew C. McLaughlin, ed., "Letters of John Quincy Adams to Alexander Hamilton Everett, 1811–1837, II," *American Historical Review,* 11 (1906), 111.

23. Brooks and Usher, *Medford,* p. 135, 142; *Bangor Historical Magazine,* 6 (1890–1891), iii. Patronage considerations also played a role in the Federalists' pursuit of moderation. See Shaw Livermore, Jr., *The Twilight of Federalism: The Disintegration of the Federalists Party, 1815–1830* (Princeton, 1962), pp. 35, 81.

24. Brooks made a public profession of Christianity in 1817. See Brooks and Usher, *Medford,* p. 139. The association of Brooks with western Orthodoxy was strongly implied by Otis supporters in 1823. See, e.g., a letter by a "Descendant of the Pilgrims," in the Northampton *Hampshire Gazette,* Apr. 2, 1823.

25. C. Gore, Waltham, 2 June 1822, to Rufus King, VI, Charles R. King, ed., *The Life and Correspondence of Rufus King,* III (New York, 1900), 473.

26. Gore first lost to Sullivan in 1808, then to Gerry in 1810 and 1811. Gore was characterized as a "transitional figure" between old-school and young Federalists by David Hackett Fischer, *The Revolution in American Conservatism: The Federalist Party in the Era of Jeffersonian Democracy* (New York, 1965), pp. 259–60.

27. *Columbian Centinel,* Feb. 16, 1811. An anonymous tract claimed that at the Revolution Gore was a "FIRM AND DECIDED WHIG, AND HE WAS ACTIVE IN THE CAUSE OF HIS COUNTRY." *Who Shall Be Governor? The Contrast . . .* (Worcester, 1809), p. 4.

28. Helen R. Pinkney, *Christopher Gore: Federalist of Massachusetts, 1758–1827* (Waltham, Mass., 1969), pp. 117–18; Morse, *Federalist Party,* p. 21.

29. Samuel Ripley, "Memoir of Hon. Christopher Gore," in *Massachusetts Historical Society Collections,* 3rd ser., 3 (1833), 191–209; James H. Stark, *The Loyalists of Massachusetts and the Other Side of the American Revolution* (Boston, 1910), p. 393. Regarding Samuel Gore, see Oliver Ayer Roberts, *History of the Ancient and Honorable Artillery Company of Massachusetts,* II (Boston, 1897), 205.

30. Pinkney, *Christopher Gore,* pp. 31–32; Goodman, *Democratic-Republicans,* pp. 31–32, 42.

31. Pinkney, *Christopher Gore,* pp. 33–50; James M. Banner, Jr., *To the Hartford Convention: The Federalists and the Origins of Party Politics in Massachusetts, 1789–1815* (New York, 1970), p. 136.

32. Pinkney, *Christopher Gore,* pp. 81, 84; Samuel Eliot Morison, *The Maritime History of Massachusetts, 1783–1860* (Boston, 1921), p. 127.

33. Fischer, *Revolution in American Conservatism,* p. 260. Pinkney, *Christopher Gore,* pp. 102–15. John Adams, 4 Mar. 1809, to Benjamin Rush, in Schutz and Adair, eds., *Fame,* p. 132; see also T. Pickering, Washington, to George Cabot, 11 Mar. 1808, and G. Cabot, Boston, 12 Mar. 1808, to T.P., in Lodge, ed., *George Cabot,* pp. 382, 385.

34. Boston *Independent Chronicle,* quoted in Pinkney, *Christopher Gore,* p. 116. For Federalist attempts to counter, see *Centinel,* Apr. 17, 1811; New Bedford *Mercury,* Mar. 29, 1811.

35. Pinkney, *Christopher Gore,* pp. 109, 121–22, 137.

36. *Resolves, 1807,* p. 17; Goodman, *Democratic-Republicans,* p. 130; Robert Kelley, *The Cultural Pattern in American Politics: The First Century* (New York, 1979), pp. 109–31.

37. John Daniel Cushing, "Notes on Disestablishment in Massachusetts, 1780–1833," *William and Mary Quarterly,* 26 (1969), 175, 183–84.

38. Thomas Coffin Amory, *Life of James Sullivan* (Boston, 1859), II, 143; John Bernard, *Retrospections of America, 1797–1811,* ed. Mrs. William Bayle (New York, 1830), p. 338. Sullivan had interests in several other corporations. Gerald G. Gawalt, *The Promise of Power: The Emergence of the Legal Profession in Massachusetts, 1760–1840* (Westport, Conn., 1979), p. 177.

39. Amory, *Sullivan,* II, 76–78.

40. The quotation is from ibid., pp. 107–8; see also ibid., I, 190–203, II, 67–68. Most of the information about Sullivan for the two different views presented here comes from the same sources, primarily ibid., and *DAB,* XVIII, 190–91.

41. McLoughlin, *New England Dissent, 1630–1833: The Baptists and the Separation of Church and State* (Cambridge, Mass., 1971), II, 1077.

42. McLoughlin, *New England Dissent,* II, 1078; see also 1065–83 and passim.

43. J. Sullivan, 13 Jan. 1802, to William Eustis, quoted in Amory, *Sullivan,* II, 95. Opposition could be quieted, he implied, if at least "the seed of an army" be maintained, and New England especially would be pleased with the maintenance of "an armed naval force," which was needed in any case to enforce revenue laws ("and the pride of the people, conversant on the ocean, is delighted with the idea"). New Englanders would appreciate also, he said pointedly, the president's making no more speeches about aliens' being admitted freely: "We are full of people, and want no accession. We know no way to open the door, without the admission of the very dregs of Europe." He added that he was doing his best to explain away this proposal of Jefferson's. Ibid. pp. 95–96.

44. Christopher Gore, Boston, 25 Dec. 1807, to Rufus King, in King, ed., *King Life and Correspondence,* V, 41–42; and C. Gore, 8 Apr. 1808, to R. King, ibid.,

p. 92. For other negative views, see James S. Dunning, 10 June 1805, to Leverett Saltonstall, and "Leverett Saltonstall Dairy," entry for Apr. 2, 1804, in Robert E. Moody, ed., *The Saltonstall Papers, 1607–1815,* II (Boston, 1974), 254, 196.

45. J. Sullivan, 13 Jan. 1802, to W. Eustis, quoted in Amory, *Sullivan,* II, 94; William Bentley, *The Diary of William Bentley,* III (Salem, Mass., 1911), 343, for complaint; Richard E. Ellis, *The Jeffersonian Crisis: Courts and Politics in the Young Republic* (New York, 1971), pp. 221–22.

46. Nathaniel Saltonstall, Jr., 5 June 1808, to Nathaniel Saltonstall, in Moody, ed., *Saltonstall Papers,* II, 445; C. Gore, 28 May 1808, to R. King, in King, ed., *King Life and Correspondence,* V, 99; Thomas Jefferson, Monticello, 22 Aug. 1808, to Levi Lincoln, photostat of original, and T. Jefferson, Washington, 13 Nov. 1808, to L. Lincoln, Lincoln Papers, MWA; see also Levi Lincoln, 10 Sept. 1808, to T. Jefferson, ibid.

47. Amory, *Sullivan,* I, 110, 347, 350.

48. J. Sullivan, 13 Jan. 1802, to W. Eustis, quoted in ibid., II, 93–94; and J.S., 17 Jan. 1802, to W. E., quoted in ibid., 97.

49. George Athan Billias, *Elbridge Gerry: Founding Father and Republican Statesman* (New York, 1976), p. 218. Billias stressed that Gerry was an antiparty man and that political parties were slow to develop.

50. Abigail Adams quoted in ibid., p.. 292; see also pp. 218, 220–21, 236, 245, 249, 251, 289, 298–99.

51. Ibid., p. 301; Goodman, *Democratic-Republicans,* pp. 104–5; and see below, Chapter V. Federalist opponents appreciated the help which Adams's support lent to Gerry. See George Cabot, 27 Mar. 1800, to Christopher Gore, in Lodge, ed., *George Cabot,* p. 271; Stephen Higginson, Boston, 16 Apr. 1800, to T. Pickering, "Letters of Stephen Higginson, 1783–1804," *Annual Report of the American Historical Association, 1896,* I, 836; Boston *Columbian Centinel,* Apr. 16, 1800.

52. Fisher Ames, 9 Feb. 1801, to Dwight Foster, in Seth Ames, ed., *The Works of Fisher Ames* (Boston, 1854), I, 291; Boston *Independent Chronicle,* Feb. 24, 1801.

53. The first quotation is from New Bedford *Old Colony Gazette,* Mar. 1, 1811; *National Ægis,* Feb. 21, 1810, quoted in Billias, *Elbridge Gerry,* p. 313; *Resolves, 1810–1812,* p. 23. See also Newburyport *Independent Whig,* Mar. 16, 23, 1811; Pittsfield *Sun,* Mar. 30, 1811; Levi Heywood, *An Oration Delivered at Worcester, Massachusetts, on the Anniversary of American Independence, July 4th, 1810* (Worcester, 1810), p. 14; Boston *Patriot,* Mar. 16, 1811.

54. *Resolves, 1810–1812,* pp. 14–15, 17. Billias, *Elbridge Gerry,* pp. 314–15. On Republican fears, see J. Wingate, Jr., Portland, 31 May 1810, to William King, and B. Porter, Topsham, 21 Feb. 1811, to W. King, Boston, William King Correspondence, Maine Historical Society. William Bentley echoed Republican complaints of Gerry as *"so trusting a Republican Gov.," Dairy,* III, 522. This was on June 4, 1810.

55. James T. Austin, *The Life of Elbridge Gerry: From the Close of the American Revolution,* II (Boston, 1829), 346–47.

56. Billias, *Elbridge Gerry,* pp. 316–18. Billias attributed the measures of Gerry's second term to pressure from Republican "radicals" interested in both patronage and issues. Some Federalists believed Gerry to be "the tool of bad men" and reluctant on his own to remove men from office for political reasons. See the unusual newspaper of political satire *The Scourge* (Boston), Aug. 12, 28, Nov. 25, 1811, MWA. The Republican offensive is described fully in Billias, *Elbridge Gerry,* pp. 315–22. For disapproving nineteenth-century accounts by friends and foes, see Bradford, *History,* III, 113–22; and Austin, *Elbridge Gerry,* II, 333–42.

57. Billias, *Elbridge Gerry,* pp. 321–23.

58. Ibid., pp. 315–16. Gerry seized on the trumped-up "Henry Letters"—forgeries regarding a Federalist plot against the Union—and sent them with envoys to President Madison, Carl Seaburg and Stanley Patterson, *Merchant Prince of Boston: Colonel T. H. Perkins, 1764–1854* (Cambridge, Mass., 1971), p. 228.

59. *Resolves, 1810–1812,* pp. 179–80, 183, 184.

60. Ibid., pp. 185, 186.

61. Ibid., pp. 271–72, 273.

62. Ibid., p. 279.

63. For biographical information on Lincoln, see *DAB,* XI, 263–64; AHA, *Encyclopedia of Biography: Massachusetts* (New York, 1916), pp. 57–58; Amory, *Sullivan,* II, 193. In the 1780s Lincoln also acted as John Hancock's Worcester agent. Gawalt, *Promise of Power,* p. 115; also pp. 39, 55, 112.

64. Thorp Lanier Wolford, "Democratic-Republican Reaction in Massachusetts to the Embargo of 1807," *New England Quarterly,* 15 (1942), 53.

65. Adams, 4 Mar. 1809, to B. Rush, in Schutz and Adair, eds., *Fame,* p. 132.

66. Thomas Jefferson, Washington, 25 Oct. 1802, to L. Lincoln, photostat, Lincoln Family Papers. Lincoln himself had earlier recommended that "the proposed removals should take place, but not at present, not all at once, but gradual, perhaps in the course of a year." L. Lincoln, Worcester, 15 June 1801, to T. Jefferson, photostat, ibid. Other Republicans took a much harder line: William T. Whitney, "The Crowninshields of Salem, 1800–1808," *Essex Institute Historical Collections,* 94 (1958), 20.

67. L. Lincoln, Worcester, 5 July 1801, to T. Jefferson, Lincoln Family Papers.

68. A Farmer [Levi Lincoln], *Letters to the People* (Salem, 1802); also published in Philadelphia as *A Farmer's Letters to the People* (1802).

69. Levi Lincoln, Worcester, 16 Oct. 1802, to T. Jefferson; L.L., 2 June 1805, to T.J., Lincoln Family Papers. In another letter along the same lines, Lincoln criticized men who were "looking for a Union with a third party" and who injured the Republican cause by courting popularity with the Federalists and by their "silence and scruples." L.L., Worcester, 30 July 1805, to T.J., ibid.

70. Boston *Independent Chronicle,* Feb. 24, Mar. 3, 17, 31, 1817. Dearborn was an investor in the Boston and Roxubry Mill along with several prominent Federalists. See *Independent Chronicle and Patriot,* Mar. 4, 1818.

71. "Lesser" figures of the Revolutionary Center: General William Heath, a prominent farmer of Roxbury, had promoted military preparedness well before the Revolution. In the General Court in 1774, he moved quickly into service on Revolutionary committees, then rose during the war to top command in the eastern sector. After the war he returned to his farm, supported the federal Constitution, and served in minor offices. He received various Republican nominations for governor and lieutenant governor and in 1806 was elected, with bipartisan support, lieutenant governor, but declined to serve. In 1812 Heath did permit his name to be put on the ballot of presidential electors pledged to Clinton of New York, whom the Federalists were backing as a "peace candidate." Roberts, *Artillery Company,* II, 129–30; AHA, *Encyclopedia of Biography: Massachusetts,* p. 178; Amory, *Sullivan,* II, 117.

William Gray was Salem's richest merchant and a moderate Federalist up to 1808, when he broke with the Federalists and supported the Embargo, though it hurt his interests. Gray was primarily a nationalist who made money privateering during the Revolution. His personal relations in Salem soured by Federalist reaction to his "apostasy," he moved to Boston and by 1815 owned at least 113 vessels. In 1810 and 1811 he was lieutenant governor with Governor Gerry, but in 1812 declined to run. He did, however, agree to stand as a presidential elector that year, and accepted subsequent nominations. By 1816 he was a popular choice for president of the Boston branch of the Bank of the United States, and remained active in local politics. E. Gray, *William Gray of Salem, Merchant* (Boston, 1914), passim, quoted, p. 78; *DAB*, VII, 523–24; Bentley, *Diary*, III, 359, 364, 375, 376–77.

Samuel Dexter, a prominent Boston lawyer and former cabinet officer, remained nominally a Federalist but in 1814 and 1815, accompanied by howls of rage from Federalists, accepted nomination as governor from the Republicans–or rather, did not decline. Dexter had been an active Federalist through his career as state representative (1788–1790), congressman (1792–1795), senator (1799–1800), secretary of war (1800), and secretary of the treasury (1800–1802). Dexter made such vehement arguments in the courts against the embargo that he had risked contempt of court. As the War of 1812 dragged on, however, Dexter parted company with the Federalists and supported the war. On the other hand, after Republicans nominated him, Dexter declared that he differed "radically from the party called Republicans" with respect to their "system of restriction on our commerce." But he regarded it as an indispensable duty of every citizen "to hold sacred the union of this country." This opinion, he guessed, probably accounted for "the singular fact of his being nominated, for the first office in the Commonwealth, by a political party, TO WHICH HE DOES NOT BELONG." [Lucius Manlius Sargent], *Reminiscences of Samuel Dexter* (Boston, 1857), passim, quotation from p. 92; *DAB*, V, 280–81. In 1816 the Republicans again nominated Dexter for governor and Dexter again pointed out he was not a Republican but accepted the nomination by not declining it. See Boston *Independent Chronicle*, Feb. 12, 1816.

72. *Independent Chronicle and Patriot*, Mar. 15, 1823.

73. Ibid., Apr. 26, 1823. The house of representatives later replied to Eustis's inaugural as it had to similar figures of the Revolutionary past.

74. Jacob C. Meyer, *Church and State in Massachusetts, from 1740 to 1833: A Chapter in the History of the Development of Individual Freedom* (Cleveland, 1930), p. 136; Eugene Perry Link, *Democratic-Republican Societies, 1790–1800* (New York, 1942), p. 202.

75. *Columbian Centinel*, May 14, 17, 1800; Goodman, *Democratic-Republicans*, p. 105; Levi Lincoln, 30 July 1805, to T. Jefferson, Lincoln Family Papers.

76. During this time Eustis married, appropriately enough, Caroline Langdon, daughter of Governor John Langdon of New Hampshire, discussed in Chapter 1. AHA, *Encyclopedia of Biography: Massachusetts* (New York, 1916), pp. 44–45.

77. Boston *Statesman*, Feb. 3, 6, 1823. The Pittsfield *Sun* called him "a soldier of the revolution," Mar. 27, 1823; in 1824 "Revolutionary Republicanism" was the campaign theme of the Essex County Republican address to the electors, in Salem *Essex Register*, Feb. 16, 1824.

78. Daniel Sharp, *A Sermon, Preached at the Funeral of His Excellency William Eustis Esq. . . . February 11, 1825* (Boston, 1825), p. 21. Even more stress on Eustis as a "distinguished son of the revolution" is in James Barnaby, *A Sermon, Delivered at Salisbury, Mass., on the Death of His Excellency William Eustis, February 13, 1825 . . .* (Newburyport, 1825), pp. 18–19.

79. William H. Sumner, "Reminiscences of LaFayette's Visit to Boston–Gov. Eustis–Gov. Brooks and Others," *New England Historical and Genealogical Register*, 13 (1859), 104, 105–6. With his obvious desire to be liked by everyone, Eustis not surprisingly found the "subject of appointments . . . the most difficult to manage." Though he recognized that "past services" could give a candidate "superior claims on the Republican party," he also told Levi Lincoln, Jr., that he knew no other guide "than to take the best man with the chances of pleasing or offending." William Eustis, Roxbury, 22 June 1824, to Levi Lincoln, [Jr.,] Lincoln Papers, MHi.

80. Sumner, "Reminiscences," pp. 103–6; G. W. Porter, "A Sketch of the Life and

Character of the Late William Eustis," *Proceedings of the Lexington Historical Society,* 1 (1887), 106, 108–9. Eustis recalled, "It was once objected to me as a candidate . . . that I did not live in a splendid house like the other gentlemen." Quoted in Goodman, *Democratic-Republicans,* p. 101. Reacting to Republican claims that Eustis was "a farmer," the *Centinel* replied that it was not likely that either Eustis or Otis would "get a living by farming. A Boston gentleman retiring to a country villa does not thereby become metamorphosed into a farmer." Mar. 26, 1823.

81. The quoted phrase is from George Dangerfield, *The Awakening of American Nationalism, 1815–1828* (New York, 1965), pp. 103–4.

82. Even more remarkable was the fact that another son of the elder Levi, Enoch Lincoln, was elected governor of Maine in 1829 "with great unanimity" as a nonpartisan, popular figure, who after re-election in 1827 and 1828 died in office while serving his third term. See "Governor Enoch Lincoln," *Collections of the Maine Historical Society,* ed. William Willis, I (Portland, 1865), 408–11.

83. Emory Washburn, *Memoir of Hon. Levi Lincoln* (Cambridge, Mass., 1869); *DAB,* XI, 264–65; AHA, *Encyclopedia of Biography: Massachusetts,* pp. 123–35; McLoughlin, *New England Dissent,* II, 1158, 1172; C. C. Baldwin, Barre, 7 June 1825, to Isaac Davis, Davis Papers, MWA.

## IV. "Party Spirit" and Party

1. Ronald P. Formisano, "Political Character, Antipartyism, and the Second Party System," *American Quarterly,* 21 (1969), 683–709; Richard Hofstadter, *The Idea of a Party System: The Rise of Legitimate Opposition in the United States, 1780–1840* (Berkeley, 1969); Roy F. Nichols, *The Invention of the American Political Parties* (New York, 1967).

2. Walter Dean Burnham, *Critical Elections and the Mainsprings of Politics* (New York, 1970); Austin Ranney, *Curing the Mischiefs of Faction: Party Reform in America* (Berkeley, 1975).

3. See below, Chapter VIII.

4. See below, Chapter XI.

5. The notion of "attitudes" is controversial in social science, yet it seems indispensable. Many social scientists believe attitudes to be the key to motivation and thus to any explanations of behavior. "Attitude" will be used here as referring to predispositions imbedded in individual personalities and shaped by a common culture. It is conceded that attitudes are discovered by inference, but assumed that any inquiry into political culture must probe to a deeper level, to what Robert D. Putnam labeled "habits of thought" and to what Harry Eckstein called "internalized expectations about politics." Putnam, *The Beliefs of Politicians: Ideology, Conflict, and Democracy in Britain and Italy* (New Haven, 1973), p. 3; Eckstein, "A Perspective on Comparative Politics, Past and Present," in Eckstein and David Apter, eds., *Comporative Politics: A Reader* (New York, 1963), p. 26; see also Young C. Kim, "The Concept of Political Culture in Comparative Politics," *Journal of Politics,* 26 (1964), 313–36; William Theodore Bluhm, *Ideologies and Attitudes: Modern Political Culture* (Englewood Cliffs, N.J., 1974). Donald Fleming, "Attitude: The History of a Concept," *Perspectives in American History,* 1 (1967), 285–365.

6. William DeLoss Love, *The Fast and Thanksgiving Days of New England* (Boston,, 1895); William Gribbin, *The Churches Militant: The War of 1812 and American Religion* (New Haven, 1973), pp. 20–24. For proclamations, see Commonwealth of Massachusetts, By His Excellency Caleb Strong . . . A Proclamation for a Day of Public Fasting and Prayer. February 17, 1804. Boston. Broadside Collection, MWA; Boston *Independent Chronicle,* Mar. 9, 1833; Boston *Patriot,* Mar. 12, 1834.

Even the Lowell mills shut down on a fast day; only three holidays—the Fourth of July, Thanksgiving, and Christmas (besides Sundays)—were so honored: *House Documents, 1845,* no. 50, p. 9.

7. Thomas Coffin Amory, *Life of James Sullivan* (Boston, 1859), II, 153.

8. Regarding the 1812 celebration, see Benjamin Thomas Hill, ed., *The Diary of Isaiah Thomas, 1805–1828,* Transactions and Collections of the American Antiquarian Society, vols. 9 and 10 (Worcester, 1909), I, 143–45; for details of 1805, see Boston *Columbian Centinel,* June 1, 1805. General accounts include Nathaniel Bradstreet Shurtleff, "Negro Election Day," *Massachusetts Historical Society Proceedings* (1873), pp. 45–46; Paul Gustaf Faler, "Workingmen, Mechanics and Social Change: Lynn, Massachusetts, 1800–1860" (Ph.D. diss., University of Wisconsin, 1970), pp. 156–59; Hiram Barrus, *History of the Town of Goshen, Hampshire County, Massachusetts* (Boston, 1881), p. 130; Charles Nutt, *History of Worcester and Its People* (New York, 1919), I, 485–86.

9. Oliver Ayer Roberts, *History of . . . the Ancient and Honorable Artillery Company of Massachusetts, 1637–1888,* II (Boston, 1897), 458–59. The actual selection of officers was itself an elaborate ritual. Zachariah G. Whitman, *The History of the Ancient and Honorable Artillery Company* (Boston, 1842), pp. 448–50; Amory, *Sullivan,* II, 197–99.

10. Election Day was moved again later to the Tuesday after the first Monday in November. Albert Bushnell Hart, ed., *Commonwealth History of Massachusetts,* IV (New York, 1930), 7. For a description of the difficulties encountered because of the frigid weather in which the 1832 Election Day ceremonies were held, see Jonathan Messerli, *Horace Mann: A Biography* (New York, 1972), pp. 151–53.

11. Richard D. Birdsall, *Berkshire County: A Cultural History* (New Haven, 1959), p. 243. The old custom of Boston merchants and public men gathering on the Exchange or "Change" at midday every working day also endured until well into the nineteenth century. Samuel Eliot Morison, *The Maritime History of Massachusetts, 1783–1860* (Boston, 1921), p. 239.

12. Ranney, *Curing the Mischiefs of Faction,* p. 52.

13. David Hackett Fischer, *The Revolution in American Conservatism: The Federalist Party in the Era of Jeffersonian Democracy* (New York, 1965), pp. 37–38; Joseph W. Cox, *Champion of Southern Federalism: Robert Goodloe Harper of South Carolina* (Port Washington, N.Y., 1972), pp. 87–88. Yet evidence for a different view of Harper can be found in Cox's biography, in which there is little to suggest that Harper acted in conformity with a partisan ethos. On the contrary, Harper's actions as a promoter of the Alien and Sedition Acts, and of even more extreme measures of repression against Jeffersonian opponents, suggest a man in step with his contemporaries in rejecting the concept of legitimate opposition. Ibid., esp. pp. 141–56. Moreover, soon after delivering his often quoted speech, Harper wrote to his constituents in eager anticipation of war with France and of the collapse of partisan opposition because "the time is now arrived when we shall forget all our party divisions and concur heartily in defending our country." R. Goodloe Harper, Circular Letter, March 9, 1798, in Noble E. Cunningham, Jr., ed., *Circular Letters of Congressmen to Their Constitutents,* (Chapel Hill, 1978), 109. In 1800 Harper criticized party men "who are heated by constant opposition . . . and view everything with a prejudiced eye." R. G. H. Circular Letter, May 15, 1800, in ibid., p. 220.

14. Fisher Ames, 5 Nov. 1799, to Timothy Pickering, in Seth Ames, ed., *Works of Fisher Ames* (Boston, 1854), I, 260–61; F. Ames, 19 Mar. 1801, to Theodore Dwight, in ibid., p. 293; F.A., 14 Dec. 1801 to Jeremiah Smith, in ibid., p. 313; and F.A., 29 Nov. 1803, to Thomas Dwight, in ibid., p. 334.

15. William W. Story, *Life and Letters of Joseph Story* (Boston, 1851), p. 81;

Charles Warren, ed., *Jacobin and Junto: or Early American Politics as Viewed in the Diary of Dr. Nathaniel Ames, 1758–1822* (New York, 1968; first ed., 1931), p. 234; George Cabot, 27 Mar. 1800, to C. Gore, in Henry Cabot Lodge, *Life and Letters of George Cabot* (Boston, 1877), p. 271; S. Higginson, 12 Oct. 1803, to T. Pickering, quoted in Hervey Putnam Prentiss, *Timothy Pickering as the Leader of New England Federalism, 1800–1815* (Evanston, Ill., 1934), p. 12; T. Pickering, 7 Feb. 1801, to his wife, quoted in Charles W. Upham, *The Life of Timothy Pickering*, IV (Boston, 1873), 30–31; Leverett Saltonstall, Salem, 8 July 1808, to Nathaniel Saltonstall, in Robert E. Moody, ed., *The Saltonstall Papers, 1607–1815*, II (Boston, 1974), 447; Amory, *Sullivan*, II, 191; John Adams, 23 Jan. 1809, to Benjamin Rush, in John A. Schutz and Douglass Adair, eds., *The Spur of Fame: Dialogues of John Adams and Benjamin Rush, 1805–1813* (San Marino, Calif., 1966), p. 128.

16. Joseph Edward Adams Smith, *The History of Pittsfield, Massachusetts: From the Year 1800 to the Year 1876* (Springfield, Mass., 1876), pp. 90–91; Story, *Joseph Story*, p. 86.

17. Abijah Bigelow, *The Voters' Guide: or, The Power, Duty & Privileges of the Constitutional Voters in the Commonwealth of Massachusetts* (Leominster, Mass., 1807), pp. 155–56, 139–41; the quotation about Burgh is from Caroline Robbins, *The Eighteenth-Century Commonwealthman* (Cambridge, Mass., 1961), p. 365. Burgh hated electioneering and bribery, approved of deference, and recommended the secret ballot. Carla H. Hay, "The Making of a Radical: The Case of James Burgh," *Journal of British Studies*, 18 (1979), 93–94.

18. "Party Spirit," Worcester *Massachusetts Spy*, Feb. 27, 1811; a Republican paper criticized "party spirit" while it also stressed that the election choice lay between "*Federal* or *Republican* candidates." New Bedford *Old Colony Gazette*, Mar. 22, 1811.

19. Salem *Observer*, Mar. 29, 1823; and Apr. 5, 1823.

20. Bruce Kuklick's warning that speeches by public persons cannot be assumed to be indicators of popular belief is pertinent: "Myth and Symbol in American Studies," *American Quarterly*, 24 (1972), 444. The history of the sermons from their origin in 1634 through the middle of the nineteenth century is covered in Lindsay Swift, "The Massachusetts Election Sermons," *Publications of the Colonial Society of Massachusetts*, I (1892–1894), 388–451. A decided political turn in the sermons after 1800 is pointed out in Rollo Gabriel Silver, "Government Printing in Massachusetts, 1751–1801," *Sudties in Bibliography*, 16 (1963), 179–80.

21. The 1800 Election Sermon contained no references to politics: Joseph McKeen, *A Sermon Delivered May 28, 1800, Being the Day of the General Election* (Boston, 1800). Since the Election Sermons all had identical or nearly identical titles, they shall hereafter be entitled *Election Sermon* with the appropriate year.

22. Fears of catastrophe emerged early. In 1802 Thomas Baldwin noted that "many well-informed persons had been seriously alarmed at the progress of party disaffection; and have feared lest some untoward circumstance should provoke the mad attempt to divide our hitherto happy Republic. . . ." *Election Sermon, 1802*, p. 28. (Baldwin was a conservative Baptist leader from Boston: William G. McLoughlin, *New England Dissent, 1630–1833: The Baptists and the Separation of Church and State* (Cambridge, Mass., 1971), II, 1114.) The next year Reuben Puffer feared for the day, still distant, when "Happy America" might have fallen from grace: "Agitated by party, and rent by internal dissentions. . . . The days of darkness are upon thee. . . . Lost is that freedom, which cost thee so dear." *Election Sermon, 1803*, p. 12. (Puffer was a spellbinding Orthodox preacher from a little country parish in Berlin, Worcester County: *History of Worcester County, Massachusetts* (Boston, 1879), I,

277–78.) Yet in 1804 Samuel Kendall asked, "Have we not fallen already . . . divided in the zeal of triumph of parties, [and] lost sight of the public good . . . ?" *Election Sermon, 1804,* p. 29.

23. Edmund Foster, *Election Sermon, 1812,* p. 21; William Allen, *Election Sermon, 1813,* p. 21; James Flint, *Election Sermon, 1815,* pp. 18–19.

24. Thomas Thacher, *Election Sermon, 1811,* p. 20; Allen, *Election Sermon, 1813,* p. 20; Aaron Bancroft, *Election Sermon, 1802,* p. 19.

25. David Osgood, *Election Sermon, 1809,* p. 20.

26. Massachusetts Election Sermons (Boston, 1880), Broadside. A copy of the sermon in the T. Waterman bound volume of *Election Sermons, 1801–10,* p. 2, contains a note about the incident. The house also passed a resolution "Containing high charges against the sermon." The Federalists had it printed by raising their own funds: William B. Sprague, *Annals of the American Pulpit,* II (New York, 1857), 268.

27. John T. Kirkland, *Election Sermon, 1816,* pp. 6, 22; Thomas Snell, *Election Sermon, 1817,* passim; Zephaniah Swift Moore, *Election Sermon, 1818,* p. 24; Peter Eaton, *Election Sermon, 1819,* p. 3.

28. Nathaniel Thayer, *Election Sermon, 1823;* Daniel Sharp, *Election Sermon, 1824.* When Levi Lincoln took office as a consensus governor in 1825, William B. Sprague congratulated him, observing that "in all the measures which have resulted in this high testimony of public respect, the voice of party has been dumb." *Election Sermon, 1825,* p. 33.

29. James Walker, *Election Sermon, 1828,* pp. 12–13.

30. William E. Channing, *Election Sermon, 1830,* pp. 28, 29. A government which sacrifices the many to the few or the state to a party "becomes the public preacher of a crime" (p. 33).

31. Paul Dean, *Election Sermon, 1832,* pp. 29–30.

32. William Peabody, *Election Sermon, 1833,* p. 24.

33. Ibid., p. 25.

34. One minister even urged as late as 1838 that voting should be confined to those who owned property: Richard Storrs, *Election Sermon, 1838,* p. 17.

35. Andrew Bigelow, *Election Sermon, 1836,* pp. 22–23.

36. Ibid., p. 25; Daniel Dana, *Election Sermon, 1837,* pp. 29, 33.

37. This silence on parties probably resulted in part from the clergy's more general retreat from political life. As politics became more professional, so too did religion. As Election Day preachers themselves became part of a profession, the Election Sermons registered indirectly their ambivalence about that process. Their wholesale involvement earlier in politics must be seen not as a departure from but as a continuation of their traditional role, a last gasp of the role expectations of earlier centuries. In 1831 Leonard Withington said he could remember "the time when preachers were most violent in their political style." He acutely observed that the ministers then were doing only what they had done in the eighteenth century, especially before and during the Revolution, when their "political interference" was most welcome. The clergy assumed quite naturally, when great public questions and divisions again arose, that they would continue "in the path in which you had always encouraged them to walk." Unfortunately they chose the wrong side, said Withington, and in doing so lost status. Simultaneously, they acquired a good deal of caution with respect to further plunging into politics. Withington, *Election Sermon, 1831,* pp. 36–37. Regarding the professionalization of the clergy, see Daniel H. Calhoun, *Professional Lives in America: Structure and Aspiration, 1750–1850* (Cambridge, Mass., 1965); and Donald M. Scott, *From Office to Profession: The New England Ministry, 1750–1850* (Philadelphia, 1978).

38. John Codman, *Election Sermon, 1840,* pp. 7, 8, 10, 11.

39. Ibid., p. 23. Codman was the son of a wealthy Charlestown merchant and well off. He was initially a hard-line Orthodox Congregationalist who refused to have open exchanges of pulpits with Unitarians. William Allen, *Memoir of John Codman, D.D.* (Boston, 1853), pp. 13, 31–32, 383–84. In 1833, however, the "ultra Calvinist" Codman spoke to a high Unitarian audience at Brattle Street Church. Boston *Post,* March 19, 1833.

40. David Damon, *Election Sermon, 1841,* pp. 15, 22, 26, 27, 28–32.

41. Ezra S. Gannett, *Election Sermon, 1842,* pp. 31–32. "What! a man put himself in chains, that he may plead passivity as an excuse for sin? Shall the partisan with his own hand efface the prerogatives of his humanity, and dare to trample the laws of God . . . *because* he has not the courage to break the leash in which he is led along like a hound watching his master's eye?" (pp. 32–33).

42. Samuel C. Jackson, *Election Sermon, 1843,* pp. 38–43.

43. Ibid., pp. 40, 42.

44. E. H. Chapin, *Election Sermon, 1844,* p. 25.

45. Ibid., pp. 27, 28–29.

46. *Resolves, 1802,* pp. 7, 8; *Resolves, 1803,* p. 33; *Resolves, 1805,* p. 12; *Resolves, 1806,* p. 3; (Gore) *Resolves, 1809,* pp. 305, 313.

47. *Resolves, 1810–1812,* pp. 16, 179–80, 185–86, 271–73, 279. See above, Chapter III. Thomas Thacher's Election Sermon of 1811 had denounced party in a way similar to the one found in Gerry's first inaugural. *Election Sermon, 1811,* p. 23.

48. *Resolves, 1812–1815,* pp. 18, 19, 20, 20–21. A Fourth of July orator, speaking to a Federal audience in 1812, made this argument more candidly. In our government it was repugnant "to hurl from office every incumbent, who shall dare to dissent from the dominant party" and bestow places on those subscribing to "the prevalent dogmas." The orator added, however, that "we are far from condemning in any administration that honest partiality towards political friends, which operates to bestow on them an equal share of the honors and emoluments of the state; *provided that it does not introduce a system of expulsion and proscription, but only a system of partial exclusion.*" William C. Jarvis, *An Oration, Delivered at Pittsfield (Mass.) before the Washington Benevolent Society of the County of Berkshire, on the 4th of July, 1812* (Stockbridge, 1812), p. 12, italics mine.

49. Caleb Strong, 20 June 1812, to Lewis Strong, quoted in Lodge, *Studies in History,* pp. 246–47; Joel Harris, Harvard, 28 June 1812, to Thomas W. Ward, and L. Eastman, Hardwick, 29 June 1812, to T. W. W., Ward Family Papers, MWA. Ward's removal and reappointment, as well as his attitudes toward patronage, may be traced in these papers, especially box 7, folder 1.

50. In 1822 Brooks said, fittingly, that "virtue is the vital principle of a republic, though a trite observation, is one, nevertheless, that can hardly be too often repeated." *Resolves, 1819–1824,* p. 508.

51. *Resolves, 1823,* p. 635. See below, Chapter V.

52. *Resolves, 1836,* p. 300.

53. *Acts and Resolves, 1843, 1844, 1845,* pp. 368–69.

54. I consulted orations for almost every year from 1800 through 1844, and for some years read several, but the notes below mention only those quoted or especially representative of trends discussed. Many of these were brought to my attention by Carol Kanis of the MWA.

In 1805 the Republicans of Boston, believing that Federalists monopolized the official Fourth of July festivities, established a partisan association and appointed their own orator. In other towns the same thing was happening. Washington Society, *An Historical View of the Public Celebrations of the Washington Society, and Those of the Young Republicans: 1805–1822* (Boston, 1823), p. iii; Warren, ed., *Diary of Nathaniel Ames*, pp. 185, 186, 187, 234–35.

55. William Charles White, *An Oration, Pronounced in the Meeting-House at Rutland, July 5th 1802 . . .* (Worcester, 1802), p. 12; Daniel Adams, *Oration, Pronounced at Leominster, July 4, 1804 . . .* (Leominster, 1804), p. 11; Moses Hall, Jr., *An Oration Pronounced at Saugus, July Fourth, 1815 . . .* (Boston, 1815), p. 12. For an extensive antipartisan treatment of "party spirit," see Jeremiah Everts, *An Oration, Delivered in Charlestown, on the Fourth of July, 1812 . . .* (Charlestown, 1812), pp. 23–24.

56. Edward D. Bangs, *An Oration Pronounced at Springfield, Mass., on the Fourth of July, 1823 . . .* (Springfield, 1823), p. 11. This Republican effort was unusual for a positive note: "Under a government like ours, the strife of parties is no evil, whilst they are restrained from outrage and excess."

57. Nathaniel Emmons, *A Discourse Delivered July 5, 1802 . . .* (Wrentham, 1802), pp. 18–21; and John Danforth Dunbar, *An Oration, Pronounced on the 4th of July, 1805, at Pembroke . . .* (Boston, 1805), p. 15. William A. Fales urged his audience to put aside party spirit for at least one day and in a spirit of unanimity to "look with joyful anticipation to that day, when the names of Republican and Federalist shall be forgotten in that of American." *An Oration, Pronounced at Lenox, July 4th, 1807 . . .* (Pittsfield, 1807), p. 22. Along the same lines, see Isaac Braman, *The Union of All Honest Men: An Oration, Delivered at Rowley, West Parish, July 4th, 1805* (Newburyport, 1805), pp. 11–14; and Israel Hildreth, *An Oration, Pronounced at Dracut, 1st Parish, on the 4th of July 1818 . . .* (Concord, 1818), pp. 14–15, 17. James D. Richardson, ed., *A Compilation of the Messages and Papers of the President, 1789–1847* (Washington, D.C., 1900), I, p. 322.

58. John Davis, *An Oration, Pronounced at Worcester (Mass.) on the Fortieth Anniversary of American Independence* (Worcester, 1816); Francis Bassett, *An Oration, Delivered on Monday, the Fifth of July, 1824, . . . before the Supreme Executive of the Commonwealth, and the City Council and Inhabitants of the City of Boston* (Boston, 1824), pp. 20–21. Another sign of changed attitudes appeared in William C. Jarvis, *The Republican* (Pittsfield, 1820), p. 141.

59. Even the images began to be reversed: "The canting cry of no party is the poisonous deadly charm of the political reptile that creeps upon the unguarded genius of the constitution. . . ." Joseph H. Prince, *An Address, Delivered at Faneuil Hall, July 4, 1828, at the Jackson Celebration in Boston* (Boston, 1828), p. 15. This oration to Jackson's friends was viciously hostile to President John Quincy Adams. For the view that parties will exist but be of "temporary importance," see James T. Austin, *An Oration, Delivered on the Fourth of July, 1829, . . . in the City of Boston* (Boston, 1829), pp. 13–15. For a more traditional view, see Oliver Everett, *An Address Delivered at Fitchburgh on the Fifty-fifth Anniversary of the Declaration of the Independence of the United States of America* (Fitchburg, 1830), pp. 12, 21.

60. Edward Everett, *Oration Delivered on the Fourth Day of July, 1835, before the Citizens of Beverly, without Distinction of Party* (Boston, 1835), pp. 11–16, quotation from p. 12.

61. Alexander H. Everett, *A Defence of the Character and Principles of Mr. Jefferson: Being an Address Delivered at Weymouth, Mass., at the Request of the Anti-Masonic and Democratic Citizens of that Place, on the 4th of July, 1836* (Boston, 1836), p. 9.

62. Ibid., pp. 9–14, 21–27, quotations from pp. 27, 28. For the acceptance of party with a lingering antipartisan bias, see Jonathan Chapman, *An Oration Delivered before the Whigs of Bristol County at Taunton, July 4, 1839* (Taunton, 1839). Other defenses of party were couched in more traditional terms of seeing party as

something which could be carried to extremes but whose "commotion was healthy." Ivers James Austin, *An Oration Delivered by Request of the City Authorities, before the Citizens of Boston, . . . July 4, 1839* (Boston, 1839), pp. 30–33.

## V. Organization and Elections, 1800–1824

1. V. O. Key, Jr., *Southern Politics: In State and Nation* (New York, 1949), p. 15.

2. While I used many sources, I read newspapers extensively in the three periods to gauge the degree of organization in each. Though the files available for each period varied, I was able for each year to find papers in different parts of the state and to concentrate on the "snake season" from late January to early May. The papers were either weeklies or biweeklies, and I read sixteen for 1800, twenty-four for 1811, twelve for 1812, twenty-three for 1823, twenty-one for 1824, and several for years in between. Most of these papers are at the MWA, and Ms. Joyce Tracy was of great assistance in making them available.

3. Paul Goodman, *The Democratic-Republicans of Massachusetts: Politics in a Young Republic* (Cambridge, Mass., 1964), pp. 51, 62–64, 67–68; David H. Fischer, "The Myth of the Essex Junto," *William and Mary Quarterly,* 21 (1964), 216–17; idem, *The Revolution in American Conservatism: The Federalist Party in the Era of Jeffersonian Democracy* (New York, 1965), passim; James M. Banner, Jr., *To the Hartford Convention: The Federalists and the Origins of Party Politics in Massachusetts 1789–1815* (New York, 1970), pp. 216ff; Frederick M. Dallinger, *Nominations for Elective Office in the United States* (New York, 1897), pp. 23–25. In studies taking a different view, there is evidence to support the contention made here. Anson Ely Morse, *The Federalist Party in Massachusetts to the Year 1800* (Princeton, 1909), pp. 140–45, 148–49, 163–65; Richard E. Welch, Jr., *Theodore Sedgwick, Federalist: A Political Portrait* (Middletown, Conn., 1965), pp. 213–20; and Benjamin W. Labaree, *Patriots and Partisans: The Merchants of Newburyport, 1764–1815* (Cambridge, Mass., 1962), p. 106.

4. Goodman, *Democratic-Republicans,* pp. 122–24; George Cabot, 14 Mar. 1800, to Rufus King, in Charles R. King, ed., *The Life and Correspondence of Rufus King,* III (New York, 1896), 210; and Theodore Sedgwick, Philadelphia, 11 May 1800, to R. King, in ibid., pp. 238–39.

5. The quotation is from Boston *J. Russell's Gazette,* Mar. 28, 1800; Salem *Gazette,* Mar. 7, 18, 21, 28, 1800; Boston *Columbian Centinel,* Mar. 12, 19, Apr. 2, May 3, 1800; Boston *Constitutional Telegraph,* Apr. 12, 30, May 7, 1800; Dedham *Columbian Minerva,* Mar. 27, 1800; Northampton *Hampshire Gazette,* Jan. 8, Mar. 19, 26, Apr. 2, 1800; Greenfield *Gazette,* Apr. 4, 1800; Newburyport *Herald and Country Gazette,* Apr.–May 1800.

6. For Federal views, see *J. Russell's Gazette,* Feb. 10, 1800; Salem *Gazette,* Feb. 11, 1800. For Republican views, see Leominister *Telegraph,* Feb. 20, 25, 27 and Mar. 6, 1800; the Boston *Independent Chronicle,* gave both sides of the issue, Feb. 3, 13, 17, 1800; letter from Worcester *Massachusetts Spy* in Greenfield *Gazette,* Apr. 4, 1800; Worcester *Independent Gazette,* Mar. 18, Apr. 1, 1800; Boston *Constitutional Telegraph,* Feb. 12, 15, 22, Mar. 12, 1800.

7. *J. Russell's Gazette,* Apr. 7, 1800; Boston *Constitutional Telegraph,* Apr. 2, 1800.

8. *Columbian Centinel,* May 3, 10, 14, 1800; *Constitutional Telegraph,* May 10, 1800; Newburyport *Herald,* May 13, 1800; Salem *Gazette,* May 6, 1800. In Newburyport a "Federal ticket" of seven received votes ranging from 2,417 to 1,552 while a "Democratic list" of three garnered a low of 886 and a high of 911, according to labels in the *Herald,* May 16, 1800.

9. "Never was there a more singular and mysterious state of parties," exclaimed Fisher Ames; "the plot of an old Spanish play is not more complicated with underplot." Fisher Ames, Boston, 15 July, to Rufus King, in King, ed., *King Life and Correspondence,* III, 275; T. Sedgwick, Stockbridge, 26 Sept. 1800, to R. King, in ibid., p. 308; Northampton *Hampshire Gazette,* Oct. 29, 1800; Stephen Higginson, Boston, 12 Jan. 1800, to T. Pickering, "Letters of Stephen Higginson, 1783–1804," *Annual Report of the American Historical Association,* 1896, I, 835.

10. Papers examined include, New Bedford *Columbian Centinel;* Dedham *Columbian Minerva;* Boston *Gazette;* Stockbridge *Western Star;* Salem *Gazette;* Leominster *Telescope,* Worcester *Independent Gazette;* Worcester *Independent Intelligencer;* Greenfield *Gazette;* Boston *Constitutional Telegraph.*

11. Carl E. Prince, *The Federalists and the Origins of the U.S. Civil Service* (New York, 1977), pp. xi–xii; see also pp. 1–44, 143–44, 150, 152–53, 163, 168, 169, 171–72, 183, 184–85, 200, 203, 204, 206, 209, 212–13, 215–18, 231–33. In February 1800 a Federalist judge's charge to the Norfolk County grand jury amounted to electioneering for Federalism. W. P. Cresson *Francis Dana: A Puritan Diplomat at the Court of Catherine the Great* (New York, 1930), pp. 378–79.

12. H. G. Otis, Boston, 29 Aug. 1804, to W.S., Portland, Miscellaneous Bound Manuscripts, MHi.

13. This interpretation of the *Palladium* is indebted to Robert Edson Lee, "Timothy Dwight and the Boston *Palladium,*" *New England Quarterly,* 35 (1962), 231–34; also, Fisher Ames, 19 Mar. 1801, to Thomas Dwight, in Seth Ames, ed., *Works of Fisher Ames* (Boston, 1854), I, 295. George Cabot, 11 Oct. 1800, to C. Gore, and G. Cabot, 11 Oct. 1800, to Alexander Hamilton, in Henry Cabot Lodge, *Life and Letters of George Cabot* (Boston, 1877), pp. 292–93, 294. Thomas Jefferson, Monticello, 26 Aug. 1801, to Levi Lincoln, Levi Lincoln Papers, MHi.

14. Federal State Central Committee to chairmen of county committees, Boston, Apr. 14, 1806, Broadside Collection, MWA. Scholars who have attempted to determine the relationship between a paper's influence and voting generally found it difficult to do. See, e.g., Frederick Gardiner Fassett, Jr., *A History of Newspapers in the District of Maine, 1785–1820* (Orono, 1932), pp. 199–201.

15. On Federal lack of organization, see Fisher Ames, 19 Mar. 1801, to Theodore Dwight, in Ames, ed., *Works,* I, 293; Josiah Quincy, 23 Nov. 1804, to John Quincy Adams, quoted in Robert A. McCaughey, *Josiah Quincy, 1772–1864: The Last Federalist* (Cambridge, Mass., 1974), p. 35.

16. The Federal State Committee's increasing devotion to organization may be traced in State Central Committee Circular, Boston, 13 June 1805 (to Dwight Foster, North Brookfield); Federal Central Committee Circular Letter, Boston, February, 1806; and Circular letters, Boston 14 Apr. 1806, all in Broadside Collection MWA. "A Winter Evening's Amusement: or Democracy Upright," Jan. 17, 1805, Northampton, Broadside Collection, MWA, is a satire on Republican organization in Hampshire County which includes a Republican circular of Jan. 1, 1805. [Worcester Republican Committee], 12 Mar. 1806 letter attached to Circular from Republican Central Committee, Boston, ibid. On the intensity of the 1805 and 1806 elections, see Charles Warren, ed., *Jacobin and Junto: or Early American Politics as Viewed in the Diary of Dr. Nathaniel Ames, 1758–1822* (New York, 1968; first ed., 1931), p. 242; Fisher Ames, 10 Mar. 1806, to T. Pickering, in Ames, ed., *Works,* I, 370.

17. Warren, ed., *Dairy of Nathaniel Ames,* Aug. 28, 1808, p. 226. The Berkshire County Republican Committee operated in like manner: Pittsfield Republican Proceedings, March 4, 1809, Broadside Collection, MWA.

18. Edward Stanwood, "The Massachusetts Election in 1806," *Massachusetts Historical Society Proceeedings,* 2nd ser., 20 (1906), 12–19; [Federal Central Commit-

tee] Circular Letter, Boston, Apr. 14, 1806, and Worcester County Republican Committee Circular, Oct. 15, 1808, both in Broadside Collection, MWA. In Salem the debate over the number of representatives to be sent was always warmly contested. See, e.g., William Bentley, *The Diary of William Bentley,* III (Salem, Mass., 1911), 158, 226, 227. The attention paid to the representatives' election meant that increasing attention would be given to the election of town officers: George Cabot, 20 Mar. 1808, to T. Pickering, in Lodge, *George Cabot,* pp. 389–90.

A detailed study of Federal and Republican organization in Worcester concluded that more elements of organization existed than is conceded here, but also provided evidence of both sides' interest in secrecy. Mike Quarry, "Political Party Organization in Worcester, 1800–1809" (American Studies Seminar paper, American Antiquarian Society, 1980).

19. Thomas F. Wingate, Boston, 12 May 1810, to William King, Bath, King Correspondence, Maine Historical Society; and J. D. Forbes, *Israel Thorndike: Federalist Financier* (New York, 1953), p. 104. There are many letters in the King Correspondence, 1809–1810, which show the activities of the Republican Central Committee in organizing support in Maine, and also of local efforts: e.g., "To the Chairman of the Committee of the County of Lincoln," from A. W. Hill, Boston, Mar. 9, 1809; Francis Douglas, Portland, Mar. 19, 1810, to W. King; Joseph Farley, Waldoborough, Mar. 20, 1810, to W. King; A. W. Hill, on behalf of the Central Committee, Boston, Mar. 20, 1810, to W. King.

20. Samuel Eliot Morison, *The Maritime History of Massachusetts, 1783–1860* (Boston, 1921), p. 191; Thorp Lanier Wolford, "Democratic-Republican Reaction in Massachusetts to the Embargo of 1807," *New England Quarterly,* 15 (1942), 42. Although the complaints of Federal merchants about the embargo were filled with distress, at least one firm used the period of partial inactivity to great advantage. Carl Seaburg and Stanley Patterson, *Merchant Prince of Boston: Colonel T. H. Perkins, 1764–1854* (Cambridge, Mass., 1971), pp. 198–99.

21. Irving Brant, "Election of 1808," in Arthur M. Schlesinger, Jr., and Fred L. Israel, eds., *History of American Presidential Elections, 1789–1968,* I (New York, 1971), 185–221. On the importance of national issues, see George Cabot, 9 Apr. 1808, to T. Pickering, in Lodge, *George Cabot,* pp. 391–92; George Ulmer, Lincolnville, 6 Apr. 1808, to W. King, Daniel Granger, Wm. Moody, Saco, 23 Mar. 1810, to W. King, and E. Foot, Camden, 24 Mar. 1810, to W. King, King Correspondence.

22. Nathaniel Groton, 12 Feb. 1812, to Wm. King, Bath, King Correspondence. Regarding committee assignments, see Thomas Lawrence Davis, "Aristocrats and Jacobins in Country Towns: Party Formation in Berkshire County, Massachusetts, 1775–1816" (Ph.D. diss., Boston University, 1975), pp. 90–92, 96. An 1805 fight over printing contracts is described in Leverett Saltonstall, "Diary," in Robert E. Moody, ed., *The Saltonstall Papers, 1607–1815,* II (Boston, 1974), 213–32. In 1806 Caleb Strong found "the two Houses . . . uncommonly tranquil and good-humored, and I am told that but little of party spirit appeared in either of them." Quoted in Henry Cabot Lodge, *Studies in History* (Boston, 1884), p. 243. In 1809 the legislature handled judges' salaries in a nonpartisan manner. Theophilus Parsons, *Memoir of Theophilus Parsons* (Boston, 1859), pp. 232–33. Most evidence of each party's legislative caucuses comes from their opponents, e.g., "Rehoboth Election," *Columbian Centinel,* Feb. 26, 1812. For direct evidence of Federal caucusing, see T. H. Perkins, Letters to John Phillips, 1811–1813, n.d., Blagden Collection, Houghton Library, Harvard University.

23. The first quotation is from Leverett Saltonstall, 10 Jan. 1812, to Nathaniel Saltonstall, in Moody, ed., *Saltonstall Papers,* II, 508. The second from Josiah Dwight, Northampton, 19 Apr. 1813, to Harrison G. Otis, Blagden Collection (Letters to

John Phillips). The gerrymander stimulated intense partisan voting. Elmer C. Griffith, *The Rise and Development of the Gerrymander* (Chicago, 1907), pp. 67, 70.

24. Members of state central committees frequently had some say in the selection of senate candidates as well. Remarks that decisions about Republican senate candidacies in Maine were being made "in Boston" appeared frequently in the William King Correspondence, 1808–1811. See, e.g., Paul Dudley Sargent, Boston, 19 Mar. 1808, to W. King; and Joseph Farley, Waldoborough, 24 Feb. 1809, to W. King.

25. Pittsfield *Sun,* Mar. 9, 23, 1811; Worcester *National Aegis,* Mar. 27, 1811; Springfield *Hampshire Federalist,* Mar. 14, 1811. On other conventions or meetings, see (Berkshire Federalists) Pittsfield *Recorder,* Mar. 2, 9, 1811; (Bristol Co. Republicans) New Bedford *Old Colony Gazette,* Feb. 8, 1811, and New Bedford *Mercury,* Mar. 22, 1811; (Worcester Federalists) *Massachusetts Spy,* Mar. 27, 1811; (Essex Republicans) Newburyport *Independent Whig,* Mar. 16, 1811; (Essex Federalists) *Columbian Centinel,* Mar. 16, 1811; (Suffolk Republicans) Boston *Patriot,* Mar. 20, 1811; (Norfolk and several Maine counties, Republicans), *Patriot,* Feb. 16, Mar. 23, 1811. A Maine Republican in the Kennebec district doubted that the Federalists would "publicly announce their senatorial candidates." John Chandler, Monmouth, 16 Mar. 1811, to W. King, King Correspondence.

26. Essex *Register,* Mar. 4, 1812. In Maine the "Federal Republicans" of Lincoln County held a "convention" described as "a number of citizens according to previous notice." Portland *Gazette,* Mar. 9, 16, 1812. Pittsfield Republicans issued the call for a Berkshire County "Republican Convention," but it was not clear how it was constituted. *Sun,* Feb. 29, Mar. 14, 1812. Other meetings consisted of "delegates from several towns" (Worcester South) and "respectable . . . Inhabitants of Thirty-eight towns," (Middlesex South), *Centinel,* Mar. 12, 23, 1812; or simply of "independent electors," (Worcester North), *Spy,* Mar. 18, 1812.

27. Both parties depended heavily on their inner circles of prominent men to raise funds. In 1811 the Federal leaders in Boston decided that Madison's policies needed to be counteracted by diffusing "correct information" among the people "in a manner more efficacious than that of the ordinary newspaper." They therefore appointed a dozen collectors among themselves who divided a list of some 150 well-off Federalists with varying sums of money designated for collection from each man. H. G. Otis, T. H. Perkins, L. Sargent, J. Phillips, P. C. Brooks, "Committee Appointed for This Application, May 4, 1811"; "Memorandum Collection for 1811," (Letters of John Phillips) Blagden Collection. Several letters and documents in these papers pertain to fund raising in 1811 and shed light on a similar effort in 1808. In 1811 Berkshire County Federalists also raised money for electioneering through the private donations of local leaders, the most prominent giving the most. Davis, "Aristocrats and Jacobins in Country Towns," pp. 18–20. The Maine merchant prince and Republican politician William King, besides playing a key role in appointments and nominations, contributed freely from his own pocket to support the Republican cause in Maine. Nathaniel Cheever, Hallowell, 17 Apr. 1810, to W. King, King Papers.

28. See, e.g., "To the Republican Voters of Bristol County," New Bedford *Old Colony Gazette,* Mar. 29, 1811; *Centinel,* Mar. 6, 1811; Northampton *Democrat,* Mar. 26, 1811.

29. Boston *Gazette,* Apr. 1, 1811; *Centinel,* Mar. 30, 1811; *Independent Chronicle,* Apr. 4, 1811. For Republican organization, see *Patriot,* Mar. 30, 1811.

30. Some other towns: (Charlestown) *Patriot,* Mar. 27, 1811; (Newburyport) *Independent Whig,* Mar. 16, 28, 1811; (Northampton) *Hampshire Gazette,* Mar. 27, 1811.

31. The *Centinel* entitled the Federal address of 1811 the "American Address." Feb. 23, 1811. The Republicans in 1812 entitled theirs "To the Republicans of Massa-

chusetts." Pittsfield *Sun,* Feb. 6, 1812. Resolutions and statements of county conventions throughout the period and especially in 1811 and 1812 discussed national issues.

32. Pittsfield *Reporter,* Mar. 16, 1811. In 1812 the parties focused even more attention on town elections because the Republican legislature had broadened the suffrage in town elections so that almost all males twenty-one and over could vote. For a Republican defense of the law, see New Bedford *Gazette,* Feb. 28, 1812. Federalists claimed that it backfired. *Centinel,* Mar. 7, 25, 1812.

33. For Boston, see *Gazette,* Mar. 14, 1811; for Dedham and Norfolk Co., Warren, ed., *Diary of Nathaniel Ames,* p. 239, and *Centinel,* Mar. 9, 1811; for Salem, *New-England Palladium,* Mar. 29, 1811, and *Essex Register,* Feb. 9, Mar. 2, 6, 9, 27; for Newburyport, *Herald,* Mar. 12, 1811; for Bristol Co., James Thomas, New Bedford, 22 Mar. 1810, to W. King, King Correspondence, and New Bedford *Mercury,* Feb. 22, Mar. 1, 1812; for Haverhill, 1811 and 1812, *Essex Register,* Mar. 25, 1812; for compromise in Marblehead, ibid., Mar. 21, 1812; for Bridgewater, 1811 and 1812, *Herald,* Apr. 3, 1812.

34. The quotation is from Leverett Saltonstall, Salem, 4 May 1811 to Nathaniel Saltonstall, in Moody, ed., *Saltonstall Papers,* II, 502. Newburyport *Independent Whig,* Mar. 16, 23, 1811. New partisan papers were established throughout 1811 and 1812: e.g., (Northampton) *Democrat,* Mar. 12, 1811; New Bedford *Gazette,* Oct. 18, 1811, and prospectus for *The Yankee,* ibid., Jan. 3, 1812. Partisan rancor stayed in the air after the May election and into the summer: Greenfield *Traveller,* June 18, July 9, 1811.

35. *Centinel,* Apr. 24, 27, May 8, 1811; resolutions of Apr. 17 meeting of "Federal Republicans" of Worcester, ibid., May 1; Pittsfield *Sun,* Apr. 20, 1811; Springfield *Hampshire Federalist,* Apr. 24, 1811; Northampton *Democrat,* May 7, 1811; Northampton *Hampshire Gazette,* Apr. 24, 27, May 1, 1811; Pittsfield *Reporter,* May 18, 25, 1811; (Bristol Co. Republicans) *Patriot,* Apr. 17, 1811; New Bedford *Mercury,* May 3, 17, 1811; New Bedford *Old Colony Gazette,* Apr. 26, May 10, 1811; Worcester *National Ægis,* Apr. 24, May 1, 1811; Worcester *Massachusetts Spy,* May 1, 1811.

36. Thomas H. Perkins et al., Boston, Apr. 19, 1811, Circular letter to town committees, Broadsides, Essex Institute; Newburyport *Independent Whig,* May 2, 1811; *Patriot,* Apr. 27, 1811.

37. North District Central Committee (Samuel Ward et al., letters of Mar. 2 and 13 Apr. 1812 to Committee for Princeton, William Dodds, Esq., et al.), Worcester Historical Museum.

38. Warren, ed., *Diary of Nathaniel Ames,* p. 248.

39. The quotation is from *Centinel,* Feb. 19, 1812; see also Feb. 26; Greenfield *Franklin Herald,* Mar. 10, 1812. On Republican removals in Worcester County, see Lovell Walker, Templeton, 29 Feb. 1812, to Abijah Bigelow, Abijah Bigelow Papers, MWA. Walker complained of "two parties in this county whose measures and policy are totally opposite in everything." For a retrospective Federal view of the "new order of things" under Gerry, see the house of representatives' official reply to Governor Strong, May 1813, in *Resolves, May, 1812–March, 1815,* pp. 233–34.

40. Davis, "Aristocrats and Jacobins in Berkshire County," p. 39; the 1812 "address" appeared in the *Centinel,* Feb. 12, 1812, and the *Palladium,* Feb. 14, 1812, and other papers. For the antiparty theme, see Newburyport *Herald,* Feb. 11, 1812, Portland *Gazette,* Mar. 16, 1812. Examples of Federal eclecticism in names are in *Palladium,* Feb. 26, Mar. 1, 5, 12, Apr. 30, 1811, Feb. 11, Mar. 31, 1812; Boston *Independent Chronicle,* Mar. 7, 1811; Pittsfield *Reporter* Mar. 9, 16, 1811; *Centinel,* Feb. 16, 23, Mar. 6, 27, 30, 1811; Feb. 19, 26, Mar. 25, 1812; Newburyport *Herald,* Mar. 19, 26, 29, 1811, Feb. 21, 1812; New Bedford *Mercury,* Mar. 27, 31, Apr. 3,

1812; Portland *Gazette,* Feb. 24, Mar. 9, 1812; Worcester *Massachusetts Spy,* Mar. 25, 1812. Barnstable County Federalists stressed issues and not party in the 1812 congressional election: "To the free and independent electors of the first Southern or Barnstable Congressional District. . . ." Lemuel Shaw Papers (Microfilm, reel 3B), MHi.

41. Fischer, *Revolution in American Conservatism,* pp. 115, 127, 128.

42. Harlan Ballard, "A Forgotten Fraternity," in *Collections of the Berkshire Historical and Scientific Society,* 3 (1913), 292, 293; William Alexander Robinson, "The Washington Benevolent Society in New England: A Phase of Politics during the War of 1812," *Massachusetts Historical Society Proceedings,* 49 (1916), 279, 280. Notices of society meetings appeared frequently in newspapers during election seasons.

43. Washington Benevolent Society Constitution, Bye Laws, and Journal [1812–1824], MHi. The Republicans of Boston had a similar club. In the 1820s its members were mostly National Republicans who later tended to become Jacksonian Democrats. Washington Society, Proceedings, 1811–1833, and Washington Society, Boston. Record 1805–1821, MHi. [Washington Society], *Historical View* (1823), p. iv.

44. Salem *Essex Register,* May 22, 1811, contained a vivid account of the Rehoboth melee; the Greenfield *Franklin Herald,* Mar. 3, 1812, printed the report of the house committee on the case with its editorial comments.

45. In Newburyport a Republican effort to get the town to declare support of the war was voted down at town meeting by 10 to 1. In the 1812 presidential poll the "Peace Ticket" received 695 votes to 135 for Madison, and by the fall of 1814 the Republican candidates for Congress received no votes at all. Labaree, *Patriots and Partisans,* pp. 186, 190. On the war's unpopularity, see Theodore Dwight, *History of the Hartford Convention* (New York, 1833), pp. 277–78; Seaburg and Patterson, *Merchant Prince,* p. 246; Christopher Gore, Waltham, 28 July 1814, to R. King, in King, ed., *King Life and Correspondence,* V, 403; Morison, *Maritime History,* pp. 195–97.

46. Hervey Putnam Prentiss, *Timothy Pickering as the Leader of New England Federalism, 1800–1815* (Evanston, Ill., 1934), pp. 87–89; Warren, ed., *Diary of Nathaniel Ames,* pp. 251–52, 256; Dr. Ames said that in presenting coalition peace tickets, the Federalists tended "to break and divide like the Devil." Ibid., p. 258. See also William Gribbin, *The Churches Militant: The War of 1812 and American Religion* (New Haven, 1973), pp. 24–60.

47. [Federal] North District Central Committee, Lancaster, Mar. 14, 1813, to Dr. Ephraim Wilson, Princeton, for Princeton Town Committee, Lancaster Town Papers, Worcester Historical Museum. "Federalist Party Organization in 1814," table 15, in Fischer, *Revolution in American Conservatism,* p. 80. Not all Republicans hid under rocks during the war; see, e.g., John Leland, "Address to the Association of the Sons of Liberty, Cheshire, March 4, 1813," in L. F. Greene, ed., *The Writings of the Late Elder John Leland* (New York, 1845), pp. 373–75.

48. Banner, *Hartford Convention,* pp. 294–350, passim. Morison, *Maritime History,* p. 210; see also Labaree, *Patriots and Partisans,* p. 199.

49. Edmund Quincy, *Life of Josiah Quincy* (Boston, 1868), p. 360.

50. Samuel S. Conner, Circular Letter, Apr. 22, 1816, in Noble E. Cunningham, Jr., ed., *Circular Letters of Congressmen to Their Constituents 1789–1829,* II (Chapel Hill, 1978), 973; Daniel Webster, Washington, 21 Apr. 1816, to Samuel Ayer Bradley, in Charles M. Wiltse and Harold D. Moser, eds., *The Papers of Daniel Webster: Correspondence,* I (Hanover, N.H., 1974), 197; Jeremiah Mason, Portsmouth, 24 Dec. 1817, to C. Gore, in George S. Hilliard, ed., *Memoir and Correspondence of Jeremiah Mason* (Cambridge, Mass., 1873), p. 178; C. Gore, Waltham, 26 Jan. 1817, to R. King, in King, ed., *King Life and Correspondence,* VI, 48; Harry William

Fritz, "The Collapse of Party: President, Congress, and the Decline of Party Action, 1807–1817" (Ph.D. diss., Washington University, 1971).

51. Seaburg and Patterson, *Merchant Prince,* p. 274; Shaw Livermore, Jr., *The Twilight of Federalism: The Disintegration of the Federalist Party, 1815–1830* (Princeton, 1962), pp. 44–51; compare Samuel Eliot Morison, *Harrison Gray Otis, 1765–1848: Urbane Federalist* (Boston, 1969), p. 543.

52. Joseph T. Buckingham, *Specimens of Newspaper Literature: With Personal Memoirs, Anecdotes, and Reminiscences* (Boston, 1850), II, 96–98; Livermore, *Twilight,* pp. 48–49; C. Gore, Waltham, 15 May 1817, to Rufus King, in King, ed., *King Life and Correspondence,* VI, 71; Samuel Eliot Morison, *The Life and Letters of Harrison Gray Otis, Federalist, 1765–1848* (Boston, 1913), II, 207–8; J. Hopkinson, Philadelphia, 20 Nov. 1817, to Daniel Webster, in Wiltse and Moser, eds., *Papers of Daniel Webster: Correspondence,* I, 214; William Sullivan, 1 Jan. 1819, to John Phillips, Letters to John Phillips, Blagden Collection.

53. H. G. Otis, Washington, 23 Dec. 1818, to John Phillips (Letters to John Phillips), Blagden Collection; Livermore, *Twilight,* pp. 56–57; Morison, *Harrison Gray Otis* (1913), II, 209; C. Gore, 20 Jan. 1819, to Jeremiah Mason, in Hilliard, ed., *Mason,* p. 210.

54. These factions suggest the "Boston office-holders" vs. "country" division that was to appear in the Democratic party in the 1830s.

55. A. H. Everett, Boston, 15 June 1818, to John Bailey, Washington, vol. 20, Washburn Collection, MHi.

56. The Federal caucus was discussed in H. G. Otis, Washington, 23 Dec. 1818, to John Phillips (Letters to John Phillips), Blagden Collection; Federal organization, in "List of the County Committees, as corrected in a meeting holden at Boston on Tuesday Evening, February 13, 1821," ibid.; the 1822 partisan division of the house and senate was given by county in New-England *Palladium,* June 7, 1822. Calculation of party supremacy could also figure in nonpartisan gestures. See, e.g., Livermore, *Twilight,* p. 55; and John Quincy Adams, Washington, 23 Nov. 1817 to Alexander H. Everett, Boston, in Andrew C. McLaughlin, ed., "Letters of John Quincy Adams to Alexander Hamilton Everett, 1811–1837," *American Historical Review,* 11 (1905), 109–11.

57. Banner, *Hartford Convention,* p. 349, held that Hartford made the Federalists stronger at the polls; this was true for the short run, but not in 1823–1824.

58. *Centinel,* Feb. 26, 1823. Consensus prevailed in the Salem March meeting; see *Essex Register,* Mar. 20, 1823, and *Observer,* Mar. 22, 1823. It also prevailed in Beverly; see Salem *Gazette,* Mar. 14, 1823. In Worcester, Republicans caucused for the March meeting; see *National Ægis,* Feb. 26, 1823. In the Boston city election, now in April, Federalists and Republicans both elected city officers on a "Union" ticket; see Boston *Evening Gazette,* Apr. 12, 1823.

59. *Centinel,* Feb. 22, 1823. Federal convention, ibid., Feb. 12; notices of Middlesex, Norfolk, and Bristol county Federal meetings, ibid., Mar. 12. Worcester County "Federal Republicans" assembled from "various parts" of the county, and their address gave little sense of the differences between the parties, *Spy,* Mar. 19, 1823; Berkshire County Republican convention and address, Pittsfield *Sun,* Mar. 20, 1823. Republican convention and state address, *Independent Chronicle,* Feb. 5, 1823; calls for various Republican county meetings in Boston *Statesman,* Jan. 13, Feb. 13, 17, 24, Mar. 6, and various election eve caucuses, Apr. 3, 1823. In Hampden County politicking by both parties appeared to be mild, Springfield *Hampden Journal,* Mar. 26, 1823. In Hampshire County Federalists held a "meeting of Gentlemen" to nominate senators and endorse the state ticket, Boston *Repertory,* Apr. 5, 1823. Federal Essex County convention, Salem *Gazette,* Mar. 11, 1823; in Haverhill Feder-

alists and Republicans caucused together for town purposes, Haverhill *Gazette* and *Essex Patriot,* Mar. 22, 29, and Apr. 5, 1823.

60. Isaac Parker, Jan. 1823, to H. G. Otis, Otis Papers, MHi; John Lowell, 25 Feb. 1823, to H. G. Otis, and J. Lowell, 26 Feb. 1823, to H. G. Otis, ibid.; Morison, *Harrison Gray Otis* (1913), II, 251–53; For a glowing appreciation of Otis by a young Federalist in 1829, see Josiah Quincy, *Figures of the Past: From the Leaves of Old Journals* (Boston, 1884), pp. 266–70. Regarding clubs among the Federal business-political elite after 1815, see Frances W. Gregory, *Nathan Appleton: Merchant and Entrepreneur, 1779–1861* (Charlottesville, 1975), pp. 194–96.

61. Douglas Shaw, "Unitarians, Trinitarians, and the Massachusetts Establishment, 1820–1834" (Master's thesis, Brown University, 1967), p. 74; Boston *Repertory,* Jan. 27, 1823; Morison, *Otis* (1969), pp. 440–41, and Morison, *Harrison Gray Otis* (1913), II, 241–42. One Federal leader later said he expected Eustis's victory "when I saw both Orthodoxy and the Hartford Convention invoked to his aid." Jeremiah Mason, Portsmouth, 17 Apr. 1823, to C. Gore, in Hilliard, ed., *Mason,* p. 270.

62. Though the Orthodox were concentrated in western Massachusetts, they also threw their weight against Otis in Boston and Essex County. Shaw, "Unitarians, Trinitarians," pp. 44–45; Morison, *Otis* (1969), pp. 440–41; John L. Withrow, *Seventy-Fifth Anniversary of Park Street Congregational Church* (Boston, 1884), p. 37. Samuel Hubbard of Park Street Church, Boston, was one of the Amherst petitioners. *Repertory,* Jan. 23, 1823.

63. Otis had recently been certified a member of the Brattle Square Church, November 8, 1822: "Covenant between Members of the Church in Brattle Square," in 1824 folder, Otis Papers, MHi. Federal defenses are in *Centinel,* Mar. 26, 1823; Address of the Federal State Central Committee, in ibid., Apr. 2, 1823; *Repertory,* Mar. 29, 1823. Republican attacks are in Boston *Stateman,* Feb. 16, Mar. 6, 24, 27, 1823, and *Independent Chronicle and Patriot,* Apr. 2, 1823.

64. Dedham *Village Register,* Mar. 7, 1823; Worcester *National Ægis,* Mar. 19, 1823; Salem *Gazette,* Feb. 28, 1823.

65. In 1824 Worcester County Federalists complained of this Republican tactic of the year before as "glittering bait." *Spy,* Mar. 17, 1824; and *Spy* broadside, Mar. 31, 1824. For the Federalists earlier controversy with the national administration, see Dwight, *Hartford Convention,* pp. 273–74. There is extensive information regarding the claim negotiations in W. Edwin Hemphill, ed., *The Papers of John C. Calhoun,* VIII (Columbia, S.C., 1975), 268–69, 351, 360–61, 364–65, 405, 411, 419, 422, 551, 565.

66. Edward D. Bangs, *An Oration Pronounced at Springfield, Mass., on the Fourth of July, 1823* . . . (Springfield, 1823), pp. 8, 14. Republican efforts to make "Hartford" an odious shibboleth are covered in Dwight, *Hartford Convention:* "No political subject . . . of these United States has ever been the theme of more gross misrepresentation, or more constant reproach . . ." (p. 3). "Revilings of the convention have been continued in common conversation, in newspapers, in Fourth of July orations, in festive toasts, in baccanalian revelries and songs" (pp. 4, 382).

67. Several speeches of Republican leaders given just before the election were printed in the Boston *Statesman,* Apr. 10, 1823; *Patriot,* Feb. 22, Mar. 8, 1823; *Spy,* Mar. 12, 1823; *Centinel,* Feb. 1, 12, 1823. The *Repertory* began electioneering by running a biography of the Revolutionary hero James Otis even before discussing H. G. Otis's candidacy, Feb. 6, 23, 1823. One ardent young Federalist warned his mother after the election that they could now "expect to see the scenes of 1811–12 revived in all their blighting influence." William Lloyd Garrison, in Walter M. Merrill, ed., *The Letters of William Lloyd Garrison* I (Cambridge, Mass., 1971), 10.

68. *Hampden Journal,* Mar. 12, 1823.

69. Nantucket *Inquirer,* Jan. 7, Feb. 4, 1823; Haverhill *Gazette and Essex Patriot,* formed from two papers earlier in the year, copied the *Inquirer,* Mar. 8, 1823. A low-key Republican paper was the Dedham *Village Register,* Feb. 21, Mar. 7, 1823, passim. Two neutrals: Worcester *Massachusetts Yeoman,* Sept. 3, 1823, and Salem *Observer,* Jan. 6, 1823. A new paper established late in 1823 went in the opposite direction: Taunton *Free Press,* Nov. 21, 1823.

70. Daniel Webster, Washington, 30 Nov. 1823, to Jeremiah Mason, and same to same, 15 Feb. 1824, and same to same, 9 May 1824, in Wiltse and Moser, eds., *Papers of Daniel Webster: Correspondence* I, 336, 354, 358. Jeremiah Mason, Portsmouth, 17 Apr. 1823 to C. Gore, in Hilliard, ed., *Mason,* p. 271. New Bedford *New-England Gazette,* June 3, 1823.

71. Boston *Daily Advertiser,* Apr. 3, 1824.

72. Worcester *Massachusetts Yeoman,* Jan. 21, 28, 1824.

73. Taunton *Free Press,* Apr. 9, 1824.

74. Salem *Essex Register,* Apr. 8, 1824; *Massachusetts Yeoman,* Apr. 7, 1824.

75. On the Amherst charter, see Shaw, "Unitarians, Trinitarians," pp. 74–76; Northampton *Hampshire Gazette,* Feb. 18, Mar. 3, 1824; Greenfield Franklin *Herald and Public Advertiser,* Feb. 24, Mar. 16, 23, 1824; *Spy,* Feb. 25, Mar. 31, 1824; *Centinel,* Feb. 11, Mar. 20, 1824. Republican papers also pointed out that the Amherst vote had not been along party or sectarian lines. Taunton *Free Press,* Feb. 6, 1824. The *Massachusetts Yeoman* could not understand why good men in the house opposed Amherst and believed "there was a mystery about this business too deep for our penetration." The paper's excerpts from the legislative debate showed the nonpartisan nature of opposition. Feb. 11, 1824.

76. Federal State "Address," *Centinel,* Feb. 11, 1824. Otis's letters, in ibid., Feb. 24–Apr. 21, 1824; see also *Hampshire Gazette,* Mar. 3, 1824; *Repertory,* Apr. 1, 1824. Federalists tried hard to aid their cause by recalling the peace and prosperity of the reigns of Strong and Brooks. See [Federal Party, Mass.,] To the Electors of Massachusetts [1824].

77. On various Federal conventions or caucuses, see Salem *Gazette,* Mar. 19, 30, Apr. 1, 1824; *Centinel,* Mar. 10, 23, 27, Apr. 3; Boston *Daily Advertiser,* Apr. 5, 1824; Concord *Gazette and Middlesex Yeoman,* Mar. 13, 1824. Regarding Massachusetts's claim, and inaugural, see Boston *Evening Gazette,* Apr. 3, 1824; *Daily Advertiser,* Mar. 24, 25, 26, 27; *Centinel,* Mar. 27, 1824; and esp. address of Worcester County Federal Republicans of Mar. 12, in *Spy,* Mar. 17, and broadside, Mar. 31, and editorial, Apr. 14, 1824: William Eustis, Roxbury, 22 June 1824, to Levi Lincoln, Levi Lincoln Papers, MHi.

78. Boston *American Statesman and City Register* (hereafter *Statesman*), Feb. 26, Mar. 15, 25, Apr. 22, 26, May 3, 10, 1824; New Bedford *New-England Gazette,* Mar. 23, 1824; *National Ægis,* Mar. 17, 1824; Taunton *Free Press,* Mar. 26, Apr. 2, 1824; Dedham *Village Register,* Mar. 9, 1824.

79. The Taunton *Reporter* indulged in some electioneering but also praised the "Era of Good Feelings," Mar. 24, 1824; Concord *Gazette and Yeoman,* Jan. 31, Mar. 13, 1824; Boston *Telegraph,* Jan. 1, Mar. 25, Apr. 1, 8, 15, 1824; Boston *Evening Gazette,* Apr. 3, 1824; *Massachusetts Yeoman,* Sept. 3, 1823; Mar. 10, 17, 24, 1824. The *Patriot,* however, favored "amalgamation" only through Federalist conversion, Mar. 10, Apr. 3, 1824.

80. *Patriot,* Apr. 14, 1824; *Massachusetts Yeoman,* Mar. 31, 1824. Though Hampshire County went strongly Federal for governor as always, in senate elections party lines dissolved in local squabbles; see *Hampshire Gazette,* Mar. 17, 24, Apr. 7, 21, 1824. In Bristol County regular ticket voting was apparent; see Taunton *Columbian Reporter,* Apr. 7, 1824.

81. The evidence for the statements in this paragraph is impressionistic. Analysis of roll calls has become a convenient way to measure party-in-the-legislature, but, as noted above, there were few roll calls during the era. There are, however, many references to patronage and some revealing of attitudes about patronage in public and especially in private papers.

82. "The Federalists . . . did not publicly confess the existence of the Central Committee nor publish its letters in newspapers until 1810." See Banner, *Hartford Convention,* p. 242. Fischer, *Revolution in American Conservatism,* presented a table describing "Federal Organization in 1807," including caucus, caucus committee, central committee, county committees, ward and town committees, subcommittees, and runners: "All committees were appointed from above and were top secret" (p. 65).

83. *Patriot,* Apr. 27, 1811; *Independent Whig,* May 2, 1811.

84. Quincy, *Josiah Quincy,* pp. 308–9. For plans for the Washington Birthday celebration in Hampshire County, see Greenfield *Franklin Herald,* Feb. 25, 1812. For a description of a Boston celebration, see *Palladium,* Apr. 23, May 1, 1812. See also Fischer, *Revolution in American Conservatism,* pp. 123–25. Regarding Washington Benevolent Society activities in Worcester, see Benjamin Thomas Hill, ed., *The Diary of Isaiah Thomas, 1805–1828,* Transactions and Collections of the American Antiquarian Society, vols. 9 and 10 (Worcester, 1909), I, 148–50.

85. William C. Jarvis, *An Oration, Delivered at Pittsfield (Mass.) before the Washington Benevolent Society of the County of Berkshire, on the 4th July, 1812* (Stockbridge, 1812), p. 23.

## VI. Deference, Influence, and Balloting

1. For discussion of this point, see Ronald P. Formisano, "Deferential-Participant Politics: The Early Republic's Political Culture, 1789–1840," *American Political Science Review,* 68 (1974), 483–85.

2. Richard D. Brown, *Modernization: The Transformation of American Life 1600–1865* (New York, 1976), p. 81; on the background, see Gorden S. Wood, *The Creation of the American Republic, 1776–1787* (Chapel Hill, 1969). Wood observed that the Antifederalists of the 1780s had greatly feared the habit of deference: the "authority of names" and "the influence of the great" among ordinary people were too evident to be denied. Ibid., pp. 489–90.

3. George Briggs, Whig governor during the 1840s, became a lawyer in Lanesboro in 1818, and shortly afterward his name was suggested at a local caucus as a possible nominee for the office of state representative, but a political leader objected that "George owned no property." (Representatives needed a freehold of one hundred pounds or any ratable estate of two hundred pounds.) William C. Richards, *Great in Goodness: A Memoir of George N. Briggs* (Boston, 1866), p. 66.

4. See, e.g., Paul Goodman, "Social Status of Party Leadership: The House of Representatives, 1797–1804," *William and Mary Quarterly,* 25 (1968), 465–74; Whitman H. Ridgway, *Community Leadership in Maryland, 1790–1840: A Comparative Analysis of Power in Society* (Chapel Hill, 1979).

5. Nor were Americans themselves as deferential, in the opinion of a British merchant of the Baring Brothers firm in 1832: though he had met a good many clever young men from America, "with most there is the same fault of want of deference to age and the opinions of others. They want that retiring diffidence (a studied manner, I grant you) of the English. . . . I have just left one who is about to return home. He squeezed my hand so hard that I can scarcely hold the style, but it being out of

an excess of good feeling I could not cry out." Joshua Bates, London, 21 June 1832, to Thomas Wren Ward, Ward Papers, MHi.

6. The quotation is from Samuel H. Beer, "Great Britain: From Governing Elite to Organized Mass Parties," in Sigmund Neumann, ed., *Modern Political Parties: Approaches to Comparative Politics* (Chicago, 1956), p. 16; see also H. J. Hanham, *Elections and Party Management: Politics in the Time of Gladstone and Disraeli* (London, 1959); James Cornford, "The Adoption of Mass Organization by the British Conservative Party," in Erik Allardt and Yrjö Littunen, eds., *Cleavages, Ideologies and Party Systems: Contributions to Comparative Political Sociology* (Turku, Finland, 1964), pp. 400–24; T. J. Nossiter, *Influence, Opinion and Political Idioms in Reformed England: Case Studies from the North-east, 1823–74* (Sussex, 1975); D. C. Moore, *The Politics of Deference: A Study of the Mid-Nineteenth Century English Political System* (Hassocks, England, 1976).

7. Suggestive for this discussion are D. A. Hamer, *The Politics of Electoral Pressure: A Study in the History of Victorian Reform Agitations* (Sussex, 1977); Eric A. Nordlinger, "Political Development: Time Sequences and Rates of Change," in Nordlinger, ed., *Politics and Society: Studies in Comparative Political Sociology* (Englewood Cliffs, N.J., 1970), pp. 329–47, esp. p. 346; Stein Rokkan, "The Comparative Study of Political Participation: Notes toward a Perspective on Current Research," in Austin Ranney, ed., *Essays on the Behavioral Study of Politics* (Urbana, 1962), p. 70; see also Eric A. Nordlinger, *The Working-Class Tories: Authority, Deference and Stable Democracy* (London, 1967).

8. Though there is no adequate study on this subject, it appears that in 1800 American society was pervaded by consciousness of different "orders," "ranks," or "class." In Washington, as Henry Adams put it, an "imposing presence had much to do with political influence." *History of the United States in America during the First Administration of Thomas Jefferson* (New York, 1889), I, p. 188. The same held for the smallest hamlet. On the point generally, see Timothy Dwight, *Travels in New England and New York,* ed. Barbara Miller Solomon with Patricia M. King, 4 vols. (Cambridge, Mass., 1969; first ed., 1821); Percy Wells Bidwell, "Rural Economy in New England at the Beginning of the Nineteenth Century," *Transactions of the Connecticut Academy of Arts and Sciences,* 20 (1916), 370–76; Frederick Marryat, *Dairy in America,* ed. Jules Zanger (Bloomington, 1960; first ed., 1839); Joseph Edward Adams Smith, *The History of Pittsfield, Massachusetts,* II (Springfield, Mass., 1976), 51.

9. John B. Kirby, "Early American Politics—The Search for Ideology: An Historiographical Analysis and Critique of the Concept of 'Deference,'" *Journal of Politics,* 32 (1970), 808–38; David Hackett Fischer, *The Revolution in American Conservatism: The Federalist Party in the Era of Jeffersonian Democracy* (New York, 1965), p. 4; J. G. A. Pocock, "The Classical Theory of Deference," *American Historical Review,* 81 (1976), 516–23, takes a slightly different view.

10. Winfred E. A. Bernhard, *Fisher Ames: Federalist and Statesman, 1758–1808* (Chapel Hill, 1965), p. 283; D. Hamilton Hurd, comp., *History of Plymouth County, Massachusetts* (Philadelphia, 1884), p. 266.

11. William Michael Weber, "Before Horace Mann: Elites and Boston Public Schools, 1800–1822" (Ed.D. diss., Harvard University Graduate School of Education, 1974), pp. 7–8. Similarly, in 1808 Salem Federalists at their Fourth of July dinner "divided their guests into 3 classes requiring of one class 6 D., of another 5, & of another 3½ D. It gave great opportunity to laugh at such men as felt small in the last class. The populace called it Nobles, gentry, & commons." William Bentley, *The Diary of William Bentley,* III (Salem, Mass., 1911), 373.

12. Basil Hall, *Travels in North America* (Edinburgh, 1829), II, 80–81; Sedgwick is quoted in Richard D. Birdsall, *Berkshire County: A Cultural History* (New Haven, 1959), p. 26. In Hampshire County in the period 1790s–1820s, "the usual form of salutation to a superior in social position, or when it was desired to show respect, was 'Your sarvant, sir,' or 'Your sarvant, marm,' with a lifting of the hat if by a gentleman, or a courtesy if by a lady," Charles W. Dyer, *History of the Town of Plainfield, Hampshire County, Mass.* (Northampton, 1891), p. 124. In the 1820s, and for most of the century, Boston's wealthy "demanded deferential social conduct from domestics" employed as servants in their homes. Blaine Edward McKinley, " 'The Stranger in the Gates': Employer Reactions toward Domestic Servants in America, 1825–1875" (Ph.D. diss., Michigan State University, 1969), p. vi. See also Henry Cabot Lodge, *Life and Letters of George Cabot* (Boston, 1877), pp. 576–77; and Robert Hallowell Gardiner, *Early Recollections of Robert Hallowell Gardiner, 1782–1864* (Hallowell, Maine, 1936), pp. 66–67.

13. Adams is quoted in J. R. Pole, *Political Representation in England and the Origins of the American Republic* (New York, 1966), p. 218; Bentley, *Diary,* III, 15, also 13.

14. This point has been made many times, e.g., in Anson Ely Morse, *The Federalist Party in Massachusetts to the Year 1800* (Princeton, 1909), pp. 69–70.

15. Samuel Eliot Morison, *The Maritime History of Massachusetts, 1783–1860* (Boston, 1921), p. 153. Federal success in role playing was suggested by a critical Maine Republican: "I would not give a cent for Massachusetts Republicans, they are not up to the mark, and never will be, as long as they consider federalists as Demogods, here they are only men and some of them very bad ones." James C. Jewett, Portland, 11 Apr. 1812, to Gen. Henry A. S. Dearborn, Boston, Dearborn Papers, MWA.

16. Fischer, *Revolution in American Conservatism,* pp. 2–3. At the height of political strife a correspondent named Lucius showed the Federal concern for gentlemanly manners, "better company," and "gentlemanly diction." See Boston *Columbian Centinel,* May 8, 1811.

17. The quotation is from Claude M. Fuess, "Massachusetts in the Union (1789–1812)," in Albert Bushnell Hart, ed., *Commonwealth History of Massachusetts,* III (New York, 1929), 413; Theophilus Parsons, *Memoir of Theophilus Parsons* (Boston, 1859), pp. 109, 131–32. According to James M. Banner, Jr., Parsons was of "respectable but moderate origins." *To the Hartford Convention: The Federalists and the Origins of Party Politics in Massachusetts, 1789–1815* (New York, 1970), p. 185, also pp. 124, 136; Fischer, *Revolution in American Conservatism,* p. 254.

18. The quotations are from [Lucius Manlius Sargent] *Reminiscences of Samuel Dexter* (Boston, 1857), p. 53, and Samuel Shapiro, *Richard Henry Dana, Jr., 1815–1882* (East Lansing, Mich., 1961), p. 3; see also Hart, ed., *Commonwealth History,* III, 413; Fischer, *Revolution in American Conservatism,* 247, and W. P. Cresson, *Francis Dana: A Puritan Diplomat at the Court of Catherine the Great* (New York, 1930), pp. 156–57, 344.

19. Pocock, "Classical Theory of Deference," p. 522; Bernhard, *Fisher Ames,* pp. 322, 352.

20. Fisher Ames, 1 Jan. 1801, to Thomas Dwight, and same to same 19 Mar. 1801, in Seth Ames, ed., *Works of Fisher Ames* (Boston, 1854), I, 290, 294–95; also F. Ames, 13 Dec. 1802, to C. Gore, in ibid., p. 310. A typical Federal view of 1795 was that "when the expediency of a measure is clear to those who have the means of forming a right Judgement, and who alone are the regular constituted Judges of it, there can not be such a deference due to popular Opinion, still less to a Clamour

only, which is known to originate in party spirit." Stephen Higginson 13 Aug. 1795, to T. Pickering, "Letters of Stephen Higginson, 1783–1804," *Annual Report of the American Historical Association, 1896*, I, 789.

21.. F. Ames, 14 Dec. 1802, to J. Smith, in Ames, ed., *Works*, I, 316.

22. On the importance of militias elsewhere, see Eugene Perry Link, *Democratic-Republican Societies, 1790–1800* (New York, 1942), p. 181; Frank A. Cassell, *Merchant Congressman in the Young Republic: Samuel Smith of Maryland, 1752–1839* (Madison, Wisc., 1971), pp. 71, 87–89, 92; Richard R. Beeman, *The Old Dominion and the New Nation, 1788–1801* (Lexington, Ky., 1972), pp. 106–10; George F. Taylor, "Suffrage in Early Kentucky," *Register of the Kentucky Historical Society*, 61 (1962), 23, 28.

23. Commonwealth of Massachusetts, *Laws, 1780–1800*, II (1801), 828–29. Nathaniel Colburn, 29 Apr. 1809, to William King; Samuel Thatcher, 23 Mar. 1810, to W. King; and Benjamin Porter, 25 Mar. 1811, to W. King, Collection 165, King Correspondence, Maine Historical Society. In Salem the militia was much engaged in politics in 1801. Bentley, *Diary*, II, 372. In 1809 Bentley described a man moving up rapidly in the Second Artillery as "very busy with politics." Ibid., III, 452–53. See also William Goold, "Governor Christopher Gore and His Visit to Maine," *Collections and Proceedings of the Maine Historical Society*, 2nd ser., 5 (1894), 80; *Columbian Centinel*, Feb. 27, Mar. 30, 1811.

24. Dorothy Ann Lipson, *Freemasonry in Federalist Connecticut, 1789–1835* (Princeton, 1977); John F. Kutolowski and Kathleen S. Kutolowski, "Commissions and Canvasses: The Militia and Politics in Western New York, 1800–1845," *New York History*, 63 (1982): 5–38.

25. William H. Sumner, "Reminiscences of LaFayette's Visit to Boston—Gov. Eustis—Gov. Brooks and Others," *New England Historical and Genealogical Register*, 13 (1859), 103; Edmund Quincy, *Life of Josiah Quincy* (Boston, 1868), p. 377. See also Boston *Gazette*, Nov. 3, 1800; Samuel Eliot Morison, "Elbridge Gerry, Gentleman-Democrat," *New England Quarterly*, 2 (1929), 29–30; John Mills, 21 Nov. 1826, to Levi Lincoln, in "Letters to John Brazer Davis, 1819–1831," *Massachusetts Historical Society Proceedings*, 49 (1916), 194; Charles W. Upham, *The Life of Timothy Pickering*, IV (Boston, 1873), 51.

26. George Ulmer, Lincolnville, 22 Feb. 1809, to W. King, King Correspondence.

27. Francis M. Thompson, *History of Greenfield, Shire Town of Franklin County, Massachusetts* (Greenfield, 1904), I, 317; Commonwealth of Massachusetts, *Reports of Contested Elections in the House of Representatives* (Boston, 1812), pp. 23–25. A Republican paper complained of Federalists' abuse of drink and spoke of several men "much *started*, as they say." Worcester *National Ægis*, Apr. 17, 1811.

28. Sumner, "Reminiscences," p. 106. In 1792 Governor Hancock ordered that Boston's new theater be closed, and some of the young gentlemen present protested vociferously, pulled down a portrait of the governor, and trampled it. Later that night a crowd of men, mostly sailors, appeared at Hancock's door and requested "if it was his honor's wish that the playhouse be pulled down." In 1808, when the embargo was throwing men out of work, some hundred seamen marched with a half-masted flag to Governor Sullivan's house and demanded work or bread. "A tactful speech from the Governor," said Mark A. DeWolfe, "chanced to send them away good-natured." These stories are told in several sources, including Mark A. DeWolfe Howe, *Boston: The Place and the People* (New York, 1903), pp. 134, 142.

29. Though the English scene was quite different, H. J. Hanham's discussion of "influence" as it operated after 1832 is suggestive. Hanham, introd. to Charles R. Dod, *Electoral Facts: From 1832 to 1853 Impartially Stated* (Sussex, 1972; first ed., 1853), pp. xxii–xxiii.

30. One observer in 1799 asserted that "not one fift [sic] part of the common farmers and laborers that are the most interested in the measures of the times, that git any information from them [newspapers], for they cannot be at the expence of the time and money they cost." William Manning 15 Feb. 1799, to Abijah Adams, in Samuel Eliot Morison, ed., *The Key of Liberty* (Billerica, Mass., 1922), pp. x–xi. Of the election of 1808 Henry Adams observed: "In Massachusetts the modern canvass was unknown . . . and the public opinions of men in high official or social standing weighed heavily." *History of the United States of America during the Second Administration of Thomas Jefferson* (New York, 1890), II, 242.

31. Bentley, *Diary,* II, 423.

32. Levi Lincoln, [Sr.], Worcester, 2 June 1805, to Thomas Jefferson, Lincoln Papers, MWA.

33. That Republican moderation in wielding influence in Massachusetts proper sometimes reflected their lesser resources was candidly admitted by a Republican who told William Eustis in 1811 that conducting business and hiring men exclusively on political grounds was bad policy, "for if retaliated by the Federalists we should suffer the most, as the mechanics must secure their employment generally from the Federalists." [J. Eustis ?], Boston, 3 Jan. 1811, to William Eustis, vol. 2 (1808–1815), William Eustis Papers, LC. The writer added that all things being equal, employment should be given to those who supported the Madison administration.

34. Nathan Hale and Charles Hale, eds., *Journal of Debates and Proceedings in the Convention of Delegates, Chosen to Revise the Constitution of Massachusetts . . . 1820 . . . 1821* (Boston, 1853; first ed., 1821), pp. 247–48, 251–52.

35. Carl Seaburg and Stanley Patterson, *Merchant Prince of Boston: Colonel T. H. Perkins, 1764–1854* (Cambridge, Mass., 1971), p. 123; Carl E. Prince, *The Federalists and the Origins of the U.S. Civil Service* (New York, 1977), p. 40; Benjamin W. Labaree, *Patriots and Partisans: The Merchants of Newburyport, 1764–1815* (Cambridge, Mass., 1962), p. 40; Bentley, *Diary,* III, 287. In 1808 Bentley again stressed the importance of "influential men" (p. 399). Also indicating the same were Boston *J. Russell's Gazette,* Apr. 7, 1800; Boston *Constitutional Telegraph,* Mar. 29, 1800, and Salem *Gazette,* Oct. 28, 1800.

36. Federal State Central Committee Circular Letter, Boston, Feb. 1806, Broadside Collection, MWA; Christopher Gore, Boston, 25 Mar. 1807, to Bristol Co. Committee, Miscellaneous Bound Manuscripts, MHi. References to influence are implicit in Republican communications, e.g., in E. Foote, Camden, 24 Mar. 1810, to William King, and James Thomas, Brickstown, 26 Mar. 1812, to W. King, King Correspondence.

37. "I blushed for Old Haverhill," said one of its native-son Federalists in 1808, "when I observ'd she was represented by a Democrat and astonished, when almost every man of property and respectability are federal, that their influence does not regulate the Election." Nathaniel Saltonstall, Jr., Baltimore, 5 June 1808, to Nathaniel Saltonstall, in Robert E. Moody, ed., *The Saltonstall Papers, 1607–1815,* II (Boston, 1974), 445.

38. Bentley objected to Salem Federalists soliciting signatures by "alarming the dependent citizens with apprehensions that all aid will be withdrawn." *Diary,* III, 227. A Federal petition campaign similarly gathered "a greater number than they had obtained at any town meeting & encouraged their hopes. But they forget that timidity overawed many & this day the friends of the Government obtained a majority. . . ." Ibid., p. 279.

39. Cf. ibid., pp. 402, 545.

40. Edward Lewis Ballantyne, "The Incorporation of Boston 1784–1822" (Honors thesis, Harvard College, 1955), pp. 98, 99; William Sullivan, Boston, 13 Jan. 1822, to

Harrison Gray Otis, Otis Papers, MHi. A Republican paper asked, "Are our mechanics, our men of middling life, those who are compelled to labor . . . willing to submit to be debarred from the right of suffrage, because they cannot afford to spend hours in 'shoving and pushing' their way up to the ballot boxes in Faneuil Hall?" Boston *Patriot,* Jan. 7, 1822. For Federal opinion, see Boston *New-England Palladium,* Feb. 26, Mar. 1, 5, 1822.

41. H. G. Otis, 8 Jan. 1822, to W. Sullivan, Otis Papers, MHi (original in New York Public Library).

42. H. G. Otis, Washington, 19 Jan. 1822, to W. Sullivan, Otis Papers (original in New York Public Library). On the general situation, see below, Chapter VIII.

43. Boston *Statesman,* Feb. 27, 1823. By no means did ward voting eliminate influence from elections, especially if Republican charges are given any credence. See, e.g., *Patriot,* Apr. 7, 1824.

44. Boston *Independent Chronicle,* Apr. 11, 1811.

45. The dramatic increase in voting from 1800 to 1812 occurred although property and other qualifications remained unchanged. Paul Goodman, *The Democratic-Republicans of Massachusetts: Politics in a Young Republic* (Cambridge, Mass., 1964), pp. 138–40; Banner, *Hartford Convention,* pp. 276–77. An 1805 law indicated that in many towns of 500 qualified voters the town meeting might be opened before 11:00 A.M. and that in towns of 1,000 voters or more the selectmen must be in session at some convenient place on the day preceding the meeting for as long as they judged necessary to pass on voters' qualifications. Abijah Bigelow, *The Voters' Guide: or, The Power, Duty & Privileges of the Constitutional Voters in the Commonwealth of Massachusetts* (Leominster, Mass., 1807), pp. 75–76.

46. *Journal of Debates of Convention to Revise Constitution, 1820–1821,* pp. 247, 248.

47. Ibid., pp. 246, 252.

48. J. R. Pole, "Suffrage and Representation in Massachusetts: A Statistical Note," *William and Mary Quarterly,* 14 (1957), 560–92, as corrected in "Letters to the Editor," ibid., 15 (1958), 412–16; Labaree, *Patriots and Partisans,* p. 104; Hart, ed., *Commonwealth History,* III, 204–5; *Journal of Debates of Convention to Revise Constitution, 1820–1821,* pp. 246–57.

49. Joseph P. Harris, *Registration of Voters in the United States* (Washington, D.C., 1929), p. 67; Bigelow, *Voters' Guide,* p. 72. Republicans sometimes complained that registration methods placed too much power in the hands of tax collectors. Northampton *Anti-Monarchist,* Jan. 31, 1810. For a young voter's concern about residency, see Francis Davis, W. Boylston, 25 Mar. 1823, to I. Davis, Isaac Davis' Papers, MWA.

In 1831 the Massachusetts law was challenged in the courts, on the ground that it constituted "a restraint upon the right of voting." In a landmark decision, the court held (*Capen* v. *Foster,* 1832) that a registration law was well within the legislature's power and was "highly reasonable and useful, calculated to promote peace, order and celerity in the conduct of elections." Frederick C. Brightly, *A Collection of Leading Cases on the Law of Elections in the United States* (Philadelphia, 1871), p. 59.

50. David Syrett, "Town-Meeting Politics in Massachusetts, 1776–1786," *William and Mary Quarterly,* 21 (1964), 363–73.

51. In the November 1800 congressional election in Boston, one observer supposed that "near one thousand of the voters were illegal." H. Jackson, Boston, 5 Nov. 1800, to David Cobb, in Frederick S. Allis, ed., *William Bingham's Maine Lands, 1790–1820,* Publications of the Colonial Society of Massachusetts, vols. 36 and 37, Collections (Boston, 1954), II, 1085. In 1800, too, Republicans complained of "negroes and other unqualified persons" being allowed to vote in Norfolk County. Boston *In-*

*dependent Chronicle,* Oct. 9, 1800. Bentley believed that bribery occurred in Salem in 1808. *Diary,* III, 359. In 1809 Republicans complained that many illegal votes had been cast in the Newburys: Nathaniel Cogswell, Newburyport, 11 Apr. 1809, to William King, King Correspondence. The Salem *Essex Register,* Apr. 11, 1812, charged that illegal voting took place in several major towns. In 1811 the Federalists had charged that voters in some palces were allowed "to put in their votes doubled." *Centinel,* May 22, Nathaniel Ames thought the Federalists cheated heavily in Boston in 1812. Warren, ed., *Diary of Nathaniel Ames,* p. 249. Since 1812 was a Republican defeat, they seem to have complained most that year about fraud. See, e.g., New Bedford *Gazette,* May 1, 1812. Federal concern for illegality accordingly reawakened in 1823, e.g., in Boston *New-England Palladium,* May 20, 1823. In 1820 a Salem Federalist claimed that the large towns had often experienced "the evil . . . of hundreds of men coming in from New Hampshire in the spring and voting in our elections, just after they had voted in elections in their own state." *Journal of Debates of Convention to Revise Constitution, 1820–1821,* p. 555.

52. Howard A. Allen, "Vote Fraud and the Validity of Election Data" (Paper presented to the Annual Meeting of the Organization of American Historians, Atlanta, Apr. 7, 1977).

53. William Stickney, ed., *Autobiography of Amos Kendall* (Boston, 1872), p. 79; Bentley, *Diary,* II, 429. Farm laborers were challenged on the basis not of property but of residence; in large towns college students, blacks, apprentices, sailors, and others commonly voted. Goodman, *Democratic-Republicans,* p. 138. For a strict construction of election laws in a closely fought contest in Weston in which several voters were challenged on grounds of residence, age, and property, see House Journal Manuscript Copy, vol. 31, May 1810–Mar. 1811, Massachusetts State Archives, pp. 154–56.

54. William C. Jarvis, *The Republican* (Pittsfield, 1820), pp. 137–38.

55. Federal State Central Committee, Circular Letter, Boston, Feb. 1806, Broadside Collection, MWA. Bentley's comments on elections frequently revealed election conditions varying with the posture of selectmen: e.g., "The Selectmen were firm. The seats were kept entirely clear in which they were placed. The votes were given in without crowding near the boxes, & any impositions. . . ." *Diary,* II, 452; see also III, 18, and 222. Salem selectmen's actions, however, were frequently controversial: *Centinel,* May 18, 22, 1811; *Essex Register,* Apr. 8, 15, 1812.

56. A. Wood, Wiscasset, 9 Apr. 1809, to William King, King Correspondence. *Independent Chronicle,* Feb. 10, 24, 1817.

57. In 1839 the town of Warren, Worcester County, divided over the selectmen's running of an election, and there is extensive eyewitness testimony about the dispute in box 2, folder 6, Massachusetts Collection, MWA. As partisan competition revived, so did complaints that selectmen were arbitrarily running elections. Otis Batchelor, Upton, 21 Nov. 1839, to I. Davis, Isaac Davis Papers, MWA.

58. Ezra S. Stearns, *History of Ashburnham, Massachusetts* (*1734–1886*) (Ashburnham, 1887), p. 220. Commonwealth of Massachusetts, *Laws of Massachusetts, 1780–1800,* II (1801), p. 716; "Commonwealth of Massachusetts. To the Selectmen of the Town of Pelham in Hampshire North District: Greeting." [1802] Broadside Collection, MWA. An account of an election dispute in Cambridge in 1800 revealed the openness of voting. *Centinel,* May 7, 1800. So did a selectman's discovery of trick ballots. Salem *Gazette,* Oct. 21, 1800.

59. Nossiter, *Influence, Opinion and Political Idioms;* Moore, *Politics of Deference;* Paul F. Bourke and Donald A. DeBats, "Identifiable Voting in Nineteenth-Century America: Toward a Comparison of Britain and the United States before the Secret Ballot," *Perspectives in American History,* 9 (1977–1978), 259–88.

60. Phillip E. Converse, "Change in the American Electorate," in Angus Campbell and Converse, eds., *The Human Meaning of Social Change* (New York, 1972), p. 277; James L. Sundquist, *Dynamics of the Party System: Alignment and Realignment of Political Parties in the United States* (Washington, D.C., 1973), p. 4.

61. Stein Rokkan et al., *Citizens, Elections, Parties: Approaches to the Comparative Study of the Processes of Development* (New York, 1970), pp. 34–35; Rokkan, "Comparative Study of Political Participation," pp. 77–78.

62. A New York law of 1787 declared that "an opinion hath long prevailed among divers of the good people of this State that voting at elections by ballot would tend more to preserve the liberty and equal freedom of the people than voting *viva voce.*" Quoted in Spencer D. Albright, *The American Ballot* (Washington, D.C., 1942), p. 18; see also p. 19, and Wood, *Creation of the American Republic*, p. 170.

63. Albright, *American Ballot*, pp. 17–19; Simeon E. Baldwin, "The Early History of the Ballot in Connecticut," *Papers of the American Historical Association*, 4 (1890), 407–22; Robert M. Ireland, "Aristocrats All: The Politics of County Government in Antebellum Kentucky," *Review of Politics*, 32 (1970), 367–68. David P. Peltier, "Party Development and Voter Participation in Delaware, 1792–1811," *Delaware History*, 14 (1970), 86–87. In 1802 New Hampshire voting was open. Mark D. Kaplanoff, "From Colony to State: New Hampshire, 1800–1815" (unpublished ms., Cambridge University, England, 1974), p. 204.

64. Bourke and DeBats, "Identifiable Voting," pp. 269–75; see also Ballot Society, *The Ballot in America*, Tracts on the Ballot, no. 1 (London, 185?), pp. 7–9, Widener Library, Harvard University.

65. The statutes of 1795 and 1798 mentioned "written votes" and "votes in writing," Henshaw v. Foster, 9 Pickering, 314, 315. Brightly, *Leading Cases of Laws of Elections*, p. 56. John Adams is quoted in Baldwin, "Connecticut Ballot," p. 416. Bentley, *Diary*, III, 118. In 1804 Attorney General James Sullivan ruled in favor of printed ballots: 9 Pickering, 320–31.

66. Stockbridge *Western Star* quoted in Thomas Lawrence Davis, "Aristocrats and Jacobins in Country Towns: Party Formation in Berkshire County, Massachusetts, 1775–1816" (Ph.D. diss., Boston University, 1975), p. 66. Having votes written and on hand in plenty of time was a key element of political organization. See William Widgery, Portland, 16 Apr. 1809, to William King, Bath, King Correspondence; see also Circular Letter, March 12, 1806, Broadside Collection, MWA; Bigelow, *Voters' Guide*, pp. 61, 63, 77, 83.

67. *Journal of Debates of Convention to Revise Constitution, 1820–1821*, p. 521; *Book for Massachusetts Children* (1829), p. 24. *Centinel*, May 9, 1829.

68. The young William Lloyd Garrison complained that "as there is something particularly attractive to vulgar minds, in a brave picture, this trick was not without its effect." Boston, 26 July 1827, to the editor of the Newburyport *Herald*, in Walter M. Merrill, ed., *The Letters of William Lloyd Garrison*, I (Cambridge, Mass., 1971), 58.

69. Boston *Statesman*, Mar. 29, 1827; Henshaw v. Foster, 9 Pickering, 312–22; *Statesman*, Jan. 23, 1830; Northampton *Hampshire Gazette*, Apr. 14, 1830. Parker also said that the reason given in the 1820 convention against printed ballots, namely, that they might be marked with pictures, and so on, was an abuse common to written ballots. Henshaw v. Foster, 9 Pickering, 321. Eldon Cobb Evans, *A History of the Australian Ballot System in the United States* (Chicago, 1917), p. 4. Maine authorized printed ballots in 1831 by law, but Connecticut did not do so until 1844 and then by a constitutional amendment. Albright, *American Ballot*, p. 19.

70. Nathan Brooks, 10 Nov. 1831, to John B. Davis, in "Letters to John Brazer Davis, 1819–1831," *Massachusetts Historical Society Proceedings*, 49 (1916), 254,

and Solomon Lincoln, Jr., Hingham, 11 Nov. 1831, to J. B. Davis, in ibid., 255; Concord *Yeoman's Gazette,* Mar. 12, 1836.

71. The commonness of voting by hand in town meetings in small towns was implied in remarks made in the 1820 constitutional convention. *Journal of Debates,* p. 601.

72. Full accounts appeared in both parties' papers in an unusual coverage of town affairs. Salem *Gazette,* Mar. 12, 15, 22, 1811, and Salem *Essex Register,* Mar. 13, 16, 1811; the quotation is from the *Register,* Mar. 16. As early as 1806, men voted in Salem by filing through different doors. Bentley, *Diary,* III, 227; compare ibid., III, 422.

73. Nathaniel Cogswell, Newburyport, 5 Apr. 1809, to W. King, King Correspondence; Bentley, *Diary,* III, 418, 422, 425.

74. *Resolves, 1810–1812,* pp. 188, 200; The Greenfield *Traveller,* Aug. 6, 1811, printed the law; Goodman, *Democratic-Republicans,* pp. 138–40; Banner, *Hartford Convention,* pp. 276–77.

75. Dedham *Columbian Minerva,* Nov. 24, 1801. Judge Parker in *Henshaw* v. *Foster* claimed retrospectively that even hand or viva voce voting in town meetings for representatives was not "thought calculated to ensure an independent suffrage." 9 Pickering, 319.

76. *House Documents, 1834,* no. 51, pp. 2–3; Albright, *American Ballot,* pp. 19, 20; Evans, *Australian Ballot System,* pp. 6–7.

77. Harriet Martineau, *Society in America* (London, 1837), I, 159. Ballot Society, *Ballot in America,* p. 5.

78. *House Documents, 1839,* no. 22, An Act Concerning Elections; *Acts and Resolves, 1840,* pp. 311–12. There were ample grounds for Morton's fears that partisan leaders took it for granted that they could inform themselves as to how voters cast their ballots. See William Edwards, Southbridge, 10 Nov. 1840, to I. Davis, Issac Davis Papers, MWA. For various practices before 1850, see the letter of Amasa Walker, printed in Edward Capel Whitehurst, ed., *"The Test of Experience: or The Working of the Ballot in the United States,* Ballot Society, Tracts on the Ballot, no. 5 (London, 1855).

## VII. Social Bases of Federalism and Republicanism, 1800–1824

1. Michael Hechter, *Internal Colonialism: The Celtic Fringe in British National Development, 1536–1966* (Berkeley, 1975), pp. 50–51. In this passage, Hecter quoted frequently from Fernand Braudel, *The Mediterranean and the Mediterranean World in the Age of Philip II* (New York, 1972), II.

2. Paul Goodman, *The Democratic-Republicans of Massachusetts: Politics in a Young Republic* (Cambridge, Mass., 1964), p. xi.

3. On the discontinuity of political alignments in the last part of the eighteenth century, see Oscar Handlin and Mary Handlin, "Radicals and Conservatives in Massachusetts after Independence," *New England Quarterly,* 18 (1944), 343–55.

4. Hampshire won this honor before and after 1811, when its northern and southern thirds were set off as Hampden and Franklin counties. Franklin was also Federal while Hampden was weakly Federal. In 1812 the Federal banner counties were Hampshire 76.1, Suffolk 67.2, Franklin 64.2, Worcester 59.8, Essex 59.5. In 1824, when Federalism fell forever, only Hampshire and Franklin gave strong Federal votes, 67 percent and 58.2 percent.

5. Margaret Elizabeth Martin, *Merchants and Trade of the Connecticut River Valley, 1780–1820,* Smith College Studies in History, vol. 24 (Northampton, 1939). Both

the eastern and western Centers formed parts of larger bands of Federal strength: the North Shore of New England, and the Connecticut Valley into New Hampshire and Vermont and south into Connecticut. David Hackett Fischer, *The Revolution in American Conservatism: The Federalist Party in the Era of Jeffersonian Democracy* (New York, 1965), p. 211.

6. *Moby Dick: or, The Whale,* ed. Alfred Kazin (Cambridge, Mass., 1956), p. 67.

7. Samuel Eliot Morison, *The Maritime History of Massachusetts, 1790–1861* (Boston, 1921), p. 211.

8. Ibid., p. 4.

9. Moses Greenleaf, *A Statistical View of the District of Maine* (Boston, 1816), pp. iii, 46, 55.

10. Richard D. Birdsall, *Berkshire County: A Cultural History* (New Haven, 1954), p. 2. "The imposing Berkshire Barrier, a range of mountains stretching a distance of thirty miles between the Connecticut and Housatonic Rivers, mutely proclaimed that nature had not intended this western region to be a part of Massachusetts."

11. James M. Banner, Jr., *To the Hartford Convention: The Federalists and the Origins of Party Politics in Massachusetts, 1789–1815* (New York, 1970), p. 169.

12. Obed Macy, *The History of Nantucket* (Boston, 1835), pp. 8, 13–15, 39. David Benedict, *A General History of the Baptist Denomination of America* (New York, 1850), pp. 367, 413, 414. Charles Edward Banks, *The History of Martha's Vinyard, Dukes County, Massachusetts,* II (Boston, 1911), 31–33, 39–40, 172. Samuel Deyo, ed., *History of Barnstable County, Massachusetts* (New York, 1890), pp. 157, 163, 165. There is a list of Barnstable County churches dated after 1799 in the Thomas Walcutt MSS, MWA.

Quakerism grew on Nantucket not just because Quakers sought refuge there but also because Nantucket residents who had no particular interest in religion could avoid the extension of church taxes to the island: "What better way . . . to counteract Massachusetts religious expansion than to adopt a congenial faith that opposed the taxes?" Arthur J. Worrall, *Quakers in the Colonial Northeast* (Hanover, N.H., 1980), p. 73.

13. Birdsall, *Berkshire County,* pp. 75–102; Albert Bushnell Hart, ed., *Commonwealth History of Massachusetts,* IV (New York, 1930), 354; Benedict, *Baptists,* p. 415; Joseph Hooper, "The Protestant Episcopal Church in Berkshire," in *Berkshire Book: Historical and Scientific Society,* I (Pittsfield, Mass., 1892), 187, 189, 201–2. In 1822 a Federalist complained that "there is a strong *country party* in our General Court headed by W. C. Jarvis [of Berkshire] who propose to abolish all direct taxation and exact all the support of the Commonwealth from the seaports—by duties on auctioneers, licenses, Insurance Companies, etc. A Bill for this purpose has been under debate . . . but . . . [probably] will not pass. It however indicates the hostility of the country to the town." Quoted in Birdsall, *Berkshire County,* p. 100, n. 42.

14. Goodman, *Democratic-Republicans,* p. 125; Jonathan Greenleaf, *Sketches of the Ecclesiastical History of the State of Maine* (Portland, 1821), pp. 221 and 224, regarding Congregationalists and Baptists; see also pp. 26, 223–33, 245–62, 273, and app., pp. 34, 50ff.

15. John Daniel Cushing, "Notes on Disestablishment in Massachusetts, 1780–1833," *William and Mary Quarterly,* 26 (1969), pp. 169–83; Theophilus Parsons, *Memoir of Theophilus Parsons* (Boston, 1859), p. 201.

16. For examples, see *Salem Gazette,* Aug. 15, 19, 22, Oct. 21, 1800; Northampton *Hampshire Gazette,* Mar. 27, 1811; Portland *Gazette,* Mar. 30, Apr. 4, 1812; Governor Caleb Strong's June 3, 1800, inaugural address, reprinted in *Patriotism and Piety: The Speeches of His Excellency Caleb Strong, Esq.* (Newburyport, 1808), p. 16.

17. William G. McLoughlin, *New England Dissent, 1630–1833: The Baptists and the Separation of Church and State* (Cambridge, Mass., 1971), II, 1067.

18. Ibid., p. 1083; Jacob C. Meyer, *Church and State in Massachusetts: From 1740 to 1833* (Cleveland, 1930), p. 140. William Bentley recorded the established clergy's opposition to Sullivan's election and their vindictiveness against him in 1808. *The Diary of William Bentley*, III (Salem, Mass., 1907), 298, 302.

19. Regarding the bill of 1807–1808, see McLoughlin, *New England Dissent*, II, 1079–82; and Birdsall, *Berkshire County*, pp. 88, 97. Bentley hinted at Republican uncertainty, in *Diary*, III, 345. This measure anticipated the 1811 law dissolving parish boundaries.

20. McLoughlin, *New England Dissent*, II, 1084–89, 1091, 1097–98, 1101, 1102; Cushing, "Disestablishment," pp. 185–86; *Resolves, 1810–1812*, p. 189; Salem *Essex Register*, Apr. 6, May 4, 7, 11, 15, 1811; Northampton *Democrat*, May 14, 1811, and esp. May 21, 1811, containing an editorial from the *Register;* Boston *Independent Chronicle*, May 2, 13, 1811, and especially the report of an April 17 meeting in Reading, Apr. 25. For an example of an indirect Republican approach, see New-Bedford *Old Colony Gazette*, Mar. 1, 1811; for Republican outrage at pulpit interference, see Worcester *National Ægis*, Jan. 23, Apr. 17, May 1, 1811. Federal papers complained of Republican efforts to get Baptist votes by making irresponsible charges of oppression. Worcester *Massachusetts Spy*, May 15, 1811. In 1812 the Republican William King of Bath, a candidate for lieutenant governor, was seen as a strong backer of dissenters' rights. Daniel Merrill, Sedgwick, 17 Mar. 1812, to William King, King Papers, col. 165, box 10, Maine Historical Society.

21. Donald M. Scott, *From Office to Profession: The New England Ministry, 1750–1850* (Philadelphia, 1978), pp. 24, 27; Banner, *Hartford Convention*, p. 152. "At no time before 1825 could the Republicans boast of support from more than half a dozen of the 200 to 250 Standing ministers in Massachusetts." McLoughlin, *New England Dissent*, II, 1074. This estimate was probably too low; cf. Goodman, *Democratic-Republicans*, pp. 90, 227, n. 43.

22. Anson Ely Morse, *The Federalist Party in Massachusetts to the Year 1800* (Princeton, 1909), pp. 93–101, 107–8, 116–25, 216–19; Gary B. Nash, "The American Clergy and the French Revolution," *William and Mary Quarterly*, 22 (1965), 392–412; Kerber, *Federalists in Dissent*, pp. 208–11; Banner, *Hartford Convention*, pp. 159–60.

23. Edward Craig Bates and Heman Packard DeForest, *The History of Westborough, Massachusetts* (Westborough, 1891), pp. 212–14; Bentley, *Diary*, III, 513. See also Boston *Gazette*, Dec. 15, 1800; McLoughlin, II, 1078, n. 35; Bentley, *Diary*, III, 298, 364, 390, 400, 412, 419; Charles Warren, ed., *Jacobin and Junto: or Early American Politics as Viewed in the Diary of Dr. Nathaniel Ames, 1758–1822* (New York, 1968; first ed., 1931); William Stickney, ed., *Autobiography of Amos Kendall* (New York, 1949; first ed., 1872), pp. 72–73.

24. McLoughlin, *New England Dissent*, II, 1158. By 1820, however, dissenters were closer to parity. In the constitutional convention of that year, a Federalist claimed there were 450 Congregational churches to 150 dissenting churches. Enoch Mudge disagreed and counted 373 Congregational and 325 dissenting churches. McLoughlin thought Mudge "more nearly correct." Ibid., p. 1175.

25. Banner has an excellent discussion of the problems involved, in *Hartford Convention*, pp. 197–215.

26. Bentley, *Diary*, III, 342.

27. Fisher Ames, Dec. 7, 1798, to Thomas Dwight, in Seth Ames, ed., *Works of Fisher Ames* (Boston, 1854), I, 224. Bentley referred to the "parties which mix

in . . . congregations," in *Diary,* III, 279; and an incident in Newburyport showed divisions, in ibid., pp. 390, 397, 417. See also Benjamin W. Labaree, *Patriots and Partisans: The Merchants of Newburyport, 1764–1815* (Cambridge, Mass., 1962), pp. 144–45.

28. Joseph Edward Adams Smith, *The History of Pittsfield, Massachusetts: From the Year 1800 to the Year 1876* (Springfield, Mass., 1876), pp. 104–7, 117–19, 128; William Allen, *An Account of the Separation of the Church and Town of Pittsfield* (Pittsfield, Mass., 1809). The Berkshire town of Sheffield also had a Republican Congregational minister, but it usually voted Federal. Smith, *Pittsfield,* p. 71.

In 1814 the town of Worcester held two Fourth of July celebrations, the Federal at the North meeting house and the Republican at the South meeting house. Benjamin Thomas Hill, ed., *The Diary of Isaiah Thomas, 1805–1828,* Transactions and Collections of the American Antiquarian Society, vols. 9 and 10 (Worcester, 1909), I, 233.

29. Samuel Adams Drake, *History of Middlesex County, Massachusetts* (Boston, 1880), II, 280–81. For a similar story regarding Cambridge and West Cambridge, see Banner, *Hartford Convention,* pp. 206–7. Another Middlesex town, Littleton, was united behind one minister for most of his forty-six-year tenure (1782–1826), and was strongly Republican. Drake, *Middlesex County,* pp. 49–50. In 1802 the minister of Eastham, Barnstable County, claimed there was "not an individual in town that does not belong to the Cong'l Society." Quoted in Deyo, ed., *Barnstable,* p. 732. Eastham voted generally Republican from 1800 to 1812. In Worcester County, North Brookfield was created in 1812 out of Brookfield, a strong Federal town. North Brookfield immediately voted Republican, but during the unpopular war it soon swung to Federal majorities: Republican leaders in North Brookfield were Congregationalists. J. H. Temple, *History of North Brookfield, Massachusetts* (Boston, 1887), pp. 267–68, 270–75, 287, 612.

30. The Congregationalists' sense of denominationalism began to grow after 1800. A. H. Quint, "Historical Sketch of the General Association of Massachusetts," in *Massachusetts General Association* (Boston, 1859), pp. 39–40.

31. John J. Valenti, Jr., "The Social Bases of Party Voting in Hampshire and Hampden Counties, Massachusetts, 1800–1840" (Honor's thesis, Clark University, 1979); *History of Worcester County, Massachusetts* (Boston, 1879), I, 277; Abijah P. Marvin, *History of the Town of Lancaster, Massachusetts* (Lancaster, 1879), pp. 412, 456–57, 463, 479; Francis H. Underwood, *Quabbin: The Story of a Small Town with Outlooks upon Puritan Life* (Boston, 1893), pp. 34–35; Banner, *Hartford Convention,* p. 203; Douglas Shaw, "Unitarians, Trinitarians, and the Massachusetts Establishment, 1820–1844" (M.A. thesis, Brown University, 1967), pp. 27, 32–37.

32. Leonard Bliss, Jr., *The History of Rehoboth, Bristol County, Massachusetts* (Boston, 1836), pp. 2, 10, 16–19.

33. The quotation is from Bliss, *Rehoboth,* p. 217; see also McLoughlin, *New England Dissent,* II, 682–83. On Baptist growth, see ibid., p. 113; Banner, *Hartford Convention,* pp. 198–99. In 1801 Bentley observed that the Baptists "grow not rapidly in great towns." *Diary,* III, 4–5; In 1808 he counted some 200 Baptist congregations in the state and believed that their strength and that of other dissenters was underestimated by the *Massachusetts Register.* Ibid., pp. 345–46.

34. McLoughlin, *New England Dissent,* II, 1066, 1077, 1158, 1172; Banner, *Hartford Convention,* pp. 213–15; Smith, *Pittsfield,* p. 103; Bentley, *Diary,* II, 409; Birdsall, *Berkshire County,* p. 97; and L. F. Greene, ed., *The Writings of the Late Elder John Leland* (New York, 1845), pp. 51, 257–70, 353–58. In Worcester the Baptists were "all Democrats or Republicans." B. D. Marshall, *Historical Sketch of the First Baptist Church of Worcester, Mass.* (Worcester, 1877), p. 8; see also Samuel Austin,

*The Apology of Patriots: or The Heresy of the Friends of the Washington Peace Policy Defended* (Worcester, 1812), p. 8. These statements are also based on examinations of voting returns and of sources describing towns with numerous Baptists. E.g., Middleboro: Benedict, *Baptists,* pp. 366–67, 412–13; Swansea: ibid., p. 407; Bellingham: ibid., pp. 416–17; Malden: Drake, *Middlesex County,* II, 130–33; West Springfield and Westfield: J. G. Warren, *A Discourse on the History of the Westfield Baptist Association* (Springfield, Mass., 1844). On Baptist, Methodist, and Universalist support for Republicans during the War of 1812, see William Gribbin, *The Churches Militant: The War of 1812 and American Religion* (New Haven, 1973), pp. 78–99; and regarding the Disciples of Christ and Freewill Baptists, pp. 99–103.

35. McLoughlin, *New England Dissent,* II, 1068, 1114; Salem *Essex Register,* May 17, 1811.

36. Smith, *Pittsfield,* pp. 149–50; McLoughlin, *New England Dissent,* II, 1067, 1073, rightly observed that Republicans also looked down on Baptists, but Republican snobbery could hardly have surpassed that of the Federalists, who seldom made any effort to disguise it.

37. Quoted in Smith, *Pittsfield,* p. 150; see also pp. 255–57. Banner, *Hartford Convention,* pp. 208–14. Banner estimated (p. 198) that the Methodists had at most some 7,000 members. Boston *New-England Palladium,* Apr. 3, 1811; Alfred S. Roe, "The Beginnings of Methodism in Worcester," *Worcester Society of Antiquity Proceedings,* 27 (1888), 44–45, 49; John A. Trickel, "Social Analysis of New England Methodism" (Unpublished ms.); Deyo, ed., *Barnstable,* p. 988.

38. Paul Gustaf Faler, "Workingmen, Mechanics and Social Change; Lynn, Massachusetts, 1800–1860" (Ph.D. diss., University of Wisconsin, 1970), pp. 88–92, 104–5. At least one of the early Methodists was a leading businessman. Parsons Cooke, *A Century of Puritanism, and a Century of its Opposites* (Boston, 1856), p. 227.

39. Smith, *Pittsfield,* p. 103; McLoughlin, *New England Dissent,* II, 1170. In Connecticut the Episcopalian minority was initially an important part of the Federal establishment. Richard J. Purcell, *Connecticut in Transition: 1775–1818* (Middletown, Conn., 1963; first ed., 1918).

40. Smith, *Pittsfield,* p. 144.

41. Ezra S. Stearns, *History of Ashburnham* (Ashburnham, Mass., 1887), pp. 321–33; D. Hamilton Hurd, comp., *History of Plymouth County, Massachusetts* (Philadelphia, 1884), pp. 265–66; McLoughlin, *New England Dissent,* I, 678; Kirk Gilbert Alliman, "The Incorporation of Massachusetts Congregational Churches, 1692–1833: The Preservation of Religious Autonomy" (Ph.D. diss., University of Iowa, 1970), p. 197; Samuel Austin, *Protest against Proceedings in the First Church in Worcester* (Worcester, 1821), pp. 6–10.

42. D. D. Field, *A History of the County of Berkshire, Massachusetts* (Pittsfield, Mass., 1829), p. 147.

43. Morison, *Maritime History,* p. 23.

44. Goodman, *Democratic-Republicans,* pp. 105–27. Carl E. Prince has argued that partisan appointments in the customshouse helped the Federalists dominate maritime Massachusetts. *The Federalists and the Origins of the U.S. Civil Service* (New York, 1977), pp. 20–22. Forty-three customs officers and nearly a hundred subordinates were "cadremen" who formed the "backbone of the Federalist establishment in the harbor towns."

45. The Boston *Columbian Centinel,* Jan. 14, 1801, published a "List of Federalists and Anti-Federalists by Professions." Republicans often charged that Federalists used intimidation on the middle and lower classes: Boston *Constitutional Telegraph,* May 7, 1800; Levi Lincoln, Worcester, 6 Nov. 1805, to Thomas Jefferson, Lincoln Papers, MWA.

46. For example, Benjamin Russell, editor of the *Centinel,* a man who worked closely with the merchant princes, also had close ties to the "mechanic interest," including artisans and journeymen. Joseph T. Buckingham, *Specimens of Newspaper Literature: With Personal Memoirs, Anecdotes, and Reminiscences* (Boston, 1850) II, 45, 110–11. The membership of Boston's lower customshouse also showed that Federal leadership "penetrated Boston's middle class of skilled artisans, mechanics, and tradesmen." Prince, *Federalists and the Civil Service,* p. 43. For Federalist election appeals to mechanics, see *Centinel,* Mar. 28, Apr. 4, 1812; New-Bedford *Mercury,* Mar. 27, 1812; Portland *Gazette,* Mar. 16, 1812.

47. Lawyers, for example, tended throughout the state to be overwhelmingly Federal. A recent study found that 70 percent were Federal; yet it must again be noted that lawyers were an important element in Republican leadership. Gerard W. Gawalt, *The Promise of Power: The Emergence of the Legal Profession in Massachusetts, 1760–1840* (Westport, Conn., 1979), pp. 95–96. For examples of Boston influence, see Smith, *Pittsfield,* pp. 193–94; J. D. Forbes, *Israel Thorndike: Federalist Financier* (New York, 1953), pp. 100–101.

48. Morison, *Maritime History,* p. 190, n. 1.

49. From 1793 to 1815 more than 115 vessels were built here; all fittings were made locally, and hundreds of skilled workers were employed. Ibid., pp. 101–102; Timothy Dwight, *Travels in New England and New York,* ed. Barbara Miller Solomon, with Patricia M. King (Cambridge, Mass., 1969), I, 315–16.

50. "Most of the leading families were but one generation removed from the plough or forecastle; but they had acquired wealth before the Revolution, and conducted social matters with the grace and dignity of an old regime." Morison, *Maritime History,* pp. 152–53; Dwight, *Travels,* I, 318–19; Percy Wells Bidwell, "Rural Economy in New England at the Beginning of the Nineteenth Century," *Transactions of the Connecticut Academy of Arts and Sciences,* 20 (1916), 279.

51. Of the twenty-five wealthiest citizens in 1807 at least sixteen were Federal while only two were definitely Republican. Labaree, *Patriots and Partisans,* pp. 139–41. Prince, *Federalists and the Civil Service,* pp. 34–37. Dwight, *Travels,* I, 317–18, praised the town for its beautiful houses and for its "morals and religion."

52. D. Hamilton Hurd, ed., *History of Essex County, Massachusetts* (Philadelphia, 1888), I, 711; Morison, *Maritime History,* p. 141; Dwight, *Travels,* I, 321–22.

53. Hurd, ed., *Essex,* I, 711–13; Edwin M. Stone, *History of Beverly, Civil and Ecclesiastical: From Its Settlement in 1630 to 1842* (Boston, 1843), pp. 123–54, 161–66. Bentley observed in 1808, "the Republicans have rich men, but not as high in reputation." *Diary,* III, 350.

54. Morison, *Maritime History,* pp. 137–40; and Samuel Eliot Morison, "Elbridge Gerry, Gentleman-Democrat," *New England Quarterly,* 2 (1929), 8–9. Dwight, *Travels,* I, 332–33.

55. George Athan Billias, *Elbridge Gerry: Founding Father and Republican Statesman* (New York, 1976), pp. 37–41; Bentley, *Diary,* III, 130.

56. Samuel Roads, Jr., *The History and Traditions of Marblehead* (Boston, 1880), pp. 226–28; Morison, "Elbridge Gerry," p. 8; Bidwell, "Rural Economy," p. 280; Warren, ed., *Diary of Nathaniel Ames,* pp. 231–32; Priscilla Sawyer Lord and Virginia Clegg Gamage, *Marblehead: The Spirit of '76 Lives Here* (Philadelphia, 1972), p. 149. On seamen voting Republican, see Bentley, *Diary,* III, 508.

57. Morison, *Maritime History,* pp. 122–23; Robert Doherty, *Society and Power: Five New England Towns* (Amherst, 1977), pp. 17–18; Bernard Farber, *Guardians of Virtue: Salem Families in 1800* (New York, 1972); Leverett Saltonstall, "Diary," July 2, 1805, in Robert E. Moody, ed., *The Saltonstall Papers, 1607–1815,* II (Boston, 1974), 256.

58. William T. Whitney, "The Crowninshields of Salem," *Essex Institute Historical Collections,* 94 (1958), 79–118.

59. Whitney, "Crowninshields of Salem," p. 31; Prince, *Federalists and the Civil Service,* pp. 31, 33, 44; Salem *Essex Register,* Mar. 18, 1812; Leverett Saltonstall, "Diary," entry of May 14, 1808, in Moody, ed., *Saltonstall Papers,* II, 430. Most of the employers of sailors in Salem were Federalists. E. Gray, *William Gray of Salem, Merchant* (Boston, 1914), pp. 75–76.

60. Dwight, *Travels,* III, 43, 44, 384; Bidwell, "Rural Economy," p. 282; Prince, *Federalists and the Civil Service,* pp. 24–25, 40–41.

61. On Dartmouth, see D. Hamilton Hurd, comp., *History of Bristol County, Massachusetts* (Philadelphia, 1883), pp. 195, 203–4. On Westport, see Dwight, *Travels,* III, 43; Bidwell, "Rural Economy," p. 282.

62. Immediately west of New Bedford, across the Acushnet River, was Fairhaven, part of New Bedford until 1812, a maritime town with a small but thriving whale fishery. Fairhaven rallied to the Republican standard, and New Bedford Federalists called them "Corsicans." Quaker influence seems to have stopped at the Acushnet, and religious influence generally was weaker and an egalitarian spirit stronger in Fairhaven. Hurd, comp., *Bristol,* pp. 267–77. The nickname came from Napoleon's birthplace, suggesting the pro-French inclinations of Republicans.

63. Josiah Quincy, *Figures of the Past: From the Leaves of Old Journals* (Boston, 1884), pp. 175, 181, 182–85; Bidwell, "Rural Economy," p. 290; Morison, *Maritime History,* p. 159; Alexander Starbuck, *History of Nantucket* (Boston, 1924), pp. 265, 267; Micajah Coffin, 5 Jan. 1808, to Jacob Crowninshield, Crowninshield Family Papers, Essex Institute.

64. Regarding the latter point, see Nantucket *Inquirer,* Jan. 19, 1824. Macy, *History of Nantucket,* pp. 160, 235; Morison, *Maritime History,* pp. 156–57, 314–15. Though Nantucket voted heavily Republican in 1808, Jefferson believed it had not obeyed the embargo. He said the island "has been so deeply concerned in smuggling, that if it wants, it is because it has illegally sent away what it ought to have retained for its own consumption." Thomas Jefferson, Washington, 13 Nov. 1808, to Lt. Gov. Levi Lincoln, Lincoln Family Papers, MWA.

65. The quotation is from Bidwell, "Rural Economy," p. 257, also pp. 245, 248, 253–56, 270–76; Christopher Clark, "The Household Economy, Market Exchange and the Rise of Capitalism in the Connecticut Valley, 1800–1860," *Journal of Social History,* 13 (1979), 170–79. For a somewhat different view, see Margaret Richards Pabst, *Agricultural Trends in the Connecticut Valley Region of Massachusetts, 1800–1900,* Smith College Studies in History, vol. 26 (Northampton, 1941), pp. 10–12, 112.

66. Tench Coxe and Brissot de Warville, quoted in Bidwell, "Rural Economy," pp. 262, 263.

67. By 1823 there seemed to be a quite clear-cut relationship between the level of social complexity and competitiveness: i.e., the more populous and developed a town, the more likely that the two-party vote was competitive. There remained, however, exceptions.

68. The most complete set of information about the socioeconomic characteristics of Massachusetts towns comes from the 1801 tax-valuation manuscript, at the Massachusetts State Archives. This provided such items for each town as number of polls; aggregate value of dwellings; value of stock; value of United States and state securities; value of silver plate; acres of tillage; acres of unimproved land; aggregate valuation; money on hand at 6 percent; and fifteen others. Multiple regression analysis of these variables, using a BMD program, with party vote in 1801 as the dependent variable, yielded no suggestion that Republican and Federal votes came from towns very

different in these characteristics. The Republican vote of 1801 seemed to have a positive correlation with higher agricultural productivity.

Similar data were available in 1811 only for Franklin County, and multiple regression analysis of several compound variables for the county's twenty-four towns yielded similar results, except for a slight positive correlation between commercial activity and Federal vote. Alan Larsen and John Blydenburgh of Clark University provided valuable assistance in performing these calculations and in interpreting them.

69. Birdsall, *Berkshire County,* pp. 27, 28; Dwight, *Travels,* II, 261–78.

70. Thomas Lawrence Davis, "Aristocrats and Jacobins in Country Towns: Party Formation in Berkshire County, Massachusetts (1775–1815)" (Ph.D. diss., Boston University, 1975). Using data from the 1798 Massachusetts direct tax and the 1801 tax valuation, Davis found that Republican towns tended to be more prosperous than Federal ones, used their land more efficiently, and contained more shops, mills, and commercial holdings. Davis also compiled information for numbers of *individual* Federalists and Republicans; he found them to be similar in mean wealth and material condition. Using lists from Stockbridge and Pittsfield, Davis concluded that Federalists included more of the "poorer" citizens, and while Republicans were more middle class, both Federalists and Republicans were among the wealthy. Ibid., pp. 170–71, 176–78, 183. Davis has an excellent discussion, on pp. 172–73, of the flaws in the 1798 data and the greater reliability of the 1801 valuation.

Davis computed such items as average wealth, comparable efficiency of land use (bushels produced divided by tillage acres), and voter turnout in several elections. I used the 1798 data and several of his computed variables in a multiple regression analysis, and found the 1801 Federal vote to have a slight negative correlation with average bushels produced, average tons of hay, and valuation of houses. Some support also existed for Davis's contention that Republican towns possessed more commercial enterprise.

71. Ibid., pp. 125, 127, 254–60, 264, 280, 284, 286, 287; Birdsall, *Berkshire County,* pp. 21–23; Smith, *Pittsfield,* pp. 53, 79.

72. Comparisons of Federal and Republican banner towns, based on the number of churches, support the claim that there was a relation between dissent and Republicanism. The number of churches comes from Davis, from the *Massachusetts Register, 1810,* and from official church sources and local histories. For the difficulties involved in making firm statements about the religious composition of towns, see Appendix XII.B.

73. Birdsall, *Berkshire County,* pp. 92–93; Lyman H. Butterfield, "Elder John Leland, Jeffersonian Itinerant," *Proceedings of the American Antiquarian Society,* 62 (1952), 202–3.

74. Ellen M. Raynor and Emma L. Petitclerc, *History of the Town of Cheshire, Berkshire County, Massachusetts* (Holyoke, Mass., 1885), pp. 18, 22, 73.

75. Butterfield, John Leland," pp. 176–97, 202, 210–11, and esp. pp. 204–7; Raynor and Petitclerc, *Cheshire,* pp. 83, 89. As a rich dairying center, Cheshire had become well known for its cheese; it thus followed that in celebration of Jefferson's election, Cheshire made a giant cheese to honor the champion of religious toleration. This famous cheese was a community project involving many men and women and, reputedly, the milk of 900 cows—not one of which was said to be a Federalist. One month from the day of its making, the cheese weighed 1,235 pounds. It was transported by sled, ship, and wagon to Washington. On New Year's Day morning 1802, Jefferson stood in his door to receive the cheese and Cheshire's greetings, read to him by Elder Leland. The Virginian privately called the cheese "an ebullition of the passion of republicanism in a state where it has been under heavy persecution." Butterfield, "John Leland," pp. 219–23; Raynor and Petitclerc, *Cheshire,* pp. 86–87.

76. Martin, *Merchants of the Connecticut Valley,* pp. 93–101, 231–40, 245–64; Hiram Barrus, *History of the Town of Goshen, Hampshire County, Massachusetts* (Boston, 1881), pp. 42–43.

77. Dwight, Travels, I, 240, 256; Valenti, "Social Bases of Party Voting," pp. 49–50; Pabst, *Agricultural Trends,* pp. 5, 7; Doherty, *Society and Power,* p. 16; Martin, *Merchants of the Connecticut Valley,* p. 251; Ellen Elizabeth Callahan, *Hadley: A Study of the Political Development of a Typical New England Town from the Official Records (1659–1930),* Smith College Studies in History, vol. 16 (Northampton, 1931), pp. 72–75. Regarding family persistence among town officers, see Sylvester Judd, *History of Hadley: Including the Early History of Hatfield, South Hadley, Amherst and Granby, Massachusetts* (Springfield, Mass., 1905), pp. 19–33.

78. Valenti, "Social Bases of Party Voting," pp. 31–34; Republican features are implicit in Alfred Noon, ed., *Ludlow: A Century and a Centennial* (Springfield, Mass., 1875), pp. 29–52.

79. Benedict, *Baptists,* pp. 415–21; Warren, *Historical Discourse* (1844).

80. Doherty, *Society and Power,* p. 15; Pabst, *Agricultural Trends,* pp. 6, 7.

81. Henry Jones Ford, *The Scotch-Irish in America* (Princeton, 1915), p. 228. Sumner Gilbert Wood, *Ulster Scots and Blandford Scouts* (West Medway, Mass., 1928).

82. Meyer, *Church and State,* pp. 160–65, 169, 172; Shaw, "Unitarians, Trinitarians," pp. 12, 53; Frank Otto Gatell, *John Gorham Palfrey and the New England Conscience* (Cambridge, Mass., 1963), pp. 33–36, 41–47; Goodman, *Democratic-Republicans,* pp. 91–92; Anson Phelps Stokes, *Church and State in the United States* (New York, 1950), II, 31. Regarding Unitarian progress in Worcester County despite opposition to it as "heresy," see John Davis, Worcester, 2 Jan. 1824, to Thomas Jefferson, Davis Papers, MWA.

83. Meyer, *Church and State,* p. 168; Warren, ed., *Diary of Nathaniel Ames,* pp. 305–7, 309; Cushing, "Disestablishment," pp. 188–89, said that the Dedham decision made the Orthodox cause hopeless; McLoughlin, *New England Dissent,* II, 1196, said it produced "the final and fatal crack in the wall of the Standing Order in Massachusetts." See also Shaw, "Unitarians, Trinitarians," pp. 19, 57–58, 67.

84. Regarding the religious issue in 1823, see McLoughlin, *New England Dissent,* II, 1197–99, 1203–5; Shaw, "Unitarians, Trinitarians," pp. 40–42; Boston *Columbian Centinel,* Mar. 26, Apr. 2, 1823; Boston *Repertory,* Mar. 29, 1823; Boston *Patriot,* Apr. 2, 1823; Boston *Statesman,* Mar. 27, 1823. On Orthodox opposition to Otis earlier, see John T. Kirkland, Boston, 10 Feb. 1810, to Josiah Quincy, in "Letters of John T. Kirkland," *Massachusetts Historical Society Proceedings,* 17 (1879), 113–14.

85. Meyer, *Church and State,* pp. 214–15; Shaw, "Unitarians, Trinitarians," pp. 46–49, 89–90; McLoughlin, *New England Dissent,* II, 1205–6; Cushing, "Disestablishment," pp. 189–90. Congregational minorities in towns had sought incorporation as "poll parishes" in distinction to the original geographical parishes ever since the 1780s. Between 1790 and 1817 sixty-eight Congregational churches had become "poll parishes." Alliman, "Massachusetts Congregational Churches," p. 170.

86. In Connecticut the collapse of the Federal political establishment followed hard upon the end of the religious establishment in 1818. Purcell, *Connecticut in Transition.*

## VIII. "Improvements" and Populism, 1820–1830

1. Fred Somkin, *Unquiet Eagle: Memory and Desire in the Idea of American Freedom, 1815–1860* (Ithaca, 1967), pp. 18–28.

2. Thomas Bender, *Community and Social Change in America* (New Brunswick, 1978), p. 76.

3. This is one of the major themes of Oscar Handlin and Mary Flug Handlin, *Commonwealth: A Study of the Role of Government in the American Economy: Massachusetts, 1774–1861* (Cambridge, 1969; first ed., 1947), and a secondary theme of George Dangerfield, *The Awakening of American Nationalism, 1815–1828* (New York, 1965).

4. Henry Adams, *History of the United States of America during the First Administration of Thomas Jefferson* (New York, 1889), I, 5–16.

5. In the 1830s Harriet Martineau told of arriving in Gloucester and observing the rapidity with which news of her visit, like other "small articles of intelligence," circulated there "as in other country places." Harriet Martineau, *Society in America* (London, 1837), I, 211. The quotation is from George S. Merriam, *The Life of Samuel Bowles* (New York, 1885), I, 30. Allan R. Pred, *Urban Growth and the Circulation of Information: The United States System of Cities, 1790–1840* (Cambridge, 1973), pp. 144–49.

6. Ibid., pp. 13–14. In the 1790s in Berkshire County, riders bringing newspapers provided some towns with their only regular contact with the outside world. Richard D. Birdsall, *Berkshire County: A Cultural History* (New Haven, 1959), p. 187; Fisher Ames, Dedham, 1 Feb. 1806, to T. Pickering, in Seth Ames, ed., *Works of Fisher Ames* (Boston, 1854), I, 357, and F. Ames, 1 Feb. 1806, to Josiah Quincy, in ibid., p. 359. See also Nathaniel Ames's appreciation of newspapers, Dec. 31, 1800, in Charles Warren, ed., *Jacobin and Junto: or Early American Politics as Viewed in the Diary of Dr. Nathaniel Ames, 1758–1822* (New York, 1968; first ed., 1931), pp. 158–59.

7. Pred, *Urban Growth and Information,* p. 24; George Rogers Taylor, *The Transportation Revolution, 1815–1860* (New York, 1951), pp. 22, 58; Caroline F. Ware, *The Early New England Cotton Manufacture: A Study in Industrial Beginnings* (Boston, 1931), p. 16; Handlin and Handlin, *Commonwealth,* pp. 108–9, 111–12; Stephen Salsbury, *The State, the Investor, and the Railroad: The Boston & Albany, 1825–1867* (Cambridge, 1967), pp. 41–42. In 1810 a stage left Boston every day at 4:00 A.M. and reached Hartford at 8:00 P.M., using relays every ten miles. Warren, ed., *Diary of Nathaniel Ames,* p. 320. The New York mail stage left Boston at 3:00 A.M. and arrived in Worcester before 8:00 "for an early breakfast." Worcester *Massachusetts Spy,* May 1, 1811.

8. The isolation of central Massachusetts lessened with the completion of the Providence-Worcester canal, but western Massachusetts still remained relatively isolated. Salsbury, *Boston & Albany,* pp. 21–24, 26–27.

9. Josiah Quincy, *Figures of the Past: From the Leaves of Old Journals* (Boston, 1884), pp. 191, 198; Pred, *Urban Growth and Information,* p. 13.

10. William Ellery Channing, "Remarks on Associations," *The Works of William E. Channing* (Boston, 1854), I, 283–84. "Through these means, men of one mind, through a whole country, can easily understand one another, and easily act together. The grand manoeuver to which Napoleon owed his victories, we mean the concentration of great numbers on a single point, is now placed within the reach of all parties and sects. . . ." Ibid.

11. George Sweet Gibb, *The Saco-Lowell Shops: Textile Machinery Building in New England, 1813–1849* (Cambridge, 1950), pp. 92–93.

12. John G. B. Hutchins, *The American Maritime Industries and Public Policy, 1789–1914: An Economic History* (Cambridge, 1941), pp. 142, 173, 184–86, 257, 272–73; Robert F. Dalzell, Jr., "The Rise of the Waltham-Lowell System and Some

Thoughts on the Political Economy of Modernization in Ante-Bellum Massachusetts," *Perspectives in American History,* 9 (1965), 252–56; Samuel Eliot Morison, *The Maritime History of Massachusetts, 1783–1860* (Boston, 1921), pp. 95–96, 188–89, 298.

13. Vera Shlakman, *Economic History of a Factory Town: A Study of Chicopee, Massachusetts,* Smith College Studies in History, vol. 20 (Northampton, 1935), pp. 28–31. For more evidence on the continuity of economic and social power, see Dalzell, "Waltham-Lowell System," pp. 248–49; Salsbury, *Boston & Albany,* pp. 7–9; Morison, *Maritime History,* pp. 241, 253; Quincy, *Figures of the Past,* pp. 302–3; Thomas G. Cary, *Profits on Manufactures at Lowell* (Boston, 1845), p. 4. Edward Pessen has also observed the high intermarriage among the rich families of Boston merchants, manufacturers, and intellectuals. *Riches, Class, and Power before the Civil War* (Lexington, Mass., 1973), pp. 54–56, 66–68, 215–16.

14. Handlin and Handlin, *Commonwealth,* p. 162. In the first part of this period, state legislatures everywhere tended to grant charters to business corporations for "activities of some community interest–supplying transport, water, insurance, or banking facilities." James Willard Hurst, *The Legitimacy of the Business Corporation in the Law of the United States, 1780–1970* (Charlottesville, 1970), pp. 14–18.

15. Lewis Mumford, *Sticks and Stones: A Study of American Architecture and Civilization* (New York, 1955; first ed., 1924), p. 75. The 1820s marked the decade in which manufacturing decisively changed many towns: Richard D. Brown, *Urbanization in Springfield, Massachusetts, 1790–1830* (Springfield, 1962), pp. 24–25.

16. Dalzell, "Waltham-Lowell System," pp. 261–62; Ware, *Cotton Manufacture,* pp. 46–47, 54–56, 66, 77, 78, 80–81, 91–93, 96; Charles L. Sanford, "The Intellectual Origins and New-Worldliness of American Industry," *Journal of Economic History,* 18 (1958), 1–16; Handlin and Handlin, *Commonwealth,* pp. 126–27, 182–83; Salsbury, *Boston & Albany,* pp. 16–18. In 1811 Nathaniel Ames noted, "Embargo has raised a spirit of factory enterprize in this country that will never be extinguished," and he also reported rumors of excellent profits made by cotton factories. Warren, ed., *Diary of Nathaniel Ames,* p. 238. Gibb, *Saco-Lowell Shops,* p. 63, said that the major reason the Boston Associates expanded was that "the Boston Manufacturing Company had been making more money than the stockholders had dreamed possible"; Dalzell, "Waltham-Lowell System," pp. 244–45, 266–68, emphasized the desire to hold on to fortunes already made. This might simply be called a case of *diversification.* On the attitudes of Boston's elite, see Paul Goodman, "Ethics and Enterprise: The Values of the Boston Elite, 1800–1860," *American Quarterly,* 18 (1966), 437–51; Seaburg and Patterson, *Merchant Prince,* pp. 341–42, 416. Regarding the distinction drawn at the time between "manufactures" and cities, see Thomas Bender, *Toward an Urban Vision: Ideas and Institutions in Nineteenth-Century America* (Lexington, Ky., 1975), pp. 23–24.

17. John Coolidge, *Mill and Mansion: A Study of Architecture and Society in Lowell, Massachusetts, 1820–1865* (New York, 1942), pp. 30–31. Ware, *Cotton Manufacture,* pp. 80–81. Shlakman, *Factory Town,* pp. 37, 43–44; Gibb, *Saco-Lowell Shops,* passim.

18. Basil Hall, *Travels in North America* (Edinburgh, 1829), II, 135; Nathan Appleton, *The Introduction of the Power Loom and the Origin of Lowell* (Lowell, 1858), p. 15; Ware, *Cotton Manufacture,* pp. 60–61, 64–65, 85; Handlin and Handlin, *Commonwealth,* pp. 186–87; Shlakman, *Factory Town,* p. 64; Allis Rosenberg Wolfe, ed., "Letters of a Lowell Mill Girl and Friends, 1845–1846," *Labor History,* 17 (1976), 96–102.

19. John R. Commons et al., eds., *A Documentary History of American Industrial*

*Society* (New York, 1958; first ed., 1909), V, pt. 1, pp. 57–61; Ware, *Cotton Manufacture,* p. 210. According to Ware (p. 202) there were some 184 cotton mills of the family type in Massachusetts.

20. Blanche Evans Hazard, *The Organization of the Boot and Shoe Industry in Massachusetts before 1875* (Cambridge, Mass., 1921), pp. 248–49, 254; Alan Dawley, *Class and Community: The Industrial Revolution in Lynn* (Cambridge, Mass., 1976), pp. 42–45; Paul Gustaf Faler, "Workingmen, Mechanics, and Social Change: Lynn, Massachusetts, 1800–1860" (Ph.D. diss., University of Wisconsin, 1970), pp. 124–33, 158–59, 161–67. Centralization also came to rope making: Samuel Eliot Morison, *The Ropemakers of Plymouth: A History of the Plymouth Cordage Company, 1824–1949* (Boston, 1950), pp. 7, 43.

21. Boston *Columbian Centinel,* Jan. 19, 1828; Henry Bass Hall, "A Description of Rural Life and Labor in Massachusetts at Four Periods" (Ph.D. diss., Harvard University, 1917), pp. 128–31. On the general subject of riparian rights, see Morton J. Horowitz, *The Transformation of American Law, 1780–1860* (Cambridge, Mass., 1977), pp. 34–53. On declining farm prices in the 1820s, see Winifred B. Rothenberg, "A Price Index for Rural Massachusetts, 1750–1855," *Journal of Economic History,* 39 (1979), 984–85.

22. Margaret Richards Pabst, *Agricultural Trends in the Connecticut Valley Region of Massachusetts, 1800–1900,* Smith College Studies in History, vol. 26 (Northampton, 1941), pp. 13–15, 30–42, 47–53, 57, 64–65, 112; Hall, "Rural Life and Labor," p. 131; Salsbury, *Boston & Albany,* pp. 9–15.

23. Martineau, *Society in America,* II, 32, 34; Harold Fisher Wilson, *The Hill Country of Northern New England: Its Social and Economic History, 1790–1930* (New York, 1936); [Robert C. Winthrop's Speech] To State Convention of Whig Young Men of Massachusetts, Worcester, Sept. 11, 1839, Massachusetts Collection, MWA (Winthrop apparently struck these lines from his speech). In 1832 the Boston *Artisan,* on Nov. 8, observed that mortgages were spreading through the countryside; see also Jan. 31, Feb. 28, and May 9, 1833. In 1834 a spokesman of the workingmen said that the so-called *"Life Office"* in Boston was known in the country among poor farmers as the "Death Office." Abel Cushing, *Oration Delivered at the Celebration of the Democratic Working-Men, in Milford, Mass., July 4, 1834* (Providence, 1834), p. 12.

24. Taylor, *Transportation Revolution,* pp. 217–19, 232–33, 267–69; Martineau, *Society in America,* II, 34, 36–37.

25. For general views, see Stuart Blumin, "Mobility and Change in Ante-Bellum Philadelphia," in Stephen Thernstrom and Richard Sennett, eds., *Nineteenth-Century Cities: Essays in the New Urban History* (New Haven, 1969), pp. 199–205; Lee Soltow, *Men and Wealth in the United States, 1859–1870* (New Haven, 1975); and Craig Buettinger, "Economic Inequality in Early Chicago, 1840–1850," *Journal of Social History,* 11 (1978), 413–18.

26. Howard M. Gitelman, *Workingmen of Waltham: Mobility in American Urban Industrial Development, 1850–1890* (Baltimore, 1974), pp. 9, 10, 12, 16–17. In 1818 the Salem Society for the Moral and Religious Instruction of the Poor formed and ascertained that there were "several hundred families of poor people in the town." Elias Cornelius, *The Moral and Religious Improvement of the Poor. A Sermon Delivered on the Evening of October 20, 1824, in the Tabernacle Church, Salem* (Salem, Mass., 1824), p. 14.

27. Ronald Story, *The Forging of an Aristocracy: Harvard & the Boston Upper Class, 1800–1870* (Middletown, Conn., 1980), pp. 41, 88–108. The class consciousness of employers of domestic servants became more intense in the 1820s: Blaine

Edward McKinley, " 'The Stranger in the Gates': Employer Reactions toward domestic Servants in America, 1825–1875" (Ph.D. diss., Michigan State University, 1969), pp. 69–70, 148–90, 281–82.

28. The quotation is from *Acts and Resolves, 1828,* p. 383; Carl Siracusa, *A Mechanical People: Perceptions of the Industrial Order in Massachusetts, 1815–1880* (Middletown, Conn., 1979), pp. 69–74. Social scientists are placing increasing emphasis on the level of economic activity of communities as the most important condition influencing vertical mobility. Michael P. Weber and Anthony E. Boardman, "Economic Growth and Occupational Mobility in Nineteenth Century Urban America: A Reappraisal," *Journal of Social History,* 11 (1977), 52–74.

29. Faler, "Workingmen, Mechanics, and Social Change," pp. 223, 235, 254, 274; David J. Rothman, *The Discovery of the Asylum: Social Order and Disorder in the New Republic* (Boston, 1971), pp. 156, 157, 175, 188; on prison problems, see Taunton *Free Press,* Feb. 6, 1824, and Boston *Evening Gazette,* Mar. 13, 1824. During the first two decades of the nineteenth century, Bostonians discovered great numbers of the poor as a "separate, deviant group threatening the values held by the majority," and by the early 1820s "reforming the poor, rather than relieving their sufferings, became the central goal." Redmond James Barnett, "From Philanthropy to Reform: Poverty, Drunkenness and the Social Order in Massachusetts, 1780–1825" (Ph.D. diss., Harvard University, 1973), pp. 245, 280–81.

30. Mary McDougall Gordon, "Patriots and Christians: A Reassessment of Nineteenth-Century School Reformers," *Journal of Social History,* 11 (1978), 554, 558–59. It was no coincidence that the American Institute moved to direct political lobbying in 1834. Gordon attributed the timing of this to the Whigs' capturing control of the state in 1834, but the same social elements largely controlled both the Whigs and the National Republicans who preceded them. Ibid., pp. 563–64. Gordon also correctly pointed to money made available when the federal government finally compensated Massachusetts the $2 million in militia claims from the 1812 war, which was used for a school fund. But the coming of disestablishment as a legal fact in 1833 was the most important impetus to the institute.

31. This was not the first occasion on which the middle and lower classes asserted themselves, though usually they managed to find middle-class and well-to-do leaders, as, e.g., in an 1817 controversy over public schools: William Michael Weber, "Before Horace Mann: Elites and Boston Public Schools, 1800–1822" (Ed.D. diss., Harvard University Graduate School of Education, 1974), pp. 94–95. Gary B. Nash, *The Urban Crucible: Social Change, Political Consciousness, and the Origins of the American Revolution* (Cambridge, Mass., 1979), argues that this kind of change began much earlier and presents a view of the eighteenth century very different from that presented here in Chapters II and III.

32. The episode is treated briefly in Robert A. McCaughey, *Josiah Quincy, 1772–1864: The Last Federalist* (Cambridge, Mass., 1974), pp. 100–6; and Samuel Eliot Morison, *Harrison Gray Otis, 1765–1848: Urbane Federalist* (Boston, 1969), pp. 436–37.

33. Roger Lane, *Policing the City: Boston, 1822–1885* (Cambridge, Mass., 1967), p. 13; John Koren, *Boston, 1822 to 1922: The Story of Its Government and Principal Activities during One Hundred Years* (Boston, 1922), pp. 7–8. Josiah Quincy, *A Municipal History of the Town and City of Boston, during Two Centuries, from September 17, 1630, to September 17, 1830* (Boston, 1852), p. 28, stressed the unmanageable size of town meetings in Faneuil Hall, a reason which must be viewed with skepticism. An anonymous critic of the change also revealed the general decline of community spirit: *Selections From the Chronicles of Boston* (Boston?, 1822),

Widener Library, Harvard University. In the 1790s opponents of a city plan had directed their appeals to the "middling people." Edward Lewis Ballantyne, "The Incorporation of Boston, 1784–1822" (Honors thesis, Harvard College, 1955), pp. 53–56.

34. Carl Wilhelm Ernst, *Constitutional History of Boston, Massachusetts: An Essay* (Boston, 1893), pp. 73, 74.

35. For debates over the change see Boston *Palladium*, Feb. 26, Mar. 1, 1822; [William Emmons], *Mr. Emmons' Speech, Delivered at the Grand Caucus, Held in Faneuil Hall, on the Evening of the Third of March, 1822, upon the Acceptance or Rejection of the City Charter* (Boston, 1822); Caleb H. Snow, *A History of Boston* (Boston, 1828), pp. 363–64, 366.

36. *Palladium*, Jan. 1, 4, 8, 1822. On Federal opposition to ward voting, see "A North End Mechanic," Boston *Columbian Centinel*, Jan. 5, 1822. Other Federalists said the measure needed to pass or the charter would fail: *Palladium*, Mar. 1, 1822. For Republican support, see *Patriot*, Jan. 7, 1822; also, see above Chapter VI, and Snow, *History of Boston*, pp. 367–68.

37. On January 7 the town approved the charter 2,805 to 2,006 and ward elections 2,611 to 2,195. On March 4 it passed the charter 2,797 to 1,881 and ward elections 2,813 to 1,887. *Palladium*, Jan. 8, Feb. 15, Mar. 5, 1822.

38. Petitions to town meetings before and after the legislature's action are in *Palladium*, Jan. 15, Mar. 5, 1822; arguments against wooden buildings, in *Palladium*, Jan. 25, 1822, and esp. "Z" in *Patriot*, Mar. 5, 1822. The 1803 law and past fires are treated in Snow, *History of Boston*, pp. 322, 325; and Walter Muir Whitehill, *Boston: A Topographical History* (Cambridge, Mass., 1968; first ed., 1959), p. 50.

39. *Palladium*, Mar. 15, 1822; McCaughey, *Josiah Quincy*, p. 102. In 1822 the elite had tried to avert such a split by including middle-class leaders on the charter planning committee. Quincy, *Municipal History*, pp. 30, 31.

40. *An Exposition of the Principles and Views of the Middling Interest: In the City of Boston* (Boston, 1822), quotation pp. 4, 5, 7: A subsequent *Defence of the Exposition of the Middling Interest* . . . (Boston, 1822) devoted itself to justifying the right of Bostonians to instruct their legislative representatives and also undergirded its argument with the same themes.

41. McCaughey, *Josiah Quincy*, pp. 89–91, 93–94, 103–4. Thomas H. Perkins sputtered that Quincy had "thrown himself into the hands of the 'Middling or Medling Interest' " and would be supported by some "Democrats." T.H.P., Boston, 5 Apr. 1822, to Harrison Gray Otis, Otis Papers, MHi.

42. McCaughey, *Josiah Quincy*, pp. 104–5; Speech before a Federalist Caucus, spring (no date) of 1822, H. G. Otis Papers; *Palladium*, Apr. 9, 16, 1822. The Middling Interest nominated its own slate of candidates for sixteen ward offices in Ward Seven, and probably in other wards as well. *Palladium*, Apr. 2, 5, 9, 1822.

43. *Palladium*, Apr. 15, 18, 1823; Boston *Evening Gazette*, Apr. 12, 1823; *Bostonian*, Apr. 19, 1823.

44. *Palladium*, Apr. 8, 15, May 13, 16, 1823; *Bostonian*, Feb. 8, Apr. 5, 12, May 3, 1823; E. Starkweather, 29 Jan. 1823, to H. G. Otis, Otis Papers.

45. *Palladium*, May 7, 10, 14, 17, 1822; *Patriot* Apr. 1, May 3, 16, 1822.

46. The editor, Charles W. Moore, was a young man in his early twenties whose father, an English immigrant, ran a music store. Moore had served as an apprentice printer for the Federal *Palladium* and then for two Republican papers, the Haverhill *Essex Patriot* and the Boston *Statesman*. The *Bostonian* did not simply follow a Republican line, but did usually back Republican candidates, as in the November congressional elections. *Bostonian and Mechanics' Journal*, Nov. 2, 1822, June 28, 1823; Boston *Evening Gazette*, Oct. 26, 1822. Other newspapers also criticized imprisonment

for debt: Joseph T. Buckingham, *Personal Memoirs and Recollection of Editorial Life* (Boston, 1852), I, 102.

47. On the middling-class identification, and rather conservative values, of the Massachusetts Charitable Mechanics Association, see Gary J. Kornblith, "From Artisans to Businessmen: Master Mechanics in New England, 1789–1850" (Paper presented at the Annual Meeting of the Organization of American History, New York, Apr. 14, 1978).

In 1820 there lived in the city, by conservative estimate, some 10,500 males twenty-one years old or older. Thus, it was likely that several thousand of the young, transient, and poor did not vote and had little to do with town affairs. Routine town meetings often consisted of 150 to 250 citizens. *Records Relating to the Early History of Boston: Boston Town Records,* vol. 35, *1796 to 1813,* and vol. 37, *1814 to 1822* (Boston, 1906). On the relationship between the city's demography and its politics, see Peter R. Knights and Stephen Thernstrom, "Men in Motion: Some Data and Speculation about Urban Population Mobility in Nineteenth-Century America," *Journal of Interdisciplinary History,* 1 (1970), 7–35.

48. *Principles and Views of the Middling Interest,* pp. 7–8; "Middling Interest" Circular, Boston, May 15, 1822, William Smith Shaw Papers, Boston Athenaeum. William Emmons, an opponent of the charter, claimed to be a voice of the "poor," though his manner was that of a self-taught and somewhat learned eccentric of the middle class: *Mr. Emmons' Speech,* pp. 3–4.

49. The first quotation is from Samuel H. Riddel, "Mr. Charles Ewer," in *Memorial Biographies,* II, 153. Christopher Gore, Waltham, 2 June 1822, to Rufus King, in Charles R. King, ed., *Life and Correspondence of Rufus King,* VI (New York, 1900), 474. The chairman of the first Middling Interest meeting, Michael Roulstone, was indicated on an 1822 Boston tax list as possessing $6,200 in real property. The 1826 *Boston Directory* described him as a "plumber and glazier." The *Patriot,* May 16, 1822, compared the Middling and Federal candidates, emphasizing that the former were heads of families active in the community who had made their way by hard work. For an expression of elite antagonism toward middle class climbers, see William Sullivan, Boston, 6 Jan. 1822, to H. G. Otis, Otis Papers; and of the contrasting Middling views, see Andrew Dunlap, *An Oration, Delivered at the Request of the Republicans of Boston, at Faneuil Hall, on the Fourth of July, 1822* (Boston, 1822), pp. 10–11.

50. Outside of Boston a candidate for office might be identified as of the "Middling Interest," as in the case of an aspirant for town clerk in Salem (New Bedford *Gazette,* Mar. 23, 1824), but use of the term seems not to have been common outside of Boston. In 1823, lower-class groups of New Bedford came to the town meeting to oppose the old town officers but were put down by the "better and more respectable part of the inhabitants . . . to have all the children of the town to be educated together at the public expense in town schools, but they found the town too aristocratic to carry a thing of this kind into operation." Zephaniah W. Pease, ed., *Life in New Bedford a Hundred Years Ago: A Chronicle of the Social, Religious and Commercial History of the Period as Recorded in a Diary Kept by Joseph R. Anthony* (New Bedford, 1922), pp. 26, 27.

51. L. F. Greene, ed., *The Writings of the Late Elder John Leland* (New York, 1845), p. 502. There was a similar, though less widespread, impulse in the 1820s which condemned the incarceration of the mentally ill in jails: Gerald N. Grob, *The State and the Mentally Ill: A History of the Worcester State Hospital in Massachusetts, 1830–1920* (Chapel Hill, 1966), pp. 20ff.

52. Peter J. Coleman, *Debtors and Creditors in America: Insolvency, Imprisonment for Debt, and Bankruptcy, 1607–1900* (Madison, Wis., 1974), pp. 41–43.

53. Whitehill, *Boston,* p. 54; Salem *Gazette,* Jan. 17, 1823; *Palladium,* Jan. 17, 1823; George Phillip Bauer, "The Movement against Imprisonment for Debt in the United States" (Ph.D. diss., Harvard University, 1935), pp. 131–32, 214–15. In Worcester from 1785 to 1817, the jail limits changed several times. Benjamin Thomas Hill, ed., *The Diary of Isaiah Thomas, 1805–1828,"* Transactions and Collections of the American Antiquarian Society, vols. 9 and 10 (Worcester, 1909), I, 142–43. In Pittsfield in the early nineteenth century, prisoners had the privilege, unless the creditor objected, of spending the day where they pleased within the village, returning to the jail at night. Joseph Edward Adams Smith, *The History of Pittsfield, Massachusetts, from the Year 1800 to the Year 1876* (Springfield, 1876), p. 63.

54. Quoted in Redmond J. Barnett, "The Movement against Imprisonment for Debt in Massachusetts, 1811–1834" (Senior honors thesis, Department of History, Harvard University, 1965), p. 22; see also Coleman, *Debtors and Creditors,* pp. 4–5, 44. On the other hand, a spokesman for creditors observed that "the dread of a thirty days nominal confinement, the period required in Massachusetts," would not "make a rogue an honest man." [John B. Davis], *A Letter to the Senate and House of Representatives of the United States upon the Expediency of an Uniform System of Bankruptcy* (Boston, 1821), p. 26.

55. [Davis], *Letter on Bankruptcy,* pp. 12–15. In England from 1800 to 1820 the movement against imprisonment for debt was fairly continuous. Bauer, "Movement against Imprisonment for Debt," pp. 129–30.

56. Ibid., pp. 147–59, 164–65, 179–80, 225–26; Coleman, *Debtors and Creditors,* pp. 117–19; Barnett, "Movement against Imprisonment for Debt in Massachusetts," pp. 1–31; Charles Warren, *Bankruptcy in United States History* (Cambridge, Mass., 1935), p. 37. During 1810 to 1813 pressure for drastic action to help the insolvent appears to have spread rapidly through the seacoast towns, but the legislature defeated proposals for action.

57. *Bostonian and Mechanics' Journal,* March 29, 1823; Bauer, "Movement against Imprisonment for Debt," pp. 174–75. Bauer, p. 196, found no record of the society's incorporation. In his 1821 Election Sermon Henry Ware implicitly opposed imprisonment for debt. Barnett, "Movement against Imprisonment for Debt in Massachusetts," p. 33; Dedham *Village Register,* Jan. 18, 1822; Boston *Patriot,* Jan. 10, 31, Mar. 15, 1822; Salem *Essex Register,* Mar. 23, 1822; Boston *Statesman,* Jan. 30, Apr. 28, 1823; *Bostonian and Mechanics' Journal,* Oct. 12, 1822. The Howard Benevolent Society, founded in 1812 to relieve the plight of the sick and poor, became more active at this time: *Howard Benevolent Society* (Boston, 1822), and Barnett, "Movement against Imprisonment for Debt in Massachusetts," 248–53.

58. *Laws of the Commonwealth of Massachusetts, 1822–1825* (Boston, 1825), IX, 133–35, 148–52. *P. P. F. Degrand's Boston Weekly Report,* Apr. 26, 1823, and Jan. 15, 25, 1823; *Bostonian and Mechanics' Journal,* Mar. 1, 1823, which also quoted the *Mechanics' Gazette.* The jail-limits issue was debated in the *Palladium,* Jan. 17, 24, 28, Feb. 4, 1823. Samuel Upton and John A. Haven, Committee of the Society for the Relief of the Distressed, 1 Apr. 1823, to H. G. Otis, and H. G. Otis, Apr. 1823, to S. Upton and J. A. Haven, Otis Papers. Bauer, "Movement against Imprisonment for Debt," p. 196. Barnett, "Movement Against Imprisonment for Debt in Massachusetts," p. 32. W[illiam] Emmons, *An Address, Delivered This Morning, on the Western Avenue* (Boston, 1823), New Bedford *New England Gazette,* May 27, 1823. In early 1823 a legislative committee investigated prisons in the Commonwealth and found that the condition of imprisoned debtors was perhaps not as bad as reformers claimed. Boston *Howard Gazette and Evening Herald,* Jan. 24, 1824. This was a reform paper and thus not likely to make the findings more palatable than they actually were.

59. Boston *Howard Gazette,* Oct. 8, Nov. 22, 1823; Bauer, "Movement against Imprisonment for Debt," pp. 137–38, 230–31; Warren *Bankruptcy,* p. 39; *P. P. F. Degrand's Boston Weekly Report,* Jan.–Mar. 1824, passim; Boston *Independent Microscope,* Sept. 19, 1823. Theron Metcalf, ed., *The General Laws of Massachusetts 1822–1835* (Boston, 1827), III, 66–68. Over the years various Republicans had been far more conspicuous than any Federalists as critics of the system of imprisonment.

In 1825 William Emmons, who had powerfully expressed the attitudes of traditional and middling-interest Boston in the charter controversy, again raised his gadfly voice against debtors' prison, delivering a conscience-pricking harangue to clergymen, political leaders, and the rich: *An Address to the Clergy, Legislature, and Wealthy Citizens, on Imprisoning the Unfortunate Debtor* (Boston, 1824). The next year, Emmons delivered an oration at Bunker Hill the evening before Daniel Webster gave his great speech at that commemoration, and at the end of an otherwise historical speech about the Revolutionary battle Emmons burst out with a passionate denunciation of imprisonment for debt, deploring particularly the incarceration of "aged fathers," especially Revolutionary veterans in jail for debt. *An Address in Commemoration of the Battle of Bunker Hill . . . Delivered on the Evening of June 16th, 1825 . . .* (Boston, 1825). Tracts containing legal and other arguments against the practice continued to appear: e.g., Thomas Hertell, *Remarks on the Law of Imprisonment for Debt: Showing Its Unconstitutionality and Its Demoralizing Influence on the Community* (Boston, 1825).

60. Nantucket *Inquirer,* quoted in *Howard Gazette,* Mar. 20, 1824. Though the *Gazette* bore down hard on lawyers (e.g., Feb. 14, Mar. 20), it nevertheless endorsed the six Republican nominees for state senate for Suffolk, four of whom were attorneys, Mar. 27, 1824. A splinter movement in 1823 in Hampshire County had already raised an anti-elite, anticonspiratorial, and antilawyer cry, calling for candidates for the senate to be taken "from the plough, the shop, or the store," but not from the bar. Northampton *Hampshire Gazette,* Apr. 2, 1823; see also Joseph Lyman, Northampton, 27 Mar. 1823, to T. H. Perkins, Otis Papers.

61. Arthur B. Darling, *Political Changes in Massachusetts, 1824–1848: A Study of Liberal Movements in Politics* (New Haven, 1925), p. 42; Morison, *Harrison Gray Otis,* II, 245–51.

62. On the river improvement, see Boston *Courier,* Mar. 16, 1826. The Northampton *Hampshire Gazette* presented Lincoln's name as "Nominated by members of the "Legislature," and Hubbard and the rest as "Other nominations," on Mar. 29, 1826. The *Patriot,* Feb. 26, 1826, labeled Lincoln's a "Republican nomination." On Federal support for Hubbard, see *Courier,* Mar. 24, 1826, and *Palladium,* Mar. 31, 1826. On Republican comment, see *Statesman,* Mar. 16, Apr. 6, 1826, and Boston *Independent Chronicle,* Apr. 8, 1826. The *Statesman* tried to give an appearance of electioneering but finally complained of apathy, on Mar. 9, 21, 23, 28, Apr. 1, 1826. On attitudes in the west, see Greenfield *Gazette,* Apr. 11, 1826, and *Hampshire Gazette,* Apr. 25, 1827. Hubbard became a member of Park Street Church in 1821 and was also a trustee of the Andover Theological School: Elizabeth Greene Buck, "Hon. Samuel Hubbard, LL.D.," *Memorial Biographies,* I, 86–99.

63. The account here is based heavily on Whitehill, *Boston,* pp. 47–91, which is indispensable for understanding the background of the bridge controversy, though it contains, ironically, almost nothing about the Warren Bridge matter.

64. Ibid., pp. 51–52, 76, 78, 85–88, 90–91; Stanley I. Kutler, *Privilege and Creative Destruction: The Charles River Bridge Case* (Philadelphia, 1971), pp. 19–20; Snow, *History of Boston,* pp. 327, 330, 332–35.

65. Quoted in Whitehill, *Boston,* p. 92.

66. During the first six months of 1829, after the new bridge went into operation, the old bridge's receipts fell by nearly $9,000 from an intake of $15,000 for a comparable period in 1828. Kutler, *Privilege and Creative Destruction,* pp. 19, 35, 75.

67. The Warren Bridge incorporators also included Nathan Tufts, John Cofran, Nathaniel Austin, and Ebenezer Breed. *Laws of the Commonwealth of Massachusetts, 1825–1828,* X, 851, 852, 855. For the business interests and social standing of these men (a point seemingly lost in earlier interpretations of this affair), see Timothy T. Sawyer, *Old Charlestown: Historical, Biographical, Reminiscent* (Boston, 1902), pp. 107, 167–68, 173, 175–78, 217, 219, 220–22, 226, 227, 371, 957–67, 995–96; Thomas Bellows Wyman, *The Genealogies and Estates of Charlestown, in the County of Middlesex and Commonwealth of Massachusetts, 1629–1818,* II (Boston, 1879), 129–31, 870; *A Century of Banking in Historic Charlestown, 1825–1925* (Boston, 1925), pp. 7, 8, 17, 19, 21.

A recent social history of Charlestown has stressed that the Warren Bridge was a Charlestown enterprise, the struggle over which united much of the town: James Gillespie Blaine II, "The Birth of a Neighborhood: Nineteenth-Century Charlestown, Massachusetts" (Ph.D. diss., University of Michigan, 1978), pp. 44, 46.

68. *Statesman,* Apr. 1, 1826. This editorial concentrated on the alleged dealings of the "FIFTY ASSOCIATES" who manipulated city real estate to their own advantage, who had lobbied to repeal the law against excessive interest or usury, and who now controlled immense amounts of bank capital.

69. Whitehill, *Boston,* p. 76.

70. *An Appeal to the Good Sense of the Legislature* (Boston, 1825), pp. 4, 19–20. This pamphlet, probably written by Henshaw, repeated arguments from newspapers and drew an analogy between bridge ownership and the monopolistic control of banking which once existed and was "broken down by the republicans . . . in 1811" (p. 3). "Instruction" from Faneuil Hall meetings was in fact not legally binding: Ernst, *Constitutional History of Boston,* p. 111.

71. Darling, *Political Changes,* p. 49, n. 22, listed the individuals involved with Henshaw in the Boston Free Bridge Corporation. Former Middling Interest men were among those associated with the enterprise. Riddell, "Charles Ewer," p. 116.

72. *Review of the Case of the Free Bridge, between Boston and Charlestown* (Boston, 1827). For emphasis on the tolls as the heart of the matter, see the letter of William Austin, Boston *Patriot,* Apr. 3, 1827. Awareness of the old bridge's profits was widespread and well acknowledged. See Northampton *Hampshire Gazette,* Mar. 14, 1827; Kutler, *Privilege and Creative Destruction,* pp. 19–25. The Charlestown petitioners had allies in Boston among like-minded entrepreneurs and probably also among master builders and carpenters and shipbuilders. Some of the men associated with free bridges were precisely those aroused by the "ten-footer" law, and at least one Free Bridge candidate was a master ship carpenter, employing men in shipyards and looking to gain cheaper lumber and supplies from the hinterland through reduced transportation cost.

73. Handlin and Handlin, *Commonwealth,* p. 150; Kutler, *Privilege and Creative Destruction,* p. 27. On the day of Lincoln's veto the house voted to override it (99 to 45) but the senate did not manage a two-thirds majority (16 to 12), so the Warren Bridge was again blocked. For old-Federalist approval of Lincoln's veto, see Leverett Saltonstall, Salem, 10 May 1827, to Levi Lincoln, and Daniel A. White, 14 Mar. 1827, to L. L., Lincoln Papers, MHi.

74. In Suffolk County four different tickets of state-senate candidates confronted the voters. *Palladium,* Mar. 27, Apr. 3, 1827. The emergence of the various factions and the maneuvering of Henshaw may be traced in the *Statesman,* Mar. 10, 13, 15, 17, 20, 22, 24, 27, 29, 31, 1827. The Boston *Courier* backed the "Federal Republican"

ticket and accused Henshaw of inconsistency, on Mar. 26, 29, 1827. The four tickets of six candidates each overlapped, and there were actually seventeen candidates in all. *Statesman,* Apr. 3, and *Courier,* Apr. 2.

75. Huge majorities came in from Charlestown and towns in its vicinity:

| | Jarvis | Lincoln | Scattering |
|---|---|---|---|
| Charlestown | 962 | 53 | 35 |
| Medford | 210 | 2 | 2 |
| Woburn | 203 | 3 | 4 |
| Malden | 194 | 21 | 1 |
| Reading | 185 | 1 | 3 |

76. *Patriot,* May 8, 16, 18, 30, 1827; *Courier,* May 9, 1827; *Statesman,* May 10, 12, 14, 17, 19 1827. For a vivid description of the first four tickets in the field for the second election see William Lloyd Garrison, Boston, May 7, 1827, to the editor of the Newburyport *Herald,* in Walter M. Merrill, ed., *The Letters of William Lloyd Garrison,* I (Cambridge, Mass., 1971), 42.

77. Regarding Henshaw's congressional run, see "Member of Congress," July 24, 1827, Broadside, Rare Book Room, Boston Public Library, and L. Garrison, Boston, 26 July 1827, to the editor of the Newburyport *Herald,* in Merrill, ed., *Letters of Garrison,* I, 58. For a redefinition of the Union party, the precursor of the National Republicans, see David Lee Child, Boston, 24 May 1827, to Levi Lincoln, Lincoln Papers, MHi; D. L. Child, 21 July 1827, notice of meeting to Ebenezer Clough, Custom House, Rare Book Room, Boston Public Library; *Palladium,* Apr. 20, 24, May 15, 18, 1827; William Emmons, *An Oration on Bunker Hill Battle, Delivered . . . 11th June 1827, Together with a Caucus Speech . . . May 9th* (Boston, 1827), pp. 15–16.

78. The quotation is from Salsbury, *Boston & Albany,* pp. 80–81. This account relies heavily on ibid., pp. 31–81. Salsbury judged the Charles River Bridge episode to be in the long run a blessing in disguise for potential railroad investors. On the consensus in Boston on state aid, see Handlin and Handlin, *Commonwealth,* pp. 172–73. In the state-senate election Nathan Hale as a National Republican defeated the Jacksonian Republican David Henshaw, but both supported railroads. Mayor Harrison Gray Otis was a strong backer of railroads. Quincy, *Municipal History,* pp. 280–89. And most of Boston's papers had railroad fever, e.g., Boston *Columbian Centinel,* Feb. 7, 11, 14, 21, 25, Mar. 7, 18, 1829. The National Republicans of Boston made the railroad cause their own, calling their 1829 nominees the "PEOPLE'S TICKET AND RAILROAD TICKET" and featuring a picture of a horse drawn train. *Centinel,* Apr. 4, 1829.

79. There is no doubt that the railroad hurt the Middlesex Canal, which had been paying dividends (for the first time) through the 1820s. The drop in the canal's tolls was immediate in 1835–1836, and it went out of business in the 1840s. Some of the canal's owners, however, were involved with the railroads and factories; in 1846 the largest shareholder was Abbot Lawrence. Christopher Roberts, *The Middlesex Canal, 1793–1860* (Cambridge, Mass., 1938), pp. 170–71, 224, 227.

80. Contemporaries believed the railroad question had strongly affected representative elections: *Hampshire Gazette,* May 12, 1830. Charles Francis Adams reluctantly attended Boston town meetings which discussed railroads on July 12 and August 2, 1830, and both times came away disgusted: "The people were not overmuch disposed to hear those in opposition. . . . A Town Meeting is no place to hear argument or attempt discussion. And when a people are taken with such schemes as these, they will often be led, by very inconsiderable persons." Marc Friedlander and L. H. Butterfield, eds., *Diary of Charles Francis Adams,* III (Cambridge, Mass., 1968), 292.

## IX. Antimasons and Masons

1. Mill, *The Spirit of the Age,* ed. Frederick A. von Hayek (Chicago, 1942), pp. 7, 18.

2. Whitney R. Cross, *The Burned-Over District: The Social and Intellectual History of Enthusiastic Religion in Western New York, 1800–1850* (Ithaca, 1950), pp. 113–25; Lee Benson, *The Concept of Jacksonian Democracy: New York as a Test Case* (Princeton, 1961), pp. 15–17; James S. Chase, *The Emergence of the National Nominating Convention, 1789–1832* (Urbana, 1973), pp. 121–36; Michael F. Holt, "The Antimasonic and Know Nothing Parties," in Arthur M. Schlesinger, Jr., ed., *History of U.S. Political Parties,* I (New York, 1973), 575–620; Ronald P. Formisano with Kathleen Smith Kutolowski, "Antimasonry and Masonry: The Genesis of Protest, 1826–1827," *American Quarterly,* 29 (1977), 139–65.

3. These statements are based primarily on Dorothy Ann Lipson, *Freemasonry in Federalist Connecticut, 1789–1835* (Princeton, 1977); John F. Kutolowski and Kathleen S. Kutolowski, "Commissions and Canvasses: The Militia and Politics in Western New York, 1800–1845," *New York History,* 63 (1982):5–38; and my study of Masons in Rochester, New York, and Massachusetts.

4. On Isaiah Thomas's Masonic activities, see Benjamin Thomas Hill, ed., *The Diary of Isaiah Thomas, 1805–1828,* Transactions and Collections of the American Antiquarian Society, vols. 9 and 10 (Worcester, 1909), I, ix; [F. A. Currier] *Thomas Royal Arch Chapter: Historical* (Fitchburg, 1909?); and J. Hugo Tatsch, "Isaiah Thomas, Printer, Patriot, Freemason," *Grand Lodge Bulletin, Iowa Masonic Library,* 30 (1929), 74–80. The 1827 numbers are from *House Documents, 1834,* no. 73. In Worcester, Masons tended to belong to the Unitarian Church, and Thomas said of the church in 1829: "Many of our members stand high in the community. . . ." I. Thomas, Cincinnati, 4 July 1829, to E. D. Bangs, Thomas Papers, MWA.

5. In 1807 William Bentley saw no particular political ties among Masons, *The Diary of William Bentley,* III (Salem, Mass., 1911), 300. Caleb Cushing, recently elected to the state legislature and already planning to run for Congress, gave a Masonic address at Lynn, June 24, 1826. Claude M. Fuess, *The Life of Caleb Cushing* (New York, 1923), I, 71; Cushing's "cast of mind" in several respects epitomized that of men attracted to Masonry. In Pittsfield the Masons seem to have been mostly Federal, and were also involved in the Washington Benevolent Society. Joseph Edward Adams Smith, *The History of Pittsfield, Massachusetts, from the Year 1800 to the Year 1876* (Springfield, Mass., 1876), p. 9.

6. On Masons' drinking, see Bentley, *Diary,* II, 403; George S. Hilliard, ed., *Memoir and Correspondence of Jeremiah Mason* (Cambridge, Mass., 1873), pp. 24–25.

7. A description of Worcester Mason's processions on Washington's death is in Annie Russell Marble, *From 'Prentice to Patron: The Life Story of Isaiah Thomas* (New York, 1935), pp. 240–41. The Reverend Bentley was a Mason and described the order's place in public ceremonies in 1800. *Diary,* II, 325, 326, 329, 337, 359; see also Nathaniel Saltonstall, 11 June 1803, to Leverett Saltonstall, in Robert E. Moody, ed., *The Saltonstall Papers, 1607–1815,* II (Boston, 1974), 151. In 1821 a Haverhill editor avowed himself a Mason and said he hoped for a share of the fraternity's patronage; see Haverhill *Essex Patriot,* Feb. 24, 1821. For extracts from or descriptions of minister's sermons praising Masonry, see *Independent Bostonian,* July 20, 1822, Mar. 22, 1823; Concord *Gazette and Yeoman,* Mar. 13, 1824; and Greenfield *Gazette,* June 29, 1824. On Masonry's growth, see John Abbott, *An Address Delivered before the Grand Lodge of Massachusetts, at the Annual Communication, December, 1826* (Cambridge, Mass., 1826), pp. 7–8; and *Centennary of Olive Branch Lodge, Mill-*

*bury, Mass., 1897* (Millbury, 1897?), p. 42. By 1824 even the Quakers of New Bedford seemed to enjoy the Masons' "grand holiday." Pease, ed., *Diary of Joseph R. Anthony,* p. 90.

8. The quotation is from David Ludlum, *Social Ferment in Vermont, 1791–1850* (New York, 1939), p. 94. Antimasons soon pointed to the same fact, complaining that many pious men "have opened the door [of the church], and have helped in the evil with their own hands." Boston *Anti-Masonic Free Press,* Aug. 22, 1828.

9. The first quotation is from Rev. Cheever Felch, *An Address Delivered before Mount Carmel Lodge, at Lynn, June, 1821, on the Anniversary of St. John the Baptist* (Boston, 1822), p. 4; see also Rev. Thaddeus M. Harris, *A Discourse Delivered at Marblehead June 24, 1822, before the Philanthropic Lodge* (Cambridge, Mass., 1822); (Rev.) Paul Dean, *An Address at the Consecration of Mount Hope Lodge, Sept. 1, 1825* (Boston, 1825); Benjamin Huntoon and Paul Dean, *Masonic Discourses Delivered on the Festival of St. John the Baptist, June 24, 1823* (Boston, 1823). Rev. Benjamin Wood, quotation of remarks at Holden, June 24, 1825, in the Rochester *Craftsman,* Mar. 24, 1829.

10. Caleb Cushing, *An Address Delivered at Lynn, before the Associated Lodges of Salem, Lynn, Marblehead, Danvers, and Beverly: On the Festival of St. John, June 24, 1826* (Newburyport, 1826), p. 27. In 1826 a Baptist minister told Lowell Masons that while Freemasonry "most *reverentially bows* to the pure and spiritual religion of Jesus Christ, and claims only the relationship of an handmaid; [yet] she occupies an elevated stand, and holds the *key-stone* of an arch far above any mere literary or political establishment." Charles Otis Kimball, *The Claims of Free-Masonry: An Address Delivered at the Consecration and Installation of the Mount Horeb Royal Arch Chapter in Lowell, Mass., August 31, 1826* (Boston, 1827), p. 4.

11. *Proceedings of the Grand Lodge of Massachusetts, Ancient Free and Accepted Masons, 1815 to 1825,* pp. 485–95, quotations from pp. 487, 488.

12. Formisano and Kutolowski, "Antimasonry and Masonry."

13. Early notices of the New York events appeared in, e.g., Northampton *Hampshire Gazette,* Mar. 14, 21, 28, Apr. 11, 1827; for an attempt to mislead, see Boston *Statesman,* Mar. 22, 1827. Boston *Anti-Masonic Free Press,* Aug. 8, Oct. 24, 1828. On August 22 the *Free Press* observed that no Antimasonic books could be obtained in Boston and that they would sell quickly if available. The New-Bedford *Mercury* seemed sincerely to wish to remain neutral, Jan. 16, Apr. 10, 1829. In Fall River the National Republican paper opposed Antimasonry early and backed the Masons; see D. Hamilton Hurd, comp., *History of Bristol County, Massachusetts* (Philadelphia, 1883), pp. 332–33. Printed material also came in from New York, especially Henry Dana Ward's journal, *The Anti-Masonic Review* (New York, 1828). According to the *Free Press,* Oct. 19, 1831, four of Boston's six daily papers were edited by Masons, and a fifth had a "high masonic tone." For other Antimasonic comments on the press, see John B. Turner, Scituate, 29 Nov. 1832, to Samuel Breck, Esq., Plymouth "We the People" Papers, MWA; [George Allen, Jr.], *Thoughts on 'The Excitement' in Reply to a Letter to Hon. Edward Everett* (Worcester, 1833), pp. 20–21; A Freeman, *An Address to the Freemen of Massachusetts* (Worcester, 1832).

14. Antimasons made frequent efforts to prove that Illuminism and Masonry were connected. James C. Odiorne, ed., *Opinions on Speculative Masonry* (Boston, 1830), pp. 43–58; *Brief Report of the Debates in the Anti-Masonic State Convention of the Commonwealth of Massachusetts . . . December 30, 31, 1829, and January 1, 1830* (Boston, 1830), pp. 180–87; [Allen], *Thoughts on 'The Excitement,'* pp. 33–34; Boston *Masonic Mirror,* Nov. 14, Dec. 5, 1929. But this did not mean that one had led to the other.

15. Alonzo Lewis, *The History of Lynn, Including Nahant* (Boston, 1844), pp.

246–47. On January 15 a convention at Reading declared Masonry "hostile to our civil and religious institutions." Rev. P[eter] Sanborn, *Address, Delivered before the Antimasonic Convention of Reading, Mass., January 15, 1829* (Boston, 1829), p. 3.

16. Boston *Anti-Masonic Free Press,* Aug. 28, 1829, gave a list of organizers and the Suffolk Committee; the meeting and Walker's speech were also summarized in the Boston *Columbian Centinel,* Aug. 29, 1829; also *Anti-Masonic Free Press,* Oct. 2, 1829.

17. *Centinel,* Sept. 12, 1829; *Anti-Masonic Free Press,* Sept. 18, 1829; Odiorne, ed., *Opinions on Masonry,* p. 142; the handbill was quoted in Greene's highly charged account of the event, *The Broken Seal: or, Personal Reminiscences of the Morgan Abduction and Murder* (Boston, 1870), pp. 160–64; see also *Anti-Masonic Tract No. 4* (Boston, 1829), at Olin Library, Cornell University. Even Boston's Masonic newspaper reported that hissing and shouting had made it impossible for Greene to speak, and that several pro-Masonic speakers had held forth uninterrupted. *Masonic Mirror,* Sept. 12, 1829.

18. Antimasonry gained few prominent converts. The exceptions included Frederick A. Sumner, sheriff of Suffolk County, and Pliny Merrick of Worcester (a young lawyer with a prominent father), who renounced the order. Both Masons and Antimasons made much of Merrick's reversal, which underlines the point that such converts were few. Sumner's public letter of Oct. 19, 1829, was one of the milder statements of Antimasonry: *Sheriff Sumner's Letter on Speculative Masonry* (Boston, 1832). Antimasons admitted that they lacked "great men." Lynn *Record,* Dec. 15, 1830.

19. See especially Abner Phelps et al., Suffolk Committee, "Circular" to Fellow Citizens [1830], and "Worcester County Convention, November 6, 1829," in Merrick Papers, MWA.

20. *Report of the Debates in the Anti-Masonic State Convention, 1829–1830; An Abstract of the Proceedings of the Anti-Masonic State Convention of Massachusetts . . . Dec. 30 and 31, 1829, and Jan. 1, 1830* (Boston, 1830), contains the committee reports which the *Report of the Debates* does not; *Masonic Mirror,* Jan. 2, 1830.

21. *Anti-Masonic Free Press,* Mar. 5, 1830 (later called just the *Free Press*). For Antimasonry's treatment in the press, see *Free Press,* Sept. 18, 1829; *Masonic Mirror,* Dec. 29, 1829; and Boston *Evening Transcript,* on May 12, 1831. Antimasons keenly felt the need for a daily press in the early stages; see *Free Press,* Mar. 19, 1830, and Amasa Walker, Boston, 3 May 1830, to Pliny Merrick, Merrick Papers. A former Batavia, New York, editor published an Antimasonic paper in Fall River for about a year in 1830–1831. Hurd, comp., *Bristol,* p. 334.

22. S. D. Greene, Boston, 15 Apr. 1830, to Pliny Merrick, Merrick Papers; F. W. Gale, Marlborough, 16 July 1830, to Andrew J. Davis, Leicester, July 16, 1830, Gale Papers, MWA; during a speech by Amasa Walker at Stoughton, Masons fired cannon to engulf the meeting in noise and smoke, Lynn *Record,* July 10, 1830; *Free Press,* May 28, 1830; *Masonic Mirror,* June 12, 1830. On the Faneuil Hall meeting, the Boston *Courier,* Aug. 28, 1830, said 3,000 turned out in bad weather; *Free Press,* Sept. 3, 9, 31, 1830; *Mirror,* Sept. 4, 18, 1830; for a full report of the subsequent correspondence between the Antimasons and Otis, see Lynn *Record,* Oct. 6, 1830; Rochester (New York) *Anti-Masonic Enquirer,* Sept. 21, 1830. On Springfield, see *Mirror,* Sept. 18, 1830; for a later summary of the major "Masonic riots," see *Record,* Mar. 6, 1833.

23. For the armory story, see *Free Press,* Mar. 5, 1830; *Mirror,* Mar. 20, May 8, Aug. 21, 1830. Other examples are in [Henry Gassett], *Catalogue of Books on the Masonic Institution: Antimasonic, 1852* (Boston, 1852), pp. 5–9; Abner Phelps, Bos-

ton, 23 July 1830, to Pliny Merrick, Worcester, and George Odiorne, Boston, 15 Mar. 1830, to P. Merrick, Merrick Papers; Rochester *Anti-Masonic Enquirer,* Mar. 30, Apr. 6, 1830.

24. Darling, *Political Changes,* p. 91; Charles McCarthy, "The Antimasonic Party," *Annual Report of the American Historical Association, 1902,* I, 515–16; *The Proceedings of the United States Anti-Masonic Convention, Held at Philadelphia, September 11, 1830* (Philadelphia, 1830), p. 71, regarding Bristol County. By 1830 county and some town committees existed in Plymouth and Norfolk; see *Free Press,* Mar. 12, Apr. 2, 1830. Three of the five Middlesex Antimasonic nominations were also the National Republican nominees, as were four of the five in Worcester. On organization in Worcester County, see *Free Press,* Mar. 19, 26, Apr. 2, 1830, and Onslow Peters, Westboro', 18 Mar. 1830, to P. Merrick, Merrick Papers. Also, *An Abstract of the Proceedings of the Antimasonic State Convention of Massachusetts, Held in Franeuil Hall, Boston, May 19 & 20, 1831* (Boston, 1831); Lynn *Record,* Mar. 20, 27, 1830. F. A. Sumner, Boston, 10 Mar. 1829, to Levi Lincoln; C. P. Sumner, Boston, 12 Mar. 1829, to L. Lincoln, with copy of letter, Asaph Churchill, Milton, Mar. 1829, to C. P. Sumner; and L. Lincoln, Worcester, 13 Mar. 1829, to Charles P. Sumner, Lincoln Papers, MHi. Abner Phelps, Boston, 6 July 1830, to P. Merrick, Merrick Papers.

25. Amasa Walker, Boston, 9 Feb. 1830, to P. Merrick, Merrick Papers, discussed the need for a press and for delay in "carrying this question to the Ballot Boxes." On the Committee of 100, see *Free Press,* Feb. 12, 1830, and A. Walker, Boston, 25 Feb. 1830, to P. Merrick, and George Odiorne, Boston, 15 Mar. 1830, to P. Merrick, Merrick Papers.

26. *Masonic Mirror,* Mar. 27, 1830; Amasa Walker, Boston 30 June 1830, to P. Merrick, Merrick Papers. The quotations are from Jonathan Torrey, Dexter Munger, and Bela Bennett, Monson, 19 July 1830, to P. Merrick, Merrick Papers; and *Free Press,* Apr. 9, 1830.

27. Benjamin F. Hallett, Providence, 23 Dec. 1830, to P. Merrick, Merrick Papers.

28. On planning for the national convention, see Abner Phelps, Boston, 6 July 1830, to P. Merrick, Merrick Papers. On the congressional planning, see *Free Press,* Oct. 22, Nov. 5, 1830. On New York elections, see Amasa Walker, Boston, 6 Dec. 1830, to P. Merrick, Merrick Papers. On politics, see *Free Press,* Mar. 16, 23, 30, Apr. 13, May 4, 11, 18, 1830; Circular Letter, 2 Apr. 1831, "Anti-Masonry in Boston, 1831," in Politics in Boston Collection, Widener Library, Harvard University.

29. *Abstract of Proceedings of the Antimasonic State Convention, 1831,* p. 63.

30. *Free Press,* June 22, 1831; *Abstract of Proceedings of the Antimasonic State Convention, 1831,* pp. 32–33. *Adams Memoirs,* VIII, 400–401. In August, Adams told a Clay National Republican that the National Republican caucus had erred last winter in nominating Clay and that "they had further kicked and buffeted the Antimasonic party till it was impossible they should support Mr. Clay." On Clay's unacceptability, see Amasa Walker, Boston, 6 Dec. 1830, to P. Merrick, Merrick Papers. Some Antimasons, however, wanted somehow to hold on to Clay. Lynn *Record,* Nov. 3, 24, 1830.

31. Abner Phelps et al., Boston, 6 Sept. 1831, to L. Lincoln, Lincoln Papers, MHi.

32. Levi Lincoln, Worcester, 13 Sept. 1831, to A. Phelps, G. Odiorne et al., Lincoln Papers; A. Phelps, Boston 8 Sept., 1831, to P. Merrick, Merrick Papers. Some National Republicans tried to heal the breach: A. H. Everett, Boston, 23 Oct. 1831, to John Bailey, Washburn Collection, 20, MHi; see also, George Hubbard Blakeslee, "The History of the Anti-Masonic Party" (Ph.D. diss., Harvard University, 1903), chap. 7 and pp. 27–28. Blakeslee's work deals with Massachusetts.

33. Lathrop's maneuvers are described in several letters to John Brazer Davis, including, George Bliss, Springfield, 12 Oct. 1831, to J.B.D.; Samuel Bowles, Spring-

field, 27 Oct. 1831, to J.B.D.; and Caleb Rice, W. Springfield, 27 Oct. 1831, to J.B.D., in "Letters to John Brazer Davis, 1819–1831," *Massachusetts Historical Society Proceedings,* 49 (1916), 240–41, 243, 242. Lathrop had spent several terms in the state senate and four consecutive terms in Congress (1819–1827), and had most recently been president of the state senate in 1829 and 1831.

34. The 1831 fall vote for lieutenant governor indicated that Antimasonic votes came heavily from National Republicans:

| | Antimasonic | Nat. Rep. | Jack Rep. |
|---|---|---|---|
| Governor | 13,357 | 28,804 | 10,975 |
| Lieutenant Governor | – | 39,820 | 11,416 |

The Antimasons had nominated the National Republican candidate for lieutenant governor.

35. The counties with the six highest Antimasonic percentages were:

| | | | | | |
|---|---|---|---|---|---|
| Hampshire | 52.3 | 1,377 | Norfolk | 40.5 | 1,925 |
| Franklin | 48.2 | 1,431 | Plymouth | 30.6 | 1,026 |
| Bristol | 40.5 | 2,406 | Worcester | 24.5 | 1,831 |

36. *Proceedings of the Most Worshipful Grand Lodge of Ancient Free and Accepted Masons of the Commonwealth of Massachusetts, 1826–1844* (Boston, 1928?), p. 139; Gustavus F. Davis, *Free-Masonry an Honourable Institution: An Address, Delivered in Haverhill, Mass., before the Northern Association of the Second Masonic district, at the Festival of John the Baptist, June 25, 1827* (Boston, 1827). (Davis was the Baptist pastor in the town of South Reading.) DeWitt Clinton's death occasioned a Grand Royal Arch ceremony in Boston, *Centinel,* June 24, 1828, reported in Boston *Aramanth,* July 1828, 1, no. 4, and Aug., no. 5; announcement of Grand Lodge officers for the year, *Centinel,* Jan. 10, 1829. Some local lodges soon became inactive, while others did so at various times during the next several years, and still others never completely ceased to function, though most curtailed activities in some way. There is, of course, a problem in discovering the full extent of Masonic activity, since some of it now became covert. The published history of Worcester's Morning Star Lodge said that the business of the lodge suddenly ceased in June 1828: Edward S. Nason, *A Centennial History of Morning Star Lodge, 1793–1893* (Worcester, 1894), pp. 46–47. C. C. Baldwin recorded in his diary on January 30, 1830: "Annual meeting of Morning Star Lodge. Have a Full meeting. Otis Corbett made master." Nathaniel Paine, ed., *Diary of Christopher Columbus Baldwin, Librarian of the American Antiquarian Society, 1829–1835,* Transactions and Collections of the American Antiquarian Society, vol. 8 (Worcester, 1901), 43–44. Rural Lodge of Quincy decided to suspend meetings indefinitely in 1834, not resuming until 1853; see *By-Laws of Rural Lodge, of Ancient Free and Accepted Masons, 1861* (Boston, 1862), pp. 49–51. Olive Branch Lodge in Millbury curtailed activities and then resumed full operation in 1839; see *Centennary Olive Branch Lodge,* pp. 42–44.

37. The first quotation is from Paul Dean, *A Discourse Delivered before Constellation Lodge, and the Associate Lodges, Assembled at Dedham, Mass., June 24, 1829* (Boston, 1829), p. 16; Nahum Capen, *An Address Delivered before Constellation Lodge, and the Associated Lodges, Assembled at Dedham, Mass., June 24, 1829* (Boston, 1829), p. 32. In a similar vein is William Hilliard, *Address Delivered at the Annual Visitation of Amicable Lodge, in Cambridge, Mass., November 16, 1829* (Cambridge, 1829).

38. Villification of seceded Masons knew almost no limits. The *Masonic Mirror* was perhaps outdone by none in its vehemence against seceders, e.g., Jan. 9, July 31, 1830; see also *Strictures on Seceding Masons: With Reviews of the Anti-Masonic*

*Characters of Pliny Merrick, Esq., . . .* (Boston, 1830). Pressure against seceders is described in N. D. Strong, Hartford, 28 Jan. 1830, to Pliny Merrick, Merrick Papers. Several anonymous letters to Pliny Merrick were of the poison-pen variety, e.g., anonymous, 4 Jan. 1830, to Col. Pliny "Physick" Merrick. Antimasonic printed sources are also revealing, e.g., Pliny Merrick's letter to the Worcester County Convention, 1830, in Odiorne, ed., *Opinions on Masonry,* p. 88; and *Rev. H. Tatem's Reply to the Summons of the R.I. Royal Arch Chapter* (Providence, 1832).

39. *Masonic Mirror,* July 4, 11, 1829. *The Aramanth: or Masonic Garland* (Boston), 1, nos. 1–3 (Apr.–Aug. 1828), 2, no. 1 (Apr. 1829).

40. Joseph Jenkins, *An Address Delivered before the Grand Lodge of Massachusetts, December 28, 1829* (Boston, 1830).

41. *Proceedings of the Grand Lodge, 1826–1844,* pp. 193–98, 218; *Masonic Mirror,* Oct. 23, 1830; *Grand Lodge of the Most Ancient and Honorable Fraternity of Free and Accepted Masons of the Commonwealth of Massachusetts* (Boston, 1834), Widener Library, Harvard University; Isaiah Thomas, Worcester, 12 Oct. 1830, to Thomas Power, Boston, Letterbook 1828–1831, and clippings from *Massachusetts Spy,* Apr. 4, 1831, Isaiah Thomas Papers, MWA. *Adams Memoirs,* VIII, 379.

42. The declaration was bound in the *Masonic Mirror.* Charles W. Moore, former editor of the *Bostonian and Mechanics' Journal,* was the author: *Centennial Memorial: The Lodge of Saint Andrew, and the Massachusetts Grand Lodge* (Boston, 1870), p. 128.

43. Asahael Huntington, Salem, 29 Oct. 1831, to John B. Davis, in "Letters to John Brazer Davis," p. 246.

44. According to one observer, Masons voted with the Jacksonians in Bristol County but elsewhere with the Nationals: Charles T. Congdon, *Reminiscences of a Journalist* (Boston, 1880), p. 30. In Lynn, Antimasons and Nationals allied closely: Lynn *Record,* Feb. 20, Mar. 6, 1830. Regarding Plymouth, see *Adams Memoirs,* VIII, 239–43, 245–47; but for a view of Masons controlling state-senate nominations in Plymouth, see [Col. John B. Turner], "Plymouth County, for the Free Press," in Plymouth "We the People" Papers, MWA. Some Antimasons believed that Masonic electoral activity would rebound against the fraternity as it had in New York: Amasa Walker, Boston, 11 Mar. 1830, to P. Merrick, Worcester, and Henry Dana Ward, New York, 10 Nov., 1830, to P.M., Merrick Papers. But compare *Adams Memoirs,* VIII, 326.

45. *Masonic Mirror,* Feb. 20, 1830; Paul Dean, *An Address Delivered before the Boston Encampment of the Knights Templars, Feb. 28, 1832* (Boston, 1832), pp. 7–8.

46. Dean, *Election Sermon, 1832,* pp. 29–30; Dean's choice was probably a victory also for the friends of disestablishment, since he had long supported separation of government and religion. One Antimason alleged that the 1832 National Republican state convention at Worcester had chosen at least eight of thirteen presidential electors who were known Masons and that the Worcester County Convention had put up five of six senatorial candidates who were Masons: Elijah W. Brigham, Worcester, 15 Oct. 1832, to Thomas W. Ward, Shrewsbury, Ward Family Papers, MWA.

47. Henry Clay had shrewdly observed as early as 1830 that "whenever Anti-Masonry is in the minority, it will seek a connection with any other party, which . . . is also in the minority . . . for the natural tendency of all divisions of a minority, is to cohesion." Henry Clay, Ashland, 24 Nov. 1830, to John Bailhache, in Calvin Colton, ed., *The Works of Henry Clay: Comprising His Life, Correspondence and Speeches* (New York, 1904), IV, 289. This process was delayed in Massachusetts, however, for several reasons. The Jacksonian or Democratic Republicans sought to cultivate the Masons as soon as the controversy arose, and were naturally encouraged in this by the Masons in their ranks, among whom was David Henshaw. *Free Press,* Feb. 5,

1830; *Statesman,* Nov. 12, 1831; *Record,* Apr. 10, 1830; *Adams Memoirs,* VIII, 393–94; Boston *Morning Post,* Nov. 9, 12, 1832; Amasa Walker, Boston, 25 Feb. 1830, to P. Merrick, Worcester, Merrick Papers.

48. *Adams Memoirs,* VIII, 416. For National Republican hopes that Antimasons would support Clay, and Adams's doubts, see ibid., pp. 337, 358, 380. The course of the Lynn *Record* from July to November 1830 illustrated the division within Antimasonic ranks. Stephen Oliver assumed the editorship in July and soon began backing Clay and moderating the paper's Antimasonry. In November the proprietor, Jonathan Buffum, dismissed Oliver and took over the paper himself, rejecting Clay as a presidential nominee because he was a Mason and a duelist. See also Merrick Papers, MWA, 1830–31. The Antimasonic Boston *Daily Advocate,* of Benjamin F. Hallett, in 1832 supported National Republican policies while disassociating them from Clay and backing Wirt, July 6, 1832. Wirt had most recently been involved in national affairs as a humanitarian defender of the Cherokee Indians and an opponent of Jackson's Indian policy, an association which made him attractive to the evangelical public: Ronald N. Satz, *American Indian Policy in the Jacksonian Era* (Lincoln, 1975), pp. 40–42.

49. Boston *Daily Advocate,* Aug. 9, Sept. 25, Oct. 5, 1832. "Circular. To the Friends of Wirt and Ellmaker and Lathrop and Fuller, and to all friends of their country, who prefer William Wirt to Andrew Jackson." Nov. 1832, *Daily Advocate* file, MWA. When in August 1832 John Quincy Adams was urged to reconcile the National Republicans and Antimasons, he replied that the National Republicans had mismanaged the situation and that while ignoring "certain offenses" by Masons in another state they "have for two years past taken most especial care to turn out of office every Anti-Mason upon whom they could lay their hands, all the while, bitterly complaining of the persecuting and proscriptive Spirit of political Anti-Masonry." J.Q.A., Quincy, 18 Aug. 1832, to Alexander H. Everett, Boston, in Andrew C. McLaughlin, ed., "Letters of John Quincy Adams to Alexander Hamilton Everett, 1811–1837," *American Historical Review,* 11 (1906), 343–44.

50. Darling, *Political Changes,* pp. 104–5.

51. Lathrop's strength in 1832 ranked by percentage as follows:

| | | | | | |
|---|---|---|---|---|---|
| Hampshire Co. | 50.8 | 1,571 | Plymouth Co. | 29.8 | 1,256 |
| Bristol Co. | 49.5 | 2,255 | Worcester Co. | 19.7 | 2,208 |
| Franklin Co. | 42.0 | 1,418 | Middlesex Co. | 17.9 | 1,506 |
| Norfolk Co. | 40.7 | 1,904 | | | |

52. Daniel Webster, Washington, 8 Jan. 1833, to Levi Lincoln, Lincoln Papers, MHi; see also George Ticknor Curtis, *Life of Daniel Webster* (New York, 1898), I, 393–94.

53. B. F. Hallett, Boston, 7 Mar. 1833, to P. Merrick, Merrick Papers; *Record,* Mar. 6, 1833; *Free Press and Boston Weekly Advocate,* Nov. 27, 1833.

54. *Daily Advocate,* Oct. 29, 1833; *Record,* Mar. 13, 1833; Boston *Daily Atlas,* Mar. 2, 1833.

55. *Adams Memoirs,* IX, 71.

56. Adams's early views on the New York events are well developed in: John Quincy Adams, Washington, 6 Dec. 1831, to Levi Lincoln; 18 Dec. 1831, to L.L.; and J.Q.A., 1 Feb. 1832, to L.L., Lincoln Papers, MHi.

57. *Adams Memoirs,* VIII, 535, 538, 539, and IX, 6, 11, 14; J.Q.A., 23 July 1833, to A. H. Everett, in McLaughlin, ed., "Letters of John Quincy Adams," p. 345.

58. The quotations are from *Adams Memoirs,* IX, 19, 20, 28; and Alexander H. Everett, Boston, 11 Oct. 1833, to George Bancroft, Bancroft Papers, MHi. On October 5 Everett told Adams he was thinking of declining re-election to the state sen-

ate, since "the Masonic faction was so strong it was impossible to resist them, and if he should decline he thought he should leave the State." *Adams Memoirs,* IX, 21. For anti-Adams and anti-Antimasonic editorials, see *Daily Atlas,* Sept.–Oct. 1833; and Boston *Courier,* Sept. 26, 1833.

John Davis accepted the nomination most reluctantly (*Diary of Christopher Baldwin,* p. 235) and was chosen probably because he was a prominent public man who had managed to make no enemies on either side of the Masonic-Antimasonic controversy.

59. "Address to the National Republican Electors of the Commonwealth," *Columbian Centinel,* Oct. 19, 1833. Some National papers either ignored the controversy or treated it cautiously, while many others, particularly the Boston *Atlas,* denounced Antimasons and their allies without restraint and insisted that Nationals draw lines between themselves and their enemies. Some local National conventions, too, such as that in Norfolk County, supported the Masons by calling for protection of equal access to jury boxes, to the judiciary, and to church membership. Dedham *Norfolk Advertiser,* Oct. 26, 1833; *Mirror,* Oct. 31, 1829.

60. Darling, *Political Changes,* pp. 113–14; *Post,* Sept. 7, Nov. 6, 9, 1833. The Democratic leader Marcus Morton conceded only the "inutility of speculative Masonry and the injurious tendency of many of its rites and ceremonies," while treating Antimasons coldly and saying he would not make opinions on Masonry "a political test, or the basis of a political party." Marcus Morton, Boston, 14 Mar. 1833, to Abner Phelps, Morton Letterbooks, MHi.

61. Some National Republicans quickly softened their tone toward Antimasonry, e.g., *Centinel,* Nov. 20, 1833.

62. Counties with largest Antimasoic votes, 1833, ranked by percentage and number of votes:

| | | | | |
|---|---|---|---|---|
| Bristol | 51.2 | 2,338 | Middlesex | 3,162 |
| Norfolk | 50.3 | 2,830 | Norfolk | 2,830 |
| Franklin | 44.6 | 1,312 | Bristol | 2,338 |
| Plymouth | 40.8 | 1,893 | Worcester | 2,335 |
| Middlesex | 35.0 | 3,162 | Plymouth | 1,893 |
| Hampshire | 32.5 | 1,023 | Franklin | 1,312 |

63. *Record,* Feb. 5, 1825, attributed the increased vote to Adams. On organization, see Circular Letter from Abner Phelps, Boston, Mar. 25, 1833, in Plymouth "We the People" Papers; Boston *Daily Advocate,* Apr. 1, Nov. 7, 12, 1833. In Plymouth County the Antimasonic paper *We the People* had "scarcely any circulation, the zeal of which was rather to stimulate and exasperate the opposition." *Adams Memoirs,* VIII, 538. In Norfolk County, Antimasons were apparently well organized. Dedham *Norfolk Advertiser,* Oct. 26, Nov. 9, 1833.

64. *Adams Memoirs,* IX, 52, 53, 58–59; John Quincy Adams, Quincy, 24 Sept. 1833, to Alexander H. Everett, in McLaughlin, ed., "Letters of Adams to Everett," p. 346.

65. Boston *Daily Advocate: Extra,* Jan. 1, 1834.

66. *Grand Lodge of Massachusetts, 1834,* pp. 13, 14.

67. *Senate Documents, 1834,* no. 42. *House Documents, 1834, Report by a Joint Committee of the Legislature of Massachusetts on Freemasonry, March, 1834,* no. 73. One of the Antimasonic Petitions appeared as house doc. no. 7, Petition from James Tappan and 63 other Citizens of Gloucester, Mass. See also Boston *Evening Transcript,* Jan. 2, 1834.

68. *Report by a Joint Committee on Freemasonry,* pp. 7–10, "Appendix," pp. 24–

26; Lynn *Record,* Feb. 5, 1834. Cf., William L. Stone, *Letters on Masonry and Antimasonry: Addressed to the Hon. John Quincy Adams* (New York, 1832).

69. *Laws of the Commonwealth of Massachusetts, 1834–1836* (Boston, 1836), XIII, 63, 88–89. The House Judiciary Committee reported out "An Act Concerning Unlawful Oaths," *House Documents, 1834,* no. 7. *Report by a Joint Committee on Freemasonry,* pp. 71–72, 74–76. On Antimasonic skepticism, see *Record,* Feb. 5, 1834. A senate vote on terminating the powers of the Grand Lodge went twenty-five to seven against the Antimasons, and the latter alleged that eleven of those voting against the measure were Masons. Boston *Free Press,* Mar. 5, 1834.

70. *Adams Memoirs,* IX, 103–4. In early January the house had filled all the vacancies in the senate with National Republicans even when Antimasons had carried a plurality of the districts. Ibid., p. 70.

71. *Free Press,* Nov. 27, 1833; Marcus Morton, Taunton, 17 Feb. 1834, to J. K. Simpson, and M. Morton, 20 Feb. 1834, to Jubal Harrington, Esq., Morton Letterbooks, MHi. Some politicians, such as Robert Rantoul, Jr., went along with Antimasonry and bided their time before moving into the Democratic Republican party: Robert D. Bulkley, Jr., "Robert Rantoul, Jr., 1805–1852: Politics and Reform in Antebellum Massachusetts" (Ph.D. diss., Princeton University, 1975), pp. 118–19.

72. *Adams Memoirs,* IX, 71–72. Rufus Choate, Washington, 30 Jan. 1834, to John Davis, Davis Letterbook, vol. I-10, MWA.

73. Rufus Choate, Washington, 9 Feb. 1834, to John Davis, ibid., vol. I-9. One National, who later worked to placate Antimasons, said in 1831 that Antimasonry "will continue to spread until the lodge-charters are surrendured." Samuel Metcalf McKay, Pittsfield, 30 Oct. 1831, to John Brazer Davis, in "Letters to John Brazer Davis," p. 249.

74. David Bradstreet Walker, "Rufus Choate: A Case Study in Old Whiggery," *Essex Institute Historical Collections,* 94 (1958), 338; Daniel Webster, Boston, 14 Aug. 1834, to John Davis, Davis Letterbook, vol. I-12, Davis Papers; Rufus Choate, Salem, 23 Aug. 1834, to John Davis, ibid., vol. I-13; Caleb Cushing, Newburyport, 28 Aug. 1834, to J. Davis, ibid., vol. I-14, Davis Papers, MWA. Samuel Bowles, n.d., 3 Sept. 1834, in Bliss Papers, MHi. Boston *Courier,* Sept. 17, 1834.

75. J. Davis, Worcester, 1 Aug. 1834, to P. Merrick, chairman of the Antimasonic Committee for the County of Worcester, Letterbook I-11, Davis Papers; Boston *Courier,* Sept. 11, Nov. 4, 1834; Connecticut Valley Antimasons were also going into Whig ranks, ibid., Oct. 28, 1834; *Proceedings of the Grand Lodge, 1826–1844,* pp. 387–88; E. Everett, Charlestown, 13 Oct. 1834, to J. Davis, Letterbook, I-16, Davis Papers; B. F. Hallett, Boston, 17 Aug. 1834, to P. Merrick, Merrick Papers. The Antimasons would have accepted Everett as a gubernatorial nominee in 1834; he had been both favorable to them and critical of Masons. In 1833, at a Charlestown caucus, he had blamed the Masons for the division in National ranks and had urged that the Nationals needed to let Masonry go down, "utterly, openly, and without qualification." But Everett refused Antimasonic overtures and backed Davis: Darling, *Political Changes,* pp. 119–20; *Adams Memoirs,* IX, 170, 171; Lynn *Record,* Feb. 5, 1834; *Report by a Joint Committee on Freemasonry,* "Appendix," p. 34.

76. *Free Press,* Oct. 21, 1834.

77. While the state convention recommended that county committees correspond with town or ward committees "to take care that the people in all elections, are seasonably provided with antimasonic votes," several leaders still maintained that the great object of the convention was "*to spread information* before the people on . . . freemasonry." *Free Press,* Oct. 28, 1834, italics mine; McCarthy, "Anti-Masonic Party," p. 523.

78. See below, Chapters X and XI.

79. Seymour Martin Lipset and Earl Raab, *The Politics of Unreason: Right-Wing Extremism in America, 1790–1970* (New York, 1970), pp. 39–49.

80. These statements about Antimasons and Masons are based primarily on collective biographies of both groups and on a comparative study in progress whose findings initially were reported in Ronald P. Formisano, "Antimasons and Masons: Massachusetts and Western New York" (Paper delivered to the Annual Meeting of the American Historical Association, San Francisco, Dec. 28, 1978).

Amasa Walker described the Boston Committee of One Hundred (Antimasons) as made up mostly of "active and respectable young men, although we have a number who are aged, wealthy respectable men." A.W., Boston, 25 Feb. 1830, to Pliny Merrick, Merrick Papers.

81. *The Form of the Covenant of the Old South Church, in Boston, Massachusetts* (Boston, 1833), pp. 62–65.

82. H. Crosby Englizian, *Brimstone Corner: Park Street Church, Boston* (Chicago, 1968), pp. 19, 23–24, 26–31, 32–39, 41, 57–58, 60, 61, 74, 83–87, 94, 97, 121, 128–31; for examples of disciplinary and other actions revealing of the church, see Records of the Park Street Church, 1809–1834, Congregational Library, Boston, pp. 373–75, 380–83, 398, 402, 419, 421, 425, 440, and especially the committee report of April 1, 1829, pp. 409–10; see also John L. Withrow, *Seventy-Fifth Anniversary of Park Street Congregational Church* (Boston, 1884), pp. 7–8, 20–22.

Thomas W. Ward, Jr., of Shrewsbury, son of a Worcester County sheriff and brother of Henry Dana Ward, was heavily involved in Antimasonry, temperance, and antislavery: box 22, Ward Family Papers, MWA.

83. Englizian, *Brimstone Corner*, pp. 72, 86, 101–2; Darling, *Political Changes*, pp. 15, 87; State Legislative File, State Library, State House, Boston; Marcus Morton, Taunton, 13 Dec. 1825, to Hon. George Odiorne, Morton Letterbooks, MHi. Temperance, and the best way to promote it, also divided the Orthodox and the Unitarians.

84. Lewis G. Pray, *Historical Sketch of the Twelfth Congregational Society in Boston* (Boston, 1863), passim. In Northampton in 1833 it was observed that the "Unitarians, Jackson men and masons" were united on a political candidate. Entry of Aug. 29, 1833, Sylvester Judd, Journal, I, Forbes Library, Northampton. Judd was an extraordinary local historian who had been a Federalist and National Republican. He was also an Orthodox Congregationalist who was becoming disillusioned with politics generally and with the National Republicans-Whigs specifically. During 1833–1834 he was sympathetic to the Antimasons and Workingmen, voting for the former, and during 1835 he took a hand in launching an antislavery society.

85. Jacob C. Meyer, *Church and State in Massachusetts: From 1740 to 1833* (Cleveland, 1930), pp. 173–80, 202–7; Englizian, *Brimstone Corner*, pp. 90, 97, 103, 105; Douglas Shaw, "Unitarians, Trinitarians, and the Massachusetts Establishment, 1820–1834" (M.A. thesis, Brown University, 1967), pp. 81, 90–99, 100–102; William G. McLoughlin, *New England Dissent, 1630–1833: The Baptists and the Separation of Church and State* (Cambridge, Mass., 1971), II, 1210. Secular sources also recognized the Orthodox belief that "Unitarians have been intolerant and overbearing" and that this made the Orthodox politically rebellious. Northampton *Hampshire Gazette*, Mar. 31, 1830.

86. The Orthodox tendency to support Antimasonry was sometimes suggested by defenders of Masonry: John Emerson, *Letter to the Members of the Genesee Association, N.Y.* (Boston, 1829); *Masonic Mirror*, Dec. 5, 1829, Apr. 10, 17, 1830. In western Massachusetts the first Antimasonic meetings frequently assembled in Congregational churches, and where consensual Orthodoxy was strong the Antimasonic vote tended to be large: *History of the Connecticut Valley, in Massachusetts* (Philadelphia, 1879), II, 706–7; Theophilus Packard, Jr., *A History of the Churches and*

*Ministers, and of Franklin Association, in Franklin County, Mass.* (Boston, 1854), pp. 204–5. Regarding Orthodoxy and Antimasonry in an 1830 Worcester school committee election, see *Diary of Christopher Baldwin,* p. 56. On August 19, 1828, however, the Boston *Recorder,* a leading Orthodox journal, announced it would exclude all references to Masonry from its columns, and rebuked the Antimasons for lacking moderation. The Boston *Anti-Masonic Christian Herald,* on the other hand, began later in 1828 and championed all the evangelical Orthodox causes, including disestablishment, Mar. 12, May 28, June 25, 1829; McLoughlin, *New England Dissent,* II, 1221–22.

The role of Orthodoxy in Lathrop's 1831 candidacy, and its impact on National Republicanism is extensively discussed in "Letters to John Brazer Davis," pp. 241, 243–44, 246, 248–49, 254, and 256; see also George Bliss, Stockbridge, 8 Nov. 1831, to George Bancroft, Bancroft Papers, MHi. Finally, there is a good discussion of the Orthodox-Unitarian split and the appeal of Antimasonry to the Orthodox in Shaw, "Unitarians, Trinitarians," pp. 96–98.

87. The first phrase is from *Free Masonry: A Poem,* p. 167; the second from Stone, *Letters,* p. 564; see also Odiorne, ed., *Opinions on Masonry,* passim; *Proceedings of Antimasonic State Convention, 1831,* pp. 22–23; John B. Turner, Scituate, 7 May 1832, to Nathan Lazell, Jr., and N.L., Jr., Bridgewater, 13 July 1832, to Samuel Breck, in Plymouth "We the People" Papers, MWA.

88. Regarding Methodists, see Boston *Aramanth,* Aug., 1828, I, no. 5, 131 (a Masonic magazine); *Abstract of Proceedings of the Antimasonic State Convention, 1831,* p. 63; *Masonic Mirror,* July 25, 1829, discussed the Methodist conference's decision with displeasure.

Regarding Baptists, see [South Reading Baptists] *Ecclesiastical Record, 1832,* pp. 16–17; on Fall River Baptists Antimasonic tendencies, see Benjamin Wood Pearce, *Recollections of a Long and Busy Life* (Newport, R. I., 1890), p. 53.

In Lynn, where Antimasonry quickly caught on among most of the town's leaders and among Quakers and Methodists, Masons had been members and attenders of every church in town. But, if the editor of the Lynn *Record,* a prominent Quaker, may be trusted, Lynn's Masons were distributed in quite varying proportions in Lynn's churches, and their concentration in the Unitarian church was striking:

| | Number of Masons | | |
|---|---|---|---|
| Church | Members | Attenders | Total |
| First Methodist[a] | 11 | 40 (First, Second and Third Methodist) | 55 (First, Second and Third Methodist) |
| Second Methodist[b] | 2 | | |
| Third Methodist | 2 | | |
| First Congregational | 4 | 8 | 12 |
| Second Cong. (Unitarian) | 4 | 40 | 44 |
| Baptist[b] | 3 | 6 | 9 |
| Friends | 1 | 3 | 4 |
| Episcopal (no church | 1 | 1 | 2 |

[a] two resident ministers were Masons

[b] minister a Mason

(Lynn *Record,* Dec. 15, 1830)

89. The quotation is from *Trial of Moore and Sevey for a Libel on Samuel D. Greene, in the Municipal Court, Boston, July Term, 1833,* reported by Charles Locke (Boston, 1833), p. 49.

90. In the Reverend Moses Thacher's North Wrentham Church, the Antimasons led by Thacher seceded. The two groups, Antimasonic and pro-Masonic, according to Thacher's opposition, were "nearly equally divided in numbers and property," though

a number of men of property, not of the congregation, also opposed Thacher. *Report of a Committee of the Church in the North Parish . . .* (Boston, 1831), pp. 15, 16.

91. M. Morton, 20 Feb. 1834, Taunton, to Jubal Harrington, Esq., Morton Letterbooks, MHi; Boston *Daily Advocate: Extra,* Jan. 1, 1834. Martin B. Duberman's discussion of Charles Francis Adams, who entered briefly into Antimasonic politics, is revealing not only of Adams's political character but also of a movement which attracted him by its "attachment to principles." Duberman's assessment of Adams is also quite pertinent here: he found him "primarily a moralist who entered politics at the dictation of his conscience, and to whom the calculation and bargains of that realistic world were always repugnant." Duberman, *Charles Francis Adams, 1807–1886* (Boston, 1961), pp. 47–51.

92. Abner Phelps, Boston, 8 Sept. 1831, to P. Merrick, Merrick Papers.

93. Charles Francis Adams, Boston, 7 Feb. 1834, to John Quincy Adams, quoted in Samuel Flagg Bemis, *John Quincy Adams and the Union* (New York, 1956), p. 302, n. 121. Adams added, "Wealth to be sure is sometimes supercilious and in this case of Masonry has been unfortunately so. . . ." A National Republican who congratulated Governor Lincoln on his firmness with "the fanatics" said they would soon go further and attack all in high places. Edward D. Bangs, Boston, 7 Sept. 1831, to L. Lincoln, Lincoln Papers, MHi.

## X. The Workingmen's Movements and Party

1. B. L. Hutchins and A. Harrison, *A History of Factory Legislation* (New York, 1970; first ed., 1903), pp. 44–45.

2. Frederick Robinson, *An Oration Delivered before the Trades Union of Boston and Vicinity, on Fort Hill, Boston, on the Fifty-Eighth Anniversary of American Independence* (Boston, 1834), p. 15.

3. Samuel Whitcomb, Jr., *Address before the Working Men's Society of Dedham, September 7, 1831* (Dedham, 1831), p. 14.

4. An exception to this tendency is the analysis of the Workingmen's ideology presented in Edward Pessen, *Most Uncommon Jacksonians: The Radical Leaders of the Early Labor Movement* (Albany, 1967). The early study of the movement by Helen L. Sumner, "Citizenship (1827–1833)," in John R. Commons et al., *History of Labour in the United States,* I (New York, 1921), 169–332, though lacking interpretive depth and incomplete, is still useful.

5. On the influence of Workingmen's movements in Philadelphia and New York on Boston in the 1820s, see Pessen, *Most Uncommon Jacksonians,* p. 21; John R. Commons et al., eds., *A Documentary History of American Industrial Society* (New York, 1958), VI, pt. 2, p. 78. In 1829 John Greenleaf Whittier wrote a series of articles for the *American Manufacturer,* published in Essex County, in which he criticized the expanding merchant manufacturers and said that the American laborer was being subjugated. John A. Pollard, "Whittier on Labor Unions," *New England Quarterly,* 12 (1939), 100.

6. Both the journeymen's and the merchants' points of view may be found in the Lynn *Record,* May 22, June 19, 1830; see also Sumner, "Citizenship," p. 291; Paul Gustaf Faler, "Workingmen, Mechanics, and Social Change: Lynn, Massachusetts, 1800–1860" (Ph.D. diss., University of Wisconsin, 1970), pp. 396–97. Alan Dawley and Paul Faler, "Working Class Culture and Politics in the Industrial Revolution: Sources of Loyalism and Rebellion," *Journal of Social History,* 9 (1976), 466–80, emphasize the skilled workingmen's decline in status and income; there is also reason to believe that Lynn became an early center of Workingmen's agitation in part because

its artisans were better off and more cohesive compared with similar artisans elsewhere.

7. Boston *Courier,* Aug. 28, 1830; Sumner, "Citizenship," pp. 291–92, 302–3; Boston *Evening Transcript,* Aug. 30, 31, Sept. 2, 1830. This meeting of "Workingmen, Mechanics and others friendly to their interests" said it would exclude none. In Lynn, on August 4, a member of the Society of Journeymen Cordwainers urged the establishment of a general trade society and a fund to help their co-workers. Some workers were satisfied, he said, with the present rise in wages, but "the price of goods is the canker-worm that gnaws upon your vitals." The cordwainers needed to unite in order to receive only cash for their labor: "By paying the cash, the Bosses would be obliged to make a profit on their shoes . . . [rather than] depending for a living on the profits of their articles delivered out to workmen. Look, and see how they have depressed the price of female labor . . . almost to nothing! This has an effect on us as husbands, as fathers, and as brothers." Lynn *Record,* Aug. 7, 1830.

During the fall of 1830 the educated classes frequently discussed the Workingmen in public forums. Marc Friedlander and L. H. Butterfield, eds., *Diary of Charles Francis Adams,* III (Cambridge, Mass., 1968), 371, 383.

8. Edward Pessen, "Did Labor Support Jackson? The Boston Story," *Political Science Quarterly,* 64 (1949), 265, 266–67; Sumner, "Citizenship," p. 291. The Boston *Working Man's Advocate,* Dec. 4, 1830, supported the measures mentioned above and offered the wealthy merchant Theodore Lyman as the "Working Men's" candidate for mayor, though Lyman refused the nomination. *Evening Transcript,* Dec. 4, 1830. In August, spokesmen for the Workingmen included middle-class entrepreneurs, and the alleged Workingmen's representative ticket of May 1831 listed several well-off men and prominent National Republicans. Boston *Courier,* May 11, 1831. In August of 1831 the *Working Man's Advocate* said its object was to elevate the working classes, which included "artizans, farmers, traders, and merchants" (Aug. 20). In the town of Millbury, Worcester County, there appeared in 1831–1832 *The Plebeian and Millbury Workingmen's Advocate,* which discussed the Workingmen's party, usually in vague terms, and which by August 29, 1832, as *The Millbury Patriot and Worcester County Workingmen's Advocate,* had apparently become a National Republican paper.

9. *Plebeian and Millbury Workingmen's Advocate,* Feb. 9, 1831; Redmond J. Barnett, "The Movement against Imprisonment for Debt in Massachusetts, 1811–1834" (Senior honors thesis, Department of History, Harvard College, 1965), pp. 48–50; *Resolves, 1828–1831,* pp. 594–95.

10. The first quotation is from Frances S. Martin, *Lanesborough, Massachusetts: The Story of a Wilderness Settlement, 1765–1965* (Pittsfield, 1965), pp. 54–55; see also 33, 49, 52; Boston *Courier,* Mar. 11, 1831, Nov. 5, 1832. Shaw was also a patron of young George Briggs, later Whig governor: William C. Richards, *Great in Goodness: A Memoir of George N. Briggs* (Boston, 1866), p. 54. Augustus B. Reed, Ware, 10 Mar. 1831, to Pliny Merrick, Merrick Papers, MWA. The second quotation is from Alexander H. Everett, Boston, 26 Mar. 1831, to George Bancroft, Bancroft Papers, MHi; see also Daniel Wells, Greenfield, 3 Apr. 1831, to John Brazer Davis, in "Letters to John Brazer Davis, 1819–1831," *Massachusetts Historical Society Proceedings,* 49 (1916), 239. Arthur M. Schlesinger, Jr., *The Age of Jackson* (Boston, 1945), p. 149, described Shaw as "the Workingmen's candidate for Governor [in 1831] and at the same time the National Republican candidate for State Senator." Indeed, the men who nominated Shaw as "the Workingmen's candidate" were mostly the same men who in Berkshire also nominated John Davis as the National Republican candidate. Northampton *Hampshire Gazette,* Oct. 23, 1823.

11. Pawtucket *New England Artisan,* Jan. 5, 1832, no. 1, MWA. During 1832 the place of publication of this journal shifted to Providence and then to Boston.

12. *New England Artisan,* Feb. 28, 1832, Kress Library, Harvard Business School; Commons et al., eds., *Documentary History,* V, pt. 1, pp. 192–95. In March, April, and July, branches of the association came into being in Boston, Lowell, and New Bedford. Sumner, "Citizenship," p. 308.

13. Commons, et al., eds., *Documentary History,* V, pt. 1, pp. 57–61, 195–99; *Artisan,* Feb. 23, 1832.

14. *Artisan,* Feb. 23, 1832. On March 6, 1835, the Lowell *Patriot,* a Democratic paper, made the same point. "Factory time" also meant a rigid schedule by which "every man, woman, and child in a Cotton Mill, to use a homely saying, is tied to the Bell Rope." *Artisan,* Mar. 1, 1832.

15. *Artisan,* Mar. 1, 1832.

16. Commons, et al., eds., *Documentary History,* VI, pt. 2, pp. 76–81.

17. The Boston *Evening Transcript* changed its position on the ten-hour day and said that "highly respectable mechanics" were backing it. Mar. 14, 1831, and Feb. 20, 1832; *Artisan,* Mar. 8, 15, 22, Apr. 5, 1832.

18. *Transcript,* May 19, 1832; Commons et al., eds., *Documentary History,* VI, pt. 2, pp. 81–82; Pessen, *Most Uncommon Jacksonians,* pp. 17, 40; Sumner, "Citizenship," p. 310. The state of affairs in Fall River's mills may perhaps be gauged from the following story. In 1832 the satinet mill of J. and J. Eddy had a large order to fill and the owners added one-half to a thirteen-hour day without consulting the overseers. The latter met and went in a body "to the office" to resign, but the Eddys quickly came to terms. Benjamin Wood Pearce, *Recollections of a Long and Busy Life* (Newport, R.I., 1890), pp. 42–43.

19. *Laws of the Commonwealth of Massachusetts, 1822–1825* (Boston, 1825), IX, 70, act of Jan. 24, 1823.

20. The quotation is from a contemporary description of shipbuilding in the town of Duxbury, in Louis McLane, *Report of the Secretary of the Treasury, 1832: Documents Relative to the Manufactures in the United States* (Washington, 1833) (22nd Cong., 1st sess., *House Executive Documents,* no. 308), I, 414. John G. B. Hutchins, *The American Maritime Industries and Public Policy, 1789–1914: An Economic History* (Cambridge, Mass., 1941), pp. 109–11, 173–86, 257, 272–73; and Boston *Columbian Centinel,* May 2, 1831.

21. Commons et al., eds., *Documentary History,* VI, pt. 2, pp. 83–84.

22. Ibid., pp. 84–86; Providence *New England Artisan,* June 7, 21, 28, July 26, 1832; Seth Luther, *An Address to the Working Men of New England* (New York, 1833), pp. 7, 33–34; Sumner, "Citizenship," pp. 311–12; Pessen, *Most Uncommon Jacksonians,* p. 40. Among the strikebreakers, as Pessen pointed out, were men who had claimed to be "Working Men's" candidates a short time before. Pessen, "Boston Story," p. 268. For some reason Arthur M. Schlesinger, Jr., failed to mention this strike in his *Age of Jackson,* pp. 144–58.

23. Luther, *Address to Working Men,* p. 36.

24. Ibid., p. 17; the speech was apparently delivered first at Charlestown on June 21. *Artisan,* July 6, 1832. On Luther's distinctiveness among labor leaders, see Louis Hartz, "Seth Luther: The Story of a Working Class Rebel," *New England Quarterly,* 13 (1940), 401–18. Luther's speech attracted considerable notice, both friendly and hostile. Boston *New England Artisan,* Oct. 25, 1832.

25. Boston *Artisan,* Nov. 1, 1832, Aug. 22, 1833.

26. These statements are based on reports in the *Artisan,* Jan. 5, 26, Feb. 16, Mar. 8, Aug. 16, Nov. 22, 1832. In 1832 New Bedford shipyard workers earned $1.75 per day, compared with $1.50 in Charlestown and $1.25 on Cape Cod: McLane, *Documents Relative to Manufactures,* II, 188–89, 98–99, 316–17. South Shore yards also paid higher wages; see pp. 374–75. According to one who had worked as a child in

a Fall River mill, the ten-hour day was in the 1830s "undreamed" of, and overseers were cruel to children even in a factory where the owners were popular and friendly with the men. Pearce, *Recollections,* pp. 35–43.

27. *Artisan,* Sept. 27, Oct. 11, 1832. In 1833 and 1834 Masons seem to have intervened in Workingmen's politics, too: *Artisan,* Dec. 7, 1833; and Benjamin F. Hallett, Boston, 2 Nov. 1834, to George Bancroft, Bancroft Papers, MHi.

28. *Artisan,* June 7, 21, Aug. 2, 23, Sept. 6, Oct. 18, 1832. On taking over as editor of the *Artisan,* Douglas quickly stated his belief that laws had always been framed for the benefit of the rich and powerful and said he would advise "the useful classes" to prefer men whose interests were theirs and who would remember that they were agents and not masters of the people. Ibid., Nov. 15, 1832.

29. Ibid., Nov. 15, Dec. 20, 1832.

30. Ibid., Oct. 2, 1833; Sumner, "Citizenship," pp. 312–15. The electioneering did not dilute the *Artisan's* firm commitment to specific issues. Nov. 9, 1833.

31. *Artisan,* Oct. 17, 1832.

32. S. C. Allen, Northfield, 24 Oct. 1833, to Capt. A. P. Pritchard and Solomon Parsons, in Northampton *Hampshire Gazette,* Nov. 6, 1833. For Allen's background and thinking, see Herbert Collins Parsons, *A Puritan Outpost: A History of the Town and People of Northfield, Massachusetts* (New York, 1937), p. 494; and Schlesinger, *Age of Jackson,* pp. 151, 153, 154, 157. For an illustration of Allen's concern for justice and honesty in government, see S. C. Allen, Grafton, 29 Sept. 1839, to Isaac Davis, Davis Papers, MWA. The N.E.A. convention did not nominate Allen but endorsed a letter he had published in the Boston *Courier* declining to be considered for the National Republican nomination; shortly afterward a Charlestown meeting of Working Men made the nominations: *Artisan,* Oct. 10, 17, 1833; Arthur B. Darling, *Political Changes in Massachusetts, 1824–1848: A Study of Liberal Movements in Politics* (New Haven, 1925), pp. 113–14.

33. *Artisan,* Nov. 9, 1833. In Lowell two independent Workingmen's candidates for state representative received some 12 percent of the vote out of over 1,000 cast. Sumner, "Citizenship," p. 316.

34. The Democratic-Republicans appropriated the Workingmen's name, as in the Boston *Post,* Apr. 1, 1833, or claimed that the Workingmen's party was identified with the Democracy, in ibid., Oct. 2, 30, 1833; the *Post* finally said, on Nov. 5, that the Workingmen would be "ill-advised" to bypass Marton.

35. *Atlas,* Oct. 31, 1833; also Nov. 6, 7, 1833. The *Columbian Centinel* noted, on Nov. 13, 1833, "they are from us, and of us, and their dearest interests are identified with ours"; see also Boston *Patriot,* Nov. 2, 4, 9, 1833.

36. Statements of the harmony-of-interests doctrine appeared frequently in newspapers as the Workingmen's agitation began, e.g., in *Courier,* Sept. 4, Nov. 24, 1830. For a general discussion, see Carl Siracusa, *A Mechancial People: Perceptions of the Industrial Order in Massachusetts, 1815–1880* (Middletown, Conn., 1979).

37. The *Artisan* complained that most farmers and mechanics did not even know of the paper's existence. Dec. 28, 1833, Feb. 8, 1834.

38. Commons et al., eds., *Documentary History,* VI, pt. 2, pp. 87, 88, 89; Robinson, *An Oration Delivered before the Trades Union of Boston* (1834), included an appendix describing the history of the Boston Trades Union, which extended an invitation to farmers to cooperate and whose constitution also provided for male delegates from any female association; see p. 32.

39. Charles Cowley, "History of the Ten Hours Movement," in Trades and Labor Council of Lowell, Mass., *Lowell: A City of Spindles* (Lowell, 1900), pp. 245–61; Robinson, *Oration Delivered before the Trades Union,* pp. 7–8, 10, 12–15, 17–21,

28, 29. For Robinson's subsequent career as a Democrat, see Schlesinger, *Age of Jackson*, pp. 156, 167–68, 172, 261, 468, 495–96.

40. *Artisan*, Aug. 30, 1834; Summer, "Citizenship," p. 316; Darling, *Political Changes*, p. 126; Abel Cushing, *Oration Delivered at the Celebration of the Democratic Working-Men, in Milford, Mass., July 4, 1834* (Providence, 1834). Tickets to the "entertainment" accompanying Cushing's oration "admitting a gentleman and a lady" cost $1.50–a day's pay for many artisans. Dedham *Norfolk Advertiser*, July 4, 1831. Regarding Cushing, see Robert D. Bulkley, Jr., "Robert Rantoul, Jr., 1805–1852: Politics and Reform in Antebellum Massachusetts" (Ph.D. diss., Princeton University, 1975), pp. 104–5, 181.

41. Judd Journal, entry of 11 Sept. 1834.

42. Evans Woolen, "Labor Troubles between 1834 and 1837," *Yale Review*, 1 (1892), 92, 93, 96, 98; *Transcript*, Mar. 6, 1834, regarding a "turn out" of mill girls in Dover, N.H. In 1836 even the lowly hand spinners of the Plymouth ropewalks struck against a lowered wage. Samuel Eliot Morison, *The Ropemakers of Plymouth: A History of the Plymouth Cordage Company, 1824–1949* (Boston, 1950), p. 23.

43. These remarks are from the famous "Ten-hour Circular," issued on May 8, four days after the Julien Hall meeting. Written by Luther, A. H. Wood, and Levi Abell, the circular inspired a general strike in Philadelphia for a ten-hour day. Commons et al., eds., *Documentary History*, VI, pt. 2, pp. 94–99, quotations from pp. 94, 95.

44. Pessen, *Most Uncommon Jacksonians*, pp. 42–43, quotation on p. 51.

45. Robert Rantoul, Jr., "An Address to the Workingmen of the United States of America," in *The Lyceum, or Working-Men's Library* (Boston, 1834), pp. 72, 73. Similarly, Orestes Brownson, who functioned as a "radical" Democrat from 1836 to 1841, in 1836 proclaimed that if he repeated the words of Jesus in the marketplaces of Boston, "You would call me a 'radical,' an 'agrarian,' a 'trades-unionist,' a 'leveller,'" and he asserted that Jesus was "the prophet of the workingmen"; but Brownson, too, opposed the Workingmen's association and the ten-hour day. Arthur M. Schlesinger, Jr., *A Pilgrim's Progress: Orestes A. Brownson* (Boston, 1966; first ed., 1939), pp. 53, 64.

46. Boston *Daily Advertiser and Patriot*, Dec. 17, 1835.

47. James Trecothick Austin, *An Address, Delivered before the Massachusetts Charitable Mechanics Association, at the Celebration of Their Eleventh Triennial Festival, October 3, 1839* (Boston, 1839), pp. 6–7. On the master mechanics' ideology, see Gary J. Kornblith, "From Artisans to Businessmen: Master Mechanics in New England, 1789–1860" (Paper presented at the Annual Meeting of the Organization of American Historians, New York, Apr. 14, 1978), pp. 4–5. An earlier speaker before the masters had called the ten-hour idea "a mere bugbear–an unreal substance." James L. Homer, *An Address before the Massachusetts Charitable Mechanics Association at Their Tenth Triennial Festival, October 6, 1836* (Boston, 1836), p. 9.

48. The standard studies of the Workingmen, besides those of Pessen and Sumner mentioned above, include William A. Sullivan, *The Industrial Worker in Pennsylvania, 1800–1840* (Harrisburg, 1955); and Walter Hugins, *Jacksonian Democracy and the Working Class: A Study of the New York Workingmen's Movement, 1829–1837* (Stanford, 1960). See also Bruce Laurie, *Working People of Philadelphia, 1800–1850* (Philadelphia, 1980).

49. The amount of manufacturing and nonfarming activity in towns was determined by comparing McLane, *Documents Relative to Manufactures*, and John P. Bigelow, *Statistical Tables: Exhibiting the Condition and Products of Certain Branches of Industry in Massachusetts, for the Year Ending April 1, 1837* (Boston, 1838). The town of Gill had been Shaysite in sympathy and was almost wholly agricultural. *History*

*of the Connecticut Valley, in Massachusetts* (Philadelphia, 1879), II, 765, 767. For Workingmen's appeals to farmers, see *Artisan,* Aug. 8, 1833.

50. *Artisan,* Jan. 31, Feb. 28, May 9, 1833; *History of the Connecticut Valley,* II, 792–93. In Pawtucket an *Artisan* editor, a former Universalist preacher, addressed the Workingmen at the Universalist Chapel. *Artisan,* Feb. 9, Mar. 22, 1832. Douglas's two successors as editor were both ex-Universalist preachers, Theophilus Fisk and Linus S. Everett. After rejecting Calvinism, Orestes Brownson became a Universalist and shortly thereafter began to embrace Workingmen's doctrines: Schlesinger, *Pilgrim's Progress,* pp. 17–22. Adin Ballou was a leader of the Restorationists Association which had seceded from Universalism. About half of the Restorationists believed their theology meant "radical reform . . . [of] personal and social abuses and evils, and had zealously espoused the Temperance, Anti-Slavery, and Peace movements." Adin Ballou, *History of the Hopedale Community,* ed. William S. Heywood (Lowell, Mass., 1897), pp. 2–3; *DAB,* I, 556.

51. Darling, *Political Changes,* pp. 3, 97–98.

52. For reports of the Hampshire County Workingmen's meetings, see Northampton *Hampshire Gazette,* Oct. 9, 16, 1833; also Nov. 6, 1833. Biographical information on the Workingmen's leaders mentioned in these reports came from *History of the Connecticut Valley,* I; Solomon Clark, *Antiquities, Historicals and Graduates of Northampton* (Northampton, 1882); idem, *Historical Catalogue of the Northampton First Church, 1661–1891* (Northampton, 1891); *Biographical Review: The Leading Citizens of Hampshire County, Massachusetts* (Boston, 1896). Some of the Workingmen later became Free Soilers.

53. Judd Journal, I, entries of 24, 25, 26 Dec. 1833, 20 Feb. and 11 Apr. 1834; "To the Electors of Hampshire Co." [ca. 1833], and "To the Electors of Hampshire Co., Dec. 23, 1833," Northampton Historical Society. Stephen A. Aron, "The Minds of Hands: Working People of Amherst in the Mid-Nineteenth Century" (Honor's Thesis, Department of History, Amherst College, 1982), pp. 126–42.

54. Judd Journal, I, entries of 8 Jan. 1834, 13 Nov. 1833, 5 Nov. 1834; also revealing of Judd's attitudes were editorials in the *Gazette,* esp. Sept. 11, Oct. 9, and Nov. 6, 1833. For Judd's life, see Gregory H. Nobles and Herbert L. Zarov, eds., "Selected Papers from the Sylvester Judd Manuscript" (Typescript Forbes Library, Northampton, Mass., 1976), pp. 12–23.

55. The quotation is from Judd Journal, I, entry of 1 Jan. 1835; see also 17 Sept. 1834, 17, 19, 29 Oct. 1834, 5, 9, 18, Nov. 1834, 16, 17, Nov. 1835.

56. Ibid., entry of 16 Mar. 1835. The Whigs' charges of infidelity against the Workingmen angered Judd because, according to him, many Workingmen were "orthodox christians in good standing" (1 Jan. 1835).

57. Schlesinger, *Age of Jackson,* pp. 144–76, and passim.

58. George Dickinson, Deerfield, 11 May 1835, to George Bancroft, Bancroft Papers, MHi. Herman Mann, "Address to Working-Men's Society at Dedham, September 25, 1830," Lynn *Record,* Dec. 15, 22, 1830; Luther, *Address to Working Men,* pp. 5, 25–26. "The leaders of both parties and all parties," said Theophilus Fisk, "are equally fond of obtaining exclusive favors by an act of incorporation, and for supporting each other in legalized fraud." *Labor the Only True Source of Wealth* (Charleston, S.C., 1837), p. 2; see also idem, *Capital against Labor: An Address, Delivered at Julien Hall, before the Mechanics of Boston . . . May 20, 1835* (Boston, 1835). See also Pessen, *Most Uncommon Jacksonians,* p. 201; see also pp. 24–25, 26.

59. The overriding object of the Workingmen's society should be, said Herman Mann, "to hunt up, and create MERIT among ourselves and to place men of this description, as our servants in the offices of our Town, County, State and Nation."

Lynn *Record,* Dec. 22, 1830; see also Whitcomb, *Address before the Working Men's Society of Dedham,* pp. 22–23.

60. Boston *Courier,* Oct. 31, 1834; for the letter of George Bancroft, see October 22, 1834. Regarding the openness of the class structure in the United States before the Civil War, see Edward Pessen, *Riches, Class, and Power before the Civil War* (Lexington, Mass., 1973); and, for a different view, E. Digby Baltzell, *The Protestant Establishment: Aristocracy and Caste in America* (New York, 1964). Though focused differently, David Hammack, "Problems of Power in the Historical Study of Cities, 1800–1960," *American Historical Review,* 83 (1978), 323–49, discusses much of the relevant literature.

61. In the late twentieth century the historian might well wonder whether there still existed at large, and even among better-informed segments of the populace, the capacity to apprehend and appreciate Bancroft's insight as he and populists of the nineteenth century perceived and felt it.

62. *Artisan,* Feb. 2, 1832. Hence Article 4 of the N.E.A., providing that any member who submitted to any deduction unless by a decision in a court of law, or by referees, or because the bill was erroneous, would be expelled. Ibid., Feb. 23, 1832. The master mechanics of Boston, for example, had always treated apprentices in a paternalistic fashion. Caleb H. Snow, *A History of Boston* (Boston, 1828), p. 359.

63. *Artisan,* Feb. 2, 1832.

64. The first quotation is from Robinson, *Oration Delivered before the Trades Union,* p. 32; the second from Whitcomb, *Address before the Working Men's Society of Dedham,* pp. 3–5, 7, 8. The best examples of broad-gauged and specific social criticism are found in the *Artisan,* e.g., Aug. 8, 1833. At one point the *Artisan* even argued that because "labor is labor" women were entitled "to the same amount of wages as men, for the same . . . services" (Sept. 26, 1833).

65. The English radicals of the 1830s, whom R. S. Neale described as originating in a "Middling Class," resembled to some degree the Middling Interest of the 1820s, but the Workingmen's minority in the United States was much more like Neale's Middling Class, which acquired a "social class-consciousness making them receptive to the ideas of the Philosophic Radicals throughout the 1820's and 1830's." Neale, "Class and Class-Consciousness in Early Nineteenth-Century England: Three Classes or Five?" *Victorian Studies,* 12 (1968), 13 and 4–32, passim.

## XI. The Factory and the Revival

1. William O. Lynch, *Fifty Years of Party Warfare* (*1789–1837*) (New York, 1931), pp. 356–57. "Writers of history and biography as well as political leaders are almost criminally careless in carrying party names back into periods in which they were not recognized as the true designations by the members of the party involved" (p. 357, n. 36).

2. For a general account of the election which tends to posit two parties, see Robert V. Remini, *The Election of Andrew Jackson* (Philadelphia, 1963). The fullest account of the election in Massachusetts is in Arthur B. Darling, *Political Changes in Massachusetts, 1824–1848: A Study of Liberal Movements in Politics* (New Haven, 1925), pp. 56ff., to which this account is indebted but with which it frequently disagrees.

3. On the sectionalism of the 1828 election, see Richard P. McCormick, *The Second American Party System: Party Formation in the Jacksonian Era* (Chapel Hill, 1966), p. 335; and idem, "Political Development and the Second Party System," in William Nisbet Chambers and Walter Dean Burnham, eds., *The American Party Systems:*

*Stages of Political Development* (New York, 1975; first ed., 1967), pp. 98–99. Boston *Columbian Centinel*, Apr. 5, Oct. 11, 1828. In Hampden County, backers of Marcus Morton for governor said that they wholly supported the national administration. Ibid., Mar. 29.

4. Darling, *Political Changes*, pp. 7, 15, 21, 43; Andrew Henshaw Ward, "Hon. David Henshaw," *Memorial Biographies*, I, 483–99, esp. 497; Arthur M. Schlesinger, Jr., *The Age of Jackson* (Boston, 1945), pp. 147–48; Stephen Salsbury, *The State, the Investor, and the Railroad: The Boston & Albany, 1825–1867* (Cambridge, Mass., 1967), pp. 48, 49, 50, 51; John Barton Derby, *Political Reminiscences* (Boston, 1835), pp. 12–13.

5. In 1824 the *Statesman* Republicans backed Crawford against Adams for the presidency, a choice which at this distance looks perversely principled or stupid. Henshaw and company were neither. If Crawford remained healthy and won the presidency–and in 1824 smart money might easily bet on continuance of the Virginia dynasty (though a Georgian, Crawford was born in Virginia)–then Crawford's backers in Massachusetts would be in line for office, whereas if Adams won, few changes of office would occur, and the waiting lines for any vacancies were already long. In 1828–1829 the Crawford strategy, transferred to Jackson, paid off. Derby, *Political Reminiscences*, pp. 16–22. Though this source is not to be taken at face value, it is persuasive on this point.

6. Ibid., pp. 34–39; Theodore Lyman, "Hon. Theodore Lyman," *Memorial Biographies*, I, 168–98, and William Ingalls, "William Ingalls, M.D.," ibid., p. 334; George Ticknor Curtis, *Life of Daniel Webster* (New York, 1898), I, 338, 339. Henry Orne, *The Letters of Columbus* (Boston, 1829), is the bitter view of these matters by one of the Lyman group.

Henshaw's opponents and rivals often charged that the *Statesman* faction wanted to keep the Jackson party "conveniently small" as a way of keeping control of the best offices: Derby, *Political Reminiscences*, pp. 27, 31; Orne, *Letters of Columbus*, pp. 29–30; John Quincy Adams, Washington, 1 Dec. 1835, to A. H. Everett, in Andrew C. McLaughlin, ed., "Letters of John Quincy Adams to Alexander Hamilton Everett, 1811–1837," *American Historical Review*, 11 (1906), 349.

7. Wesley Everett Rich, *The History of the United States Post Office to the Year 1829* (Cambridge, Mass., 1924), pp. 134–36, emphasized that the important shift of the Post Office to a spoils system came with the Jacksonians. Dorothy Ganfield Fowler, *The Cabinet Politician: The Postmasters General, 1829–1909* (New York, 1943), also emphasized the point that the Jacksonians brought a frankly spoilsmen's rationale to the department. The account here is based in part on ibid., pp. 3–20. John Quincy Adams early observed "that sweeping proscription of postmasters which is to be one of the samples of the proposed reform." *Adams Memoirs*, VIII, 112. Regarding the Jacksonians' politicization of the Indian Service, see Ronald N. Satz, *American Indian Policy in the Jacksonian Era* (Lincoln, Neb., 1975), pp. 179, 184, 186–88.

8. These statements are based on comparisons of the lists of postmasters published in the annual *Massachusetts Register*. They describe gross change, and not all replacements necessarily resulted from political causes, but the pattern in the larger towns seems clear. Derby claimed that in 1829 he went to Washington with petitions for the removals of "obnoxious Postmasters" in Norfolk County and that in a meeting with Postmaster General Barry "We killed off *five* Postmasters of Massachusetts, in *five* minutes. . . ." *Political Reminiscences*, p. 52.

9. James Estabrook, Boston, 26 Dec. 1832, to Isaac Davis and Jubal Harrington, Davis Papers, MWA. The Davis Papers contain several letters illustrating changing

attitudes to patronage during these years. Cyrus Gale, a National Republican merchant of Northborough, enlisted the aid of Davis, a Jacksonian, in trying to preserve his postmastership; see, e.g., letters of Gale to Davis, 20 Nov. 1829, 24 Nov. 1829, 2 Jan. 1830, and 6 Mar. 1830.

10. Carl Wilhelm Ernst, *Postal Service in Boston, 1639–1893* (Boston, 1975; first ed., 1894), pp. 21–22, 25–28; Carl E. Prince, *The Federalists and the Origins of the U.S. Civil Service* (New York, 1977), pp. 189–90; Fowler, *Cabinet Politician,* pp. 14–15.

11. According to his critics, Henshaw replaced all but half a dozen of the custom staff. After the outcry reached Washington, Jackson sent word to Henshaw to slow down and to clear further appointments with a cabinet member. The administration also appointed an outsider independent of Henshaw to the post of surveyor of the port. But Henshaw and the *Statesman* group, with the tacit approval of some wealthy free-trade merchants, now commanded resources to expand their operations in both business and politics. Derby, *Political Reminiscences,* pp. 72, 91, 124–25; Darling, *Political Changes,* p. 179; Boston *Columbian Centinel,* Apr. 29, May 27, June 13, Aug. 1, Sept. 23, Oct. 24, Dec. 2, 5, 1829.

12. Roy F. Nichols, *The Invention of the American Political Parties* (New York, 1967), pp. 299, 313.

13. James S. Chase, *The Emergence of the National Nominating Convention, 1789–1832* (Urbana, 1973), pp. 136–37, 139, 151, 153, 156–81, 194–203, 216, 244–45, 263.

14. Boston *Statesman "Extra,"* Feb. 1830; *Statesman,* Jan. 22, June 29, 1831; Worcester *Republican,* Sept. 7, 1831. McCormick's statement that the Jacksonian Republicans introduced the convention into Massachusetts, *Second American Party System,* p. 94, is valid if one ignores the Antimasonic convention which preceded it.

15. Charles Edward Forbes, 4 Apr. 1831, to John Brazer Davis, in "Letters to John Brazer Davis, 1819–1831," *Massachusetts Historical Society Proceedings,* 49 (1916), 239. Many letters in this collection reveal the lack of National Republican organization in these years; see e.g., pp. 210–11, 235–36, 244, 245. Samuel Metcalf McKay of Pittsfield wrote, "I took it upon me to call a County Convention. . . . We have been without Caucus nomination for a few years back until the last spring when I called the first." 30 Oct. 1831, to J.B.D., in ibid., p. 248. In 1831 the Jacksonian Republicans could claim only seven papers in the state. Worcester *Republican,* Sept. 7, 1831.

In Essex County the old Federal organization carried over to the Nationals: "Essex National Republican Convention" and "To the Electors of Essex North District, Oct. 26, 1830," Broadsides, Essex Institute; and Reports of twenty-one towns to county convention of National Republicans, 1831, Duncan Papers, Essex Institute. Nevertheless, factionalism was rife in Essex: Gerald J. Baldasty, "Political Stalemate in Essex County: Caleb Cushing's Race for Congress, 1830–1832," *Essex Institute Historical Collections,* 117 (1981), 54–70.

16. Worcester *Republican,* Mar. 7, 21, 1832; *Journal of the Proceedings of the National Republican Convention Held at Worcester, October 11, 1832* (Boston, 1832); Boston *Courier,* Oct. 15, 1832. All three parties held numerous local caucuses and conventions, yet none possessed organizations of much permanence or depth. Each party did make its general posture known in "addresses" to voters and in published resolutions of various conventions.

17. For National Republican debates on a convention, see Boston *Daily Atlas,* Feb. 21, 25, Mar. 2, 8, 27, Oct. 5, 1833; *Centinel,* Mar. 9, 1833; the Nationals' "address" is in ibid., Oct. 19, 1833, and Boston *Courier,* Oct. 19, 1833. For National

organization, see *Atlas,* Oct. 5, 10, 30; *Centinel,* Oct.–Nov., 1833; *Courier,* Oct. 7, 11, 1833. On the Democratic convention, see Darling, *Political Changes,* pp. 112–13; an excellent history of Democratic organization can be found in the Worcester *Republican,* Apr. 12, 1835.

18. The use of the label "National Republican" by the Lincoln-Adams group gradually came into greater use during 1829, e.g., in *Centinel,* Feb. 21, Mar. 14, 18, 21, 25, Apr. 4, 1829.

19. On the Nationals' emphasis on national affairs, see Daniel Webster, "A Speech Delivered at the National Republican Convention Held at Worcester, Mass., on the 12th of October, 1832, Preparatory to the Annual Election," in *The Works of Daniel Webster* (Boston, 1851), I, 237–78; Boston *Courier,* Oct. 15, 1832; Norfolk *Advertiser and Independent Politician,* Nov. 2, 1832.

General treatments of the "Bank War" include Thomas Payne Govan, *Nicholas Biddle: Nationalist and Public Banker, 1786–1844* (Chicago, 1959); Robert V. Remini, *Andrew Jackson and the Bank War: A Study in the Growth of Presidential Power* (New York, 1967); and Jean Alexander Wilburn, *Biddle's Bank: The Crucial Years* (New York, 1967). For reviews of the literature, see Ronald P. Formisano, "Toward a Reorientation of Jacksonian Politics: A Review of the Literature," *Journal of American History,* 63 (1976), 46–49; and Edward Pessen, *Jacksonian America: Society, Personality, and Politics* (Homewood, Ill., 1978; first ed., 1969), pp. 348–67.

20. Donald B. Cole, *Jacksonian Democracy in New Hampshire, 1800–1851* (Cambridge, Mass., 1970), pp. 108–24.

21. Ward, "Henshaw," pp. 491–92; Darling, *Political Changes,* pp. 134–36; Schlesinger, *Age of Jackson,* pp. 147–48, 171; Remini, *Jackson and the Bank War,* pp. 55–64.

22. The other was the Merchant Bank, which though not Jacksonian was now willing to work with the administration and Henshaw and which eventually put both Henshaw and Marcus Morton on its board of directors. Frank Otto Gatell, "Spoils of the Bank War: Political Bias in the Selection of Pet Banks," *American Historical Review,* 70 (1964), 50–51; Darling, *Political Changes,* pp. 136–37. The Whigs frequently drew attention to Democratic political candidates' involvement with local banks. *Courier,* Nov. 8, 1834. Jackson's 1832 proclamation against South Carolina's nullification attempt won the admiration of some old Federalists, but his removal of the deposits drove them into opposition. Samuel Eliot Morison, *The Life and Letters of Harrison Gray Otis, Federalist, 1765–1848* (Boston, 1913), II, 294–95. Henshaw's newspaper, now the *Morning Post,* called removal "an excellent thing for the middling class. . . . Heretofore scarcely anyone received discounts from the Branch in this city but the great capitalists—the millionists—the Appletons, the Lawrences, etc.; but when the deposites are transferred to the State banks, men of smaller business and capital will stand as good chance to receive discounts from them as the 'big bugs.'" Quoted in Darling, *Political Changes,* p. 137.

23. U.S. Congress, *Senate Documents, 1833–1834,* 23rd Cong., 1st sess., vol. 2, no. 127; *House Documents, 1833–1834,* 23rd Cong., 1st sess., vol. 3, no. 153. The Boston memorial had over 6,600 signatures: Boston *Patriot,* Mar. 8, 1834; *House Documents, 1833–1834,* 23rd Cong., 1st sess., vol. 2, no. 54. On the resolution of the Massachusetts Legislature, see ibid., vol. 3, no. 174. For the Whig sense of crisis, see Caleb Cushing, *A Reply to the Letter of J. Fenimore Cooper, by One of His Countrymen* (Boston, 1834); John Davis, Boston, 20 Mar. 1834, to George W. Briggs, Briggs Papers, MWA; and Edward Everett, Washington, 18 Feb. 1834, to Thomas Wren Ward, Ward Papers, MHi. From January to early April the Bank question was talked of much in Northampton: Judd Journal, I, entries of 16 Jan., 10 Feb., 5 Mar., and 7 Apr.

24. In Lowell almost 860 legal voters signed the antiremoval or recharter petition and in November 893 cast Whig ballots; in Haverhill 314 legal voters signed, and in November the Whigs counted 339 ballots (Democrats 304, Antimasons 2, Workingmen 1). In some cases the number of signatures exceeded the fall Whig vote. U.S. Congress, *House Documents, 1833–1834,* 23rd Cong., 1st sess., vol. 4, nos. 251, 253, 254, 324, 325, 327; vol. 3, nos. 176, 175 (Boston); and vol. 5, no. 376. For petitions against recharter and in support of the administration, see ibid., vol. 4, nos. 255, 331, 338; a large antibank petition from Boston purported to contain 3,067 names, ibid., vol. 5, no. 382, but a group of Whigs scrutinized it and told Congress that it listed men living in other towns, counties, and states, and that some of those listed were dead, some repeated, some foreigners, and others unauthorized. They verified only 1,130 qualified voters of Boston. U.S. Congress, *Senate Documents, 1833–1834,* 23rd Cong., 1st sess., vol. 6, no. 509.

25. Boston *Courier,* Oct. 27, 28, Nov. 7, 1834; excerpt from Springfield *Republican* in *Courier,* Nov. 19, 1834.

26. *Courier,* Nov. 6, 8, 1834. The National Republicans published Davis's speeches arguing that the tariff was necessary to protect the wages of free laborers from being reduced to European levels. *Ibid.,* Nov. 7, 1833.

27. In an 1834 election-eve speech at Charlestown to a Whig rally, Everett had supported abolition of imprisonment for debt, a "less expensive and more equal law system," and a general system of education, though he would not levy a state tax to fund it. He would also reform but not abolish the militia. Like the Workingmen, he objected to "overtasking" children, but he thought that "the number of hours a man shall labor ought to be left to himself . . . a law or combination to prevent a free citizen, arrived at years of discretion, from working or employing workmen, as many hours as the parties pleased, was a most unwarrantable interference with private rights." *Courier,* Nov. 10, 1834.

28. Norman D. Brown, *Daniel Webster and the Politics of Availability* (Athens, Ga., 1969), pp. 154–55; Daniel Webster, Washington, 1 Feb. 1835, to Jeremiah Mason, in Charles M. Wiltse and Harold D. Moser, eds., *The Papers of Daniel Webster: Correspondence,* IV (Hanover, N.H., 1980), 24–25; Edward Everett, Charlestown, 26 Mar. 1835, to George Bliss, Bliss Papers, MHi.

29. George Bliss of Springfield opposed Everett's nomination, and his papers contain several letters from disaffected Whigs: Daniel Wells, Greenfield, letters of 2, 10, and 31 Mar. 1835, to G.B.; O. B. Morris, Springfield, 30 Mar. 1835; more cautious were George Ashmun, Springfield, 2 Mar. 1835, to G.B., and Samuel Bowles, Springfield, 5 Mar. 1835, to G.B.; see esp. G. B., Boston, Mar. 1835, draft of letter to E. Everett, all in Bliss Papers. Letter of William G. Bates, Springfield, quoted in Mason A. Green, *Springfield, 1636–1886: History of Town and City* (Boston, 1888), p. 432. On the continuing Masonic hostility toward Everett, see E. Everett, Charlestown, 9 Mar. 1836, to John Davis, Davis Letterbook, I-30, Davis Papers, MWA.

30. Even Everett's friend George Bancroft offered to support him in 1834, but by 1835 it was too late for him. E. Everett, Charlestown, 26 Aug. 1834, to A.. Bigelow, Jr., H. Atwill, and N. Austin, Jr., Committee, Davis Letterbook, I-18B, Davis Papers, contains Everett's reasons for refusing the Antimasons, and also his critical attitude toward Masonry. Regarding Everett's nomination pleasing the Antimasons, see Stephen White, Boston, 28 Feb. 1835, to Daniel Webster, in Wiltse and Moser, eds., *Papers of Daniel Webster: Correspondence,* IV, 24–25.

31. Boston *Daily Advocate,* Oct. 6, 1835; Edward Everett, Charlestown, 22 Oct. 1835, to John Davis, Letterbook, I-17, Davis Papers.

32. The counties with the largest differences between the Foster (lt. gov.) and Morton (gov.) votes in 1835 were the following:

| | % | No. | | % | No. |
|---|---|---|---|---|---|
| Norfolk | 32.9 | 1,209 | Suffolk | 10.6 | 706 |
| Bristol | 18.0 | 642 | Hampshire | 7.3 | 210 |
| Plymouth | 18.0 | 716 | Franklin | 5.6 | 146 |
| Middlesex | 15.4 | 1,429 | | | |

Even before this, on Feb. 18, 1835, the Worcester *Republican* had estimated that there were "no more" than 6,000 Antimasons in the Whig party. If at least 5,000 Antimasons voted for Davis in 1834 and a minimum of 5,000 to 6,000 for Everett in 1835, that meant that a majority of the Antimasons voted with the Whigs in 1835. Regarding Antimasonic support for Everett in 1835, see John Quincy Adams, Washington, 1 Dec. 1835, to A. H. Everett, in McLaughlin, ed., "Letters of John Quincy Adams," p. 349.

33. Township correlations also suggest the Whig re-creation of the Federal coalition, at least in its essentials. The 1812 Federal vote correlates negatively with the Jacksonian Republican and Democratic vote in every presidential election from 1828 through 1840 and 1844 (–.549 and –.543 in the latter), but it correlates positively with the Whig vote (1836: .468; 1840: .539; 1844: .482).

34. Marcus Morton, Taunton, 8 Dec. 1828, to John C. Calhoun, and M. M., Dedham, 21 Feb. 1829, to William Parmenter, Morton Letterbooks, MHi; A. H. Everett, Boston, 15 Apr. 1830, to John Bailey, Washburn Collection, vol. 20, MHi, said that votes for Morton came from blind opposition to "amalgamation."

35. The 1831 address of the Jacksonian Republicans is in Worcester *Republican,* Sept. 7, 1831.

36. For the 1830 address of the "Democratic Republican Convention," see Boston *Statesman* "Extra," Feb. 1830; for the spring 1831 election, see *Statesman,* Jan. 22, 1831, and for the fall 1831 election, Worcester *Republican,* Sept. 7, 1831. In 1832 the Jacksonian Republicans gave some attention to national issues, e.g., in the Worcester South Congressional District convention. *Republican,* Oct. 3, 1832. In Essex and Middlesex counties the local question of free bridges remained a live issue. Robert D. Bulkley, Jr., "Robert Rantoul, Jr., 1805–1852: Politics and Reform in Antebellum Massachusetts" (Ph.D. diss., Princeton University, 1975), pp. 111–12, 125–27; Benjamin Crowninshield, Salem, 13 Oct. 1832, to Robert Rantoul, South Reading, Rantoul Papers, Essex Institute.

37. U.S. Congress, *House Documents, 1833–1834,* 23rd Cong., 1st sess., vol. 4, no. 255; Lowell *Patriot,* Nov. 7, 1834. The anti-Bank leaders called themselves "friends of the Administration, and opponents to the U.S. Bank," and included several former leaders of the Middling Interest. Foster was born in 1772, son of a wealthy merchant who was conservative enough in the 1780s to drive off with his son in a two-horse sleigh "to put down Shays." Foster spent much of his youth abroad, witnessing scenes of the French Revolution and its aftermath while doing business in Spain and France. He returned to Boston in 1808, fluent in several languages, rich enough to pursue "no regular business," and broadened in his social views to become identified successively with Jeffersonianism, the Middling Interest, free trade, Antimasonry, the Workingmen, and Jacksonianism. In business and in politics, however, Foster pursued his own course, investing in real-estate development and in other enterprises. Foster was regarded as a friend by the Workingmen, but he was also a key member of the legislative committee that wrote the *Report on Freemasonry,* and he had supported Antimasonic objectives in the legislature. The memorial which issued from the Faneuil Hall meeting he chaired concluded by denouncing the B.U.S. as an "imperial power within the government," a phrase strongly echoing the legislative

report on Masonry which Foster helped to write. In the fall of 1834 Foster ran for Congress from the Suffolk district against the Whig manufacturer-capitalist Abbott Lawrence, nominated jointly by "Workingmen" and the Democratic-Republicans. Foster was just the type of independent, complex man who helped to draw many dissenters into the anti-Whig coalition. His wealth, character, and talents, combined with his broad social views, made him the kind of man to whom many workingmen deferred.

38. Schlesinger, *Age of Jackson,* pp. 157–58, 173–74, 176; Darling, *Political Changes,* pp. 188–91. Both Schlesinger and Darling exaggerate the extent to which Bancroft was a Workingmen's leader. Sylvester Judd of Northampton, who worked closely with Bancroft in the winter of 1834–1835, found him "in conversation very democratic" and "quite democratic in his notions." But Judd also thought Bancroft typical of those Democrats who were not "democratic" in practice, though he liked him personally. Judd Journal, I, entries of 12, 20 Aug. 1834, 11, 20 Feb. 1835, passim.

39. On the accession of Antimasons to the Democrats, see Martin B. Duberman, *Charles Francis Adams, 1807–1886* (Boston, 1961), pp. 53–54. Lawson Kingsbury, Framingham, 24 Nov., 1835, to Levi Woodbury, Levi Woodbury Papers, book 17, LC: same to same, 20 Dec. 1836, book 19, and A. H. Everett, Newton, 31 Dec. 1836, to L. Woodbury, ibid. Marcus Morton, Taunton, 9 Jan. 1836, to D. L. Pearce, Morton Letterbooks, MHi (Morton estimated that 7,000 of Everett's votes in 1835 came from Antimasons); same to same, 14 Jan. 1836, and M. Morton, 3 Aug. 1836, to B. F. Hallett, ibid; and Benjamin Franklin Hallett, *An Oration, Delivered July 4, 1836, at Palmer, in Hampden County, Massachusetts, by Request of a Committee of Democratic Citizens . . .* (Boston, 1836), p. 46. For a discussion of both Workingmen and Antimasons going to the Democrats, see B. F. Hallett, 2 Nov. 1834, to George Bancroft, Bancroft Papers, MHi; M. Morton, Greenfield, 9 Sept. 1835, to G. Bancroft, ibid.; A. H. Everett, Boston, 16 Dec. 1836, to L. Woodbury, Levi Woodbury Papers; Russell B. Nye, *George Bancroft: Brahmin Rebel* (New York, 1944), pp. 107–11; M. Morton, Worcester, 15 June 1836, to L. Woodbury, Morton Letterbooks, Morton Papers; M. Morton, Taunton, 27 Mar. 1837, to Martin Van Buren, ibid. Regarding Antimasons splitting between the Whigs and Democrats, see Julius Rockwell, Boston, 3 Mar. 1836, to John Davis, Davis Letterbook, I-28, Davis Papers; J. H. Clifford, New Bedford, 24 Sept. 1836, to Robert C. Winthrop, Winthrop Papers, MHi; Francis Baylies, Taunton, 19 Apr. 1836, to Gen. John E. Wool, in Samuel Rezneck, ed., "Letters from a Massachusetts Federalist to a New York Democrat, 1823–1839," *New York History,* 48 (1967), 268.

40. Boston *Post,* Nov. 17, 1834. Local issues were also important: Northampton's Democratic party coalesced as a haven for "radicals" unhappy with corporations, "aristocracy," and social snobbery, and also attracted some temperance men and antislavery sympathizers. See Judd Journal, I, entries of 28 Mar., 21, 25 Apr., 4 May, 1835.

41. Worcester *Republican,* Sept. 30, 1835, italics in original. Nye, *George Bancroft,* pp. 106–11, did not seem aware of Bancroft's authorship of the Democratic address. The interpretation given here differs from the one which holds that Bancroft's views of 1834–1835 made the Bank issue important to the Massachusetts Democrats. Schlesinger, *Age of Jackson,* pp. 162–63.

42. "Address to the Democratic Electors of Massachusetts," Worcester *Republican,* Oct. 21, 1835.

43. There is an excellent account of party affairs from 1829 to 1835 in the Worcester *Republican,* Apr. 12, 1835. For Morton's acceptance of the Henshaw-managed nomination and his initial regret at "a kind of organization of a party," see M.M., 11

Feb. 1830, to David Henshaw, Morton Letterbooks, Morton Papers. In 1831 Morton still distanced himself from "the Office-holders in the City of Boston." M.M., Taunton, 9 Mar. 1831, to J. C. Calhoun, ibid.

44. *Republican,* Mar. 18, 1835; "To Andrew Jackson, President of the United States," 10 Feb. 1835, Circular, Essex Institute; Bulkley, "Robert Rantoul," pp. 163–64. Henshaw's faction also had its hands full with a factional struggle within Boston: *Republican,* Sept. 30, 1835; and M. Morton, Taunton, 29 Oct. 1835, to George Bancroft, Bancroft Papers, MHi.

45. *Republican,* Dec. 2, 1835.

46. M. Morton, Taunton, 10 Feb. 1835, to J. L. Silbey, Morton Letterbooks, Morton Papers. The Bostonians, said Morton, showed "a little to much disposition to do things *covertly* and without the knowledge of, if not against the wishes of the party." See also *Republican,* Apr. 1, 1835.

47. Worcester *Republican,* Sept. 2, 9, 16, 30, Oct. 14, 1835. The *Republican* observed on Mar. 25, 1835, that at the 1833 convention 281 delegates had attended, representing 94 towns, whereas in 1835 the caucus consisted of 103 delegates, representing 61 towns.

48. *Republican,* Mar. 3, 9, 16, 1836. In September the usual round of local conventions for state-senate and congressional nominations began, and were apparently well attended. To the "Worcester Democratic [county] Convention," for example, came about seventy delegates from over thirty towns to chose a state-senatorial ticket and to endorse the state and national nominations of their party. *Republican,* Sept. 21, 28, Oct. 5, 1836; also Dedham *Norfolk Advertiser,* Aug. 27, Sept. 10, 24, Oct. 1, 8, Nov. 5, 12, 1836.

49. *Republican,* Mar. 29, 1837.

50. For the preconvention meetings, see *Republican,* Sept. 6, 1837 (Worcester and Middlesex counties, Charlestown); the Worcester County delegates caucused just before the state convention and nominated state senators then. For the state convention, see *Republican,* Sept. 27, 1837; Boston *Post,* Sept. 27, 1837. For senate-nominating conventions later in Middlesex, Bristol, Hampden, Plymouth, Berkshire, and Essex counties, see *Post,* Oct. 10, 1837. In Boston, ward caucuses were chosen preparatory to the Suffolk County meeting. *Post,* Oct. 16, Nov. 7, 1837. Town committees were the building block of the system, and the party's top leaders worried about their formation. Seth J. Thomas, 2 Nov. 1837, to George Bancroft, Bancroft Papers, MHi.

51. Boston *Bay State Democrat,* Aug. 24, Sept. 28, 1828, Apr. 12, Oct. 4, 11, 1839; Pittsfield *Sun,* Apr. 18, 1839, Mar. 26, Aug. 27, Sept. 24, 1840, Sept. 9, 1841, Sept. 15, 1842. Politicians, like historians, often remember what they wish. In 1838 Bancroft's *Bay State Democrat* labeled a state convention a "time-hallowed institution" and "the only strictly democratic method of making preparations for State Elections." Sept. 7, 1838.

52. See note 31 above. Worcester *Massachusetts Spy,* Mar. 4, 25, 1835; *Republican,* Mar. 4, 1835.

53. *Spy,* Mar. 30, Aug. 31, Sept. 21, 1836; Hingham *Gazette,* Sept. 2, 9, Oct. 7, 1836; Concord *Yeoman's Gazette,* Sept. 10, 1836; Haverhill *Gazette,* Sept. 10, 24, 1836; Dedham *Norfolk Advertiser,* Sept. 17, 1836; Salem *Observer,* Oct. 8, 1836; Newburyport *Herald,* Sept. 20, 1836; Springfield *Republican,* Sept. 17, 1836.

54. *Spy,* Mar. 22, Sept. 20, Nov. 8, 1837; *Yeoman's Gazette,* Sept. 16, 1837; Charlestown *Bunker Hill Aurora,* Oct. 14, 1837; Northampton *Hampshire Gazette,* Sept. 21, 1836; Essex County Whig towns were asked to send a number equal to the number of representatives, Haverhill *Gazette,* Oct. 6, 1837; Boston *Atlas,* Oct. 9–Nov. 13, 1837; when Hampshire County Whigs assembled, they chose a "committee of

nomination" of one member from each town, *Hampshire Gazette*, Oct. 11, 25, 1837. In 1836, meanwhile, the legislature sought to reduce its size by doubling the unit of representation. In Bristol County, nineteen towns sent eighty-one delegates: John H. Clifford, New Bedford, 12 Oct. 1837, to Robert C. Winthrop, Winthrop Papers, MHi. The certificates of Worcester County Whig town meetings in 1839 are preserved in "Worcester County Convention, October 8, 1839," Massachusetts Collection, MWA.

55. *Spy*, Mar. 7, Sept. 12, 26, 1838; Mar. 13, Sept. 18, 1839; Mar. 11, Sept. 16, 1840; Mar. 10, 17, Apr. 7, Sept. 20, Oct. 6, 1841; Mar. 9, Aug. 3, Sept. 14, 21, 1842; Mar. 1, May 10, June 14, 1843; Feb. 28, June 5, 26, 1844. [August 1839] Documents Folder 1, box 6, Young Men's Convention, Massachusetts Collection, MWA.

56. *Spy*, Sept. 21, 1842; May 10, June 14, 1843; June 26, 1844; Pittsfield *Sun*, Sept. 24, 1840, Sept. 15, 1842. In 1832 the National Republican convention assembled over 500 "delegates" to hear Daniel Webster speak. Benjamin Goddard, Jr., 31 Oct. 1832, to William A. Goddard, Springfield, Goddard Family Papers, MWA.

57. For this statement's theoretical basis see Whitman H. Ridgway, *Community Leadership in Maryland, 1790–1840: A Comparative Analysis of Power in Society* (Chapel Hill, 1979); and Robert Doherty, *Society and Power: Five New England Towns, 1800–1860* (Amherst, 1977).

58. In 1839, for example, faced with an insurgent faction of Whigs in Worcester County that was about to take control of state-senate nominations, Governor Everett wrote to John Davis, now U.S. senator, to ask that he and four or five other prominent Whigs "take matters in hand [i.e., the senate nominations], and give them a proper direction." This particular effort failed, however, and two Whig tickets appeared that year. E. Everett, Boston, 12 Aug. 1839, to John Davis, Davis Letterbook, I-53, Davis Papers, MWA; see also E. Everett, Watertown, 17 Sept. 1839, to Robert C. Winthrop, Winthrop Papers. Daniel Wells, Northampton, 26 Mar. 1835, to George Bliss, George Bliss Papers, MHi, described some unexpected factionalism in a county convention, while J. H. Clifford, New Bedford, 19 July 1839, to R. C. Winthrop, Winthrop Papers, described the selection of state-convention delegates by prominent men. In the Whig party, nominations for councillor were made by the county caucuses of state legislators: certificates of meetings, Jan. 1839, box 6, folder 4, Massachusetts Collection, MWA.

59. M. Morton, Taunton, 20 Feb. 1834, to Jubal Harrington, Morton Letterbooks, MHi. Other support for these statements is in Richard Houghton, Mar. 1836, to J. Davis; E. Everett, Charlestown, 9 Mar. 1836, to J. Davis; and same to same, 29 Mar. 1836, Davis Letterbook, I-29, 30, and 32, Davis Papers, MWA; see also M. Morton, Greenfield, 17 Sept. 1837, to G. Bancroft, Morton Letterbooks; L.H.W., ? 1840, to J. H. Clifford, Clifford Papers, MHi; J. H. Clifford, 25 Sept. 1840, to R. C. Winthrop, Winthrop Papers, and R. W. Winthrop Diary, entry of Sept. 14, 1836, Winthrop Papers, MHi.

60. Darling, *Political Changes*, pp. 182–83, is suggestive. The power of wealthy manufacturers like Abbott and Amos Lawrence in Whig councils is apparent in the biographies of most Whig leaders and in, e.g., Sidney Nathans, "Daniel Webster: Massachusetts Man," *New England Quarterly*, 39 (1966), 163–65; and Kinley J. Brauer, *Cotton versus Conscience: Massachusetts Whig Politics and Southwestern Expansion, 1843–1848* (Lexington, Ky., 1967).

61. The most complete account of the collectorship episode is in Bulkley, "Robert Rantoul," pp. 179–209; see also Darling, *Political Changes*, pp. 195–97; M. Morton, 31 May, 1836, to Martin Van Buren; M. Morton, 25 May 1836, to G. Bancroft; M.M., 1 June 1836, to David Henshaw; and M. M., 27 Mar. 1837, to M. Van Buren, Morton Letterbooks, MHi. F. P. Blair, Washington, 9 Jan. 1838, to G. B., Bancroft Papers,

C. G. Green, Boston, 10 Sept. 1836, to Levi Woodbury, and Robert Rantoul, 11 Feb. 1837, to L. W., Levi Woodbury Papers, LC. Worcester *Republican,* March 1, 8, 15, 1837.

62. John K. Simpson, Boston, 28 Apr. 1836, to L. Woodbury, Woodbury Papers. When Bancroft's appointment became known, he immediately received not only congratulations from all sides, but promises of cooperation and expressions of support which can only be called *pledges of fealty*. The Bancroft Papers, MHi, contain many such letters, e.g., B. F. Hallett, Washington, 6 Jan. 1838, to G.B., and same to same, 15 Jan. 1838.

63. The best description of Bancroft's reorganization and of the Democratic factions is in the long letter written to Bancroft by an able New Bedford journalist he hired as a consultant and editor, Jeremiah G. Harris, ? 1838, to G. Bancroft, Bancroft Papers; for discussion, see Nye, *George Bancroft,* pp. 115–16. The 1838 Democratic state address repeated the themes which had appeared earlier in Bancroft's *Bay State Democrat: Democrat,* Oct. 5, 1838, cf., Aug. 24, Sept. 7, 14, 1838.

64. The William Schouler Papers, MHi, contain much material on Schouler's and other Whig politicians' militia activities in the 1840s. Schouler's friend Henry Wilson was also active: Ernest McKay, *Henry Wilson: Practical Radical, Portrait of a Politician* (Port Washington, N.Y., 1971), p. 26; Richard H. Abbott, *Cobbler in Congress: The Life of Henry Wilson, 1812–1875* (Lexington, Ky., 1972), p. 30. A militia tour by Everett in 1836 was described in Robert C. Winthrop, Diary, entries of 4, 5, Oct. 1863, which also mentioned Daniel Webster's simultaneous appearance at the Berkshire Cattle Show. Winthrop fully revealed the political nature of these events in R. C. Winthrop, Boston, 13 Oct. 1836, to J. H. Clifford, Winthrop Papers. In September 1840 the Worcester Guards paraded through Worcester and in the evening marched to the Worcester House, where they were feted by the town's Whigs: Levi Lincoln Newton, Diary, July–Sept. 1840, Newton Family Papers, MWA. In 1839 the Bristol County Whigs scheduled their county conventions to coincide in time and place with the Agricultural Society's annual cattle show, and John H. Clifford reported that the large hall of the convention was "filled by the picked men of the County." 12 Oct. 1837, to R. C. Winthrop; also R.C.W., Boston, 22 Sept. 1838, to J.H.C., regarding the necessity of scheduling the state central committee meeting around the Worcester Cattle Show, Winthrop Papers.

65. Jonathan Chapman, Boston, 28 Oct. 1843, to Samuel Houghton, Houghton Papers, MHi.

66. Robert Rantoul, Gloucester, 14 Oct. 1838, to George Bancroft, Bancroft Papers; New Bedford *Daily Register,* Nov. 11, 1839. In 1839 the Boston *Post* printed a long list of all the Whig state officeholders with their salaries, and Democratic papers throughout the state reprinted it, e.g., the *Daily Register,* Oct. 19, 1839.

67. Regarding the forming of Bay State Associations see *Bay State Democrat,* Mar. 1, 15, 22, 29 Apr. 12, 26, June 7, 14, 1839. For Democratic views on organization, see Isaac Hill, Concord, N.H., 16 Nov. 1838, to G.B., Bancroft Papers; *Bay State Democrat,* May 31, July 5, Oct. 4, Nov. 8, 1839; *Daily Register,* Sept. 26, 1839. For Whig reaction, see J. H. Clifford, New Bedford, 11 Apr. 1839, to R.C.W.; J.H.C., 7 May 1839, to R.C.W., and same to same, 31 Oct. 1839, Winthrop Papers; *Bay State Democrat,* Oct. 11, 1839; [Robert C. Winthrop's Speech] To State Convention of Whig Young Men of Massachusetts, Worcester, Sept. 11, 1839, Massachusetts Collection, MWA; Henry O. Riverman, Newburyport, 22 May 1839, to J. H. Clifford, Clifford Papers, MHi.

68. J. H. Clifford, 17 Nov. 1839, to R. C. Winthrop, Winthrop Papers. On October 6 Clifford had reported, "We have already taken up the list of voters, *every name*

upon which will be canvassed. . . ." See also same to same, 31 Oct. 1839, Winthrop Papers.

69. Whig State Central Committee, Boston, 17 Apr. 1840, to P. Greely, Jr., see Confidential Circular, box 6, folder 4, Massachusetts Collection. Worcester had organized a Whig association in February, the names of central committee members and the state legislator William Lincoln anchoring its roster of some forty members; see "Constitution of the Worcester Whig Association," ibid. As the June convention approached, more Whig town organizations came into being across the state, and called themselves an incredible variety of names, including the Brighton Harrison Association, the Democratic Whigs of Bellingham, the Washington Whig Association, the Republican Whig Association of Dracut, the Whig Party of Marblehead, the Whig Republican Association of Plymouth, the Warren Democratic Whig Association, and the South Reading Harrisonian Association. Certificates from town committees, box 6, folder 6, and box 7, folders 1 and 3.

70. John Atkins, Provincetown, 9 June 1840, to Edwin Conant, Worcester; Jared Ward, Petersham, 15 June 1840, to E. Conant, both in box 7, folder 3; G. B. Upham, Leicester, 2 June 1840, to William Lincoln, Worcester, box 6, folder 4; —— Eaton, South Reading, 9 June 1840, to E. Conant, box 7, folder 3; Letter to Dear Sir, 10 June 1840, P. Greely, Jr., Boston, Secretary Whig State Central Committee, Massachusetts Collection. Boxes II and III, Kinnicutt Collection, Worcester Historical Museum.

71. "Great Meeting of the People," box 6, folder 4, Massachusetts Collection.

72. Ibid.; Edward Clarke, Sutton, 20 June 1840, to William Lincoln, Worcester, box 7, folder 3; Chester Davis, Webster, 19 June 1840, to Jonathan Day, Worcester, box 7, folder 4; Massachusetts Collection.

73. N. P. Denny, Leicester, 20 June 1840, to William Lincoln, Box 7, folder 3, Massachusetts Collection. Even old Federalists found little to criticize, though they originally had apprehensions. The account of the June mass meeting by crusty old Benjamin Russell is instructive. He told a friend that it was perhaps "a little too noisy," but that contrary to many reports "*It was no mob meeting*" (italics added). Salutations between the Whig ladies of Worcester and their visitors were all done "in good order, good discipline, cheerful countenance, and not an instance of Intemperance." The convention conducted its business in accord with caucus arrangements made the night before, and it came off as well as conventions "we have attended." Loud cheering and commotion were caused only by late arrivals announcing themselves and being greeted with "hearty cheers, which overflowed from all hearts." Otherwise the crowd was disciplined and utterly attentive to the speakers, with "not one mob-like or disorderly movement." There was, Russell stressed again, "as much order and decorum, as that which has ever attended the great Mechanic and Civic Processions . . . in Boston." All the business parts "were conducted with true Yankee order and decorum, and the cheerings [were] not more loud than you and I have heard in old Faneuil Hall. The *People* feel the wrongs of their tyrannical Oppressors,—and when they raise the voice to proclaim them, it is the voice of God. I hate *mobs* in the true acceptance of the term." Letter of Benjamin Russell, 24 June 1840, reprinted in Joseph T. Buckingham, *Specimens of Newspaper Literature: With Personal Memoirs, Anecdotes, and Reminiscences* (Boston, 1850), II, 113–14.

74. Leverett Saltonstall, Salem, 19 Aug. 1840, to R. C. Winthrop. See also J. H. Clifford, New Bedford, 28 Aug. 1840, to R.C.W., Winthrop Papers; Mark A. DeWolfe Howe, *The Life and Letters of George Bancroft* (New York, 1908), I, 232; Mrs. W. S. Robinson, ed., *"Warrington" Pen Portraits: A Collection of Personal and Political Reminiscences from 1848 to 1876* (Boston, 1877), p. 20.

75. *Works of Daniel Webster,* II, 39–40. Harrison's name "was upon all our lips,

his praises on all our tongues, hsi likeness upon all our breasts, in the form of badges and medallions." R.C.W., Boston, 7 Apr. 1841, to J. H. Clifford, Winthrop Papers.

76. Leverett Saltonstall, Salem, 12 Nov. 1840, to R. C. Winthrop, Winthrop Papers.

77. For a superb description of campaign excitement in the "west," see Onslow Peters, Peoria, Ill., 15 July 1840, to Isaac Davis, Davis Papers, MWA; and for excitement in Delaware, see Harold B. Hancock, ed., "William Morgan's Autobiography and Diary: Life in Sussex County, 1780–1857—Part II," *Delaware History*, 19 (1980), 108–9.

78. Richard P. McCormick, "Political Development and the Second Party System," p. 108.

79. The quotation is from Congdon, *Reminiscences of a Journalist*, p. 78. The same view emerges from Charles N. Dyer, *History of the Town of Plainfield, Hampshire County, Mass.* (Northampton, 1891), pp. 102–3; Festus C. Currier, *Reminiscences and Observations of the Nineteenth Century* (Fitchburg, 1902), pp. 18–19. Many more sources might be mentioned which recalled the campaign's peculiar intensity: e.g., Charles F. Swift, *History of Old Yarmouth: Comprising the Present Towns of Yarmouth and Dennis* (Yarmouth Port, 1975), p. 75; D. Hamilton Hurd, comp., *History of Bristol County, Massachusetts* (Philadelphia, 1883), p. 221; Lilley B. Caswell, *The History of the Town of Royalston, Massachusetts* (n.p., 1917), pp. 132–35. "Even the women took part: they named their sun-bonnets 'log-cabins,' and set their tea-cups at supper and breakfast in little glass plates with log cabins impressed on the bottom." Robinson, ed., *"Warrington" Pen Portraits*, pp. 19–20.

80. The concept of the people "seeing themselves" is central to Lawrence Goodwyn, *Democratic Promise: The Populist Moment in America* (New York, 1976). There were crucial differences between the manifestations of this phenomenon among southern and midwestern farmers in the 1880s and 1890s and among New Englanders in 1840, but recognition of some similarity in the two situations can aid in looking at the seemingly familiar election of 1840 in a new way. Also pertinent are two essays by Walter Dean Burnham, "Party Systems and the Political Process" and "American Politics in the 1970's: Beyond Party?" in Chambers and Burnham, eds., *American Party Systems*, pp. 277–307 and 308–57.

## XII. Whigs and Democrats

1. Edward Everett, "An Oration Delivered at Cambridge, on the 4th of July, 1826," *Orations and Speeches on Various Occasions* (Boston, 1895), I, 129. The Whig reformer Horace Mann thought of the state as "the parent of the people." For a discussion of Mann's "positive republicanism," see Jonathan Messerli, *Horace Mann: A Biography* (New York, 1972), pp. 104–8, 200–216. On the importance of a positive view of the state in Whig thought, see David Bradstreet Walker, "Rufus Choate: A Case Study in Old Whiggery," *Essex Institute Historical Collections*, 94 (1958), 334–55. For Choate, government was not a necessary evil "but a positive blessing" (p. 353). "Perfect liberty," said one Whig, "implies not the absence but the perfection of government." Jonathan Chapman, *An Oration Delivered before the Citizens of Boston, on the Sixty First Anniversary of American Independence, July 4, 1837* (Boston, 1837), p. 23. Cf. Edmund S. Morgan, *The Puritan Dilemma: The Story of John Winthrop* (Boston, 1958). Whig paternalism was to survive in its least-diluted form, perhaps, among the Mugwump reformers of the late nineteenth century. Geoffrey Blodgett, *The Gentle Reformers: Massachusetts Democrats in the Cleveland Era* (Cambridge, Mass., 1966), pp. 39–40.

2. See Chapter XI, notes 19, 37, and 38; see also Boston *Columbian Centinel*,

Oct. 19, 1833; Worcester *Massachusetts Spy,* Sept. 28, 1836, Mar. 22, 1837, Mar 7, 1838, Sept. 21, 1842. In 1843, out of power in the state, the Whig convention focused more than ever before on state issues. *Spy,* June 14, 1843.

3. Samuel Metcalf McKay, 30 Oct. 1831, to John Brazer Davis, in "Letters to John Brazer Davis, 1819–1831," *Massachusetts Historical Society Proceedings,* 49 (1916), 249. In 1831 Governor Lincoln noted the public concern over "excessive expenditures of the state." *Revolves, 1828–1831,* p. 607.

4. *Resolves, 1832–1834,* pp. 48–49.

5. Nationals and Whigs consistently defended tariffs as a utilitarian measure benefiting most of society. See, e.g., Jeremiah Mason, Boston, 27 May 1832, to Daniel Webster, in George S. Hilliard, ed., *Memoir and Correspondence of Jeremiah Mason* (Cambridge, Mass., 1873), pp. 337–40. John Davis's wife said that because of the tariff the poorest family in Worcester "go better dressed now than I used to when a child. Money is more plenty [sic] and clothing cheaper." Eliza Davis, Worcester, 8 Mar. 1832, to John B. Davis, Washington, John Davis Papers, MWA. Many other letters in the Davis Papers also discuss the tariff, especially in the years 1838–1841. Walker, "Rufus Choate," p. 340, aptly described Choate as defending the tariff with "egalitarianized Hamiltonian arguments." See also, in the same vein, Boston *Daily Atlas,* Mar. 4, 1833.

6. [Robert C. Winthrop's Speech] To the State Convention of Whig Young Men of Massachusetts, Worcester, Sept. 11, 1839, Massachusetts Collection, MWA. During 1839–1841 the Whig legislative leader William Lincoln of Worcester apparently gathered materials and helped draft Winthrop's and other Whigs' speeches dealing with expenditures. The spirit of Whig paternalistic activism permeates Lincoln's notes: [State Finances, 1841–1842], box 2, folder 7, Massachusetts Collection.

7. Stephen Salsbury, *The State, the Investor, and the Railroad: The Boston & Albany, 1825–1867* (Cambridge, Mass., 1967), pp. 143–47.

8. Resolutions of the Whig Young Men's Massachusetts Convention, Sept. 11, 1839, Massachusetts Collection. Daniel Webster, "Speech Delivered at the Odeon, at Boston . . . on the 12th of October, 1835," *The Works of Daniel Webster* (Boston, 1851), I, 331–32.

9. *Acts and Resolves, 1841,* p. 464. See also Martin Green, *The Problem of Boston: Some Readings in Cultural History* (New York, 1966), p. 42; and Daniel Walker Howe, *The Unitarian Conscience: Harvard Moral Philosophy, 1805–1861* (Cambridge, Mass., 1970), p. 211.

10. *Acts and Resolves, 1840,* pp. 302, 304. A representative statement of this viewpoint is George Bancroft, *An Oration Delivered before the Democracy of Springfield and Neighboring Towns, July 4, 1836* (Springfield, Mass., 1836).

11. Arthur M. Schlesinger, Jr., *The Age of Jackson* (Boston, 1945), p. 176. For a different view, see above, Chapter XI.

12. Nor was criticism of corporations, "manufacturing and monied," a new thing among Democrats in 1835. See, e.g., Jubal Harrington, Worcester, 2 Nov. 1832, to Robert Rantoul, Jr., Robert Rantoul Papers, Essex Institute.

13. Gerard W. Gawalt, "Sources of Anti-Lawyer Sentiment in Massachusetts, 1740–1840," *American Journal of Legal History,* 14 (1970), 283–307; idem, *The Promise of Power: The Emergence of the Legal Profession in Massachusetts, 1760–1840* (Westport, Conn., 1979), pp. 51, 94, 179–86; and Richard E. Ellis, *The Jeffersonian Crisis: Courts and Politics in the Young Republic* (New York, 1971), pp. 200–203. One Democrat later claimed that in the town of Groton the "spirit of Job Shattuck," a Shaysite leader of the 1780s, lived on in Democratic descendants of the 1840s who displayed a marked "devotion to liberty." George S. Boutwell, *Reminiscences of Sixty Years in Public Affairs* (New York, 1902), I, 64–66.

14. Thomas W. Dorr, Providence, 25 Nov. 1835, to George Bancroft, Bancroft Papers, MHi. I have reversed the emphasis here—Dorr placed his on the first point.

15. Robert D. Bulkley, Jr., "Robert Rantoul, Jr., 1805–1852: Politics and Reform in Antebellum Massachusetts" (Ph.D. diss., Princeton University, 1975), pp. 170–74; Worcester *Republican,* Sept. 16, 23, 30, 1835, Mar. 9, 1836.

16. Salsbury, *Boston & Albany,* pp. 91–92, 224–25, 297. Opposition in the Periphery to the building of the railroad was reflected in, for example, the belief that by the legislature's lending of the state's credit to the Western Railroad "all the farms in the state were mortgaged." Hiram Barrus, *History of the Town of Goshen, Hampshire County, Massachusetts* (Boston, 1881), p. 174.

17. Arthur B. Darling, *Political Changes in Massachusetts, 1824–1848: A Study of Liberal Movements in Politics* (New Haven, 1925), pp. 197–210; David Henshaw, *An Address Delivered before an Assembly of Citizens from All Parts of the Commonwealth, at Faneuil Hall . . . Boston, July 4, 1836* (Boston, 1836), pp. 28–31. Few Massachusetts Democrats were "hard money" purists; some wanted "bank paper based on both property and credit." New Bedford *Daily Register,* Feb. 16, 1839.

18. Darling, *Political Changes,* pp. 197–98; David Henshaw, *Remarks upon the Rights and Powers of Corporations* (Boston, 1837); Bulkley, "Robert Rantoul," p. 183; for criticism of "associated capitalists" in a Henshaw-linked paper, see Lowell *Patriot,* July 10, 1835.

19. Henshaw, *Address, July 4, 1836,* pp. 26–27; Darling, *Political Changes,* pp. 140–41, 204, 206; Harry N. Scheiber, "George Bancroft and the Bank of Michigan," *Michigan History,* 44 (1960), 82–95; and idem, "A Jacksonian as Banker and Lobbyist: New Light on George Bancroft," *New England Quarterly,* 37 (1964), 363–72. Ironically, Marcus Morton frequently assured Bancroft of his lack of interest in banks: M.M., Taunton, 29 Oct., 1835, to G. Bancroft, and M.M., 3 Feb. 1838, to G.B., Bancroft Papers, MHi. Although Morton had no personal investments in banks, he did not refrain from recommending the Hancock Bank of Boston as a "pet" to the national administration: M. Morton, Taunton, 10 Nov. 1934, to Levi Woodbury, Woodbury Papers, LC.

20. See, e.g., Boston *Post,* Oct. 29, 1834. Resentment against the "codfish aristocracy" played a powerful role in shaping the sensibilities of the young Benjamin F. Butler, who also became one of the more unprincipled demagogues to cut a swath in nineteenth-century Massachusetts politics. Butler, *Butler's Book* (Boston, 1892), pp. 37–41, 49, 81; Howard P. Nash, Jr., *Stormy Petrel: The Life and Times of Benjamin F. Butler, 1818–1893* (Rutherford, N.J., 1969), p. 32.

21. The failure of Henshaw's Commonwealth Bank in early 1838, however, benefited the Bancroft faction and ultimately helped it in its effort to reshape the party's image. Darling, *Political Changes,* pp. 224–29, on Henshaw's business deals; see also *Refutation of the Charges against Marcus Morton* (Boston?, 1845), pp. 4, 30–31.

22. Boston *Bay State Democrat,* Nov. 2, 1838; report of a speech at Lynn by B. F. Hallett, in ibid., Nov. 1, 1839, and Nov. 15, 1839; Nathan W. Littlefield, *Gov. Marcus Morton* (Taunton, 1905), pp. 9, 13, 14–16, 21.

23. M. Morton, Greenfield, 9 Sept. 1835, to G. Bancroft, Bancroft Papers. For a similar statement in nearly the same language, see M.M., Taunton, 13 Feb. 1834, to J. C. Calhoun, and M.M., Taunton, 8 Dec. 1828, to J.C.C., Morton Letterbooks, MHi.

24. See Schlesinger, *Age of Jackson,* p. 257, for an assessment quite different from the one given here.

25. *Acts and Resolves, 1840,* pp. 292–301, 301–3.

26. Ibid., pp. 308–10; see also, on this point, M.M., 13 Dec. 1828, to George Odiorne, Morton Letterbooks, MHi.

27. *Acts and Resolves, 1840,* pp. 312–13. Similarly, Alexander H. Everett com-

plained that "the principal seats of opposition [to democracy] have been and still are the commercial cities, which from their frequent communication and intimate relations with England . . . all . . . are fashioned on the aristocratic model." Everett, *An Oraton Delivered at Holliston, Mass., on the Fourth of July, 1839, at the Request of the Democratic Citizens of the Ninth Congressional District* (Boston, 1839), p. 37.

28. Morton also urged a constitutional amendment to eliminate the poll tax and proposed that in the meanwhile it be fixed so low that anyone could pay it. *Acts and Resolves,* 1840, p. 311–12.

29. Ibid., p. 307. Morton called the present "a time when factitious distinctions in society, arising from its very refinements, from education, from family, from social relations, and from wealth, are multiplying and becoming more clearly defined" (p. 310). Morton's 1843 inaugural also gathered together the ancient complaints of the Periphery, old Republicanism, and a concern for political equality and social justice. *Acts and Resolves, 1843, 1844, 1845,* pp. 116–17.

30. Carl Siracusa, *A Mechanical People: Perceptions of the Industrial Order in Massachusetts, 1815–1880* (Middletown, Conn., 1979), pp. 86–89, discussed aspects of this.

31. The Boston *Atlas* and Boston *Courier* were outdone by no other Whig papers in appealing to farmers, laborers, mechanics, merchants, and others, e.g., *Atlas,* Oct.–Nov. 1837, and *Courier,* July–November 1840. Melvyn Dubofsky, "Daniel Webster and the Whig Theory of Economic Growth: 1828–1848," *New England Quarterly,* 42 (1969), 556, 571. On the appeal of "classless" rhetoric to the middle as well as the working classes in another time and place, see Michael Rogin, "Progressivism and the California Electorate," *Journal of American History,* 55 (1968), 315.

32. *Courier,* Oct. 23, 1834; Edward Everett, "An Address Delivered before the Mercantile Library Association, at the Odeon, in Boston, 13th September, 1838," in *Orations and Speeches,* II, 294. Another classic statement of this view is Nathan Appleton, *Labor, Its Relations in Europe and the United States Compared* (Boston, 1844).

33. For an excellent demonstration of this point with reference to a Whig who held many un-Whiggish positions, see Arthur M. Schlesinger, Jr., "The Problem of Richard Hildreth," *New England Quarterly,* 13 (1940), 223–45. Recent discussions of Democratic and Whig ideology vary slightly from the one offered here, but they agree in general and, more importantly, emphasize that common denominators can be found amid the diversity in each party: Siracusa, *Mechanical People,* pp. 121–36; Daniel Walker Howe, *The Political Culture of the American Whigs* (Chicago, 1979), especially Howe's emphasis (on p. 21) on three preoccupations of the Whigs–improvement, morality, and harmony. Significantly, in his chapter on "Whig Conservatism," pp. 210–37, Howe focused on two Massachusetts Whigs, Webster and Choate.

34. The Massachusetts Collection, MWA, contains records of roll-call votes on the temperance legislation of 1838–1839 which reveal intraparty splits. On the tariff, see Darling, *Political Changes,* pp. 146–47.

35. Carl F. Kaestle and Maris A. Vinovskis, *Education and Social Change in Nineteenth-Century Massachusetts* (Cambridge, 1980), pp. 221–28.

36. Ibid., pp. 230–31. In the same legislature an earlier vote on a bill to reduce salaries of state officials and to eliminate some state offices was defeated narrowly, 222 to 232, with 95.2 percent of the Democrats in favor and 92.7 percent of the Whigs against (p. 216). On laws involving corporations these legislators "united solidly behind their parties" (p. 231).

37. Jesse Chickering calculated that from 1820 to 1840 "the agricultural class" increased by 38 percent while the number of those engaged in manufacturing and

commerce rose by 155 percent. *A Statistical View of the Population of Massachusetts, from 1765 to 1840* (Boston, 1846), p. 42, see also pp. 41–51.

38. Bristol County was the only one the Democrats carried in 1840, by a plurality; in 1836 the Democrats won four counties: Bristol, with 57.1 percent; Middlesex, with 53.4; Hampden, with 51.3; and Berkshire, with 50.1.

39. The continuity of political divisions is apparent in some counties and towns in a simple comparison of Federal and Republican banner units with Democratic and Whig banner units. Some shifted, and not all Federal strongholds were Whig enclaves, nor did all the overwhelmingly Republican towns vote Democratic. But in most counties, continuities are apparent.

40. Edmund Soper Hunt, *Reminiscences: Weymouth Ways and Weymouth People* (Boston, 1907), p. 66; Henry S. Gere, *Reminiscences of Old Northampton: Sketches of the Town as It Appeared from 1840 to 1850* (n.p., 1902), p. 69; Franklin Benjamin Sanborn, *Recollections of Seventy Years* (Boston, 1909), I, 21; George K. Tuffts, "Historical Address," in *Account of the Observance of the One Hundred and Fiftieth Anniversary of the Incorporation of the town of New Braintree, Mass., June 19, 1901* Worcester, 1902), p. 65; see also entry of 7 Nov. 1839, Levi Lincoln Newton Diary, Nov.–Dec. 1839, Newton Family Papers, MWA. Sometimes, however, political differences caused trouble in families; see, e.g., William E. Davis, Northboro', 7 Feb. 1834, to Isaac Davis, Davis Papers, MWA.

41. Paul Goodman, "The Politics of Industrialism: Massachusetts, 1830–1870," in Richard Bushman et al., eds., *Uprooted Americans: Essays to Honor Oscar Handlin* (Boston, 1979), p. 170. Despite the shortcomings inherent in the data used in this essay, Goodman's descriptions of the Democratic and the Whig parties are valuable.

42. John P. Bigelow, *Statistical Tables: Exhibiting the Condition of Industry in Massachusetts 1837* (Boston, 1838), p. 127. Louis McLane, *Report of the Secretary of the Treasury, 1832: Documents Relative to the Manufactures in the United States* (Washington, 1833) (22nd Cong. 1st sess., *House Executive Documents*, no. 308), I, 388–89, depict a similar structure in Quincy.

43. Harriet Martineau, *Society in America* (London, 1837), I, 277.

44. Bigelow, *Statistical Tables*, p. 13.

45. On the varied experiences of seaports after 1820, see Samuel Eliot Morison, *The Maritime History of Massachusetts, 1783–1860* (Boston, 1921), pp. 216–23. In 1818 Gloucester's fisheries were minor, by 1840 it surpassed Boston, and by 1860 it led all ports in fishing. Raymond McFarland, *A History of the New England Fisheries* (New York, 1911), pp. 189–90. For a good sense of the evolutionary nature of economic change, see Christopher Clark, "The Household Economy, Market Exchange and the Rise of Capitalism in the Connecticut Valley, 1800–1860," *Journal of Social History*, 13 (1979), 169–89.

46. Bigelow, *Statistical Tables*, pp. 169, 170; S. Wellington, W. Cambridge, 10 Mar. 1842, to William Schouler, Schouler Papers, MHi.

47. Thomas Dublin, "Outwork and the Economy of a Country Town" (Informal paper presented at the Charles Warren Center, Harvard University, Mar. 18, 1981); Bigelow, *Statistical Tables*, p. 181.

48. Ibid., p. 146. In the small agricultural town of Carver, in Plymouth County, iron forges began operating about 1735. In the 1830s three small furnaces, employing two dozen hands, produced bar-iron and cast-iron goods. The two cast-iron furnaces "ran" about 140 and 90 days each year, while the bar furnace worked about 16 weeks: Henry S. Griffith, *History of the Town of Carver, Massachusetts* (New Bedford, 1913), p. 196; and McLane, *Documents Relative to Manufactures*, I, 414–15.

49. Carl F. Kaestle and Maris A. Vinovskis kindly made available to me the socio-

economic variables from the 1840 census that they used in their study of legislative voting patterns on the state board of education, and reported in their *Education and Social Change,* pp. 219–30; no very significant relationship with party vote appeared, and even if one had, its meaning would be far from self-evident. As William G. Shade commented recently regarding the usual kinds of data available to historians in applying multivariate analysis to election and demographic data, "tremendous measurement problems . . . as well as troublesome multicollinearity [exist]. Such problems are not likely to go away since historians must work with data collected for other purposes, and ethnicity, religion, race, and class (the theoretically relevant categories) are hardly the independent variables the statistician's model demands." Shade, " 'New Political History,' " *Social Science History,* 5 (1981), 190–91.

50. Benjamin Waterhouse, Cambridge, 4 Dec. 1835, to Levi Woodbury, Woodbury Papers, LC.

51. Robert Rich, " 'A Wilderness of Whigs': The Wealthy Men of Boston," *Journal of Social History,* 4 (1971), 263–76.

52. The literature on the capitalist entrepreneurs and Whig leaders is extensive: a provocative recent assessment is Carl E. Prince, "Daniel Webster, the Boston Associates, and the U.S. Government's Role in the Industrializing Process, 1815–1830" (Paper prepared for the Lowell Conference on Industrial History, May 21–22, 1981). The best introduction to the relationship between state policy and entrepreneurs in Massachusetts remains Oscar Handlin and Mary Flug Handlin, *Commonwealth: A Study of the Role of Government in the American Economy: Massachusetts, 1774–1861* (Cambridge, Mass., 1969; first ed., 1947); also pertinent is Frances W. Gregory, *Nathan Appleton: Merchant and Entrepreneur, 1779–1861* (Charlottesville, 1975).

53. M. Morton, Taunton, 27 Mar. 1837, to Martin Van Buren, Morton Letterbooks; see also Worcester *Republican,* Mar. 2, 1836, which advocated keeping corporations small to increase the number of owners, otherwise the "more wealthy and smaller the number of bribers, the larger will be the number of votes bought in favor of the rich man's policy."

54. Benjamin Wood Pearce, *Recollections of a Long and Busy Life* (Newport, R. I., 1890), pp. 77–78.

55. M. Morton, E. Cambridge, 7 Dec. 1837, to G. Bancroft, Bancroft Papers; New Bedford *Daily Register,* Nov. 15, 1839; Fred Harvey Harrington, *Fighting Politician: Major General N. P. Banks* (Philadelphia, 1948), p. 7; Boston *New England Artisan,* Nov. 29, 1832.

56. George Sweet Gibb, *The Whitesmiths of Taunton: A History of Reed & Barton, 1824–1943* (Cambridge, Mass., 1943), pp. 137–50, for a discussion of personal management and strong community feeling within the firm. Also suggestive are Samuel Eliot Morison, *The Ropemakers of Plymouth: A History of the Plymouth Cordage Company, 1824–1949* (Boston, 1950); and Thomas R. Navin, *The Whitin Machine Works since 1831: A Textile Machinery Company in an Industrial Village* (Cambridge, Mass., 1950).

57. Caroline F. Ware, *The Early New England Cotton Manufacture: A Study in Industrial Beginnings* (Boston, 1931), p. 8; Arthur Harrison Cole, *The American Wool Manufacture* (Cambridge, Mass., 1926), I, 241–44, 370; Butler, *Butler's Book,* pp. 89–90. After 1840 the owners of the cotton mills became less concerned about their workers' welfare, and the system increasingly rested on exploitation of laborers, changing the nature of labor-management relations. Ware, *Cotton Manufacture,* pp. 110–13; John Coolidge, *Mill and Mansion: A Study of Architecture and Society in Lowell, Massachusetts, 1820–1865* (New York, 1942), pp. 47–48, 68–69, 73, 75, 101; Vera Shlakman, *Economic History of a Factory Town: A Study of Chicopee, Massa-*

*chusetts,* Smith College Studies in History, vol. 20 (Northampton, 1935), pp. 110–37; Thomas F. Dublin, *Women at Work: The Transformation of Work and Community in Lowell, Massachusetts, 1826–1860* (New York, 1979), pp. 86–131.

58. Charles Cowley, *History of Lowell* (Boston, 1868), pp. 89–90; George Sweet Gibb, *The Saco-Lowell Shops: Textile Machinery Building in New England, 1813–1849* (Cambridge, Mass., 1950), pp. 89, 92–93; Frederick W. Coburn, *History of Lowell and Its People* (New York, 1920), I, 150; Douglas Shaw, "Unitarians, Trinitarians, and the Massachusetts Establishment, 1820–1834" (M.A. thesis, Brown University, 1967), pp. 99–100.

59. Harriet H. Robinson, *Loom and Spindle, or Life among the Early Mill Girls* (New York, 1898), pp. 17–18, 86. In the early thirties a friend of the Democratic leader Robert Rantoul went into the Waltham factory to recruit subscriptions to a "Workingman's" paper, but met with cold indifference from the workers (which did not, it must be noted, stop publication of the paper). Bulkley, "Robert Rantoul," pp. 132–35, 150. At about the same time, on Apr. 26, 1832, the *New England Artisan* sadly observed that most factory workers voted National Republican.

60. See the sources listed in note 57.

61. *House Documents, 1852,* no. 230, pp. 48–51, 141–44, 147–48, and passim.

62. Ibid., pp. 3–4, 11–26. Earlier, Child had been an antislavery Whig in the legislature, and after his move to Lowell to manage a cotton mill his former colleagues accused him of selling out for personal gain. Kinley J. Brauer, *Cotton versus Conscience: Massachusetts Whig Politics and Southwestern Expansion, 1843–1848* (Lexington, Ky., 1967), pp. 86, 116, 132, 192.

63. Butler, *Butler's Book,* pp. 37–44; Harrington, *Fighting Politician,* p. 2. Butler's biographer erroneously called him a "swamp Yankee," missing the significance of his Scotch-Irish ancestry in his and his father's politics. Nash, *Stormy Petrel,* p. 20.

In the Whig party such men did not rise to prominence. Henry Wilson, the "Natick Cobbler," was exceptional. Wilson accepted Whig political economy, but he had gravitated to the party first because of his concern for moral issues, notably temperance, and his friendship with Natick's Congregational minister. Wilson's associates among the master shoemakers of Natick also favored Whiggery, Congregationalism, and moral causes. Elias Nason and Thomas Russell, *The Life and Public Services of Henry Wilson* (Boston, 1876), pp. 43–44; Richard H. Abbott, *Cobbler in Congress: The Life of Henry Wilson, 1812–1875* (Lexington, Mass., 1972), pp. 8, 13–16, 23; J. B. Mann, *The Life of Henry Wilson* (Boston, 1872), pp. 13, 19; Boutwell, *Reminiscences,* I, 79; Oliver N. Bacon, *A History of Natick* (Boston, 1856), p. 147.

In Lynn, a shoemaking center, the biggest shoe merchant-manufacturers tended to be Quakers, Congregationalists, and Whigs. Some Lynn shoe masters, however, were Methodists and Democrats. In North Bridgewater, later the "shoe city" of Brockton, merchant shoemakers also tended to be Whigs and Congregationalists. In both towns, however, the industry did not begin to be centralized until the 1840s, and labor was still often seasonal. Thus, for thousands of men who made shoes, the category "shoemakers" is only partly relevant to their politics. Bates Torrey, ed., *The Shoe Industry of Weymouth* (South Weymouth, 1933), pp. 55–56, is particularly good; see also Paul Gustaf Faler, "Workingmen, Mechanics, and Social Change: Lynn, Massachusetts, 1800–1860" (Ph.D. diss., University of Wisconsin, 1970), pp. 335–36, 355; Alan Dawley, *Class and Community: The Industrial Revolution in Lynn* (Cambridge, Mass., 1976), pp. 42–58; D. Hamilton Hurd, *History of Plymouth County, Massachusetts* (Philadelphia, 1884), pp. 561, 569–78; Bradford Kingman, *History of North Bridgewater, Plymouth County, Massachusetts* (Boston, 1866), pp. 399–408.

64. In 1840, Fall River voted about 53 percent Whig; in 1841 and 1842, about 53

percent Democratic; in 1843, 48.0 percent Democratic, 46.4 percent Whig, and 5.5 percent Liberty of 1,025 votes cast.

65. John Davis, Worcester, 20 Oct. 1842, to Association of Industry, Fall River, Davis Letterbook I-108, Davis Papers, MWA; Orin Fowler, *A Historical Sketch of Fall River: From 1620 to the Present Time* (Fall River, 1841), pp. 48, 51, 54–56 (this source contains excellent information about religious and economic life and is discussed further in Appendix XII.B); Thomas Russell Smith, *The Cotton Textile Industry of Fall River, Massachusetts: A Study of Industrial Localization* (New York, 1944), pp. 24–25, 28, 30, 36–37; Henry H. Earl, *A Centennial History of Fall River, Massachusetts* (New York, 1877), said that factory owners were remarkable for "affiliation with their help" (p. 33) but also that hours were "extremely long" (p. 28); cf. Philip T. Silvia, Jr., "The Spindle City: Labor, Politics, and Religion in Fall River, Massachusetts, 1870–1905" (Ph.D. diss., Fordham University, 1973), pp. 30–32. On the 1840 campaign, see J. H. Clifford, New Bedford, 25 Oct. 1840, to R. C. Winthrop, Winthrop Papers.

66. Gibb, *Saco-Lowell Shops*, pp. 73, 88–90, 747; Ware, *Cotton Manufacture*, pp. 203, 207.

67. William Hancock, Dudley, 31 July 1844, to John W. Lincoln, box 7, folder 6, Massachusetts Collection.

68. The Lancaster report of 1844 is in Letters to Stephen Salisbury, box 7, folder 6, Massachusetts Collection. Several sources pertaining to Lancaster were consulted, the most useful being Abijah P. Marvin, *History of the Town of Lancaster, Massachusetts* (Lancaster, 1879), pp. 573, 575, 765–66, 772, 773–77, 781, 784; *History of Worcester County, Massachusetts* (Boston, 1879), I, 610; D. Hamilton Hurd, *History of Worcester County, Massachusetts* (Philadelphia, 1889), I, 32, 35–37, 44, 58, 76. The data here support the argument of Paul F. Bourke and Donald A. DeBats regarding the political significance of neighborhoods and local influentials, "Identifiable Voting in Nineteenth-Century America: Toward a comparison of Britain and the United States before the Secret Ballot," *Perspectives in American History*, 11 (1977–1978), 283–86.

69. P. F. Clarke, "Electoral Sociology of Modern Britain," *History*, 50 (1972), 45.

70. Precise figures are hard to come by. In 1836 one source assigned 323 churches and 291 ministers (rather high) to the Congregationalists, 122 ministers to the Unitarians, and 189 churches and 170 ministers (probably too low) to the Baptists. See John Hayward, *The Religious Creeds and Statistics of Every Christian Denomination in the United States and British Provinces* (Boston, 1836), pp. 119, 120, 150.

71. For discussion of a similar situation in nineteenth-century England, see T. J. Nossiter, *Influence, Opinion and Political Idioms in Reformed England: Case Studies from the North-east, 1832–74* (Sussex, 1975), pp. 174–76.

72. For various approaches, see Ronald P. Formisano, "Analyzing American Voting, 1830–1860: Methods," *Historical Methods Newsletter*, 2 (1968), 1–12; Formisano, *The Birth of Mass Political Parties: Michigan, 1827–1861* (Princeton, 1971), pp. 137–64; Richard Jensen, *The Winning of the Midwest: Social and Political Conflict, 1888–1896* (Chicago, 1971), pp. 59–89, 309–15; Paul Kleppner, *The Cross of Culture: A Social Analysis of Midwestern Politics, 1850–1900* (New York, 1970), pp. 36–91, 381–83; and Paul Goodman, "A Guide to American Church Membership Data before the Civil War," *Historical Methods Newsletter*, 10 (1977), 183–90.

73. Kaestle and Vinovskis, *Education and Social Change*, p. 227, used "the presence or absence of Unitarian churches" in towns as one of their independent variables in analyzing the legislative vote on the state education board. Though recognizing that their measure of religion was "crude," the authors nevertheless decided that it had nothing to do with the vote, pp. 227–32. Given the varieties of Unitarianism, the

absence of information regarding other churches and their relative size, and the fragmentary nature of the available data (see Appendix XII.B), the measure would seem to lack any meaning at all.

74. See Appendix XII.B. Recent studies of other localities have found church participation among adult males to be far higher than would be suggested by membership figures alone. Paul E. Johnson, *A Shopkeeper's Millennium: Society and Revivals in Rochester, 1815–1837* (New York, 1978), pp. 169, 192–93, 194–95, 152–61. In Vermont's Connecticut Valley it was generally true that church *attenders* constituted a strong majority of adult males, while a significant minority of adult males were actually members. Those men who persisted in the community ten years or more were especially likely to be church members. Randolph Roth, "Whence This Strange Fire? Religious and Reform Movements in the Connecticut River Valley of Vermont, 1791–1843" (Ph.D. diss., Yale University, 1981), chaps. 2 and 6. Of course most members were women: Richard D. Shiels, "The Feminization of American Congregationalism, 1730–1835," *American Quarterly*, 33 (1981), 46–62.

75. Howe, *Unitarian Conscience*, pp. 207, 210–11. Boston's richest men were predominantly Unitarian, and rich, upper-class Unitarians were usually Whig. Rich, " 'Wilderness of Whigs,' " pp. 273–74. In 1850 the average value of churches of the major denominations was as follows: Unitarian, $14,200; Episcopal, $12,900; Trinitarian, $7,300; Baptist, $5,500; and Methodist $3,600. See *Seventh Census of the United States* (Washington, 1853), pp. 61–62.

In 1839 the Whigs held their state convention at Worcester's Unitarian Church. In 1837 Plymouth Whigs met at the First Church (Unitarian), Boston *Atlas*, Oct. 19, 1837. West Bridgewater's elite of prosperous farmers and entrepreneurs tended to be Whig and Unitarian. D. Hamilton Hurd, comp., *History of Bristol County, Massachusetts* (Philadelphia, 1883), pp. 891–92, 896–97, 924–34. In Worcester the dominant elites of the growing town tended to be Whig and Unitarian. Ronald Petrin, "Political Power in a Local Community: Worcester, Massachusetts, 1835–1843" (Seminar paper, Clark University, 1974).

76. The *Plebeian and Millbury Workingmen's Advocate* (Millbury), Mar. 23, 1831, objected that too many Unitarians were being nominated as state senators. Attacks on Harvard frequently contained at least an implied criticism of the Unitarian-Whig elite. Ronald Story, *The Forging of an Aristocracy: Harvard & the Boston Upper Class, 1800–1870* (Middletown, Conn., 1980), p. 140.

77. The quotation is from Parsons Cooke, *A Century of Puritanism and a Century of Its Opposites* (Boston, 1856), p. 400. Orthodox moralism and strictness are revealed in numerous sources, e.g., in Judd Journal, I, entry of 5 June 1833; Barbara M. Cross, ed., *The Autobiography of Lyman Beecher* (Cambridge, Mass., 1961), II, 43, 48, 108; Hurd, *Plymouth*, pp. 274–75, 345; Boutwell, *Reminiscences*, I, 74; Hurd, *Worcester*, I, 339–40, 857; Robinson, *Loom and Spindle*, pp. 48–50; F. W. Gale, Northboro', 23 July 1834, to Hannah D. Gale, Keene, N.H., Gale Family Papers, MWA; Josiah Coleman Kent, *Northborough History* (Newton, Mass., 1921), pp. 2, 47–56, 119, 132–33, 136, 173–86, 197–200. On the Orthodox connection with the National Republicans and Whigs, see *Adams Memoirs*, IX, 12; Lawson Kingsbury, Framingham, 24 Nov. 1835, to Levi Woodbury, Woodbury Papers, LC; Hurd, comp., *Bristol*, pp. 1112, 1124A–1124B; R. C. Winthrop, Boston, 28 June 1837, to J. H. Clifford, Winthrop Papers.

78. Barrus, *Goshen*, pp. 35–40, 43, 51, 66–67, 173–74; Alice Morehouse Walker, *Historic Hadley* (New York, 1906), pp. 111–12; Carpenter Morehouse, *The History of the Town of Amherst, Massachusetts: 1731–1896* (Amherst, 1896), pp. 198–234; Frank Prentice Rand, *The Village of Amherst: A Landmark of Light* (Amherst, 1958), pp. 299–302; Gere, *Northampton*, p. 27 and passim.

In 1834 George Bancroft described the Whig party taking form in Northampton: "A powerful combination was entered into with the Springfield junto; the aid of the clergy was called in; sermons were preached; and the community was made to believe, that there was a danger the bible would be taken out of their hands. Democracy was said to be a branch of atheism. . . . the Sunday night previous to the election an immense crowd was gathered in the town hall . . . and never was such an appeal to the stormy passions. The charges against their opponents were Jacksonism, infidelity, and atheism. . . . The *church,* orthodoxy was made to bear upon us." G. B., Northampton, 17 Nov. 1834, to E. Everett, Bancroft Papers. Six years later Bancroft was running the Democratic party from the Boston customshouse, and a Northampton Democrat complained to him of the "hypocrisy of orthodox deacons who go about attempting to justify falsehood." Hiram Ferry, Northampton, 28 Nov. 1840, to G.B., Bancroft Papers, MHi.

79. McLoughlin, *New England Dissent, 1630–1833: The Baptists and the Separation of Church and State* (Cambridge, Mass., 1971), II, 1263–67, 1270, 1274, 1281. The Jacksonian Republicans and Democrats worked hard, of course, to get and hold Baptist votes. M. Morton, 22 Aug. 1831, to R. Fletcher, Esq., Morton Letterbooks; Robert Rantoul, Gloucester, 14 Oct. 1839, to G. Bancroft, Bancroft Papers; and R. Spofford, Newburyport, 25 Feb. 1841, to Caleb Cushing, Cushing Papers, Special Correspondence, LC.

80. Ebenezer Thresher, Boston, 4 Nov. 1839, to Isaac Davis, Davis Papers. Thresher was secretary of the Northern Baptist Education Society in Boston from 1830 to 1845. *Historical Catalogue of Brown University, 1764–1904* (Providence, 1905), p. 151. The Davis Papers illuminate the Democratic-Baptist connection: A. G. Randall, Millbury, 29 Dec. 1839, to Isaac Davis, and Samuel Allen, Grafton, 6 Oct. 1840, to I.D.

81. McLoughlin, *New England Dissent,* II, 1231–34; 1236–37, 1268; *Massachusetts Register, 1841,* passim.

82. John G. Adams, *Memoir of Thomas Whittemore, D.D.* (Boston, 1878), p. 110; Bernard Whitman, *An Address Delivered May 30, A.D. 1832, at the Dedication of the Masonic Temple in Boston* (Cambridge, Mass., 1832), p. 29; Richard Eddy, *Universalism in America: A History* (Boston, 1894), pp. 232–59.

83. Henry Steele Commager, "The Blasphemy of Abner Kneeland," *New England Quarterly,* 8 (1935), 29–41; Octavius Pickering, *Reports of Cases Argued and Determined in the Supreme Judicial Court of Massachusetts* (Boston, 1864), XX, 242; [David Henshaw], *A Review of the Prosecution against Abner Kneeland, for Blasphemy. By a Cosmopolite* (Boston, 1835); Henshaw, *Address at Faneuil Hall, July 4, 1836,* p. 8; Ellis Gray Loring, 13 June 1838, to G. Bancroft, Bancroft Papers. Roderick S. French, "Liberation from Man and God in Boston: Abner Kneeland's Free-Thought Campaign, 1830–1839," *American Quarterly,* 32 (1980), 220.

84. McLoughlin, *New England Dissent,* II, 1232; Elias Nason, *A History of the Town of Dunstable, Mass.* (Boston, 1877), pp. 171–72; James Fletcher, *Middlesex* (Philadelphia, 1890), pp. 290–93; J. H. Temple, *History of Framingham, Massachusetts* (Framingham, 1887), p. 368. In Democratic Bellingham in Norfolk County, Baptists and Universalists were dominant: George F. Partridge, *History of the Town of Bellingham, Massachusetts, 1719–1919* (n.p., 1919), pp. 40, 43, 73–74, 117, 146, 154–55, 160–65; D. Hamilton Hurd, ed., *History of Norfolk County, Massachusetts* (Philadelphia, 1884), pp. 152–58. Baptists and Methodists also controlled the Democratic stronghold of Hanson in Plymouth County: Hurd, *Plymouth,* pp. 345–46, 351. For a case of a Whig Universalist and Freemason, see Hurd, comp., *Bristol,* pp. 228–29.

85. Josiah Gilbert Holland, *History of Western Massachusetts: The Counties of Hampden, Hampshire, Franklin and Berkshire* (Springfield, 1855), II, 393. The top

three Whig towns in Franklin were more populous but in the same class with populations of 1,022, 719, and 881. Of the two towns with the lowest total valuations in Franklin, one was Democratic and one was Whig, indicating that small farmers in hill towns were often divided in party preference.

86. Similar lists have been used previously: Formisano, *Mass Political Parties,* pp. 297–98, 318–23, 347–48, used two randomly discovered lists of voters compiled privately in Detroit (1856) and Lansing (1858), Michigan. Other studies have made use of county directories which also revealed voters' party loyalties: Jensen, *Winning of the Midwest,* pp. 59–63, 309–15; and Melvyn Hammarberg, *The Indiana Voter: The Historical Dynamics of Party Allegiance during the 1870's* (Chicago, 1977), pp. 51–61.

More reliable, perhaps, are conclusions based on the use of poll books of actual elections under viva voce voting. See, e.g., David A. Bohmer, "Stability and Change in Early National Politics: The Maryland Voter and the Election of 1800," *William and Mary Quarterly,* 36 (1979), 27–50; John Michael Rozett, "The Social Bases of Party Conflict in the Age of Jackson: Individual Voting Behavior in Greene County, Illinois, 1838–1848" (Ph.D. diss., University of Michigan, 1974); and Paul McAllister, "Missouri Voters, 1840–1856: An Analysis of Ante-Bellum Voting Behavior and Political Parties" (Ph.D. diss. University of Missouri, 1976). The subject is discussed in its broadest bearing, and a fresh interpretation appears, in Bourke and DeBats, "Identifiable Voting in Nineteenth-Century America," pp. 259–88.

87. Reply of Aug. G. Hill, Whig Town Committee Chairman, Harvard, to letter of Whig State Central Committee and Whig County Committee of Worcester, May 1, 1840, Worcester County Papers, box 6, folder 4, which includes the list of Harvard voters.

88. McLane, *Documents Relative to Manufactures,* I, 494–95. A tracing of Whigs and Democrats in the manuscript population schedules of the 1850 federal census showed similar patterns: great similarity in persistence in town, real-property ownership, and place of birth, and a slight difference in occupations: 73 percent of the Democrats were farmers compared with 66 percent of the Whigs; artisans and those engaged in commerce or manufacturing were somewhat more numerous among the Whigs. Tax lists at the Assessor's Office, Harvard, Massachusetts.

89. The surnames of the founding fathers of the Baptist Church were checked on the voter list (when no other identification was possible), and among these there were 27 Whigs, 20 Democrats, and 5 Doubtful: Katherine L. Lawrence, *The Baptist Church of Harvard–Still River, 1776–1926* (n.p., 1926). Other sources include Evangelical Church Record Book, 1840–1855; Methodist Class Records; Calvinist Congregational Society Record Books; Manuscript Records of First Universalist Church of Harvard, 1845–1866, containing 1845 list of signers of first constitution; Manuscript Records of Second Universalist Society, 1830–1843; Henry S. Nourse, *History of the Town of Harvard, Massachusetts 1732–1893* (Harvard, 1894).

90. The list of voters is in the Worcester County Papers; tax lists for the period are in the Northborough Town Hall, Northborough. Other sources are Josiah Colman Kent, *Northborough History* (Newton, Mass., 1921); Thomas W. Valentine, *Fifty Years of Pilgrimage: A Historical Discourse Delivered before the First Baptist Church in Northborough, Massachusetts* (Brooklyn, N.Y., 1877) [Valentine's name appeared on the 1840 list as a Democrat]; W. A. Houghton, *The Evangelical Congregational Church and Society* [Northborough] (Clinton, 1883); Evangelical Congregational Church, Northborough, Massachusetts, *Manual* (Hudson, Mass., 1892); Northborough Church Book of Records, 1746–1874, Northborough Town Papers, MWA; Unitarian Congregational Church Records, 1816–1858 (incomplete), Northborough; U.S. Census, 1840 Population Schedules.

Two Whigs, Cyrus Gale and Nathaniel Fisher, placed among those listed as Massachusetts's richest men in 1851: A. Forbes and J. W. Greene, *The Rich Men of Massachusetts* (Boston, 1851), p. 136.

91. The Sutton poll list of 1839 is in the Sutton Town Papers, MWA, and tax lists for 1838, 1840, and 1849 are in the Assessor's Office, Sutton. In 1851 four of the town's men made the list of *Rich Men:* two of these appeared on the 1840 list, one a Whig and the other a Democrat, pp. 138–39. Other sources used were the 1840 U.S. Census Population Schedules and vital-statistics records.

92. William A. Benedict and Hiram A. Tracy, *History of the Town of Sutton, Massachusetts: From 1704 to 1876* (Worcester, 1878), pp. 461–85 and passim.

93. Vincent Edward Powers, " 'Invisible Immigrants': The Pre-Famine Irish Community in Worcester, Massachusetts, from 1826 to 1860" (Ph.D. diss., Clark University, 1977), pp. 256–62; Lowell *Patriot,* Sept. 4, 1835; Oscar Handlin, *Boston's Immigrants: A Study in Acculturation* (New York, 1968; first ed., 1941), pp. 186–92; Boston *Statesman,* Mar. 19, 1827; *The Experimental and Office Holder's Journal,* July 4, 1834, Boston, Broadsides, Essex Institute, a satirical attack on the Democrats and the Irish; Darling, *Political Changes,* p. 309.

94. W. J. Rorabaugh, *The Alcoholic Republic: An American Tradition* (New York, 1979), p. ix; consumption peaked in the 1820s and early 1830s, p. 8. The numerous sources on the prevalence of drinking include George Faber Clark, *History of the Temperance Reform in Massachusetts, 1813–1883* (Boston, 1888), pp. 18–22; Sumner Gilbert Wood, *The Taverns and Turnpikes of Blandford, 1733–1833* (n.p., 1908), pp. 29–31; Frederick A. Currier, *Tavern Days and the Old Taverns of Fitchburg: Stage Coach Days and Stage Coach Ways* (Fitchburg, 1897), p. 25; Basil Hall, *Travels in North America* (Edinburgh, 1829), II, 79, 82–83, 90–91, 150–52; Faler, "Workingmen, Mechanics, and Social Change," pp. 216–19, 266–69. In 1812 it seemed to be routine in Worcester for landlords to provide tenant farmers with one-half pint of rum a day. Arnold Cargill agreement with Levi Lincoln, 23 Mar. 1812, Lincoln Family Papers, MWA. Even a New Bedford Quaker could in 1824 get "pretty well cut" on bottles of "June wine" and "York wine." Zephaniah W. Pease, ed., *Life in New Bedford a Hundred Years Ago: A Chronicle of the Social, Religious and Commercial History of the Period as Recorded in a Diary Kept by Joseph R. Anthony* (New Bedford, 1922), p. 74.

95. On the progress of temperance, see Faler, "Workingmen, Mechanics, and Social Change," pp. 220, 227; Northampton *Hampshire Gazette,* Apr. 21, 1830; "Circular of the State Temperance Societies, To the Citizens of the United States [1832]," Kinnicut Papers, box 2, Worcester Historical Museum; Cyrus Gale, Northboro', 26 May 1834, to Frederick W. Gale, Cambridge, Gale Family Papers, MWA; Dedham *Norfolk Advertiser,* Oct. 5, Dec. 7, 1833.

On reactions to temperance, see J. H. Temple, *Framingham,* p. 427; Boston *Statesman,* Nov. 5, 12, 1831; *Centinel,* Feb. 4, 1832; Boston *Advertiser,* Dec. 9, 1833; Worcester *Republican,* Apr. 8, 1835; *Spy,* Feb. 18, 1835; Roger Lane, *Policing the City: Boston, 1822–1835* (Cambridge, Mass., 1967), pp. 40–41; and Amos Everett Jewett and Emily Mabel Adams Jewett, *Rowley, Massachusetts: "Mr. Ezechi Rogers Plantation," 1639–1850* (Rowley, 1946), pp. 293, 294.

On the politics of temperance, see Ian R. Tyrell, *Sobering Up: From Temperance to Prohibition in Antebellum America, 1800–1860* (Westport, Conn., 1979), pp. 227–37.

96. The social sources of temperance and antitemperance, based on detailed study of Worcester in the 1830s, were examined in ibid., pp. 92–115. Tyrrell found religious identifications for 25 of 79 antitemperance men: 20 were Unitarian and 1 was Orthodox. He also found religion for 34 of 60 prohibitionists: 19 were Orthodox and nine

were Unitarians (p. 110). In Boston, similarly, in the late 1830s the division over temperance was more cultural than economic. "Living in the new neighborhoods located away from the eighteenth century commercial, marine environment of the waterfront; adherence to an evangelical creed; church and voluntary organization membership; participation in the moral reform movement of which the benevolent societies were a part—all coexisted in varying degrees with belief in temperance." Jill Siegal Dodd, "The Working Classes and the Temperance Movement in Ante-Bellum Boston," *Labor History*, 19 (1978), 529.

97. Edward Everett, Boston, 23 Jan. 1839, to John Davis, Davis Letterbook I-48, Davis Papers; Memorials against and for Repeal of the License Law, box 2, folder 4, Massachusetts Collection; *House Documents, 1839,* no. 37; entries of June 14, Sept. 24, 30, Oct. 31, 1839, Levi Lincoln Newton Diary, Newton Family Papers, MWA; E. Everett, 12 Aug. 1839, to J. Davis, Davis Letterbook I-53, Davis Papers. There are also many letters in the Winthrop Papers and Clifford Papers (MHi) dealing with the law of 1839, and many materials relating to the legislature's actions in the Massachusetts Collection.

98. Replies of Town Chairmen, 1840, Massachusetts Collection, MWA.

99. Though the Whigs split on the issue, they were generally thought of as the temperance party, and the Democrats as the "wets." But there was temperance sentiment in the Democracy as well: Boutwell, *Reminiscences*, I, 55–56, 66; Bulkley, "Robert Rantoul," pp. 229–31; Fall River *Patriot and Freeman*, Nov. 21, 1839; H. Chapin, Springfield, 12 Oct. 1838, to G. Bancroft, Bancroft Papers.

100. On Democratic factions, see Nye, *George Bancroft*, pp. 124–30. On Whig factions, see Robert F. Dalzell, Jr., *Daniel Webster and the Trial of American Nationalism, 1843–1852* (Boston, 1973), pp. 73–77, and Brauer, *Cotton versus Conscience*. On the Democrats' religious liberalism, see McLoughlin, *New England Dissent*, I, 1162, 1166–67; Boutwell, *Reminiscences*, I, 70; Bulkley, "Robert Rantoul," pp. 45–46, 52, 54.

101. Emerson is quoted in Darling, *Political Changes*, p. 317.

102. William C. Richards, *Great in Goodness: Memoir of George N. Briggs, Governor of the Commonwealth of Massachusetts, 1844–1851* (Boston, 1866), pp. iv, 20, 27, 33, 50–51, 54, 69, 186; A. B. Whipple, "Gov. George N. Briggs," *Collections of the Berkshire Historical and Scientific Society*, II (Pittsfield, 1894), 154–72.

103. Richards, *Great in Goodness*, pp. 116, 169, 188–89. John Greenleaf Whittier called Briggs "in many respects an estimable man," but added that as a governor he had not advanced the cause of temperance: J.G.W., Amesbury, 3 Nov. 1845, to the *Essex Transcript*, in John B. Pickard, ed., *The Letters of John Greenleaf Whittier* (Cambridge, Mass., 1975), I, 674.

104. Whipple, "Gov. George N. Briggs," pp. 171–74; Richards, *Great in Goodness*, pp. 140–41; Darling, *Political Changes*, p. 335; Brauer, *Cotton versus Conscience*, pp. 56, 62, 105–6, 110–11, 131, 143, 190, 211.

105. Richards, *Great in Goodness*, p. 210. Southern hostility to *"northern manufactures,"* such as that encountered by Henry Wilson in Congress, also helped to create a sense of harmony among Northern classes: H. Wilson, Natick, 16 Apr. 1844, to William Schouler, Schouler Papers, MHi.

## XIII. Parties and Policy

1. J. P. Healy, Boston, 7 Oct. 1841, to William Schouler, Schouler Papers, MHi.

2. J. H. Clifford, New Bedford, 16 Nov. 1839, to Robert C. Winthrop; J.H.C., 13 Nov. 1840, to R.C.W.; also J.H.C., Providence, 24 Oct. 1840, to R.C.W., Winthrop

Papers, John C. Park, Boston, 3 Oct. 1840, to Samuel Houghton, Houghton Papers, MHi.

3. Amasa Walker's reminiscence is quoted in James Phinney Munroe, *A Life of Francis Amasa Walker* (New York, 1923), p. 12; R. C. Winthrop, Boston, 22 Oct. 1840, to J. H. Clifford, Winthrop Papers. The Democratic leader Isaac Davis received numerous requests to speak in the towns of central Massachusetts; see, A. Converse, Oxford, 12 Sept. 1840, to I.D.; Anson Rice, Northborough, 18 Sept. 1840, to I.D.; Adam Hunt et al., Milford, 5 Oct. 1840, to I.D.; and many others. The Whig leaders Thomas Kinnicutt and former governor Lincoln also campaigned in Worcester County, Worcester *Massachusetts Spy,* Oct. 7, 1840. Further indications of the intensity of the campaign there are in William S. Hastings, Mendon, 6 Sept. 1840, to W. Schouler, Schouler Papers. Henry Wilson, the "Natick Cobbler," from spring to fall spoke in at least sixty towns in Massachusetts and New Hampshire. Ernest McKay, *Henry Wilson, Practical Radical: Portrait of a Politician* (Port Washington, 1971), pp. 17, 21.

4. Boston *Bay State Democrat,* Oct. 12, 1838, and Aug. 9, 1839; E. D. Beach, Springfield, 12 Oct. 1840, to George Bancroft; Grenville T. Winthrop, Boston, 27 Oct. 1840, to G.B.; and M. Morton, Taunton, 3 Nov. 1840, to G.B., Bancroft Papers, MHi. On Hallett's eloquence, see *Democrat,* Nov. 1, 1839. On Robert Rantoul's strenuous campaigning, see Robert D. Bulkley, Jr., "Robert Rantoul, Jr., 1805–1852: Politics and Reform in Antebellum Massachusetts" (Ph.D. diss., Princeton University, 1975), pp. 291–92.

5. George S. Boutwell, *Reminiscences of Sixty Years in Public Affairs* (New York, 1902), I, 61; May 25, 1840, List of pledges; Bills of receipt, and list of expenses for Log Cabin and Sundries, June 17, 1840 ($562.67 for Log Cabin), boxes II and III, Kinnicutt Collection, Worcester Historical Museum. [Salem] Whig Levee and Ball, Mar. 5, 1841, Subscription List, and Whig finance committee, Feb. 1, 1842, Nathaniel B. Mansfield, Uncatalogued Manuscripts, Salem Politics, Essex Institute.

6. See, e.g., Robert C. Winthrop, Boston, 13 Oct. 1836, to J. H. Clifford, New Bedford; J.H.C., 15 Oct. 1836, to R.C.W.; J.H.C., 30 June 1837, to R.C.W.; and J.H.C., 23 Dec. 1837, to R.C.W., Winthrop Papers. In 1833, by comparison, National Republican leaders had urged John Davis to accept their state convention's nomination, appealing to him to obey the "general voice" but making no mention of party duty: Daniel Webster, Exeter, 30 Sept. 1833, to J.D.; and Rufus Choate, Salem, 6 Oct. 1833, to J.D., Davis Letterbook I-7 and 8, Davis Papers, MWA.

7. Leavitt Thaxter, Edgartown, 11 Jan. 1841, to Caleb Cushing; and Henry Whipple, Salem, 30 Jan. 1841, to C. Cushing, Special Correspondence 145, Cushing Papers, LC. The Cushing Papers are a superb source for attitudes to patronage; they display the variety of attitudes described in this paragraph.

8. Stephen Nissenbaum, "The Firing of Nathaniel Hawthorne," *Essex Institute Historical Collections,* 114 (1978), 57–86, is, among other things, an excellent account of patronage norms in the late 1840s in Salem and shows the importance of the customshouse to both parties. On alleged Whig restraint in state offices, see George N. Briggs, Boston, 2 Mar. 1844, to ——, quoted in William C. Richards, *Great in Goodness: A Memoir of George N. Briggs* (Boston, 1866), pp. 191–92.

9. Julius Rockwell, Boston, 3 Mar. 1836, to John Davis. In contrast, the Boston *Atlas*'s editor implied a heightening of party influence by claiming to have nearly every Whig member of the legislature "on our books . . . and we spread in the country so widely that it gives us more influence than we have ever been able to exercise before." Richard Houghton, Boston, Mar. 1836, to John Davis, Davis Papers.

10. Robert C. Winthrop, Boston, 16 Apr. 1839, to J. H. Clifford, Winthrop Papers;

see also Worcester *Republican,* Jan. 18, 1837. In the Massachusetts Collection, MWA, are several complete lists of representatives to the legislature with their party identification, e.g., in box 2, folder 3, and in box 6, folder 2. A table in box 2, folder 1, gives the number of Whig and Democratic representatives in each county, with totals of 344 Whigs and 178 Democrats.

11. Attention to the party identity of legislators was growing throughout the period, however, as the lists mentioned in note 10 testify, and it was more intense than Winthrop suggests here. Newspapers more often identified newly elected legislators by party, and in the early 1840s, when the legislature was more evenly divided, the identities of representatives from even the tiniest hamlets received close scrutiny.

12. Robert C. Winthrop, Boston, 22 Apr. 1839, to J. H. Clifford, Winthrop Papers.

13. J. H. Clifford, New Bedford, 24 Oct. 1841, to R. C. Winthrop, ibid.

14. Alphonse Brooks, 16 Aug. 1844, to John W. Lincoln, Worcester, box 6, folder 6, Massachusetts Collection, MWA.

15. Marcus Morton, Taunton, 12 Nov. 1840, to George Bancroft, Bancroft Papers.

16. In new states like Michigan this was less true, though traditional practices and attitudes were also present: Ronald P. Formisano, *The Birth of Mass Political Parties: Michigan, 1827–1861* (Princeton, 1971).

17. Roy F. Nichols, *The Invention of the American Political Parties* (New York, 1967), pp. 342–43; Richard P. McCormick, *The Second American Party System: Party Formation in the Jacksonian Era* (Chapel Hill, 1966), pp. 104–23, 134–47, 349–56.

18. For New York Politics in the early national period, see Jabez D. Hammond, *The History of Political Parties in the State of New York,* 2 vols. (Buffalo, 1850); Dixon Ryan Fox, *The Decline of Aristocracy in the Politics of New York* (New York, 1919); and Alvin Kass, *Politics in New York State, 1800–1830* (Syracuse, 1965).

19. Lee Benson, *The Concept of Jacksonian Democracy: New York as a Test Case* (Princeton, 1961), pp. 56–58; William J. Cooper, Jr., *The South and the Politics of Slavery, 1828–1856* (Baton Rouge, 1978), pp. 49–51.

20. See, e.g., Thomas Brown, "Southern Whigs and the Politics of Statesmanship, 1833–1841," *Journal of Southern History,* 19 (1980), 366–70; J. Mills Thornton III, *Politics and Power in a Slave Society: Alabama, 1800–1860* (Baton Rouge, 1978), pp. 34–39, 118–60, esp. 140, 143–45; Ronald P. Formisano, "Toward a Reorientation of Jacksonian Politics: A Review of the Literature, 1959–1975," *Journal of American History,* 63 (1976), 53–56; and Harry L. Watson, *Jacksonian Politics and Community Conflict: The Emergence of the Second American Party System in Cumberland County, North Carolina* (Baton Rouge, 1981).

21. McCormick, *Second Party System,* pp. 98, 334–35.

22. The first quotation is from W. J. Rorabaugh, *The Alcoholic Republic: An American Tradition* (New York, 1979), p. 193; the second from Ian Tyrrell, *Sobering Up: From Temperance to Prohibition in Antebellum America, 1800–1860* (Westport, Conn., 1979), p. 67.

23. Kermit L. Hall, *The Politics of Justice: Lower Federal Judicial Selection and the Second Party System, 1829–61* (Lincoln, Neb., 1979), pp. xvii, 174.

24. Newburyport *Advertiser,* June 22, 1831, quoted in Gerald J. Baldasty, "Political Stalemate in Essex County: Caleb Cushing's Race for Congress, 1830–1832," *Essex Institute Historical Collections,* 117 (1981), 66. The *Bay State Democrat* (Boston), Aug. 31, 1838, criticized a Whig congressman for "self-electioneering." The desire to avoid the appearance of "self-electioneering," is expressed in Marcus Morton, East Cambridge, 7 Dec. 1837, to George Bancroft, Springfield, Bancroft Papers.

25. Edward Pessen used the phrase "new men" but described a somewhat complex situation. *Jacksonian America: Society, Personality, and Politics* (Homewood, Ill.,

1978), pp. 171–96. The most useful work published thus far on changing patterns of leadership in this period is Whitman H. Ridgway, *Community Leadership in Maryland, 1790–1840: A Comparative Analysis of Power in Society* (Chapel Hill, 1979). See also John F. Kutolowski and Kathleen Smith Kutolowski, "Commissions and Canvasses: The Militia and Politics in Western New York, 1800–1845," *New York History* 63 (1982): 5–38.

26. Frederick Cople Jaher generously allowed me to read the portion of his then forthcoming book dealing with Boston elites, *The Urban Establishment: Upper Strata in Boston, New York, Charleston, Chicago, and Los Angeles* (Chicago, 1982); see also idem, "The Boston Brahmins in the Age of Industrial Capitalism," in Jaher, ed., *The Age of Industrial Capitalism in America: Essays in Social Structure and Cultural Values* (New York, 1968), pp. 188–262.

27. George Morey, Boston, 16 May 1850, to Samuel Houghton, Houghton Papers, MHi. In Maryland "the 'bought voter' was a common political practice." Wilbur Wayne Smith, "The Whig Party in Maryland, 1828–1856" (Ph.D. diss., University of Maryland, 1967), p. 45. Yet the evidence offered there (pp. 45–46) regarding several alleged cases of bribery before 1850 was all based on indirect testimony. The one case supported by direct evidence (an entry in a manuscript journal of the eyewitness) came from the year 1852 (pp. 46–47). Even in this instance the act of illegal voting itself was not witnessed.

28. Richard E. Dawson, "Social Development, Party Competition, and Policy," in William Nisbet Chambers and Walter Dean Burnham, eds., *The American Party Systems: Stages of Political Development* (New York, 1975; first ed., 1967), p. 237. Richard P. McCormick, "Political Development and the Second Party System," in ibid., pp. 107, 115–16.

29. Pessen, *Jacksonian America*, pp. 197–232, 240–41, quotation on p. 208; Richard L. McCormick, "The Party Period and Public Policy: An Exploratory Hypothesis," *Journal of American History*, 66 (1979), 287. Pessen also found that Whig and Democratic differences did not matter much in the governance of the nation's cities. "Who Governed the Nation's Cities in the 'Era of the Common Man'?" *Political Science Quarterly*, 87 (1972), 591–614. See also Peter D. Levine, *The Behavior of State Legislative Parties in the Jacksonian Era: New Jersey, 1829–1844* (Rutherford, N.J., 1977).

30. Herbert Ershkowitz and William G. Shade, "Consensus or Conflict? Political Behavior in the State Legislatures during the Jacksonian Era," *Journal of American History*, 58 (1971), 591–521; Rodney O. Davis, "Partisanship in Jacksonian State Politics: Party Divisions in the Illinois Legislature, 1834–1841," in Robert P. Swierenga, ed., *Quantification in American History: Theory and Research* (New York, *Atheneum*, 1970), pp. 149–62; and Benson, *Jacksonian Democracy*.

31. Oscar Handlin and Mary Flug Handlin, *Commonwealth: A Study of the Role of Government in the American Economy: Massachusetts, 1774–1861* (Cambridge, Mass., 1969; first ed., 1947), passim. Regarding corporations and personal liability, see ibid., p. 150, and Caroline F. Ware, *The Early New England Cotton Manufacture: A Study in Industrial Beginnings* (Boston, 1931), pp. 147–48. Recent research confirms these conclusions and extends them to other states as well. The literature is discussed in Harry N. Scheiber, "Government and the Economy: Studies of the 'Commonwealth' Policy in Nineteenth-Century Massachusetts," *Journal of Interdisciplinary History*, 3 (1972), 142; and idem, "Federalism and the American Economic Order, 1789–1910," *Law and Society Review*, 10 (1975), 92–96. Scheiber's discussion of the similarities and differences between Massachusetts, New York, Pennsylvania, and Ohio in the 1820s is especially pertinent.

32. Alexander James Field, "Economic and Demographic Determinants of Educa-

tional Commitment; Massachusetts, 1855," *Journal of Economic History*, 5 (1979), 453, stresses that in Massachusetts "politically active, self-conscious groups of professionals, merchants, and businessmen—in short, elite groups, were able, at both the state and local levels, to articulate and thus define the nature of the problems confronting both the economy and educational systems."

33. William E. Nelson, *Americanization of the Common Law: The Impact of Legal Change on Massachusetts Society, 1760–1830* (Cambridge, Mass., 1975), pp. 3–8; Morton J. Horowitz, *The Transformation of American Law, 1780–1860* (Cambridge, Mass., 1977), pp. 1–4. Both of these histories show in detail how the law changed, and both make clear the far-reaching social implications of that change. Both rely heavily, however, on a central theme of explanation which neither of them explains and which both, perhaps justifiably, take for granted. "Nineteenth-century society," Nelson wrote (p. 7), "was the product . . . of a final force that emerged during the revolutionary period—a desire for economic growth." Horowitz invoked (p. 31) "the spirit of economic development."

34. Nelson, *Americanization of the Common Law*, p. 174; Horowitz, *Transformation of American Law*, p. xvi.

35. Handlin and Handlin, *Commonwealth*, p. 200; the starkness of this phrase was softened by other aspects of their argument, on pp. 200–202.

36. For the 1843 inaugural, see *Acts and Resolves, 1843, 1844, 1845* (Boston, 1845), pp. 123, 128; see also *Refutation of the Charges against Marcus Morton* ([Boston?], 1845), pp. 29–30.

37. Handlin and Handlin, *Commonwealth*, p. 216; see also Merle E. Curti, "Robert Rantoul, Jr.: The Reformer in Politics," *New England Quarterly*, 5 (1932), 264–80.

38. Bulkley, "Robert Rantoul," p. 201. In this speech Rantoul blamed Whigs or "aristocrats" for fostering the evils of the paper-money system, yet still worried that it might have been too radical (pp. 202–4).

39. Ibid., pp. 159, 217–19.

40. Leonard W. Levy, *The Law of the Commonwealth and Chief Justice Shaw* (Cambridge, Mass., 1957), pp. 186–87. The Boston Journeymen Bootmakers Society had organized in 1835 and raised its wages by successive strikes between 1835 and 1840. It is difficult to tell how representative or unusual the bootmakers were. They were highly skilled and their shops small, masters employing not many more than one to six workers. At the trial, employers testified that the quality of the work had improved, that "the society men were all good workmen," that the men were steadier than before, that the wages negotiated by the society were moderate, and that nonmembers as well as members could get them. Walter Nelles, "Commonwealth vs. Hunt," *Columbia Law Review*, 32 (1932), 1131–38, which contains the most details on the background of the case.

During the same week that *Commonwealth* v. *Hunt* was decided, Chief Justice Shaw created the famous "fellow-servant rule" in *Farwell* v. *Boston and Worcester Railroad:* "By this rule American capitalism, at a critical stage in its development, was relieved of the enormous financial burden for industrial accidents which it would otherwise have incurred. The losses from injury on the job were sustained by the workers themselves." Levy, *Chief Justice Shaw*, p. 166.

## XIV. Parties and Democracy

1. John Adams, 27 Dec. 1810, to Benjamin Rush, in John A. Schutz and Douglass Adair, eds., *The Spur of Fame: Dialogues of John Adams and Benjamin Rush, 1805–1813* (San Marino, Calif., 1966), p. 174.

2. M. Ostrogorski, *Democracy and the Organization of Political Parties*, ed. Seymour Martin Lipset (Garden City, N.Y., 1964; first ed., 1902), II 40; Edward Pessen, *Jacksonian America: Society, Personality, and Politics* (Homewood, Ill., 1978), pp. 149–260; Richard P. McCormick, "Political Development and the Second Party System," in William Nisbet Chambers and Walter Dean Burnham, eds., *The American Party Systems: Stages of Political Development* (New York, 1975; first ed. 1967), pp. 106, 107; and McCormick, *The Second American Party System: Party Formation in the Jacksonian Era* (Chapel Hill, 1966).

3. Among historians the trend setter in this, and in many other respects, was William Nisbet Chambers, *Political Parties in a New Nation: The American Experience, 1776–1809* (New York, 1963). From among the many examples of works by political scientists that might be chosen to illustrate the point here, see Gerald M. Pomper, "The Decline of the Party in American Elections," *Political Science Quarterly*, 92 (1977), 21–41. For Pomper, parties and mass politics are the hallmarks of modern popular democracy, their relationship being "obvious, even tautological" (p. 21).

4. *Massachusetts Resolves, 1836*, p. 276; [Robert C. Winthrop Speech] To the State Convention of Whig Young Men of Massachusetts, Worcester, Sept. 11, 1839, Massachusetts Collection, MWA.

5. *Acts and Resolves, 1843, 1844, 1845* (Boston, 1845), p. 116.

6. In a similar vein Vivien Hart has studied recent "widespread misgivings" in Britain and the United States "among the general public about an apparant contradiction between the professed ideals of democracy and the day to day activities of government." Hart calls *political distrust* "this perception of a discrepancy between the ideals and realities of the political process itself." *Distrust and Democracy: Political Distrust in Britain and America* (London, 1978), p. xi. Unlike Samuel P. Huntington, who views the gap between institutions and ideals as a "problem" for the governing elite—*American Politics: The Promise of Disharmony* (Cambridge, Mass., 1981)—I agree with Hart that distrust is necessary for the survival of democratic institutions, and especially for the maintenance of some degree of justice and equity.

7. "The mass parties formed in the Jacksonian era," one historian recently asserted, "were viewed as instruments with which the people could control government, and because each party offered a different way to secure equal rights and protect liberty from power and privilege, voters believed in the legitimacy of a political procss that manifestly preserved republicanism." Michael F. Holt, *The Political Crisis of the 1850s* (New York, 1978), p. 5; also pp. 34, 35.

My thinking here has been influenced by Walter Dean Burnham, "The Changing Shape of the American Political Universe," *American Political Science Review*, 59 (1965), 7–28; idem, *Critical Elections and the Mainsprings of American Politics* (New York, 1970); idem, "Theory and Voting Research: Some Reflections on Converse's 'Change in the American Electorate,' " *American Political Science Review*, 68 (1974), 1002–23; and Lawrence Goodwyn, *Democratic Promise: The Populist Moment in America* (New York, 1976).

8. Harriet Martineau criticized the American press for "profligacy" and told of a newpaper editor "who began his professional course by making an avowed distinction between telling lies in conversation and in a newspaper, where everybody looks for them." *Society in America* (London, 1837), I, 147, 149. Newpaper accusations against prominent men were not taken as fact, since everyone, as Horace Greely testified in an 1843 libel trial, understood them merely as "expressions of the Editor's opinions." Norman L. Rosenberg, "The Law of Political Libel and Freedom of Press in Nineteenth Century America: An Intetrpretation," *American Journal of Legal History*, 17 (1973), 343.

9. John Barton Derby, *Political Reminiscences* (Boston, 1835), p. 76; *Democrat,* May 3, 1839.

10. E. Everett, Charlestown, 15 Mar. 1836, to R. C. Winthrop, Winthrop Papers, MHi; A. H. Everett, 16 Oct. 1834, to George Bancroft, Bancroft Papers, MHi. Richard Houghton, the flamboyantly partisan editor of the Boston *Atlas,* spelled out his assumptions and his need for regular, rapid information from Washington: "It is a very easy matter to give a right direction to popular feeling and opinion, if you take it in its incoate [sic] state. But if you delay until it acquires a wrong formation, you have an herculean labor." R. Houghton, Boston, 6 June 1836, to John Davis, Davis Letterbook I-37, Davis Papers, MWA. Also revealing is R. C. Winthrop, Boston, 22 May 1838, to J. H. Clifford, Winthrop Papers; and R. Houghton, Boston, 1838 or 1839, to J. H. Clifford, Clifford Papers, MHi.

11. Robert D. Bulkley, Jr., "Robert Rantoul, Jr., 1805–1852: Politics and Reform in Antebellum Massachusetts" (Ph.D. diss., Princeton University, 1975), pp. 292–93; George S. Boutwell, *Reminiscences of Sixty Years in Public Affairs* (New York, 1902), I, 62–63, for the story about the wood, and p. 63 for the last-quoted phrases. The Boston *Workman,* a Whig campaign sheet of 1840, parried extreme Democratic thrusts while delivering its own folderol against Van Buren, June 11 and Sept. (no. 18) 1840.

12. J. Mills Thornton III, *Politics and Power in a Slave Society: Alabama, 1800–1860* (Baton Rouge, 1978), pp. 81, 161, 162.

13. Neil Harris, *Humbug: The Art of P. T. Barnum* (Boston, 1973). Richard D. Brown called my attention to the relevance of Harris's biography to this chapter.

14. The 1844 campaign letters of Whig town chairmen in Worcester County, in the Massachusetts Collection, MWA, are particularly revealing in this respect: Hiram Wheelock, Warren, 15 Aug. 1844, to John W. Lincoln, Worcester, box 7, folder 6; Sullivan Fay, Southboro, 31 Oct. 1844, to Stephen Salisbury, Worcester, ibid; John G. Thurston, 30 July 1844, to J. W. Lincoln, ibid; J. Goulding, Phillipston, 5 Nov. 1844, to Whig County Committee, ibid; and Jared Weed, Petersham, 15 June 1840, to Edwin Conant, Worcester, box 7, folder 3.

15. In Worcester County, for example, an abolitionist minority had been agitating for almost a decade. James Eugene Mooney, "Antislavery in Worcester County, Massachusetts: A Case Study" (Ph.D. diss., Clark University, 1971), pp. 6–10, 21–23.

16. Whitney R. Cross, *The Burned-Over District: The Social and Intellectual History of Enthusiastic Religion in Western New York, 1800–1850* (New York, 1965; first ed., 1950), pp. 113–25, 211–37; Lee Benson, *The Concept of Jacksonian Democracy: New York as a Test Case* (Princeton, 1961), pp. 21–46, 110–12.

17. Lynn *Record,* June 5, 19, 1830. My examination of the careers of Antimasonic and Masonic state leaders, and of groups of Antimasons and Masons in Boston, revealed a tendency for Antimasons, but not Masons, to become active in antislavery. "Antimasons and Masons in New York and Massachusetts, 1830" (Paper delivered at the Annual Meeting of the American Historical Association, San Francisco, Dec. 27, 1978).

18. W. L. Garrison, Worcester, 7 Sept. 1832, To the Liberator, in Walter M. Merrill, ed., *The Letters of William Lloyd Garrison,* I (Cambridge, Mass., 1971), 164.

19. For other indications of openness before 1834–1835, see Boston *Columbian Centinel,* Aug. 9, 1828; Martineau, *Society in America,* I, 119–20; Priscilla Hawthorne Fowle, "Boston Daily Newspapers: 1830–1850" (Ph.D. diss., Radcliffe College, Harvard University, 1920), p. 157; Martin L. Stow, Northboro', 18 Jan. 1834, to Frederick W. Gale, Cambridge, Gale Family Papers, MWA; Judd Journal, I, entries of 14 July, 9, 10, 12 Aug. 1834. In 1833 when the Boston *Post* circulated a handbill calling for

Garrison to be tarred and feathered, the Boston *Transcript* rebuked the *Post* for provoking mobs. *Post,* Oct. 8, 1833, and *Transcript,* Oct. 8, 1833. Notice the change in attitude toward abolitionists in the Lowell *Democrat* between Nov. 28 and Dec. 19, 1834. The changing climate is also revealed in John B. Pickard, ed., *The Letters of John Greenleaf Whittier: 1828–1845* (Cambridge, Mass., 1975), I, in numerous letters in the years 1833–1836.

20. On Worcester, see Alfred S. Roe, "The Beginnings of Methodism in Worcester," *Worcester Society of Antiquity Proceedings,* 27 (1888), 62; Worcester *Republican,* Aug. 12, 1835. On Faneuil Hall, see *Republican,* Aug. 26, 1835; Paul Revere Frothingham, *Edward Everett: Orator and Statesman* (Boston, 1925), pp. 132–34. The quotations regarding the Garrison mob are the words of Maria Weston Chapman, quoted in Albert Bushnell Hart, ed., *Commonwealth History of Massachusetts,* IV (New York, 1930), 323; also pertinent is Theodore Lyman, ed., *Papers Relating to the Garrison Mob* (Cambridge, Mass., 1870), p. 5; Henry Cabot Lodge, *Boston* (London, 1891), pp. 214–17; and Vincent Yardley Bowditch, *Life and Correspondence of Henry Ingersoll Bowditch* (Boston, 1902), I, 100–02. The role of party leaders and partisanship in anti-abolition mobs has been well established by Leonard L. Richards, *"Gentlemen of Property and Standing": Anti-Abolition Mobs in Jacksonian America* (New York, 1970).

21. For elite reaction to the convent mob, see Boston *Evening Transcript,* Aug. 12, 13, 1834; Boston *Patriot,* Oct. 1, 1834; Theodore M. Hammett, "Two Mobs of Jacksonian Boston: Ideology and Interest," *Journal of American History,* 62 (1976), 549–56. Violence in Charlestown involving Irish Catholic and native workers began in 1833. *Transcript,* Nov. 29, 30, 1833. See also Wilfred Joseph Bisson, "Some Conditions for Collective Violence: The Charlestown Convent Riot of 1834" (Ph.D. diss., Michigan State University, 1974).

22. Martineau, *Society in America,* I, 168–69; the comment on slavery and Masonry is on p. 178. For fear of an anti-abolition mob in Northampton, see Judd Journal, I, 13 Jan. 1836. For a similar point of view, see David Grimsted, "Rioting in Its Jacksonian Setting," *American Historical Review,* 77 (1972), 361–97.

23. Boston *New England Artisan,* Aug. 15, 1833. The comments regarding abolitionists referred to here were made mostly by historians writing about the causes of the Civil War. For related discussions of the literature, see Thomas J. Pressly, *Americans Interpret Their Civil War* (Princeton, 1954); Thomas N. Bonner, "Civil War Historians and the 'Needless War' Doctrine," *Journal of the History of Ideas,* 17 (1956), 193–216; and especially William G. McLoughlin, introd. to Gilbert Hobbs Barnes, *The Antislavery Impulse, 1830–1844* (New York, 1964; first ed., 1933), pp. vii–xxxi.

24. See, e.g., Kinley J. Brauer, *Cotton versus Conscience: Massachusetts Whig Politics and Southwestern Expansion, 1843–1848* (Lexington, Ky., 1967); Robert F. Dalzell, Jr., *Daniel Webster and the Trial of American Nationalism, 1843–1852* (Boston, 1973); and Martin B. Duberman, *Charles Francis Adams, 1807–1886* (Boston, 1961).

25. Samuel Shapiro, "The Conservative Dilemma: The Massachusetts Constitutional Convention of 1853," *New England Quarterly,* 33 (1960), 207–24; Oscar Handlin, *Boston's Immigrants: A Study in Acculturation* (New York, 1968; first ed., 1941), pp. 192–97; Martin B. Duberman, "Behind the Scenes as the Massachusetts 'Coalition' of 1851 Divides the Spoils," *Essex Institute Historical Collections,* 99 (1963), 152–60. One conservative Whig called the convention a "body of destructionists." James Savage, Lunenburg, 27 June 1853, to William Barton Rogers, in *Letters of James Savage to His Family* (Boston, 1906), p. 185.

26. Shapiro, "Convention of 1853," quotation on p. 224; William G. Bean, "Puritan

versus Celt, 1850–1860," *New England Quarterly,* 7 (1934), 70–79; Handlin, *Boston's Immigrants,* pp. 197–201; Ray Allen Billington, *The Protestant Crusade: 1800–1860* (Chicago, 1964; first ed., 1938).

27. For similar interpretations, see Ronald P. Formisano, *The Birth of Mass Political Parties: Michigan, 1827–1861* (Princeton, 1971), pp. 217–38; Holt, *Political Crisis,* pp. 101–38.

28. Ian R. Tyrrell, *Sobering Up: From Temperance to Prohibition in Antebellum America, 1800–1860* (Westport, Conn., 1979), pp. 261–63.

29. This emphasis differs in part from Tyrrell's in *Sobering Up,* who stressed more the hostility between nativism and temperance. George Richardson, e.g., elected Know-Nothing mayor of Worcester in 1854, after having been a prominent anti-prohibitionist in the 1830s, said that the voters who elected him were "tired of talk about rum and talk about niggers" (pp. 266, 267). Yet new prohibition laws in Maine and Massachusetts passed in 1854–1855 with nativist appeals and nativist political support (p. 268).

30. Bean, "Puritan versus Celt," p. 78. In November 1854 Charles Francis Adams wrote in his diary that it was the Catholic vote against the 1853 constitution "which has gone far to bring about in Quincy the present state of things, as many of my friends in disgust at this combined religious action had gone into the new combination to resist that dangerous influence." The quotation is from John Raymond Mulkern, "The Know Nothing Party in Massachusetts" (Ph.D. diss., Boston University, 1963), p. 111.

31. Virginia Cardwell Purdy, "Portrait of a Know-Nothing Legislature: The Massachusetts General Court of 1855" (Ph.D. diss., George Washington University, 1970), pp. 148, 149; Handlin, *Boston's Immigrants,* p. 202. Though new, the 1855 legislators returned to the General Court at about the same rate as legislators elected in earlier and later years during the period. Purdy, "Know-Nothing Legislature," pp. 151–53.

32. This partial list is compiled from several sources, the most complete of which is Mulkern, "Know Nothing Party," pp. 143–46, 151–52; see also Handlin, *Boston's Immigrants,* pp. 202–3; Purdy, "Know-Nothing Legislature," pp. 95–96. Governor Gardner's inaugural revealed the eclectic and wide-ranging nature of Know-Nothing interests. Boston *Daily Bee,* Jan. 10, 1855. One scholar recently noted the remarkably "strong affirmation of support for the public school system" by the Know-Nothings. Alexander James Field, "Economic and Demographic Determinants of Educational Commitment: Massachusetts, 1855," *Journal of Economic History,* 39 (1979), 51; see also *Bee,* March 31, 1855.

Imprisonment for debt, despite the reforms of the thirties, had remained a weapon of lawyers, apparently routinely resorted to by creditors. See, e.g., Welcome Young, E. Bridgewater, 27 Feb. 1839, to Charles E. Forbes, and Browning Hall, Springfield, 11 Feb. 1842, to C.E.F., Forbes Papers, Forbes Library, Northampton.

33. Purdy, "Know-Nothing Legislature," pp. 94–96; Handlin, *Boston's Immigrants,* p. 204. The nativists also petitioned for removal of the local judge who had presided over fugitive-slave cases. The 1855 desegregation law, which passed "with a shout" in the house, is reprinted in Leonard W. Levy and Douglas L. Jones, eds., *Jim Crow in Boston: The Origins of the Separate But Equal Doctrine* (New York, 1974), pp. 261–62.

That the Know-Nothing law prohibited the exclusion of children from schools on grounds of religion as well as race probably had something to do with conflicts between Irish Catholics and native Americans over Irish children who wanted to attend public schools and had been prevented by families or Irish community pressure from doing so. In Lawrence, where such trouble had occurred, a Know-Nothing school committee during this period raised per-pupil expenditure and the school-tax rate to their highest levels, demonstrating that the Know-Nothings "must have cared considerably for the schools." Michael B. Katz, *The Irony of Early School Reform: Educational Innovation in Mid-Nineteenth Century Massachusetts* (Cambridge, Mass., 1968), pp. 103–7, quotation on p. 107.

34. Mulkern, "Know Nothing Party," pp. 146, 148, 151–54, 237, 294–96; Handlin, *Boston's Immigrants*, pp. 202–4. In 1855 the government ran an operating deficit of $244,000 and spent over $300,000 more than its predecessor: it was the third-longest session ever, and legislators voted themselves a pay raise. Mulkern, "Know Nothing Party," pp. 157–58. Yet the senate also changed its rules to exclude senators with an interest in particular measures being debated to be excluded from voting. Purdy, "Know-Nothing Legislature," p. 97.

35. Eli A. Glasser, "Government and the Constitution (1820–1917)," in Hart, ed., *Commonwealth History*, IV, 26. Other Know-Nothing proposals which did not come to law include removal of the toll from the Charles River Bridge for pedestrians; court appointed counsel for destitute prisoners, to be paid by the state; repeal of the death penalty; and reform of loan-and-fund associations. Purdy, "Know-Nothing Legislature," pp. 97–98.

36. For a recent example of this tendency, see Dale Baum, "Know-Nothingism and the Republican Majority in Massachusetts: The Political Realignment of the 1850s," *Journal of American History*, 64 (1978), 959–86. The Know-Nothings were aware of the criticisms leveled at them by the established press and defended themselves against it. *Bee*, Mar. 29, 1855. Ironically, many of the accusations brought against the Know-Nothing legislatures were almost the same ones leveled against the Whig-dominated legislature of 1853, indicating in part that these were stock partisan charges.

37. Robert Kelley, *The Transatlantic Persuasion: The Liberal-Democratic Mind in the Age of Gladstone* (New York, 1969); Handlin, *Boston's Immigrants*, pp. 124–50. The controversy over representation had constituted a constant drain on the body politic, consuming enormous amounts of time in the constitutional conventions of 1820 and 1853 and in legislatures in the interim. The Know-Nothings simply untied the Gordian knot. They also made final the disestablishment of the church by removing all aid from sectarian schools, abolished property qualifications for a seat in the legislature and council, abolished the test oath, and incorporated machinery into the constitution for amending it. Glasser, "Government and the Constitution," p. 26.

38. Bean, "Puritan versus Celt," pp. 73–74; Oscar Handlin and Mary Flug Handlin, *Commonwealth: A Study of the Role of Government in the American Economy: Massachusetts, 1774–1861* (Cambridge, Mass., 1969; first ed., 1947), p. 205; Handlin, *Boston's Immigrants*, pp. 194, 195. The Coalition also tried, unsuccessfully, to pass a personal-liberty law, bills to liberalize divorce, to protect the property rights of women, and to extend the power of juries. In 1851 came the first of a series of general incorporation laws (1851, 1852, 1854, then two in 1855) allowing any group of individuals to organize as a manufacturing, banking, insurance, or gaslight company by a "simple process" of registration open to public view, much as Marcus Morton had recommended in 1843. Handlin and Handlin, *Commonwealth*, pp. 218, 221. Few areas of commerce escaped attention. In 1856 the power of examining and licensing marine pilots was taken from private marine societies and given to a state board of pilot commissioners, Ibid., p. 209.

39. Purdy, "Know-Nothing Legislature," pp. 96–98; Handlin and Handlin, *Commonwealth*, pp. 212, 213; Stephen Salsbury, *The State, the Investor, and the Railroad: The Boston & Albany, 1827–1867* (Cambridge, Mass., 1967), p. 287. Though he was a Boston merchant close to the financial community, even Governor Gardner could be sharply critical of banking practices: *Written for the Governor's Reply to a Letter Addressed to Him by "A Practical Banker"* (Boston, 1855).

40. Estimates of the support have varied: e.g., three-fourths of the Free Soilers, two-thirds of the Democrats, and over half of the Whigs; or, the 1854 Know-Nothing vote of over 81,000 consisted of 39 percent former Whigs, 33 percent former Democrats, and 28 percent former Free Soilers. Mulkern, "Know Nothing Party," p. 114. The most recent and systematic estimates: 56 percent of the Free Soil voters of 1852 (25 percent abstained), 60 percent of the 1852 Democratic voters, and (by deduction from the foregoing) about 65 percent of the Whig voters in 1852. Baum, "Know-Nothingism and the Republican Majority," pp. 965–66; according to Baum, former Free Soilers composed slightly over one-fifth of the Know-Nothing total, and "former Whigs and Democrats made up the bulk of the Know-Nothing vote."

41. Handlin and Handlin, *Commonwealth,* p. 231; Thomas Franklin Currier, "Whittier and the Amesbury-Salisbury Strike," *New England Quarterly,* 8 (1935), 110.

42. Henry A. Miles, *Lowell, As It Was, and As It Is* (Lowell, 1845), p. 101. Thomas A. Dublin estimated that the ten-hour day was rare in the 1840s. *Women at Work: The Transformation of Work and Community in Lowell, Massachusetts, 1826–1860* (New York, 1979), p. 113. According to Charles E. Persons, a ten-hour day was common for skilled workers in some large towns by 1853. "The Early History of Factory Legislation in Massachusetts: From 1825 to the Passage of the Ten Hour Law in 1874," in Susan M. Kingsbury, ed., *Labor Laws and Their Enforcement* (New York, 1911), pp. 75–76. The legislative minority report of 1852 asserted that many master workmen had adopted the system. *House Documents,* no. 185, pp. 8–9. In 1858 in the successful silversmith firm of Reed and Barton of Taunton, the eleven-hour day was standard, with overtime for hours beyond eleven. George S. Gibb, *The Whitesmiths of Taunton: A History of Reed & Barton, 1824–1943* (Cambridge, Mass., 1943), p. 144.

43. Persons, "Factory Legislation," pp. 29–54; John Davis, Worcester, 20 Oct. 1842, to Association of Industry, Fall River, Davis Letterbook, I-108, MWA; Philip T. Silvia, "The Spindle City: Labor, Politics, and Religion in Fall River, Massachusetts, 1870–1905" (Ph.D. diss., Fordham University, 1973), pp. 30–34; *House Documents, 1845,* no. 50; *House Documents, 1850,* no. 153.

44. Carl Siracusa, *A Mechanical People: Perceptions of the Industrial Order in Massachusetts, 1815–1880* (Middletown, Conn., 1979), p. 134; Robert J. Topitzer, "Values about Industrialization: The Case of Lowell, Massachusetts, 1840–1860" (Ph.D. diss., University of New Hampshire, 1976), pp. 105–13; *House Documents, 1844,* no. 48. On the incident in the legislature, see George Frisbee Hoar, *Autobiography of Seventy Years* (New York, 1903), I, 163–64. Free Soilers seem, in fact, to have been far more resolute in support of ten hours than were any other politicians. Perhaps the most prominent advocate of "short hours" in the state was the Free Soiler William S. Robinson, editor of the *Lowell American* (1849–1853); Siracusa, *Mechanical People,* pp. 202, 217.

45. Persons, "Factory Legislation," pp. 63–67; Currier, "Whittier," pp. 109–10; Dublin, *Women at Work,* pp. 115–16, 125–31, 201–2.

46. Ibid., p. 200; Edward Capel Whitehurst, ed., *"The Test of Experience": or The Working of the Ballot in the United States* (London, 1855), pp. 15–16. The secret ballot was a principal common bond for Democratic and Free Soil Coalitionists. Hoar, *Autobiography,* I, 171. Charges that Whigs intimidated workers became frequent by the early 1850s. Siracusa, *Mechanical People,* pp. 185–86. The persistence of open voting is revealed in a report of a contested representative's election in 1850 in Ashfield; see *House Documents, 1850,* no. 49, pp. 5–9.

47. *House Documents, 1852,* no. 177; Hoar, *Autobiography,* I, 174; Michel Brunet, "The Secret Ballot Issue in Massachusetts Politics from 1851 to 1853," *New England Quarterly,* 25 (1952), 354–61; Shapiro, "Convention of 1853," pp. 221–24;

Benjamin F. Butler, *Butler's Book* (Boston, 1892), pp. 91–93, 98–106; Whitehurst, ed., *"Test of Experience"; Journal of the Constitutional Convention, 1853* (Boston, 1853), p. 503.

48. Purdy, "Know-Nothing Legislature," p. 97.

49. *Bee,* Mar. 27, 28, Apr. 4, 9, 11, 1855. See esp. the *Bee*'s support, on Apr. 10, 1855, of striking caulkers at the Charlestown navy yard.

50. *Transcript,* Mar. 9, 1855; see also Apr. 7, 1855. This was hardly unusual, since "Political spokesmen repeatedly stressed that the worker in Massachusetts was 'free.' " Siracusa, *Mechanical People,* p. 90. For another view of Free Labor, see Eric Foner, *Free Soil, Free Labor, Free Men: The Ideology of the Republican Party before the Civil War* (New York, 1970).

51. *House Documents, 1852,* no. 185, p. 7.

52. Currier, "Whittier," pp. 105–12; Dublin, *Women at Work,* p. 147. In the Boston Bootmakers' Society of the 1830s, of *Commonwealth* vs. *Hunt,* Irish Catholics had been quite active. Walter Nelles, "Commonwealth vs. Hunt," *Columbia Law Review,* 32 (1932), 1132.

53. *House Documents, 1850,* no. 153, p. 19; J. G. Whittier wrote the resolutions and circular of the Amesbury workers and said that if manufacturers continued present practices they would "drive from our manufacturing villages the best portion of the native population, and . . . fill their places with a vagrant, dependent and irresponsible class." Quoted in Currier, "Whittier," p. 111. Back in 1845 Whittier had already given moderate support to the "ten hour system." John G. Whittier, *The Stranger in Lowell* (Boston, 1845), pp. 117–19.

54. *Transcript,* Mar. 9, 1855; Lawrence, during 1855–1856, was also supporting the free-soil agitation in Kansas, though in 1860 he became conciliatory to the South. Barry A. Crouch, "Amos A. Lawrence and the Formation of the Constitutional Union Party: The Conservative Failure in 1860," *Historical Journal of Massachusetts,* 8 (1980), 46–58. While the ten-hour law was being considered in 1855, the workers of Manchester, New Hampshire, staged a huge strike and attracted much attention in Massachusetts.

55. *Bee,* Mar. 26, Apr. 4, 11, 13, 17, 1855; the *Transcript* reported the senate margin as 26 to 11, Apr. 16, 1855; the Northampton *Hampshire Gazette* asserted that the senate's rejection "was expected by many who voted for it in the House . . . for political effect. . . . The truth is that our manufacturing corporations are not now in a condition to bear a further reduction in the hours of labor below the 11 hours generally adopted. . . ." Apr. 17, 1855.

56. Charles Cowley, *History of Lowell* (Boston, 1868), p. 148; and idem, "History of the Ten Hours Movement," in Trades and Labor Council of Lowell, Mass., *Lowell: A City of Spindles* (Lowell, 1900), pp. 245–61.

57. Caroline F. Ware, *The Early New England Cotton Manufacture: A Study in Industrial Beginnings* (Boston, 1931), pp. 228–35; Hannah Josephson, *The Golden Threads: New England Mill Girls and Magnates* (New York, 1949), pp. 288–99; Dublin, *Women at Work,* pp. 147–64.

58. Robert G. Layer, *Earnings of Cotton Mill Operatives, 1825–1914* (Cambridge, Mass., 1955), p. 23. Regarding mismanagement of the mills in the 1850s, see James Cook Ayer, *Some of the Uses and Abuses in the Management of Our Manufacturing Corporations* (Lowell, 1863).

59. David Montgomery, *Beyond Equality: Labor and the Radical Republicans, 1862–1872* (New York, 1972; first ed., 1967), pp. 261–95.

60. J. Rockwell, Boston, 3 Mar. 1836, to John Davis, Letterbook, I-28, Davis Papers, MWA; for a description of Rockwell, see Worcester *Massachusetts Spy,* Jan.

14, 1835. Rockwell later served in Congress (1843–1851) and the U.S. Senate (1854–1855) and was an unsuccessful Republican candidate for governor in 1855, losing to the Know-Nothing Gardner.

61. Before encountering the phrase "democratic moment" in Lawrence Goodwyn, *Democratic Promise: The Populist Moment in America* (New York, 1976), I had used it (in the plural, as here) in "Parties and Social Movements, 1800–1860" (Paper delivered at the University of Connecticut History Department Colloquium, Oct. 30, 1975).

62. Robert W. Jackman, "Political Elites, Mass Publics, and Support for Democratic Principles," *Journal of Politics*, 34 (1972), 753–73; D. A. Hamer, *The Politics of Electoral Pressure: A Study in the History of Victorian Reform Agitations* (Hassocks, Sussex, 1977), p. viii.

63. On the relationship between distrust and participation based on a sense of efficacy, see Hart, *Distrust and Democracy*.

## Appendix VII

1. Bidwell, "Rural Economy," pp. 288–89; Dwight, *Travels*, III, 57–64, 71.

2. In 1814 Falmouth defied the British and withstood a bombardment of cannonballs, and an entrenched militia prevented the redcoats from landing. Morison, *Maritime History*, p. 209.

3. On Yarmouth, see Deyo, *Barnstable*, pp. 467–68, 479; Dwight, *Travels*, III, 51; on Dennis, see Deyo, *Barnstable*, pp. 515, 524–29; Dwight, *Travels*, III, 55–56. The pastors of Dennis's original and Calvinist church had tenures of 1764–1804 and 1804–1813, both dying in office. Deyo, *Barnstable*, pp. 517–18. On Falmouth, see Bidwell, "Rural Economy," p. 289. On Sandwich, see Dwight, *Travels*, III, 48–49, 385. On Barnstable, see Deyo, *Barnstable*, p. 367; Dwight, *Travels*, III, 50; Donald B. Trayser, *Barnstable: Three Centuries of a Cape Cod Town* (Hyannis, Mass., 1939), pp. 58, 63–65. The Osterville branch of the Baptist Church of Barnstable included the maritime entrepreneur and Baptist leader Captain Benjamin Hallett, father of the later reformer and Democratic politician of the same name. Ibid., pp. 69–70.

4. Deyo, ed., *Barnstable*, pp. 825, 839–44, 855, 899, 901; Frederick Freeman, *The History of Cape Cod: The Annals of the Thirteen Towns of Barnstable County* (Boston, 1862), II, 523–26; McLoughlin, *New England Dissent*, I, 675–77; Dwight, *Travels*, III, 56.

## Appendix XI.A.

1. Whig State Central Committee, Boston, 17 Apr. 1840, P. Greely, Jr., Secretary, Confidential Circular, box 6, folder 4, Massachusetts Collection, MWA. Democratic organization in Worcester County in 1840 is fairly well illuminated by letters in the Davis Papers, MWA, e.g., Nathan Richardson, 3 Sept. 1840, to Isaac Davis, and Anson Rice, Northboro, 23 Sept. 1840, to I. Davis.

2. Worcester *Massachusetts Spy*, Oct. 11, 1837. In 1844 all town officers were nominated and elected by party ticket, with Whigs dominating. *Spy*, Mar. 6, 1844.

3. The most extreme case of partisanship in a town reported in these letters appeared four years later when the Warren Whig chairman complained that the Democrats there held power by an overwhelming margin and used *"that power for their own exclusive party purposes."* H. Wheelock, 12 Nov. 1844, to John W. Lincoln, Worcester, box 7, folder 6, Letters to Stephen Salisbury, Massachusets Collection.

4. Circular of Whig State Central Committee, Boston, 15 July 1844, "Private and Confidential," Jonathan Chapman, Chairman, box 7, folder 6, Massachusetts Collec-

tion. Isaac Stevens, Athol, 25 July 1844, to J. W. Lincoln, Worcester; Mark Haskell, Oakham, 7 Aug. 1844, to J.W.L.; William Hancock, Dudley, 31 July 1844, to J.W.L., and other letters to John Waldo Lincoln from Whig Town Committee chairmen, box 7, folder 6, Massachusetts Collection.

5. Edwin Conant, Worcester, 18 Oct. 1844, to Samuel Houghton, Sterling; and George Morey, Boston, 1 May 1851, to Samuel Houghton, Houghton Papers, MHi.

## Appendix XII.B.

1. Hurd, comp., *Bristol,* pp. 451, 457, 568–69, 765; Barrus, *Goshen,* p. 174; Abbott, *Cobbler in Congress,* p. 8. John Langdon of New Hampshire was not a "religious man" but always a "church-going man," who late in life became a church member: Lawrence Shaw Mayo, *John Langdon of New Hampshire* (Concord, 1937), p. 285.

2. Ina Mansur, *A New England Church, 1730–1834* (Freeport, Maine, 1974), pp. 157, 161, 188–89. Lynn's Congregational Church in 1818 consisted of 8 male and 32 female members and a congregation of from 150 to 200 persons. Cooke, *Century of Puritanism,* p. 366.

3. A story of moderates who fought and compromised against division is in Griffith, *History of Carver,* pp. 115–16.

4. The first quotation is from John Fessenden, Dedham, 8 Feb. 1841, to Caleb Cushing, Cushing Papers, LC; Joseph Allen, *To the Members of the First Parish in Northborough, May 27, 1833* (n.p., n.d.), pp. 1–2; John Fiske, *A Half-Century and Dedicatory Discourse, Delivered in New Braintree, Mass., October 26, 1846* (Greenfield, Mass., 1846), pp. 6–15.

5. Elias Cornelius, *The Moral and Religious Improvement of the Poor: A Sermon Delivered on the Evening of October 20, 1824, in the Tabernacle Church, Salem* (Salem, Mass., 1824), p. 14.

6. In 1837 a Worcester County town was described as having three churches, an Orthodox, Methodist, and "Congregational, a mixt multitude without any particular discrimination." Worcester Statistics, 1837, Worcester County Papers, MWA.

7. Fowler, *Historical Sketch of Fall River,* pp. 29–30, 56. According to Benjamin Wood Pearce, Fall River citizens took their religion seriously, *Recollections,* pp. 50–56.

8. Worcester County Papers, MWA; the manuscript list of churches is in the oversize box, folder 2.

# Index